Poetry of Charles d'Orléans and His Circle

MEDIEVAL AND RENAISSANCE
TEXTS AND STUDIES

VOLUME 383

ARIZONA STUDIES IN THE
MIDDLE AGES AND THE RENAISSANCE

VOLUME 34

Poetry of Charles d'Orléans and His Circle

A Critical Edition of BnF MS. fr. 25458, Charles d'Orléans's personal manuscript

Edited by
John Fox and Mary-Jo Arn

English translations by
R. Barton Palmer

With an excursus on literary context by
Stephanie A. V. G. Kamath

ACMRS
(Arizona Center for Medieval and Renaissance Studies)
Tempe, Arizona
in collaboration with
BREPOLS
2010

Published by ACMRS (Arizona Center for Medieval and Renaissance Studies)
Tempe, Arizona
and Brepols Publishers, n.v., Turnhout, Belgium.

ASMAR Volume 34: ISBN 978-2-503-53382-7   D/2010/0095/183

Library of Congress Cataloging-in-Publication Data
Charles, d'Orléans, 1394-1465.
  [Poems. English & French (Middle French). Selections]
  Poetry of Charles d'Orléans and his circle : a critical edition of BnF MS. fr. 25458,
Charles d'Orléans's personal manuscript / edited by John Fox and Mary-Jo Arn ;
English translations by R. Barton Palmer ; with an excursus on literary context by
Stephanie A. V. G. Kamath.
      p. cm. -- (Medieval and Renaissance texts and studies ; v. 383)
  Texts in Middle French with English translations.
  Includes bibliographical references and index.
  ISBN 978-0-86698-431-7 (alk. paper)
  1. Charles, d'Orléans, 1394-1465--Manuscripts. 2. Charles, d'Orléans,
1394-1465--Translations into English. 3. Bibliothèque nationale de France.
Manuscript. Français 25458. I. Fox, John, 1925- II. Arn, Mary-Jo. III. Palmer, R.
Barton, 1946- IV. Kamath, Stephanie A. V. G. V. Bibliothèque nationale de France.
Manuscript. Français 25458. VI. Title.
  PQ1553.C5A28 2010
  841'.2--dc22

                                                                              2010041270

Cover Art:
Charles d'Orléans and Marie de Clèves
Image courtesy of Les Arts Decoratifs, Paris
Photo by Laurent Sully Jaulmes. All rights reserved.

∞

This book is made to last. It is set in Adobe Caslon Pro,
smyth-sewn and printed on acid-free paper to library specifications.
Printed in the United States of America.

Paix est tresor qu'on ne peut trop louer.

Charles d'Orléans, *Ballade* 114

The Committee's emblem indicates that this volume is based on an examination of all available relevant textual sources, that it is edited according to principles articulated in the volume, that the appropriate texts, both source and edited texts, are fully described, that the editorial principles, the text, and the apparatus have undergone a peer review, that a rigorous schedule of verification and proof reading was followed to insure a high degree of accuracy in the presentation of the edition, and that the text is accompanied by appropriate textual, critical, and other historical information.

TABLE OF CONTENTS

Preface

The text in this edition, as well as the glossary and the innovative Notes on Narrative and Verse Forms, are entirely the work of John Fox, who has devoted a significant part of his scholarly career to the study of the poetry of the duc d'Orléans. His *Lyric Poetry of Charles d'Orléans* remains one of the best studies of the duke's French *œuvre,* and his long article, "Charles d'Orléans: Poète anglais?" was the first strong and detailed scholarly argument for the duke's authorship of the English poetry in British Library MS. Harley 682 (put forward by Robert Steele and Mabel Day in the first modern edition of the collection, for which see Bibliography).

John and I were very pleased when R. Barton Palmer agreed to provide a translation to accompany John's text. We are grateful for his close and serious involvement in many aspects of this project. Stephanie A. V. G. Kamath kindly agreed to contribute a short excursus on the late medieval literary context for those users not well versed in the forms of poetry Charles would have known. My task has been to see to a new analysis of the manuscript and, on the basis of that, to construct a more accurate account of the history of the production of the manuscript on which our edition is based, and thus a new ordering of its contents. I have written most of the introduction and appendices, contributed to the explanatory notes, edited the volume, and seen the project through the publication process (initials in the table of contents indicate who is responsible for which texts). The careful reader will discern some differences in our work, differences of style, a few of terminology, and yet others of opinion. We have tried to minimize these inconsistencies, but we have stopped short of pretending that they do not exist.

It would be curmudgeonly not to acknowledge here the learned work of those who have gone before us in the study of the life and work of the duc d'Orléans, among them great bibliographer/librarians such as Leopold Delisle and le comte de Laborde; the first great scholar of matters Carolian in the early twentieth century, Pierre Champion; another in the mid-twentieth century, Daniel Poirion; and one whose work spans the most recent half-century, Gilbert Ouy. Many others before and since have devoted (and are devoting) long and serious attention to the work of the duke, with excellent results. This edition can be seen as a companion to an earlier volume in the MRTS series, my edition of the duke's English poetry

(*Fortunes Stabilnes*, MRTS 138) which, like this edition, was awarded a seal from the Modern Language Association's Committee on Scholarly Editions.

The edition breaks new ground in a number of ways. The new text, notes, and glossary include many corrections of Pierre Champion's text, new information on the poet's language, and a new analysis of the *chançon* and *rondel* forms (see §6 and §7 below). The translation, the first ever made of the entire corpus, makes the edition available to those who do not read medieval French easily as well as suitable for a variety of teaching purposes. The reordering of the individual lyrics will give readers for the first time the opportunity to read the poems in something more like the order in which they were composed. In this edition the organization of the lyrics is less like that found in the works of many other medieval French poets and in modern editions, instead offering a reading experience that preserves some of the immediacy and displays some of the messiness of a manuscript that was compiled over a period of a quarter-century and copied by dozens of different scribes (and authors), including the duke himself. We hope that this new order will appeal to those who are interested in the development of Charles's poetic art and his shifting interest in verse form.

Because the publisher felt a translation was a desideratum, we have taken the opportunity, not only of including one, but of offering some other aids for the reader who requires an English text. In providing a bit more support than will be needed by those who specialize in the language, literature, or history of medieval France, we trust that our colleagues in Middle French studies will not begrudge some extra help to those like myself who come from other scholarly disciplines or who have varying language competencies.

Mary-Jo Arn

Acknowledgments

We are grateful to the following libraries for providing documents and scholarly hospitality: the Bibliothèque nationale de France, Paris; the Archives nationales, Paris; Bibliothèque Inguimbertine, Carpentras; and the British Library, London. The libraries of Harvard University have opened the riches of their resources to a researcher from outside the university; I am especially grateful to the staffs of the Houghton Library, the Isham (music) Library, and above all Widener Library, whose peerless reference librarians have provided invaluable bibliographic support to this project. The staff of Child Library have offered support of other kinds and I am most grateful for it.

We are all grateful to James Laidlaw for his careful reading of the entire text for the MLA Committee on Scholarly Editions. He provided perspective when ours failed and suggested improvements in both concept and detail. John Niles, too (who coordinated the committee's review of the edition), read the whole and made many useful suggestions.

Our editors at ACMRS have been unfailingly gracious and patient with us, as we revised, corrected, and revised again our own and each others' texts. Prof. Johan Gerritsen (University of Groningen, emeritus) has been, as always, forthcoming with his expertise in the ways of manuscripts, and the edition is better for it.

Mary-Jo Arn

ABBREVIATIONS

BL	British Library
BnF	Bibliothèque nationale de France
CFMA	Classiques français du Moyen Age
CHFMA	Classiques de l'histoire de France au Moyen Âge
CNRS	Centre national de la recherche scientifique
CTHS	Comité des travaux historiques et scientifiques
FEW	*Französisches etymologisches Wörterbuch*
i	infra
MED	*Middle English Dictionary*
MRTS	Medieval and Renaissance Texts and Studies
OED	*Oxford English Dictionary*
PRF	Publications romanes et françaises
R-H	Jean Rychner and Albert Henry, eds., *Le Testament Villon*.
SATF	Société des anciens textes français
s	supra
TLF	*Trésor de la langue française*
B	*Ballade* (as in B74)
Bal	one of seven narrative *ballades*
Co	*Complainte*
Ch	*Chançon*
R	*Rondel*
Ca	*Carole*

Note: In the apparatus to this edition, French words and phrases are generally italicized. When a French word or phrase is flanked by quotation marks, they indicate that the word or phrase represents exactly what appears in the manuscript (e.g., "hancon" for the word *Chançon* sans its initial letter). Longer quotations of French text are flanked by quotation marks or blocked.

CONTRIBUTORS

John Fox, Chevalier dans l'Ordre des Palmes Académiques, published his first book in 1950: *Robert de Blois, son oeuvre didactique et narrative.* This has been followed by many articles and books on medieval French language and literature, including *The Poetry of Villon* (1962), *The Lyric Poetry of Charles d'Orléans* (1969), and *The Middle Ages. A Literary History of France.* (1974). He is Professor Emeritus of French in the University of Exeter.

Mary-Jo Arn is the editor of *Fortunes Stabilnes: Charles of Orleans's English Book of Love* (a critical edition, 1994), and the author of the entry on the duc d'Orléans for the new *Oxford Dictionary of National Biography.* More recently, she has published a codicological study of the manuscript edited here, *The Poet's Notebook: The Personal Manuscript of Charles d'Orléans (Paris, BnF MS. fr. 25458)* (2008). She manages the book reviewing process for *Speculum: A Journal of Medieval Studies* and edits the *Medieval Academy News* at the Medieval Academy of America.

R. Barton Palmer has published many editions and translations of the work of late medieval French authors, including Guillaume de Machaut and Jean Froissart. Among his translations for classroom use are *Medieval Epic and Romance* and (with Barbara Altmann) *Medieval Love Debate Poetry.* He is Calhoun Lemon Professor of Literature and director of Film Studies at Clemson University.

Stephanie A. V. G. Kamath has published studies of medieval allegory and its vernacular translation, with special attention to Christine de Pizan, Jean d'Outremeuse, and Guillaume de Deguileville. She has coauthored a bilingual edition of René d'Anjou's *Livre du cuers d'amours espris* (2001) and is currently preparing an analysis of Guillaume de Deguileville's allegory with the support of the British Academy's Neil Ker Memorial Fund. She is an assistant professor at the University of Massachusetts, Boston.

Introduction

This is an edition of Charles d'Orléans's personal copy of his poetry (BnF MS. fr. 25458), made up largely of lyrics but containing some narrative, together with lyrics composed by members of his household, his family, his friends, and his peers. The manuscript was probably commissioned in London near the end of the duke's English captivity (1439–1440). Into it went most or all of the poetry the duke had written (he was about forty-six at this time), which did not begin to fill its many blank leaves. He returned to France with it and continued to add lyrics until his death in 1465.[1] No manuscript can thus have any higher authority than this one (though a handful of lyrics that were not copied into it turn up in other manuscripts). What this edition does not contain is two religious works found elsewhere, the short poem he composed at the age of ten, "Le livre contre tout péché," and a later work composed during his captivity, *Canticum amoris*.[2] Although this collection contains eleven lyrics in Middle English, the bulk of his English poetry can be found in another manuscript, BL MS. Harley 682 (published under the title *Fortunes Stabilnes: Charles of Orleans's English Book of Love* [Binghamton, NY: MRTS, 1994]) edited by Mary-Jo Arn.

This edition's function is twofold. First of all it is intended to replace Pierre Champion's 1923 edition of the same manuscript. Before Champion's day, editions of the duke's poetry simply reproduced the poems in manuscript order, but his edition contained a new order based on his close observations of the manuscript. The second function of this edition is to correct Champion's order by basing it on Mary-Jo Arn's codicological study of the manuscript, *The Poet's Notebook*.[3]

---

[1] Twice he was forced to add new vellum to accommodate his steady output of poetry and that of other poets.

[2] The former is printed in Pierre Champion's edition (*Charles d'Orléans, Poésies. I. La Retenue d'Amours; ballades, chançons, complaintes et caroles. II. Rondeaux*, 2 vols., CFMA 34 and 56 [Paris: Honoré Champion, 1923, 1927]), 545–50; the latter is reproduced in Gilbert Ouy's book, *La librairie des frères captifs: Les manuscrits de Charles d'Orléans et Jean d'Angoulême*, Texte, Codex & Contexte 4. (Turnhout: Brepols, 2007), 145–76.

[3] *The Poet's Notebook: The Personal Manuscript of Charles d'Orléans (Paris, BnF MS. fr. 25458)*, Texts and Transitions 3 (Turnhout: Brepols, 2008). In 1803 the duke's French poetry was published by Vincent Chalvet (*Poésies de Charles d'Orléans, père de Louis XII et oncle de François Ier, rois de France* [Grenoble: Giroud, 1803], based on G (for which

This edition could be described as a best-text edition, but it is something more than that both because of its provable physical connection with the author over a period of decades and because it contains work from hands other than the poet's. This collection is demonstrably unified by shared ideas, motifs, and individual lines (usually the first). In light of the new interest in *social* poetry by scholars such as Jane H. M. Taylor,[4] this manuscript contains precious evidence of literary collaboration on many levels.

Today Charles de Valois, duc d'Orléans (1394–1465), is known to literary scholars and readers of his poetry chiefly as a writer of *rondels* and *ballades*,[5] in large part because scholars have found his later work more interesting than his early work, even though the early poetry is written in a wider variety of forms. It is these later lyrics that are most often anthologized and collected. His earliest known work (apart from "Le livre contre tout péché") may be the first line of a *chançon* he had embroidered in pearls on a *robe* in 1414.[6] Only that line and

---

see Appendix 1); it also includes some of the Latin. This was followed in 1842 by two completely independent editions: one by Aimé Champollion-Figeac (*Les poésies du duc Charles d'Orléans publiées sur le manuscrit original de la Bibliothèque de Grenoble* [G] *conféré avec ceux de Paris et de Londres* [Paris: Belin-Leprieur and C. de Batines]), the other by J. Marie Guichard (*Poésies de Charles d'Orléans publiées avec l'autorisation de M. le ministre de l'instruction publique, d'après les manuscrits des bibliothèques du Roi et de l'Arsenal* [Paris: Gosselin] based primarily on O). In 1874, Charles Héricault edited the poetry once again (*Poésies complètes de Charles d'Orléans revues sur les mss. avec préface, notes et glossaire*, 2 vols. [Paris: Jannet; repr. Paris: Flammarion, 1896] also based primarily on O). Finally, Pierre Champion re-edited the entire text of O (*Charles d'Orléans, Poésies*. CFMA 34 and 56. Paris: Honoré Champion, 1923, 1927). There have been too many partial editions of the duke's poetry to mention, except for two recent editions with translations (into modern French): Jean-Claude Mühlethaler, ed. and trans., *Charles d'Orléans, Ballades et rondeaux*, Lettres Gothiques 4531 (Paris: Livre de Poche, 1992) (arranged in manuscript order); and Gérard Gros, ed. and trans., *Charles d'Orléans: En la forêt de longue attente et autres poèmes*, Postface by Jean Tardieu [1962], Poésie 365 (Paris: Gallimard, 2001).

    [4] *The Making of Poetry: Late-Medieval French Poetic Anthologies,* Texts and Transitions 1 (Turnhout: Brepols, 2007). See especially chapter 2: "Preserved as in a Violl: Charles d'Orléans' Circle and His Personal Manuscript." In fact the edition of *ballades* and *rondels* by Jean-Claude Mühlethaler, though admirable in many ways, is incomplete in exactly this social sense, excluding as it does work by poets other than Charles.

    [5] The spelling "rondel(s)" will be used in this edition, as it is in the manuscript; the spelling "rondeau(x)" will, however, be retained in quoted material.

    [6] For the sleeves, 960 pearls were purchased to spell out the lyric (with musical notation) beginning *Madame je suis plus joyeulx* (the remainder of the text is lost). The garment was clearly an extraordinary one, produced at the cost of 276 pounds, 7 shillings, and six deniers Tournois (Le comte de Laborde, *Les ducs de Bourgogne* [Paris: Plon frères, 1852], vol. 3, #6241). Such extravagances were in this period *de rigueur* for the royal family (which is easy to see by browsing through the inventories, e.g., those edited by de Laborde, Henwood, or Stratford, for which see the bibliography).

the exchange of lyrics with Jean de Garencières (see Appendix 3) survive among the duke's accounts to indicate that he may have written any number of lyrics in *chançon* or other forms before his capture at Agincourt in 1415. Some of this early poetry was conserved, however, and brought to him in England by one of his retainers (including the exchange with Garencières, *ballades* 116 and 117).[7] However, it is impossible to pick all these early lyrics out from among those written in the early years of his captivity. It is possible that the opening narrative that recounts the duke's first encounter with the God of Love was also written before his fateful twenty-first year. While in England, Charles continued to write not only *chançons* but *ballades*, *complaintes*, *caroles*, and verses in various other forms.[8] He also wrote narrative verse, including his vision of Age and withdrawal from the service of Love (*Songe en complainte*).

The duke gradually lost interest in the *complainte* and *carole*, but, once back in France, he wrote *rondels* in ever-increasing numbers, so that, by the time his collection was complete, the number of *rondels* far exceeded the number of lyrics in all other forms combined. Only the *ballade* seemed to hold its interest beside that of the shorter *rondel*. It was not just the verse forms that changed as the years passed. His earlier poetry is written largely on courtly themes of love and loss (with political or patriotic poetry running a poor second); his later work addressed the love question less frequently and took in a variety of other subjects, including melancholy and the preoccupations of old age.

Following his return to France in 1440, he seems quite naturally to have drawn to him men who were poets or who were at least accustomed to writing verse. Some were noblemen whose names we recognize (Jean, duc de Bourbon, Jean, duc d'Alençon, René d'Anjou); a few are known to us as authors in their own right (François Villon, Vaillant, Gilles Des Ourmes, Georges Chastellain); others were members of the duke's household: (?Guillaume) Fredet, apparently simply a friend, or Jacques Caillau, the duke's physician. Pierre Champion noted that it is from among the *écuyers* (squires) and the *échansons* (cupbearers), those offices filled by young men, that we find the greatest number of *rimeurs*.[9] This

---

[7] Garencières (see Index of Medieval Authors) died at Agincourt. On the various retainers of the duke and their duties, see Elizabeth Gonzalez, *Un prince en son Hôtel* (Paris: Publications de la Sorbonne, 2004).

[8] In fact he seems to have set himself the task of composing various pseudo-documents and connecting bits of narrative verse in as many different verse forms as he could. One of these swathes of verse, the *Departie d'amours*, also contains the seven narrative *ballades*, marked out from his other *ballades* in three ways: he did not number them, they have no *envois*, and they are surrounded by narrative verse.

[9] Pierre Champion, *Vie de Charles d'Orléans (1394–1465)* (Paris: Honoré Champion, 1911), 600. It is also interesting that he included such people in his *Ordre du Camail* (Order of the Camail, also called the Order of the *Porc-Épic*) (see Gonzalez, *Un prince*, 220; Champion, *Vie*, 137, 324, 395, 414).

varied company seems to have met at a kind of literary centerpoint, and it is possible to trace a fine thread from one to the other as we read lyrics that respond to one another or build on the same first line. It is unusual to find a serious poet who took pains to have a manuscript of his own work copied and decorated asking others to record their work in his book—not just those who wrote excellent poetry, but those whose production was decidedly mediocre. In this sense, his manuscript became something more like a journal or notebook than an example of medieval *belles-lettres* like the author-supervised manuscripts of the work of Guillaume de Machaut or Christine de Pizan. It is a unique chronicle not only of poetic inspiration but of social practice.

§1 The manuscript

Paris, Bibliothèque nationale de France, MS. fr. 25458 is a vellum manuscript of 299 leaves, with modern, perhaps eighteenth-century, pagination (except for a number of blank leaves, which remain unnumbered). It contains sections of narrative verse, a collection of *ballades* and *complaintes*, a collection of *chançons* and *rondels*, and four *caroles* (of which nine lyrics are in English,[10] one in Latin, and a few macaronic). Most of the poetry was composed by Charles de Valois, duc d'Orléans, the nephew of Charles VI. In addition to the duke's poetry, the manuscript contains lyrics from the hands of many people, most of them visitors to or residents of the court of the duke at Blois.

The pages are ruled for 31 lines per page. Written space is c. 125 mm. x 82 mm.[11] One of the primary keys to understanding the construction of the manuscript is the four different ruling patterns, which reveal a series of additions to the original manuscript.[12] The other, corroborative feature of the manuscript is the repeatedly changing style of the decorative initials, some limned (i.e., illuminated, the earliest by an English limner, the later by French limners), some painted very simply (i.e., later still, with alternating red and blue lombards), some

---

[10] These consist of 2 lyrics in *rondel* form, 6 in *chançon* form (see §6, below), and 1 in *ballade* form.

[11] If we imagine a leaf with nearly identical margins on the three unbound sides (which, judging from the decoration, would be adequate, the lower margin at this point being wider than the other two), the original manuscript might have measured something like 195 x 135mm (7.7" x 5.4").

[12] It was Johan Gerritsen (who provided invaluable help in sorting through codicological evidence for Arn's study, *The Poet's Notebook*) who first noticed the differences in ruling pattern in different parts of the manuscript. That discovery has had a profound impact on the amount we can learn from the physical manuscript about the history of its composition. Because Pierre Champion was apparently unaware of this series of patterns, his analysis of the manuscript contains a number of inaccuracies (*Le manuscrit autographe des poésies de Charles d'Orléans* [Paris: Honoré Champion, 1907; repr. Geneva: Slatkine, 1975].

initialed in ink by the scribe who copied the lyric, some with blank spaces left for initials that were never added.[13]

The text is written in various (mostly cursive) French hands of the fifteenth century, usually in black ink. Punctuation is almost entirely absent. The first, French scribe, who worked in England during the closing months of Charles's captivity, copied more lines than any of the later scribes. The last scribes probably copied lyrics into it in the year of Charles's death in 1465. The second most frequent hand is that of the duke himself, who frequently copied his own lyrics or those of others into his manuscript, entered corrections and revisions, and numbered many of his poems, in two series:[14] 107 *ballades* in the first and then, in a single series, 164 *chançons* and *rondels*.[15] The rest of the manuscript is filled with hands of dozens of French scribes, probably belonging in large part to the duke's chancery or to the authors of various lyrics. This plethora of hands gives the manuscript an irregular look that is belied by the structural evidence from analysis of other of its features (see below). As the wear on the outsides of some quires and especially of the first written page shows, the work lay unbound for some time after it was written.

§2 Ordering the texts

Editing the duke's manuscript is not as straightforward as transcribing the lyrics, constructing an apparatus, and sending the resulting text to a publisher. Representing the manuscript in print (inasmuch as that can even be done) presents many challenges. Editors of earlier centuries saw their job as presenting an accurately transcribed text accompanied by an apparatus in which they solved puzzles and explained what was going on in the manuscript(s) in order to clarify the meaning of the texts. Such editions, while extremely useful, occlude certain kinds of information more recently summed up in the phrase "manuscript context."

This manuscript began as an unbound collection of lyrics and narrative poetry copied by a single scribe, with initials painted by a single limner, but from the beginning the poet imagined a book with room for expansion, building into

---

[13] Pierre Champion noticed this progression of initials and based much of his analysis of the manuscript on it (in *Le manuscrit autographe*). There are many errors in the initials, most in the work of the third limner, perhaps because the scribes were not consistent in supplying directors.

[14] See Champion, *Le manuscrit autographe*, 11, 31. Lines 8–12 of the lyric on the lower half of page 365 (see frontispiece) are in the duke's hand. A list of autograph lyrics can be found in Appendix 1.

[15] See the frontispiece. On the identification of the duke's handwriting, see Champion, *Le manuscrit autographe*, 30–31, and Gilbert Ouy, "À propos des manuscrits autographes de Charles d'Orléans identifiés en 1955 à la Bibliothèque nationale," *Bibliothèque de l'Ecole des Chartes* 118 (1961): 179–88.

even this first stage of copying a number of blank leaves following each verse form, waiting to receive yet-to-be-composed lyrics. Patricia Stirnemann was the first to recognize that the limner of this earliest poetry was English and that the manuscript must therefore have been made in England before the duke's release in 1440.[16] Through the years, the manuscript grew, in part because the duke continued to compose lyrics, in part because he began encouraging others to record their poetry in it, until he found that more vellum would be needed if he were to continue collecting poetry in the same manuscript. In the course of time, some of the quires became displaced and the individual bifolia in some had become shuffled. To complicate matters, the poet had begun recording his short lyrics (*chançons*) only on the lower portions of leaves, but later thought better of it and began having short lyrics copied on the upper portions. Because the short lyrics are generally copied two to a page, the upper and lower halves of the page are indicated in this edition by page number [the manuscript is paginated, not foliated] followed by *i* [infra] or *s* [supra]. Lyrics were transcribed sometimes by their authors, sometimes by one or another scribe in the household. The result looks very much like a patchwork of hands and decoration (or lack of it).[17] But there is more: because the manuscript was unbound, perhaps when a second batch of vellum was added to the book, some of the quires and some leaves within quires became displaced from their original positions. This state of affairs makes sorting out the development of the poet's craft difficult. A few of the lyrics can be dated approximately, which is some help, as is the fact that some refer to other lyrics or are written on the same first line. However, other criteria often prove more useful in this venture, most of which are codicological and textual.

Before the twentieth century, editors generally published poetry in more or less the order in which they found it in the manuscript,[18] but in 1907, Pierre Champion published a slim volume entitled *Le manuscrit autographe*, in which he analyzed the physical manuscript, identifying a number of production layers by the work of a succession of different initial makers (limners or lombard makers). Putting that information to work, together with paleographical observations, he provided a new rationale for the poem order of the duke's whole *œuvre*, which he followed (more or less) in his edition of the poems in 1923.[19] In his day, however,

---

[16] "Français 25458," in François Avril and Patricia Dans Stirnemann, *Manuscrits enluminés d'origine insulaire, VIIe–XXe siècle* (Paris: Bibliothèque nationale, 1987), 181. Pierre Champion dated the *fonds primitif* as late as 1450. See Arn, *The Poet's Notebook*.

[17] Many dozens of hands of all levels of proficiency are represented. Three limners and more than one rubricator worked on the manuscript at various points.

[18] E.g., Vincent Chalvet (1803), Aimé Champollion-Figeac (1842), J.-Marie Guichard (1842), and Charles d'Héricault (1874). For publication details, see the bibliography.

[19] Many people who used his edition were apparently unaware of the 1907 volume and so did not understand why he undertook such a radical re-ordering of the poems.

codicology had not yet emerged as a method of working with manuscripts, and, like other scholars of his age, Champion lacked a conception of the manuscript as an object that could be mined for information. He based his work on two assumptions that do not square with what the makeup of the manuscript tells us: he thought that the manuscript was first made in 1450 and that the primary principle of organization in the manuscript was verse form running in this order: *ballades, chançons, complaintes, caroles, rondels.*

In fact, the poet has left clear evidence that he conceived of lyric form differently than did other lyric poets of his day. Rather than simply sorting his lyrics by form, he envisioned two large categories or kinds of poems, each containing more than one form. Following his introductory narrative, he placed the longer lyrics (the *complainte* and the *ballade*), which were "weightier" than the shorter ones, first.[20] The shorter (the *chançon*, the *carole*, and the *rondel*) followed. How do we know this? Because the poet numbered his *chançons* and *rondels* in one long series. His *ballades* he numbered in a separate series. The *complaintes* (there are only seven, plus the *Songe en complainte*) appear in various places in the manuscript as it now stands (with some intruding in the midst of the shorter lyrics, where they do not belong). There is textual evidence that they belong among the *ballades*, which we can easily see because the poet gave us two instances of quires that contain both forms. The first is the *Songe en complainte* (quire H), in which narrative verse is followed by a *complainte*, which is in turn followed by a series of seven *ballades* (unlike other of the duke's *ballades* in that they are narrative in content, though lyric in form). The other example of the mixing of the two forms is in quire Q, where the *Complainte de France* is followed by two *ballades* and then by a blank leaf with only the heading "Complainte."[21] Though unnumbered, the *caroles* appear at two points in the *chançon/rondel* series.[22] In this edition, then, the reader should expect to encounter *complaintes* among the *ballades* or *caroles* and *chançons* cheek by jowl with *rondels*.

There are a number of departures in his edition from the results he obtained from his analysis, some of them major. Jean-Claude Mühlethaler reverted to the present manuscript order in his edition of the duke's *ballades* and *rondels*.

[20] This idea is borne out by the ordering of the lyrics in the Latin translation of his poems, produced under his watchful eye and copied into Grenoble MS. 873 (see A.E.B. Coldiron, "Translation, Canons, and Cultural Capital: Manuscripts and Reception of Charles d'Orléans's English Poetry," in *Charles d'Orléans in England*, 183–214.).

[21] Words intended to represent scribal practice are flanked by quotation marks, as here. Charles also left evidence that subject matter sometimes trumped verse form. He separated his *ballades* on the subject of love from his *ballades de pluseurs propos*, and he seems to have included his *complaintes* in this same category.

[22] The *chançon* being identified by a two-line refrain at mid-point, the *rondel*, by a one-line refrain.

Because it is not possible in the space of an introduction to rehearse all the evidence and arguments for this new ordering of the duke's poetry, the reader is referred to the more exhaustive analysis of the manuscript in Arn, *The Poet's Notebook*. What follows here is a summary of the more essential arguments presented there to explain some of the differences between this edition and the Champion edition (for a concordance of this poem order with that of Champion's edition, the reader can consult the index of first lines).

The chief tool in sorting out the correct order of the manuscript is the work of successive initial makers, three limners in succession, then two or more rubricators who added red and blue (lombard) initials to the scribes' work. Finally, there is a group of lyrics without any decoration at all, some with scribal initials (for which the scribe left no space for a larger, decorative initial) and some with spaces left for initials that were never added. In all, as Champion determined, there were four major layers or stints (he called them *campaigns*) of copying, each distinguished in large part by the decoration of initials or lack of it.

The homogeneity of the work copied by the first scribe in the late 1430s (what Champion called the *fonds primitif*) makes it difficult to say anything definite about the possible composition order of these poems. The first 121 pages of the manuscript contain a narrative that begins with the speaker's entry into the service of the God of Love and ends with his withdrawal from that service after the death of his lady (the *Songe en complainte*). In addition to this work (if we can call it that) on the subject of love, the stint or run of the first scribe also comprises another series of *ballades* on miscellaneous subjects, *Balades de plusieurs propos* (*ballades* on many subjects), as well as a number of *complaintes*. The name attached to the first two *ballades de plusieurs propos* is "Garencière," so these must have been among the earliest *ballades* the poet composed. An exchange of *ballades* with Philippe le Bon datable to 1439–1440 stands at the other end of this series. This suggests that the early lyrics, copied in the course of the first stint, may have been composed in more or less the order in which they appear in the manuscript, but many may have been arranged more artfully, to serve the narrative impulse. The *chançon* series, also copied by the first scribe, seems to run more or less parallel to the first series of *ballades*; they deal with many of the same themes and comprise a similarly coherent set, but nothing absolute can be said about the composition order of individual poems. Here, however, are some of the more striking differences from Champion's edition to be found in the remainder of the collection.

(1)   At first sight, the headings in the manuscript that identify the shorter forms (*chançon* and *rondel*) look inconsistent, the word "Chançon" sometimes appearing above a *rondel*, the word "rondel" above a *chançon*. The confusion is only apparent, however. The first scribe, writing in England before 1440, was instructed to write the heading ("Chançon") at the top of the leaf but to copy the lyric itself on the lower portion of the leaf. Why? That we do not know for

certain, though a number of reasons have been put forward by scholars. Much later, other scribes were instructed to write their *rondels* in the spaces left above those *chançons*. At this point, then, the page contained the heading "Chançon," beneath it a *rondel*, and at the bottom of the page a *chançon*. Some scribes (of which there were dozens) confused the issue further by writing a heading above the *chançon* (i.e., between the *rondel* supra and the *chançon* infra). Since the term poets customarily used at that point was "rondel," that is what they wrote. The result of this sequence of acts is that each lyric is provided with a label that applies to the other.[23]

Pierre Champion understood this and printed most of the short lyrics in the right verse form collection, but a few (fifteen, in fact) of the *rondels* in quires BB and CC he printed among his *chançons*.[24] In these cases, Champion relied on the headings in the manuscript to identify the *chançons*, whether they contained a one- or two-line refrain in the middle (though he certainly recognized this difference and mentioned it elsewhere). However, though the heading (generally) at the top of the page was "Chançon," the lyric on the lower part of the page was a *rondel* (the opening at pages 354–355 contains four headings that read "Chançon" but four *rondels* beneath them). How could this have happened? It is most likely that the scribe was inattentive, writing headings either on blank pages that had not received lyrics or on pages that contained *rondels* which he was (quite naturally) not reading as he worked. (Although Champion claims to recognize Charles's hand in some of these headings, the letter forms are far too common and the sample far too small to allow for even near-positive identification.)[25] We have sorted the poems by the form on the page (about the interpretation of that form, see John Fox's analysis, §6: Notes on *chançons* and *rondels*). In this edition, those lyrics copied with a one-line refrain remain with the *rondels* (with which they are surrounded), regardless of what heading the scribe wrote above the lyric.

(2)   The reader will encounter a single, undivided run of short lyrics: *chançons*, *caroles*, and *rondels*. The poet included the *chançons* and *rondels* in a single numbering system (1 through 164, at which point the numbering ceases).[26] Though he did not number the *caroles* (there are only four), they are to be found in two places, in both of which they are surrounded by *chançons* and *rondels*, and so they remain here. Moreover, there is here no clean break between a series of *chançons* followed by a series of *rondels* (not to speak of printing them in separate

---

[23] In this edition, such headings are presented in one of two ways: without comment if correct, within square brackets if missing, or simply wrong (see textual notes).

[24] They are R19–R27, R33–R36, and R135–R136.

[25] A list of the autograph poems can be found in Appendix 1.

[26] These numbers entered by the duke can be found in square brackets following each lyric.

volumes, as Champion did). After his return to France, the duke seems to have experimented with the *rondel* form (MS. pages 318 *infra* to 328 *infra*; R1 to R18), revisited for a short time the *chançon* form (MS. pages 329 *infra* to 337 *infra*; Ch64 to Ch72—a group of lyrics that takes up themes in the *rondels* surrounding them), and finally turned his back on the *chançon* form to devote himself to the writing of *rondels,* short lyrics with a one-line central refrain, for the rest of his days.

John Fox offers the following thoughts on this final group of *chançons* surrounded by *rondels:*

> At first sight this appears to be an ill-placed series of *chançons,* coming as it does after several rondels complaining about love: his loyalty to it has been ill rewarded, and he is tired of it all (*Je suis desja d'amour tanné*). However, these nine *chançons* are not in praise of love. Six of them share a common theme related to the love theme with which the main body of *chançons* is concerned, but different all the same: they are all about looks (*Regard*), looking at, and admiring (and in Ch64 desiring) a beautiful woman. This is not a pleasure allotted only to the young. Ch67 continues the theme of the preceding *rondels:* for too long, he says, his heart has been his master; now he is reversing the roles. Ch66 is on a different theme, one that comes in time and time again in the rondels: the promise of Hope that has never been fulfilled. Here he seems disillusioned and certainly no longer young and full of the hope expressed in the *ballades.*
>
> Although headed "Chançon" and given a two-line central refrain, like the first group they can equally well be read with a single-line refrain in both instances. Also, it is noticeable that the last two of the series have very short lines: Ch71, lines of four syllables only, Ch72, five. Such poems occur frequently among the *rondels* (e.g., R131, R139, R149, R153, R172, R337, etc.), but never amongst the earlier *chançons.* It seems that, in this transitional period on his return to France after such a long absence, Charles hesitated for a time as to the best way of recording his shorter poems, while at the same time turning to new subject matter and new verse forms. Whatever the truth concerning Ch64 to Ch72, they are in their right place, not only toward the middle of the manuscript, but also toward the middle years of Charles's life. Beneath its thick veneer of convention and allegory, Charles's poetry charts well enough everyman's journey through life: the callowness, the earnestness and idealism of the early years, the growing disillusionment of the middle years, though the interest in love and beauty has not yet died, the cynicism of the later years (lovers should have their urine examined), and finally the weariness of the last years, the melancholy, the looking back and feeling that it could all have been so much better. These are common experiences.

(3)   Just as the reader will not find the *caroles* presented in a separate section of this edition, so he or she will not find a section devoted to the *complainte.* The *Complainte de France* is surrounded in the manuscript by *ballades,* and it is printed

that way here (as is the *complainte* that forms part of the *Songe en complainte*, which Champion did not extract from the larger whole). The remainder of the *complaintes* currently intrude in the manuscript among the *chançons* and the *caroles*. This is one of the most difficult problems the manuscript presents: where were these lyrics displaced from? Since there is no codicological evidence to point the way, it is necessary to resort to textual evidence to locate them properly. The first *complainte*, which begins on page 299 of the manuscript (on the subject of love), copied by the first scribe, finds its place here at the end of the stint-1 copying of the *ballades*. The rest of the *complaintes*, copied in the third stint, can be found among the *balades de plusieurs propos*, in the vicinity of the *Complainte de France*.[27]

(4)   Two large groups of *rondels* are here in an order different from that of Champion: those on pages 318 *supra* to 429 *supra* of the manuscript (R108–R419, copied only on the upper portions of the page) and those on pages 430 *supra/infra* to 481 *supra/infra* (R210–R211 to R307–R308, copied two to a page). The coherence of each of these blocks of lyrics is easily demonstrable, but their relation to one another is more vexed. The series of lyrics written on the first line *En la forest de Longue Actente* are grouped in two places in the manuscript. One group falls between pages 413 and 417 (R193–R197, in the first of these two groups); the other, between pages 447 and 450 (R244–R247, in the second). Read in Champion's order (MS. pages 430–482 before 318–429),[28] the *rondels* by Thignonville, Philippe Pot, Antoine de Lussay, Guiot Pot, Gilles des Ormes, and Jacques, bâtard de la Tremoille (pages 447si–448si, 450i; R244–R247; see Appendix 3) come first, followed some thirty lyrics later by those of Nevers (413s; R193), Charles himself (414s and 417s; R194 and R197), his wife Marie (415s; R195), and Fredet (416s; R196). This suggests that the duke was a latecomer to the competition rather than its originator. We have restored the order—but not for this reason alone.

There is other, stronger evidence for this new poem order as well. It is generally agreed that, after his return from captivity, the duke attracted many poets and versifiers to himself and to his court at Blois and began to let them copy or have copied their own lyrics into his manuscript. In the course of time, the names of these people were added to identify the authors, sometimes by the scribe, sometimes by the author, sometimes by the duke. It is possible to chart the gathering momentum of this custom. On the lower halves of pages 318 through 428 (over 100 lyrics, copied first; R1–R107), eight authors (other than the duke) are identified. On the upper halves of those leaves (R108–R209), copied next, a further eight names are to be found. But then, on pages 430si through 481si (the second group, with a run of only a little over fifty lyrics; R210–R309), the

---

[27] For a more detailed argument on the placement, see Arn, *The Poet's Notebook*.

[28] He held to this order both in the study that paved the way for his edition (*Le manuscrit autographe*) and in the edition itself.

number jumps to thirty-nine. Parallel to this development, we can see the grad-
ual withdrawal of the duke from the actual copying of lyrics into his manuscript.
On pages 318i through 428i (group 1; R1–R107), fifty autograph lyrics; above
those lyrics (R108–R209), a further twenty-four autograph lyrics; on pages 429si
through 482 (group 2), only three.[29] The evidence points clearly to a progression
of copying that runs 318i–428i, 318s–428s, 430si–482si, and that is the order in
which we have printed the lyrics here.

(5)   The reader will also find a run of *rondels* in this edition (247s–291s;
R310–R357) in reverse order from Champion's edition. These lyrics, written
on the upper halves of pages (above lyrics copied much earlier), begin at an odd
spot in the manuscript, near the end of the first quire of *chançons* (T), which runs
from manuscript pages 235 to 250. The first *chançons*, copied in England by the
first scribe, are limned with initials bearing long, graceful sprays in the margins.
Why didn't the scribe simply begin at the beginning of those blank spaces on
page 235, instead of leaving twelve empty spaces and starting only on page 247?
Champion himself noted that this series of *rondels* appeared in reverse order in
the Carpentras manuscript belonging to Marie de Clèves, copied from her husband's manuscript in the mid- to late 1450s.[30] What apparently happened is this:
his vellum was filling up and the poet was uncertain how many lyrics would
have to be accommodated. Still not quite willing to see all the spaces above
the original *chançons* filled with later lyrics (and those opening *chançons* give us
some of the most beautiful work of the first limner of the manuscript), the poet
decided to have the scribe begin in the *last* available space, on page 250, and work
back toward the beginning of the *chançon* series. He then, at some point, added
the final four quires of new vellum to the manuscript and at that point asked
the scribe(s) to begin working near the end of the manuscript. The copyists of
Marie's manuscript, knowing nothing of the progression of copying in his exem-
plar, simply copied the lyrics in order as they appeared to them.

(6)   Finally, we have found no compelling reason to follow Champion in
excluding either seven of the nine English lyrics or the three final lyrics in the
manuscript from the text. Champion printed all of them in the notes to his edition
because he was not convinced that they were copied under the duke's direction.[31]
The two English roundels printed in his collection of *chançons* were, he claimed,
copied by the duke;[32] the remaining seven lyrics (six *rondels* and a *ballade*) he was

---

[29] See Appendix 1 and Champion's list of lyrics in the duke's hand in *Le manuscrit
autographe*, 8–11.

[30] See Champion, *Le manuscrit autographe*, 49–50.

[31] See Champion, *Poésies*, 569–72 and 594–95.

[32] Johan Gerritsen has disputed this; Gilbert Ouy has confirmed it. The question
remains open. I am most grateful to both for invaluable help in analyzing the manuscript.

inclined to ascribe to some Englishman traveling in the entourage of the duke of Suffolk in 1444, on his journey to escort Margaret of Anjou, Henry VI's bride, to England.[33] Whoever the author(s) of these poems may be, we feel that they should take their place in the main body of the text. Of the last three *rondels*, one is unascribed; the other two open with the same phrase (*Gardez vous bien*), one of them by the duc de Bourbon, the other by Pierre Danche.[34] Though they follow the last lyric composed by the duke, and though the duke's final lyric has a strong valedictory tone, we have no reason to believe that they were composed and copied long after the preceding poetry. We see no reason, therefore, to remove these three lyrics from the end of the edited text.

∼

We hope that this revised and improved order of lyrics will make possible a somewhat clearer picture of the development of the poet's art.[35] Because Charles ordered his manuscript both by verse form and by time period, adding new lyrics to each section as he wrote them, it is possible to read his poetry in a number of quite different ways. The reader can read the early work as a narrative, beginning with the induction of the poet into the service of Love and ending soon after the lover's retrieval of his heart from Love and withdrawal to the *château* of *Nonchaloir* (the castle of indifference), a narrative that then ceases. The story, sketchy as it is, gives way to a purely lyric spirit, but that body of lyric has its own structural principles. The reader can divide the poetry mentally into two categories: poems about love of the *fin'amor* variety and poems on miscellaneous subjects. The poet laid the groundwork for such a reading when he had some of his *ballades* copied under the rubric "Balades de plusieurs propos" to distinguish them from the love poetry that precedes them. On the other hand, reading horizontally across the forms can produce a picture of a poet at a certain stage in his artistic life. To do so, the reader would read three parallel collections: one beginning at the beginning, one beginning with the *Complainte de France*, and one beginning with the *chançons*. Reading vertically in a single form can illuminate the poet's development in that form. Most readers, of course, will simply pick and choose, sampling what interests them most.

---

[33] See Champion, *Poésies*, 569. He thought mistakenly that the scribe was English.

[34] Bourbon (Clermont) contributed nine other lyrics to the duke's collection (see Appendix 3). Danche is otherwise unrepresented in this collection, though his work appears in other fifteenth-century collections (see, e.g., Françoise Fery-Hue, *Au grey d'amours*, special issue of *Le moyen français*, 27–28 [1991]).

[35] A list of individual lyrics in Champion's order and in this new order can be found in *The Poet's Notebook*, pp. 194–197, and a synoptic table with more detailed information can be found on the CD-Rom that accompanies the volume.

§3 Charles de Valois, duc d'Orléans: historical background

The life of Charles d'Orléans (1394–1465) can be read in a variety of ways. The historian's duke and prince is a shrewd man of political importance at a critical point in French history who lived through great misfortune — a prisoner of war, a diplomat, a politician, a political prisoner; an able administrator. The duke of the bibliographer and the manuscript specialist is a book collector and bibliophile both learned and devout, a man of many serious interests. The literary historian sees Charles, the host of the "salon" at his favorite château in the Loire valley, offering hospitality to other poets. The literary scholar deals with Charles the narrator/lover, who trades the passion of youth for the resignation of *nonchaloir*, an author of great imagination and prodigious linguistic and technical skills. The paragraphs that follow are an attempt to sketch briefly the rich human contexts of the poetry he wrote.

Charles was born in the palace of St.-Pol in Paris in November of 1394 to Louis d'Orléans, brother of Charles VI, and Valentina Visconti of Milan, daughter of Giangaleazzo Visconti, the duke of Milan, and Isabelle de Valois. He was reared in surroundings of fabulous wealth that included an exceptionally large and growing library to which both of his parents contributed. He seems to have been given his first illuminated manuscript, a *petit livre* bound in *cuir de Cordoan vermeil* (red leather from Cordoba), in 1401; this was followed in 1403 by a psalter.[36] In May of 1404, his father Louis installed his own secretary, Nicolas Garbet, a fine Latinist and a theologian, as tutor to his three sons: Charles, then comte d'Angoulême, aged ten; Philippe, comte de Vertus, aged eight; and little Jean, about four (a daughter, Margaret, was born in 1401).[37] At about the same time, Valentina acquired another child, also named Jean. He was the son of Louis d'Orléans and Mariette d'Enghien, dame de Cany, but Valentina reared him as her own. Louis later made him comte de Dunois. To the Frenchmen of his day, however, he became known as the companion of Jeanne d'Arc and most loyal defender of his half-brother Charles. He wore as a badge of honor the name of Bâtard d'Orléans.

---

[36] *Deux petis livres pour MS. d'Angoulesme et pour Philippe* (two little books for Charles, lord of Angoulême, and for Philippe). The content of this first book is not specified, but it was described at the time as *enluminé d'or et d'azur et de vermeillon* (illuminated with gold, azure, and red) — an extraordinarily fine book for a small child, purchased for *lx s. p.* (60 sols of Paris; de Laborde, *Les ducs de Bourgogne*, #5941). The psalter purchased for him must have been even more lavish, for it cost twenty-one *écus* (Léopold Delisle, *Le cabinet des manuscrits de la Bibliothèque impériale* [Paris: Imprimerie Impériale, 1868–1881], 1:103). The psalter cost Louis d'Orléans something in the neighborhood of 4 times the price of the first book, itself adorned with gold.

[37] See Joseph de Croÿ, "Notices biographiques," in *Cartulaire de la ville de Blois (1196–1493)*, ed. Jacques Soyer and Guy Trouillard, Extrait des *Mémoires de la Société des Sciences et Lettres de Loir-et-Cher* 17 (1903–1907) (Paris: C. Migault, 1907): 298–99.

In 1396, Valentina was banished from the court because the queen, Isabeau (or someone close to her), was jealous of her influence over the mentally unbalanced Charles VI. She withdrew with her children, their tutor, and a large train to the domains of her husband on or near the Loire river, far (in those days) from the overheated atmosphere of royal Paris. For eleven years she moved from château to château: Asnières, Coucy, Villers-Cotterêts, Châteauneuf, Crépy, Montils, Blois, and her favorite, Château-Thierry.

Meanwhile, in the capital the periodic incapacity of the king intensified the rivalry between Louis d'Orléans and Jean sans Peur, duc de Bourgogne, who both seem to have put their own interests ahead of those of their people. Hostilities among these three were exacerbated by Jean sans Peur's alliance with England. Then in November of 1407, the imprudent Jean arranged to have Louis assassinated in a dark Paris street by his henchmen. Going even further, he had Louis denounced from the pulpit by Jean Petit as a vile man, guilty of every vice, including murder and necromancy. Valentina embarked immediately and tirelessly on an attempt to clear her husband's name. Aided by Guillaume Cousinot, the chancellor of the duchy and a staunch supporter of her rights, she tried to exact some form of justice from the king on his murderers, but her attempts were largely fruitless and she died only a year later, in December of 1408. Thus Charles inherited a new title, duc d'Orléans, at the age of fourteen.[38]

In June of 1406, Louis had married his eldest son to the boy's cousin Isabelle (five years his senior), the eldest daughter of Charles VI. The unfortunate bride, already the young widow of Richard II of England, bore Charles one child, a daughter Jeanne, in September 1409, and died in childbirth. Charles was fifteen. In 1410, the young duke, realizing his need for allies in a land where the king was sane only intermittently, took as his second wife the eleven-year-old Bonne d'Armagnac, daughter of Bernard VII, comte d'Armagnac and later *connestable* of France.[39] Bernard was a warrior of reputation who had been in the pay of Charles's father, and his men were feared both for their fighting abilities and for their ruthlessness. By sealing an alliance with the Gascons, Charles hoped to balance the ever-increasing power and aggression of Jean sans Peur, whose lands in the Low Countries, at the time a flourishing center of the trade in northern Europe and beyond, had greatly expanded his wealth and the length of his political arm. Charles became the head of the Orléans faction before his twentieth

---

[38] It was not until January of 1413 that Louis d'Orléans was exonerated (the king having recovered his senses for a time). Jean Gerson, chancellor of the University of Paris, preached at the obsequies in the presence of Louis's children and les ducs de Berry, d'Alençon, de Bourbon, Louis de Bavière, le comte de Richemont, and a host of clerics, nobles, and lesser people (Champion, *Vie*, 131; Enguerrand de Monstrelet, *The Chronicles of Enguerrand de Monstrelet*, trans. Thomas Johnes [London: W. Smith, 1840], 1.319–21).

[39] For a definition of these and other terms applied to household functionaries, see Gonzalez, *Un prince*.

birthday. His own forces and those of Bernard were augmented by those of Jean, duc de Berry, Jean, duc de Bretagne, Jean, comte d'Alençon, Jean, comte de Clermont, and Jean, duc de Bourbon. The ensuing hostilities brought the country to the verge of civil war.

The duc d'Orléans felt a desperate need for more troops, and it was his misfortune to look to England for help in the winter of 1412. Negotiations with the English went on for some months, and when the treaty was signed on 18 May it seemed the English made out very well. The timing was in all respects unfortunate for *les frères Orléans*. The king took a turn for the better just in time to realize that a foreign army was about to invade his country and that it was all the fault of the duc d'Orléans. Charles's allies abandoned him, leaving him to face the problem of a very large force of Englishmen about to arrive, fully armed, on his shores, soldiers that he no longer had any way of paying. Forced to attend a gathering at Auxerre in August attended by all the French factions, Charles and his brother Philippe had no option but to sign a new treaty renouncing their treaty with the English. The terms were punishing. In addition to a staggering amount of money (210,000 *écus*), one of the parties, John Cornwall, demanded hostages who were to remain in his hands until the money owed him (some 21,375 *écus*) was received. Because it was customary that at least one of the hostages be a member of the debtor's family, the young duke sent his twelve-year-old brother, Jean d'Angoulême, to England as a hostage, never guessing that it would be thirty-three years till he would stand again on French soil. Throughout this period, Charles was attempting to clear his father's name of Jean sans Peur's false accusations and to see Jean punished for Louis's murder. At least the second of these he succeeded in seeing in 1413, at the age of nineteen. In a remarkably symmetrical turn of events, Jean was himself assassinated in 1419 — whether at the behest of the king or not is unclear — and was succeeded by his son, Philippe le Bon.[40]

Then in 1415 the battle against the English at Agincourt changed everything. Against an English army under Henry V, Charles took the field as part of a force made up of an exceptionally large number of nobles who faced a proportionally large corps of longbowmen led by a smaller group of English nobles. When the battle ended Charles was taken prisoner, along with the duc de Bourbon and a number of other French noblemen. In the standard retelling of the

---

[40] There is evidence that dynastic pressures did not entirely occlude the young duke's pleasure in literature, which was always at hand. Eustache Deschamps, Oton de Granson, Christine de Pizan, and Jean, duc de Bourbon, were all part of his parents' world and thus to some extent of his own (see, e.g., I. S. Laurie, "Eustache Deschamps, 1340(?)–1404," in *Eustache Deschamps, French Courtier-Poet*, ed, Deborah M. Sinnreich-Levi [New York: AMS Press, 1998], 22–31; Champion, *Vie*, 26–28 and 236–37; Charity Cannon Willard, *Christine de Pizan* [New York: Persea Books, 1984], 51–53, 66, 82, 165–69, and passim).

story, the young duke (he was almost twenty-one)[41] is knighted on the eve of battle,[42] takes the field in the vanguard,[43] falls early in the fight, and is later hauled unhurt from under a pile of corpses and taken off to England by Henry V, who taunts him with the bitterness of the French defeat.[44] What the reader of these sometimes oversimplified and sometimes biased accounts may overlook is that, as the head of the Armagnac coalition, the duke was no stranger to arms, despite his youth. If he was indeed made commander of the forces at Agincourt, this was in recognition of the skills he had already demonstrated.[45] He had headed the Armagnac party for some five years, fortifying towns and castles, recruiting troops, and marching more than once to battle with his forces. The fact that these campaigns ended in disadvantageous settlements does not diminish the fact that the duke knew what it meant to put himself in armor at the head of an army. That he fell early in the battle points to his being in the crush of bodies and horses in the first attack, which is confirmed by that fact that he was discovered by the English (as were many others) under a pile of corpses. Though he probably did not consider himself fortunate at the time, his survival can probably be attributed to the protection his plate armor afforded; many others were suffocated in the crush of human and animal bodies at the battle line.

On 11 November 1415, the king embarked for Dover with some of the most valuable captives, the ducs d'Orléans and de Bourbon being the greatest prizes. Henry was received with a grand display by the English as he paraded his captives through the London streets. So began Charles's twenty-five years of captivity in England, during which, after a short stay in the Tower of London and another at Windsor Castle, he was handed on from the custody of one nobleman

---

[41] Monstrelet, *Chronicles*, chap. 147, in Anne Curry, *Battle of Agincourt* (Woodbridge and Rochester: Boydell and Brewer, 2000), 156; trans. Johnes, 1.339.

[42] This detail is mentioned in only one of the many accounts of the battle (*La chronique d'Enguerran de Monstrelet*, ed. L. Douët-D'Arcq [Paris: Renouard, 1857–1862], 3.89–124; see Anne Curry, *Agincourt* [Stroud: Tempus, 2005], 180, and eadem, *The Battle of Agincourt*, 156).

[43] le Héraut Berry (?1450s), in *Les Chroniques du roi Charles VII*, ed. Henri Couteault and Léonce Celier (Paris: C. Klincksieck, 1979), 64–71; see Curry, *Battle of Agincourt*, 181.

[44] See Champion, *Vie*, 152–53, for the imagined conversation between the duke and Henry on the way to England by Le Fèvre de Saint-Rémy (*Chronique de Jean le Fèvre*, ed. François Morand [Paris: Renouard, 1877]).

[45] This is maintained in at least two of the French sources, one anonymous, the other by Jean Juvenal des Ursins: *Chronique anonyme du règne de Charles VI*, ed. J. Fr. Michaud (Paris: Editeur du commentaire analytique du code civil, 1836), in Douët-D'Arcq, ed., *Enguerran de Monstrelet*, 6.228–30 (see Anne Curry, *The Battle of Agincourt: Sources and Interpretations* [Woodbridge and Rochester: Boydell Press, 2000], 114–15), and Jean Juvenal des Ursins, *Histoire de Charles VI*, ed. Fr. Michaud. (Paris: Editeur du commentaire analytique du code civil, 1836), ser. 1, 2.518–20 (see Curry, *Sources*, 132).

to another.[46] He did not, however, live in isolation. He had a number of French servants around him, including a French secretary; he received delegations from his French estates regularly; and he travelled frequently in the company of one or other of his keepers on various kinds of business.[47] One that occupied him constantly was the raising of money to pay the ransoms for both himself and his brother Jean, and for a second time money flowed from the duke's coffers into English pockets, this time in a more or less steady stream.

The first half of the fifteenth century was a period of upheaval in both France and England. Charles VI's intermittent insanity, and the rivalry between Louis d'Orléans and Jean sans Peur, the usurpation of Richard II's throne and the early death of Henry IV, the short reign of Henry V, which left a nine-month-old child on the throne, and the rivalry of Humphrey, duke of Gloucester, and John, duke of Bedford, each attempting to wrest power from the other during Henry VI's minority—all resulted in dramatic swings in policy depending on who held power at any given time. Charles was involved in peace negotiations between the English and the French as early as 1433, travelling up and down the country and across the Channel to Normandy, but, despite his best efforts, he was caught up in forces much greater than any single man could control, or even influence very much. Gloucester and his adherents feared that the return of Charles to France would result in a reunification of that country and put an end to England's hopes for wealth and dominion on the Continent.[48] In a document in which Humphrey set out his objections just prior to the release of the duke in 1440, he wrote,

> First, it is not unknown to *my Lord* and all his Counseill, as be comune reporte and fame, the Indysposition [i.e., insanity] of *my said Lord's Adversarie* [the French king] that he neither hath Wisdom nor Discretion to

---

[46] One of the most well-known and oft-reprinted of all medieval miniatures is that of the duke in the Tower of London, taken from a late fifteenth-century manuscript of his poetry (London, British Library, MS. Royal 16.F.ii) owned by the English royal family. For some of the reasons for the long duration of the duke's captivity, see Michael K. Jones, "'Gardez mon corps, sauvez ma terre'—Immunity from War and the Lands of a Captive Knight," in *Charles d'Orléans in England*, ed. Mary-Jo Arn (Woodbridge and Rochester: Boydell and Brewer, 2000), 9–26. It was claimed that on his deathbed Henry V had forbidden his release until Henry VI (at this point nine months old) came of age. For a fuller account of his years in England, see William Askins, "The Brothers Orléans and Their Keepers," in *Charles d'Orléans in England*, ed. Arn, 27–45; Mary-Jo Arn, *Fortunes Stabilnes* (Binghamton: MRTS, 1999), 12–26; and Lucy de Angulo, "Charles and Jean d'Orléans," in *Miscellanea di studi e ricerche sul quattrocento francese* (Turin: Giappichelli, 1967), 52–92.

[47] For his movements around England, see Champion, *Vie*, "Itinéraire," 663–72. This chronology is undoubtedly incomplete.

[48] It is worth remembering that in 1422 Charles was second in line for the throne of France.

Governe himselfe, but must be led, for defaut of Naturell Raison, aftur th'entent of theym that have hym for the tyme in Governance; and his Eldest Sonne also in the same wise disposed: Wherefore me thinketh, considering the grete Subtilte and Cauteleux [wily] Disposition of *the said Duc of Orlians*, whch is so well know to all my said Lordes Conseil, they shuld never conseille, advise, nor assent to his said Deliveraunce or Enlargissement [release]: for it is to presume that he, beyng so nyghe of the [royal] Blode, and of such Discretion as he is named, that *the Adverse Partie* [the French], by the Advis of the Lordes, with assent of the Three Estates ther, wul yif hym the Governaunce and make hym their Regent; and he, knowyng the disposition here, that he wulde labour to ony Meene of Peas [kind of peace] that shuld be worshipfull or profitable to *my said Lord*, I cannot think it.[49]

In the late 1420s, a young French girl named Jeanne d'Arc had hoped for the same outcome Gloucester feared and made the release of the good duke from his captivity in England one of the major goals of her mission. She knew that God loved the duc d'Orléans because she had more revelations concerning him than of any man living, except the king himself.[50] She was determined to deliver him from English captivity. When asked how, she replied that she would first try to exchange him for English prisoners but, if that failed, she would cross the sea and take him by force. Asked whether Saints Margaret and Katherine had told her absolutely and without condition that she would have enough prisoners to exchange for the duke, she said yes, and she added that if she had had three years to accomplish this, she would have succeeded.[51] She was never given the opportunity to try.

As the years passed, though Bedford and his followers were interested in peace, they found it difficult to negotiate with the French nobility, whose position kept changing with the shifts of power and health of the king. The result, at least as far as Charles was concerned, was stasis — twenty-five years of

---

[49] Thomas Rymer, *Foedera conventiones* (London: Joannes Neaulme, 1841), vol. 5, parts 1–2, 76–77; orig. ed. 10:764–68 (2 June 1440).

[50] 22 February 1431 (*Procès de condamnation de Jeanne d'Arc*, ed. Pierre Tisset [Paris: C. Klincksieck, 1960], 1:50–51).

[51] 12 March 1431 (*Procès*, ed. Tisset, 1:128–29). Years later, in 1443, the duke gave the Ile aux Bœufs, on the shores of the Loire, to Pierre d'Arc *en faveur et contemplation de Jeanne la Pucelle, sa sœur* (in favor and remembrance of Joan the Maid, his sister) (*Procès*, ed. Tisset, 2.54, n. 1). The fact that the duke never mentioned Jeanne in his poetry is unremarkable. He did not mention Dunois, either, or write mourning poems about any of his family (his parents, his first two wives, or his brothers) or of Garencières, with whom he had a strong literary relationship. He reserved his mourning for "the lady," who may or may not have been a real person. The generous provisions he made for the Arc family were at least a tacit acknowledgment of all that was owed to Jeanne.

intermittent but fruitless negotiation.[52] Philippe le Bon eventually took an interest in peace between England and France, perhaps influenced by his wife, Isabelle de Portugal.[53] She seems to have taken an exceptional interest in bringing the duc d'Orléans home. Following intensive negotiations with the English in the late 1430s, she was instrumental in forging an agreement acceptable to both sides. Despite Gloucester's fury, Charles returned to France in November 1440 at the age of forty-six (by one account speaking better English than French) and was almost immediately married to the fourteen-year-old niece of Philippe and Isabelle, Marie de Clèves.[54]

Though finally free, Charles was burdened with raising an enormous ransom, an obligation which, after the payment of the English army and raising of ransom during his captivity, constituted the third great impoverishment of the house of Orléans.[55] From his seat at Blois, he crisscrossed northern France, visiting other noble households and in the process raising money, meeting younger noblemen, negotiating informal alliances, and firming up his position in a France that must have seemed in many ways strange to him, after a quarter of a century spent abroad.[56] In the ensuing years he worked tirelessly to forge a peace agreement between France and England, which he brought to partial fruition with the Treaty of Tours (in fact a five-year truce rather than an outright cessation of hostilities, but no less welcome for that).

The years that followed were filled with activity, both diplomatic and administrative. He never again played a major role in politics, but as the third person of the kingdom, he had meetings to attend and negotiations to further; there were renovations to be made at Blois and his much-enlarged library to install there;[57] as the heir of the lands of Asti, and the dukedom of Milan from

---

[52] See Jones, "'Gardez mon corps'."

[53] Her parents were John of Gaunt's daughter, Philippa of Lancaster and King João I of Portugal.

[54] His second wife, Bonne d'Armagnac, died childless in the 1430s. Marie, his third wife, was the daughter of Adolf I, duc de Clèves, who married Philippe's sister, Marie de Bourgogne (she was also the sister of Catherine de Clèves, whose book of hours is available in a modern facsimile edition [*The Hours of Catherine of Cleves* (New York: George Braziller, n.d.)] and the granddaughter of Charles V). She was reared in the household of Philippe and Isabelle. The comment on Charles's fluency in English is found in Edward Hall, *Hall's Chronicle* (London: J. Johnson, 1809, 193), written some two centuries after the fact and probably fantasy or folklore.

[55] On 2 July 1440 the ransom was set at 100,000 nobles, of which 40,000 was to be paid at once.

[56] See Claudio Galderisi, "Charles d'Orléans et l''autre' langue," in *Charles d'Orléans in England*, ed. Arn, 79–87; and *Fortunes Stabilnes*, ed. Arn, 39–45.

[57] L. Jarry, *Le châtelet d'Orléans* (Orléans : H. Herluison, 1873), 8, 13–19; Pascale Thibault, *La bibliothèque de Charles dOrléans et de Louis XII*. Blois: Les Amis de la Bibliothèque de Blois, 1989.

his mother Valentina, he felt an obligation to maintain his claim and to act as a good lord to the Astesan people (he led an army to Italy in an unsuccessful attempt to reclaim his mother's lands but finally gave the dukedom up for lost in 1449). Finally, there would be, belatedly, a new family to enjoy—Marie (b. 1457), Louis (b. 1462, who took the throne in 1498 as Louis XII), and Anne (b. 1464). After 1451, he seems to have settled down at Blois to give his full attention to his domestic life, his library, his friends, and poetry. Not that poetry had ever *not* been part of his life, in good times and bad, but the lyrics of his last years are ripe with the kind of reflection that comes only when the distractions of dynasty, of politics, and of care are stilled. He died in January 1465 at the age of seventy.

For an estimate of the man, his enemies provide (not without a touch of irony) a clearer picture than do his countrymen, who were more likely to comment on his poetic or rhetorical skills than his character.[58] In the royal document drawn up to counter the furious outburst of Humphrey, duke of Gloucester, at the plan to release the duke in 1440, Henry VI refers to the duc d'Orléans as "a grete and a felle-witted [very intelligent/acute/shrewd/subtle] man."[59] As we have seen, the king's uncle recognized Charles's "cautelous disposition."[60]

§4 Charles d'Orléans, reader, book collector, patron

The duke's literary life was multifaceted. He loved books, was an avid reader, had a keen sense of bibliographic beauty, enjoyed the company of other writers, was proficient in more than one language, and enjoyed intensely verbal play in his own and in other languages, experimenting with a variety of metrical and verse forms. His book-collecting habits were influenced by those of his father, whose library he inherited in his youth. He undertook, for instance, to continue (though he never finished) the great project to produce a French translation of the Bible in eleven volumes that Charles V had begun and his father Louis had carried on,[61] and he bought books or had them copied throughout his life. Finding himself in England, he began asking for books to be brought to him by members of

---

[58] See, e.g., Jean-Claude Mühlethaler, ed., *Charles d'Orléans*, 14–16. For Martin Le Franc's estimate of the duke, see Gérard Gros's excellent article, "Le livre du prince et le clerc," in *L'ecrivain éditeur*, ed. François Bessire (Geneva: Droz, 2001), 43–58 (in which he argues for Martin le Franc's attentive scrutiny of Charles's opening narrative); see also Champion, *Vie*, 235.

[59] Joseph Stevenson, ed., *Letters and Papers* (London: Longman, 1864), 2:459.

[60] The word "cautelous" can mean "wise" or "prudent," but it also carries the implication of "crafty" or "wily," especially when Humphrey couples it with reference to the duke's "grete Subtilte." For *rondels* in praise of the duke from the pens of Robertet and Cadier, see Champion, *Poésies*, 603–4.

[61] See A.-J.-V. Le Roux de Lincy, *Les quatre livres des rois* (Paris: Imprimerie royale, 1841), xx–xxi, and, for example, de Laborde, *Les ducs de Bourgogne*, #6175.

his household from his library at Blois, but he did not hesitate to acquire other books in his more immediate vicinity.[62] He employed both French and English scribes, artists, and limners to produce books for him, whether for his own use or for gifts to others. The elegant book of prayers the copying of which he commissioned (BnF MS. lat. 1196), decorated by English artists, is an especially fine example.[63] No books in English can be associated with his period of captivity, unless Kathleen Scott is correct in her surmise that he was the commissioner of Corpus Christi College Cambridge MS. 61, a copy of Geoffrey Chaucer's *Troilus and Criseyde*, which contains the famous frontispiece in which Chaucer is represented speaking to a group of high noblemen, the central (standing) figure being the duke himself.[64] In any case, Charles certainly read English poetry, including that of Chaucer, Gower, and others,[65] and there were quantities of French poems circulating in England during his captivity, to which he certainly had access.[66]

The fact that he owned many copies of some books (as many as seven of the *Consolatio philosophiae* of Boethius) suggests that, at least on occasion, he acquired a book for its physical characteristics (or as a potential gift, which is not entirely a separate purpose), rather than as a reading text. We know that he had copies of his French poetry made as gifts to other people.[67] That he was interested in his

---

[62] Probably when his library at Blois was sent away for safekeeping, first to Saumur, then to La Rochelle between the siege of Orléans (1428) and 1436 (see Mary-Jo Arn, "A Need for Books: Charles d'Orléans and His Travelling Libraries in England and France." *Journal of the Early Book Society* 12 [2009], 77–98).

[63] See Kathleen Scott, "Limner-Power," in *Prestige, Authority and Power*, ed. Felicity Riddy (York: York Medieval Press, 2000), 55–75; for plates, see Kathleen Scott, *Later Gothic Manuscripts* (London: Harvey Miller, 1996), 1:227, 228, 232–35, 237, 238, and 2:178–82.

[64] Scott, "Limner-Power," 73–75, and eadem, *Later Gothic Manuscripts*, 1:242, and 2:182–85. See also the facsimile of Geoffrey Chaucer's *Troilus*, in the bibliography. The miniature is frequently reproduced. There is evidence in the duke's English poetry that he knew Chaucer's poem (see *Fortunes Stabilnes*, ed. Arn, 42).

[65] See Galderisi, "Charles d'Orléans et l'"autre" langue," and *Fortunes Stabilnes*, ed. Arn, 39–45.

[66] See Julia Boffey, *Manuscripts of English Courtly Love Lyrics* (Woodbridge and Rochester: Boydell and Brewer, 1985); Ardis Butterfield, "Chaucerian Vernaculars," Biennial Chaucer Lecture. *Studies in the Age of Chaucer* 31 (2009), 25–51; and the monographs of Jane H. M. Taylor: *The Poetry of François Villon* (Cambridge: Cambridge University Press, 2001) and *The Making of Poetry*.

[67] His wife Marie de Clèves's manuscript was copied from his; he had a copy made for Madame d'Argueil (see Pierre Champion, *La librairie de Charles d'Orléans* [Paris: Honoré Champion, 1910]), lx; and Françoise Robin, "Le luxe des collections aux XIVe et XVe siècles," in *Les bibliothèques médiévales*, ed. André Vernet [Paris: Promodis, 1989], 1: 193–214, here 194); and there are various entries in his accounts of payments to scribes to copy "ballades," a generic term for poems. It has been suggested that the Harley manuscript of his English poetry was made for the same purpose (i.e., as a gift). For a useful

books both as a collection and as a valuable financial resource is evidenced in the inventories that survive from various periods.[68] Back at Blois after his release he set about constructing in the tower a new library to hold his collection.[69]

Charles had been surrounded by poetry and poets all his life. For the young prince, poets were not a breed apart from other men and women; they were often members of the household, retainers of one sort or another, visiting nobles or dignitaries, or people who hoped to gain the favor of the duke by what they wrote. Works by Christine de Pizan were in the household, as were those of Jean Froissart and Eustache Deschamps (a staunch friend of Valentina's and steward of Louis's).[70] In fact, Louis himself contributed a *ballade* to *Les cent ballades* (under the title Monseigneur de Touraine), by Jean le Seneschal,[71] and he almost certainly composed other lyrics that do not survive. Prior to Agincourt, Charles exchanged *ballades* with his father's *chambellan/maître d'hotel*, Jean de Garencières.[72] Poetry was a common (if highly constructed) form of communication, witness his exchange with Philippe le Bon (who was no poet) in the year or so prior to his release from English captivity.[73] The epistolary *ballade* was one of the duke's favorite forms.[74]

---

table that allows comparison between libraries of fifteenth-century noble and royal book owners, see Geneviève Hasenohr, "L'Essor des bibliothèques privées," in *Les bibliothèques médiévales*, ed. Vernet, 214–63, here 249.

[68] See de Laborde, *Les ducs de Bourgogne*; Pierre Champion, *Un inventaire des papiers de Charles d'Orléans*. (Paris: Honoré Champion, 1912).

[69] See Jarry, *Le chatelet d'Orléans*, 8, 13–19.

[70] On all three, see Champion, *Vie*, passim. For Deschamps's role in the household of Louis, see Gonzalez, *Un prince en son Hôtel*, and Willard, *Christine de Pizan*, 169. On Froissart, see le baron de Joursanvault, *Catalogue analytique des archives de M. le baron de Joursanvault* (Paris: J. Techener, 1838), #833; on Deschamps, #837, #844, #846, 142–43. Christine dedicated a number of her early works to Louis: her *Epistre d'Othéa* (Willard, *Christine*, 166), her *Dit de la Rose* in 1402 (82, 167), the *Débat de deux amants*, in which the debate was to be judged by Louis d'Orléans (65, 166), and a series of *ballades* (166).

[71] *Les cent ballades*, ed. Gaston Reynand. SATF. Paris: Firmin-Didot, 1905. Charles owned a copy (probably his father's), and it seems to have gone to England and come back with him (Champion, *La librairie*, 30).

[72] See B116 and B117 (Champion, *Vie*, 245 and note; Champion, *Poésies*, 2.620). Champion is mistaken, however, when he writes that Garencières contributed to *Les cent ballades* (*Vie*, 237).

[73] See B127 to B131.

[74] For which see Martin Camargo, *The Middle English Verse Love Epistle* (Tübingen: Max Niemeyer, 1991), 98–121.

Charles composed poetry in at least three languages, French, English, and Latin,[75] sometimes mixing them in his macaronic lyrics.[76] He spent many years in England, had an Italian mother, and inherited from her lands in the region of Asti and Milan. The few Italian words in his poetry he used to express his exasperation at the lack of cooperation he faced when trying to reclaim those lands (see R140). In addition to the nine English lyrics in this volume (if indeed they are from his pen), the poet composed during his captivity a work that has been titled *Fortunes Stabilnes*, a collection of English lyrics (two series of *ballades* and one of roundels) framed by narrative sections that include, among other things, two dream visions.[77] During his captivity, in addition to the Latin *carole* in this volume (*carole* 4), the poet composed *Canticum amoris* a religious poem in the Franciscan mold.[78]

The duke was widely read in theology and religion, science and medicine, ethics, chess, history, and literature (classical and modern). He owned works by Jean Gerson, Virgil, Gaston Phébus, Jean de Meun, Sallust, Joachim de Fiore, Cicero, John Mandeville, Alain Chartier, Nicholas of Lyra, Ovid, Guillaume de Deguilleville, Vegetius, and Petrarch, to name a few. He owned a *Tacuinum sanitatis* (a health handbook), a *Legende dorée* (Golden Legend), and many saints' lives, as well as work by Aristotle and Anselm, Bartholomaeus Anglicus and Brunetto Latini.[79] The duke himself was an excellent Latinist (evidently a good pupil of Nicholas Garbet, his tutor), as the high percentage of Latin texts among

---

[75] Valentina owned a few German (or Flemish) manuscripts, and one wonders whether Charles may have known at least a few words in that language as well. The duke was only twenty-one when he was taken to England, and it was certainly in his interest to know what his English captors were saying or writing to one another.

[76] See note to B106.

[77] The work runs to 6531 lines. Some scholars and critics have questioned the authorship of these poems. For details, see the bibliography by Claudio Galderisi, *Charles d'Orléans* (Bari: Adriatica, [1994]); see also "Bibliographical Supplement," in *Charles d'Orléans in England*, ed. Arn, 215–25. His English poetry is edited in *Fortunes Stabilnes*, ed. Arn. For a discussion of his *anglicisation*, see Galderisi, "Charles d'Orléans et l'"autre' langue."

[78] Gilbert Ouy, "Un poème mystique de Charles d'Orléans: le *Canticum amoris*," *Studi francesi* 7 (1959): 64–84; de Angulo, "Charles et Jean d'Orléans"; see also Gilbert Ouy, "Recherches sur la librairie de Charles d'Orléans et de Jean d'Angoulème," in *Académie des inscriptions et belles-lettres* (1955): 273–88. A speech the duke made in defence of his son-in-law, the duc d'Alençon, who was accused of treason, is replete with Latin quotations from a wide variety of sources. It is interesting to note that he always provides a translation (rather like a schoolmaster teaching his pupils!), evidently not expecting all his audience to understand the Latin. The speech also reveals that he was more of a scholar than an orator. Not surprisingly, it was completely ineffective in saving the man's life (see Champion, *Vie*, 534–51).

[79] See Champion, *La librairie*.

his manuscript acquisitions (rather than the French translations of the sort preferred by his bibliophile father) attest, including his prayerbook (BnF MS. lat.
1196), in which some of the prayers were of his own composition.

It is worth wondering why the duke never employed the new poetic forms
coming out of Italy. He was nominally the duke of Milan, he travelled to Italy
himself, his mother was Italian, he knew at least some colloquial Italian, members
of his court travelled to and fro between Blois and Milan, the brothers Astesano
came north to make manuscripts for him at Blois. Surely he was not unaware of
the constellation of poetic forms and subject matters that mark the Renaissance
in southern Europe.[80] Yet he never wrote a sonnet, and attempts to locate Italian
material in his thought or his poetic practice have not been very successful.[81]

The Pléiade poets of the French Renaissance argued forcefully that the
sonnet was on an altogether higher plane than the *rondel*, and that view has
been accepted among students of French literature ever since. Some have taxed
Charles with having a "blind spot," but just because we know what ensued does
not mean that he should have been able to foresee it (and the sonnet did not
appear in French until the early sixteenth century).[82] With hindsight, we know
that he was one of the last to write a certain kind of poetry, and so we may
employ terms like "backward-looking" to his work, but he did not see the end of
the *rondel* form. For him it was filled with life, capable of adapting to changes in
thought and fashion.

The very fluidity of the *rondel*—revealed in the many forms it assumes
in his large collection—allowed him more variety and scope than would the
more rigid sonnet. It is doubtful that he would ever have viewed the sonnet as
in any way superior to the *rondel*. Moreover, the poet was not writing to please a
patron, who might demand the latest fad or poetic trend, or to immortalize his
name. Charles and his court enjoyed the challenge of finding a suitable refrain,
often proverbial (something the sonnet did not offer), and adapting it to the
framework of the whole, and then, quite often, writing variations on that same
refrain in other poems. The fact that the duke and those around him for the

---

[80] The works in his library by Petrarch, according to Pierre Champion, were *De
viris illustribus* (BnF MS. lat. 6069 K) and *Epistole* (BnF, MS. lat. 8570); about a third
work, identified only as *le livre de Francoys Petrac en françoys*, we know nothing (Ouy, *La
librairie des frères captifs,* 131; de Laborde, *Les ducs de Bourgogne,* #6776, #6777, #6780,
#6781). The duke also owned more than one book by Boccaccio: two copies of *De casibus
virorum illustrium* and two of *De mulieribus claris* (Ouy, *La librairie,* 121).

[81] See, for example, Mia Cocco, "The Italian Inspiration in the Poetry of Charles
d'Orléans," *Mid-Hudson Language Studies* 2 (1979): 46–60; or Concetta Mera Cisternino,
Charles d'Orléans, il Petrarca francese (Bari: Resta, 1969).

[82] Jacques Charpentreau names Mellin de Saint-Gelais (c. 1478–1558) as the poet
who introduced the sonnet into France (in *Dictionnaire de la poésie* [Paris: Fayard, 2006],
s.v. Sonnet).

last twenty-five years of his life wrote in the forms they did seems to confirm (unless we think of him as dictating what others should write) that the forms that had appealed to their ancestors appealed likewise to them. The duke and those around him found the interplay of formal variation, of sally and response, both satisfying and aesthetically meaningful.

§5 Literary context and poetic form

Charles's *œuvre* is defined by the physical object that most completely contains it: his personal manuscript, BnF MS. fr. 25458, a collection of verse in a variety of genres and lyric forms. Such author-centered collections were a significant development of the late Middle Ages in France. Charles's influential predecessor, Guillaume de Machaut (c. 1300–1377), famously referred to his personal copy of his collected works as the "livre ou je mes toutes mes choses" (the book in which I have put all my compositions), reflecting the way in which the collection in manuscript, like Charles's, grew incrementally as Machaut continued to compose.[83] Jean Froissart (c. 1337–1404) also commissioned the production of manuscripts containing extensive selections of his poetical works (BnF MSS fr. 830 and fr. 831), probably intended for presentation to noble patrons. The works of Eustache Deschamps (c. 1340–1404), Machaut's disciple and a member of Louis's household when Charles was a child, were collected into a manuscript a few years after his death (BnF MS. fr. 840). Deschamps's contemporary, Oton de Grandson (c. 1340–1396), introduces a collection of verse forms and prose, surviving only in manuscripts produced after his lifetime, with the declaration "je veuil ung livre encommencier / Et a ma dame l'envoyer, / Ainsi que je luy ay promis, / Ou seront tous mes faiz escriptz" (I wish to begin a book, in which all I do will be written, and to send it to my lady, just as I have promised).[84] Charles's involvement in the physical production of a manuscript of poetry during his lifetime perhaps most closely resembles the efforts of Christine de Pizan (c. 1364–1430). A poet directly connected to the Orléans household, Christine played a significant role in the material creation of multiple manuscript collections of her works, although her dedications of the manuscripts to different patrons suggest a different purpose for her efforts. Her first poetic collection, the *Cent Balades*, imitates the structure of an earlier, collaboratively authored, *Livre de cent balades*, a work to which Charles's father had contributed a *ballade*.[85] Charles's crafting

---

[83] *Le livre dou Voir Dit*, ed. Daniel Leech-Wilkinson (New York: Garland, 1998), 430–31.

[84] "Le livre messire Ode," in *Oton de Grandson; sa vie et ses poésies*, ed. A. Piaget, Mémoires et documents publiés par la Société d'histoire de la Suisse romande, 3rd ser., vol. 1. (Lausanne: Librairie Payot, 1941), 383, ll. 1–4.

[85] See p. xxxvii, above. Christine de Pizan's connections to the Orléans household are also visible in other aspects of her poetry: she dedicated multiple *ballades* to Charles's

of a personal manuscript thus represents his inheritance from preceding generations of poets.

Like Charles's manuscript collection, the range of his verse forms, in particular his frequent use of the *ballade* and *rondel*, also reflects a taste Charles shared with his predecessors and contemporaries.[86] Yet Charles's manner of combining forms is distinct. In contrast to the *ballade* collection to which his father contributed, Charles's manuscript uses layout and numbering systems to connect a variety of forms, rather than simply offering variations within the shared form of a *ballade*.[87] The choice to begin the collection with an allegorical narrative of entry into Love's service reflects the seminal influence of the allegorical *Prologue*

---

father and added a lament for his assassination to her *Oraison Nostre-Dame*. See Christine de Pisan, *Oeuvres poétiques*, ed. Maurice Roy, 3 vols. (Paris: Firmin-Didot, 1886–1896; repr. New York: Johnson Reprint, 1965). On the contribution of Jean de Garencières to the *Livre de cent balades* and to the poetry of Charles d'Orléans, see Young Abernathy Neal, *Le chevalier poète, Jean de Garencières, sa vie et sa poésies complètes, 1372–1415*, 2 vols. (Paris: Nizet, 1953), 1:203–15, 2:xxxv.

[86] Machaut offered an important model for late medieval poetic forms, particularly in his *Remède de Fortune*, which embeds examples of the *lai, chançon royale, ballade, virelai, rondel, complainte*, and *balladelle*. Deschamps defined a similar but not identical group of seven forms in his 1392 treatise, *L'Art de dictier*: the *ballade, serventois, virelai, rondel, sotte chançon, pastourelle*, and *lai*. The common elements—the *lai, ballade, virelai*, and *rondel*—were the most popular and, among these, the *ballade* and *rondel* were most frequently employed. The *ballade* was the favorite form for Machaut as well as for Deschamps and Christine de Pizan. After the *ballade*, the *rondel* was the form most frequently employed by all three. In contrast, Machaut represents the apogee in popularity of the lyric *lai*; the production of Deschamps and Froissart put together barely equals his, and Christine de Pizan writes only three. Later in the fifteenth century, Alain Chartier is almost alone in his use of the form, and the term *lai* itself became increasingly general in meaning (on Villon's use, see R-H, 2:144). Similarly, as Pierre Bec noted, although the poets just mentioned do create *virelais*, they create far fewer of this form and in general terms, "le virelai s'éteint peu à peu" (the *virelai* slowly dies out) in France after its separation from musical composition in the fourteenth century (in R-H 1.239–40). Some of Charles's *rondels* resemble *virelais*, but he never identified a poem as such (see Daniel Poirion, *Le poète et le prince* [Paris: Presses universitaires de France, 1965], 351). In contrast to contemporaries, Charles also did not use typical, thematically defined formal terms such as the *pastourelle*, the *jeu-parti*, or the *sotte chançon*, nor did Charles craft prose compositions, unlike other late medieval writers including Christine, Froissart, and René d'Anjou.

[87] Collections of *ballades* were nonetheless a popular model on both sides of the Channel in the fifteenth century; John Gower's *Cinkante Ballades* was dedicated to Henry IV. See R. F. Yeager, "John Gower's Audience: The Ballades," *Chaucer Review* 40 (2005): 81–105. The largest number extant in Middle English are those in the duke's collection of English poetry, composed before 1440 (see Arn, *Fortunes Stabilnes*), and one English *ballade* finds its way into the present collection (B144).

created by Machaut as an introduction to all of his works, but Charles stops short of making the claims of poetic skill found Machaut's *Prologue*, which depicts Machaut receiving the gifts of rhetoric, wisdom, and music from Nature prior to his entry into Love's service.[88] Moreover, despite the narrative nature of its introductory allegory, Charles's collection as a whole does not set forth a coherent dramatic plot in the manner of many other late medieval assemblies of narrative verse and lyrics (and on occasion prose), including Machaut's *Voir dit*, Oton de Granson's "Le livre messire Ode", Jean Froissart's *La prison amoureuse*, or Christine de Pizan's *Livre du Duc des Vrais Amants*, all of which envision extended interaction between different composing characters.[89] Charles's collection features fewer clearly differentiated subject positions, despite being the product of far more contributors. Indeed, the number of authors appearing in this edition's collection (more than forty) demonstrates the extent to which the practice of poetry served Charles as a vehicle for actual rather than fictive social exchange.

Charles's collection also displays the new distinctions the late Middle Ages had begun to draw between the interrelated arts of music and poetry. Surviving manuscripts exhibit Machaut's compositions of melodies as well as verses, but we have no evidence that Charles composed such musical accompaniment for his lines, despite the awareness of musical forms evident in his language.[90] Unlike Machaut's beloved *ballade layée*, in which the shorter line after the opening quatrain drew attention to a new musical phrase, Charles's *ballades* all feature isometric stanzas. Charles's practice demonstrates the influence of Deschamps, who differentiated a writer of metered verse, or *musique naturele* (natural music), from a composer of instrumental music, or *musique artificiele* (artificial music).[91] In Deschamps's *ballades*, the *oultrepassé* (continuation) section plays the dominant role rather than the balancing role it had played when the form was more closely tied

---

[88] On the innovative nature of Machaut's *Prologue*, its relation to the *Roman de la rose,* and its later influence, see Kevin Brownlee, *Poetic Identity in Guillaume de Machaut* (Madison: University of Wisconsin Press, 1989), 20.

[89] For a relevant analysis of the powerful relationship between form and perspective in Charles's English poetry, see Mary-Jo Arn, "Poetic Form as a Mirror of Meaning in the English Poems of Charles of Orleans," *Philological Quarterly* 69 (1990): 13–29. Although less directly focused upon Charles, useful explorations of the interrelation of melody, lyric, and narrative are also found in such works as Sylvia Huot, *From Song to Book* (Ithaca: Cornell University Press, 1987); Ardis Butterfield, *Poetry and Music in Medieval France* (Cambridge: Cambridge University Press, 2002); Maureen Boulton, *The Song in the Story* (Philadelphia: University of Pennsylvania Press, 1993); and Christopher Page, *The Owl and the Nightingale: Musical Life and Ideas in France, 1100–1300* (London: Dent, 1989).

[90] See the musical settings reproduced in Guillaume de Machaut, *La Louange des Dames,* ed. Nigel Wilkins (Edinburgh: Scottish Academic Press, 1972), 121–70.

[91] See Eustache Deschamps, *L'Art de dictier,* ed. and trans. D. Sinnreich-Levi (East Lansing: Colleagues Press, 1994), 60–67.

to musical composition. Deschamps both expands the *oultrepassé* of the *ballade* and helps to popularize the addition of a final *envoi*. Christine de Pizan created a greater number of *envois* for *ballades* in her collection from the early fifteenth century than she had in her fourteenth-century collection.[92] Charles's manuscript shows a similar development, since the number of *envois* before 1440 is limited to three, whereas an *envoi* is assigned to nearly every one of his *ballades* thereafter. With the addition of the *envoi* and expansion of the *oultrepassé*, the *ballades* of Charles and his contemporaries become, on average, almost ten to twenty lines longer than their fourteenth-century models.[93] Charles also employed the *rondel* form with a longer opening stanza of five lines, found first in the poetry of Jean de Garencières and later widely adopted.[94] Such significant changes in poetic forms over time, as well as variations in individual poetic practice, contribute to the growing dissatisfaction of modern scholars with the perhaps misleading late nineteenth-century term *formes fixes* for medieval lyric forms.[95]

Within the changing forms of his poems, Charles also varies thematic concerns, employing a range of religious, military, and amatory imagery, as well as parodies of legal processes and medical formulas. As Deschamps's *ballade* on the price of Parisian cabbage suggests, *ballades* on almost any subject appear to have been welcome to late medieval French readers.[96] The *complaintes* interspersed among the *ballades* are rarer as forms, but also encompass thematic range, discovering moral and political woes as well as the sentiments of a lover. The *Complainte de France* merits individual mention for its celebrated sound play, featuring an almost unrivaled number of rhyme words ending in –*esse*.[97] Charles's display of skilled invention on a single rhyme in this *complainte* inverts the virtuoso variety of rhymes contained in works like Machaut's *Fonteinne amoureuse*: in Machaut's *Fonteinne*, a noble character ends a lengthy *complainte* with the boast that "Cent rimes ay mis dedens ceste rime, qui bien les conte" (I have put

---

[92] James C. Laidlaw, "The *Cent balades:* The Marriage of Content and Form," in *Christine de Pizan and the Medieval French Lyric*, ed. E. J. Richards (Gainesville: University Press of Florida, 1998), 53–82, here 53.

[93] See Laidlaw, "The *Cent balades*," 57. See also p. lv, below.

[94] On Garenciéres's innovation and Charles's adoption of the form, see Neal, *Le chevalier poète, Jean de Garencières*, 213.

[95] Proposed alternative terms include *forme limitée*, from Suzanne Bagnoly, "Christine de Pizan et l'art de 'dictier' ballades," *Moyen Âge* 92 (1986): 41–47, here 43, or *poèmes enroulés*, from W. D. Paden, "Christine de Pizan and the Transformation of Late Medieval Lyric Genres," in *Christine de Pizan*, ed. Richards, 27–49, here 38.

[96] I. S. Laurie, "Deschamps and the Lyric as Natural Music," *Modern Language Review* 59 (1964): 561–90, here 569. Maurice Roy similarly notes that "les pensées d'amour ne forment pas exclusivement les sujets de toutes les ballades de Christine de Pisan" (amorous ideas do not serve exclusively as the subjects of all Christine de Pisan's *ballades*) (Christine de Pisan, *Oeuvres poétiques*, ed. Roy, 1:xxx).

[97] Poirion, *Le poète*, 432, n. 19.

a hundred rhymes into this verse, whoever numbers them right).[98] Charles does not appear to have been attracted by variety in rhymes or by complex sound devices such as the forms described by Deschamps as *equivoque* (placing rhyming homonyms at the end of each line and the start of the next line) or *retrograde* (beginning each line with the preceding end rhyme sound, so that each strophe's word order could be inverted without disturbing the rhyme scheme).[99] In general, Charles incorporated fewer rhyme-scheme variations in his poetry than did poets such as Machaut, Deschamps, and Christine, and he also eschewed his contemporaries' use of visual devices like the acrostic or anagram.[100] Yet Charles's more sustained uses of rhyme sounds and patterns produced a remarkable level of complexity rather than stagnation. Charles's *rondels*, for example, employ fewer rhyme pattern variations than those of Machaut, Christine, or Deschamps, but display greater rhythmic variation than was exercised by Machaut or other contemporaries who favored the form, including Jean Froissart.[101]

While varied in theme, Charles's poetry places emphasis on "personal emotions and experiences," a trend already visible in the poems of Machaut.[102] Charles's *rondels* often appear to address the poet's psyche rather than a listener, and the subjects of Charles's *caroles* similarly include not only communal holiday festivities but the allegorical figures of interior thought, such as *Merancolie*, *Espoir*, and *Soussy*.[103] Daniel Poirion attributes this combination of introspective allegory and a deepening sensitivity to communal life at least in part to the

---

[98] Guillaume de Machaut, *The Fountain of Love*, ed. and trans. R. Barton Palmer (New York: Garland, 1993), 144–45.

[99] See Deschamps, *L'Art de dictier*, 74–79.

[100] One English lyric in the duke's manuscript contains an acrostic: the initial letters of R363 spell out "Anne Molins."

[101] On form, see below, §6. No other individual poet of the time produced much more than a third of the number of *rondels* produced by Charles. Poirion speculates that the *rondel* attracted Charles because its relative ease in composition meant that a *rondel* could move from conception to completion in a single stream of thought (*Le poète*, 353). Kristen Figg suggests that Froissart's similarly heightened production of *ballades* and *rondels* could be explained by these forms' adaptability to many subjects (*The Short Lyric Poems of Jean Froissart* [New York: Garland, 1994], 17).

[102] Nigel Wilkins, "Guillaume de Machaut," in Guillaume de Machaut, *La Louange des Dames*, ed. idem, 5.

[103] In particular, Charles's use of Valentine's Day as an occasion for romantic address reflects the influence of Oton de Granson, who appears to have been the first to produce multiple *ballades* and *complaintes* as well as other forms of poetry on the subject. See Piaget, *Oton de Grandson*, 132, 479–86. Granson's poetry had a notable effect in England as well as in France: Geoffrey Chaucer's *Parliament of Fowls* imitates Granson's dream vision of birds debating on Valentine's Day and Chaucer also adapted and translated three of Granson's *ballades* as *The Complaint of Venus*.

influence of Alain Chartier (c. 1380–1429).[104] Certainly, fifteenth-century readers saw a resemblance: Chartier's poems were copied together with the poems of
Jean de Garencières and Charles d'Orléans (see BnF MS. fr. 19139), and Martin
le Franc (c. 1410–1461) depicts the allegorical protagonist of his *Champion des
dames* defending female virtue through repeated citation of Charles and "le livre
qu'il fit en Inglant" (the book that he made in England) (line 11914) as well as
Alain Chartier's *Le breviaire des nobles*.[105] *Le champion des dames* reflects clearly
the continued influence of the earlier generation of poets on Charles and his suc-
cessors, as it cites the poets named above in the context of reopening the debate
about fidelity raised in Machaut's *Jugement du roy de Behainge* and challenging
the conflicting portrayal of love in the widely popular late thirteenth-century
Roman de la rose.

Indeed, in Charles's collection, the two most extended narrative pieces, the
Songe en complainte and the opening narrative, visibly borrow the personifications and themes of earlier allegories including the *Roman de la rose*. In these,
Charles deploys one of the most fascinating poetic devices that late medieval
French narrative took from the lyric: a complex first-person voice, identified
with the poet by use of the poet's proper name or individual attributes but set
within an imaginary realm peopled by mythic figures and personifications.[106]

---

[104] Poirion, *Le poète*, 260–63, 286. The relationship of the two poets in terms of
manuscript circulation is also noteworthy: Chartier's poetry appears in manuscripts created for Charles's wife, Marie de Clèves, and for his brother's wife, Marguerite de Rohan
(BnF MS. fr. 20026 and BnF MS. fr. 2230, respectively), and Charles's brother Jean is
known to have owned a manuscript of Chartier's complaint in 1467. See *The Poetical
Works of Alain Chartier*, ed. J. C. Laidlaw (London: Cambridge University Press, 1994),
71, 108–9, 111–112.

[105] Line number citation for Martin le Franc's poem refers to *Le Champion des Dames*,
ed. Robert Deschaux, 5 vols. (Paris: Champion, 1999). The allegorical protagonist of the
Champion, *Franc Voloir*, reflects a debt to Eustache Deschamps's *Miroir de mariage*, which
features the same protagonist. (R. Barton Palmer, Ian S. Laurie, and Deborah Sinnreich-
Levi are currently preparing a bilingual edition of the *Miroir* for Pegasus Press.) Other
contempories, including Oton de Granson and Christine de Pizan, are also praised in
the *Champion*.

[106] This narrative style is notably indebted to Boethius's sixth-century *Consolatio
philosophiae*, a work richly represented (seven copies) in Charles's library, but its first major
vernacular incarnation appeared in the *Roman de la rose*. On late medieval responses to
the *De consolatione*, see Glynnis Cropp, "Fortune and the Poet in Ballades of Eustache
Deschamps, Charles d'Orléans, and François Villon," *Medium Aevum* 58 (1989): 125–32;
Jean-Claude Mühlethaler, "Récrire *Le roman de la rose* au XVe siècle: Les commandements d'amour chez Charles d'Orléans et ses lecteurs," in *'Riens ne m'est seur que la chose
incertaine'*, ed. Jean-Claude Mühlethaler and Denis Billotte (Geneva: Slatkine, 2001),
105–19; Sarah Kay, *The Place of Thought* (Philadelphia: University of Pennsylvania Press,
2007); and Winthrop Wetherbee, "The *Consolation* and Medieval Literature," in *The

Like the simultaneously authorial and figurative *je* of these poems, the names of personifications show a fluidity in identity, at times representing figures with dramatic agency and at other times slipping back into abstract nouns. The shadowy presence of m/Melancholy, looming with unprecedented frequency over the collection, has held particular interest for later readers of Charles's poetry.[107] Seemingly autobiographical pieces, the opening and the *Songe* propose a kind of chronological progression—each in fact rhymes Charles's name "Orlians" with "ans" (years)—but these pieces of narrative are equally important as explorations of lyric form, ranging from the *quatrain renversé* pattern (abab + baab or bccb) of the *Songe* to the chancery style adopted with different rhyme schemes in the appended letter of homage and letter of request.[108] Charles's most intimate language of self-exploration thus represents his sustained interest in poetic form.

This edition's inclusion of the contributions of other poets in the places Charles created for them among his own creations offers insight into the ways Charles defined his own literary context. The network of textual relations cannot receive detailed discussion here, but a sense of its range and significance can be conveyed through consideration of two contributors from opposite ends of Charles's elite social spectrum, each of whom has been the subject of scholarly attention in his own right: François Villon (c. 1431–c. 1463) and René d'Anjou (1409–1480). Villon and René each composed a notable response to one of the two long sequences of overtly inter-referential poems within the collection—the ten poems that elaborate the paradox *Je meurs de soif en couste la fontaine* and the eleven others that explore what transpires *En la forest de Longue Actente*.

Villon, who characterizes himself in his *Testament* as an ungentle rogue and criminal, makes a contribution to the series of fountain poems that stands out as a response to the "dauntingly high standards" Charles set in his initiatory *ballade* (B75).[109] One of only two participants to expand the seven-line stanza employed by Charles into the symmetrical *dizain carré* (a ten-line stanza of decasyllabic lines), Villon extends the tension of the initial paradox rather than resolving it.

Cambridge Companion to Boethius, ed. John Marenbon (Cambridge: Cambridge University Press, 2009), 279–302. On the reception and circulation of the *Rose*, see Pierre-Yves Badel, *Le "Roman de la rose" au XIVe siècle* (Geneva: Droz, 1980); Sylvia Huot, *The "Romance of the Rose" and Its Medieval Readers* (Cambridge: Cambridge University Press, 1993); and eadem, "'Ci parle l'aucteur': The Rubrication of Voice and Authorship in the *Roman de la Rose* Manuscripts," *SubStance* 56 (1988): 42–48.

[107] In the poems of Alain Chartier, for example, Melancholy makes only two appearances.

[108] On the form and relation of the introductory narrative and the *Songe en complainte*, see §6 The introductory narrative and the valentine poems.

[109] Jane Taylor, *The Poetry of François Villon* (Cambridge: Cambridge University Press, 2001), 59. Taylor's book offers an informative discussion of the collection's exchange on the fountain theme, 58–68.

His practice in this poem, save for its enjambement, closely resembles Charles's own. [110] Copied nearby, Villon's less celebrated poem praising Charles's daughter Marie finds an alternative fount of poetic inspiration, inscribing a direct connection between Charles's life and his literary collection. The density of Villon's scholastic allusions within this poem—beginning with a Vergilian epigraph and naming Caesar, Cato, Clovis, the Psalmist, St. John, St. Andrew, Judith, Lucretia, Cassandra, Dido, and Echo—reflects a crucial difference between Villon and Charles as poets. Charles was undoubtedly learned—his play upon Latin grammar in his exchange with Estienne le Gout (R28–29) is delightful—but he never quite adopts the poetic persona of *escolier* in the manner of *povre Françoys*, as Villon calls himself (*Jam nova*, 132). Charles does explore the possibilities of posturing as a pupil in R419, but the pupil of this poem attends a metaphorical school under the discipline of *Soussy*. Charles's avoidance of overt displays of learning marks a difference not only from Villon but also from other late medieval writers: Charles never composed a treatise on poetic art like Deschamps or historical chronicles in the manner of Froissart, and none of Charles's works feature detailed biography resembling Machaut's attention to Pierre I of Cyprus in *La prise d'Alixandrie*. Rather than establishing his literary context with a profusion of classical, patristic, and historical referents, Charles gathers his poetic circle around figurative landmarks set within visionary landscapes—the thirst-increasing Fountain, the Forest of Long Waiting, the Prison of Thought.

Charles's younger noble cousin, René d'Anjou, was particularly attracted to this use of the visionary landscape as a vehicle for reflecting socio-literary context: René weaves together the theme of the Forest of Long Waiting and the figure of Charles himself within his own volume in mixed forms, the *Livre du cuers d'amours espris*. This prose romance with inset verses is framed by a dream vision in verse and by a courtly prose epistle addressed to Jean II, duc de Bourbon, kinsman of both René and Charles, who contributed no fewer than eight poems to Charles's manuscript. Charles's *rondel* on the subject of the Forest of Long Waiting warns against the danger of an abstraction, *Dure Rigueur*, by whom "a esté robbé vostre cueur" (your heart has been abducted) (R197, 4). René's *Livre du cuers* enacts the same danger, as the poet loses his heart to the personification Desire in the dream vision. In the prose romance section, the Heart acts as an independent knight, and his first adventure is wandering into the dark Forest of Long Waiting.

---

[110] Taylor advances this argument (*The Poetry of François Villon*, 65–68). Adrian Armstrong, among other scholars, similarly insists that there is less distance between practice of 'courtly poets' and Villon than is frequently suggested: "François Villon: Rhétoriqueur?" in *Villon at Oxford*, ed. Michael Freeman and Jane H. M. Taylor (Amsterdam: Rodopi, 1999), 51–84. Certainly, the sort of innuendo and slang considered characteristic of Villon also appears in a number of Charles's poems (see Explanatory Notes on B125, and B133, 16).

René's poem retains the sense of a shared poetic landscape found in Charles's interchange of *ballades* on the subject of the dreadful Forest by having the Heart carefully observe the coats of arms decorating the hospital of the *Dieu d'Amors*. Here, Charles's coat of arms is described as suspended on high along with those of other lovers; below Charles's arms appears first-person verse declaring:

> . . . par mon hault couraige,
> Tins pié coy en bataille, dont souffry maint dommaige,
> Car prins fuz des Anglois et mené en servaige,
> Et tant y demouray qu'en aprins le langaige,
> Par lequel fus acoint de dame belle et saige
> Et d'elle si espris qu'a Amours fis hommaige,
> Dont mains beaux ditz dictié bien prisez davantaige.
> S'ay mis mon blazon cy cloué en cest estaige.[111]

> . . . by my high courage,
> [I] held my ground in battle, thus suffered many woes,
> For I was taken by the English and led into servitude,
> And stayed there so long I learned the language,
> By which means I encountered a lady beautiful and wise
> And was so smitten by her that I did homage to Love.
> On this subject I composed many beautiful and well-received compositions.
> So I placed my arms here, pegged at this level.

These lines have been cited in past debates over Charles's composition of English poetry, but literary scholars have not reached a critical consensus on their reliability as evidence. However, their context in René's poem reveals not only a cross-linguistic interest but also the thoroughly interpersonal and intertextual nature of Charles's literary tradition. René's imaginary armorial vault plays upon the *rondel* Charles addressed to him, in which Charles claims that long ago "me suis aux armes rendu" (I have surrendered myself to arms) in his struggle with *Amors* (R5, 14);[112] in René's poem, the vault bears shields and verses representing not only Charles but René himself and others of their circle.[113] In addition to such

---

[111] BnF MS. fr. 24399, fol. 85v. René later changed the shields represented in his work; the recension omits mention of Charles, Louis XI, and Louis de Beauvau. See *Le livre de coeur d'amour épris*, ed. Florence Bouchet (Paris: Le Livre de Poche, 2003), 338–40. Stephanie Gibbs [Kamath] and Kathryn Karczewska provide an edition of the recension text from the Vienna manuscript with a facing-page English translation (*The Book of the Love-Smitten Heart*, by René of Anjou [New York and London: Garland, 2001]).

[112] It may also owe something to the tomb the lover has built for his dead lady in B69.

[113] Those featured include Charles's father; the seneschal, Pierre de Brézé, who contributes two *ballades* to Charles's manuscript; and Philippe II, whose grandson, Philippe le Bon, duc de Bourgogne, exchanged with Charles a *ballade* sequence on his captivity.

armorial representation, René's vision features elaborate descriptions of tombs inscribed with verses. Three of the tombs memorialize French poets—Guillaume de Machaut, Alain Chartier, and the *Rose* poet, Jean de Meun—reflecting sources of poetic inspiration shared by René and Charles.[114]

The conclusion of the Heart's adventures reveals another resemblance in the poetic practice of Charles and René, as it reminds readers of the close connection between the poet and his household. At the close of René's work, the poet's fears are calmed by the laughing touch of his chamberlain, who demonstrates the lack of any visible wound through which his heart might have departed.[115] We know that Charles received the service of Jean de Garencières as a chamberlain, and that the two were close enough to exchange *ballades* jesting about suffering in Love's service, and its suspected imaginary nature. Garencières's poetry remained, as John Fox has remarked, the greatest single influence on Charles's later compositions.[116] The grand literary tributes paid to poets like Jean de Meun should not obscure our attention to the household circle as an important context for poetic creation in Charles's lifetime.

In looking at domestic influences, we should also remember the time Charles involuntarily spent in the proximity of cultured English noblemen and churchmen: Sir Thomas Comberworth, Sir John Cornwall, Fr. Thomas Winchelsey, and Sir John Stourton, among others.[117] The English nobility of the fifteenth century read French poetry as intently as their counterparts across the Channel, and read it in relation to poetic production in English.[118] One important site

---

[114] The distinction implied between the noble lovers represented by shields and the poets given tombs is nonetheless interesting, as is the fact that the tombs of the three French poets are interspersed among the tombs of Ovid, Giovanni Boccaccio, and Francis Petrarch. René's vision of Love's hospital refers directly to a poem that Achilles Caulier wrote in response to Alain Chartier's *Belle dame sans merci*, a poem which responds in its opening lines to the *Livre de cent ballades* to which Charles's father had contributed.

[115] Beyond the tale of the dream, the closeness of the chamberlain's relation to the poet is also evident in the archive. René ordered a manuscript of Guillaume de Deguileville's *Pèlerinage* trilogy to be created for his chamberlain Louis Martel in 1437, as recorded in its colophon. See Philadelphia, Rosenbach Library MS. 722, fol. 204r. These allegories, the first to respond directly to the *Rose*, citing the work by name and borrowing personifications, were another interest that René shared with Charles, who also owned a manuscript copy of Deguileville's allegories (see §2, 16).

[116] "No other influence on Charles was as immediate, as personal and direct as that of Garencières" (John Fox, *The Lyric Poetry of Charles d'Orléans* [Oxford: Clarendon Press, 1969], 69). For more extended analysis of the nature of the influence, see Neal, *Le chevalier poète*, 1:203–15.

[117] For further information see Askins, "The Brothers Orléans," in Arn, *Charles d'Orléans in England*.

[118] Nor was complex cross-Channel linguistic exchange new to the English readership of Charles's day, as current scholarship demonstrates. See, for example, Ardis

of linguistic poetic exchange for Charles during his captivity was the circle of William de la Pole, the marquis (later duke) of Suffolk. A manuscript copied by John Shirley, a book-collector and translator who took an active role in Suffolk's household, clearly demonstrates the place of French poetry as the inspiration, and at times the competition, for English writers' creations: it features the side-by-side presentation of a French *ballade* and its English translation, with a prefatory note in which Shirley urges his contemporaries *regardez et lysez* (examine and read) the French poem by Deschamps and declares John Lydgate's accompanying creation "a balade of þe same sentence," worthy of comparison.[119] Of course, Suffolk's own experience as a captive in Charles's native land may offer an instructive parallel to Charles's later experience in English captivity. According to John Shirley, Suffolk wrote and copied French lyrics during his time as a prisoner in the castle of Charles's half-brother, the comte de Dunois, in France (1430–32).[120] United as well as divided by the era's cross-Channel conflict, both French courts and English households such as Suffolk's promoted a literary culture of comparative reading. Charles's experience of these contexts may well have encouraged the mixed nature of his own collection, which incorporates nine poems in English as well as macaronic compositions employing Latin and Italian. The collection's linguistic play, so often obscured by the selectiveness of earlier editions of Charles's poetry, thus has as much to teach us about Charles's response to his literary environment as other salient formal features of the collection, including its author-centered focus, its record of collaborative contributors, its development of the language of interiority, and its use of poetic forms and particular variations in theme, rhythm and rhyme.

Butterfield's *The Familiar Enemy: Chaucer, Language, and Nation in the Hundred Years War* (Oxford and New York: Oxford University Press, 2009).

[119] See London, BL, Add. MS. 16165, fol. 49r. For discussion of Shirley's relation to the Suffolk household, see Derek Pearsall, "The Literary Milieu of Charles of Orléans and the Duke of Suffolk, and the Authorship of the Fairfax Sequence," in *Charles dOrléans in England*, ed. Arn, 150–51. Of Shirley and Suffolk's role in the English reading of poetry by Eustache Deschamps, Alain Chartier, and Christine de Pizan, see Margaret Connolly and Yolanda Plumley, "Crossing the Channel: John Shirley and the Circulation of French Lyric Poetry in England in the Fifteenth Century," in *Patrons, Authors and Workshops: Books and Book Production in Paris around 1400*, ed. Godfried Croenen and Peter Ainsworth. Synthema 4 (Leuven: Peeters, 2006), 311-32. David Fallows's intriguing study ("Words and Music in Two English Songs of the Mid-Fifteenth Century: Charles d'Orléans and John Lydgate," *Early Music* 5 [1997]: 38–43) of two fifteenth-century melodic settings for the respective verses of Charles and Lydgate also reflects the importance of reading lyrics composed in French and in English comparatively.

[120] Susan Crane draws attention to this suggestive parallel in "Anglo-Norman Cultures in England, 1066–1460," in the *Cambridge History of Medieval English Literature*, ed. David Wallace (Cambridge: Cambridge University Press, 1999), 35–61, here p. 59.

Errata

Despite countless hours of diligent editing, after printing this book we discovered that a vital portion of text was omitted from the last paragraph on page li of the Introduction. This omission creates confusion for the reader and therefore the last paragraph of this page is reproduced below, with the missing text included in bold. Please accept our sincere apology for this error.

Whereas the *Songe en complainte* is "dated" 1437 (line 413), three years before Charles's release from imprisonment in England, the introductory narrative is not dated. In his *Vie*, Champion (23) regards it as a late addition: "De son enfance, Charles d'Orléans conserva un souvenir attendri. Beaucoup plus tard, dans la grande allégorie qu'il ajouta en guise de préface à la collection de ses premières poésies, il dira: Ou temps passé . . ." (whole of first stanza quoted). Of his childhood, he kept a tender memory. Much later, in the great allegory which he added as a preface to the collection of his first poems, he will say: In times past . . . **In this edition, however, he has evidently changed his mind, relying on the reference "Charles, a present jeune d'ans" (line 406) to suggest that it was an early work, composed around 1414, the year before Agincourt (2:551). In itself that is insufficient evidence, occurring, as it does, in the *lettre de retenue*, like the entire work, from the past, but other factors do point in that direction.** The juvenile work by Charles, not included in his personal manuscript, entitled *Le livre contre tout péché*, written with the aid of a tutor when he was ten years old (Champion, *Poésies*, 2.604–5) is, naturally enough, composed in the simplest rhyme scheme possible: aabb, etc. This pattern of rhyming couplets is retained in the introductory narrative, whereas the corresponding verses of the *Songe en complainte* follow one of the intersecting rhyme patterns—such patterns being an integral part of the *ballade* form—occurring in the series of poems to which it forms the conclusion: ababbcbc, reverting to the simpler pattern only in the last 61 of its 550 lines, very likely a deliberate harking-back to the introductory narrative, to which these lines make reference.

§6 Notes on narrative and verse forms

The introductory narrative and the Valentine poems

This first work (457 lines) portrays the young Charles's entry into the service of Love. It introduces a series of 77 *ballades* which progress, *grosso modo*, from the conventional praise of the lady's beauty (9 poems), to the pain and tribulation of separation (46 poems), to his emotions on learning of her illness and death (22 poems), leading finally to the narrative counterpart to the first poem, a farewell to Love (550 lines). While this concluding poem has a title, *Songe en complainte*, the opening one does not. In his *Vie de Charles d'Orléans*, Champion (23) simply refers to it as the preface, whereas in his edition, published twelve years later, he provides a title in brackets, *La Retenue d'Amours*, with no indication of its provenance. No doubt an invention of Champion's, it is certainly an appropriate choice given the two meanings of "retenue" in the poem: (1) in line 45 of the opening narrative and in B119, 6, "retinue," a meaning the word no longer has in modern French; (2) in line 388 and the heading following line 400, "lettre de retenue" means "retainer," i.e., a letter retaining Charles in Love's service. It was a legal term also used in R237, 8. Champion's title can accordingly be read in two ways. However appropriate, since Charles did not see fit to add a title in his personal manuscript, to which this new edition adheres as far as modern editing practices permit, none has been used here.

Whereas the *Songe en complainte* is "dated" 1437 (line 413), three years before Charles's release from imprisonment in England, the introductory narrative is not dated. In his *Vie*, Champion (23) regards it as a late addition: "De son enfance, Charles d'Orléans conserva un souvenir attendri. Beaucoup plus tard, dans la grande allégorie qu'il ajouta en guise de préface à la collection de ses premières poésies, il dira: Ou temps passé . . ." (whole of first stanza quoted). Of his childhood, he kept a tender memory. Much later, in the great allegory which he added as a preface to the collection of his first poems, he will say: In times past . . . In itself that is insufficient evidence, occurring, as it does, in a *lettre de retenue*, like the entire work, from the past, but other factors do point in that direction. A juvenile work by Charles, not included in his personal manuscript, entitled *Le livre contre tout péché*, written with the aid of a tutor when he was ten years old (Champion, *Poésies*, 2.604–5) is, naturally enough, composed in the simplest rhyme scheme possible: aabb, etc. This pattern of rhyming couplets is retained in the introductory narrative, whereas the corresponding verses of the *Songe en complainte* follow one of the intersecting rhyme patterns — such patterns being an integral part of the *ballade* form — occurring in the series of poems to which it forms the conclusion: ababbcbc, reverting to the simpler pattern only in the last 61 of its 550 lines, very likely a deliberate harking-back to the introductory narrative, to which these lines make reference.

In his later works there are seven poems (longer than the *ballades* and *rondels*) that could have been written in rhyming couplets but are not, so the only longer works making extensive use of this elementary pattern are *Le livre contre tout péché* and the introductory narrative, suggesting that both were written early in Charles's career, before he embarked on the *ballade* and *rondel* forms. A third factor: the introductory narrative, along with the first nine *ballades*, is entirely conventional; it includes praise of the God of Love and the promise to be his faithful servant, followed in the *ballades* by lavish praise of the lady's beauty. With the tenth *ballade*, however, an entirely different note appears, repeated in poem after poem, even though these themes also are conventional: separation from the lady, necessitating the need to remain loyal, and the plea not to forget him, all strongly suggesting that from the tenth *ballade* onwards Charles is a prisoner in England, whereas the introductory narrative and the first nine *ballades* give not the slightest hint of this. (That he was writing *ballades* before Agincourt is shown by B116, in which he teases a fellow-poet, Garencières, for exaggerating his suffering in love, and receives a reply [B117]). A fourth and last factor: two lines, B65, 2 and *Songe*, 550 refer back to the introductory narrative as having been written some time in the past (*pieça–jadis*), showing that it was written *before* them and not after. It seems reasonable to conclude that Charles had already composed the introductory narrative, followed by the first nine *ballades*, while still in France, before Agincourt, very likely in the brief spell of happiness he enjoyed in 1414, when the troubles consequent upon his father's assassination in 1407 had been settled, and when he wore the message, picked out in pearls on his sleeve: *Madame, je suis plus joyeulx* (see p. xvii). In the following years he was to know far more melancholy than joy.

The choice of St. Valentine's Day for the young Charles's introduction to the God of Love is all the more appropriate as his father before him had celebrated that day, of particular interest to courtly circles (Intro., 24, 453; see Champion, *Vie*, 26–27). A further seventeen poems are written on or concerning St. Valentine's Day, all but four by Charles. Only one dates from his years in England (B66, 1, 25). It refers to the birds choosing their mates on that day, a traditional belief mentioned by Chaucer in his *Parlement of Foules* ("For this was on Seynt Valentyne's day whan every foule cometh ther to chese his make"), but death has claimed Charles's *per* (peer, mate) and there can be no rejoicing for him. Back in France (aged forty-six), St. Valentine brings him no more joy than it did in England. He is simply not interested, and prefers to stay in bed (R3 and R74). He is too old anyway (R6), his valentines are *Pluye, vent et mauvais chemin* (R223, 4), or *Penser* (R263, 4), evidently of the gloomy kind because he would rather it be *Espoir*, which it is in R292, though even that brings him precious little comfort, while *Soussy et Penance* (R127, 5) bring him only care and worry.

In R263, exceptionally, he has fought off Soussy and at least given thought to the games played on St. Valentine's Day, while in the following poem he urges young poets to get on with their writing verses in French or Latin, observing that some will be lucky with their valentines, others not so. In R128, St. Valentine actually addresses the court, urging them to choose their mates, though Charles does no such thing, and all he wants in his last poem on the subject (R377) is good food and wine. Only one poem (R270) takes the subject seriously, and of the entire manuscript collection it is the most overtly biographical, and the most revealing. Charles has been allotted as his valentine—it does not appear to have been his choice—his sister-in-law Marguerite de Rohan, wife of his brother Jean d'Angoulême—and it is to her that Charles addresses the poem. His advice to her is crude, with nothing "courtly" or romantic about it: make love with your husband (*hutin*, lit. noise, racket, frenzy, is frequent in a sexual sense) until your belly is swollen (*pense levee*, line 6, cf. B134, 15, "ce qui fait le ventre lever"). As for me, I prefer to sleep on, and shall give scant pleasure to my wife on this St. Valentine's Day.

Throughout the entire collection the numerous references to his "Dame" are so circumspect that one can never be absolutely certain whether she is his wife or some lady at court, or whether she is English or French, or even if the poem is an exercise on a well-worn theme and nothing more, but in this poem there can be no doubt: *assené* meant "married" (Godefroy, 1.434), so *ma malassenee* (R270, 10) is literally "my badly married wife," the context suggesting "badly" from her point of view, hence "my unfortunate (or unhappily married) wife." There can hardly be a greater contrast than that between the callow young poet, timorously entering the service of the God of Love in the opening work, and this world-weary cynic who quite literally turns his back on love and whatever pleasures it may bring. This one poem may be said to sound the death knell of *amour courtois*, which in any case by the latter half of the fifteenth century had run its course.

Of the four remaining Valentine poems, two are by Fredet, certainly an intimate of Charles judging by the number (11) and the tone of the poems by him in Charles's personal manuscript. Co5 is a long poem about the indifference of Fredet's valentine, and the consequent pangs of unrequited love he has to endure. Charles replies in Co6, also at length, that he too has known such pangs, but that is in the past and now he suffers from *Soussy*, one of the several words for his melancholy. Fredet replies (Co7) offering some consolation, then reverts to his first subject, but it is now about a friend suffering love's torments. The interest of these two long-drawn-out poems for the protagonists was no doubt partly in their varied verse and rhyme patterns, and the variations they give on standard themes. In R228 Fredet complains to *Amour* about the suffering love gave him, while in the following poem Simonnet Caillau gives details of herbal remedies which will get rid of the woes caused by love (see note to R151). In R5, René d'Anjou ("le Roi René") assures his valentine that he will serve her loyally, with, however, one exception—presumably his wife. In R271, Tignonville (Guillaume de Monceau) reveals that, to maintain the St. Valentine tradition, his heart has chosen his damsel.

Note on *ballade* form

A striking feature of the 71 *ballades* between the Introduction and the *Songe* is
the variety of forms in what is generally assumed to have been a fairly rigid pattern. Within the usual framework of 3 verses ending in a refrain, with the first
5 lines of each following the same rhyme pattern: ABABB (with only 2 exceptions), Charles introduces a total of 20 variations, the variants being the number
of lines in each verse, the number of syllables in each line, the rhyme patterns
following the first 5 lines of each verse. As the following tables show, 3 patterns
clearly dominate, between them accounting for over a third of the series, while
11 are limited to a single poem. There are only 5 instances of consecutive poems
using the same pattern: B5–B7, B13–B14, B19–B20, B31–B32, B48–B50. Variety within a given pattern, and also within a given theme, appears to have been
one of Charles's aims.

LINES PER VERSE	LENGTH OF LINES	RHYME AFTER ABABB	POEMS INVOLVED
7	10	CC	B4
8	7	AAB	B26
8	8	CBC	B2, B8, B16, B22, B24, B29, B31, B32, B34, B41, B45, B48, B49, B50, B53, B59, B64
8	8	CCB	B15, B36, B46, B60
8	10	ABA	B23
8	10	CBC	B1, B10, B12, B19, B20, B63
8	10	CCB	B66
9	8	CDCD	B5, B6, B7, B13, B14, B17, B33, B35, B37, B39, B47, B52, B70
9	8	CDDC	B25, B57, B65
9	8	CCDD	B30
9	10	CDCD	B27
9	10	CDDC	B9, B58
10	8	CCDCD	B3, B18, B21, B40, B51, B54, B56
10	10	CCDCD	B11, B62
11	8	CCDEDE	B28, B43
11(9)*	8	CCDEDE	B67

11	8	CCDEED	B61, B69
11	10	CCDEDE	B42
11	10	CCDEED	B38
15	8	CCDDEEFGFG	B44

* The 3rd verse lacks 2 lines, but makes good sense without them.

Exceptions are B55, with 9 lines per verse, 10 syllables per line, a third rhyme being introduced in the fifth line instead of the usual sixth: ABABCCDDC (it is perhaps coincidental that this is the most emotionally charged poem of the series, in which he has just received news of the lady's death), and the last poem of the series, B71, quite different from all the rest, with only 5 syllables per line and rhyme pattern ABABABABABA.

Of the 71 ballades in the series, 51 have *envois*, the traditional conclusion to a *ballade* directly addressing the person to whom the poem is dedicated. Charles, however, introduces variations here as everywhere else. While 19 are addressed to the lady, variously called *Ma Dame, Belle, Bonne, Douce Amie, Princesse,* and *Toutes Dames,* 15 are addressed to abstractions—*Amour, Loyauté, Espoir, Souvenir, Advis, Dieu*—while 13 provide a conclusion to the poem with no dedication. Length varies between 4 and 6 lines, the rhyme pattern always repeating that of the concluding lines of the verses. The 20 poems lacking *envois* have no particular features that account for the absence.

In Charles's time there was as yet no convention requiring alternating masculine and feminine rhymes. The clear predominance of masculine rhymes was no doubt owed more to the nature of the language than any deliberate choice on Charles's part. The frequency of rhymes such as the following indicates that there was no preoccupation with rich rhyme: *dy:mercy; puy:suy; a:va; rigueur:doleur; tours:rebours; per:tarder:conter; tort:reconfort.*

Note on *chançon* and *rondel* form

The third series of *ballades*[121] is followed by a long series of shorter lyrics (beginning with *chançons*), occupying the last two-thirds of the MS. The first bear the heading "Chançon," eventually replaced by "Rondel." Several *chançons,* having no characteristic distinguishing them from the rest, have had the second title, "Rondel," added in a later hand beneath the first. These are detailed in the textual notes.

Most of the *chançons* (Ch1–Ch74), consist of 13 lines (octosyllabics are the favoured length, see below), the first two repeated at the end of the second verse, the first line only at the end: *ABBA ABAB ABBAA.* Nine have 17 lines (Ch9,

---

[121] The first series preceding the *Songe en complainte* and the second following it.

Ch13, Ch17, Ch39, Ch41, Ch44, Ch45, Ch53, and Ch60), the first verse containing 5 lines, the first 3 of which are repeated at the end of the second verse: *AAB*BA AAB*AAB* AABBA*A*. The scribes' addition of the new heading "Rondel" to some of the *chançons* is apparently random. It was certainly applied to them after the duke's return from England. Towards the mid-century, not only had the term *rondel* become the norm for all such poems, the central refrain was also being reduced to one line. One manuscript, BnF nouv. acq. fr. 15771, the *terminus ad quem* of which is 1453, contains 97 *rondels* by different authors.[122] Of these, 58, as printed by its modern editor, have a one-line central refrain, 24 have no central refrain, only 15 have a two-line central refrain. Another collection of *rondels*, from about the same period, contains 40 *rondels*, 24 of which have the one-line central refrain, 14 have no central refrain, and only 2 the longer refrain.[123] Already in the second half of the fifteenth century the first examples appeared of what was to become the ultimate reduction, in which the refrain was limited to the first word or two of the poem's first line.[124]

The *chançons* also lead into the *rondels* in another way: line length. Octosyllabics dominate very clearly, the only exceptions being Ch3, Ch15, and Ch32 with lines of seven syllables, and Ch11, Ch14, Ch26, Ch31, Ch38, Ch69 with lines of ten syllables. Ch71 has lines of four syllables while Ch72 has lines of five syllables.. The pattern is set for the *rondels* that follow. Octosyllabics still dominate, and, as in the *chançons*, variations occur, from the shortest lines of four syllables to the longest of ten. However, in well over 80% of all these poems, whether headed *chançon* or *rondel*, and whatever the length of line, a regular pattern is followed in the two opening lines: the first is end-stopped since it concludes the poem. The second qualifies the first without being essential to it and is also end-stopped:

> Dieu, qu'il l'a fait bon regarder
> La gracïeuse, bonne et belle . . . (Ch6)

> Se ma doleur vous saviés,
> Mon seul joyeux pensement . . . (Ch15)

> Pour le don que m'avez donné,
> Dont tresgrant gré vous doy savoir . . . (Ch24)

> Pour les grans biens de vostre renommee
> Dont j'oy parler a vostre grant honneur . . . (Ch26)

---

[122] Barbara L. S. Inglis, ed., *Le manuscrit B. N. nouv acq. fr. 15771* (Paris: Honoré Champion, 1985).

[123] See Robert Deschaux, ed., *Les œuvres de Pierre Chastellain* (Geneva: Droz, 1982).

[124] See Margaret Zsuppán, ed., *Jean Robertet: oeuvres* (Geneva: Droz; Paris: Minard, 1970), 47–48, 158; also Inglis, *Le manuscrit*, 68–69, 124 (poem by Meschinot); Fox, *Lyric Poetry*, 116–31.

It is for this reason that the middle refrain can equally well be of one line or two. Characteristic examples are the first *chançon* (Ch1) and the last *rondel* by Charles (R457). In each case here, the first version of each poem is as it appears in the MS., except that there only the first one or two words of the refrain lines are written:[125]

Chançon 1:

Ce may, qu'Amours pas ne sommeille	Ce may, qu'Amours pas ne sommeille
Mais fait amans eslïesser	Mais fait amans eslïesser,
De riens ne me doy soussïer,	De riens ne me doy soussïer,
Car pas n'ay la pusse en l'oreille.	Car pas n'ay la pusse en l'oreille.
Ce n'est mie doncques merveille	Ce n'est mie doncques merveille
Se je vueil joye demener,	Se je vueil joye demener,
Ce may, *qu'Amours pas ne sommeille*	Ce may, *qu'Amours pas ne sommeille.*
Mais fait *amans eslïesser.*	
Quant je me dors, point ne m'esveille,	Quant je me dors, point ne m'esveille,
Pour ce que n'ay a quoy penser.	Pour ce que n'ay a quoy penser.
Sy ay vouloir de demourer	Sy ay vouloir de demourer
En ceste vie nompareille,	En ceste vie nompareille,
Ce may, *qu'Amours pas ne sommeille.*	Ce may, *qu'Amours pas ne sommeille.*

Rondel 457:

Salués moy, toute la compaignie	Salués moy, toute la compaignie
Ou a present estez a chiere lye,	Ou a present estez a chiere lye,
Et leur dites que voulentiés seroye	Et leur dites que voulentiés seroye
Avecques eulx, mais estre n'y pourroye,	Avecques eulx, mais estre n'y pourroye,
Pour Viellesse qui m'a en sa ballie.	Pour Viellesse qui m'a en sa ballie.
Au temps passé, Jennesse sy jolie	Au temps passé, Jennesse sy jolie
Me gouvernoit.Las! Or n'y suy ge mye,	Me gouvernoit. Las! Or n'y suy ge mye,
Et pour cela, pour Dieu, que escuzé soye:	Et pour cela, pour Dieu, que escuzé soye:
Salués moy, *toute la compaignie*!	Salués moy, *toute la compaignie*
	Ou a present estez a chiere lye.

---

[125] The final line of "Salués moi" is (unusually) written out in the MS. Theoretically at least, there is a third possibility. In both these poems, and several others, the first two words could stand alone as the refrain. That this was not the intention, however, is shown by the scribe's "etc." which follows them.

Me gouvernoit. Las! Or n'y suy ge mye,
Et pour cela, pour Dieu, que escuzé soye:
Salués moy, *toute la compaignie!*

Amoureus fus, or ne le suy ge mye,
Et en Paris menoye bonne vie.
Adieu bon temps, ravoir ne vous saroye.
Bien sanglé fus d'une estrete courroye,
Que par Age, convient que la deslie.
Salués moy, *toute la compaignie!*

Me gouvernoit. Las! Or n'y suy ge mye,
Et pour cela, pour Dieu, que escuzé soye.
Salués moy, *toute la compaignie,*
Ou a present estez a chiere lye.

Amoureus fus, or ne le suy ge mye,
Et en Paris menoye bonne vie.
Adieu bon temps, ravoir ne vous saroye.
Bien sanglé fus d'une estrete courroye,
Que par Age convient que la deslie.
Salués moy, *toute la compaignie!*

However, there are exceptions. In 22 cases, amounting to a little over 7% of the total, the central refrain cannot consist of the first two lines, e.g., R45:

Cueur, a qui prendrez vous conseil?
A nul ne pouez descouvrir . . .

The complete list is as follows: R12, R29, R45, R130, R145, R146, R149, R154, R193, R196, R215, R230, R238, R242, R243, R254, R302, R386, R398, R424, R431, R453. Eighteen of these are by Charles, the rest by various contributors to the MS. In complete contrast, an even smaller number can be said to read better with the first two, occasionally three, first lines as the central refrain, but even here the single-line refrain is always possible. In all these cases we have supplied the second line in brackets, so the poem can be read either way, e.g., R59:

Faignant de sousrire
Quant suis tres dolent,
Plus penser que dire
[Me couvient souvent.]

cf. R61, R70, R79, R80, R123, R124, R160, R313, R340. There is a note to R59, to which all these refer.

Finally, nearly three times this number are written with no central refrain: R143, R144, R224, R225, R227, R232, R234, R235, R236, R260, R277, R291, R320, R346, R367, R377, R379 through to R385, R395, R427, R434. Half of these have quite a distinctive pattern: either 4-2-2-5 (R260, R346, R380, R381, R383, R385), or 5-3-3-6: (R143, R144, R377, R382, R384, R427), while R434 has 7-3-3-8. Also unique is R173 with 4-2-4, but this is probably owed to omission of the central refrain. This has been added in brackets to match the surrounding rondels.

In conclusion, the peculiarity is not that the second line of the chançons has disappeared from the central refrain. Its superfluity there made its eventual demise inevitable. The peculiarity is that the second line of the vast majority of the *rondels* continued to be end-stopped when there was no longer any need for this, so enabling these poems to be read, like the earlier *chançons*, with a central refrain of either one or two lines. Why was this so? Possibly it was the result of long-established habits dying hard, and perhaps a touch of nostalgia for the far-off traditions of Charles's early, pre-Agincourt years. Since this is the case with most *rondels*, it is surely a deliberate, inbuilt ambiguity. The close attention to detail essential in the composition of such poems surely means that Charles cannot have been unaware of the obvious ambiguity in hundreds of them. They offer a choice. Well over 80% can be read with either a one-line central refrain, or two. This is far too large a figure for the matter to be dismissed as coincidental. It was surely intended to be so by Charles, part, no doubt, of the pleasure he found in composing these poems, which are a good deal more complex than has hitherto been believed.

Champion has often been criticized for printing the *rondels* sometimes with a two-line central refrain where the manuscript invariably indicates one only, and on other occasions retaining the single-line refrain. So he has made his own choice, which is exactly what the poems invite the reader to do. He was, however, wrong to put his personal stamp on the poems. He should have reproduced them with the length of refrains shown in the manuscript, leaving his readers to make up their own minds, and that is how they have been reproduced here.

Although differences between *chançon* form and *rondel* form are more apparent than real, there is a difference of subject matter. While the *chançon's* principal concern is with variations on the traditional courtly love theme, the *rondels* open the floodgates to practically any subject that catches Charles's attention, mostly of a topical nature: the seasons (B17, R44, R320), a thwarted lover who had to jump out of a window (R28), a cosy bed (R51), spotty-faced, noisy children (R138), foolish young lovers (R277), good food and wine (R377), an old pet dog (R415), and so much else. It is poetry of an intensely private nature, written for the entertainment of a narrow court circle, and as an expression of his innermost thoughts and feelings.

§7 The language

The main features distinguishing late medieval French from the modern language, as revealed by Bibliothèque nationale manuscript fr. 25458, are summarised as follows:

Frequent omission of personal pronouns
As examples, the first person singular, present indicative of three common verbs are quoted here: *Avoir, être, vouloir*:

J'ai/ai (alternative spelling ay)

Omission of the pronoun is frequent in the interior of a line: *Un mirouer qu'ay acheté*, B35, 2. This ellipsis, *qu'ay*, occurs frequently, depending on syllable count. Here, *que j'ai acheté*, as in Modern French, would give a syllable too many. Occasionally the pronoun is omitted where it could equally well have been used: *Et ay esté*, B13, 25; *com en vous ay fiance*, B22, 26. At the beginning of a sentence *J'ai* is regularly used: *J'ay en Espoir . . .* B14, 24 ; *J'ay aucune fois le vouloir . . .* B7, 2 ; etc. *Ai (Ay)* may only appear at the beginning of a line in two circumstances:

1) As an overflow from the preceding line:
 . . . par vostre commandement
 Ay despendu de ma jeunesse   B54, 37–38, etc.

2) As an interrogative:
 Ay je bien dit . . .?   R327, 6, etc.

Je suis/suis (alternative spellings: sui, suy, suys)

Numbers are fairly evenly divided between use and omission of the pronoun, syllable count again being the deciding factor: *Puis qu'ainsi est que de vous suis loingtains . . .* B10, 8 (decasyllabic); *A l'estude je suis venu . . .* B 94, 2 (octosyllabic). Here too, the full form *Je suis* is used at the beginning of a sentence: *Je suis alé . . .* B55, 10; *Je suis gouverné . . .* B82, 22; etc. This contrasts with *Desarmé suis . . .* B87, 7; *Ygnorant suis . . .* B102, 22; etc. As with *ai*, *suis* can begin a line in only two circumstances:

1) As an overflow:
 En douleur et merencolie
 Suis . . .   R62, 8–9

 Entre les amoureux fourrez . . .
 Suis . . .   Ch60, 1–3

2) As an interrogative:
 Suis je destiné en ma vie
 D'estre tousjours en tel hutin?   R301, 10–11

 Suis je enchanté . . .?   R327, 13

Je vueil/vueil

Vueil without pronoun predominates in the interior of a line. Once more the form with pronoun regularly begins a sentence: *Je ne vueil pas . . .* B83, 17; *Je vueil endurer . . .* Ch29, 9. Again, *vueil* can only appear at the beginning of a line as an overflow:

> *Se may, le plus plaisant des moys,*
> *Vueil servir, ce present Esté . . .*   R402, 3–4

As with *ai* and *suis*, *vueil* could not be confused with any other form of the verb, so the pronoun was redundant. In this instance, the second person singular eventually took the place of this isolated form, hence modern *je veux, tu veux*, etc. The circumstances described above with these three common verbs apply equally well to other verbs, though with many, imperative and optative forms are also found at the beginning of lines and sentences: *Chantez ce que vous pensés . . .* R49, 7; *Pleust a Dieu . . .* B5, 15; etc.

Omission of definite and indefinite articles before nouns

This occurs less frequently than is the case with pronouns before verbs. Usage does not differ greatly from modern French. However: *. . . Il dessert bon guerdonnement . . .* B21, 19 (Modern French: *il mérite une bonne récompense*) *Non pas amans qui congnoissent qu'est joye* Intro., 65 (Modern French: *Non pas les amants qui savent ce que c'est que la joie*).

Word order

This quite often differs from modern usage: *. . . j'ay loyaument lui promis . . .* (Intro., 168) (Modern French: *je lui ai loyalement promis*). Two regular orders differing from Modern French are:

1) direct and indirect object pronouns before a verb: *se le me commandés . . .* Intro., 38; *Le me baillant . . .* Bal 4, 367; etc.

2) direct object pronoun before the auxiliary rather than the infinitive: *. . . je ne le puis celer . . .* B1, 5; *. . . cuide qu'il le doye faire* R158, 9. In each case grammarians eventually decided that the direct object pronoun should immediately precede the verb, hence: *me le donnant, je ne peux pas le cacher . . .*, etc.

Spelling

Many words have more than one spelling in medieval French. In one of Charles's poems, the scribe appears to be having a little fun when he spells the same word three different ways in one line: *Alez vous ant, allez, alés . . .* R68, 1. Spellings such as *scavoir, moult, veult* are common and are due to misunderstanding on the part of the scribes. *Scavoir* was thought to derive from Latin *scire*, hence the addition of the *-c-*. In fact it derived from Latin *sapere*. The *-l-* in *moult* etc. should not have been added since it was already present in the vocalised *-u-*, while *-s-* in *estre, feste*, etc., had become silent, later to be replaced in spelling by an accent over the preceding vowel: *être, fête*, etc.

Vocabulary

Numbers of words in common use in Charles's time have since disappeared, e.g., *cuider* has been replaced by *penser*, *moult* by *très* or *beaucoup* depending on the context, *pieça* by *il y a longtemps*, etc. All such words are included in the Glossary.

In conclusion, despite the numerous differences in syntax, spelling, and vocabulary, Charles's language and that of his fellow poets should not be beyond the comprehension of anybody reasonably familiar with the modern language, the more so as the Glossary, Notes, and Translation are there to facilitate understanding.

§8 Editorial principles and presentation of the text

This is a complete edition of Charles d'Orléans's personal copy of his poetry, Paris, Bibliothèque nationale de France, MS. fr. 25458 (O). This edition does not present the poetry in the order of the manuscript's present state but in something like the order in which it was composed (see §2, above). The fact that it is Charles's own copy, partially copied and corrected in his own hand, makes it the necessary basis for any edition that pretends to represent the work closest to the poet's act of writing. No other manuscript can match its authority, though other manuscripts are interesting for a variety of reasons (see Appendix 2). Carpentras, Bibliothèque Inguimbertine, MS. 375 (M), copied from his own manuscript for his wife Marie, may reveal something of her taste and helps on occasion to sort out a textual puzzle. Bibliothèque de Grenoble MS. 873 (G), which contains a selection of the duke's lyrics in a completely new order and in Latin, may shed light on a view of his work that does not emerge from a reading of BnF MS. fr. 25458, revealing a literary posture that produced what A. E. B. Coldiron has called "world poetry."[126] London, BL. MS. Royal 16.F.2 (C) may reveal more about the tastes of English kings and courts in the late fifteenth century than about the duc d'Orléans but is none the less precious for that.

The poet himself copied a number of lyrics into the manuscript and corrected the texts the scribes produced, though not consistently or always as carefully as he might have. He also numbered a series of *ballades* and another series of *chançons* and *rondels*.[127] It is an interesting exercise to consider what he thought in need of correction and what he could overlook or live with (such as erroneous

---

[126] A. E. B. Coldiron, *Canon, Period, and the Poetry of Charles of Orleans: Found in Translation* (Ann Arbor: University of Michigan Press, 2000). In the early 1450s, his Italian secretary, Antonio Astesano, copied many of the lyrics he found in O (reorganized, most likely by the duke) and provided a Latin translation, which was then copied in parallel columns by his brother Nicolas into what is now Grenoble MS. 873 (see Appendix 2).

[127] These numbers are bracketed and placed below each lyric in this edition. The *chançons* and *rondels* the duke numbered without any distinction, so that our number of a *chançon* or *rondel* may differ from that of the duke's (bracketed) number.

headings that indicate verse form or errors made by limners in the decorative initials). Marginal comments and corrections are detailed in the textual notes.

The headings for the *chançons* and *rondels* present a complex problem. It is likely that at least some of them were not written at the same time as was the lyric being titled (some headings being written earlier, some later). They are of course scribal, and it is unlikely that anyone told any of the dozens of scribes who wrote in this book what the headings ought to be (many of these short lyrics have no heading at all).

The few scribal errors that do occur have been corrected; the original readings can be found in the textual notes, as can the errors of limners who provided the wrong decorative initial at various points. In accordance with standard practice, punctuation and accents have been added to facilitate reading, hence *ales > alés, scavoir > sçavoir, oy* (past participle) *> oÿ,* etc. Consonantal *u* and *i* have been changed, the former to *v*, the latter to *j: auoir > avoir, sauez > savez, tousiours > tousjours, iusques > jusques.* Asterisks signal comments on specific words, phrases, or lines in the explanatory notes.

Translator's Preface

The translation is meant to serve two purposes: first, to provide some help with unfamiliar vocabulary and difficult constructions for those reading the lyrics in the original French; and second, to offer to those readers without a working knowledge of Middle French accurate, readable English versions that reproduce something of Charles's elegant and fluent style. Because Middle French syntax and grammar do not differ radically from those of Modern English, it has often, perhaps most often, proven possible to reconcile these two aims. The reader will notice that generally the English corresponds line by line and sometimes even word by word to the original French. However, to produce a readable translation it has occasionally been necessary to alter the line division in the translation and otherwise depart somewhat from strict faithfulness to the original. In doing so, I have been guided by my deep appreciation for Charles's gracefulness, intellectual sophistication, and close attention to verbal texture, attempting to the best of my ability to suggest something of these qualities in the translation. A huge debt of gratitude is owed to this text's editor, John Fox, who not only helpfully surveilled the translation, correcting numerous errors, but also provided me with the benefits of his unrivaled knowledge of Charles, his connections with other poets, and, more generally, of late medieval French literature.

The Text and Translation

Note on the Text

Manuscript page numbers (the manuscript is paginated, not foliated) are indicated in square brackets to the right of the first line of text.

Material in square brackets, whether italicized or not, does not appear in the manuscript.

Lowercase *s* and *i* (*supra* and *infra*) refer to page position (e.g., MS. p. 352i). Below each *chançon* or *rondel*, forms that occupy only half the space on the page, is indicated what, if anything, is written on the other half.

An asterisk (*) refers the reader to an explanatory note. The number in square brackets at the end of each lyric (if there is one) is the number the duke assigned to the poem.

Note on the Translation

Four words call for brief comment here: two ordinary nouns, *belle* and *biens*, and two that are often personified, *cuer* and *danger*. In French the word *belle* contains both the idea of "beautiful" and "lady," a combination without an obvious single equivalent in English, so we have chosen to stick for the most part with the English word "belle." The literal translation of *biens* as "goods" smacks of the mercantile. We have therefore opted for a variety of alternatives (virtues, benefits, good things, etc.). We have likewise tailored the use of contractions to the situation in which the lover/poet finds himself. In conversation with the God of Love, the lady, or other august personages, speech is more formal; in his dealings with his heart and eyes, with various personifications (especially his enemies), and in his "internal" musings, his language is more colloquial.

Personifications, and the allegories within which they often move, were central to much medieval thinking, very often providing the writer with ways both to think about and to demonstrate intangibles such as feelings and ideas as well as relationships between them. This technique of writing and of thinking operated in many different kinds of writing (didactic, devotional, literary, etc.) in the late Middle Ages, and it was an integral part of Charles's literary inheritance. One such "character," *Danger,* is often translated into English as "Haughtiness," but the English word does

not carry the additional sense of threat or power to harm, which is often appropriate in the context in which is it found here. To quote John Fox, "Dangier . . . plays a
prominent part, signifying any factor that comes between the poet and his desires, or
any melancholy thoughts that assail him, for Dangier changes shape and substance,
and passes from concrete to abstract as readily as do his other allegorical creations.
Only the fundamental essence of the particular abstraction remains constant" (*Lyric
Poetry*, 82). We have therefore translated it here with its English cognate, "Danger."
The heart, *cuer*, is referred to with neuter pronouns when it is treated as an object or an
organ. When it acts in any way (weeps, waits, etc.), it calls for masculine pronouns.

[Introductory narrative*]

Ou temps passé, quant Nature me fist   [MS. p. 1]
En ce monde venir, elle me mist
Premierement tout en la gouvernance
D'une dame qu'on appelloit Enfance
5   En lui faisant estroit commandement
De me nourrir et garder tendrement
Sans point souffrir Soing ou Merencolie
Aucunement me tenir compaignie,
Dont elle fist loyaument son devoir.
10   Remercier l'en doy, pour dire voir.

En cest estat par un temps me nourry,
Et aprés ce, quant je fu enforcy,
Ung messagier, qui Aage s'appella,*
Une lettre de creance bailla
15   A Enfance de par Dame Nature
Et si lui dist que plus la nourriture
De moy n'auroit et que Dame Jennesse
Me nourriroit et seroit ma maistresse.
Ainsi du tout Enfance delaissay
20   Et avecques Jennesse m'en alay.

Quant Jennesse me tint en sa maison
Un peu avant la nouvelle saison
En ma chambre s'en vint un bien matin
Et m'esveilla le jour Saint Valentin*
25   En me disant : «Tu dors trop longuement,
Esveille toy et aprestes briefment,
Car je te vueil avecques moy mener
Vers un seigneur dont te fault acointer,
Lequel me tient sa servante treschiere.
30   Il nous fera sans faillir bonne chiere.»

Je respondy : «Maistresse gracïeuse,   [p. 2]
De lyé cueur et voulenté joyeuse
Vostre vouloir suy content d'acomplir,
Mais humblement je vous vueil requerir
35   Qu'il vous plaise le nom de moy nommer
De ce seigneur dont je vous oy parler,
Car s'ainsi est que sienne vous tenés,
Sien estre vueil, se le me commandés,
Et en tous fais vous savez que desire
40   Vous ensuïr, sans en riens contredire.»

Long ago, when Nature had me
Come into this world, she put me
First under the sole authority
Of a lady whose name was Childhood,
5   Strictly commanding her
To nourish and care tenderly for me
Without allowing Worry or Melancholy
Ever to be my companions,
And she faithfully discharged this duty.
10   I should give her thanks, if truth be told.

In this state she sustained me for some time
And afterward, when I had grown in strength,
A messenger whose name was Age
Presented to Childhood a testimonial
15   Letter on behalf of Lady Nature
Saying she was to be charged
No longer with my upbringing, and Lady Youth
Should care for me and be my mistress.
In this way I abandoned Childhood completely
20   And ventured forth with Youth.

While Youth was keeping me in her house,
A little before springtime,
She came into my room early one morning
And awoke me on this St. Valentine's day,
25   Saying to me: "You sleep too long.
Get up and get dressed at once,
For I will take you along
To a lord you should meet,
Who retains me as his much esteemed servant.
30   He will treat us kindly, of this there is no doubt."

I answered: "Gracious mistress,
With a happy heart and eager goodwill
I'm pleased to do whatever you desire,
But, with humility, I'd like to ask you
35   To please name for me the name
Of that lord whom I heard you mention.
For if you consider yourself his,
I wish to be his, if you so command me,
And in all things you know my desire is
40   To follow your lead, offering no opposition."

«Puis qu'ainsi est», dist elle, «mon enfant,
Que de savoir son nom desirez tant,
Sachiez de vray que c'est le Dieu d'Amours
Que j'ay servy et serviray tousjours,
45   Car de pieça suy de sa retenue
Et de ses gens et de lui bien congneue.
Oncques ne vis maison jour de ta vie
De plaisans gens si largement remplie.
Je te feray avoir d'eulx accointance,
50   La trouverons de tous biens habondance.»

Du Dieu d'Amours quant parler je l'oÿ,
Aucunement me trouvay esbahy.
Pour ce lui dis : «Maistresse, je vous prie
Pour le present que je n'y voise mie,
55   Car j'ay oÿ a plusieurs raconter
Les maulx qu'Amour leur a fait endurer.
En son dangier bouter ne m'oseroye,
Car ses tourmens endurer ne pourroye.
Trop jenne suy pour porter si grant fais,
60   Il vault trop mieulx que je me tiengne en pais.»

«Fy», dist elle, «par Dieu! Tu ne vaulx riens!   [p. 3]
Tu ne congnois l'onneur et les grans biens
Que peus avoir, se tu es amoureux.
Tu as oÿ parler les maleureux,
65   Non pas amans qui congnoissent qu'est joye,
Car raconter au long ne te sauroye
Les biens qu'Amours scet aux siens departir.
Essaye les, puis tu pourras choisir
Se tu les veulx ou avoir ou laissier.
70   Contre vouloir nul n'est contraint d'amer.»

Bien me revint son gracieux langage
Et tost muay mon propos et courage
Quant j'entendy que nul ne contraindroit
Mon cueur d'amer, fors ainsy qu'il vouldroit.
75   Si lui ay dit : «Se vous me promettés,
Ma maistresse, que point n'obligerés
Mon cueur ne moy contre nostre plaisir,
Pour ceste fois je vous vueil obeir
Et a present vous suivray ceste voye.
80   Je prie a Dieu qu'a honneur m'y convoye!»

«Ne te doubtes», se dist elle, «de moy.
Je te prometz et jure, par ma foy,
Par moy ton cueur ja forcé ne sera,

She said: "My child, since you desire
So much to learn his name,
Know truly he is the God of Love,
Whom I've served and will serve always,
45   For I've long been of his company
And am well known to him and his people.
Never, on any day of my life, have I seen
A house so filled with pleasant folk.
I'll introduce you to them;
50   There we'll find all goods in abundance."

When I heard him mention the God of Love,
I found myself a bit taken aback.
And so I said to her: "Mistress, my request
Is that I should on no account go to him,
55   For I have heard several recount
The ills Love made them suffer.
I shouldn't dare put myself under his tyranny,
For I could not endure his torments.
I'm too young to bear so great a burden.
60   Much better I remain at peace."

"Oh no," said she, "By God, you are worthless!
You don't recognize the honor and great benefits
That might be yours if you give yourself to love.
You've heard the unfortunate speak,
65   Not the lovers who know what a joy this is,
For I could not recount to you in full
The benefits Love can bestow on his own people.
Put them to the test; you can then choose
If you wish such things or will leave them be.
70   No one is forced to love against his will."

Her gracious speech greatly pleased me,
And my purpose and intention both changed
When I heard no one would compel
My heart to love unless it was its wish.
75   So I said to her: "If you promise,
Mistress mine, that you'll obligate
Neither my heart nor me against our wishes,
I'll obey you this one time
And for the present follow you on this path.
80   I pray God in honor convey me along it!"

"Have no fear of me," she said,
"I promise and swear to you, upon my faith,
Your heart will never be compelled by me.

Mais garde soy qui garder se pourra,
85   Car je pense que ja n'aura povoir
De se garder, mais changera vouloir
Quant Plaisance lui monstrera a l'ueil
Gente Beaulté plaine de doulx acueil,
Jeune, sachant, et de maniere lye
90   Et de tous biens a droit souhait garnie.»

Sans plus parler, sailli hors de mon lit,   [p. 4]
Quant promis m'eut ce que devant est dit,
Et m'aprestay le plus joliement
Que peu faire, par son commandement,
95   Car jennes gens qui desirent honneur,
Quant veoir vont aucun royal seigneur,
Ilz se doivent mettre de leur puissance
En bon array, car cela les avance
Et si les fait estre prisiez des gens,
100   Quant on les voit netz, gracïeux et gens.

Tantost aprés tous deux nous en alasmes
Et si longtemps ensemble cheminasmes
Que venismes au plus pres d'un manoir
Trop bel assis et plaisant a veoir.
105   Lors Jennesse me dist : «Cy est la place
Ou Amour tient sa court et se soulace.
Que t'en semble, n'est elle pas tresbelle?»
Je respondy : «Oncque mais ne vi telle.»
Ainsi parlant approchasmes la porte
110   Qui a veoir fut tresplaisant et forte.

Lors Jennesse si hucha le portier
Et lui a dit : «J'ay cy un estrangier
Avecques moy. Entrer nous fault leans :
On l'appelle Charles, Duc d'Orlians.»
115   Sans nul delay le portier nous ouvry,
Dedens nous mist et puis nous respondy :
«Tous deux estes cyens les bien venus.
Aler m'en vueil, s'il vous plaist, vers Venus
Et Cupido, si leur raconteray
120   Qu'estes venuz et ceans mis vous ay.»

Ce portier fu appellé Compaignie   [p. 5]
Qui nous receu de maniere si lye.
De nous party, a Amour s'en ala.
Briefment aprés devers nous retourna
125   Et amena Bel Acueil et Plaisance
Qui de l'ostel avoient l'ordonnance.

But let the man who can protect himself do so!
85   For I think the heart will not have the power
To restrain itself, but rather heart's desire will alter
When to the eyes Pleasure reveals
Noble Beauty, replete with fair welcome,
Youthful, lively, her manner joyful,
90   And charged with all good things one might properly wish."

Without saying more, I jumped from my bed
As she promised me what has been said above,
And I dressed myself as attractively
As I could manage, according to her commandment,
95   For young people who are eager for honor,
When they go to see any royal lord,
Should dress finely, as best
They can manage, for it will advance
And further them with people
100   If they appear well groomed, gracious, and elegant.

Very soon thereafter, we two made our way
And for a long time proceeded
Till we came very close to a manor
Very handsomely sited and pleasant in appearance.
105   Then Youth said to me: "Here is the place
Where Love holds his court and disports himself.
What do you think? Is it not very beautiful?"
I answered: "Never have I seen the like."
Speaking thus, we approached the gate
110   Which, in appearance, was very attractive and strong.

Then Youth called over the porter
And said: "I have a stranger here
With me. We are to go inside.
Charles is his name, the duke of Orleans."
115   Without delay, the porter opened to us,
Allowed us inside, and then answered us:
"You two are welcome here.
If you please, I would like to go to Venus
And Cupid and tell them
120   That you have come and I have let you in."

Company was the name of the porter
Who received us so pleasantly;
He left us at the spot and went off to Love.
Soon thereafter he returned
125   And brought along Fair Welcome and Pleasure,
Who had charge of administering the house.

Lors, quant de nous approuchier je les vy,
Couleur changay et de cueur tressailly.
Jennesse dist : «De riens ne t'esbahys.
130   Soies courtois et en faiz et en dis.»

Jeunesse tost se tira devers eulx.
Aprés elle m'en alay tout honteux,
Car jennes gens perdent tost contenance
Quant en lieu sont ou n'ont point d'acointance,
135   Si lui ont dit : «Bien soiez vous venue.»
Puis par la main l'ont liement tenue.
Elle leur dit : «De cueur vous en mercy.
J'ay amené ceans cest enfant cy
Pour lui moustrer le tresroyal estat
140   Du Dieu d'Amours et son joyeux esbat.»

Vers moy vindrent me prenant par la main
Et me dirent : «Nostre roy souverain,
Le Dieu d'Amours, vous prie que venés
Par devers lui, et bien venu serés.»
145   Je respondy humblement : «Je mercie
Amour et vous de vostre courtoisie.
De bon vouloir iray par devers luy.
Pour ce je suy venu cy au jourd'uy,
Car Jennesse m'a dit que le verray
150   En son estat et graciëux array.»

Bel Acueil print Jennesse par le bras,   [p. 6]
Et Plaisance si ne m'oublia pas,
Mais me pria qu'avec elle venisse
Et tout le jour pres d'elle me tenisse.
155   Si alasmes en ce point jusqu'au lieu
La ou estoit des amoureux le dieu.
Entour de lui son peuple s'esbatoit,
Dançant, chantant, et maint esbat faisoit.
Tous a genoulz nous meismes humblement,
160   Et Jennesse parla premierement,

Disant : «Treshault et noble puissant prince,
A qui subgiet est chascune province
Et que je doy servir et honnorer
De mon povair, je vous vien presenter*
165   Ce jenne filz qui en moy a fiance,
Qui est sailly de la maison de France,
Creu ou jardin semé de fleur de lis,*
Combien que j'ay loyaument lui promis

Then, as we saw them approach,
My color changed, and my heart skipped a beat.
Youth said: "Fear nothing.
130   Let your words and deeds be courteous."

At once Youth drew beside them.
I followed her, very embarrassed,
For young people lose all composure
When they are some place unfamiliar.
135   And they said to her: "You are welcome."
Then they gladly took her by the hand.
She said to them: "I thank you from the heart.
I have brought this young man here
To show him the very regal state
140   Of the God of Love and his pleasant amusement."

With her in hand, they came my way
And said to me: "Our sovereign king,
The God of Love, asks you to make your way
Before him, and you will be welcome."
145   I answered humbly: "I thank
You and Love for your courtesy.
Willingly, I will go to him.
That is why I came here today,
For Youth told me I would see him
150   In his gracious estate and array."

Fair Welcome took Youth by the arm,
And Pleasure did not neglect me,
But begged that I go with her
And stay by her side all that day long.
155   So in this fashion we went as far as the place
Where resided the God of those who love.
All around him his people were making merry,
Dancing, singing, and playing at many games.
We all got down humbly on our knees,
160   And Youth was the first to speak,

Saying: "Mighty prince, exalted and noble,
To whom every province is subject
And whom I should serve and honor
As I am able, I come to present to you
165   This young man, who trusts in me,
Who sprang from the house of France,
Grew up in the garden planted with the lily flower;
In the event, I have faithfully promised

Qu'en riens qui soit je ne le lyeray,
170   Mais a son gré son cueur gouverneray.»

Amour respond : «Il est le bien venu.
Ou temps passé j'ay son pere congneu,*
Plusieurs autres aussi de son lignage
Ont maintes foiz esté en mon servage,
175   Par quoy tenu suy plus de lui bien faire,
S'il veult aprés son lignage retraire.»
«Vien ça,» dist il, «mon filz, que penses tu?
Fus tu oncques de ma darde feru?
Je croy que non, car ainsi le me semble.
180   Vien pres de moy, si parlerons ensemble.»

De cueur tremblant pres de lui m'aprochay,   [p. 7]
Si lui ay dit : «Sire, quant j'acorday
A Jennesse de venir devers vous,
Elle me dist que vous estiez sur tous
185   Si trescourtois que chacun desiroit
De vous hanter, qui bien vous congnoissoit.
Je vous suply que je vous treuve tel.
Estrangier suy venu en vostre hostel,
Honte seroit a vostre grant noblesse
190   Se fait m'estoit ceans mal ou rudesse!»

«Par moy contraint,» dist Amour, «ne seras,
Mais de ceans jamais ne partiras
Que ne soies es las amoureux pris.
Je m'en fais fort, se bien l'ay entrepris.
195   Souvent mercy me vendras demander
Et humblement ton fait recommander,
Mais lors sera ma grace de toy loing,
Car a bon droit te fauldray au besoing.
Et si feray vers toy le dangereux
200   Comme tu fais d'estre vray amoureux.»

«Venez avant,» dist il, «Plaisant Beauté,
Je vous requier que sur la loyauté
Que vous me devez, le venez assaillir.
Ne le laissiez reposer ne dormir
205   Ne nuit ne jour, s'il ne me fait hommage.
Aprivoisiez ce compaignon sauvage.
Ou temps passé vous conqueistes Sampson*
Le fort, aussi le sage Sal[e]mon.
Se cest enfant surmonter ne savez,
210   Vostre renon du tout perdu avez.»

170   To constrain him to do nothing at all,
But govern his heart according to his wish."

Love answers: "He is welcome.
In times past I knew his father;
Several others as well of his line
Have many times been in my service,
175   So I am bound even more to treat him well
If he will follow the path of his lineage."
"Come here," said he, "my son, what do you think?
Have you ever been struck by my arrow?
I think not, or so it seems.
180   Draw close, and we will speak."

With trembling heart, I went up to him
And said: "Lord, when I agreed
With Youth to come to you,
She told me you are so much courtlier
185   Than all others that all who know you well
Are eager to be of your company.
I pray I find you such.
I have come as a stranger to your house.
It would dishonor your exalted estate
190   For any ill or rudeness to befall me here."

Love said: "I shall do nothing to compel you.
Yet you will not leave this place
Save as one bound by the ties of love.
I am certain of that, provided I've undertaken it well.
195   Often you will come to ask for mercy
And humbly beg consideration of your case.
But my mercy will be withheld,
For it is my right to fail you in your time of need
And treat you with arrogance
200   Even as you act the true lover."

"Come forward," he said, "Pleasant Beauty,
I require you, by the loyalty
You owe me, to assault the man.
Allow him neither rest nor sleep,
205   Night and day, if he does not render me homage.
Tame this savage companion.
In times past, you conquered Samson
The strongman, also wise Solomon.
If you cannot get the better of this child,
210   You will forfeit all your renown."

Beauté lors vint, decoste moy s'assist.   [p. 8]
Un peu se teut, puis doulcement m'a dit :
«Amy, certes, je me donne merveille
Que tu ne veulx pas que l'en te conseille.
215   Au fort saches que tu ne peuz choisir,
Il te couvient a Amour obeir.»
Mes yeulx prindrent fort a la regarder,
Plus longuement ne les en peu garder.
Quant Beauté vit que je la regardoye,
220   Tost par mes yeulx un dard au cueur m'envoye.

Quant dedens fu, mon cueur vint esveillier
Et tellement le print a catoillier
Que je senti que trop rioit de joye.
Il me despleut qu'en ce point le sentoye,
225   Si commençay mes yeulx fort a tenser
Et envoyay vers mon cueur un penser
En lui priant qu'il giectast hors ce dard.
Helas! Helas! g'y envoiay trop tard,
Car quant Penser arriva vers mon cueur,
230   Il le trouva ja pasmé de doulceur.

Quand je le sceu, je dis par desconfort :
«Je hé ma vie et desire ma mort,
Je hé mes yeulx, car par eulx suy deceu,
Je hé mon cueur qu'ay nicement perdu,
235   Je hé ce dard qui ainsi mon cueur blesse.
Venez avant, partués moy, Destresse,
Car mieulx me vault tout a un cop morir
Que longuement en desaise languir!
Je congnois bien, mon cueur est pris es las
240   Du Dieu d'Amours, par vous, Beauté, helas!»

Adonc je cheu aux piez d'Amours malade   [p. 9]
Et semblay mort, tant euz la coleur fade.
Il m'apperceu, si commença a rire,
Disant : «Enfant, tu as besoing d'un mire!
245   Il semble bien par ta face palie
Que tu seuffres tresdure maladie.
Je cuidoye que tu fusses si fort
Qu'il ne fust riens qui te peust faire tort,
Et maintenant, ainsi soudainement,
250   Tu es vaincu par Beauté seulement!

Ou est ton cueur pour le present alé?
Ton grant orgueil est bientost ravalé.
Il m'est advis tu deusses avoir honte

Beauty came to sit beside me.
She was silent a while, then said softly:
"Friend, certainly I am amazed
You do not want anyone to advise you.
215 Know you cannot choose in the end.
You must obey Love."
My eyes looked at her intently;
I could not long restrain them.
Seeing me stare, Beauty at once
220 Sent an arrow through my eyes to my heart.

Lodging there, it aroused my heart
And began to excite it so much
I felt myself smile broadly from joy.
This feeling did not please my heart,
225 So I began arguing fiercely with my eyes,
Sending my heart the thought
That it pluck out the arrow, so I begged.
Alas! Alas! I sent the message too late,
For coming to my heart, Thought found it
230 Already swooned from sweetness.

Realizing this, I said, discouraged:
"I hate my life and long for death.
I hate my eyes, for they've undone me.
I hate my heart, which I've foolishly lost.
235 I hate this arrow, which wounds my heart.
Come on, Distress, finish me off,
For I'd be better off dying at one stroke
Than languishing long in misery.
I see clearly, Beauty, that you hold my heart
240 Fast in the bonds of the God of Love, alas!"

Then, sick, I fell at the feet of Love
As if dead, my color had faded so.
He noticed, then began to smile,
Saying: "Child, you need a physician!
245 It is very evident from your pallid face
You suffer from a very grave illness.
I thought you so strong
Nothing could injure you,
And now, all of a sudden,
Beauty, all alone, has conquered you!

Where has your heart now fled?
Your great pride was humbled in a flash.
You should be ashamed, I think,

Si de legier quant Beauté te surmonte
255   Et a mes piez t'a abatu a terre.
Revenge toy, se tu vaulx riens pour guerre,
Ou a elle il vault mieulx de toy rendre,
Se tu ne scez autrement te deffendre,
Car de deux maulx, puis que tu peuz eslire,
260   C'est le meillieur que preignes le moins pire.»

Ainsi de moy fort Amour se mocquoit,
Mais non pourtant de ce ne me challoit,
Car de doleur je estoie si enclos
Que je ne tins compte de tous ses mos.
265   Quant Jennesse vit que point ne parloye,
Car tout advis et sens perdu avoye,
Pour moy parla et au Dieu d'Amours dist :
«Sire, vueilliez qu'il ait aucun respit.»
Amour respont : «Jamais respit n'aura
270   Jusques a tant que rendu se sera!»

Beauté mist lors en son giron ma teste   [p. 10]
Et si m'a dit : «De main mise t'arreste,*
Rens toy a moy et tu feras que sage,
Et a Amours va faire ton hommage.»
275   Je respondy : «Ma dame, je le vueil,
Je me soubzmetz du tout a vostre vueil.
Au Dieu d'Amours et a vous je me rens.
Mon povre cueur a mort feru je sens,
Vueilliez avoir pitié de ma tristesse,
280   Jeune, gente, nompareille princesse!»*

Quant je me fu ainsi rendu a elle,
«Je maintendray,» dist elle, «ta querelle
Envers Amour et tant pourchasseray
Qu'en sa grace recevoir te feray.»
285   A brief parler et sans faire long compte,
Au Dieu d'Amours mon fait au vray raconte
Et lui a dit : «Sire, je l'ay conquis,
Il s'est a vous et a moy tout soubzmis.
Vueilliez avoir de sa doleur mercy,
290   Puis que vostre se tient et mien aussi.

S'il a meffait vers vous, il s'en repent
Et se soubzmet en vostre jugement.
Puis qu'il se veult a vous abandonner,
Legierement lui devez pardonner.
295   Chascun seigneur qui est plain de noblesse
Doit departir mercy a grant largesse.

That Beauty has so easily conquered you
255   And forced you to the ground at my feet.
If you are at all battleworthy, take revenge;
Otherwise better surrender
If you cannot otherwise defend yourself,
For of two ills, since you can choose,
260   Better to take the one less grievous."

Love had much fun with me in this way,
But even so it did not worry me,
For I was so beset by misery
I took no account of his words.
265   When Youth saw I wasn't speaking,
But had lost all wit and sense,
She spoke for me to the God of Love:
"Lord, please let there be some respite!"
Love answered: "He shall have no respite
270   Until he surrenders himself!"

Then Beauty put my head in her lap
And said: "This hand arrests you;
Surrender and you will act wisely.
And go give Love your homage."
275   I answered: "My lady, that is my wish.
I submit myself completely to your will.
To the God of Love and you I surrender.
I feel my poor heart fatally struck.
Please take pity on my sadness,
280   Peerless princess, young and noble."

After I had surrendered to her,
She said: "I will take your part
Against Love and argue until
I have you received in his good graces."
285   Speaking briefly, and not telling a long tale,
She truthfully explained my case to the God of Love
And saying: "Lord, I have conquered the man.
He has submitted completely to both me and you.
Please have mercy on his suffering
290   Since he thinks himself yours, and mine as well.

If he has wronged you, he repents
And submits to your judgment.
Since he intends to devote himself to you,
You ought to pardon him readily.
295   Every lord full of nobility
Should very generously dispense mercy.

De vous servir sera plus obligié,
Se franchement son mal est allegié,
Et si mettra paine de desservir
300   Voz grans biensfais par loyaument servir.»

Amours respont : «Beauté, si sagement   [p. 11]
Avez parlé et raisonnablement
Que pardonner lui vueil la malvueillance
Qu'ay eu vers lui, car par oultrecuidance
305   Me courroussa quant, comme foul et nice,
Il refusa d'entrer en mon service.
Faictes de lui ainsi que vous vouldrés,
Content me tiens de ce que vous ferés.
Tout le soubzmetz a vostre voulenté,
310   Sauve, sans plus, ma souveraineté.»

Beauté respond : «Sire, c'est bien raison
Par dessus tous et sans comparaison,
Que pour seigneur et souverain vous tiengne
Et ligement vostre subgiet deviengne.
315   Premierement devant vous jurera
Que loyaument de cueur vous servira,
Sans espargnier, soit de jours ou de nuis,
Paine, soussy, dueil, courroux ou ennuis,
Et souffrera, sans point se repentir,
320   Les maulx qu'amans ont souvent a souffrir.

Il jurera aussi secondement
Qu'en ung seul lieu amera fermement,
Sans point querir ou desirer le change,
Car, sans faillir, ce seroit trop estrange
325   Que bien servir peust un cueur en mains lieux,
Combien qu'aucuns cueurs ne demandent mieulx
Que de servir du tout a la volee*
Et qu'ilz ayent d'amer la renommee,
Mais au derrain ilz s'en treuvent punis
330   Par Loyauté dont ilz sont ennemis.

En oultre plus promettra tiercement   [p. 12]
Que voz conseulx tendra secrettement
Et gardera de mal parler sa bouche.
Noble prince, ce point cy fort vous touche,
335   Car mains amans, par leurs nices paroles,
Par sotz regars et contenances folles,
Ont fait parler souvent les mesdisans,
Par quoy grevez ont esté voz servans,

He will be more obliged to serve you
If his ills are liberally relieved,
And he will take pains to merit
300   Your great benefits through loyal service."

Love answered: "Beauty, you have spoken
So wisely and reasonably
I will pardon him the ill will
I felt toward him, for through arrogance
305   He angered me when, like a fool and simpleton,
He refused to enter my service.
Do with him as you wish.
I shall be content with whatever action you take.
In all things I submit him to your will
310   Save—and this only—as regards my sovereignty."

Beauty answered: "Lord, it is entirely reasonable
He do homage to you as lord and sovereign,
Beyond all others and with no comparison to them,
Loyally becoming your subject.
315   First, in your presence he will swear
To serve you faithfully from the heart
Night and day, not hesitating because
Of pain, care, misery, anger, or worry,
And he will endure, not begrudging at all,
320   The ills lovers often have to endure.

And, second, he will also swear
To bestow his love unhesitatingly in one place
Not seeking or wanting any change at all
Since, no doubt, it would be shocking
325   For a heart to serve ably here and everywhere,
Though some hearts demand no better
Than to serve indiscriminately
So as to garner renown as lovers.
Yet in the end they find themselves punished
330   By Loyalty, whose enemies they are.

Moreover, and third, he will promise
To keep secret your counsels,
Taking care his mouth utter no villainy.
Noble prince, this point very much concerns you,
335   For many lovers, through their foolish speech,
Through their incautious glances and reckless looks,
Have often encouraged scandalmongers to tell tales;
And thus your servants have been aggrieved,

Et ont receu souventesfois grant perte
340   Contre raison et sans nulle desserte.

Avecques ce il vous fera serment
Que s'il reçoit aucun avancement
En vous servant, qu'il n'en fera ventance.
Cestui meffait dessert trop grant vengeance,
345   Car quant dames veulent avoir pitié
De leurs servans, leur moustrant amitié
Et de bon cueur aucun reconfort donnent,
En ce faisant leurs honneurs abandonnent
Soubz fiance de trouver leurs amans
350   Secrez, ainsi qu'en font les convenans.

Ces quatre poins qu'ay cy devant nommez
De tous amans doivent estre gardez,
Qui a honneur et avancement tirent
Et leurs amours a fin mener desirent.
355   Six autres pointz aussi accordera,
Mais par serement point ne les promettra,
Car nul amant estre contraint ne doit
De les garder, se son prouffit n'y voit,
Mais se faire veult, aprés bon conseil,
360   A les garder doit mettre son traveil.

Le premier est qu'il se tiengne jolis,   [p. 13]
Car les dames le tiennent a grant pris.
Le second est que trescourtoisement
Soy maintendra et gracïeusement.
365   Le tiers point est que, selon sa puissance,
Querra honneur et poursuivra vaillance.
Le quatriesme qu'il soit plain de largesse,
Car c'est chose qui avance noblesse.
Le cinquiesme qu'il suivra compaignie
370   Amant honneur et fuiant villenie.

Le siziesme point et le derrenier
Est qu'il sera diligent escolier,
En aprenant tous les gracïeux tours
A son povair, qui servent en amours :
375   C'est assavoir a chanter et dansser,*
Faire chançons et ballades rimer,
Et tous autres joyeux esbatemens.
Ce sont ycy les dix commandemens
Vray Dieu d'Amours, que je feray jurer
380   A cest enfant, s'il vous plaist l'apeller.»
Lors m'appella et me fist les mains mettre

Many times suffering great loss
340   Unreasonably and with no justification.

And in addition he will swear
That, should he receive any preferment
From serving you, he will not boast of it.
Such a misstep deserves great punishment,
345   For when ladies wish to pity
Their servants, showing them friendship,
And goodheartedly giving them some comfort,
They forfeit their honor doing so,
Trusting they will find their lovers
350   Discreet, just as they have agreed to be.

The four rules I have mentioned
Should be observed by all lovers
Pursuing honor and advancement,
And eager to bring their affairs to a proper end.
355   He will obey six other rules as well,
But not promise this with any oath,
For no lover should be constrained
To keep them should he see no profit there.
But if after sound reflection he agrees to obeying them,
360   He should devote all his energies thereto.

The first is that he should groom himself well,
For ladies put great value on this.
The second is that he should behave
In a very courtly and gracious manner.
365   The third rule is that, as he can,
He should seek honor and pursue valor.
The fourth is that he be full of generosity,
For that is what promotes nobility.
The fifth is that he should keep to a company,
370   Loving honor and fleeing discourtesy.

The sixth rule and the last
Is that he should be a diligent student,
Learning all the graceful accomplishments,
As he is able, which are of use in love.
375   That is to say, singing and dancing,
Composing songs and rhyming ballades,
As well as all other pleasant diversions.
These are the ten commandments
Of the true God of Love, to which I shall have
380   This child swear, if you will please summon him."
Then he called and had me place my hands

Sur ung livre en me faisant promettre
Que feroye loyaument mon devoir
Des poins d'amours garder a mon povair.
385   Ce que je fis de bon vueil lyement.
Adonc Amour a fait commandement
A Bonne Foy, d'Amours chief secretaire,
De ma lettre de retenue faire.*
Quant faicte fut, Loyauté la seella
390   Du seel d'Amours et la me delivra.

Ainsi Amour me mist en son servage,   [p. 14]
Mais pour seurté retint mon cueur en gage,
Pour quoy lui dis que vivre ne pourroye
En cest estat, s'un autre cueur n'avoye.
395   Il respondit : «Espoir, mon medecin,
Te gardera de mort soir et matin,
Jusques a tant qu'auras en lieu du tien
Le cueur d'une qui te tendra pour sien.
Gardes tousjours ce que t'ay commandé,
400   Et je t'auray pour bien recommandé.»

Copie de la lettre de retenue

Dieu Cupido et Venus la deesse,
Ayans povair sur Mondaine Lïesse,
Salus de cueur, par nostre grant humblesse
A tous amans.
405   Savoir faisons que le Duc d'Orlians,
Nommé Charles, a present jeune d'ans,
Nous retenons pour l'un de noz servans
Par ces presentez,
Et lui avons assigné sur noz rentes
410   Sa pensïon en joyeuses attentes
Pour en joïr par noz lectres patentes
Tant que vouldrons,
En esperant que nous le trouverons
Loyal vers nous, ainsi que fait avons
415   Ses devanciers, dont contens nous tenons
Tresgrandement.
Pour ce donnons estroit commandement
Aux officiers de nostre parlement
Qu'ilz le traittent et aident doulcement   [p. 15]
420   En tout affaire
A son besoing, sans venir au contraire,
Si chier qu'ilz ont nous obeir et plaire,
Et qu'ilz doubtent envers nous de forfaire

On a book, while making me promise
To faithfully carry out my duty
And obey the rules of love to my ability,
385   Which I did happily, with a good will.
Then Love issued an order
To Good Faith, chief secretary of Love,
To compose my letter of homage.
When it was done, Loyalty sealed it
390   With Love's seal and gave it over to me.

This was how Love enrolled me in his service,
But as a safeguard kept my heart as a pledge,
And when I told him I could not live
In such a state had I not another heart,
395   He answered: "Hope, my physician,
Will keep you from death day and night
Until you have in place of your own
The heart of a lady who will accept you as hers.
Keep always the commandments I have given you,
400   And I will retain you as one highly recommended."

Copy of the letter of homage

The god Cupid and goddess Venus
Having power over Earthly Happiness,
Greetings from the heart, in our great humility,
To all lovers.
405   We make known that the duke of Orleans,
Charles by name, presently young in years,
We retain as one of our servants
By these presents,
And we have assigned him from our rents
410   His pension in joyful expectations
So he may enjoy them by these letters patent
As long as we wish,
In the hope we will find him
Loyal to us, just as we have found
415   His forebears, with whom we have been pleased
Beyond measure.
For this reason we issue a strict commandment
To the officers of our parliament
To treat and assist him kindly
420   In every circumstance
So gently according to his need, and not to oppose him,
Because they are concerned to obey and please us,
And because they fear harming

En corps et biens,
425　　Le soustenant, sans y espargnier riens,
　　　　Contre Dangier avecques tous les siens :*
　　　　Malle Bouche, plaine de faulx maintiens,
　　　　Et Jalousie,
　　　　Car chascun d'eulx de grever estudie
430　　Les vrais subgietz de nostre seigneurie,
　　　　Dont il est l'un et sera a sa vie,
　　　　Car son serment
　　　　De nous servir devant tous ligement
　　　　Avons receu, et pour plus fermement
435　　Nous asseurer qu'il fera loyaument
　　　　Entier devoir,
　　　　Avons voulu en gage recevoir
　　　　Le cueur de lui, lequel de bon vouloir
　　　　A tout soubzmis en noz mains et povoir,
440　　Pour quoy tenus
　　　　Sommes a lui par ce de plus en plus.
　　　　Si ne seront pas ses biens fais perdus,
　　　　Ne ses travaulx pour neant despendus,
　　　　Mais pour moustrer
445　　A toutes gens bon exemple d'amer
　　　　Nous le voulons richement guerdonner
　　　　Et de noz biens a largesse donner,
　　　　Tesmoing noz seaulx
　　　　Cy atachiez devant tous noz feaulx,   [p. 16]
450　　Gens de conseil et serviteurs loyaulx,
　　　　Venuz vers nous par mandemens royaulx
　　　　Pour nous servir.

　　　　Donné le jour saint Valentin martir*
　　　　En la cité de Gracïeux Desir,
455　　Ou avons fait nostre conseil tenir.
　　　　Par Cupido et Venus souverains,
　　　　A ce presens plusieurs Plaisirs Mondains.

B1　　　　　　　**[Ballade]**   [p. 17]

　　　　Belle, bonne, nompareille, plaisant,*
　　　　Je vous suppli, vueilliez me pardonner,
　　　　Se moy, qui sui vostre grace actendant,
　　　　Viens devers vous pour mon fait raconter.
5　　　　Plus longuement je ne le puis celer
　　　　Qu'il ne faille que sachiés ma destresse
　　　　Comme celle qui me peut conforter,
　　　　Car je vous tiens pour ma seule maistresse.

Our persons and goods,
425 Sustaining him, sparing nothing,
Against Danger and all his folk:
Evil Tongue, who is replete with false conduct,
And Jealousy,
For each is intent on harming
430 The true subjects of our dominion,
Of whom he is one and will be for life,
For his oath
To serve us loyally above all else
We have accepted, and so as to more certainly
435 Assure us he will faithfully carry out
All his obligations,
We have been pleased to take as a pledge
His heart, which with good will
He has submitted completely to our hands and power;
440 And so by this
We are bound to him evermore.
And thus his good deeds will not be in vain,
Nor his labors undertaken for nothing,
But for setting
445 A good example of loving to everyone
We will richly reward the man
And generously bestow our goods upon him,
With our seals as a witness
Here attached in the presence of all our faithful,
450 The members of the council and loyal servants,
Who have come by royal command
To serve us.

Granted the day of Saint Valentine, martyr,
In the city of Gracious Desire,
455 Where we had our council convened.
On behalf of sovereign Cupid and Venus,
Several worldly pleasures to this man present.

Ballade

Belle, virtuous, peerless, cheerful,
I beg you, please pardon me,
If I, who attend your grace,
Come before you to tell my story.
5   No longer can I keep secret
That you must learn of my distress
As the lady who can comfort me,
For I consider you my only mistress.

        Se si a plain vous vois mes maulx disant,
10   Force d'Amours me fait ainsi parler,
        Car je devins vostre loyal servant
        Le premier jour que je peuz regarder
        La grant beauté que vous avez sans per,
        Qui me feroit avoir toute lïesse
15   Se serviteur vous plaisoit me nommer,
        Car je vous tiens pour ma seule maistresse.

        Que me donnez en octroy don si grant
        Je ne l'ose dire ne demander,
        Mais s'il vous plaist que de cy en avant
20   En vous servant puisse ma vie user,
        Je vous supply que, sans me refuser,
        Vueilliez souffrir qu'y mette ma jeunesse.
        Nul autre bien je ne vueil souhaidier,
        Car je vous tiens pour ma seule maistresse.

[1] (This is the numbering added by the poet.)

B2   **[Ballade]**   [p. 18]

        Vueilliez voz yeulx emprisonner
        Et sur moy plus ne les giettés,
        Car, quant vous plaist me regarder,
        Par Dieu, belle, vous me tués
5   Et en tel point mon cueur mettés
        Que je ne sçay que faire doye.
        Je suis mort se vous ne m'aidiés,
        Ma seule souveraine joye.

        Je ne vous ose demander
10   Que vostre cueur vous me donnés,
        Mais, se droit me voulés garder,
        Puis que le cueur de moy avés,
        Le vostre fault que me laissiés,
        Car sans cueur vivre ne pourroye.
15   Faictes en comme vous vouldrés,
        Ma seule souveraine joye.

        Trop hardy suy d'ainsi parler,
        Mais pardonner le me devés
        Et n'en devés autruy blasmer
20   Que le gent corps que vous portés,
        Qui m'a mis, comme vous veés,
        Si fort en l'amoureuse voye

If I come before you confessing all my woes,
10   The force of Love makes me speak,
For I became your loyal servant
The first day I laid eyes upon
The great beauty you possess unrivaled,
Which would give me every happiness
15   Were you pleased to name me your servant,
For I consider you my only mistress.

That you bestow upon me such a gift,
I dare not mention or request,
But if you are pleased that henceforth
20   I might spend my life serving you,
I beg you please do not refuse me;
Let me please spend my youth in this fashion.
I wish for no other benefit,
For I consider you my only mistress.

Ballade

Please take your eyes prisoner
And do not let them look upon me,
For, when you are pleased to gaze at me,
By God, belle, you kill me
5   And bring my heart to such a pass
I know not what I should do.
I am dead unless you help me,
My only sovereign joy.

I do not dare demand
10   You grant me your heart,
But, if you wish to treat me justly,
Since you possess my heart,
You should leave me with yours,
For without a heart I could not live.
15   Do what you wish about this,
My only sovereign joy.

In speaking thus I am too bold,
But you must pardon me
And blame no one else,
20   For the noble form that is yours,
As you see, has so forcefully
Put me on the path of love

Qu'en vostre prison me tenés,
Ma seule souveraine joye.

L'envoy

25　Ma dame, plus que ne savés,
　　Amour si tresfort me guerroye
　　Qu'a vous me rens. Or me prenés,
　　Ma seule souveraine joye.

[2]

B3　　　　　　　**[Ballade]**　　　　　　　[p. 19]

　　C'est grant peril de regarder
　　Chose dont peut venir la mort,
　　Combien qu'on ne s'en scet garder
　　Aucunes fois, soit droit ou tort.
5　Quant Plaisance si est d'accord
　　Avecques un jeune desir,
　　Nul ne pourroit son cueur tenir
　　D'envoyer les yeulx en messaige.
　　On le voit souvent avenir
10　Aussi bien au foul com au sage.

　　Lesquelz yeulx viennent raporter
　　Ung si tresgracïeux raport
　　Au cueur, quant le veult escouter,
　　Que, s'il a eu d'amer l'effort,
15　Encores l'aura il plus fort,
　　Et le font du tout retenir
　　Ou service, sans departir,
　　D'Amours, a son tresgrant dommage.
　　On le voit souvent avenir
20　Aussi bien au foul comme au sage.

　　Car mains maulx lui fault endurer
　　Et de Soussy passer le port
　　Avant qu'il puisse recouvrer
　　L'acointance de Reconfort,
25　Qui plusieurs fois au besoing dort
　　Quant on se veult de lui servir,
　　Et lors il est plus que martir,
　　Car son mal vault trop pis que rage.
　　On le voit souvent avenir
30　Aussi bien au foul comme au sage.

That you hold me in your prison,
My only sovereign joy.

Envoy
25   My lady, more than you know,
Love makes such fierce war upon me
I surrender to you. Now take me,
My only sovereign joy.

Ballade

It is very dangerous to look at
Something that can bring death,
Though one cannot help doing so
Sometimes, right or wrong.
5   When Pleasure is in accord
With a youthful desire,
No man can keep his heart
From sending the eyes as a messenger.
Often this is seen to happen
10   As much to the fool as the wise man.

And these eyes come and deliver
So very gracious a message
To the heart, when he is inclined to listen,
That, were his impulse then to feel love,
15   He would do so henceforth more strongly,
And the eyes make the heart wholly devoted
To the service (never to withdraw)
Of Love—to his very great harm.
Often this is seen to happen
20   As much to the fool as the wise man.

But the heart must suffer many ills
And pass through the gate of Care
Before regaining
The company of Comfort,
25   Who often sleeps at those times of need
When his help is desired.
And at such times the heart is more than a martyr,
For his distress is much worse than pain.
Often this is seen to happen
30   As much to the fool as the wise man.

L'envoy   [p. 20]
Amour, ne prenés desplaisir
S'ay dit le mal que fault souffrir
Demourant en vostre servage.
On le voit souvent avenir
35   Aussi bien au foul comme au sage.

[3]

B4   **Balade**

Comment se peut un povre cueur deffendre,
Quant deux beaulx yeulx le viennent assaillir?
Le cueur est seul, desarmé, nu et tendre,
Et les yeulx sont bien armez de plaisir.
5   Contre tous deux ne pourroit pié tenir,
Amour aussi est de leur alïance.
Nul ne tendroit contre telle puissance.

Il lui couvient ou mourir ou se rendre,
Trop grant honte lui seroit de fuïr.
10   Plus baudement les oseroit attendre
S'il eust pavais dont il se peust couvrir,
Mais point n'en a, si lui vault mieulx souffrir
Et se mettre tout en leur gouvernance.
Nul ne tendroit contre telle puissance.

15   Qu'il soit ainsi bien le me fist aprandre
Ma maistresse, mon souverain desir.
Quant il lui pleut ja pieça entreprandre
De me vouloir de ses doulx yeulx ferir.
Oncques depuis mon cueur ne peut guerir,
20   Car lors fut il desconfit a oultrance.
Nul ne tendroit contre telle puissance.

[4]

B5   **Balade**   [p. 21]

Espargniez vostre doulx actrait
Et vostre gracïeux parler,
Car Dieu scet les maulx qu'ilz ont fait
A mon povre cueur endurer.
5   Puis que ne voulés m'acorder
Ce qui pourroit mes maulx guerir,
Laissiez moy passer ma meschance

Envoy

Love, be not displeased
If I have mentioned the ill I must endure
While remaining in your service.
Often this is seen to happen
35   As much to the fool as the wise man.

Ballade

How can a poor heart defend itself
When two beautiful eyes come to assault it?
The heart is alone, unarmed, naked, and unprotected,
And well armed with pleasure are the eyes.
5   Against these two the heart cannot stand fast.
Love is their ally as well.
No one could hold out against such might.

He must die or surrender;
Taking flight would be too shameful.
10   The heart would dare take a bolder stand
Had he a shield to take cover behind,
But there is none, so he had better endure
And put itself wholly in their power.
No one could hold out against such might.

15   That this is so, my mistress, my sovereign desire
Brought me to know very well
When some time ago she was pleased to feel
The urge to strike me with her sweet eyes.
Since then my heart has been unable to heal,
20   Being completely overwhelmed.
No one could hold out against such might.

Ballade

Restrain your sweet allure
And your gracious speech,
For God knows the ills they have made
My poor heart suffer.
5   Since you will not grant me
What could cure my ills,
Let me endure my bad fortune

Sans plus me vouloir assaillir
Par vostre plaisant accointance!

10   Vers Amours faictes grant forfait,
Je l'ose pour vray advouer,
Quant me ferez d'amoureux trait
Et ne me voulez conforter.
Je croy que me voulez tuer.
15   Pleust a Dieu que peussiez sentir
Une fois la dure grevance
Que m'avez fait long temps souffrir
Par vostre plaisant accointance!

Helas! que vous ay je meffait
20   Par quoy me doyez tourmenter?
Quant mon cueur d'amer se retrait,
Tantost le venez rappeller.
Plaise vous en paix le laissier
Ou lui accordez son desir.
25   Honte vous est, non pas vaillance,
D'un loyal cueur ainsi meurdrir
Par vostre plaisant accointance!

[5]

B6   **Balade**   [p. 22]

N'a pas long temps qu'alay parler
A mon cueur tout secrettement
Et lui conseillay de s'oster
Hors de l'amoureux pensement,
5   Mais me dist bien fellement :
«Ne m'en parlez plus, je vous prie.
J'ameray tousjours, se m'aist Dieux,
Car j'ay la plus belle choisie.
Ainsi m'ont raporté mes yeulx.»

10   Lors dis : «Vueilliez me pardonner,
Car je vous jure mon serement
Que conseil vous cuide donner
A mon povair, tresloyaument.
Voulez vous sans allegement
15   En doleur finer vostre vie?»
«Nennil dya,» dist il, «j'auray mieulx.
Ma dame m'a fait chiere lie :
Ainsi m'ont raporté mes yeulx.»

Without your seeking to assault me more
Through your pleasant acquaintance!

10   You do Love great wrong
(I dare swear this is true)
When you deal me an amorous blow
And feel no desire to comfort me.
Killing me is what you intend, I believe.

15   May it please God you feel
One time the cruel torment
You have made me long suffer
Through your pleasant acquaintance!

Alas! Have I done you some wrong
20   That you must torture me?
When my heart demurs from loving,
At once you come to summon it back.
Please leave my heart in peace
Or grant what it desires!

25   It is a disgrace for you, not bravery,
Thus to murder a loyal heart
Through your pleasant acquaintance!

Ballade

Not long ago I went to speak
All in secret to my heart
And advised him to free himself
From these thoughts of love;

5   But quite bitterly he told me:
"Speak no more of this to me, I beg you.
Always will I love, so help me God,
For I chose the most beautiful of women.
This is what my eyes have reported."

10   Then I said: "Please pardon me,
For I swear to you, on my oath,
My intention is to give you counsel
As trustworthy as I can.
Do you want to end

15   Your life in pain with no relief?"
"No, in truth," he said, "I shall have better.
My lady has given me a friendly look.
This is what my eyes have reported."

«Cuidez vous savoir, sans doubter,
20   Par un regart tant seulement,»
Se dis je, «du tout son penser,
Ou par un doulx acointement?»
«Taisiez vous,» dist il, «vraiement,
Je ne croiray chose qu'on die,
25   Mais la serviray en tous lieux,
Car de tous biens est enrichie :
Ainsi m'ont raporté mes yeulx.»

[6]

B7   **Balade**   [p. 23]

De jamais n'amer par amours
J'ay aucune fois le vouloir
Pour les ennuieuses dolours
Qu'il me fault souvent recevoir,
5   Mais en la fin, pour dire voir,
Quelque mal que doye porter,
Je vous asseure par ma foy
Que je n'en sauroye garder
Mon cueur qui est maistre de moy.

10   Combien qu'ay eu d'estranges tours,
Mais j'ay tout mis a Nonchaloir,*
Pensant de recouvrer secours
De Confort ou d'un doulx Espoir.
Helas! se j'eusse le povoir
15   D'aucunement hors m'en bouter
Par le serement qu'a Amours doy,
Jamais n'y lairoye rentrer
Mon cueur qui est maistre de moy.

Car je sçay bien que par doulçours
20   Amour le scet si bien avoir
Qu'il vouldroit ainsi tous les jours
Demourer sans ja s'en mouvoir,
N'il ne veult oïr ne savoir
Le mal qu'il me fait endurer.
25   Plaisance l'a mis en ce ploy,
Elle fait mal de le m'oster,
Mon cueur qui est maistre de moy.

"Do you think to know beyond doubt
20   Only by a single look,"
So I said, "All that she thinks?
Or by a sweet greeting?"
"Be quiet," he said, "truly
I shall believe nothing anyone says,
25   But will serve her everywhere,
For she's enriched with all manner of good things.
This is what my eyes have reported."

Ballade

To never love in a lover's fashion
Is sometimes the wish I have
Because of the painful ills
I must often endure,
5   Yet in the end, to tell the truth,
Whatever pain I must bear,
I assure you upon my faith
That from so doing I cannot restrain
My heart, which is master over me.

10   Though suffering many a terrible turn,
I've made a bargain with Indifference,
Thinking to regain the help
Of Comfort or Sweet Hope.
Alas! Had I the power
15   To withdraw somewhat,
By the pledge I owe Love,
Never to return there would I allow
My heart, which is master over me.

For I know well that by gentle touches
20   Love can so firmly possess the heart
It would always be eager
There to remain and never leave,
Nor does it wish to hear or learn about
The ill it makes me suffer.
25   Pleasure put the heart in this fix.
She does wrong in taking from me
My heart, which is master over me.

L'envoy
Il me desplaist d'en tant parler,
Mais par le Dieu en qui je croy,
30   Ce fait desir de recouvrer
Mon cueur qui est maistre de moy.

[7]

B8   **Balade**   [p. 24]

Quant je suy couschié en mon lit,
Je ne puis en paix reposer,
Car toute la nuit mon cueur lit
Ou rommant de Plaisant Penser
5   Et me prie de l'escouter.
Si ne l'ose desobeir
Pour doubte de le courroucer :
Ainsi je laisse le dormir.

Ce livre si est tout escript
10   Des fais de ma dame sans per.
Souvent mon cueur de joye rit
Quand il les list ou oyt compter,
Car certes tant sont a louer
Qu'il y prent souverain plaisir.
15   Moy mesmes ne m'en puis lasser :
Ainsi je laisse le dormir.

Se mes yeulx demandent respit
Par Sommeil qui les vient grever,
Il les tense par grant despit
20   Et si ne les peut surmonter.
Il ne cesse de soupirer
A part soy. J'ay lors, sans mentir,
Grant paine de le rapaiser :
Ainsi je laisse le dormir.

L'envoy
25   Amour, je ne puis gouverner
Mon cueur, car tant vous veult servir
Qu'il ne scet jour ne nuit cesser :
Ainsi je laisse le dormir.

[8]

Envoy

I'm displeased to say much about this,
But by the God in whom I believe,
30   It's because of the desire to recover
My heart, which is master over me.

Ballade

When lying on my bed,
I cannot rest peacefully,
For all night long my heart
Reads in the Book of Pleasant Thought
5   And begs me to listen.
Then I dare not disobey
For fear of angering him.
So I forget about sleep.

In this book is written all about
10   The deeds of my peerless lady.
Often my heart rejoices
When he reads or hears them recited,
For surely they are so praiseworthy
My heart takes the greatest pleasure there.
15   I myself cannot weary of them:
So I forget about sleep.

If my eyes ask for respite
Because of Sleep, which weighs heavy on them,
The heart offers a bitter opposition
20   And yet cannot defeat them.
He does not stop sighing
When alone. I have then, and no lie,
Great trouble calming him.
So I forget about sleep.

Envoy

25   Love, I cannot rule my heart,
So eager is he to serve you,
He does not rest night or day.
So I forget about sleep.

B9   **Balade***

Fresche beauté, tresriche de jeunesse,
Riant regard trait amoureusement,
Plaisant parler gouverné par sagesse,
Port femenin en corps bien fait et gent,

5   Haultain maintien, demené doulcement,
Acueil humble, plain de maniere lye,
Sans nul dangier, bonne chiere faisant
Et de chascun pris et los emportant :
De ces grans biens est ma dame garnie.

10   Tant bien lui siet a la noble princesse
Chanter, dancer et tout esbatement
Qu'on la nomme de ce faire maistresse.
Elle fait tout si gracïeusement
Que nul n'y scet trouver amendement;

15   L'escolle peut tenir de courtoisie.
En la voyant aprent qui est sachant
Et en ses fais qui va garde prenant :
De ces grans biens est ma dame garnie.

Bonté, Honneur avecques Gentillesse

20   Tiennent son cueur en leur gouvernement,
Et Loyaulté nuit et jour ne la laisse.
Nature mist tout son entendement
A la fourmer et faire proprement.
De point en point c'est la mieulx acomplie

25   Qui au jour d'uy soit ou monde vivant,
Je ne dy riens que tous ne vont disant :
De ces grans biens est ma dame garnie.

Elle semble, mieulx que femme, deesse,
Si croy que Dieu l'envoya seulement

30   En ce monde pour moustrer la largesse
De ces haultz dons, qu'il a entierement
En elle mis abandonneement.
Elle n'a per, plus ne sçay que je dye.
Pour foul me tiens de l'aler devisant,

35   Car moy ne nul n'est a ce souffisant.
De ces grans biens est ma dame garnie.

S'il est aucun qui soit prins de tristesse
Voise veoir son doulx maintenement,
Je me fais fort que le mal qui le blesse

40   Le laissera pour lors soudainnement
Et en oubly sera mis plainement.

Ballade

Fresh beauty, so enriched by youth,
A smiling look lovingly sent,
Pleasant speech ruled by wisdom,
Womanly ways in a body shapely and elegant,
5   Proud bearing, displayed with kindness,
Friendly greeting, with a very jolly manner,
Showing good cheer with no danger,
And winning the esteem and praise of every man:
With such great goods is my lady endowed.

10   So well do singing, dancing, and every
Diversion suit the noble princess
She is called the mistress of such entertainments,
Engaging in them all with such grace
No one could find anything to improve.
15   She could instruct in the school of courtesy.
The wise man learns from looking at her,
As does he who considers her accomplishments.
With such great goods is my lady endowed.

Goodness, Honor, along with Nobility
20   Hold her heart under their dominion,
And Loyalty does not abandon her night or day.
Nature put all her intelligence
Into shaping and properly creating her.
She is in every way the most accomplished lady
25   Living today in our world.
I affirm nothing others do not go about saying:
With such great goods is my lady endowed.

She seems much more goddess than lady,
So I believe God for one purpose only sent her
30   Into this world: to manifest the generosity
Of the great gifts He has bestowed
Upon her with complete abandon.
The lady is unrivaled; I know not what else to say.
I think myself foolish for describing her,
35   For neither I nor any man is equal to the task.
With such great goods is my lady endowed.

If there is any man oppressed by sadness,
Let him go look upon her sweet demeanor!
I firmly contend he will be
40   Delivered at once from the ill that harms him,
And his lamenting will all be forgotten.

C'est Paradis que de sa compaignie,
A tous complaist, a nul n'est ennuiant,
Qui plus la voit plus en est desirant.
45   De ces grans biens est ma dame garnie.

L'envoy

Toutes dames qui oyez cy comment
Prise celle que j'ayme loyaument
Ne m'en sachiez maugré, je vous en prie.
Je ne parle pas en vous desprisant,
50   Mais comme sien je dy en m'acquittant :
De ces grans biens est ma dame garnie.

[9]

B10   **Balade***   [p. 27]

A ma dame je ne sçay que je dye
Ne par quel bout je doye commencer
Pour vous mander la doloreuse vie
Qu'Amour me fait chascun jour endurer.
5   Trop mieulx vaulsist me taire que parler,
Car proufiter ne me peuent mes plains,
Ne je ne puis guerison recouvrer,
Puis qu'ainsi est que de vous suis loingtains.

Quanque je voy me desplaist et ennuye
10   Et n'en ose contenance moustrer,
Mais ma bouche fait semblant qu'elle rie,
Quant maintefoiz je sens mon cueur plourer.
Au fort, martir on me devra nommer
Se Dieu d'Amours fait nulz amoureux saints,
15   Car j'ay des maulx plus que ne sçay compter
Puis qu'ainsi est que de vous suy loingtains.

Et non pourtant, humblement vous mercie,
Car par escript vous a pleu me donner
Ung doulx confort que j'ay a chiere lie
20   Receu de cueur et de joyeux penser,
Vous suppliant que ne vueilliez changier,
Car en vous sont tous mes plaisirs mondains,
Desquelz me fault a present deporter,
Puis qu'ainsi est que de vous suy loingtains.

[10]

Her company is a paradise
Pleasing all men, displeasing none.
Whoever sees her, desires to do so again.
45   With such great goods is my lady endowed.

Envoy

All you ladies who hear how
I esteem the one I faithfully love,
Feel no bitterness toward me—I beg you.
I do not speak to diminish you,
50   But, fulfilling my duty as her man, affirm that
With such great goods is my lady endowed.

Ballade

I know not what to tell you, my lady,
Or how I should undertake
Informing you of the painful life
Love makes me endure every day.
5   Much better I keep silent than speak,
For my complaints cannot profit me,
Nor can I recover my well-being
Since I am distant from you.

Whatever I see displeases and annoys me,
10   And I dare not let my face display it.
Instead my mouth pretends to smile
When often I sense my heart weeping.
In the end, I should be called a martyr
If the God of Love makes any lovers saints,
15   For I suffer more ills than my words can express
Since I am distant from you.

And yet, I humbly thank you,
For it pleased you to send me in writing
A sweet bit of comfort I received with a smile,
20   Rejoicing in heart and mind,
Begging you please do not alter,
For all my worldly pleasures are in you.
And at present I must do without them
Since I am distant from you.

B11   **Balade**   [p. 28]

    Loingtain de vous, ma tresbelle maistresse,
    Fors que de cueur que laissié je vous ay,
    Acompaignié de Dueil et de Tristesse,
    Jusques a tant que reconfort auray
5   D'un doulx plaisir, quant reveoir pourray
    Vostre gent corps plaisant et gracïeux,
    Car lors lairay tous mes maulx ennuieux
    Et trouveray, se m'a dit Esperance,
    Par le pourchas du regard de mes yeulx,
10   Autant de bien que j'ay de desplaisance.

    Car s'oncques nul sceut que c'est de destresse,
    Je pense bien que j'en ay fait l'essay
    Si tresavant et a telle largesse
    Qu'en dueil pareil nulluy de moy ne sçay,
15   Mais ne m'en chault, certes j'endureray
    Au desplaisir des jaloux envïeux
    Et me tendray par semblance joyeux,
    Car, quant je suy en greveuse penance,
    Ilz reçoyvent—que mal jour leur doint Dieux!—
20   Autant de bien que j'ay de desplaisance.

    Tout prens en gré, jenne, gente Princesse,
    Mais qu'en sachiés tant seulement le vray
    En attendant le guerdon de Lïesse
    Qu'a mon povair vers vous desserviray,
25   Car le conseil de Loyauté feray
    Que garderay prés de moy en tous lieux :
    Vostre toujours soye, jennes ou vieulx,
    Priant a Dieu, ma seule desirance,
    Qu'il vous envoit, s'avoir ne povez mieulx,
30   Autant de bien que j'ay de desplaisance.

[11]

B12   **Balade**   [p. 29]

    Puis qu'ainsi est que loingtain de vous suis,
    Ma maistresse, dont Dieu scet s'il m'ennuie,
    Si chierement vous requier que je puis
    Qu'il vous plaise de vostre courtoisie,
5   Quant vous estes seule sans compaignie,
    Me souhaidier un baisier amoureux
    Venant du cueur et de pensee lie,
    Pour alegier mes griefs maulx doloreux.

Ballade

I am far from you, my most beautiful mistress,
Save for the heart I left,
Misery and Sadness for my companions,
Until I take comfort
5   In a sweet pleasure, looking again upon
Your noble body, pleasant and gracious,
For I will be delivered of all my painful ills
And find, so Hope has told me,
From the eager glance of my eyes,
10   As much benefit as I have affliction.

For if any man ever learned what distress is,
I certainly think to have experienced it
To such a degree and with such intensity
I know no one feels the pain I do.
15   Yet I care not; surely I will endure,
To the displeasure of the jealous who envy,
And show myself disguised with joy,
For, while I am punished so grievously,
They receive—may God send them a dark day—
20   As much benefit as I have affliction.

All this I accept willingly, noble young Princess,
(Provided you alone should know the truth),
As I await the reward of Happiness,
Which I will merit from you as best I can,
25   For I follow the advice of Loyalty,
Whom I will keep everywhere by my side.
Always may I be yours, young or old
(You my sole desire), praying God
He sends you, if you cannot have better,
30   As much benefit as I have affliction.

Ballade

Since I find myself far from you,
My mistress (and God knows this pains me),
I ask you as lovingly as I can,
That you will please in your courtesy
5   When you are alone without companions
Send me a lover's kiss
From the heart, and with a happy thought,
And thus alleviate my grievous, painful ills.

Quant en mon lit doy reposer de nuis,
10   Penser m'assault et Desir me guerrie,
Et en pensant maintesfois m'est advis
Que je vous tiens entre mes bras, m'amye.
Lors acolle mon oreillier et crie
«Mercy, Amours, faictes moy si eureux
15   Qu'avenir puist mon penser en ma vie
Pour alegier mes griefs maulx doloreux!»

Espoir m'a dit et par sa foy promis
Qu'il m'aydera et que ne m'en soussie,
Mais tant y met q'un an me semble dix,
20   Et non pour tant, soit ou sens ou folie,
Je m'y attens et en lui je m'afie
Qu'il fera tant que Dangier, le crueux,
N'aura briefment plus sur moy seigneurie,
Pour alegier mes griefs maulx doloreux.

L'envoy
25   A Loyauté de plus en plus m'alye
Et a Amours humblement je supplie
Que de mon fait vueillent estre piteux
En me donnant de mes vouloirs partie
Pour alegier mes griefs maulx doloreux.

[12]

B13   Balade   [p. 30]

Pour tant se souvent ne vous voy,*
Pensez vous plus que vostre soye?
Par le serement que je vous doy,
Si suis autant que je souloye,
5   N'il n'est ne plaisance ne joye,
N'autre bien qu'on me puist donner,
Je le vous prometz loyaument,
Qui me puist ce vouloir oster
Fors que la mort tant seulement.

10   Vous savés que je vous feis foy
Pieça de tout ce que j'avoye,
Et vous laissay, en lieu de moy,
Le gage que plus chier j'amoye,
C'estoit mon cueur que j'ordonnoye
15   Pour avecques vous demourer,
A qui je suis entierement.

        When in my bed at night I am to take my rest,
10   Thought assaults and Desire wars upon me,
        And many times, deep in thought, it seems
        I hold you in my arms, my beloved.
        I embrace my pillow and cry out:
        "Mercy, Love, give me happiness
15   By making my dreams come true in life
        And thus alleviate my grievous, painful ills!"

        Hope has promised upon his faith
        To help me, and I should not worry,
        But he delays so long one year seems ten,
20   And yet all the same, be it sense or madness,
        My hope lies in him, and I trust he will
        Bring it about that cruel Danger
        Will soon no longer hold sway over me,
        And thus alleviate my grievous, painful ills.

Envoy

25   More and more I join forces with Loyalty,
        Humbly asking Love
        To please take pity on my case,
        Granting me some part of my desires,
        And thus alleviate my grievous, painful ills.

Ballade

        Though I do not see you often,
        Do you think I am still yours?
        By the oath binding me to you,
        Indeed I am, as much as I was wont,
5   And there is no pleasure, no joy,
        No other benefit I could be granted
        (This I faithfully promise you)
        That could steal this desire from me,
        Save only death alone.

10   You know I pledged you my troth
        Some time ago with all that is mine,
        And left you, taking my place,
        The surety dearest to me:
        This was my heart, which I ordained
15   Would remain with you,
        Whose I am completely.

Nul ne m'en pourroit destourber
Fors que la mort tant seulement.

Combien certes que je reçoy
20   Tel mal que, se le vous disoye,
Vous auriés, comme je croy,
Pitié du mal qui me guerroye,
Car de tout dueil suis en la voye,
Vous le povez assez penser,
25   Et ay esté si longuement
Que je ne doy riens desirer
Fors que la mort tant seulement.

    L'envoy
Belle que tant veoir vouldroye,
Je prie a Dieu que brief vous voye,
30   Ou s'il ne le veult accorder,   [p. 31]
Je lui suply treshumblement
Que riens ne me vueille donner
Fors que la mort tant seulement.

[13]

B14   **Balade**

Quelles nouvelles, ma maistresse?
Comment se portent noz amours?
De ma part je vous fais promesse
Qu'en un propos me tiens tousjours
5   Sans jamais penser le rebours.
C'est que seray toute ma vie
Vostre du tout entierement,
Et pource, de vostre partie,
Acquittez vous pareillement.

10   Combien que Dangier et Destresse*
Ont fait longuement leurs sejours
Avec mon cueur, et par rudesse
Luy ont moustré d'estranges tours,
(Helas! en amoureuses cours
15   C'est pitié qu'ilz ont seigneurie),
Si mettray paine que briefment
Loyaulté sur eulx ait maistrie.
Acquittés vous pareillement.

Quoy que la nue de Tristesse
20   Par un long temps ait fait son cours,

Nothing could deter me
Save only death alone.

Though I surely suffer from
20   An ill such that, if I told you of it,
You would have (so I believe)
Pity for the misery that assails me,
For the path I am on is all pain,
You can readily understand,
25   And I have been there so long
I should desire nothing
Save only death alone.

Envoy
Belle, whom I would so much like to see,
Pray God I see you soon,
30   Or if He will not so allow,
I beg Him in all humility
To please grant me nothing
Save only death alone.

Ballade
What news, mistress mine?
How goes our love affair?
For my part I promise you
Always to pursue but one desire
5   And never intend the opposite.
All my life I will be
Yours completely in everything,
And that is why, for your part,
May you acquit yourself the same.

10   Although Danger and Distress
Have sojourned long
Within my heart, and in their harshness
Given it many a cruel turn
(Alas! A pity it is they have
15   Dominion in the courts of love),
I'll take pains to make sure that soon
Loyalty will be their master.
May you acquit yourself the same.

Although the cloud of Sadness
20   Has long traversed the sky,

Aprés le beau temps de Lÿesse
Vendra, qui donnera secours
A noz deux cueurs, car mon recours
J'ay en Espoir, en qui me fie,   [p. 32]
25   Et en vous, belle, seulement,
Car jamais je ne vous oublie.
Acquittés vous pareillement.

L'envoy
Soiés seure, ma doulce amie,
Que je vous ayme loyaument.
30   Or vous requier et vous supplie,
Acquittiez vous pareillement.

[14]

B15   Balade

Belle que je tiens pour amye,
Pensés, quelque part que je soye,*
Que jamais je ne vous oublie,
Et pource prier vous vouldroye
5   Jusques atant que vous revoye
Qu'il vous souviengne de cellui
Qui a trouvé peu de mercy*
En vous, se dire je l'osoye.

Combien que je ne dye mie
10   Que n'aye receu bien et joye
En vostre doulce compaignie
Plus que desservir ne sauroye,
Non pourtant, voulentiers j'auroye
Le guerdon de loyal amy
15   Qu'oncques ne trouvay jusqu'a cy
En vous, se dire je l'osoye.

Je vous ay longuement servie,
Si m'est advis qu'avoir devroye
Le don que, de sa courtoisie,   [p. 33]
20   Amour a ses servans envoye.
Or faittes qu'estre content doye
Et m'accordez ce que je dy,
Car trop avez refus nourry
En vous, se dire je l'osoye.

[15]

Afterward Happiness's fine weather
Comes to provide help
To our two hearts, for my recourse
Lies with Hope, in whom I trust,
25 And in you alone, belle,
For never do I forget you.
May you acquit yourself the same.

Envoy

Be certain, my sweet friend,
I faithfully love you.
30 Now I beg and pray
May you acquit yourself the same.

Ballade

Belle, whom I think my friend,
Bear in mind that wherever I might be
I'll never forget you,
And this is why I would pray,
5 Till the moment I see you again,
That you will remember the man
Who has found so little mercy
In you, if I dare say so.

Although I do not say at all
10 I have received no goods or joy
From your sweet companionship,
More than I could merit,
Even so I would gladly receive
A true lover's reward,
15 Which I have never found till now
In you, if I dare say so.

I have served you a long time,
So it seems I should possess
The gift that, in his courtliness,
20 Love sends his servants.
Now do what should satisfy me
And grant my request,
For you have too long nourished refusal
In you, if I dare say so.

B16   Balade

        Ma dame, vous povez savoir
        Les biens qu'ay euz a vous servir,
        Car, par ma foy, pour dire voir,
        Oncques je n'y peuz acquerir
5   Tant seulement un doulx plaissir
        Que, sitost que je le tenoye,
        Dangier le me venoit tolir,
        Ce peu de plaisir que j'avoye.

        Je n'en savoye nul avoir*
10   Qui peust contenter mon desir,
        Se non quant vous povoye voir,
        Ma joye, mon seul souvenir.
        Or m'en a fait Dangier banir,
        Tant qu'il fault que loing de vous soye,
15   Par quoy a fait de moy partir
        Ce peu de plaisir que j'avoye.

        Non pas peu, car de bon vouloir
        Content m'en devoye tenir
        En esperant de recevoir
20   Un trop plus grant bien avenir.
        Je n'y cuidoye point faillir
        A la paine que g'y mettoye.   [p. 34]
        Cela me faisoit enrichir
        Ce peu de plaisir que j'avoye.

              L'envoy
25   Belle, je vous vueil requerir :
        Pensés, quant serés de loisir,
        Qu'en grant mal, qui trop me guerroye,
        Est tourné, sans vous en mentir,
        Ce peu de plaisir que j'avoye.

[16]

B17   Balade*

        En ce joyeux temps du jourd'uy
        Que le mois de may ce commence
        Et que l'en doit laissier Ennuy
        Pour prendre joyeuse Plaisance,
5   Je me treuve, sans recouvrance,
        Loingtain de Joye conquester
        De Tristesse si bien renté

Ballade

My lady, you can recognize
The benefits I have had from your service,
For, by my faith, to tell the truth,
Never could I gain thereby
5   Even a single sweet pleasure,
Which, the moment I grabbed it,
Danger came to steal from me—
This little bit of pleasure I have had.

No possession I have ever known
10   Could satisfy my desire,
Save seeing you when I could,
My joy, my only remembrance.
Now Danger has had me banished
(And I must be distant from you)
15   And has thus made depart from me
This little bit of pleasure I have had.

Not little at all, for with a good will
I should keep myself content
In the hope of receiving
20   A much greater good to come.
My intention is not to fail at all,
Such pains I will take.
It has enriched me,
This little bit of pleasure I have had.

Envoy

25   Belle, I ask you:
Bear in mind when you are at ease
That into a great ill, which mightily assails me,
Has turned (I tell you no lie)
This little bit of pleasure I have had.

Ballade

In this day's joyous season,
When the month of May commences,
And Misery should be put aside
So that joyous Pleasure might be embraced,
5   I find myself beyond recourse,
Far from conquering Joy,
So well provided with Sadness,

Que j'ay, je m'en puis bien vanter,
Le rebours de ma voulenté.

10   Las! Amours, je ne voy nulluy
Qui n'ait aucune souffisance
Fors que moy seul qui suis celluy
Qui est le plus dolent de France.
J'ay failli a mon esperance,
15   Car, quant a vous me voulz donner
Pour estre vostre serementé
Jamais ne cuidoye trouver
Le rebours de ma voulenté.

Au fort, puis qu'en ce point je suy,   [p. 35]
20   Je porteray ma grant penance
Ayant vers Loyauté refuy
Ou j'ay mis toute ma fiance,
Ne Dangier, qui ainsi m'avance,
Quelque mal que doye porter,
25   Combien que trop m'a tourmenté
Ne pourra ja en moy bouter
Le rebours de ma voulenté.

L'envoy

D'aucun reconfort accointer
Plusieurs foys m'en suy dementé,
30   Mais j'ay tousjours, au par aler,
Le rebours de ma voulenté.

[20 erased]

B18   Balade

Quant je party derrainnement
De ma souveraine sans per,
(Que Dieu gard et lui doint briefment
Joye de son loyal penser)
5   Mon cueur lui laissay emporter.
Oncques puis ne le peuz ravoir,
Si m'esmerveille main et soir
Comment j'ay vesqu tant de jours
Depuis sans cueur, mais pour tout voir
10   Ce n'est que miracle d'Amours.

That I have, of this I can well boast,
The opposite of my wish.

10   Alas! Love, I see no one
Without plenty of everything
Save me alone, who am the man
In France with the greatest sorrow.
I have failed in my hope,
15   For, determined to give myself to you
And become your sworn servant,
I never thought to find
The opposite of my wish.

In the end, since I am in this fix,
20   I will bear up under my great punishment,
Having fled to Loyalty,
In whom I've put all my trust,
And Danger, who worsens my plight,
No matter what ill I am to endure,
25   Though he has terribly tormented me,
Can never force me to do
The opposite of my wish.

Envoy

Several times I have striven hard
To find some consolation,
30   But always in the end I get
The opposite of my wish.

Ballade

When last I made my way
From my sovereign, peerless lady
(May God keep her and soon give
Her joy in her faithful thoughts),
5   I left my heart for her to take.
I've never since been able to regain it
And so marvel morning and night
How I've lived on so many days
Afterward lacking a heart, but truly
10   It's nothing but a miracle of Love.

Qui est cellui qui longuement
Peut vivre sans cueur ou durer
Comme j'ay fait en grief tourment?
Certes nul, je m'en puis vanter.   [p. 36]
15   Mais Amours ont voulu moustrer
En ce leur gracïeux povair
Pour donner aux amans vouloir
D'eulx fier en leur doulx secours,
Car bien peuent appercevoir
20   Ce n'est que miracle d'Amours.

Quant Pitié vit que franchement
Voulu mon cueur abandonner
Envers ma dame, tellement
Traitta que lui fist me laisser
25   Son cueur, me chargeant le garder
Dont j'ay fait mon loyal devoir
Maugré Dangier qui recevoir
M'a fait chascun jour de telz tours
Que sans mort en ce point manoir
30   Ce n'est que miracle d'Amours.

B19   Balade   [p. 37]

Douleur, Courroux, Desplaisir et Tristesse,
Quelque tourment que j'aye main et soir,
Ne pour doubte de mourir de destresse,
Ja ne sera en tout vostre povoir
5   De me changier le tresloyal vouloir
Qu'ay eu tousjours de la belle servir
Par qui je puis et pense recevoir
Le plus grant bien qui me puist avenir.

Quant j'ay par vous aucun mal qui me blesse,
10   Je l'endure par le conseil d'Espoir
Qui m'a promis qu'a ma seule maistresse
Lui fera brief mon angoisse savoir,
En lui mandant qu'en faisant mon devoir
J'ay tous les maulx que nul pourroit souffrir.
15   Lors trouveray, je ne sçay s'il dit voir,
Le plus grant bien qui me puist avenir.

Ne m'espargniez donc en rien de rudesse,
Je vous feray bien brief appercevoir
Qu'auray secours d'un confort de Lÿesse.

What kind of man can live
Long without a heart or suffer
The grievous torment I do?
Surely no one—I can boast of it.
15   But Love has wished in this way
To manifest the gracious power he has
To make lovers desire
To trust in his kind assistance,
For they can clearly see
20   It's nothing but a miracle of Love.

When Pity saw that freely
I intended to abandon my heart
To my lady, Pity struck a bargain
With her so she'd leave me
25   Her heart, ordering me to watch over it,
And I've faithfully discharged this duty
Despite Danger, who's made me
Endure every day such twists and turns
That to remain in this fix and yet not die,
30   It's nothing but a miracle of Love.

Ballade

Pain, Distress, Misery, and Sadness,
I suffer such torture morning and night,
But since I fear anguish will kill me,
I hope you will never prove strong enough
5   To alter the very faithful intention
I have to serve always that belle
From whom I can and think to receive
The greatest benefit that could be mine.

When some ill comes upon me for your sake,
10   I endure it, as Hope counsels,
Who's promised she will quickly
Reveal this anguish to my only mistress,
Giving her the message that while doing my duty
I suffer such divers ills no man could endure.
15   Then I'll find (if he speaks truth I know not)
The greatest benefit that could be mine.

Don't spare me rough treatment;
Soon I'll make you see clearly
I'll be helped by the comfort Happiness brings.

20   Long temps ne puis en ce point remanoir;
      Pour ce je metz du tout a Nonchaloir
      Les tresgrans maulx que me faittes sentir.
      Bien aurez dueil, se me voyez avoir
      Le plus grant bien qui me puist avenir.

L'envoy
25   Je suy cellui au cueur vestu de noir
      Qui dy ainsi, qui que le vueille ouÿr.
      J'auray briefment, Loyauté m'en fait hoir,
      Le plus grant bien qui me puist avenir.

[18]

B20   Balade

      Jeune, gente, plaisant et debonnaire,   [p. 38]
      Par un prier, qui vault commandement,
      Chargié m'avez d'une ballade faire.
      Si l'ay faicte de cueur joyeusement;
5   Or la vueilliez recevoir doulcement.
      Vous y verrés, s'il vous plaist a la lire,
      Le mal que j'ay, combien que vrayement
      J'aymasse mieulx de bouche le vous dire.

      Vostre doulceur m'a sceu si bien atraire
10   Que tout vostre je suis entierement,
      Tresdesirant de vous servir et plaire.
      Mais je seuffre maint doloreux tourment
      Quant a mon gré je ne vous voy souvent*
      Et me desplaist quant me fault vous escrire,
15   Car, se faire ce povoit autrement,
      J'aymasse mieulx de bouche le vous dire.

      C'est par Dangier, mon cruel adversaire,
      Qui m'a tenu en ses mains longuement.
      En tous mes fais je le treuve contraire
20   Et plus se rit quant plus me voit dolent.
      Se vouloye raconter plainnement
      En cest escript mon ennuieux martire,
      Trop long seroit. Pource certainnement
      J'aymasse mieulx de bouche le vous dire.

20   I cannot long remain in such a fix.
        This is why I bring to Indifference
        All the terrible ills you make me feel.
        You'd surely be displeased to see me possess
        The greatest benefit that could be mine.

Envoy
25   I'm the man, heart clothed in black,
        Who speaks in this way, no matter who cares to listen.
        Soon I'll have (Loyalty named me as heir)
        The greatest benefit that could be mine.

Ballade

        Lady, young, elegant, graceful, and genteel,
        With a request (the same as a command)
        You commissioned me to compose a ballade.
        So I happily wrote it from the heart.
5   Now please receive it kindly.
        Written there you will see, if you would please read,
        The misery I endure, though in truth
        I'd rather you'd have it from my lips.

        Your sweetness had such power to attract me
10   I am completely yours,
        Eager to serve and please you.
        Yet I suffer many painful torments,
        Not seeing you as often I wish,
        And I am displeased to write you,
15   For, could this be done differently,
        I'd rather you'd have it from my lips.

        Danger, my cruel enemy, is at fault,
        Who has long had me in his hands.
        I find him opposing all I do,
20   And the sadder he sees me, the more he smiles.
        If I intended telling the entire tale of
        My painful martyrdom in this writing,
        It should be too long. And surely this is why
        I'd rather you'd have it from my lips.

B21   **Balade**   [p. 39]

       Loué soit cellui qui trouva
       Premier la maniere d'escrire.
       En ce, grant confort ordonna
       Pour amans qui sont en martire,
5   Car, quant ne peuent aler dire
       A leurs dames leur grief tourment,
       Ce leur est moult d'alegement
       Quant par escript peuent mander
       Les maulx qu'ilz portent humblement
10   Pour bien et loyaument amer.

       Quant un amoureux escrira
       Son dueil qui trop le tient de rire,
       Au plus tost qu'envoyé l'aura
       A celle qui est son seul mire
15   S'il lui plaist a la lectre lire,
       Elle peut veoir clerement
       Son doloreux gouvernement,
       Et lors Pitié lui scet moustrer
       Qu'il dessert bon guerdonnement
20   Pour bien et loyaument amer.

       Par mon cueur je congnois pieça
       Ce mestier, car, quant il souspire,
       Jamais rapaisié ne sera
       Tant qu'il ait envoyé de tire
25   Vers la belle que tant desire.
       Et puis, s'il peut aucunement
       Oïr nouvelles seulement
       De sa doulce beauté sans per,
       Il oublie l'ennuy qu'il sent
30   Pour bien et loyaument amer.

                L'envoy   [p. 40]
       Ma dame, Dieu doint que briefment
       Vous puisse de bouche compter
       Ce que j'ay souffert longuement
       Pour bien et loyaument amer.

[21]

Ballade

Praised be the man who was the first
To discover the art of writing.
So doing, he ordained a great consolation
For lovers who suffer,
5   Since, when they cannot go and
Tell their ladies of their grievous torment,
It greatly relieves them
To send a written message
Of the ills they humbly endure
10   For loving well and faithfully.

When a man in love writes of
His pain, which surely keeps him from smiling,
As soon as he has sent the message
To the lady who is his only physician,
15   If pleased to read the letter,
She can clearly see
How painful his life is,
And then Pity can show her
He deserves a fine reward
20   For loving well and faithfully.

Some time ago my heart made me familiar with
This kind of life, for, sighing,
He'll never again be at peace
Until he's sent a message in haste
25   To the belle he so much desires.
And then, if he can only hear
Some news of any kind
Of her sweet, peerless beauty,
He forgets the misery he has felt
30   For loving well and faithfully.

Envoy

My lady, may God grant that soon
My lips can tell you
What I have suffered a long time
For loving well and faithfully.

B22   **Balade**

     Belle, combien que de mon fait
     Je croy qu'avez peu souvenance,
     Toutesfois se savoir vous plait
     Mon estat et mon ordonnance,
5   Sachiés que, loingtain de Plaisance,
     Je suis de tous maulx bien garny
     Autant que nul qui soit en France,
     Dieu scet en quel mauvais party.

     Helas! Or n'ay je riens forfait
10   Dont porter je doye penance,
     Car tousjours je me suis retrait
     Vers Leauté et Esperance
     Pour acquerir leur bien vueillance,
     Mais au besoing ilz m'ont failly
15   Et m'ont laissié sans recouvrance
     Dieu scet en quel mauvais party.

     Dangier m'a joué de ce trait,
     Mais se je puis avoir puissance,
     Je feray, maugré qu'il en ait,
20   Encontre lui une alïance,
     Et si lui rendray la grevance,
     Le mal, le dueil et le soussy
     Ou il m'a mis, jusqu'a oultrance,
     Dieu scet en quel mauvais party.

         L'envoy   [p. 41]
25   Aydiez moy a l'outrecuidance
     Vengier, com en vous ay fïance,
     Ma maistresse, je vous supply,
     De ce faulx Dangier qui m'avance
     Dieu scet en quel mauvais party.

[23]

B23   **Balade**

     Loyal Espoir, trop je vous voy dormir.
     Resveilliez vous, et Joyeuse Pensee,
     Et envoyez un plaisant souvenir
     Devers mon cueur, de la plus belle nee
5   Dont au jourd'ui coure la renommee.
     Vous ferez bien d'un peu le resjoïr,
     Tristesse s'est avecques lui logiee;
     Ne lui vueilliez a son besoing faillir.

Ballade

Belle, though I think you give
Little thought to my lot,
Still if you are pleased to learn something of
My situation and condition
5   Know that, far from Pleasure,
I am well furnished with all kinds of miseries,
As much as any man in France,
God knows in what unfortunate state.

Alas! Now I have done no wrong
10   For which I should endure penance,
Having always taken the side
Of Loyalty and Hope,
In order to gain their good will,
But in my need they failed me
15   And left me without recourse,
God knows in what unfortunate state.

Danger gave me this unfortunate turn,
But if I can gain the power,
I'll forge, no matter what he thinks,
20   An alliance to oppose him,
Requiting him for the misery,
The ill, the pain, and the worry
Into which he's sunk me (and with interest),
God knows in what unfortunate state.

Envoy

25   Help me punish
The arrogance (because I trust in you,
My mistress, I beg you)
Of this false Danger, who puts me
God knows in what unfortunate state.

Ballade

Loyal Hope, I see you sleep too long.
Rouse yourself and Joyful Thought as well,
And send my heart a pleasant
Reminiscence of the lady born most fair,
5   Whose renown swells in our age.
You could make him rejoice somewhat.
Sadness has made her home there.
Please don't fail him in this time of need.

    Car Dangier l'a desrobé de Plaisir
10 Et que pis est, a de lui eslongnee
    Celle qui plus le povoit enrichir :
    C'est sa dame tresloyaument amee.
    Oncques cueur n'eut si dure destinee.
    Pour Dieu, Espoir, venez le secourir,
15 Il a en vous sa fiance fermee,
    Ne lui vueilliez a son besoing faillir.

    Par Povreté lui fault son pain querir
    A l'uis d'Amours par chascune journee,
    Or lui vueilliez l'aumosne departir
20 De Lÿesse, que tant a desiree.
    Avancés vous, sans faire demouree,
    Pensez de lui, vous savez son desir,
    Par vous lui soit quelque grace donnee,   [p. 42]
    Ne lui vueilliez a son besoing faillir.

L'envoy
25 Seulle sans per, de toutes gens louee
    Et de tous biens entierement douee,
    Mon cueur ces maulx seuffre pour vous servir.
    Sa loyauté vous soit recommandee,
    Ne lui vueilliez a son besoing faillir.

[24]

B24   Balade*

    Mon cueur au derrain entrera
    Ou paradis des amoureux;
    Autrement tort fait lui sera,
    Car il a de maulx doloreux
5   Plus d'un cent, non pas un ou deux,
    Pour servir sa belle maistresse,
    Et le tient Dangier, le crueulx,
    Ou purgatoire de Tristesse.

    Ainsi l'a tenu, long temps a,
10 Ce faulx traistre, vilain, hideux.
    Espoir dit que hors le mettra
    Et que n'en soye ja doubteux,
    Mais trop y met, dont je me deulx.
    Dieu doint qu'il tiengne sa promesse
15 Vers lui, tant est angoisseux
    Ou purgatoire de Tristesse.

For Danger has deprived him of Pleasure
10   And, worse, has distanced him
From the lady most able to enrich him,
Who is his lady most loyally loved.
No heart ever endured such a hard fate.
For God's sake, Hope, go to his aid.
15   In you he has firmly placed his trust;
Please don't fail him in this time of need.

Because of Poverty, he must beg his bread
Every day at the gate of Love.
Please give him now the alms
20   Of Happiness, which he has long desired.
Come forward, without delay,
Think of him; you know what he desires;
Let some grace be granted him through you,
Please don't fail him in this time of need.

Envoy
25   You alone are peerless, praised by all,
And with every fine quality fully endowed.
Through serving you my heart suffers these ills.
May his loyalty be commended to you.
Please don't fail him in this time of need.

Ballade

My heart in the end will enter
The paradise for lovers.
Otherwise, he will be wronged,
For of grievous ills he has suffered
5   More than a hundred, not one or two,
Through serving his beautiful mistress,
And cruel Danger keeps him
In the purgatory of Sadness.

He has kept him there a long time,
10   This traitor false, low-born, hideous.
Hope says he will release him,
And that I should never doubt,
But he takes too long, and so I sorrow.
May God grant he keeps his promise,
15   So anguished is the heart
In the purgatory of Sadness.

Amour grant aumosne fera
En ce fait cy d'estre piteux
Et bon exemple moustrera   [p. 43]
20   A toutes celles et a ceulx
Qui le servent, quant desireux
Le verront par sa grant humblesse
D'aidier ce povre soufreteux
Ou purgatoire de Tristesse.

L'envoy
25   Amour, faittes moy si eureux
Que mettez mon cueur en lïesse.
Laissiez Dangier et Dueil tous seulx
Ou purgatoire de Tristesse.

[27]

B25   Balade

Mon cueur a envoyé querir
Tous ses bienvueillans et amis.
Il veult son grant conseil tenir
Avec eulx pour avoir advis
5   Comment pourra ses ennemis,
Soussy, Dueil et leur alïance,
Surmonter et tost desconfire,
Qui desirent de le destruire
En la prison de Desplaisance.

10   En desert ont mis son plaisir
Et joye tenue en pastis,*
Mais Confort lui a sans faillir
De nouvel loyaument promis
Qu'ilz seront deffais et bannis.
15   De ce se fait fort Esperance
Et plus avant que n'ose dire.   [p. 44]
C'est ce qui estaint son martire
En la prison de Desplaisance.

Briefment voye le temps venir,
20   J'en prie a Dieu de Paradis,
Que chascun puist vers son desir
Aler sans avoir saufconduis.
Adonc Amour et ses nourris
Auront de Dangier moins doubtance,
25   Et lors sentiray mon cueur rire

Love will do great charity
By taking pity in this case,
And set a good example
20   To all men and women
Who serve him when they
See him eager in his great humility
To help this poor unfortunate
In the purgatory of Sadness.

Envoy

25   Love, make me so fortunate
As to deliver my heart to happiness.
Leave Danger and Pain all alone
In the purgatory of Sadness.

Ballade

My heart has summoned
All his friends and well-wishers.
He will convene a great council
So as to be advised
5   How to overcome and
Utterly defeat his enemies,
Care, Pain, and their allies,
Who are bent on his destruction
In the prison of Misery.

10   They forced his pleasure into the wild
And kept his Joy near meager grazing.
But Comfort, without fail, has
Faithfully promised the heart yet again
They will be defeated and banished.
15   Hope struggles hard with this
And more than I dare say.
This is what puts an end to the heart's suffering
In the prison of Misery.

Soon may I see the time come
20   (So I pray God in Paradise)
When each man can go
To his desire without a safe-conduct.
And then Love and his disciples
Will fear Danger less.
25   And then I will feel my heart laugh,

Qui a present souvent souspire
En la prison de Desplaisance.

L'envoy

Pource que veoir ne vous puis,
Mon cueur se complaint jours et nuis,
30   Belle, nompareille de France,*
Et m'a chargié de vous escrire
Qu'il n'a pas tout ce qu'il desire
En la prison de Desplaisance.

B26   **Balade**   [p. 45]

Desploiez vostre banniere,
Loyauté, je vous en prie,
Et assailliez la frontiere
Ou Deuil et Merencolie
5   A tort et par felonnie
Tiennent Joye prisonniere.
De moy la font estrangiere.
Je pri Dieu qu'il les maudie!

Quant je deusse bonne chiere
10   Demener en compaignie,
Je n'en fais que la maniere,
Car, quoy que ma bouche rie
Ou parle parolle lye,
Dangier et Destresse fiere
15   Boutent mon plaisir arriere.
Je pry Dieu qu'il les maudie!

Helas! Tant avoye chiere,
Ja pieça, joyeuse vie.
Se Raison fust droicturiere,
20   J'en eusse quelque partie.
Or est de mon cueur bannie
Par Fortune losengiere,
Et Durté, sa conseilliere.
Je pry Dieu qu'il les maudie!

L'envoy

25   Se j'avoye la maistrie
Sur ceste faulse mesgnie,
Je les meisse tous en biere,
Si est telle ma priere.
Je pry Dieu qu'il les maudie!

[25]

Who at present often sighs
In the prison of Misery.

Envoy

Because I cannot see you,
My heart laments day and night,
30   Belle, in France unrivaled,
And charges me with writing you
That he does not possess his desire
In the prison of Misery.

Ballade

Unfurl your banner,
Loyalty, I beg you,
And assault the borderland
Where Pain and Melancholy
5   Wrongly and criminally
Hold Joy prisoner.
They have estranged her from me.
I pray God curse them!

When I was obliged to show
10   A pleasant manner among others,
I offered only its appearance,
For, though my mouth smiles
And utters pleasant words,
Danger and proud Distress
15   Suppress my pleasure.
I pray God curse them!

Alas! Some time ago, very dear
To me was a life filled with joy.
Had Reason been fair-minded,
20   I would have possessed some share.
Now that life is exiled from my heart
By mendacious Fortune,
And Hard-Heart, her advisor,
I pray God curse them!

Envoy

25   Had I dominion
Over this false retinue,
I would put them all on the bier,
Such is my request.
I pray God curse them!

B27   **Balade**   [p. 46]

Ardant desir de veoir ma maistresse
A assailly de nouvel le logis
De mon las cueur, qui languist en tristesse,
Et puis dedens par tout a le feu mis.
5   En grant doubte certainement je suis
Qu'il ne soit pas legierement estaint
Sans grant grace. Si vous pry, Dieu d'Amours,
Sauvez mon cueur, ainsi qu'avez fait maint :
Je l'oy crier piteusement secours.

10   J'ai essayé par lermes a largesse
De l'estaindre, mais il n'en vault que pis.
C'est feu gregeois, ce croy je, qui ne cesse*
D'ardre, s'il n'est estaint par bon avis.
Au feu! au feu! Courez, tous mes amis!
15   S'aucun de vous, comme lasche, remaint
Sans y aler, je le hé pour tousjours.
Avanciez vous, nul de vous ne soit faint,
Je l'oy crier piteusement secours.

S'il est ainsi mort par vostre peresse,
20   Je vous requier au moins, tant que je puis,
Chascun de vous, donnez lui une messe,
Et j'ay espoir que brief ou paradis
Des amoureux sera moult hault assis
Comme martir et treshonnoré saint
25   Qui a tenu de Loyauté le cours.
Grant tourment a, puis que si fort se plaint.
Je l'oy crier piteusement secours.

B28   **Balade**   [p. 47]

En la nef de Bonne Nouvelle
Espoir a chargié Reconfort
Pour l'amener de par la belle
Vers mon cueur qui l'ayme si fort.
5   A joye puist venir au port
De Desir, et pour tost passer
La mer de Fortune, trouver
Un plaisant vent venant de France,
Ou est a present ma maistresse,
10   Qui est ma doulce souvenance
Et le tresor de ma lÿesse.

Ballade

Burning Desire to see my mistress
Has once again attacked the fortress
Of my weary heart, who languishes in sadness,
Setting ablaze every bit of him.
5   Surely I doubt very much
This fire could be easily extinguished
Without great mercy. So I beg you, God of Love,
Do save my heart, as you have many others.
I hear him cry out piteously for help.

10   With a generous portion of tears, I've tried
To extinguish it, but that only makes matters worse.
This is Greek Fire, I believe, which never stops
Burning if not craftily extinguished.
Fire! Fire! Run, my friends, one and all!
15   If any of you, like a coward, lags behind
And does not hurry there, I'll always hate him.
Come forward, let none of you be faint-hearted.
I hear him cry out piteously for help.

If he dies from your negligence,
20   I beg, as much as I can, that each of you
At least has Mass said for him.
And I hope that soon in the paradise
Of lovers he'll find his seat on high
Like a martyr and exalted saint
25   Who has kept to the path of Loyalty.
He's greatly pained, given to terrible laments.
I hear him cry out piteously for help.

Ballade

In the ship of Good News
Hope has taken Comfort on board
So as to take him, in that beauty's name,
To my heart, who loves her so fiercely.
5   May he come with joy to the port
Of Desire and traverse quickly
Fortune's sea, come upon
A pleasant wind blowing from France,
Where at present is my mistress,
10   Who is my sweet thought
And the treasure of my happiness.

Certes, moult suy tenu a elle,
Car j'ay sceu, par loyal raport,
Que contre Dangier, le rebelle,
15   Qui maintesfois me nuist a tort,
Elle veult faire son effort
De tout son povair de m'aidier,
Et pource lui plaist m'envoyer
Ceste nef plaine de Plaisance
20   Pour estoffer la forteresse
Ou mon cueur garde l'Esperance
Et le tresor de ma lïesse.

Pource ma voulenté est telle
Et sera jusques a la mort
25   De tousjours tenir la querelle
De Loyauté ou mon ressort
J'ay mis. Mon cueur en est d'accort,
Si vueil en ce point demourer
Et souvent Amour mercier
30   Qui me fist avoir l'acointance
D'une si loyalle princesse   [p. 48]
En qui puis mettre ma fiance
Et le tresor de ma lïesse.

L'envoy
Dieu vueille celle nef garder
35   Des robeurs escumeurs de mer*
Qui ont a Dangier alïance,
Car, s'ilz povoient, par rudesse
M'osteroient ma desirance
Et le tresor de ma lïesse.

[28]

B29   Balade

Je ne crains Dangier ne les siens,
Car j'ay garny la forteresse
Ou mon cueur a retrait ses biens
De Reconfort et de Lÿesse,
5   Et ay fait Loyaulté maistresse,
Qui la place bien gardera.
Dangier deffy et sa rudesse,
Car le Dieu d'Amours m'aydera.

Surely, I'm tightly bound to her,
For trustworthy report has given me to know
That against rebellious Danger,
15 Who has often wrongly harmed me,
She'll make an effort
To help me with all her power.
And this is why she's pleased to send me
This boat full of Pleasure
20 In order to strengthen the fortress
Where my heart stands guard over Hope
And the treasure of my happiness.

This is why I'm determined
(And will be till I die)
25 Always to take the part
Of Loyalty, whom I've made
My recourse. My heart concurs.
So I wish to stand fast here
And often thank Love,
30 Who has arranged for me to receive the affection
Of a princess so faithful
That in her I can place my trust
And the treasure of my happiness.

Envoy

May God please keep this ship safe
35 From the pirates who scour the seas
And are allied with Danger,
For, if they could, in their harshness
They would take from me what I desire
And the treasure of my happiness.

Ballade

I do not fear Danger or his troop,
For I've strengthened the fortress
Where my heart has concealed the benefits
Of Comfort and Happiness.
5 And I've made Loyalty mistress there,
Who will ably guard the place.
I defy Danger and his brutality,
For the God of Love will help me.

Raison est et sera des miens,
10   Car ainsi m'en a fait promesse,
Et Espoir mon chier amy tiens,
Qui a maintesfois par proesse
Bouté hors d'avec moy Destresse,
Dont Dangier dueil et despit a,
15   Mais ne me chault de sa tristesse,
Car le Dieu d'Amours m'aidera.   [p. 49]

Pource requerir je vous viens,
Mon cueur, que prenez hardïesse.
Courez lui sus, sans craindre riens,
20   Dangier qui souvent vous blesse.
Si tost que vous prandrez l'adresse
De l'assaillir, il se rendra.
Je vous secourray sans peresse,
Car le Dieu d'Amours m'aidera.

L'envoy
25   Se vous m'aidiez, gente princesse,
Je croy que brief le temps vendra
Que j'auray des biens a largesse,
Car le Dieu d'Amours m'aydera.

[30]

B30   Balade

Belle, bien avez souvenance,
Comme certainement je croy,
De la tresplaisant alïance
Qu'Amour fist entre vous et moy.
5   Son secretaire Bonne Foy
Escrist la lectre du traittié
Et puis la seella Loyauté,
Qui la chose tesmoingnera
Quant temps et besoing en sera.

10   Joyeux Desir fut en presence
Qui alors ne se tint pas coy,
Mais mist le fait en ordonnance
De par Amour, le puissant roy,   [p. 50]
Et selon l'amoureuse loy
15   De noz deux vouloirs pour seurté
Fist une seule voulenté.
Bien m'en souvient et souvendra
Quant temps et besoing en sera.

Reason is and will remain on my side,
10   For he's made me this promise.
And I cling to Hope as my dear friend,
Who many times in his prowess
Has shoved Distress away from me.
Danger feels pain at this, also chagrin,
15   But his sadness does not concern me,
For the God of Love will help me.

This is why I come and ask you,
My heart, to be courageous.
Fearing nothing, you should attack
20   Danger, who often wounds you.
As soon as you take up a position
To assault him, he'll surrender.
With no hesitation I'll fly to your aid,
For the God of Love will help me.

Envoy
25   If you help me, noble princess,
I believe the time will soon come
When I possess happiness in abundance,
For the God of Love will help me.

Ballade

Belle, you remember clearly,
As I firmly believe,
The very pleasant alliance
Love concluded between you and me.
5   His secretary Good Faith
Wrote the letter of the treaty,
And then Loyalty sealed it,
Who will testify to the matter
When time and need arise.

10   There present was Joyous Desire,
Who then did not remain quiet,
But promulgated this decree
On behalf of Love the mighty king,
And according to the law of lovers,
15   Of our two wills he made
One single will as a guarantee.
I remember and will remember
When time and need arise.

Mon cueur n'a en nullui fiance
20   De garder la lectre qu'en soy,
Et certes ce m'est grant plaisance
Quant si tresloyal je le voy
Et lui conseille comme doy
De tousjours haïr Faulseté,
25   Car quiconque l'a en chierté,
Amour chastïer l'en fera,
Quant temps et besoing en sera.

L'envoy

Pensez en ce que j'ay compté,
Ma dame, car en verité
30   Mon cueur de foy vous requerra
Quant temps et besoing en sera.

B31   **Balade**   [p. 51]

Venés vers moy, Bonne Nouvelle
Pour mon las cueur reconforter.
Contez moy comment fait la belle.
L'avez vous point oÿ parler
5   De moy et amy me nommer?
A elle point mis en oubly
Ce qu'il lui pleut de m'acorder,
Quant me donna le nom d'amy?

Combien que Dangier le rebelle
10   Me fait loing d'elle demourer,
Je congnois tant de bien en elle
Que je ne pourroye penser
Que tousjours ne vueille garder
Ce que me promist sans nul sy,
15   Faisant nos deux mains assembler,
Quant me donna le nom d'amy.

Pitié seroit, se dame telle,
Qui doit tout honneur desirer,
Failloit de tenir la querelle
20   De bien et loyaument amer.
Son sens lui scet bien remoustrer
Toutes les choses que je dy
Et ce qu'Amour nous fist jurer
Quant me donna le nom d'amy.

My heart trusts no man
20 Save himself to keep the letter safe,
And surely the heart gives me great pleasure
When I see he is so very faithful,
And I counsel him, as I should,
To hate Falsehood always.
25 For no matter who holds Falsehood dear,
Love will have him punished
When time and need arise.

Envoy
Think about what I have said,
My lady, for in truth
30 My heart will summon you on your sworn faith
When time and need arise.

Ballade

Come to me, Good News,
And comfort my weary heart.
Tell me how that beauty is doing.
Have you heard her say anything
5 About me and call me friend?
Has she forgotten somewhat
What she was pleased to grant me
When she gave me the name of sweet friend?

Though that rebel Danger
10 Makes me remain far distant from her,
I see this lady possesses so much virtue
I cannot imagine
She will not always keep to
What she promised me with no "buts,"
15 As we put our two hands together,
When she gave me the name of sweet friend.

It would be a pity if such a lady,
Who should be eager for every honor,
Were to fail at the enterprise
20 Of loving faithfully and well.
Her mind can readily rehearse for her
All the things I speak of
And what Love made us pledge
When she gave me the name of sweet friend.

25   Loyauté, vueilliez asseurer
     Ma dame que sien suy, ainsy
     Qu'elle me voulu commander
     Quant me donna le nom d'amy.

[31]

B32   Balade   [p. 52]

     Belle, s'il vous plaist escouter
     Comment j'ay gardé en chierté
     Vostre cueur qu'il vous pleut laissier
     Avec moy, par vostre bonté,
5   Sachiés qu'il est enveloppé
     En ung cueuvrechief de Plaisance
     Et enclos pour plus grant seurté
     Ou coffre de ma souvenance.

     Et pour nettement le garder
10   Je l'ay souventesfois lavé
     En larmes de Piteux Penser,
     Et regrettant vostre beauté
     Aprés ce sans delay porté
     Pour sechier au feu d'Esperance
15   Et puis doulcement rebouté
     Ou coffre de ma souvenance.

     Pource, vueilliez vous acquittier
     De mon cueur que vous ay donné,
     Humblement vous en vueil prier
20   En le gardant en loyauté
     Soubz clef de Bonne Voulenté,
     Comme j'ay fait de ma puissance
     Le vostre que tiens enfermé
     Ou coffre de ma souvenance.

                    L'envoy
25   Ma dame, je vous ay compté
     De vostre cueur la gouvernance,
     Comment il est et a esté
     Ou coffre de ma souvenance.

[32]

25   Loyalty, please assure
My lady I am hers, just as
She was pleased to command me
When she gave me the name of sweet friend.

Ballade

Belle, please hear
How lovingly I have watched over
Your heart, which you were pleased to leave
With me in your goodness.
5   Know that it is wrapped
In one of Pleasure's kerchiefs
And, for the sake of greater safety, locked
In the treasure chest of my memory.

And for the sake of cleanliness,
10   I have oftentimes bathed it
In the tears of Piteous Thought,
And, mourning for your beauty,
I bore it afterward without delay
To Hope's fire, there to dry,
15   Softly replacing it
In the treasure chest of my memory.

And so please fulfill your obligation
Toward my heart, which I gave you.
I would humbly ask you
20   To keep it safe in faithfulness,
Under Good Will's key,
Just as I have done, as I could,
With yours, which I keep locked
In the treasure chest of my memory.

25   My lady, I have told you
How your heart is cared for,
How it is now and has been
In the treasure chest of my memory.

B33   Balade   [p. 53]

	Se je vous dy bonne nouvelle,	L'amant
	Mon cueur, que voulez vous donner?	
	Elle pourroit bien estre telle	Le cueur
	Que moult chier la vueil acheter.	
5	Nul guerdon n'en quier demander.	L'amant
	Dittes tost doncques, je vous prie,	Le cueur
	J'ay grant desir de la savoir.	
	C'est de vostre dame et amye	L'amant
	Qui loyaument fait son devoir.	
10	Que me savez vous dire d'elle	Le cueur
	Dont me puisse reconforter?	
	Je vous dy, sans que plus le celle,	L'amant
	Qu'elle vient par deça la mer.*	
	Dittes vous vray, sans me moquer?	Le cueur
15	Ouïl, je le vous certiffie,	L'amant
	Et dit que c'est pour vous veoir.	
	Amour humblement j'en mercie,	Le cueur
	Qui loyaument fait son devoir.	
	Que pourroit plus faire la belle	L'amant
20	Que de tant pour vous se pener?	
	Loyauté soustient ma querelle,	Le cueur
	Qui lui fait faire sans doubter.	
	Pensez doncques de bien l'amer.	L'amant
	Si feray je toute ma vie,	Le cueur
25	Sans changier, de tout mon povair.	
	Bien doit estre dame chierie	L'amant
	Qui loyaument fait son devoir.	

[33]

B34   Balade   [p. 54]

	Mon cueur, ouvrez l'uis de Pensee
	Et recevez un doulx present
	Que la tresloyaument amee
	Vous envoye nouvellement,
5	Et vous tenez joyeusement,
	Car bien devez avoir lïesse
	Quant la trouvez sans changement
	Tousjours tresloyalle maistresse.
	Bien devez prisier la journee
10	Que fustes sien premierement,

Ballade

	If I tell you good news,	The Lover
	My heart, what will you give?	
	It could very well be the kind	The Heart
	I'll purchase at a high price.	
5	I intend seeking no reward.	The Lover
	Speak quickly then, I beg you.	The Heart
	I'm very eager to learn it.	
	It's about your lady and sweet friend	The Lover
	Who faithfully fulfills her obligation.	
10	What can you tell me of her	The Heart
	That might comfort me?	
	I tell you, keeping this secret no longer,	The Lover
	That she travels over the sea.	
	Do you speak the truth, not mocking me?	The Heart
15	Yes, I so pledge,	The Lover
	And say it is to see you.	
	I humbly thank Love,	The Heart
	Who faithfully fulfills his obligation.	
	What more could that beauty do,	The Lover
20	Who takes such trouble for your sake?	
	Loyalty takes my part,	The Heart
	Who doubtless made her do so.	
	Think then to love her well.	The Lover
	I will do so all my life,	The Heart
25	Not altering, with all my strength.	
	Well cherished should be the lady	The Lover
	Who faithfully fulfills her obligation.	

Ballade

	My heart, open the door of Thought
	And receive a sweet present,
	Which she, so faithfully loved,
	Sends you at this time;
5	And be filled with joy,
	For happiness should be yours
	When you find her, without changing,
	Always a very faithful mistress.
	You should much prize the day
10	When first you became hers,

Car sa grace vous a donnee
Sans faintise tresloyaument.
Vous le povez veoir clerement,
Car elle vous tient sa promesse,
15   Soy moustrant vers vous fermement
Tousjours tresloyalle maistresse.

Par vous soit doncques honnouree
Et servie soingneusement
Tant comme vous aurez duree
20   Sans point faire departement,
Car vous aurez certainement
Par elle de biens a largesse,
Puis qu'elle est si entierement
Tousjours tresloyalle maistresse.

L'envoy
25   Grans mercis des fois plus de cent,
Ma dame, ma seule Princesse,
Car je vous treuve vrayement
Tousjours tresloyalle maistresse.

B35   **Balade**   [p. 55]

J'ay ou tresor de ma pensee
Un mirouer qu'ay acheté.
Amour en l'annee passee
Le me vendy de sa bonté,
5   Ou quel voy tousjours la beauté
De celle que l'en doit nommer
Par droit la plus belle de France.
Grant bien me fait a m'y mirer
En attendant Bonne Esperance.

10   Je n'ay chose qui tant m'agree
Ne dont tiengne si grant chierté,
Car en ma dure destinee
Maintesfoiz m'a reconforté,
Ne mon cueur n'a jamais santé
15   Fors quant il y peut regarder
Des yeulx de Joyeuse Plaisance.
Il s'y esbat pour temps passer
En attendant Bonne Esperance.

Advis m'est chascune journee
20   Que m'y mire qu'en verité
Toute doleur si m'est ostee.

       For she's bestowed her favor upon you
       Very faithfully without hesitation.
       This you can clearly see,
       For she keeps her promise to you,
15   Steadfastly showing herself toward you
       Always a very faithful mistress.

       Let her then be honored by you
       And carefully served
       As long as you might last;
20   And never abandon her,
       For you'll certainly have
       An abundance of gifts through her
       Since so completely is she
       Always a very faithful mistress.

Envoy

25   Many thanks, a hundredfold and more,
       My lady, my only Princess,
       For truly I find you
       Always a very faithful mistress.

Ballade

       In the treasure chest of my thought
       I have a mirror I bought.
       In this past year Love
       Sold it to me in her goodness;
5   In it I always see the beauty
       Of the lady one should call
       Rightfully France's greatest beauty.
       It does me great good to see myself in it
       While waiting for Good Hope.

10   Nothing else I have pleases me as much
       Or makes me hold it as dear,
       For in the troubled time of my destiny
       It has often comforted me;
       Nor is my heart ever in good condition
15   Save when gazing upon it
       With the eyes of Joyous Pleasure.
       There it disports itself to pass the time
       While waiting for Good Hope.

       It seems every day
20   I look therein that truly
       All my pain is relieved.

Pource de bonne voulenté
Par le conseil de Leauté
Mettre le vueil et enfermer
25   Ou coffre de ma souvenance
Pour plus seurement le garder
En attendant Bonne Esperance.

[35]

B36   **Balade**   [p. 56]

Je ne vous puis ne sçay amer,
Ma dame, tant que je vouldroye,
Car escript m'avez pour m'oster
Ennuy qui trop fort me guerroye :
5   «Mon seul amy, mon bien, ma joye,*
Cellui que sur tous amer veulx,
Je vous pry que soyez joyeux
En esperant que brief vous voye.»

Je sens ces motz mon cueur percer
10   Si doulcement que ne sauroye
Le confort au vray vous mander
Que vostre message m'envoye,
Car vous dictes que querez voye
De venir vers moy. Se m'aid Dieux,
15   Demander ne vouldroye mieulx
En esperant que brief vous voye.

Et quant il vous plaist souhaidier
D'estre emprés moy, ou que je soye,*
Par Dieu, nompareille sans per,
20   C'est trop fait, se dire l'osoye.
Se suy ge qui plus le devroye
Souhaidier de cueur tressoingneux.
C'est ce dont tant suis desireux
En esperant que brief vous voye.

[36]

B37   **Balade**   [p. 57]

L'autrier alay mon cueur veoir
Pour savoir comment se portoit,
Si trouvay avec lui Espoir
Qui doulcement le confortoit

And so with good will,
As Loyalty counsels,
I'll put and enclose it
25 In the treasure chest of my memory
So as to guard it more securely
While waiting for Good Hope.

Ballade

I cannot, know not, how, to love you,
My lady, in the way I would like,
For you have written this to lift me out of
Suffering, then fiercely warring on me:
5 "My only sweet friend, my good, my joy,
The man I intend to love above all others,
I beg you to be joyful,
Hoping I will see you soon."

I feel these words piercing my heart
10 So sweetly I cannot
Truly tell you the comfort
Your message affords me;
For you say you are seeking some way
To come to me. So help me God,
15 I would not ask for anything better,
Hoping I will see you soon.

And since you are pleased to want
To be at my side wherever I might be,
By God, lady peerless and with no rival,
20 You do too much, if I dare say so.
For I should be the one desiring
This more, my heart full of love.
This is what I want so much,
Hoping I will see you soon.

Ballade

The other day I went to see my heart
To learn how he was doing.
And there I found Hope
Gently comforting him

5   Et ces parolles lui disoit :
      «Cueur, tenez vous joieusement,
      Je vous fais loyalle promesse
      Que je vous garde seurement
      Tresor d'amoureuse richesse.

10   Car je vous fais pour vray savoir
      Que la plus tresbelle qui soit
      Vous ayme de loyal vouloir
      Et voulentiers pour vous feroit
      Tout ce qu'elle faire pourroit
15   Et vous mande que vrayement
      Maugré Dangier et sa rudesse
      Departir vous veult largement
      Tresor d'amoureuse richesse.»

      Alors mon cueur pour dire voir
20   De joye souvent soupiroit,
      Et combien qu'il portast le noir,
      Toutesfoiz pour lors oublioit
      Toute la doleur qu'il avoit
      Pensant de recouvrer briefment
25   Plaisance, Confort et Lïesse
      Et d'avoir en gouvernement
      Tresor d'amoureuse richesse.

                  L'envoy
      A Bon Espoir mon cueur s'atent
      Et a vous, ma belle maistresse,
30   Que lui espargniez loyaument
      Tresor d'amoureuse richesse.

[37]

B38   **Ballade**   [p. 58]

      Haa, Doulx Penser, jamais je ne pourroye
      Vous desservir les biens que me donnez,
      Car, quant Ennuy mon povre cueur guerroye
      Par Fortune, comme bien le savés,
5   Toutes les fois qu'amener me voulés
      Un souvenir de ma belle maistresse,
      Tantost Doleur, Desplaisir et Tristesse
      S'en vont fuiant. Ilz n'osent demourer,
      Ne se trouver en vostre compaignie,
10   Mais se meurent de courrous et d'envie,
      Quant il vous plaist d'ainsi me conforter.

5   And speaking these words:
"Heart, be joyful.
I promise you faithfully
I'll keep safely for you
A treasure of lovers' riches.

10   "For I give you to know truly
That the most beautiful lady alive
Loves you, faithful in her intentions,
And would gladly do for you
All she's able to do;
15   And I tell you that truly,
Despite Danger and his cruelty,
She intends generously to share out to you
A treasure of lovers' riches."

Then my heart, to speak the truth,
20   Often sighed from joy,
And though dressed in black,
From that moment he forgot
All the pain he was feeling,
Thinking shortly to recover
25   Pleasure, Comfort, and Happiness,
And to have under his power
A treasure of lovers' riches.

Envoy

My heart depends on Good Hope
And on you, my beautiful mistress,
30   That faithfully and for his sake you will be frugal with
A treasure of lovers' riches.

Ballade

Aha, Sweet Thought, never could I
Deserve the goods you bestow upon me,
For, when Misery wars upon my heart,
On Fortune's behalf (this you well know),
5   You think every time to bring me
Some memory of my beautiful mistress.
At once Pain, Misery, and Sadness
Take flight. They dare neither remain
Nor find themselves in your company.
10   Instead they die of anger and envy
When you are pleased thus to comfort me.

L'aise que j'ay dire je ne sauroye,
Quant Souvenir et vous me racontés
Les tresdoulx fais plaisans et plains de joye
15   De ma dame, qui sont congneuz assés
En plusieurs lieux et si bien renommés
Que d'en parler chascun en a lïesse.
Pource, tous deulx, pour me tollir Destresse,
D'elle vueilliez nouvelles m'aporter
20   Le plus souvent que pourrés, je vous prie.
Vous me sauvez et maintenez la vie
Quant il vous plaist d'ainsi me conforter.

Car lors Amour par vous deux si m'envoye
Un doulx espoir que vous me presentés,
25   Qui me donne conseil que joyeux soye,
Et puis aprés tous trois me promectés
Qu'a mon besoing jamais ne me fauldrés.
Ainsi m'atens tout en vostre promesse,
Car par vous puis avoir a grant largesse
30   Des biens d'Amour plus que ne sçay nombrer,
Maugré Dangier, Dueil et Merencolie
Que je ne crains en riens, mais les deffie,   [p. 59]
Quant il vous plaist d'ainsi me conforter.

L'envoy
Jeune, gente, nompareille Princesse,*
35   Puis que ne puis veoir vostre jeunesse,
De m'escrire ne vous vueilliez lasser,
Car vous faictes, je le vous certiffie,
Grant aumosne, dont je vous remercie,
Quant il vous plaist d'ainsi me conforter.

[38]

B39   Balade

Se je povoye mes souhais
Et mes soupirs faire voler
Si tost que mon cueur les a fais,
Passer leur feroye la mer
5   Et vers celle tout droit aler
Que j'ayme du cueur si tresfort
Comme ma lïesse mondaine
Que je tendray jusqu'a la mort
Pour ma maistresse souveraine.

I dare not confess the relief I feel
When you and Memory recount to me
The doings, so gracious, pleasant, and joyful,
15 Of my lady, which are known well
In many places and are so renowned
Every man is pleased to speak of them.
And so, to relieve me of Distress,
Both of you please bring me news of her
20 As often as you can—this I beg you.
You save me and preserve my life
When you are pleased thus to comfort me.

For then Love sends through you two
The offer of a Sweet Hope
25 Who counsels me to be joyful;
And afterward you—all three—promise
Never to fail me in my time of need.
So I count completely on your pledge,
For through you I can gain in abundance
30 More of Love's benefits than I can number,
Despite Danger, Pain, and Melancholy,
Whom I fear not, but instead defy
When you are pleased thus to comfort me.

Envoy
Princess young, elegant, and unrivaled,
35 Since I cannot look upon your youth,
Please do not be slow to write me
Because you will perform, I assure you,
A work of great charity, for which I thank you,
When you are pleased thus to comfort me.

Ballade

If I could make my wishes
And my sighs take flight
As soon as my heart gives rise to them,
I would have them traverse the sea
5 And make their way straight to the lady
I love so very much from the heart
As my earthly happiness,
Whom I will take, till death comes,
For my sovereign mistress.

10   Helas! La verray je jamais?
        Qu'en dictes vous, tresdoulx Penser?
        Espoir m'a promis ouïl, mais
        Trop long temps me fait endurer.
        Et quant je luy viens demander
15   Secours a mon besoing, il dort.
        Ainsi suis chascune sepmaine
        En maint ennuy sans reconfort   [p. 60]
        Pour ma maistresse souveraine.

        Je ne puis demourer en paix,
20   Fortune ne m'y veult laissier.
        Au fort, a present je me tais
        Et vueil laissier le temps passer
        Pensant d'avoir, au par aler,
        Par Leauté ou mon ressort
25   J'ay mis, de Plaisance l'estraine
        En guerdon des maulx qu'ay a tort
        Pour ma maistresse souveraine.

[39]

B40   Balade

        Fortune, vueilliez moy laissier
        En paix une fois je vous prie.
        Trop longuement, a vray compter,
        Avés eu sur moy seigneurie.
5   Tousjours faictes la rencherie
        Vers moy et ne voulez ouïr
        Les maulx que m'avez fait souffrir
        Il a ja plusieurs ans passez.
        Doy je tousjours ainsi languir?
10   Helas! et n'est ce pas assés?

        Plus ne puis en ce point durer
        Et a Mercy mercy je crie.
        Soupirs m'empeschent le parler.
        Veoir le povez sans mocquerie,
15   Il ne fault ja que je le dye.
        Pource vous vueil je requerir
        Qu'il vous plaise de me tollir
        Les maulx que m'avez amassez,   [p. 61]
        Qui m'ont mis jusques au mourir.
20   Helas! et n'est ce pas assez?

10   Alas! Will I never see her?
        What do you have to say, Thought so sweet?
        Hope has promised me a yes, but
        Makes me suffer so long.
        And when I come to ask for
15   Assistance in my time of need, he sleeps on.
        So every week I'm
        In terrible distress, disconsolate,
        For my sovereign mistress.

        I cannot remain at peace;
20   Fortune will not let me be.
        Now in the end I'm silent
        And let the time pass,
        Thinking of finally obtaining
        Through Loyalty, in whom I've taken
25   Refuge, the gift of Pleasure
        As a reward for the miseries I wrongly suffer
        For my sovereign mistress.

Ballade

        Fortune, please leave me
        In peace this one time, I beg you.
        Too long, if truth be told,
        You've held dominion over me.
5   Always you act the disdainful woman,
        Not wishing to hear
        The ills you've made me suffer.
        Now several years have passed.
        Am I to always suffer in this way?
10   Alas! And is this not enough?

        I can go on no longer this way,
        And from Mercy I beg mercy.
        Sighs prevent me from speaking.
        You can see it—this is no jest.
15   I've no need to tell that one.
        And so I intend asking you,
        Please alleviate the miseries
        You've brought that put me
        At the point of death.
20   Alas! And is this not enough?

Tous maulx suy contant de porter
Fors un seul, qui trop fort m'ennuye :
C'est qu'il me fault loing demourer
De celle que tiens pour amye,
25   Car pieça en sa compaignie
Laissay mon cueur et mon desir.
Vers moy ne veulent revenir,
D'elle ne sont jamais lassez.
Ainsi suy seul sans nul plaisir.
30   Helas! et n'est ce pas assez?

L'envoy
De ballader j'ay beau loisir,
Autres deduis me sont cassez.
Prisonnier suis, d'Amour martir.
Helas! et n'est ce pas assez?

[40]

B41   **Balade**   [p. 62]

Espoir m'a apporté nouvelle
Qui trop me doit reconforter.
Il dit que Fortune la felle
A vouloir de soy raviser
5   Et toutes faultes amender
Qu'a faittes contre mon plaisir
En faisant sa roe tourner.*
Dieu doint qu'ainsi puist avenir!

Quoy que m'ait fait guerre mortelle,
10   Je suy content de l'esprouver,
Et le debat qu'ay et querelle
Vers elle je vueil delaissier
Et tout courrous lui pardonner,
Car d'elle me puis bien servir,
15   Se loyaument veult s'acquitter.
Dieu doint qu'ainsi puist avenir!

Se la povoye trouver telle
Qu'elle me voulsist tant aidier
Qu'en mes bras je peusse la belle
20   Une fois a mon gré trouver,
Plus ne vouldroye demander,
Car lors j'auroye mon desir
Et tout quanque doy souhaidier.
Dieu doint qu'ainsi puist avenir!

I'm content to endure all miseries
Save one, which terribly distresses me:
I must remain far distant
From the lady I consider my sweet friend,
25   For some time ago in her company
I left behind my heart and my desire.
They'll not return
And never weary of her.
So I'm alone and find no pleasure.
30   Alas! And is this not enough?

Envoy

I have leisure enough to write ballades.
Other sport is denied me.
I'm a prisoner, a martyr to Love.
Alas! And is this not enough?

Ballade

Hope has brought news
That should greatly comfort me.
He says traitorous Fortune
Intends to change her mind
5   And amend every wrong
She's committed against my pleasure
By turning her wheel.
May God grant it happen thus!

Though she's made deadly war on me,
10   I'm content to put up with it;
And the disputes and complaints I hold
Against her I intend laying aside,
Pardoning her for all my grief.
For she can be of much use to me
15   If she'll acquit herself faithfully.
May God grant it happen thus!

If I find her
Eager enough to help me
Discover that beauty one time
20   In my arms, as I wish,
I'd ask for nothing more.
For then I'd have my desire
And my every wish would be fulfilled.
May God grant it happen thus!

25   Amour, s'il vous plaist commander
      A Fortune de me chierir,
      Je pense joye recouvrer.
      Dieu doint qu'ainsi puist avenir!

[41]

B42   **Balade**   [p. 63]

      Je ne me sçay en quel point maintenir,
      Ce premier jour de may plain de lïesse,
      Car d'une part puis dire sans faillir
      Que, Dieu mercy, j'ay loyalle maistresse,
5   Qui de tous biens a trop plus qu'a largesse,
      Et si pense que, la sienne mercy,
      Elle me tient son servant et amy.
      Ne doy je bien donques joye mener
      Et me tenir en joyeuse plaisance?
10   Certes ouïl, et Amour mercïer
      Treshumblement de toute ma puissance.

      Mais d'autre part il me couvient souffrir
      Tant de douleur et de dure destresse
      Par Fortune qui me vient assaillir
15   De tous costez, qui de maulx est princesse.
      Passer m'a fait le plus de ma jennesse
      Dieu scet comment, en doloreux party,
      Et si me fait demourer en soussy,
      Loings de celle par qui puis recouvrer
20   Le vray tresor de ma droitte esperance,
      Et que je vueil obeir et amer
      Treshumblement de toute ma puissance.

      Et pource, May, je vous viens requerir :
      Pardonnez moy de vostre gentillesse,
25   Se je ne puis a present vous servir
      Comme je doy, car je vous fais promesse.
      J'ay bon vouloir envers vous, mais Tristesse
      M'a si long temps en son dangier nourry
      Que j'ay du tout Joye mis en oubly,
30   Si me vault mieulx seul de gens eslongier.
      Qui dolent est ne sert que d'encombrance.   [p. 64]
      Pource, reclus me tendray en penser
      Treshumblement de toute ma puissance.

Envoy

25   Love, if you are pleased to command
Fortune to hold me dear,
I think joy will again be mine.
May God grant it happen thus!

Ballade

I know not what to do
On this first day of May, full of happiness,
Since I can say without fail, on the one hand,
That, thank God, I have a faithful mistress,
5   Who possesses all virtues more than abundantly.
And too I think that—thanks to her—
She considers me her servant and friend.
Should I not then make merry
And lead a life of joyous pleasure?
10   Surely yes, and I thank Love
Very humbly with all my might.

But, on the other hand, I must suffer
So much pain and bitter distress
Because of Fortune, who assaults
15   Me so at every turn, this princess of ills.
That she's made me spend most of my youth
(God knows how much) in a state of pain,
And has left me full of worries,
Far from the lady from whom I can recover
20   The true treasure of my rightful hope,
And whom I intend to obey and love
Very humbly with all my might.

And so, May, I come to make this request:
Pardon me, through the kindness of your spirit,
25   If I cannot at present serve you
As I should, nonetheless I make such a promise.
I am well disposed toward you, though Sadness
Has kept me so long in her dominion
I've forgotten Joy completely.
30   So I had better stay far from people.
The sad serve only as a burden.
And so I shall remain a hermit who thinks
Very humbly with all my might.

L'envoy

Doulx Souvenir, chierement je vous pry,
35   Escrivez tost ceste ballade cy.
De par mon cueur la feray presenter
A ma dame, ma seule desirance,
A qui pieça je le voulu donner
Treshumblement de toute ma puissance.

[42]

B43   **Balade**

Mon cueur est devenu hermite
En l'ermitage de Pensee,
Car Fortune la tresdespite,
Qui l'a haÿ mainte journee,
5   S'est nouvellement alïee
Contre lui aveques Tristesse,
Et l'ont banny hors de Lÿesse.
Place n'a ou puist demourer
Fors ou boys de Merencolie.
10   Il est content de s'i logier,
Si lui dis je que c'est folie.

Mainte parolle luy ai ditte,
Mais il ne l'a point escoutee.
Mon parler riens ne lui proufite,
15   Sa voulenté y est fermee,
De legier ne seroit changee.
Il se gouverne par Destresse,   [p. 65]
Qui contre son prouffit ne cesse
Nuit et jour de le conseillier.
20   De si prés lui tient compaignie
Qu'il ne peut ennuy delaissier,
Si lui dis je que c'est folie.

Pource sachiez, je m'en acquitte,
Belle tresloyaument amee,
25   Se lectre ne lui est escripte
Par vous ou nouvelle mandee,
Dont sa doleur soit allegee,
Il a fait son veu et promesse
De renoncer a la richesse
30   De Plaisir et de Doulx Penser
Et aprés ce toute sa vie
L'abit de Desconfort porter,
Si lui dis je que c'est folie.

Envoy

Sweet Memory, fervently I beg you,
35   Quickly write down this ballade here.
On my heart's behalf I shall have it presented
To my lady, my one desire,
To whom some time ago I wished to give it
Very humbly with all my might.

Ballade

My heart has become a recluse
In the hermitage of Thought,
For Fortune, the being so odious
Who's shown him hatred many a day,
5   Has recently allied with
Sadness to oppose my heart,
Banning him from Happiness.
He has no place to live
Save in the forest of Melancholy.
10   There he's content to take lodging,
So I tell him this is madness.

I've spoken many a word,
But he's not listened at all.
My speech does him no good,
15   His desire is set against it;
Not easily will this change.
He follows the advice of Distress,
Who, opposing his advantage, never ceases
Night and day to counsel him.
20   Distress is such a close companion
He cannot lay aside his misery,
So I tell him this is madness.

Know this is why (thus I do my duty),
Belle so faithfully loved,
25   If a letter is not written or
News sent to him
To alleviate his pain,
He's vowed and promised
To renounce the riches
30   Of Pleasure and Sweet Thought,
And, after, to wear the habit
Of Discomfort all his life,
So I tell him this is madness.

<h3 style="text-align:center">L'envoy</h3>

Se par vous n'est, Belle sans per,
35   Pour quelque chose que lui die,
Mon cueur ne se veult conforter,
Si lui dis je que c'est folie.

[43]

B44   **Ballade**   [p. 66]

Dangier, je vous giette mon gant
Vous apellant de traïson
Devant le Dieu d'Amours puissant
Qui me fera de vous raison,
5   Car vous m'avez mainte saison
Fait douleur a tort endurer
Et me faittes loings demourer
De la nompareille de France,
Mais vous l'avez tousjours d'usance
10   De grever loyaulx amoureux,
Et pource que je sui l'un d'eulx,
Pour eulx et moy prens la querelle.
Par Dieu, vilain, vous y mourrés
Par mes mains, point ne le vous celle,
15   S'a Leauté ne vous rendés.

Comment avez vous d'orgueil tant
Que vous osez sans achoison
Tourmenter aucun vray amant
Qui de cueur et d'entencïon
20   Sert Amours sans condicïon?
Certes moult estes a blasmer.
Pensez doncques de l'amender
En laissant vostre mal vueillance
Et par treshumble repentance
25   Alez crier mercy a ceulx
Que vous avés fais douloureux
Et qui vous ont trouvé rebelle.
Autrement pour seur vous tenez
Que de gage je vous appelle,*
30   S'a Leauté ne vous rendés.

Vous estes tous temps mal pensant   [p. 67]
Et plain de faulse soupeçon.
Ce vous vient de mauvais talant
Nourry en courage felon.

Envoy

If not by you, unrivaled Belle,
35 Then not for anything I might say to him
Does my heart intend to take comfort.
So I tell him this is madness.

Ballade

Danger, I cast down my glove as a challenge,
Accusing you of treason
Before the mighty God of Love,
Who will have you give me satisfaction,
5 For you've wrongly caused me
To suffer pain many a season,
And you have made me remain
Distant from the lady with no peer in France,
But yours is always the custom
10 To make faithful lovers suffer distress,
And since I am one such,
For them and myself I take up this quarrel.
By God, you low-born creature, you'll suffer death
At my hands—I don't keep it from you at all—
15 If you do not surrender to Loyalty.

How is it you are arrogant
Enough to dare, without cause,
Tormenting every true lover
Who with heart and intention
20 Serves Love unconditionally?
Surely, you're very much to blame.
Consider, then, making amends
By abandoning your ill will
And, by way of a humble repentance,
25 Go beg mercy from those
You've made suffer
And who have found you a traitor.
Otherwise be very sure
I'll shall formally challenge you
30 If you do not surrender to Loyalty.

At all times you're evil-minded
And filled with false suspicions.
This comes from your foul desire,
Nourished by a criminal heart.

35   Quel mal ou ennuy vous fait on,
        Se par amours on veult amer
        Pour plus aise le temps passer
        En lyee, joyeuse Plaisance?
        C'est gracïeuse desirance.
40   Pource, faulx vilain orgueillieux,
        Changiez voz vouloirs oultragieux,
        Ou je vous feray guerre telle
        Que sans faillir vous trouverés
        Qu'elle vauldra pis que mortelle
45   S'a Leauté ne vous rendés.

[44]

B45   Balade

        Se Dieu plaist, briefment la nuee   [p. 68]
        De ma tristesse passera,
        Belle tresloyaument amee,
        Et le beau temps se moustrera,
5   Mais savez vous quant ce sera?
        Quant le doulx souleil gracïeux
        De vostre beauté entrera
        Par les fenestres de mes yeulx.

        Lors la chambre de ma pensee
10   De grant plaisance reluira
        Et sera de joye paree.
        Adonc mon cueur s'esveillera,
        Qui en dueil dormy long temps a.
        Plus ne dormira, se m'aid Dieux,
15   Quant ceste clarté le ferra
        Par les fenestres de mes yeulx.

        Helas! Quant vendra la journee
        Qu'ainsi avenir me pourra?
        Ma maistresse tresdesiree,
20   Pensez vous que brief avendra?
        Car mon cueur tousjours languira
        En ennuy, sans point avoir mieulx,
        Jusqu'a tant que cecy verra
        Par les fenestres de mes yeulx.

35   What ill or injury do you suffer
           If someone intends to love in a lover's fashion
           And thus pass the time more at ease
           In happy, joyous Pleasure?
           This is a gracious desire.
40   And so, traitor haughty and of low degree,
           Abandon your outrageous ways,
           Or I'll wage such war against you
           That, without fail, you'll find
           It worse than mortal
           If you do not surrender to Loyalty.

Ballade

      Please God, the cloud of my
      Sadness will soon pass over,
      Belle, so faithfully loved,
      And good weather will show itself,
5   But do you know when this will be?
      When the sweet, gracious sun
      Of your beauty enters
      Through the windows of my eyes.

      Then the chamber of my thought
10   Will shine again with great pleasure
      And be replete with joy.
      Then my heart will awaken,
      Which has long slept in pain.
      No more will it sleep, so help me God,
15   When this brightness strikes it
      Through the windows of my eyes.

      Alas! When will the day come
      That this might be my lot?
      Mistress mine, so desired by me,
20   Do you think this will come soon?
      For my heart will languish always
      In distress, without the least improvement,
      Until the time it sees this
      Through the windows of my eyes.

L'envoy

25 De reconfort mon cueur aura
    Autant que nul dessoubz les cieulx,
    Belle, quant vous regardera
    Par les fenestres de mes yeulx.

[45]

B46   Balade   [p. 69]

    Au court jeu de tables jouer*
    Amour me fait moult longuement,
    Car tousjours me charge garder
    Le point d'atentte seulement*
5   En me disant que, vrayement,
    Se ce point lyé sçay tenir*
    Qu'au derrain je doy, sans mentir,
    Gaangnier le jeu entierement.

    Je suy pris et ne puis entrer
10 Ou point que desire souvent.
    Dieu me doint une fois gietter
    Chance qui soit aucunement
    A mon propos, car autrement
    Mon cueur sera pis que martir,
15 Se ne puis, ainsi qu'ay desir,
    Gaangnier le jeu entierement.

    Fortune fait souvent tourner
    Les dez contre moy mallement,
    Mais Espoir, mon bon conseillier,
20 M'a dit et promis seurement
    Que Loyauté prochainnement
    Fera Bon Eur vers moy venir,
    Qui me fera a mon plaisir
    Gaangnier le jeu entierement.

L'envoy

25 Je vous supply treshumblement,
    Amour, aprenez moy comment
    J'asserray les dez sans faillir,*
    Par quoy puisse, sans plus languir,
    Gaangnier le jeu entierement.

[46]

Envoy

25   My heart will have as much comfort
As any other under heaven,
Belle, when it looks upon you
Through the windows of my eyes.

Ballade

At backgammon Love
Makes me play a very long time,
Always stopping me
At enter point, with only
5   These words, that
If I knew how to score a good point
In the end I should, and no lie,
Win the game altogether.

I'm taken and cannot enter
10   Where I often desire to do so.
May God grant that one time
The dice I throw land
Favorably, or else
My heart will do worse than suffer,
15   If I cannot, as is my desire,
Win the game altogether.

Fortune often makes the dice
Land to my misfortune,
But Hope, my able counselor,
20   Has said (and promised me firmly)
That Loyalty soon
Will make Good Luck come my way,
Who will, to my pleasure, have me
Win the game altogether.

Envoy

25   I beg you very humbly,
Love, teach me how
I can make the dice roll my way,
And then, languishing no more, I could
Win the game altogether.

B47   Balade   [p. 70]

        Vous, soiés la tresbien venue
        Vers mon cueur, Joyeuse Nouvelle,
        Avez vous point ma dame veue?
        Contez moy quelque chose d'elle.
5   Dittes moy, n'est elle pas telle
        Qu'estoit, quant derrenierement,
        Pour m'oster de merencolie,
        M'escrivy amoureusement :
        «C'estes vous de qui suis amye.»

10   Son vouloir jamais ne se mue,
        Ce croy je, mais tient la querelle
        De Leauté qu'a retenue
        Sa plus prochainne damoiselle.
        Bien le moustre, sans que le celle,
15   Qu'elle se maintient léaument,
        Quant lui plaist, dont je la mercie,
        Me mander si tresdoulcement :
        «C'estes vous de qui suis amye.»

        Pour le plus eureux soubz la nue
20   Me tiens, quant m'amye s'appelle,
        Car en tous lieux ou est congneue
        Chascun la nomme la plus belle.
        Dieu doint que maugré le rebelle
        Dangier, je la voye briefment,
25   Et que de sa bouche me die :
        «Amy, pensez que seulement
        C'estes vous de qui suis amye.».

                          L'envoy
        J'ay en mon cueur joyeusement
        Escript, afin que ne l'oublie,
30   Ce refrain qu'ayme chierement :   [p. 71]
        C'estes vous de qui suis amye.

[47]

B48   Balade*

        Trop long temps vous voy sommeillier,
        Mon cueur, en dueil et desplaisir.
        Vueilliez vous ce jour esveillier.
        Alons au bois le may cueillir
5   Pour la coustume maintenir.

Ballade

You, you're very welcome
To my heart, Joyous News;
Have you seen anything of my lady?
Tell me something more about her.
5   Tell me, does she not feel the same
As she did, when not long ago
To take my melancholy from me,
She wrote me in a loving way:
"It is you by whom I am loved"?

10   Her intention never alters,
So I believe, but takes the part
Of Loyalty, who has retained her
As a handmaiden of highest rank.
She does not conceal, but shows clearly
15   She is behaving faithfully
Since it pleases her (for which I thank her)
Very graciously to send me the message:
"It is you by whom I am loved."

I think myself the happiest man
20   Under the clouds when she calls herself my sweet friend,
For in all the places where she is known
Every man calls her the most beautiful.
May God grant that, despite that traitor
Danger, I will see her soon
25   And that with her own lips she will say to me:
"Friend, think this one thought:
'It is you by whom I am loved.'"

Envoy

With joy have I written
In my heart, so I do not forget,
30   This refrain I dearly love:
"It is you by whom I am loved."

Ballade

I see you slumber too long,
My heart, in pain and misery.
Please awaken yourself this day.
Let us go to the woods to gather May flowers
5   And in this way follow the custom.

Nous orrons des oyseaulx le glay
Dont ilz font les bois retentir
Ce premier jour du mois de may.

Le Dieu d'Amours est coustumier,
10   A ce jour, de feste tenir
Pour amoureux cueurs festier,
Qui desirent de le servir.
Pource fait les arbres couvrir
De fleurs et les champs de vert gay
15   Pour la feste plus embellir,
Ce premier jour du mois de may.

Bien sçay, mon cueur, que faulx Dangier
Vous fait mainte paine souffrir,
Car il vous fait trop eslongnier
20   Celle qui est vostre desir.
Pour tant vous fault esbat querir.
Mieux conseillier je ne vous sçay
Pour vostre douleur amendrir
Ce premier jour du mois de may.

                    L'envoy   [p. 72]
25   Ma dame, mon seul souvenir,
En cent jours n'auroye loisir
De vous raconter tout au vray
Le mal qui tient mon cueur martir
Ce premier jour du mois de may.

[48]

B49   **Balade**

J'ay mis en escript mes souhais
Ou plus parfont de mon penser,
Et combien, quant je les ay fais,
Que peu me peuent proufiter,
5   Je ne les vouldroie donner
Pour nul or qu'on me sceust offrir,
En esperant qu'au paraler
De mille l'un puist avenir.

Par la foy de mon corps! jamais
10   Mon cueur ne se peut d'eulx lasser,
Car si richement sont pourtrais
Que souvent les vient regarder

We'll hear the warbling of the birds,
Which makes the woods resound
This first day of the month of May.

The God of Love is accustomed
10   On this day to hold a feast
To make the hearts of lovers rejoice,
Those eager to serve him.
And so he has the trees covered
With flowers, and the fields with cheerful green
15   To much embellish the feast,
This first day of the month of May.

I know well, my heart, that false Danger
Has made you suffer many a pang
Because he's forced you to remain too far
20   From the lady who is your desire.
Even so, you should seek some diversion.
I cannot offer you better advice
To alleviate your pain
This first day of the month of May.

Envoy
25   My lady, my only remembrance,
Even a hundred days would not be time enough
For me to recount truthfully
All the ills that keep my heart suffering
This first day of the month of May.

Ballade

I've put my wishes in writing
In the deepest region of my thought,
And even though, having made them,
They may profit me little,
5   I'd not exchange them
For any gold I might be offered,
Hoping that in the end
From a thousand one might come true.

Upon the faith of my body! Never
10   Might my heart weary of these wishes,
For so richly are they represented
The heart often comes to look upon them,

Et s'i esbat pour temps passer
En disant par ardant desir :
15   «Dieu doint que pour me reconforter
De mille l'un puist avenir.»

C'est merveille quant je me tais
Que j'oy mon cueur ainsi parler,
Et tient avec Amour ses plais,
20   Que tousjours veult acompaignier,
Car il dit que des biens d'amer
Cent mille lui veult departir.
Plus ne quier, mais que sans tarder   [p. 73]
De mille l'un puist avenir.

L'envoy

25   Vueilliez a mon cueur accorder
Sans par parolles le mener,
Amour, que, par vostre plaisir
Des biens que lui voulez donner
De mille l'un puist avenir.

[49]

B50   Balade

Par le commandement d'Amours
Et de la plus belle de France
J'enforcis mon chastel tousjours
Appellé Joyeuse Plaisance,
5   Assis sur roche d'Esperance.
Avitaillié l'ay de Confort.
Contre Dangier et sa puissance
Je le tendray jusqu'a la mort.

En ce chastel y a trois tours,
10   Dont l'une se nomme Fïance
D'avoir briefment loyal secours,
Et la seconde Souvenance,
La tierce Ferme Desirance.
Ainsi le chastel est si fort
15   Que nul n'y peut faire grevance.
Je le tendray jusqu'a la mort.

Combien que Dangier par faulx tours
De le m'oster souvent s'avance,
Mais il trouvera le rebours,   [p. 74]
20   Se Dieu plaist, de sa malvueillance.

Disporting himself there to pass the time
And saying through burning desire:
15   "May God grant that in order to comfort me
From a thousand one might come true."

It's a wonder I'm silent,
Hearing my heart speak this way
And pleading with Love,
20   Whom he wishes always to accompany,
For Love says he intends sharing
Out to it the hundred thousand benefits of love.
I seek no more save that without delay
From a thousand one might come true.

Envoy

25   Please, Love, grant this boon to my heart
(But not fooling it with fair speech)
That, according to your pleasure,
Of the benefits you intend giving him
From a thousand one might come true.

Ballade

By the command of Love
And of France's most beautiful lady,
Every day I strengthen my castle
Called Joyous Pleasure,
5   Seated above the cliff of Hope.
I've provisioned it with Comfort.
Against Danger and his great force
I will hold it to the death.

In this castle are three towers:
10   One is called Trust
To acquire faithful assistance quickly,
And the second Remembrance,
The third Firm Desire.
Thus the castle is so impregnable
15   No man could do it any harm.
I will hold it to the death.

Although with deceptive tricks Danger
Often moves to take the castle from me,
He will instead, should God please,
20   Find the opposite of his evil intention.

Bon Droit est de mon alïance,
Loyauté et lui sont d'accort
De m'aidier. Pource, sans doubtance,
Je le tendray jusqu'a la mort.

L'envoy

25 Faisons bon guet sans decevance
Et assaillons par ordonnance,
Mon cueur, Dangier qui nous fait tort.
Se prandre le puis par vaillance,
Je le tendray jusqu'a la mort.

[50]

B51   Balade

La premiere fois, ma maistresse,
Qu'en vostre presence vendray,
Si ravy seray de lïesse
Qu'a vous parler je ne pouray.
5 Toute contenance perdray,
Car, quant vostre beauté luira
Sur moy, si fort esbloïra
Mes yeulx que je ne verray goutte.
Mon cueur aussi se pasmera,
10 C'est une chose que fort doubte.

Pource, nompareille Princesse,
Quant ainsi devant vous seray,
Vueilliez, par vostre grant humblesse,
Me pardonner se je ne sçay   [p. 75]
15 Parler a vous comme devray,
Mais tost aprés s'asseurera
Mon cueur et puis vous contera
Son fait, mais que nul ne l'escoute.
Dangier grant guet sur lui fera,
20 C'est une chose que fort doubte.

Et se mettra souvent en presse
D'ouïr tout ce que je diray,
Mais je pense que par sagesse
Si tresbien me gouverneray
25 Et telle maniere tendray
Que faulx Dangier trompé sera,
Ne nulle riens n'appercevra.
Si mettra il sa painne toute

Good Justice is my ally.
He and Loyalty have agreed
To assist me. And so, without a doubt,
I will hold it to the death.

Envoy

25 Let us keep good watch, my heart,
Without deception and in an orderly fashion.
Let us assail Danger, who wrongs us.
If in my valor I can bring about this capture,
I will hold it to the death.

Ballade

The first time, my mistress,
I come into your presence,
Bliss shall so ravish me that
I will not be able to speak.
5 I will lose all composure,
For, when your beauty shines upon
Me, my eyes will be so dazzled
That I will see nothing.
My heart will swoon as well,
10 That is something I fear greatly.

And so, Princess unrivaled,
When I come before you,
Please, in your great humility,
Pardon me if I cannot
15 Speak to you properly,
But my heart will be reassured
At once and tell you of its condition,
Provided no one is listening.
Danger will certainly lie in ambush for him,
20 That is something I fear greatly.

Danger will often be eager
To hear all I will say,
But I think I will ably
And wisely conduct myself,
25 Acting in such a manner that
False Danger will be deceived.
He will see nothing
And so put all his energy

D'espïer tout ce qu'il pourra.
30   C'est une chose que fort doubte.

[51]

B52   **Balade**   [p. 76]

Me mocqués vous, Joyeux Espoir?
Par parolles trop me menés,
Pensez vous de me decevoir?
Chascun jour vous me promettés
5   Que briefment veoir me ferés
Ma dame, la gente princesse,
Qui a mon cueur entierement.
Pour Dieu, tenés vostre promesse,
Car trop ennuie qui attent.

10   Il a long temps, pour dire voir,
Que tout mon estat congnoissés.
N'ay je fait mon loyal devoir
D'endurer, comme bien savés?
Ouïl, ce croy je, plus qu'assés.
15   Temps est que me donnez lïesse,
Desservie l'ay loyaument.
Pardonnez moy se je vous presse,
Car trop ennuie qui attent.

Ne me mettez a nonchaloir,
20   Honte sera se me failliés,
Veu que me fie main et soir
En tout ce que faire vouldrés.
Se mieulx faire ne me povés,
Au moins moustrez moy ma maistresse
25   Une fois, pour aucunement
Allegier le mal qui me blesse,
Car trop ennuie qui attent.

L'envoy
Espoir, tousjours vous m'asseurés
Que bien mon fait ordonnerés.
30   Bel me parlés, je le confesse,   [p. 77]
Mais tant y mettés longuement
Que je languis en grant destresse,
Car trop ennuie qui attent.

30   Into taking account of whatever he can.
        That is something I fear greatly.

Ballade

        Joyous Hope, are you mocking me?
        You serve me with too many words.
        Are you bent on deceiving me?
        Every day you promise you'll soon
5   Make it possible for me to see
        My lady, the noble princess
        Who possesses all my heart.
        For God's sake, keep your promise,
        For the one who waits is too distressed.

10   For a long time, to tell the truth,
        You've known everything of my condition.
        Have I not faithfully performed my duty
        To endure? Well you know it!
        Yes, I believe, more than enough.
15   It's time you give me happiness.
        I've earned it with my faithfulness.
        Pardon me if I press you about it,
        For the one who waits is too distressed.

        Don't stop caring about me.
20   I'll be shamed should you abandon me,
        Since I trust day and night
        In all you intend doing for my sake.
        If you can do no better for me,
        At least let me see my mistress
25   One time and thus lessen
        Somewhat the ill that injures me,
        For the one who waits is too distressed.

Envoy
        Hope, you assure me time after time
        You'll put my affairs in good order.
30   You speak prettily to me, this I confess,
        But you take so long
        I languish in great misery,
        For the one who waits is too distressed.

B53   Balade

    Le premier jour du mois de may*
    S'acquitte vers moy grandement,
    Car, ainsi qu'a present je n'ay
    En mon cueur que dueil et tourment,
5   Il est aussi pareillement
    Troublé, plain de vent et de pluie.
    Estre souloit tout autrement
    Ou temps qu'ay congneu en ma vie.

    Je croy qu'il se mect en essay
10   De m'acompaignier loyaument.
    Content m'en tiens, pour dire vray,
    Car meschans en leur pensement
    Reçoivent grant allegement,
    Quant en leurs maulx ont compaignie.
15   Essayé l'ay certainement
    Ou temps qu'ay congneu en ma vie.

    Las! J'ay veu May joyeux et gay
    Et si plaisant a toute gent
    Que raconter au long ne sçay
20   Le plaisir et esbatement
    Qu'avoit en son commandement,
    Car Amour en son abbaÿe
    Le tenoit chief de son couvent
    Ou temps qu'ay congneu en ma vie.

L'envoy   [p. 78]
25   Le temps va je ne sçay comment,
    Dieu l'amende prouchainnement,
    Car Plaisance est endormie,
    Qui souloit vivre lÿement
    Ou temps qu'ay congneu en ma vie.

[53]

B54   Balade*

    Pour Dieu, gardez bien Souvenir
    Enclos dedens vostre pensee,
    Ne le laissiez dehors yssir,
    Belle, tresloyaument amee.
5   Faictes que chascune journee
    Vous ramentoive bien souvent
    La maniere, quoy et comment,

Ballade

The first day of the month of May
Does magnificently by me,
For, just as at present I've
Nothing in my heart save pain and torment,
5   So May is troubled much the same,
Full of wind and rain.
Things used to be very different
In the days I have seen in my life.

I believe May makes the attempt
10   To accompany me in a faithful fashion.
I truly feel content with this.
For the unfortunate discover
Great relief from their thoughts
When they've companions in their troubles.
15   Such indeed has been my experience
In the days I have seen in my life.

Wretched me! I've seen May joyous and gay,
And so pleasant for everyone
I cannot describe all
20   The pleasure and diversion
I experienced under his dominion.
For Love in his abbey
Used to think May the head of the Order
In the days I have seen in my life.

Envoy
25   Time passes, I don't know how.
May God soon remedy this,
For Pleasure sleeps,
Who used to live happily
In the days I have seen in my life.

Ballade

For God's sake, keep Memory well
Enclosed within your thoughts;
Do not let it emerge,
Belle, loved so faithfully.
5   Make sure that every day
You frequently recall
The how, the why, and the wherefore

Ja pieça, me feistes promesse,
Quant vous retins premierement
10   Ma dame, ma seule maistresse.

Vous savez que par Franc Desir
Et Loyal Amour conseillee
Me deistes que, sans departir,
De m'amer estiés fermee
15   Tant comme j'auroye duree.
Je metz en vostre jugement
Se ma bouche dit vray ou ment.
Si tiens que parler de princesse
Vient du cueur sans decevement,
20   Ma dame, ma seule maistresse.

Non pour tant me fault vous ouvrir
La doubte qu'en moy est entree,
C'est que j'ay paeur, sans vous mentir,   [p. 79]
Que ne m'ayez, tresbelle nee,
25   Mis en oubly, car mainte annee
Suis loingtain de vous longuement
Et n'oy de vous aucunement
Nouvelle pour avoir lïesse.
Pourquoy vis doloreusement,
30   Ma dame, ma seule maistresse.

Nul remede ne sçay querir
Dont ma doleur soit alegee,
Fors que souvent vous requerir
Que la foy que m'avez donnee
35   Soit par vous loyaument gardee,
Car vous congnoissiez clerement
Que par vostre commandement
Ay despendu de ma jeunesse
Pour vous attendre seulement,
40   Ma dame, ma seule maistresse.

Plus ne vous couvient esclarsir
La chose que vous ay comptee.
Vous la congnoissiez sans faillir.
Pource soyez bien advisee
45   Que je ne vous treuve muee,
Car, s'en vous treuve changement,
Je requerray tout haultement
Devant l'amoureuse Deesse
Que j'aye de vous vengement,
50   Ma dame, ma seule maistresse.

Of the promise you made me some time ago,
When I first took you as
10   My lady, my only mistress.

With Liberal Desire and Faithful Love
As your counselors, you know
You told me that, never altering,
You were determined to love me
15   As long as I live.
I leave it for you to judge
If my mouth utters truth or lies.
And I trust that the words of a princess
Issue from her heart with no deception,
20   My lady, my only mistress.

Not for nothing do I confess
The doubt that has entered me.
I fear (and this is no lie) that somehow
You, born so beautiful, have
25   Forgotten about me, because for many
A long year I've been distant from you,
And hearing no news from you
At all to bring me happiness.
So I live on in pain,
30   My lady, my only mistress.

No remedy can I seek
To relieve my pain,
Save that I often request
The pledge given me
35   You'll faithfully keep,
Clearly recognizing
That, as you commanded,
I've spent my youth
Waiting for you alone,
40   My lady, my only mistress.

No need is there for me to explain
Further the matter I have related to you.
Doubtless you know about it.
And so, be well advised
45   That I do not find you altered,
For, should I discover some change in you,
I will request very solemnly
Before the Goddess of Love
That I might revenge myself on you,
50   My lady, my only mistress.

L'envoy

Se je puis veoir seurement
Que m'amés tousjours loyaument, [p. 80]
Content suis de passer destresse
En vous servant joyeusement,
55   Ma dame, ma seule maistresse.

[54]

B55   **Balade**

Helas! Helas! Qui a laissié entrer
Devers mon cueur Doloreuse Nouvelle?
Conté lui a plainement, sans celer,
Que sa dame, la tresplaisant et belle,
5   Qu'il a long temps tresloyaument servie,
Est a present en griefve maladie,
Dont il est cheu en desespoir si fort
Qu'il souhaide piteusement la mort
Et dit qu'il est ennuyé de sa vie.

10   Je suis alé pour le reconforter
En lui priant qu'il n'ait nul soussy d'elle,
Car, se Dieu plaist, il orra brief conter
Que ce n'est pas maladie mortelle
Et que sera prochainement guerye,
15   Mais ne lui chault de chose que lui dye,
Ainçois en pleurs a tousjours son ressort
Par Tristesse, qui asprement le mort,
Et dit qu'il est ennuyé de sa vie.

Quant je lui dy qu'il ne se doit doubter,
20   Car Fortune n'est pas si trescruelle
Qu'elle voulsist hors de ce monde oster
Celle qui est des princesses l'estoille,
Qui par tout luist des biens dont est garnie,
Il me respond qu'il est foul qui se fie [p. 81]
25   En Fortune qui a fait a maint tort.
Ainsi ne voult recevoir reconfort
Et dit qu'il est ennuyé de sa vie.

L'envoy

Dieu tout puissant, par vostre courtoisie
Guerissez la, ou mon cueur vous supplie
30   Que vous souffrez que la mort son effort
Face sur lui, car il en est d'accort
Et dit qu'il est ennuyé de sa vie.

[55]

Envoy

If I can see for certain
That you still love me,
I will be content to pass through distress
While serving you joyfully,
55   My lady, my only mistress.

Ballade

Alas! Alas! Who has allowed
Painful News to enter my heart?
It plainly told my heart, holding back nothing,
That his lady, very pleasant and beautiful,
5   Very faithfully served a long time by him,
Is now suffering a grievous ill,
And for this reason he fell into such deep
Despair that he pitifully hopes for death
And says he has wearied of his life.

10   I came to comfort the heart,
Begging him to pay that one no attention,
For, please God, he will soon hear it said
This is no fatal illness
And she will quickly be cured,
15   But he pays no attention to anything I say,
Always takes refuge instead in tears
Because of Sadness, which bitterly gnaws at him,
And says he has wearied of his life.

When I say he should not be afraid,
20   For Fortune is not so very cruel
That she would take from this world
The lady who is the star of princesses,
Who shines everywhere because of the virtues that are hers,
He answers me that the man's a fool to trust
25   In Fortune, who has done many wrong.
And so he expects to find no comfort,
And says he has wearied of his life.

Envoy

Almighty God, heal her
In your graciousness; if not, my heart begs
30   You to let death seize
Him, for he agrees to this,
And says he has wearied of his life.

B56   **Balade**

Sitost que l'autre jour j'ouÿ
Que ma souveraine sans per
Estoit guerie, Dieu mercy,
Je m'en alay sans point tarder
5   Vers mon cueur pour le lui conter,
Mais, certes, tant le desiroit
Qu'a paine croire le povoit
Pour la grant amour qu'a en elle,
Et souvent a par soy disoit :
10   «Saint Gabriel, bonne nouvelle!»

Je lui dis : «Mon cueur, je vous pry,
Ne vueilliez croire ne penser
Que moy, qui vous suy vray amy,
Vous vueille mensonges trouver
15   Pour en vain vous reconforter,
Car trop mieulx taire me vaudroit
Que le dire, se vray n'estoit,   [p. 82]
Mais la verité si est telle :
Soyez joyeulx, comment qu'il soit.
20   Saint Gabriel, bonne nouvelle!»

Alors mon cueur me respondy :
«Croire vous vueil sans plus doubter,
Et tout le courrous et soussy
Qu'il m'a convenu endurer,
25   En joye le vueil retourner.»
Puis aprés, ses yeulx essuyoit
Que de plourer moilliez avoit,
Disant : «Il est temps que rappelle
Espoir, qui delaissié m'avoit :
30   Saint Gabriel, bonne nouvelle!»

         L'envoy
Il me dist aussi qu'il feroit
Dedens l'amoureuse chappelle
Chanter la messe qu'il nommoit
«Saint Gabriel, bonne nouvelle!»

[56]

Ballade

The other day, as soon as I heard
That my sovereign lady unrivaled
Had been healed, God be thanked,
I went forth without delay
5   To my heart to tell him about it,
Yet, so eager for this,
The heart could hardly believe
Because of the great love he feels for her,
And often said under his breath:
10   "Saint Gabriel, good news!"

I said to him: "My heart, I beg you,
Please do not think or believe
That I, who am your true friend,
Intend to concoct some lie
15   So as to offer you vain comfort,
For it would be better for me to keep silent
Than to say something that was not true,
But such indeed is the truth:
Be joyful, whatever it might be.
20   Saint Gabriel, good news!"

Then my heart answered me:
"I am eager to believe you with no further doubt,
And all the anxiety and care
I have been forced to endure,
25   I will transform into joy."
After this, he wiped his eyes,
Which were moist with tears,
Saying: "It is time I summon back
Hope, who had abandoned me:
30   Saint Gabriel, good news!"

Envoy

He told me that he would ask
To be sung in the Chapel
Of Love the mass he named
"Saint Gabriel, good news!"

B57   Balade

Las, Mort! qui t'a fait si hardie
De prendre la noble princesse
Qui estoit mon confort, ma vie,
Mon bien, mon plaisir, ma richesse!
5   Puis que tu as prins ma maistresse,
Prens moy aussi, son serviteur,
Car j'ayme mieulx prouchainnement   [p. 83]
Mourir que languir en tourment,
En paine, soussi et doleur!

10   Las! de tous biens estoit garnie
Et en droitte fleur de jeunesse.
Je pry a Dieu qu'il te maudie,
Faulse Mort, plaine de rudesse.
Se prise l'eusses en vieillesse,
15   Ce ne fust pas si grant rigueur,
Mais prise l'as hastivement,
Et m'as laissié piteusement
En paine, soussi et doleur.

Las! Je suy seul, sans compaignie.
20   Adieu ma dame, ma lÿesse!
Or est nostre amour departie.
Non pour tant, je vous fais promesse
Que de prieres a largesse,
Morte, vous serviray de cueur
25   Sans oublier aucunement,
Et vous regretteray souvent
En paine, soussi et doleur.

L'envoy
Dieu, sur tout souverain Seigneur,
Ordonnez par grace et doulceur
30   De l'ame d'elle, tellement
Qu'elle ne soit pas longuement
En paine, soussy et doleur.

[57]

B58   Balade   [p. 84]

J'ay aux eschés joué devant Amours
Pour passer temps, avecques faulx Dangier,
Et seurement me suy gardé tousjours,
Sans riens perdre jusques au derrenier

Ballade

Wretched Death! Who has made you bold enough
To take away the noble princess
Who was my comfort, my life,
My good, my pleasure, my riches!
5   Since you took my mistress,
Take me, her servant, as well,
For I prefer to die
At once than to languish in torment,
In pain, anxiety, and suffering!

10   Wretched! She was replete with all virtues
And in the proper flower of youth.
I pray God curse you,
Traitorous Death, full of cruelty.
Had you taken her in old age,
15   It should not have been so terribly harsh,
But you took her before her time,
And abandoned pitiful me
In pain, anxiety, and suffering!

Wretched! I am alone, no companions.
20   Good-bye, my lady, my happiness!
Now our love has been taken from us.
Yet even so, I promise you
That with generous prayers
I will serve you, dead, from the heart
25   And never forget you in the least,
And often I will mourn you
In pain, anxiety, and suffering!

Envoy

God, Sovereign Lord over all things,
Provide in your grace and kindness
30   For her soul, in such fashion
That she will not remain long
In pain, anxiety, and suffering!

Ballade

In the presence of Love, I played at chess
With false Danger to pass the time,
And I always kept myself safe
Without losing a piece until the very last

5   Que Fortune lui est venu aidier,
       Et par meschief, que maudite soit elle!
       A ma dame prise soudainnement.
       Par quoy suy mat, je le voy clerement,
       Se je ne fais une dame nouvelle.

10   En ma dame j'avoye mon secours
       Plus qu'en autre, car souvent d'encombrier
       Me delivroit, quant venoit a son cours,
       Et en gardes faisoit mon jeu lier.
       Je n'avoye pïon ne chevalier,
15   Auffin ne rocq qui peussent ma querelle
       Si bien aidier. Je y pert vrayement,
       Car j'ay perdu mon jeu entierement
       Se je ne fais une dame nouvelle.

       Je ne me sçay jamais garder des tours
20   De Fortune, qui maintesfoiz changier
       A fait mon jeu et tourner a rebours.
       Mon dommage scet bien tost espïer,
       Elle m'assault sans point me deffïer.
       Par mon serement, oncques ne congneu telle.
25   En jeu party suy si estrangement
       Que je me rens et n'y voy sauvement,
       Se je ne fais une dame nouvelle.

[58]

B59   **Balade**   [p. 85]

       Je me souloye pourpenser
       Au commencement de l'annee
       Quel don je pourroye donner
       A ma dame la bien amee.
5   Or suis hors de ceste pensee,
       Car Mort l'a mise soubz la lame,
       Et l'a hors de ce monde ostee.
       Je pry a Dieu qu'il en ait l'ame.

       Non pourtant, pour tousjours garder
10   La coustume que j'ay usee,
       Et pour a toutes gens moustrer
       Que pas n'ay ma dame oubliee,
       De messes je l'ay estrenee,
       Car ce me seroit trop de blasme
15   De l'oublier ceste journee.
       Je pry a Dieu qu'il en ait l'ame.

5   As Fortune came to his aid,
       And, what mischance (may she be cursed!),
       Suddenly took off my queen.
       And by this I am mated—I see this clearly—
       If I don't make a new queen.

10   In my lady I found consolation
       More than in any other, for often she delivered me
       From a tight spot when her turn did come,
       And, protecting me, she firmly kept me in the game.
       No pawn or knight did I have,
15   No bishop or rook who could quite so ably assist
       My cause. Truly I am losing,
       But I have lost my game utterly
       If I don't make a new queen.

       I can never protect myself from the maneuvers
20   Of Fortune, which many times has altered
       The course of my game, reversed my luck.
       Very quickly can she spot my disadvantage;
       She attacks me without any warning.
       I swear it—never have I known her like.
25   In my game I am put in such a desperate fix
       That I surrender and see no means of salvation,
       If I don't make a new queen.

Ballade

       It was my custom to consider,
       At the beginning of the year,
       What gift I could give
       My lady so well loved.
5   Now this thought has fled from me,
       For Death has laid her under the slab,
       And has taken her from this world.
       I pray God to keep her soul.

       Yet nonetheless, to observe faithfully
10   The custom I have followed,
       And in order to show everyone
       That I have not forgotten my lady,
       I have bestowed masses upon her for a New Year's gift,
       For I should go too far wrong
15   To forget this day.
       I pray God to keep her soul.

　　　　Tellement lui puist prouffiter
　　　　Ma priere que confortee
　　　　Soit son ame, sans point tarder,
20　　　Et de ses bienfais guerdonnee
　　　　En Paradis, et couronnee
　　　　Comme la plus loyalle dame
　　　　Qu'en son vivant j'aye trouvee.
　　　　Je pry a Dieu qu'il en ait l'ame.

　　　　　　　　　　L'envoy
25　　　Quant je pense a la renommee
　　　　Des grans biens dont estoit paree,
　　　　Mon povre cueur de dueil se pasme.
　　　　De lui souvent est regrettee.
　　　　Je pry a Dieu qu'il en ait l'ame.

[59]

B60　　　　　　　　**Balade**　　　　　　　　　　[p. 86]

　　　　Quant Souvenir me ramentoit
　　　　La grant beauté dont estoit plaine,
　　　　Celle que mon cueur appelloit
　　　　Sa seule dame souveraine,
5　　　　De tous biens la vraye fontaine,
　　　　Qui est morte nouvellement,
　　　　Je dy, en pleurant tendrement :
　　　　«Ce monde n'est que chose vaine!»

　　　　Ou vieil temps grant renom couroit
10　　　De Creseïde, Yseud, Elaine
　　　　Et maintes autres qu'on nommoit
　　　　Parfaittes en beauté haultaine,
　　　　Mais au derrain en son demaine
　　　　La Mort les prist piteusement.
15　　　Par quoy puis veoir clerement
　　　　Ce monde n'est que chose vaine.

　　　　La Mort a voulu et vouldroit,
　　　　Bien le congnois, mettre sa paine
　　　　De destruire, s'elle povoit,
20　　　Lïesse et Plaisance Mondaine,
　　　　Quant tant de belles dames maine
　　　　Hors du monde, car vrayement
　　　　Sans elles, a mon jugement,
　　　　Ce monde n'est que chose vaine.

May my prayer accomplish
Such good that her soul
Be comforted without delay,
20   And also rewarded in Paradise
For her good deeds, crowned, too,
As the most faithful lady
In her life whom I have found.
I pray God to keep her soul.

Envoy

25   When I think about the fame
Of the great virtues with which she is replete,
My poor heart swoons from grief.
Often it laments her.
I pray God to keep her soul.

Ballade

When Memory recalls for me
The great beauty with which she overflowed,
The lady my heart calls
Its one and sovereign lady,
5   The true fountain of every good thing,
Who has just died,
I say this, as I tenderly weep,
"This world is but vanity!"

In times past spread the great renown
10   Of Criseyde, Iseut, Helen,
And many others who were said to be
Perfect in their exalted beauty.
But in the end Death took them off
To his realm, and this is pitiful,
15   And makes me clearly see:
This world is but vanity.

Death would have and would
(Well I know it) take pains
To destroy, could she have compassed it,
20   Happiness and Worldly Pleasure
Since she conducts so many beauties
Out of this world; for truly
Without them, in my view,
This world is but vanity.

L'envoy

25 Amours, pour verité certaine,
    Mort vous guerrie fellement.
    Se n'y trouvez amendement,
    Ce monde n'est que chose vaine.

[60]

B61   Balade   [p. 87]

    Le premier jour du mois de may*
    Trouvé me suis en compaignie
    Qui estoit, pour dire le vray,
    De gracïeuseté garnie,
5   Et pour oster merencolie
    Fut ordonné qu'on choisiroit,
    Comme Fortune donneroit,
    La fueille plaine de verdure,
    Ou la fleur pour toute l'annee.
10 Si prins la fueille pour livree
    Comme lors fut mon aventure.

    Tantost aprés je m'avisay
    Qu'a bon droit je l'avoye choisie,
    Car, puis que par Mort perdu ay
15 La fleur de tous biens enrichie
    Qui estoit ma dame, m'amie,
    Et qui de sa grace m'amoit
    Et pour son amy me tenoit,
    Mon cueur d'autre flour n'a plus cure.
20 Adonc congneu que ma pensee
    Acordoit a ma destinee,
    Comme lors fut mon aventure.

    Pource la fueille porteray
    Cest an, sans que point je l'oublie,
25 Et a mon povair me tendray
    Entierement de sa partie.
    Je n'ay de nulle flour envie
    (Porte la qui porter la doit),
    Car la fleur que mon cueur amoit
30 Plus que nulle autre creature
    Est hors de ce monde passee,   [p. 88]
    Qui son amour m'avoit donnee,
    Comme lors fut mon aventure.

Envoy

25   Love, and this is certain truth,
Death makes cruel war upon you.
If you find no way to better that,
This world is but vanity.

Ballade

The first day of the month of May
I found myself in a company
Which was, to speak the truth,
Blessed with graciousness,
5   And to do away with melancholy
It had been so arranged to choose,
In accord with Fortune's wishes,
The leaf full of green
Or the flower for that whole year,
10   And so for my livery I took the leaf,
As the chance befell me.

Immediately after, I concluded
I'd made a most fitting choice,
For, since through Death I'd lost
15   The flower, enriched by every virtue,
Who'd been my lady, my sweet friend,
And had in her mercy loved me,
Retaining me as her lover,
My heart felt no desire for any other flower.
20   So I realized my thought
Was in accord with my destiny,
As the chance befell me.

I will then wear the leaf
This year, never neglecting it
25   And, as I can, keeping myself
One of its party in every way.
I've no wish for any flower
(Let him wear it who must),
For the flower my heart, loved
30   More than any other creature,
Has passed away from this world,
She who made me a present of her love,
As the chance befell me.

L'envoy

Il n'est fueille ne fleur qui dure
35   Que pour un temps, car esprouvee
J'ay la chose que j'ay contee,
Comme lors fut mon adventure.

[61]

B62   **Balade**

Le lendemain du premier jour de may*
Dedens mon lit ainsi que je dormoye,
Au point du jour m'avint que je songay
Que devant moy une fleur je veoye,
5   Qui me disoit : «Amy, je me souloye
En toy fier, car pieça mon party
Tu tenoies, mais mis l'as en oubly
En soustenant la fueille contre moy.
J'ay merveille que tu veulx faire ainsi,
10   Riens n'ay meffait, se pense je, vers toy.»

Tout esbahy alors je me trouvay,
Si respondy au mieulx que je savoye :
«Tresbelle fleur, oncques je ne pensay
Faire chose qui desplaire te doye.
15   Se pour esbat Aventure m'envoye
Que je serve la fueille cest an cy,
Doy je pour tant estre de toy banny?
Nennil certes, je fais comme je doy,
Et se je tiens le party qu'ay choisy,   [p. 89]
20   Riens n'ay meffait, ce pense je, vers toy.

Car non pour tant honneur te porteray
De bon vouloir quelque part que je soye,
Tout pour l'amour d'une fleur que j'amay
Ou temps passé. Dieu doint que je la voye
25   En Paradis aprés ma mort en joye.
Et pource, fleur, chierement je te pry,
Ne te plains plus, car cause n'as pourquoy,
Puis que je fais ainsi que tenu suy.
Riens n'ay meffait, ce pense je, vers toy.

L'envoy

30   La verité est telle que je dy,
J'en fais juge Amour, le puissant roy.
Tresdoulce fleur, point ne te cry mercy.
Riens n'ay meffait, se pense je, vers toy.»

[62]

Envoy

There is no leaf or flower that endures
35   More than one season, for what I've related
Has been my experience
As the chance befell me.

Ballade

The day after May's first day,
In my bed, just as I was sleeping,
As day broke I happened to dream
I saw before me a flower
5   Who said: "Friend, I was accustomed
To have faith in you, for some time ago you
Held to my party, yet you've forgotten this
In supporting the leaf against me.
I marvel that this is your intention,
10   I have done nothing, so I think, against you."

I then found myself completely bewildered
And answered as best I could:
"Most beautiful flower, never did I think
To do anything to displease you.
15   If, in game, Chance charges me
With serving the flower this year,
Should I for this reason be banished by you?
Surely, not in the least. I do as I should,
And if I keep to the party I've chosen,
20   I have done nothing, so I think, against you.

"Nevertheless I'll honor you
With a good will wherever I might be,
All out of love for a flower I loved
In days gone by. God grant I see her
25   In the joy of Paradise after my death.
And this is why, flower, I beg you with affection
Do not complain further, for you've no justification
Since I'm doing just what I'm bound to do.
I have done nothing, so I think, against you.

Envoy

30   "The truth is as I say
(I make Love, the powerful king, judge in this).
I do not beg your mercy, flower so sweet.
I have done nothing, so I think, against you."

B63   **Balade**

En la Forest d'Ennuyeuse Tristesse,
Un jour m'avint qu'a par moy cheminoye,
Si rencontray l'Amoureuse Deesse,
Qui m'appella, demandant ou j'aloye.
5   Je respondy que par Fortune estoye
Mis en exil en ce bois, long temps a,
Et qu'a bon droit appeller me povoye
L'omme esgaré qui ne scet ou il va.

En sousriant par sa tresgrant humblesse
10   Me respondy : «Amy, se je savoye   [p. 90]
Pourquoy tu es mis en ceste destresse,
A mon povair voulentiers t'ayderoye,
Car ja pieça je mis ton cueur en voye
De tout plaisir, ne sçay qui l'en osta.
15   Or me desplaist qu'a present je te voye
L'omme esgaré qui ne scet ou il va.»

«Helas!» dis je,«souverainne princesse,
Mon fait savés, pourquoy le vous diroye?
C'est par la mort qui fait a tous rudesse,
20   Qui m'a tollu celle que tant amoye,
En qui estoit tout l'espoir que j'avoye,
Qui me guidoit, si bien m'acompaigna
En son vivant que point ne me trouvoye
L'omme esgaré qui ne scet ou il va.

             L'envoy
25   Aveugle suy, ne sçay ou aler doye.
De mon baston, affin que ne forvoye,
Je vois tastant mon chemin ça et la.
C'est grant pitié qu'il couvient que je soye
L'omme esgaré qui ne scet ou il va.»

[63]

B64   **Balade**   [p. 91]

J'ay esté de la compaignie
Des amoureux moult longuement,
Et m'a Amour, dont le mercie,
Donné de ses biens largement,
5   Mais au derrain, ne sçay comment,
Mon fait est venu au contraire,
Et, a parler ouvertement,
Tout est rompu, c'est a refaire.

Ballade

In the forest of Painful Sadness,
It happened one day I made my way alone,
And so encountered the Goddess of Love,
Who hailed me, asking where I was going.
5   I answered that because of Fortune I had
Long ago been exiled to this wood
And could justly call myself
The bewildered man who knows not where he goes.

Smiling with very great humility,
10   She answered: "Friend, if I knew
Why you're put in this distress,
As I am able, I would gladly help you,
For some time ago I launched your heart on the path
Of every pleasure; I know not who diverted you.
15   It displeases me then to see you now,
The bewildered man who knows not where he goes."

"Alas!" said I, "sovereign princess,
You know my circumstances, why should I tell you?
At fault is death, which is harsh to all,
20   Taking from me the lady I loved so much,
In whom resided all the hope I had,
Who guided me, accompanied me so well
While she lived that I never at all found myself
The bewildered man who knows not where he goes.

Envoy
25   "I'm blind, know not where I ought go.
With my staff, to avoid going wrong,
I walk along tapping on my path here and there.
It's a great pity that I must be
The bewildered man who knows not where he goes."

Ballade

I've been one of the company
Of lovers for a very long time,
And Love, and I thank him, has
Bestowed his goods generously upon me.
5   But in the end, I know not how,
My affair has gone wrong,
And, to speak openly,
All was broken off and must be done again.

       Certes, je ne cuidoye mye
10   Qu'en amer eust tel changement,
       Car chascun dit que c'est la vie
       Ou il a plus d'esbatement.
       Helas! j'ay trouvé autrement,
       Car, quant en l'amoureux repaire
15   Cuidoye vivre seurement,
       Tout est rompu, c'est a reffaire.

       Au fort, en Amour je m'affye
       Qui m'aidera aucunement
       Pour l'amour de sa seigneurie
20   Que j'ay servie loyaument.
       N'oncques ne fis par mon serement
       Chose qui lui doye desplaire,
       Et non pourtant estrangement
       Tout est rompu, c'est a refaire.

                        L'envoy
25   Amour, ordonnez tellement
       Que j'aye cause de me taire
       Sans plus dire de cueur dolent :
       Tout est rompu, c'est a reffaire.

[64]

B65   **Balade**   [p. 92]

       Plaisant Beauté mon cueur nasvra
       Ja pieça si tresdurement
       Qu'en la fievre d'Amours entra
       Qui l'a tenu moult asprement,
5   Mais de nouvel presentement
       Un bon medecin qu'on appelle
       Nonchaloir, que tiens pour amy
       M'a guery, la sienne mercy,
       Se la playe ne renouvelle.

10   Quant mon cueur tout sain se trouva,
       Il l'en mercia grandement
       Et humblement lui demanda
       S'en santé seroit longuement.
       Il respondy tressagement :
15   «Mais que gardes bien ta fourcelle
       Du vent d'Amours qui te fery,
       Tu es en bon point jusqu'a cy,
       Se la playe ne renouvelle.

To be sure, I didn't believe at all
10   That Love might allow such a change,
For everyone says this is the life
In which more enjoyment is to be found.
Alas! My experience is the opposite,
For, while in the lovers' refuge,
15   I thought I was living in security,
All was broken off and must be done again.

In the end, I trust in Love,
Who will give me some help
Out of love for his dominion,
20   Which I've served loyally.
On my oath, I never did
Anything to displease him,
And yet surprisingly, even so,
All was broken off and must be done again.

Envoy
25   Love, bring it about
That I have reason to hold my tongue,
Saying nothing more, my heart painful:
All was broken off and must be done again.

Ballade

Pleasant Beauty struck my heart
So very grievously some time ago
That he caught the Love fever,
Which has affected him very harshly,
5   But just a short time ago
A good physician named
Indifference, whom I consider a friend,
Has healed him, my thanks to him,
If the wound does not reopen.

10   Finding himself completely healed,
The heart heartily thanked him
And asked humbly
If he would stay healthy for long.
Very wisely he answered:
15   "Save that you must protect your chest well
From Love's wind, which strikes you,
You're in good condition now,
If the wound does not reopen.

L'embusche de Plaisir entra
20   Parmy tes yeulx soutivement.
      Jennesse ce mal pourchassa,
      Qui t'avoit en gouvernement,
      Et puis bouta priveement
      Dedens ton logis l'estincelle
25   D'Ardant Desir qui tout ardy.
      Lors fus nasvré, or t'ay guery,
      Se la playe ne renouvelle.»

B66   **Balade**   [p. 93]

      Le beau souleil, le jour saint Valentin,
      Qui apportoit sa chandelle alumee
      N'a pas long temps, entra un bien matin
      Priveement en ma chambre fermee.
5   Celle clarté qu'il avoit apportee
      Si m'esveilla du somme de Soussy
      Ou j'avoye toute la nuit dormy
      Sur le dur lit d'Ennuieuse Pensee.

      Ce jour aussi, pour partir leur butin
10   Des biens d'Amours, faisoient assemblee
      Tous les oyseaulx, qui, parlans leur latin,
      Crioyent fort, demandans la livree
      Que Nature leur avoit ordonnee :
      C'estoit d'un per comme chascun choisy,
15   Si ne me peu rendormir pour leur cry
      Sur le dur lit d'Ennuieuse Pensee.

      Lors en moillant de larmes mon coessin
      Je regrettay ma dure destinee,
      Disant : «Oyseaulx, je vous voy en chemin
20   De tout plaisir et joye desiree.
      Chascun de vous a per qui lui agree,
      Et point n'en ay, car Mort, qui m'a trahy,
      A prins mon per, dont en dueil je languy
      Sur le dur lit d'Ennuieuse Pensee.»

                          L'envoy
25   Saint Valentin choisissent ceste annee
      Ceulx et celles de l'amoureux party.
      Seul me tendray, de Confort desgarny
      Sur le dur lit d'Ennuieuse Pensee.

[66]

"Pleasure's troop, lying in ambush,
20   Will enter your eyes stealthily.
This is the misery pursued by Youth,
Who had dominion over you,
And then Pleasure slyly tossed
Inside your dwelling the spark
25   Of Ardent Desire, which burns everything.
Then you felt yourself hurt, but now I've healed you,
If the wound does not reopen."

Ballade

On St. Valentine's day, the beautiful sun,
Carrying its lighted candle,
Not long ago made its way on a fine morning
Secretly into my locked room.
5   The brightness it brought
Woke me from the sleep of Care,
In which I'd drowsed all night long
On the hard bed of Painful Thought.

This day also, in order to share their booty
10   Of the goods of Love, all the birds
Assembled, who, speaking in their language,
Cried out loud, asking for the provision
Nature had ordained:
Which was a companion, just as each did choose.
15   Their noise did not let me fall back asleep
On the hard bed of Painful Thought.

Then, wetting my pillow with tears,
I bemoaned my bitter destiny,
Saying: "Birds, I see you on the path
20   Of all things pleasurable, expectant with joy.
Each of you has a fitting companion,
And I have none, for Death, who's betrayed me,
Has taken my companion, so I languish in pain
On the hard bed of Painful Thought."

Envoy
25   Let the men and women of Love's party
Choose their St. Valentine this year!
I remain alone, comfort stolen from me
On the hard bed of Painful Thought.

B67   **Balade**   [p. 94]

  Mon cueur dormant en Nonchaloir,
  Reveilliez vous joyeusement,
  Je vous fais nouvelles savoir
  Qui vous doit plaire grandement.
5 Il est vray que presentement
  Une dame treshonnoree
  En toute bonne renommee
  Desire de vous acheter,
  Dont je suy joyeux et d'accort.
10 Pour vous son cueur me veult donner
  Sans departir, jusqu'a la mort.

  Ce change doy je recevoir
  En grant gré tresjoyeusement.
  Or vous charge d'entier povair
15 Si chier et tant estroittement
  Que je puis, plus que loyaument
  Soit par vous cherie et amee,
  Et en tous lieux, nuit et journee,
  L'acompaignez sans la laissier
20 Tant que j'en aye bon rapport.
  Il vous couvient sien demourer
  Sans departir, jusqu'a la mort.

  Alez vous logier ou manoir
  De son tresgracïeux corps gent
25 Pour y demourer main et soir
  Et l'onnourer entierement,
  Car par son bon commandement
  Lieutenant vous veult ordonner
  De son cueur en joyeux deport.
30 Pensés de bien vous gouverner
  Sans departir, jusqu'a la mort.   [p. 95]

       [Blank]

[67]

B68   **Balade**

  Belle, se ne m'osez donner
  De voz doulx baisiers amoureux,
  Pour paour de Dangier courroucer,
  Qui tousjours est fel et crueux,
5 J'en embleray bien un ou deux,

Ballade

My heart asleep in Indifference,
Now wake up and rejoice!
I bring news you should know about
That should afford you much pleasure.
5   Truly at this moment
A lady of high honor,
Renowned for great virtue,
Wishes to conclude a bargain with you
I find agreeable and a cause for joy.
10   She'll give me her heart in exchange for you
Until death, never deserting.

This exchange — I should accept it
Willingly and very happily.
Now with all my strength I charge you,
15   With all the vigor and affection
I can muster, to faithfully
Cherish and love her.
And everywhere, night and day,
Be her companion never to depart,
20   Until I hear it well spoken of.
You must remain hers
Until death, never deserting.

Go take up residence in the manor house
Of her body, so noble and very gracious,
25   Remaining there morning and night
Doing everything to her honor,
For, by her commandment,
She'll have you commissioned officer
Of her heart with a joyous celebration.
30   Make sure you comport yourself well
Until death, never deserting.

Ballade

Belle, if you dare not give me
Any of your sweet and loving kisses
For fear of angering Danger,
Who is always cruel and mean-spirited,
5   I'll make off with one or two,

Mais que n'y prenez desplaisir
Et que le vueilliez consentir
Maugré Dangier et ses conseulx.

De ce faulx vilain aveugler,
10   Dieu scet se j'en suy desireux.
Nul ne le peut aprivoiser,
Tous temps est si soupeçonneux
Qu'en penser languist doloreux
Quant il voit Plaisance venir,
15   Mais elle se scet bien chevir
Maugré Dangier et ses conseulx.

Quant estroit la cuide garder,
Hardy Cueur, secret et eureux,
S'avecques lui scet amener
20   Avis Bon et Aventureux
Desguisé soubz Maintien Honteux,   [p. 96]
Bien peuent Dangier endormir.
Lors Plaisance fait son desir
Maugré Dangier et ses conseulx.

L'envoy
25   Bien dessert guerdon plantureux
Advis, qui scet si bien servir
Au besoing et trouver loisir
Maugré Dangier et ses conseulx.

[6]

B69   **Balade**

J'ay fait l'obseque de ma dame
Dedens le moustier amoureux,
Et le service pour son ame
A chanté Penser Doloreux.
5   Mains sierges de Soupirs Piteux
Ont esté en son luminaire.
Aussi j'ay fait la tombe faire
De Regrez, tous de lermes pains,
Et tout entour moult richement
10   Est escript : Cy gist vrayement
Le tresor de tous biens mondains.

Dessus elle gist une lame
Faicte d'or et de saffirs bleux,
Car saffir est nommé la jame

But only if you're not displeased
And give your consent
Despite Danger and his counsels.

     To blind this false villain
10   Is what I'm eager to do, God knows.
No man can tame him.
He's always so suspicious
That he languishes, pained by thought,
Whenever he spies Pleasure approach,
15   But she knows how to do well
Despite Danger and his counsels.

     The intrepid heart thinks to guard her,
Closely and discreetly, with a bit of luck.
If he knows enough to bring along
20   Advice Able and Adventurous,
Disguised by Timid Manner,
These two could put Danger to sleep.
Then Pleasure will do what she wants
Despite Danger and his counsels.

Envoy

25   Advice very much deserves a bountiful reward,
Knowing well how to be useful
In times of need and how to find the moment,
Despite Danger and his counsels.

Ballade

     I have held the funeral service for my lady
In the lovers' church,
And the mass for her soul
Has been sung by saddened Thought.
5   Many candles of tears shed in pity
Are mounted in her candelabra.
And I have also had her tomb, fashioned
From Regret, painted all over with tears,
And around it, very richly inscribed,
10   Were these words: "Here, in truth, lies
The treasure of every earthly good."

     Atop her has been placed a tomb
Made of gold and blue sapphires,
For sapphire is called the gem

15   De Loyauté, et l'or eureux.
        Bien lui appartiennent ces deux,
        Car Eur et Loyauté pourtraire
        Voulu, en la tresdebonnaire,   [p. 97]
        Dieu qui la fist de ses deux mains
20   Et fourma merveilleusement.
        C'estoit, a parler plainnement,
        Le tresor de tous biens mondains.

        N'en parlons plus : mon cueur se pasme
        Quant il oyt les fais vertueux
25   D'elle qui estoit sans nul blasme,
        Comme jurent celles et ceulx
        Qui congnoissoyent ses conseulx.
        Si croy que Dieu la voulu traire
        Vers lui pour parer son repaire
30   De paradis ou sont les saints,
        Car c'est d'elle bel parement
        Que l'en nommoit communement
        Le tresor de tous biens mondains.

L'envoy
        De riens ne servent plours ne plains.
35   Tous mourrons ou tart ou briefment.
        Nul ne peut garder longuement
        Le tresor de tous biens mondains.

[69]

B70   Balade

        Puis que Mort a prins ma maistresse,
        Que sur toutes amer souloye,
        Mourir me convient en tristesse.
        Certes, plus vivre ne pourroye.
5   Pource, par deffautte de joye,   [p. 98]
        Tresmalade, mon testament
        J'ay mis en escript doloreux,
        Lequel je presente humblement
        Devant tous loyaulx amoureux.

10   Premierement, a la haultesse
        Du Dieu d'Amours donne et envoye
        Mon esperit, et en humblesse
        Lui supplie qu'il le convoye
        En son paradis et pourvoye,
15   Car je jure que loyaument

15   Of Faithfulness, gold of those with luck.
      These two suit her well,
      For God, Who made her with His two hands,
      Wished to portray Luck and Faithfulness
      In that lady of such high estate,
20   And He shaped her in a marvelous fashion,
      That was, to speak plainly,
      The treasure of every earthly good.

      Let us say no more! My heart fails me
      Hearing of the virtuous deeds
25   Of the lady who was without blame,
      As bore witness the women and men
      Who came to know the things she said.
      So I think God wished to bring her
      To Him and thus beautify His dwelling
30   In Paradise, where all the saints reside,
      For she is a being of great beauty
      And is called by one and all
      The treasure of every earthly good.

                    Envoy
      Weeping and wailing are of no avail.
35   We will all die soon or late.
      No one can for long hold onto
      The treasure of every earthly good.

Ballade

      Since Death has taken my mistress,
      Whom I was wont to love above all others,
      I must die in sadness.
      Surely, I can live no longer.
5   And so, lacking joy,
      Terribly ill, I have written
      Down my testament in letters of pain,
      And present it humbly
      Before all faithful lovers.

10   First, to his highness
      The God of Love, I give and bequeath
      My soul and humbly
      Beg him to convey it
      To his paradise, there to guard,
15   For I swear I've

L'a servi de vueil desireux.
Advouer le puis vrayement
Devant tous loyaulx amoureux.

Oultre plus, vueil que la richesse
20　Des biens d'Amours qu'avoir souloye
Departie soit a largesse
A vrais amans, et ne vouldroye
Que faulx amans par nulle voye
En eussent part aucunement.
25　Oncques n'euz amistié a eulx.
Je le prans sur mon sauvement
Devant tous loyaux amoureux.

L'envoy

Sans espargnier or ne monnoye,
Loyauté veult qu'enterré soye
30　En sa chappelle grandement,
Dont je me tiens pour bien eureux,
Et l'en mercie chierement
Devant tous loyaux amoureux.

[70]

B71　　　　　　　　　**Balade**　　　　　　　　[p. 99]

J'oy estrangement
Plusieurs gens parler
Qui trop mallement
Se plaingnent d'amer,
5　Car legierement,
Sans paine porter,
Vouldroyent briefment
A fin amener
Tout leur pensement.

10　C'est fait follement
D'ainsy desirer,
Car qui loyaument
Veulent acquester
Bon guerdonnement,
15　Maint mal endurer
Leur fault, et souvent
A rebours trouver
Tout leur pensement.

Served him loyally and very willingly.
I can testify to this
Before all faithful lovers.

Furthermore, I wish the richness
20   Of Love's goods I once possessed
Be shared out generously
To faithful lovers, and I would not like
False lovers to have
Any of these at all.
25   I have never felt love for these people,
So I swear on my salvation
Before all faithful lovers.

Envoy

Sparing neither gold nor money,
That is how Faithfulness wishes I be buried
30   Within her chapel in a grand fashion,
And so I count myself very fortunate,
Thanking her with great affection
Before all faithful lovers.

Ballade

I've heard many people
Speak out in a strange fashion,
Complaining too petulantly
About love,
5   For without difficulty,
Not forced to suffer any pain,
They'd like to quickly
Bring to completion
All their intentions.

10   It's a foolish thing
To desire in such fashion,
For whoever in good faith
Wants to obtain
A fine reward,
15   Must endure much
Unpleasantness—and often
Find just the opposite of
All their intentions.

S'Amour humblement
20 Veulent honnourer,
Et soingneusement
Servir, sans fausser,
Des biens largement
Leur fera donner,
25 Mais premierement
Il veult esprouver
Tout leur pensement.

[71]

Songe en complainte [p. 100]

Aprés le jour qui est fait pour traveil
Ensuit la nuit pour repos ordonnee.
Pource m'avint que chargié de sommeil
Je me trouvay moult fort une vespree
5 Pour la peine que j'avoye portee
Le jour devant, si fis mon appareil
De me couschier, sitost que le souleil
Je vy retrait et sa clarté mussee.

Quant couschié fu, de legier m'endormy,
10 Et en dormant, ainsi que je songoye,
Advis me fu que devant moy je vy
Ung vieil homme que point ne congnoissoye,
Et non pour tant autresfois veu l'avoye,
Ce me sembla, si me trouvay marry
15 Que j'avoye son nom mis en oubly,
Et pour honte parler a luy n'osoye.

Un peu se teut, et puis m'araisonna,
Disant : «Amy, n'avez vous de moy cure?
Je suis Aage qui lettres apporta
20 A Enfance, de par Dame Nature,
Quant lui chargeay que plus la nourriture
N'auroit de vous. Alors vous delivra
A Jeunesse qui gouverné vous a
Moult longuement, sans raison et mesure.

25 «Or est ainsi que Raison, qui sus tous
Doit gouverner, a fait tresgrant complainte
A Nature de Jeunesse et de vous,
Disant qu'avez tous deux fait faulte mainte.
Avisez vous, ce n'est pas chose fainte,

If in humility they
20   Wish to honor Love,
And serve him well
Without proving false,
He'll have them
Given good things generously.
But in the first place
He'll put to the test
All their intentions.

A Dream in Complaint Form

After the day made for work
Follows the night ordained for rest.
And so it happened one evening
I found myself so much in need of sleep,
5   Because of the pain I'd suffered
The day before, I made my bed
In order to take my rest as soon as I saw
The sun go down, and its brightness hidden.

After I lay down, I fell asleep easily,
10   And while I slept, in a dream,
It seemed I saw before me
An old man I did not recognize.
And yet I'd seen him some time before,
It seemed, and I felt chagrined
15   To have forgotten his name
And from shame did not dare speak to him.

He was silent a while and then addressed me,
Saying: "Friend, do you care nothing about me?
I am Age, who brought letters
20   To Childhood on behalf of Lady Nature
When I charged her to be concerned no longer
With your maturing. Then I put you in the care
Of Youth, who has governed you
Very long, and with neither reason nor moderation.

25   "Now it has come about that Reason, who should
Govern everyone, has lodged a very serious complaint
With Nature against you and Youth,
Saying you both have done many wrongs.
Take this to heart, it is no laughing matter,

30   Car Vieillesse, la mere de Courrous,
       Qui tout abat et amaine au dessoubz,   [p. 101]
       Vous donnera dedens brief une atainte.

       «Au derrenier, ne la povez fuïr.
       Si vous vault mieulx, tantdis qu'avez Jennesse,
35   A vostre honneur de Folie partir,
       Vous eslongnant de l'amoureuse adresse,
       Car en descort sont Amours et Vieillesse :
       Nul ne les peut a leur gré bien servir.
       Amour vous doit pour escusé tenir,
40   Puis que la Mort a prins vostre maistresse.

       «Et tout ainsi qu'assés est avenant
       A jeunes gens en l'amoureuse voye
       De temps passer, c'est aussi mal seant
       Quant en amours un vieil homme folloye.
45   Chascun s'en rit, disant : Dieu, quelle joye!
       Ce foul vieillart veult devenir enfant!
       Jeunes et vieulx du doy le vont moustrant,
       Moquerie par tous lieux le convoye.

       «A vostre honneur povez Amours laissier
50   En jeune temps, comme par nonchalance.
       Lors ne pourra nul de vous raconter
       Que l'ayez fait par faulte de puissance,
       Et dira l'en que c'est par desplaisance
       Que ne voulés en autre lieu amer,
55   Puis qu'est morte votre dame sans per,
       Dont loyaument gardez la souvenance.

       «Au Dieu d'Amours requerez humblement
       Qu'il lui plaise de reprandre l'ommage
       Que lui feistes, par son commandement,
60   Vous rebaillant vostre cueur qu'a en gage.
       Merciez le des biens qu'en son servage   [p. 102]
       Avez receuz. Lors gracïeusement
       Departirés de son gouvernement,
       A grant honneur, comme loyal et sage.

65   «Puis requerés a tous les amoureux
       Que chascun d'eulx tout ouvertement die
       Se vous avez riens failly envers eulx,
       Tant que suivy avez leur compaignie,
       Et que par eulx soit la faulte punie,

30   For Age, the mother of Anger,
Who humbles and subdues everyone,
Will come forward soon enough to assault you.

"In the end, you cannot flee her.
And, while Youth is yours, it would be better
35   To abandon Folly to your honor,
Distancing yourself from the lovers' path,
For Love and Age are not in accord.
No man can serve both to their satisfaction.
Love should consider you excused,
40   Since Death has taken your mistress.

"And though it's fitting enough
For young people to pass their time
On the byways of Love, it's just as
Unsuitable that an old man be a fool for love.
45   Everyone has a laugh, saying: 'God, what fun!
This crazy old man acts like a young person!'
Young and old alike will point a finger at him.
Mockery will accompany him everywhere.

"You can abandon Love to your honor
50   In youth, as if you do not care.
Then no one can charge you with doing so
Because of some unsuitability.
And they'll say that, being afflicted,
You do not want to love another
55   Since your lady, who had no rival, has died,
And you're faithful to her memory.

"Make this humble request of the God of Love,
To please render invalid the homage
You made at his command,
60   Returning your heart, which he's held in warrant;
Thank him for the benefits you've received
While in his service. Thus you'll
Gracefully depart from his rule,
In great honor, as a man faithful and wise.

65   "Then beg all those who love
To say, each and every one, in all frankness
If you've done any person wrong
While you were of their company
   —They should punish any such fault—

70   Leur requerant pardon de cueur piteux,
        Car de servir estiés desireux
        Amours et tous ceulx de sa seigneurie.

        «Ainsi pourrez departir du povair
        Du Dieu d'Amours sans avoir charge aucune.
75   C'est mon conseil. Faictes vostre vouloir,
        Mais gardez vous que ne croyez Fortune
        Qui de flater est a chascun commune,
        Car tousjours dit qu'on doit avoir espoir
        De mieulx avoir, mais c'est pour decevoir.
80   Je ne congnois plus faulse soubz la lune.

        «Je sçay trop bien, s'escouter la voulez,
        Et son conseil plus que le mien eslire,
        Elle dira que, s'Amours delaissiez,
        Vous ne povez mieulx vostre cueur destruire,
85   Car vous n'aurés lors a quoy vous deduire,
        Et tout plaisir a Nonchaloir mettrés.
        Ainsi le temps en grant ennuy perdrés,
        Qui pis vauldra que l'amoureux martire.

        «Et puis aprés, pour vous donner confort,
90   Vous promettra que recevrez amende
        De tous les maulx qu'avez souffers a tort,   [p. 103]
        Et que c'est droit qu'aucun guerdon vous rende,
        Mais il n'est nul qui a elle s'atende,
        Qui tost ou tart ne soit, je m'en fais fort,
95   Deceu d'elle : a vous je m'en raport,
        Si pry a Dieu que d'elle vous deffende.»

        En tressaillant, sur ce point m'esveillay,
        Tremblant ainsi que sur l'arbre la fueille,
        Disant : «Helas! oncques mais ne songay
100   Chose dont tant mon povre cueur se dueille,
        Car, s'il est vray que Nature me vueille
        Abandonner, je ne sçay que feray.
        A Vieillesse tenir pié ne pourray,
        Mais couvendra que tout ennuy m'acueille.»

105   Et non pour tant, le vieil homme qu'ay veu
        En mon dormant, lequel Aage s'apelle,
        Si m'a dit vray, car j'ay bien aperceu
        Que Vieillesse veult emprandre querelle
        Encontre moy. Ce m'est dure nouvelle
110   Et ja soit ce qu'a present suy pourveu

70 Even as you beg them to pardon you with pitying heart.
    For yours was the desire to serve
    Love and all who follow his command.

    "In this way you can withdraw from the sovereignty
    Of the God of Love and not be charged with any wrong.
75 This is what I advise; do what you will,
    But take care not to put your trust in Fortune,
    Whose wont is to flatter everyone,
    For she always says a person should have hopes
    Of having better, but that's to deceive him.
80 I know no woman falser under the moon.

    "I know only too well that if you listen to her
    And choose her advice rather than mine,
    She'll say, if you abandon Love,
    You could find no better way to destroy your heart.
85 Then you'll have nothing to delight you,
    And you'll forget every kind of pleasure,
    Wasting your time in great pain
    Much worse than the sufferings of love.

    "And then, in order to console you,
90 She'll promise you compensation
    For all the ills you wrongly suffer,
    Saying it's right to offer you a reward.
    But no man trusts her
    Who is not, soon or late (so I affirm),
95 Deceived by her; all this I tell you.
    So I pray God protect you from her."

    Trembling, at this point I woke up,
    Shaking like some leaf on a tree,
    And said: "Alas! Never before did I have
100 A dream that pains my poor heart this terribly.
    For, if Nature truly intends
    To abandon me, I don't know what I'll do.
    I cannot stand up to Old Age,
    But must accustom myself to every ill."

105 Yet even so the old man I saw
    While dreaming, the one called Age,
    Did tell me the truth; for I clearly perceived
    That Old Age wished to file a complaint
    Against me. I took that news hard.
110 And even though then I was still full of

De jeunesse, sans me trouver recreu,
Ce n'est que sens de me pourvoir contr'elle.

A celle fin que, quant vendra vers moy,
Je ne soye despourveu comme nice.
115   C'est pour le mieulx, s'avant je me pourvoy,
Et trouveray Vieillesse plus propice,
Quant congnoistra qu'ay laissié tout office
Pour la suïr. Alors, en bonne foy
Recommandé m'aura, comme je croy,
120   Et moins soussy auray en son service.

Si suis content, sans changier desormais,   [p. 104]
Et pour tousjours entierement propose
De renoncer a tous amoureux fais,
Car il est temps que mon cueur se repose.
125   Mes yeulx cligniez et mon oreille close
Tendray, afin que n'y entrent jamais
Par Plaisance les amoureux atrais :
Tant les congnois qu'en eulx fier ne m'ose.

Qui bien se veult garder d'amoureux tours,
130   Quant en repos sent que son cueur sommeille,
Garde les yeulx emprisonnez tousjours.
S'ilz eschappent, ilz crient en l'oreille
Du cueur qui dort, tant qu'il fault qu'il s'esveille,
Et ne cessent de lui parler d'Amours,
135   Disans qu'ilz ont souvent hanté ses cours,
Ou ilz ont veu Plaisance nompareille.

Je sçay par cueur ce mestier bien a plain,
Et m'a long temps esté si agreable
Qu'il me sembloit qu'il n'estoit bien mondain
140   Fors en Amours, ne riens si honnorable.
Je trouvoye par maint conte notable
Comment Amour, par son povair haultain,
A avancié, comme roy souverain,
Ses serviteurs en estat prouffitable.

145   Mais en ce temps, ne congnoissoye pas
La grant doleur qu'il couvient que soustiengne
Un povre cueur pris es amoureux las.
Depuis l'ay sceu, bien sçay a quoy m'en tiengne.
J'ay grant cause que tousjours m'en souviengne.
150   Or en suis hors, mon cueur en est tout las.
Il ne veult plus d'Amours passer le pas,   [p. 105]
Pour bien ou mal que jamais lui adviengne.

Youth, not finding myself wearied,
It's only good sense to protect yourself from her.

To this end, when Old Age comes my way,
I won't be empty-handed like some fool.
115   It's best I take precautions,
And I'll find Old Age more congenial
If she learns I've given up all responsibilities
In order to follow her. Then in good faith
She'll have recommended me, or so I believe,
120   And I'll find serving her less troublesome.

So I'm content henceforth not to change
Ever again; I intend to renounce completely
Everything that touches on love,
For it's time my heart gets some rest.
125   I'll keep my eyes cast down, my ears
Shut fast, so that the attractions of love
Will never, through Pleasure, find their way in.
I know too much to dare trusting them.

Whoever would guard himself well from Love's tricks,
130   When he feels his heart rests in sleep,
Let him always keep his eyes prisoner.
If they escape, they'll cry in the ear
Of the sleeping heart until forced to wake,
And they'll not stop speaking to it of Love,
135   Saying they've always frequented his court,
Where they saw pleasure beyond compare.

I know everything of this service by heart,
And for a long time it was so agreeable
I thought there was no earthly good
140   Save in love, nothing else as honorable.
I remember well that I found in many a tale
How Love, in his exalted power,
Had advanced, in the manner of a sovereign king,
His servants to a rank that profited them.

145   But then I did not know
The great suffering a poor heart was forced
To endure trapped by love's bonds.
I've since learned; I know very well what I'm talking about.
I've good reason to remember it always.
150   Now I'm free, and my heart is wearied.
It no longer wishes to tilt lances with Love,
No matter if harm or good come of it.

Pource tantost, sans plus prandre respit,
Escrire vueil en forme de requeste,
155   Tout mon estat comme devant est dit,
Et quant j'auray fait ma cedule preste,
Porter la vueil a la premiere feste
Qu'Amours tendra, lui moustrant par escript
Les maulx qu'ay euz et le peu de prouffit
160   En poursuivant l'amoureuse conqueste.

Ainsi d'Amours, devant tous les amans,
Prandray congié en honneste maniere,
En estouppant la bouche aux mesdisans
Qui ont langue pour mesdire legiere,
165   Et requerray par treshumble priere
Qu'il me quitte de tous les couvenans
Que je luy fis, quant l'un de ses servans
Devins pieça de voulenté entiere.

Et reprendray hors de ses mains mon cueur
170   Que j'engagay par obligacïon
Pour plus seurté d'estre son serviteur
Sans faintise ou excusacïon,
Et puis, aprés recommandacïon,
Je delairay, a mon tresgrant honneur,
175   A jeunes gens qui sont en leur verdeur
Tous fais d'Amours par resignacïon.

La Requeste

Aux excellens et puissans en noblesse,
Dieu Cupido et Venus la deesse,

Supplie presentement,   [p. 106]
180   Humblement,
Charles, le duc d'Orlians,
Qui a esté longuement,
Ligement,
L'un de voz obeissans,
185   Et entre les vrais amans,
Voz servans,
A despendu largement
Le temps de ses jeunes ans
Tresplaisans
190   A vous servir loyaument.

And so at once, taking no more time for rest,
I intend to write down, in the form of a request,
155   The whole of my situation, as spelled out above.
And after finishing my writ,
I think to bring it to the first feast
Love holds, making clear to him in the text
The ills I've suffered, how little I profited
160   Pursuing the conquest of love.

Thus from Love, before all those who love,
I'll take my leave in an honest fashion,
Shutting the mouths of evil gossips,
Whose tongues are ready to utter calumny,
165   And I'll ask, in my very humble prayer,
That he acquit me of all the agreements
Made with him, when I became, with a whole heart,
One of his servants some time ago.

And I'll take back my heart from his hands,
170   Which I was obliged to hand over,
The better to warrant being his servant,
Without any weakness or excuses.
And then, after being recommended,
I'll abandon, to my very great honor,
175   To the young people who are in their prime,
All that pertains to love, having myself resigned.

The petition

To their Excellencies, powerful in their nobility,
The god Cupid and the goddess Venus,

Charles, the duke of Orleans,
180   At this time humbly
Makes this request,
He who for a long time has been
In faithfulness
One of your subjects,
185   Among those who love truly,
And are your servants;
He's spent a good many
Of his youthful years,
A very pleasant time,
190   In serving you faithfully.

Qu'il vous plaise regarder
Et passer
Ceste requeste presente
Sans la vouloir refuser,
195   Mais penser
Que d'umble vueil la presente
A vous, par loyalle entente,
En attente
De vostre grace trouver,
200   Car sa fortune dolente
Le tourmente
Et le contraint de parler.

Comme ainsi soit que la Mort,
A grant tort,
205   En droicte fleur de jeunesse
Lui ait osté son deport,
Son ressort,
Sa seule dame et lïesse,
Dont a fait veu et promesse,   [p. 107]
210   Par destresse,
Desespoir et desconfort,
Que jamais n'aura princesse
Ne maistresse,
Car son cueur en est d'accort,

215   Et pource que ja pieça
Vous jura
De vous loyaument servir,
Et en gage vous laissa
Et donna
220   Son cueur par leal desir,
Il vient pour vous requerir
Que tenir
Le vueilliez, tant qu'il vivra,
Escusé, car sans faillir,
225   Pour mourir,
Plus amoureux ne sera.

Et lui vueilliez doulcement,
Franchement,
Rebaillier son povre cueur,
230   En lui quittant son serment,
Tellement
Qu'il se parte a son honneur
De vous, car bon serviteur,
Sans couleur,

Please examine
And endorse
This present request,
Not considering any refusal.
195   Instead, please bear in mind
That it is presented with a humble will
To you, with faithful intentions,
In the expectation
Of obtaining your favor.
200   For his miserable fortune
Torments him
And forces the man to speak out.

Since it is that Death,
Very wrongfully,
205   Has taken from him his joy,
In the true flower of youth,
His refuge,
His only lady and happiness,
To whom he promised and vowed
210   That in distress,
Despair, and discomfort
He would never have a lady
Or mistress,
For so was his heart disposed;

215   And because formerly
He swore
To serve you faithfully,
And as a warrant left and
Bestowed upon you
220   His heart in loyal desire,
He comes to ask you
To please,
While he lives, hold him
Excused since without fail,
225   Even should he die,
He would no longer be a lover.

And please with gentleness
And liberality
Return his poor heart to him,
230   Releasing him from his oath
In such a fashion
That he honorably depart
From you, for he has truly
Been your good

235   Vous a esté vrayement.
     Moustrez lui quelque faveur,
     En doulceur,
     Au meins a son partement.

     A Bonne Foy, que tenez   [p. 108]
240   Et nommez
     Vostre principal notaire,
     Estroictement ordonnez
     Et mandez
     Sur peine de vous desplaire,
245   Qu'il vueille, sans delay traire,
     Lettre faire,
     En laquelle affermerez
     Que congié de soy retraire
     Sans forfaire,
250   Audit cueur donné avez,

     Afin que le suppliant
     Cy devant
     Nommé, la puisse garder
     Pour sa descharge et garant,
255   En moustrant
     Que nul ne le doit blasmer,
     S'Amours a voulu laissier,
     Car d'amer
     N'eut oncque puis son talant
260   Que Mort lui voulu oster
     La nomper
     Qui fust ou monde vivant.

     Et s'il vous plaist faire ainsi
     Que je dy,
265   Ledit suppliant sera
     Allegié de son soussy
     Et ennuy
     D'avec son cueur bannira,
     Et aprés, tant que vivra,   [p. 109]
270   Priera
     Pour vous, sans mettre en oubly
     La grace qu'il recevra
     Et aura
     Par vostre bonne mercy.

235   Servant, without pretext.
Show the man some favor
In your kindness,
At least as he takes his leave.

To Good Faith, whom you consider
240   And call
Your chief notary,
Expressly order
And instruct,
On the pain of your displeasure,
245   To please draw up
Without delay a letter
In which you will affirm
Your grant to
The aforesaid heart of permission
250   To withdraw without penalty,

So that the suppliant,
Named there
Above might retain it
As his discharge and warrant,
255   And thus demonstrate
That no man should blame him
For abandoning Love;
For he feels
No more desire to love
260   Since Death was pleased to steal
From him the lady most unrivaled
Of those who have lived in this world.

And if you are pleased to do just as
I have asked,
265   The aforesaid suppliant will be
Relieved of his cares,
And he will banish
Worry from his heart.
And afterward, as long as he lives,
270   He will pray
For you, never forgetting
The favor he receives
And enjoys
Through your good graces.

LA DEPARTIE D'AMOURS EN BALADES

Bal 1   **Balade**

275   Quant vint a la prochaine feste
       Qu'Amours tenoit son parlement,
       Je lui presentay ma requeste,
       Laquelle leut tresdoulcement
       Et puis me dist : «Je suy dolent
280   Du mal qui vous est avenu,
       Mais il n'a nul recouvrement,
       Quant la mort a son cop feru.

       «Eslongnez hors de vostre teste
       Vostre douloureux pensement,
285   Moustrez vous homme, non pas beste,
       Faictes que sans empeschement
       Ait en vous le gouvernement
       Raison, qui souvent a pourveu
       En maint meschief tressagement,
290   Quant la mort a son cop feru.

       «Reprenez nouvelle conqueste,
       Je vous aideray tellement
       Que vous trouverés dame preste   [p. 110]
       De vous amer tresloyaument,
295   Qui de biens aura largement.
       D'elle serez amy tenu :
       Je n'y voy autre amendement,
       Quant la mort a son cop feru.»

Bal 2   **Balade**

       «Helas! sire, pardonnez moy,»
300   Se dis je, «car toute ma vie,
       Je vous asseure par ma foy,
       Jamais n'auray dame n'amie.
       Plaisance s'est de moy partie
       Qui m'a de Liësse forclos.
305   N'en parlez plus, je vous supplie,
       Je suis bien loings de ce pourpos.

       Quant ces parolles de vous oy,
       Vous m'essaiez. Ne faictes mye!
       A vous dire vray, je le croy,

THE DEPARTURE FROM LOVE IN BALLADES

Ballade

275 When Love came to the next feast
   Where he was holding his parliament,
   I presented my request to him,
   The which he very kindly read,
   Saying: "I'm sorrowed
280 By the miseries that have come upon you,
   And yet there's no recovery
   After Death has struck his blow.

   "Banish from your head
   Your sorrowful thoughts.
285 Show yourself a man, not a beast.
   Make sure that Reason
   Enjoys unimpeded sovereignty
   Over you, who often has kept watch
   With great wisdom in times of terrible fortune
290 After Death has struck his blow.

   "Undertake a new conquest.
   I will assist you
   So you can find a lady quickly
   Who will faithfully love you,
295 Possessing virtue in abundance.
   The lady will consider you her lover.
   I see no other remedy
   After Death has struck his blow."

Ballade

   "Alas, sir, pardon me,"
300 I said, "for never in my life,
   I assure you upon my faith,
   Will I have a lady or beloved.
   Pleasure has fled from me,
   Excluding me from Happiness.
305 Speak no more of it, I beg you.
   I am very far from such business.

   "When I hear you speak such words,
   You try me. Do nothing of the sort!
   To tell you the truth, I believe what you say,

310   Ou ce n'est dit qu'en moquerie.
        Ce me seroit trop grant folie,
        Quant demourer puis en repos,
        De reprandre merencolie :
        Je suis bien loings de ce pourpos.

315   Acquittié me sui, comme doy,
        Vers vous et vostre seigneurie.
        Desormais me vueil tenir coy.
        Pource, de vostre courtoisie,
        Accordez moy, je vous en prie,
320   Ma requeste, car a briefs mos,   [p. 111]
        De plus amer, quoy que nul dye,
        Je suis bien loings de ce pourpos.»

76

Bal 3   **Balade**

        Amour congnu bien que j'estoye
        En ce pourpos sans changement.
325   Pource respondy : «Je vouldroye
        Que voulsissiez faire autrement,
        Et me servir plus longuement,
        Mais je voy bien que ne voulés,
        Si vous accorde franchement
330   La requeste que faicte avés.

        Escondire ne vous pourroye,
        Car servy m'avez loyaument,
        N'onques ne vous trouvay en voye
        N'en voulenté aucunement
335   De rompre le loyal serement
        Que me feistes, comme savés.
        Ainsi le compte largement
        La requeste que faicte avés.

        Et afin que tout chascun voye
340   Que de vous je suis trescontent,
        Une quittance vous octroye,
        Passee par mon parlement,
        Qui relaissera plainement
        L'ommage que vous me devés,
345   Comme contient ouvertement
        La requeste que faicte avés.»

310   Unless you speak only in mockery.
        It would be terribly foolish for me
        When I can remain at rest
        To take up again with Melancholy.
        I am very far from such business.

315   "I have acquitted myself as I should
        Toward you and your lordship.
        Henceforth I intend to remain at rest.
        And so, out of your courtesy,
        Do grant, I beg you,
320   My request: in brief,
        To love no longer—no matter what is said—
        I am very far from such business."

Ballade

        Love recognized clearly that I would
        Not change my mind,
325   And so he answered: "I would like
        You to take a different path
        And remain longer in my service,
        But I see well it is not your wish,
        And so I grant freely
330   The request you have made.

        "I can bring no shame upon you,
        For you have faithfully served me.
        Never have I seen you set about,
        Or show any intention of,
335   Violating the oath of loyalty
        You swore, as you know.
        So I look with favor upon
        The request you have made.

        "And so that everyone might witness
340   How very content I am with you,
        I will grant you a release,
        As passed by my parliament,
        Which will render completely void
        The homage you owe me,
345   As expressly spelled out in
        The request you have made."

Bal 4   Balade   [p. 112]

       Tantost Amour en grant arroy
       Fist assembler son parlement.
       En plain conseil mon fait contay,
350   Par congié et commandement.
       La fut passee plainement
       La quitance que demandoye,
       Baillee me fut franchement
       Pour en faire ce que vouldroye.

355   Oultre plus, mon cueur demanday,
       Qu'Amour avoit eu longuement,
       Car en gage le lui baillay,
       Quant je me mis premierement
       En son service ligement.
360   Il me dist que je le rauroye,
       Sans refuser aucunement,
       Pour en faire ce que vouldroye.

       A deux genoulz m'agenoillay,
       Merciant Amour humblement
365   Qui tira mon cueur sans delay
       Hors d'un escrin priveement,
       Le me baillant courtoisement
       Lyé en un noir drap de soye.
       En mon sain le mist doulcement
370   Pour en faire ce que vouldroye.

Copie de la quittance dessusdicte

       Sachent presens et avenir
       Que nous, Amours, par Franc Desir
       Conseilliez, sans nulle contrainte,
       Aprés qu'avons oÿ la plainte   [p. 113]
375   De Charles, le duc d'Orlians,
       Qui a esté par plusieurs ans
       Nostre vray loyal serviteur,
       Rebaillié lui avons son cueur
       Qu'il nous bailla pieça en gage,
380   Et le serement, foy et hommage
       Qu'il nous devoit, quittié avons
       Et par ces presentes quittons.
       Oultre plus, faisons assavoir,
       Et certiffions, pour tout voir,
385   Pour estoupper aux mesdisans
       La bouche, qui trop sont nuisans,

Ballade

At once Love with great ceremony
Had the parliament assemble.
Before the entire council I told my tale,
350   By their leave and at their command.
The release I had asked for
Was there approved easily by them.
It was generously granted me
To do with just as I wished.

355   And in addition I asked for my heart,
Which Love had possessed so long,
For I gave it to him as a warrant
When first enrolling myself
As a liegeman in his service.
360   He told me I would have it back
Without any refusal
To do with just as I wished.

I fell down on my knees,
Humbly thanking Love,
365   Who drew out my heart without delay
Discreetly from a case,
Courteously handing it to me,
Wrapped in some black silk cloth.
He put it softly on my breast,
370   To do with just as I wished.

Copy of the aforesaid release

Let those present and in the future know
That we, Love, advised by Generous
Desire, under no compulsion at all,
After we heard the complaint
375   Of Charles, the duke of Orleans,
Who has been for many years
Our true, loyal servant,
Have returned to him his heart,
Which, a long time ago, he gave us as a pledge;
380   And from the oath, faith, and homage
That he owed us, we have released him
And by these present documents hold him quit.
Furthermore, we make known
And attest, in all truth,
385   In order to put a gag in the mouths
Of evil gossips, who do too much harm,

Qu'il ne part de nostre service
Par deffaulte, forfait ou vice,
Mais seulement la cause est telle :
390   Vray est que la mort trop cruelle
A tort lui est venu oster
Celle que tant souloit amer,
Qui estoit sa dame et maistresse,
S'amie, son bien, sa lëesse,
395   Et pour sa loyauté garder,
Il veult desormais ressembler
A la loyalle turturelle
Qui seule se tient a par elle,
Aprés qu'elle a perdu son per.

400   Si lui avons voulu donner
Congié du tout de soy retraire
Hors de nostre court sans forfaire.
Fait par bon conseil et advis
De noz subgiez et vrais amis,   [p. 114]
405   En nostre present parlement
Que nous tenons nouvellement.
En tesmoing de ce avons mis
Nostre seel, plaqué et assis
En ceste presente quittance.

410   Escripte par nostre ordonnance
Presens mains notables recors,
Le jour de la Feste des Mors,
L'an mil quatre cent trente et sept,
Ou chastel de Plaisant Recept.

Bal 5   Balade

415   Quant j'euz mon cueur et ma quittance,
Ma voulenté fu assouvie,
Et non pour tant, pour l'acointance
Qu'avoye de la seigneurie
D'Amour et de sa compaignie,
420   Quant vins a congié demander,
Trop mal me fist la departie,
Et ne cessoye de pleurer.

Amour vit bien ma contenance,
Si me dist : «Amy, je vous prie,
425   S'il est riens dessoubz ma puissance
Que vueilliez, ne l'espargniez mie.»

That he does not leave our service
Through some fault, wrong, or crime.
Instead, the only cause is this:
390   True it is that death, so cruel,
Has come to wrongfully take from him
The lady whom he loved so much,
His lady and mistress,
His beloved, his good, his happiness.
395   And, to hold onto his loyalty,
He intends henceforth to resemble
The faithful turtledove,
Who keeps alone and by herself
After she has lost her mate.

400   And so it is our wish to give
Him leave to recuse himself completely
From our court, committing no wrong thereby.
Done according to the good counsel and advice
Of all our subjects and true friends
405   In our present parliament,
Which we have just recently assembled,
In witness of which we have placed
Our seal, attached and joined to
This present document of release.

410   Written according to our authority,
In the presence of many notable witnesses,
On All Souls' Day,
In the year fourteen hundred and thirty-seven,
In the Castle of Pleasant Refuge.

Ballade

415   Once I had my heart and my release,
My desire was satisfied.
Yet even so, because of the friendship
I'd received from the dominion
Of Love and his company,
420   When the time came to take my leave,
The departure proved difficult for me,
And I could not stop weeping.

Love noted well how I felt,
And said: "Friend, I beg you,
425   If there's anything I have in my power
That you wish, please do not hesitate at all."

Tant plain fu de merencolie
Que je ne peuz a lui parler
Une parolle ne demye,
430   Et ne cessoye de pleurer.

Ainsi party en desplaisance   [p. 115]
D'Amour, faisant chiere marrie,
Et, comme tout ravy en transse,
Prins congié sans que plus mot dye.
435   A Confort dist qu'il me conduye,
Car je ne m'en savoye aler.
J'avoye la veue esbluye
Et ne cessoye de pleurer.

Bal 6   Balade

Confort, me prenant par la main,
440   Hors de la porte me convoye,
Car Amour, le roy souverain,
Luy chargea moy moustrer la voye
Pour aler ou je desiroye.
C'estoit vers l'ancïen manoir
445   Ou en enffance demouroye,
Que l'en appelle Nonchaloir.

A Confort dis : «Jusqu'a demain
Ne me laissiez, car je pourroye
Me forvoier, pour tout certain,
450   Par desplaisir vers la saussoye*
Ou est Viellesse rabat joye.
Se nous travaillons fort ce soir,
Tost serons au lieu que vouldroye,
Que l'en appelle Nonchaloir.»

455   Tant cheminasmes qu'au derrain
Veismes la place que queroye.
Quant de la porte fu prouchain,
Le portier qu'assez congnoissoye,   [p. 116]
Si tost comme je l'appelloye
460   Nous reccu, disant que, pour voir,
Ou dit lieu bien venu estoye,
Que l'en appelle Nonchaloir.

So overcome with melancholy,
I could say nothing to him,
Not utter a word or even a sound,
430   And I could not stop weeping.

And so I departed from Love
With no pleasure, my face showing pain,
As if dazed by a trance, taking my leave,
And not saying a single word.
435   I asked Comfort to bear me company,
For I knew not how to proceed.
My eyes could see only with difficulty,
And I could not stop weeping.

Ballade

Comfort, taking my hand,
440   Escorted me out the door,
But Love, the sovereign king,
Charged him to show me the way
To proceed where I wished,
Which was toward the ancient manor
445   Where I'd spent my childhood,
Which is called Indifference.

To Comfort I said: "Do not leave
Me before tomorrow. For I could well
Take the wrong path because of grief,
450   This is certain, toward the weeping willow
Where Old Age keeps herself, that killjoy.
If we travel hard this evening,
We'll soon be in the place that pleases me,
Which is called Indifference."

455   We traveled far enough until in the end
We spied the place I was seeking.
When we approached the door,
The porter, whom I knew well enough,
As soon as I summoned him,
460   Greeted us, saying that, in truth,
I was welcome to the aforesaid place,
Which is called Indifference.

Bal 7   Balade

      Le gouverneur de la maison,
      Qui Passe Temps se fait nommer,
465   Me dist : «Amy, ceste saison
      Vous plaist il ceans sejourner?»
      Je respondy qu'a brief parler,
      Se lui plaisoit ma compaignie,
      Content estoie de passer
470   Avecques lui toute ma vie.

      Et lui racontay l'achoison
      Qui me fist Amour delaissier.
      Il me dist qu'avoye raison,
      Quant eut veu ma quittance au cler
475   Que je lui baillay a garder.
      Aussi de ce me remercie
      Que je vouloie demourer
      Avecques lui toute ma vie.

      Le lendemain lettres foison
480   A Confort baillay a porter
      D'umble recommendacïon,
      Et le renvoiay sans tarder
      Vers Amour, pour lui raconter
      Que Passe Temps a chiere lye
485   M'avoit receu pour reposer
      Avecques luy toute ma vie.   [p. 117]

      A tresnoble, hault et puissant seigneur
      Amour, prince de mondaine doulceur.

      Tresexcellent, treshault et noble prince,
490   Trespuissant roy en chascune province,
      Si humblement que se peut serviteur
      Recommander a son maistre et seigneur,
      Me recommande a vous, tant que je puis,
      Et vous plaise savoir que tousjours suis
495   Tresdesirant oïr souvent nouvelles
      De vostre estat, que Dieu doint estre telles
      Et si bonnes comme je le desire,
      Plus que ne sçay raconter ou escrire,
      Dont vous supli que me faictes sentir
500   Par tous venans, s'il vous vient a plaisir,
      Car d'en oïr en bien et en honneur,
      Ce me sera parfaitte joye au cueur,
      Et s'il plaisoit a vostre seigneurie

Ballade

The master of the house,
Who calls himself Pass Time,
465 Said to me: "Friend, does it please you
To spend the season here within?"
I answered, keeping my speech short,
That if my company pleased him
I was content to spend
470 All my life with him.

And I recounted to him the reason
Why I had abandoned Love.
He said I was right,
After he carefully checked my release,
475 Which I gave over to his keeping.
And he also expressed his thanks
That my wish was to spend
All my life with him.

The next day I gave Comfort
480 A sheaf of letters to carry,
Recommending myself humbly.
And I sent him back without delay
To Love, in order to tell him
That Pass Time had welcomed me
485 With good cheer and I could spend
All my life with him.

To the most noble, exalted, and mighty Lord
Love, prince of worldly delight

Most excellent, most exalted and noble prince,
490 Lord whose great power extends to every land,
As humbly as a servant can
Commend himself to his master and lord,
I recommend myself to you, with all my power.
And may it please you to know I am always
495 Most eager to hear from time to time the news
Of how you are, and may God grant this news
Be as good as I would like,
Better than I can report or write down,
And so I beg that all who come this way
500 Will tell me your news, if such is your wish,
For to hear this, in goodness and in honor,
Would be a perfect joy to my heart.
And if your lord would be pleased,

Vouloir oïr, par sa grant courtoisie,
505 De mon estat, je suis en tresbon point,
Joyeux de cueur, car soussy n'ay je point,
Et Passe Temps, ou lieu de Nonchaloir,
M'a retenu pour avec lui manoir
Et sejourner tant comme me plaira,
510 Jusques atant que Vieillesse vendra,
Car lors fauldra qu'avec elle m'en voise
Finer mes jours. Ce penser fort me poise   [p. 118]
Dessus le cueur, quant j'en ay souvenance,
Mais, Dieu mercy, loing suis de sa puissance,
515 Presentement je ne la crains en riens,
N'en son dangier aucunement me tiens.
En oultre plus, sachiés que vous renvoye
Confort, qui m'a conduit la droite voye
Vers Nonchaloir, dont je vous remercie
520 De sa bonne, joyeuse compaignie.
En ce fait a vostre commandement,

De bon vouloir et tressoingneusement,*
Auquel vueilliez donner foy et fiance
En ce que luy ay chargié en creance
525 De vous dire plus plainnement de bouche,
Vous suppliant qu'en tout ce qui me touche,
Bien a loisir le vueillez escouter,
Et vous plaise me vouloir pardonner
Se je n'escris devers Vostre Excellence,
530 Comme je doy, en telle reverence
Qu'il appartient, car c'est par Non Savoir
Qui destourbe d'acomplir mon vouloir.
En oultre plus, vous requerant mercy,
Je congnois bien que grandement failly,
535 Quant me parti derrainement de vous,
Car j'estoye si raempli de courrous
Que je ne peu un mot a vous parler,
Ne mon congié au partir demander.
Avecques ce, humblement vous mercie
540 Des biens qu'ay euz soubz vostre seigneurie.
Autre chose n'escris quant a present,
Fors que je pry a Dieu le Tout Puissant,   [p. 119]
Qu'il vous ottroit honneur et longue vie,
Et que puissiez tousjours la compaignie
545 De faulx Dangier surmonter et deffaire,
Qui en tous temps vous a esté contraire.
Escript ce jour troisiesme, vers le soir,
En novembre, ou lieu de Nonchaloir.

In his great courtesy, to hear
505 How I am doing, I am very well,
My heart full of joy, for I have no worries.
And Pass Time in the dwelling of Indifference
Has retained me to remain with him
And sojourn there as long as I please,
510 Until Old Age comes along,
Because I then must go along with her
To finish my days. This thought pains my heart
Grievously whenever it comes to mind.
But, thank God, I am far from her power;
515 At this point I do not fear her at all,
And she has no dominion over me.
Know further that I am sending back
Comfort, who has guided me along the true path
To Indifference, and I thank you for
520 His fine, pleasant company.
And he executed your command in this,

Competently and with a good will;
Please put your faith and trust in him,
Concerning what I told him, which he assured me
525 He would tell you plainly with his own mouth,
And I beg you please listen to him,
As you find the time, in everything that touches me.
Please extend a pardon to me
If I have not written to Your Excellency
530 As I should, with the kind of respect
Required, for Not Knowing
Makes it hard for me to do as I wish.
And furthermore, begging your mercy,
I firmly acknowledge failing miserably
535 When I left you some time ago,
For grief so ruled me then,
Not a single word could I speak,
And, departing, I could not ask for leave.
Moreover, I humbly thank you
540 For the benefits I received under your dominion.
I shall write you no more at this time,
Save that I beg God Almighty
Grant you honor and a long life,
Always allowing you to overcome
545 And defeat the host of that traitor Danger,
Who has forever been your foe.
Written on the third day, toward evening,
Of November in the dwelling of Indifference.

Le bien vostre, Charles, duc d'Orlians,
550   Qui jadis fut l'un de voz vrais servans.

B72   **Balade***

Balades, chançons et complaintes
Sont pour moy mises en oubly,
Car ennuy et pensees maintes
M'ont tenu long temps endormy.
5   Non pour tant, pour passer soussy,
Essaier vueil se je sauroye
Rimer ainsi que je souloye.
Au meins j'en feray mon povoir,
Combien que je congnois et sçay
10   Que mon langage trouveray
Tout enroillié de Nonchaloir.

Plaisans parolles sont estaintes
En moy qui deviens rassoty.
Au fort, je vendray aux attaintes
15   Quant beau parler m'aura failly.
Pour quoy pry ceulx qui m'ont oÿ
Langagier, quant pieça j'estoye
Jeune, nouvel et plain de joye,   [p. 120]
Que vueillent excusé m'avoir.
20   Oncques mais je ne me trouvay
Si rude, car je suis pour vray
Tout enroillié de Nonchaloir.

Amoureux ont parolles paintes
Et langage frois et joly.
25   Plaisance dont ilz sont accointes
Parle pour eulx. En ce party
J'ay esté, or n'est plus ainsi.
Alors de beau parler trouvoye
A bon marchié tant que vouloye,
30   Si ay despendu mon savoir,
Et s'un peu espargnié en ay,
Il est, quant vendra a l'essay,
Tout enroillié de Nonchaloir.

L'envoy
Mon jubilé faire devroye,*
35   Mais on diroit que me rendroye
Sans coup ferir, car Bon Espoir
M'a dit que renouvelleray.

Yours truly, Charles, duke of Orleans,
550 Who was formerly one of your true servants.

Ballade

Ballades, songs, and complaints
I have neglected them all,
For worry and many a thought
Have kept me slumbering a long time.
5 Nonetheless, in order to expel care,
I intend to attempt, as I can,
To compose verse, as was my custom.
At least I'll do so as best I'm able,
Though I know and realize
10 I'll find my words
All rusty with Indifference.

Pleasant words have lost their voice
For me, now become a fool.
In the end, I'll achieve my goal,
15 Though pretty language fails me.
So I beg those who heard the words
I spoke some time ago when I was
Young, fresh, and joyful,
To please hold me excused.
20 Never before have I found myself
So ill at ease, for truly I am
All rusty with Indifference.

Those in love utter fancy words
And speech both novel and elegant.
25 Pleasure, whose friends they are,
Speaks for them; I've been
Of that party—but no longer so.
Then I found beautiful words
At a cheap price, as many as I wished.
30 I paid out what I came to know
And, if I've hoarded some, they'll
Be seen to be, when put to the proof,
All rusty with Indifference.

Envoy

I ought to celebrate my jubilee,
35 But they'd say I am surrendering
Without striking a blow, for Good Hope
Has said I'll rediscover my youth

Pource mon cueur fourbir feray
Tout enroillié de Nonchaloir.

[7]

B73   **Balade**   [p. 121]

L'emplastre de Nonchaloir
Que sus mon cueur pieça mis,
M'a guery, pour dire voir,
Si nettement que je suis
5   En bon point, ne je ne puis
Plus avoir jour de ma vie
L'amoureuse maladie.

Si font mes yeulx leur povoir
D'espïer par le pays
10   S'ilz pourroient plus veoir
Plaisant Beauté, qui jadis
Fut l'un de mes ennemis
Et mist en ma compaignie
L'amoureuse maladie.

15   Mes yeulx tense main et soir,
Mais ilz sont si treshastis
Et trop plains de leur vouloir.
Au fort, je les metz au pis,
Facent selon leur advis.
20   Plus ne crains, dont Dieu mercie,
L'amoureuse maladie.

L'envoy
Quant je voy en doleur pris
Les amoureux, je m'en ris,
Car je tiens pour grant folie
25   L'amoureuse maladie!

[73]

Co1   **Complainte**

Amour, ne vous vueille desplaire,   [p. 299]
Se trop souvent a vous me plains,
Je ne puis mon cueur faire taire,
Pour la doleur dont il est plains.
5   Helas! vueilliez penser au meins

For I'll have my heart scraped clean, which is
All rusty with Indifference.

Ballade

The poultice of Indifference,
Applied at some time to my heart,
Has in truth healed me
So completely I'm
5   In good health and will no longer
Suffer for the rest of my life
The malady of love.

Yet my eyes do their utmost
To search through the countryside
10   And catch sight once again of
Pleasant Beauty, formerly
One of my enemies,
Who made me companion to
The malady of love.

15   With my eyes I debate morning and night,
For they're so impatient
And filled with their own desire.
In the end, I pay them no heed.
Let them do as they think best.
20   Thank God, I no longer fear
The malady of love!

Envoy
When I see lovers afflicted
With pain, I find it humorous,
For it seems a great madness,
25   The malady of love!

Complaint

Love, do not be displeased
If I often complain to you;
I cannot keep my heart silent,
He is so filled with pain.
5   Alas! At least please consider

Au(s) services qu'il vous a fais,
Je vous empry a jointes mains,
Car il en est temps, ou jamais.

Moustrez qu'en avez souvenance,
10   En lui donnant aucun secours,
Faisant semblant qu'avez plaisance
Plus a son bien qu'a ses doulours,
Ou me dittes, pour Dieu, Amours,
Se le lairez en cest estat,
15   Car d'ainsi demourer tousjours,
Cuidez vous que ce soit esbat?

Nennil, car Dangier qui desire
De le mectre du tout a mort,
L'a mis, pour plus tost le destruire,
20   En la prison de Desconfort,
Ne jamais ne sera d'accort
Qu'il en parte par son vouloir,
Combien que trop, et a grant tort,
Long temps lui a fait mal avoir.

25   Et pour la tresmauvaise vie
Que lui fait souffrir ce villain,
Il est encheu en maladie,
Car de tout ce qui lui est sain
A le rebours, j'en suy certain.
30   En ceste dolente prison,   [p. 300]
Ne sçay s'il passera demain
Qu'il ne meure sans guerison,

Car il n'a que poires d'angoisse
Au matin pour se desjeuner,
35   Qui tant le refroidist et froisse
Qu'il ne peut santé recouvrer.
D'eaue ne lui fault point donner,
Il en a de larmes assés.
Tant a de mal, a vray parler,
40   Que cent en seroient lassés.

Et n'a que le lit de Pensee
Pour soy reposer et gesir,
Mais Plaisance s'en est alee,
Qui plus ne le povoit souffrir.
45   A peine l'a peu retenir,
S'Espoir ne fust jusques a cy.

The service he has performed for you,
I beg you, my hands joined,
For it is now or never.

Show that you recall this service,
10   As you afford him some kind of help,
Making clear you take pleasure
More in his benefit than in his distress.
If not, Love, for God's sake, tell me
If you will abandon him in such a state,
15   For if he remains forever thus,
Do you think it good sport?

It is not so, since Danger, eager
To put him to death, has confined
The heart, for his speediest destruction,
20   In the prison of Desolation,
And Danger will never agree
That he should depart the place as he wishes,
Though it is unjust and excessive
To have made the heart suffer so long such ill.

25   Now because of the very miserable life
This villain has made the heart endure,
He has fallen ill,
For if he once in everything enjoyed good health,
He now finds the opposite, I'm certain,
30   In this distressing prison.
I know not if he will live past tomorrow,
Dying for lack of a cure.

For the heart has only the fruit of anguish
In the morning on which to breakfast,
35   Which chills and harms him so much
He will never recover his health.
No need at all to give him water,
He has enough from tears.
So much misery does he feel, in truth,
40   That it would bring low a hundred such.

And he has only the bed of Thought
Where he can lie down and take his rest,
For Pleasure has taken flight,
Who could no longer endure him.
45   He could hardly have retained her
Had Hope not been present until that time.

N'a il donc raison, sans mentir,
S'il fait requeste de Mercy?

Il porte le noir de Tristesse
50 Pour Reconfort qu'il a perdu,
N'oncques hors des fers de Destresse
N'est party, pour mal qu'il ait eu.
Toutesfois vous avez bien sceu
Qu'a vous s'estoit du tout donné,
55 Quelque doleur qu'il ait receu,
Et vous l'avez abandonné.

Par m'ame c'est donner courage
A chascun de voz serviteurs
De vous laissier, s'il estoit sage,
60 Et querir son party aillieurs.
Car tant qu'aurés telz gouverneurs   [p. 301]
Comme Dangier, le desloyal,
Vous n'aurés que plains et clameurs,
Car il ne fist oncque que mal.

65 A mon cueur le conseilleroye
Qu'il vous laissast, mais, par ma foy,
Ja consentir ne lui feroye,
Car tant de son vueil j'aperçoy,
Quelque doleur qu'il ait en soy,
70 Qu'il est vostre, pardevant tous,
Et, par mon serement, je le croy,
Qu'autre maistre n'aura que vous.

Or regardez, n'est ce merveille
Qu'il vous ayme si loyaument,
75 Quant toute doleur nompareille
A receu sans allegement?
Et si le porte lÿement,
Pensant une fois mieulx sera.
A vous s'en attent seulement
80 Ne ja autrement ne fera.

Si m'a chargié que vous requiere,
Comme pieça vous a requis,
Que vueilliez oïr sa priere :
C'est qu'il soit hors de prison mis,
85 Et Dangier et les siens bannis,
Qui jamais ne vouldront son bien,
Ou au meins qu'aye saufconduis
Qu'ilz ne lui mesfacent de rien.

Is he not right, this is no lie,
To have petitioned Mercy?

He wears the black of Sadness
50 Because of Consolation, whom he has lost,
Nor has he ever fled the irons of Distress
Because of the ill he has received.
However, you know well
How completely he has been devoted to you,
55 No matter what pain was his to suffer,
Yet you have abandoned him.

Upon my soul, this encourages
Every one of your servants
To abandon you, if they are wise men,
60 And to embrace some other allegiance.
For while you have such governors
As Danger, the faithless,
You will have only pain and complaint,
For Danger never did anything but ill.

65 I would counsel my heart
To leave you, but, upon my faith,
I would never gain his consent,
For I know this much of his intent:
No matter what pain he feels,
70 He belongs to you beyond all others,
And, on my oath, I assert
He will accept no other master but you.

Consider this, is it not a marvel that
He loves you so faithfully
75 When unbelievable pain of all kinds
He has suffered with no relief?
No matter what, he bears it joyfully,
Thinking it will be alleviated sometime.
His mind is set on you
80 And never will it be otherwise.

So he has charged me to beg this of you,
Just as some time ago he asked
You to please listen to his prayer:
It is that he be released from prison,
85 And that Danger and his people be banished,
Who would never intend his benefit,
Or at least that he might have a safe-conduct
So they would do him no harm,

90   Afin qu'il puist oïr nouvelle
De celle dont il est servant,
Et souvent veoir sa beaulté belle,   [p. 302]
Car d'autre rien n'est desirant
Que la servir, tout son vivant,
Comme la plus belle qui soit,
95   A qui Dieu doint de biens autant
Que son loyal cueur en vouldroit.

Co2   Complainte

Ma seule Dame et ma maistresse,
Ou gist de tout mon bien l'espoir
Et sans qui plaisir ne lïesse
Ne me peuent en riens valoir,
5   Pleust a Dieu que peussiez savoir
Le mal, l'ennuy et le courrous
Qu'a toute heure me fault avoir
Pour ce que je suy loings de vous.

Helas! or ay je souvenance
10   Que je vous vy derrainement
A si tresjoyeuse plaisance
Qu'il me sembloit certainement
Que jamais ennuieux tourment
Ne devoit pres de moy venir,
15   Mais je trouvay bien autrement
Quant me faillu de vous partir,

Car, quant ce vint au congié prandre,
Je ne savoye pour le mieulx,
Auquel me valoit plus entendre,
20   Ou a mon cueur, ou a mes yeulx,
Car je trouvay, ainsi m'ayd Dieux,
Mon cueur courroucié si tresfort   [p. 303]
Q'oncques ne le vy, en nulz lieux,
Si eslongnié de Reconfort.

25   Et d'autre part, mes yeulx estoient
En un tel vouloir de pleurer
Qu'a peine tenir s'en povoient,
N'ilz n'osoient riens regarder,
Car, par un seul semblant moustrer
30   En riens d'en estre desplaisans,
C'eust esté pour faire parler
Les jalous et les mesdisans.

In order that he might have news
90 Of the lady whose servant he is,
And often look upon her fine beauty,
For he desires nothing but
Serving her all his life,
As the most beautiful lady who might be,
95 Upon whom may God bestow as many good things
As his faithful heart would wish for.

Complaint

My only lady and mistress,
On whom rests all my hope for benefit,
And without whom no kind of pleasure
Or happiness is worth a thing to me,
5 May it please God you recognize
The ill, the misery, and the sorrow
I must endure at every hour,
Being far distant from you.

Alas! For I remember
10 That when last I saw you
My pleasure was so filled with joy
It surely seemed
No miserable torment
Should ever descend on me,
15 But it was very different, I found,
When I had to depart from you,

For, when the time came for leave-taking,
I could not decide what might serve me best,
Whether to attend to
20 My heart or my eyes,
For I found, so help me God,
My heart so terribly troubled
I have never seen it anywhere
So far from Consolation.

25 And yet my eyes felt
Such an urge to weep
They could hardly restrain themselves,
Nor did they gaze on anything,
For to reveal in a single look
30 That they were somehow distressed
Would have given the jealous
And the evil gossipers reason to gab,

Et de la grant paour que j'avoie
Que leur dueil si ne fust congneu,
35 Auquel entendre ne savoye,
Oncques si esbahy ne fu,
Si dolent ne si esperdu,
Car, par Dieu, j'eusse mieulx amé,
Avant que l'en l'eust apperceu,
40 N'avoir jamais jour esté né,

Car, se par ma folle maniere,
J'eusse moustré, ou par semblant
Venant de voulenté legiere,
L'amour dont je vous ayme tant,
45 Parquoy eussiez eu, tant ne quant,
De blasme ne de deshonneur,
Je sçay bien que tout mon vivant,
Je fusse langui en doleur.

En ce point et encore pire,
50 Alors de vous je me party,
Sans avoir loisir de vous dire
Les maulx dont j'estoye party. [p. 304]
Toutesfois, Belle, je vous dy
Qu'il vous pleust de vouloir penser
55 Que je vous avoie servy
Et serviroye sans cesser,

Tant comme dureroit ma vie,
Et quant de mort seroye pris,
De m'ame seriés servie,
60 Priant pour vous en Paradis,
S'il en estoit en son devis,
Et mes biens, mon cueur et mon corps,
Je les vous ay du tout soubzmis,
Mais ç'a esté de leurs accors,

65 Car il n'est nulle que je clame,
Ne qui se puist nommer de vray,
Ma seule souveraine Dame,
Fors que vous, a qui me donnay
Le premier jour que regarday
70 Vostre belle plaisant beauté,
De qui vray serviteur mourray,
En gardant tousjours loyauté.

Or, vueilliez donc avoir pensee,
Puis que lors j'avoye tel dueil,

And this great fear came over me
That their great pain might be noticed, to which
35   I could not attend,
Never having been so flustered,
So pained, or so lost,
For, by God, I would have preferred,
Before this could have been remarked upon,
40   To never have been born.

For if my crazed behavior
Would have shown or given any indication
(The result of my weak will)
Of the love I feel so strongly for you,
45   And should you then have suffered
Any blame or dishonor at all,
I know well that the rest of my life
I would have languished ever more in pain.

In such a state, which worsened,
50   I departed from you,
Not enjoying the leisure to tell you
Of the miseries I have come to share.
Nonetheless, Belle, I tell you
You should be pleased to think
55   How I have served you
And will serve you, never ceasing,

As long as I live,
And after death takes me prisoner,
You will be served by my soul,
60   Praying for you in Paradise,
For this was its intention,
And my goods, my heart, and my body,
I have put all these under your control,
To which they have given their assent,

65   For there is no other lady whom I call,
Who could be accorded the title of,
My sole and sovereign lady,
Save only you, to whom I surrendered
The first day I gazed upon
70   Your elegant and compelling beauty,
As whose true servant I will remain till death,
Guarding always my faithfulness.

Please let this then be your thought,
That since I feel such misery,

75   Belle, tresloyaument amee,
      Qu'encore plus grant le recueil,
      Maintenant que contre mon vueil
      Me fault estre de vous loingtains,
      Et que veoir ne puis a l'ueil
80   Voz belles, blanches, doulces mains,

      Et vostre beauté nompareille
      Que veoye si voulentiers,   [p. 305]
      Plaine de doulceur a merveille,
      Dont tous voz fais sont si entiers
85   Qu'ilz ont esté les messagiers
      De me tollir et pres et loing
      Mes vouloirs et mes desiriers.
      Ainsi m'aid Dieu a mon besoing.

      Si vous suppli, tresbonne et belle,
90   Qu'ayez souvenance de moy,
      Car a tousjours vous serez celle
      Que serviray comme je doy.
      Je le vous prometz, par ma foy,
      Du tout a vous me suis donné.
95   Se Dieu plaist, je feray pourquoy
      J'en seray tresbien guerdonné.

B74   **Balade**

      Mon cueur m'a fait commandement
      De venir vers vostre jeunesse,   [p. 122]
      Belle que j'ayme loyaument
      Comme doy faire ma princesse.
5   Se vous demandés pour quoy esse?
      C'est pour savoir quant vous plaira
      Alegier sa dure destresse.
      Ma dame, le sauray je ja?

      Ditez le par vostre serment.
10   Je vous fais leale promesse :
      Nul ne le saura, seulement
      Fors que lui pour avoir lëesse.
      Or lui moustrés qu'estes maistresse,
      Et lui mandez qu'il guerira,
15   Ou, s'il doit morir de destresse,
      Ma dame, le sauray je ja?

75   Belle, so truly loved,
       I will endure even worse,
       For at present and unwillingly
       I must remain a great distance from you
       And cannot lay eyes upon
80   Your beautiful, white, gracious hands,

       As well as your beauty unrivaled,
       Which I used to see gladly,
       Marvelously full of that delight
       That is so much a part of all your doings
85   That they have been the messengers
       Who bear from me both far and near
       My wishes and my desires.
       God help me in my time of need.

       Thus I beg you, lady so very fine and virtuous,
90   To remember me,
       For you will always be the lady
       I serve as I should.
       I promise you, by my faith,
       I am completely devoted to you.
95   May God please I do whatever
       Brings me a very good reward.

Ballade

       My heart has given me the command
       To approach you in your youthfulness,
       Belle, whom I love as faithfully
       As I should love my princess.
5   If you ask: "Why is this so?"
       It is to learn if you are pleased
       To alleviate the heart's dire distress.
       My lady, will I know soon?

       Tell it on your oath.
10   I make you a faithful promise.
       No one save my heart will know
       About this, so he can find happiness.
       Now show him you are the mistress
       And let me know if he will be cured
15   Or die from distress.
       My lady, will I know soon?

Penser ne porroit nullement
Que la douleur qui tant le blesse
Ne vous desplaise aucunement.
20 Or faitez dont tant qu'elle cesse,
Et le remettés en l'adresse
D'Espoir, dont il party pieça.
Respondez sans que plus vous presse;
Ma dame, le sauray je ja?

[74]

B75   Balade   [p. 123]

Je meurs de soif en couste la fontaine.
Tremblant de froid ou feu des amoureux.
Aveugle suis, et si les autres maine.
Povre de sens, entre saichans l'un d'eulx.
5   Trop negligent, en vain souvent songneux.
C'est de mon fait une chose faiee,
En bien et mal par Fortune menee.

Je gaingne temps et pers mainte sepmaine.
Je joue et ris quant me sens douloureux.
10 Desplaisance j'ay d'esperance plaine.
J'atens bon eur en regret engoisseux.
Rien ne me plaist et si suis desireux.
·Je m'esjoïs et cource a ma pensee,
En bien et mal par Fortune menee.

15 Je parle trop et me tais a grant paine.
Je m'esbaÿs et si suis courageux.
Tristesse tient mon confort en demaine.
Faillir ne puis, au mains a l'un des deulx.
Bonne chiere je faiz quant je me deulx.
20 Maladie m'est en santé donnee,
En bien et mal par Fortune menee.

L'envoy
Prince, je dy que mon fait maleureux
Et mon prouffit aussi avantageux
Sur ung hasart j'asserray quelque annee,*
25 En bien et mal par Fortune menee.

[75]

He could in no way imagine how
The pain that greatly wounds him
Should not displease you somewhat.
20   Now make sure this pain ends
And that you put the heart back on the path
Of Hope, from which he wandered some time ago.
Answer without further harangues from me.
My lady, will I know soon?

Ballade

I die of thirst beside the fountain,
Tremble with cold by the lovers' fire.
I'm blind, and yet lead others.
My wit poor, one wise man among others.
5   All too negligent, often taking pains for nothing.
My life—it's too much a game of chance,
Determined for good or ill by Fortune.

I gain time and waste many a week.
I celebrate and laugh when I feel pain.
10   Full of hope I am displeased.
I wait for good fortune anguished by regret.
Nothing pleases me, yet I fill with desire.
My thoughts make me angry but I rejoice,
Determined for good or ill by Fortune.

15   I speak too much, yet with great difficulty keep silent.
I'm terrified, yet full of courage.
Sadness holds sway over my consolation.
I cannot fail to feel one way or the other.
My face shows happiness when I feel sorrow.
20   Illness descends on me in my good health,
Determined for good or ill by Fortune.

Envoy

Prince, I say that my misfortune
And my profit I will hazard
Some year on a game of dice,
25   Determined for good or ill by Fortune.

B76   **Balade**   [p. 124]

Comment voy je ses Anglois esbaÿs!
Resjoÿs toy, franc royaume de France.
On apparçoit que de Dieu sont haÿs,
Puis qu'ilz n'ont plus couraige ne puissance.
5   Bien pensoient par leur oultrecuidance,
Toy surmonter et tenir en servaige,
Et ont tenu a tort ton heritaige.
Mais a present Dieu pour toy se combat
Et se monstre du tout de ta partie.
10   Leur grant orgueil entierement abat,
Et t'a rendu Guyenne et Normandie.

Quant les Anglois as pieça envaÿs
Rien n'y valoit ton sens ne ta vaillance.
Lors estoies ainsi que fut Taÿs,*
15   Pecheresse qui, pour faire penance,
Enclouse fut par divine ordonnance.
Ainsi as tu esté en reclusaige
De Desconfort et Douleur de couraige,
Et les Anglois menoient leur sabat*
20   En grans pompes, baubans et tiranie.
Or a tourné Dieu ton dueil en esbat,
Et t'a rendu Guyenne et Normandie.

N'ont pas Anglois souvent leurs rois traÿs?
Certes ouyl, tous en ont congnoissance,
25   Et encore le roy de leur pays
Est maintenant en doubteuse balance.
D'en parler mal chascun Anglois s'avance.
Assez monstrent par leur mauvais langaige
Que voulentiers lui feroient oultraige.
30   Qui sera roy entr'eux est grant debat.
Pource, France, que veulx tu que te dye?   [p. 125]
De sa verge Dieu les pugnist et bat
Et t'a rendu Guyenne et Normandie.

Prince
Roy des Françoys, gangné as l'avantaige!
35   Parfaiz ton jeu comme vaillant et saige,
Maintenant l'as plus belle qu'au rabat.
De ton bon eur, France, Dieu remercie.
Fortune en bien avecques toy s'embat
Et t'a rendu Guyenne et Normandie.

Ballade

How I see the English confounded!
Take heart, noble kingdom of France!
It is evident they are hated by God,
For they have no power or might left.
5   In their arrogance, they very much intend
To overwhelm and enslave you,
And they have wrongly held onto your heritage.
But now God fights on your side
And shows He is entirely of your party.
10   He beats down all of their great pride,
And has returned Guienne and Normandy to you.

When some time ago you attacked the English,
Neither wisdom nor courage availed.
Then you were like Thaïs,
15   A sinner who, in order to suffer penance,
Was shut in by divine command.
Just so, you have been put in the seclusion
Of Desolation and Painful Resolve,
And the English wreaked their havoc
20   With great pomp, pride, and tyranny.
Now God has changed your suffering to joy,
And has returned Guienne and Normandy to you.

Have not the English often betrayed their kings?
Yes, indeed, as everyone knows,
25   And even now the king of their country
Finds himself in a perilous state.
Every Englishman hastens to speak ill of him.
In their ugly tongue they affirm
How they would willingly do him wrong.
30   Who will be their king is much disputed.
And so, France, what should I tell you?
With his rod God punishes and chastises them,
And has returned Guienne and Normandy to you.

Prince

King of the French, you have gained the advantage!
35   Finish the game like a man valiant and wise.
Now you have got a shot easier to retrieve.
For your good fortune, France, thanks be to God.
Fortune now works in your favor,
And has returned Guienne and Normandy to you.

B77   **Balade**   [p. 126]

On parle de religïon
Qui est d'estroicte gouvernance,
Et par ardent devocïon
Portent mainte dure penance,
5   Mais, ainsi que j'ay congnoissance,
Et selon mon entencïon,
Entre tous j'ay compassïon
Des amoureux de l'observance.*

Tousjours par contemplacïon
10   Tiennent leurs cuers raviz en transe
Pour venir par perfeccïon
Au hault Paradis de Plaisance.
Chault, froit, soif et fain d'esperance
Seuffrent en mainte nacïon.
15   Telle est la conversacïon
Des amoureux de l'observance.

Piez nuz, de Consolacïon
Quierent l'aumosne d'alegeance.
Or ne veulent ne pensïon,
20   Fors de Pitié : povre pitance
En bissacs plains de Souvenance
Pour leur simple provisïon.
N'est ce saincte condicïon
Des amoureux de l'observance?

                L'envoy
25   Des bigotz ne quiers l'acointance,
Ne loue leur oppinïon,
Mais me tiens, par affectïon,
Des amoureux de l'observance!

[78]

B78 **[Ballade] · Obligation de Vaillant***   [p. 127]

Present le notaire d'Amours,
Sans alleguer decepcïon,
En renonçant tous droiz d'Amours,
Coustume, loy, condicïon,
5   De treslealle entencïon
A vous servir sans me douloir,
Passe ceste obligacïon
Soubz le seel de vostre vouloir.

Ballade

One speaks about religious orders
In which the rule is strict
And through ardent devotion
Such people endure much hard penance.
5   But insofar as I have knowledge,
And according to my opinion,
I feel compassion for everyone
Of the order of those who love.

Every day through contemplation
10   They keep their hearts entranced
So they might arrive, perfected,
Into the exalted Heaven of Pleasure.
Heat, cold, thirst, and the hunger for hope
Is what they suffer among many a nation.
15   Such is the way of life
Of the order of those who love.

Their feet bare, they seek out
The alms of consolation.
They wish neither gold nor nourishment,
20   Save from Pity: a poor pittance
In bags full of remembrance
For their plain provisioning.
Isn't it sanctified, the condition
Of the order of those who love?

Envoy

25   I don't seek the company of fanatics,
Nor do I praise their opinions.
But with a warm heart I think myself one
Of the order of those who love!

The engagement agreement of Vaillant

In the presence of the notary of Love,
Without intending any deception,
And renouncing all the rights of Love,
The customs, law, condition
5   With very faithful intention
To serve you [my lady] without complaint,
I affirm this contract
Under the seal of your will.

De cuer, corps, biens, sans nul recours,
10 Vous fais renunciacïon,
Presens, advenir, a tousjours,
Et vous metz en possessïon,
Ne nulle part ne porcïon
N'y aura, et pour mieulx valoir,
15 Le jure en ma dampnacïon
Soubz le seel de vostre vouloir.

Et quant je feray le rebours
Pour recevoir pugnacïon
Me soubzmetz, sans estre ressours
20 A vostre juridicïon,
Et a bon droit et actïon
Pourrez de vostre plain povoir
Me mettre a execucïon
Soubz le seel de vostre vouloir.

L'envoy
25 En l'an de ma grant passïon,
Mettant toutes a Nonchaloir,
Feis ceste presentacïon
Soubz le seel de vostre vouloir.

[79]

B79   [Ballade]

Vidimus de la
dite obligation
par le duc d'Orlians   [p. 128]

A ceulx qui verront ces presentes,
Le bailli d'Amoureux Espoir,
Salut plain de bonnes ententes.
Mandons et faisons assavoir
5 Que le tabellïon Devoir,*
Juré des contraux en amours,*
A veu nouvellement a Tours,
De Vaillant l'obligacïon
Entiere de bien vraye sorte,
10 Dont en fait la relacïon,
Ainsi que ce vidimus porte.

A double queue, par patentes,*
En cire vert, pour dire voir,
S'oblige, soubzmectant ses rentes,

Heart, body, goods, nothing held back,
10   I hereby renounce in your favor,
For the present, future, and evermore,
And give you possession of them,
And no part or portion
Will be excepted, and to make this worth more,
15   I swear to this at the risk of damnation
Under the seal of your will.

And if I do the opposite,
I shall submit myself to
Your punishment, without any support
20   From your jurisdiction,
And, acting as is your perfect right,
You can, using your full power,
Deliver me to execution
Under the seal of your will.

Envoy

25   In the year of my great passion,
Bestowing everything on Indifference,
I made this presentation
Under the seal of your will.

[Ballade]

The confirmation of the aforementioned engagement agreement from the duke of Orleans

To those who will see this present writing,
The bailiff of lovers' Hope,
We send a greeting
Full of good intention, making known
5   That the notary Duty,
Who is the registrar of love contracts,
Has recently in Tours looked over
The engagement agreement of Vaillant,
Complete and very authentic,
10   Of which a certified copy is made,
Just as this vidimus bears witness.

Through letters patent, with their double ribbons,
With a seal of green leather, to tell the truth,
He obliges himself to pay his rents,

15   Cuer, corps et biens, sans decevoir,
       Dessoubz le seeau d'autruy vouloir,
       Pour recouvrer Joyeux Secours,
       Qu'il a desservy par mains jours,
       Faisant ratifficacïon,
20   Ledit notaire le rapporte
       Par sa certifficacïon,
       Ainsi que ce vidimus porte.

       Et deust il mettre tout en ventes
       Des biens qu'il pourra recevoir,
25   Veult paier ses debtes contentes,
       Tant qu'on pourra apparcevoir
       Qu'il fera trop plus que povoir,
       Combien qu'ait eu d'estranges tours
       Qui lui sont venuz a rebours.
30   En soit faicte informacïon,   [p. 129]
       Car a Leaulté se conforte
       Qu'en fera la probacïon,
       Ainsi que ce vidimus porte.

                    L'envoy
       Pour plus abreviacïon,
35   De l'an et jour je me deporte,
       On en voit declairacïon,
       Ainsi que ce vidimus porte.

[80]

B80   **[Ballade]**

                Intendit de la dite
           obligacion par Me J. Caillau*

       Intendit. Le nommé Vaillant
       Qui fait ceste obligacïon,
       Vous resigne tout son vaillant*
       Par simple resignacïon,
5   Ne ne fait supplicacïon
       De guerredon pour mieulx valoir,
       Fors tout a vostre oppinïon,
       Soubz le seeau de vostre vouloir.

       Lequel, d'estoc et de taillant*
10   Endure mainte passïon
       D'Amours, qui le vont assaillant,
       Mais soubz dissimulacïon

15 Heart, body, and goods, and no deception,
Under the seal of another's will
In order to recover Joyful Assistance,
Which he has deserved for many days.
In order to ratify this,
20 The aforesaid notary affirms it
By affixing his certification
Just as this vidimus bears witness.

And even if he must offer everything for sale,
With the goods he is likely to receive
25 He intends paying the debts on the nail,
Inasmuch as it could turn out
That he will do even more than he can,
Though he has been through some strange twists and turns
That have been unkind to him.
30 Let this be made public,
For he takes his comfort with Faithfulness,
Who will offer her approval,
Just as this vidimus bears witness.

Envoy
To make this shorter,
35 I will do without the day and the year.
The declaration of this matter can be seen,
Just as this vidimus bears witness.

Ballade

Intendit of the aforesaid engagement agreement by M. Jean Cailleau

Intendit. The man named Vaillant,
Who drew up this engagement agreement,
Consigns to you all his possessions
Through a simple resignation,
5 Nor does he make application
For some reward to increase his worth,
Save insofar as you might think,
Under the seal of your will.

And this man one way or another
10 Endures much suffering
For Love, who assails him,
And yet with dissimulation

Porte sa tribulacïon,
Faisant semblant de non doloir,
15   Actendant doulce pensïon,
Soubz le seeau de vostre vouloir.

Pource, ne doit estre faillant
A la remuneracïon,   [p. 130]
Car s'il y estoit deffaillant,
20   Ce seroit sa perdicïon,
Et par Dieu si bon champïon
Ne devez mectre a nonchaloir.
Si faictes qu'ait provisïon
Soubz le seel de vostre vouloir.

L'envoy
25   J'en parle par compacïon,
Mais grant bien lui devez vouloir,
Puis que met son entencïon
Soubz le seeau de vostre vouloir.

[81]

B81   Balade   [p. 131]

En la Forest de Longue Actente,
Chevauchant par divers sentiers
M'en voys, ceste annee presente,
Ou voyage de Desiriers.
5   Devant sont allez mes fourriers
Pour appareiller mon logeis
En la cité de Destinee,
Et pour mon cueur et moy ont pris
L'ostellerie de Pensee.

10   Je mayne des chevaulx quarente
Et autant pour mes officiers,
Voire, par Dieu, plus de soixante
Sans les bagaiges et sommiers.
Loger nous fauldra par quartiers,
15   Se les hostelz sont trop petis.
Toutesfoiz, pour une vespree,
En gré prendray, soit mieulx ou pis,
L'ostellerie de Pensee.

Je despens chascun jour ma rente
20   En maintz travaulx avanturiers,
Dont est Fortune mal contente

He bears up under his tribulations,
Giving the impression of not suffering,
15   Awaiting sweet provisioning
Under the seal of your will.

And so, he should not fail to receive
Remuneration,
For were he to fail at this,
20   It would be his undoing,
And, by God, to so good a champion
You should not be indifferent.
So make sure he is provided for
Under the seal of your will.

Envoy

25   Out of compassion I speak of him,
But you should want to do much to his benefit
Since he puts his intentions
Under the seal of your will.

Ballade

In the Forest of Long Waiting,
Riding down several pathways
I went along, this present year,
On a journey of Desire.
5   My harbingers preceded me
To prepare my lodging
In the city of Destiny,
Finding lodging for me and my heart at
The inn of Thought.

10   I'm taking forty horses with me,
And the same for my officers,
Truly, by God, more than sixty,
Not counting the pack and baggage animals.
We'll have to take a soldier's lodging
15   If the inn is too small.
In any case, for one night
I will gratefully accept, for better or worse,
The inn of Thought.

Each day I spend the money I have
20   On many a challenging task,
And upon these Fortune looks with disfavor,

        Qui soutient contre moy Dangiers;
        Mais Espoirs, s'il sont droicturiers
        Et tiennent ce qu'ilz m'ont promis,
25   Je pense faire telle armee
        Qu'auray, malgré mes ennemis,
        L'ostellerie de Pensee.

L'envoy

        Prince, vray Dieu de Paradis,
        Vostre grace me soit donnee,
30   Telle que treuve, a mon devis,
        L'ostellerie de Pensee.

B82   **Balade**   [p. 132]

        Je cuide que ce sont nouvelles,
        J'oy nouveau bruit, et qu'est ce la?
        Helas! pourray je savoir d'elles
        Quelque chose qui me plaira,
5   Car j'ay desiré, long temps a,
        Qu'Espoir m'estraynast de lïesse.
        Je ne sçay pas qu'il en fera,
        Le beau menteur plain de promesse.

        S'il ne sont ou bonnes ou belles,
10   Auffort, mon cueur endurera
        En actendant d'avoir de celles
        Que Bon Eur lui apportera,
        Et de l'endormye beuvra
        De Nonchaloir. En sa destresse
15   Espoir plus ne l'esveillera,
        Le beau menteur plain de promesse.

        Pource mon cuer, se tu me celles
        Reconfort, quant vers toy vendra,
        Tu feras mal, car tes querelles
20   J'ay gardees, or y perra.
        Adviengne qu'avenir pourra!
        Je suis gouverné par Vieillesse,
        Qui de legier n'escoutera
        Le beau menteur plain de promesse.

L'envoy

25   Ma bouche plus n'en parlera,
        Raison sera d'elle maistresse,
        Mais, au derrain, blasmé sera
        Le beau menteur plain de promesse.

Who supports Danger in opposing me.
But Hopes—if they are just
And keep their promises to me—
25   Will constitute such an army
That I'll have, despite my enemies,
The inn of Thought.

Envoy

Prince, true God of paradise,
May your mercy be granted me
30   So I find, as I'd like,
The inn of Thought.

Ballade

I think this is news,
I hear some rumor, and what is it?
Alas! Could I but learn something
Therein to please me,
5   For I've desired a long time
For Hope to bestow happiness on me.
I do not know if he'll do so,
This fine liar, full of promises.

If the news is neither fine nor pleasing,
10   My heart will endure its suffering in the end,
Waiting for some tidings
Happiness will bring,
And the heart will down the sleeping potion
Of Indifference. In its distress
15   Hope will not wake the heart again,
This fine liar, full of promises.

And so, my heart, if you keep Comfort
Hidden when he comes your way,
You do wrong, for I've taken
20   Your part—so it will appear.
Then let happen whatever might!
I'm governed by Old Age,
Who will not readily listen to
This fine liar, full of promises.

Envoy

25   My mouth will speak no more of this.
Reason will be its mistress,
But in the end blame will fall upon
This fine liar, full of promises.

B83   **Balade**   [p. 133]

N'a pas longtemps qu'escoutoye parler
Ung amoureux qui disoit a s'amye :
«De mon estat plaise vous ordonner
Sans me laissier ainsi finer ma vie.
5   Je meurs pour vous, je le vous certiffie.»
Lors respondit la plaisante aux doulx yeulx :
«Assez le croy, dont je vous remercie,
Que m'aymez bien, et vous encores mieulx.

Il ne fault ja vostre pousse taster;
10 Fievre n'avez que de merencolie,
Vostre orine ne aussi regarder.
Tost se garist legiere maladie.
Medecine devez prendre d'oublye,
D'autres ay veu trop pis, en plusieurs lieux,
15 Que vous n'estes, et pource je vous prie
Que m'aymez bien, et vous encores mieulx.

Je ne vueil pas de ce vous destourber
Que ne m'amiez de vostre courtoysie,
Mais que pour moy doyez mort endurer,
20 De le croire ce me seroit folye.
Pensez de vous, et faictes chiere lye.
J'en ay ouÿ parler assez de tieulx
Qui sont tous sains, quoyque point ne desnye
Que m'aimez bien, et vous encores mieulx.

L'envoy
25 Telz beaulx parlers ne sont en compaignie
Qu'esbatemens, entre jeunes et vieulx.
Contente suis, combien que je m'en rye,
Que m'aymez bien et vous encores mieulx.»

B84   **Balade**   [p. 134]

Portant harnoys rouillé de Nonchaloir
Sus monture foulee de Foiblesse,
Mal abillé de Desireus Vouloir,
On m'a croizé aux montres de Lïcsse,*
5   Comme cassé des gaiges de Jeunesse.
Je ne congnois ou je puisse servir.
L'arriereban a fait crier Vieillesse.
Las! fauldra il son soudart devenir?

Ballade

Not long ago I listened to
A man in love say to his beloved:
"Please decide what to do about me,
Without letting my life end this way.
5   I die for you—I tell you this is the truth."
Then she answered, her eyes filled with kindness:
"I believe this is the truth and give thanks
That you love me well, and yourself even more.

"No need to take your pulse
10   (You have no fever save melancholy)
Nor to examine your urine.
Those barely ill quickly improve.
You must take the medicine of forgetfulness,
I have a worse view of others elsewhere
15   Than I have you, and so I beg you
That you love me well, and yourself even more.

"I don't intend to prevent you
From loving me in your courtly fashion,
But I'd be a fool to believe
20   You're bound to die because of me.
Think of yourself and be of good cheer.
Often enough I've heard tell of such men
Who've been healed, though I don't deny at all
That you love me well, and yourself even more.

Envoy

25   "Such fine words are meant only to entertain
Companies of the young and old.
I'm satisfied, even though I might make fun,
That you love me well, and yourself even more."

Ballade

Since my mailshirt's rusty with Indifference,
And I ride a horse feverish with weakness,
Since I can hardly think about willful desire,
I was dismissed from Joy's troops on parade
5   As a man whom Youth had scent packing.
I don't understand where I might serve.
Old Age has summoned her army:
Alas, am I to become her soldier?

Le bien que puis avecques elle avoir
10   N'est que d'un peu d'atrempee sagesse.
En lieu de ce me fauldra recevoir
Ennuy, Soussy, Desplaisir et Destresse.
Par Dieu! Bon Temps, mal me tenez promesse!
Vous me deviez contre elle soustenir,
15   Et je voy bien qu'elle sera maistresse.
Las! fauldra il son soudart devenir?

Foibles jambes porteront Bon Vouloir,
Puis qu'ainsi est endurant en humblesse,
Prenant confort d'un bien joyeux espoir,
20   Quant, Dieu mercy, Maladie ne presse,
Mais loing se tient, et mon corps point ne blesse,
C'est ung tresor que doy bien chier tenir,
Veu que la fin de menasser ne cesse.
Las! fauldra il son soudart devenir?

L'envoy

25   Prince, je dy que c'est peu de richesse
De ce monde ne de tout son plaisir.
La mort depart ce qu'on tient a largesse.
Las! fauldra il son soudart devenir?

B85   **Balade**   [p. 135]

Dieu veuille sauver ma galee
Qu'ay chargee de marchandise
De mainte diverse pensee
En pris de Loyaulté assise.*
5   Destourbee ne soit, ne prise
Des robeurs escumeurs de mer.
Vent ne maree ne lui nuyse,
A bien aler et retourner.

A Confort l'ay recommandee
10   Qu'il en face tout a sa guise,
Et pencarte lui ay baillee*
Qui estranges pays devise,
Affin que dedens il advise
A quel port pourra arriver,
15   Et le chemin a chois eslise,
A bien aler et retourner.

Pour acquitter joye empruntee
L'envoye, sans espargner mise.
Riche deviendray quelque annee,

The good I can obtain from her
10   Is nothing save a bit of temperate wisdom.
       And, as part of this exchange, I must accept
       Worry, Care, Misery, and Distress.
       By God, Good Times, your promise is ill kept!
       You were to further me against her,
15   And I see well she'll be mistress:
       Alas, am I to become her soldier?

       Feeble legs support Good Will
       Since he endures in humility,
       Taking comfort from a joyous hope
20   When, thank God, Illness does not overtax him.
       But he keeps his distance, doing my body no harm.
       This treasure I should hold very dear,
       Seeing how life's end never stops threatening.
       Alas, am I to become her soldier?

Envoy

25   Prince, I say there are few riches
       In the world or all its pleasures.
       Death disposes of our abundant goods.
       Alas, am I to become her soldier?

Ballade

       God please safeguard our galley
       That I've loaded up with the merchandise
       Of many a strange thought
       Chosen for its Loyalty value.
5   May it not be attacked or captured
       By pirates who scour the seas.
       May wind and tide do it no harm
       While voyaging fair and then returning.

       I've commended the galley to Comfort
10   So he will do everything in his power,
       And I've furnished him with a map
       That images strange lands,
       So he might spy on that map
       What port it could make,
15   And thus set a true course
       While voyaging fair and then returning.

       To requite the joy I've borrowed,
       I dispatch the galley, sparing no expense.
       Some year I'll be rich

20   Se mon entente n'est surprise.
        Conscience n'auray reprise
        De gaing a tort. Au paraler,
        En eur viengne mon entreprise,
        A bien aler et retourner.

                    L'envoy
25   Prince, se maulx Fortune atise,
        Sagement s'i fault gouverner.
        Le droit chemin jamais ne brise,
        A bien aler et retourner.

B86   **Balade de Jacques,**   [p. 136]
            bastart de la Tremoille*

        Pour la conqueste de Mercy
        Ou les vaillans hommes et sages
        Ont esté pris et mors aussy
        En acquerant leurs avantages,
5   Amours, accroissant les courages
        Des mieulx venuz, lectre patente
        A tous a donné leurs usages,
        En la Forest de Longue Actente.

        Les piteux s'arment de Soussy,
10   Les francs se mectent en servages,
        Maigres de corps, le cuer noircy
        De dueil et pales les visages,
        A tant pour services et gages
        Auront iiic maulx jours de rente
15   Par an avec les arrerages,
        En la Forest de Longue Actente.

        Ceulx qui Amours servent ainsy,
        En lui faisant foys et homages,
        Il les fait aprés eureux sy
20   Qu'ilz s'eschappent des brigandages
        De Dangiers par petiz boucages,
        Puis les duit en la droicte sente,
        Mais premier paient leurs truages
        En la Forest de Longue Actente.

                    L'envoy
25   Prince, pour duire cuers volages,
        Affin que nul ne s'en exempte,
        Mectez les tous en hermitages
        En la Forest de Longue Actente.

20 If my plans do not go awry.
  I'll not feel any guilt
  For taking improper gain. In the end,
  May my enterprise find good fortune
  While voyaging fair and then returning.

Envoy

25 Prince, if Fortune stirs up trouble,
  A man must rule himself wisely:
  May the right course never take a wrong turn
  While voyaging fair and then returning.

Ballade by Jacques,
the bastard of La Tremoille

  For the sake of the conquest of Mercy,
  In which men wise and valiant
  Have been captured and killed as well
  In order to obtain what might advantage them,
5 Love, giving braver heart
  To the best comers, has granted a letter patent
  To these men for their use
  In the Forest of Long Waiting.

  Compassionate people arm themselves with Care.
10 The generous put themselves in service,
  Their bodies wasted, their hearts black
  From pain, faces gone pale,
  Inasmuch as for their services and wages
  They'll have three hundred unpleasant days paid
15 Every year, along with other required labors
  In the Forest of Long Waiting.

  Those who serve Love in this fashion,
  Rendering him faith and homage,
  He makes afterward so fortunate
20 They escape the brigandage
  Of Danger hiding in the woods,
  Then Love shows them the right path,
  But first they pay their dues
  In the Forest of Long Waiting.

Envoy

25 Prince, in order to direct flighty hearts,
  So that none makes excuses,
  Set them all up in hermitages
  In the Forest of Long Waiting.

B87   **Balade**   [p. 137]

Ha! Dieu d'Amours, ou m'avez vous logié?
Tout droit ou trait de Desir et Plaisance,
Ou, de legier, je puis estre blecié
Par Doulz Regart et Plaisant Atraiance,
5   Jusqu'a la mort, dont trop suis en doubtance.
Pour moy couvrir prestez moy ung pavaiz.
Desarmé suis, car pieça mon harnaiz
Je le vendy par le conseil d'Oiseuse,
Comme lassé de la guerre amoureuse.

10   Vous savez bien que me suis esloingné,
Des long temps a, d'amoureuse vaillance,
Ou j'estoye moult fort embesoingné
Quant m'aviez en vostre gouvernance.
Or en suis hors. Dieu me doint la puissance
15   De me garder que n'y rentre jamais,
Car, quant congneu j'ay les amoureux faiz,
Retrait me suis de vie si peneuse,
Comme lassé de la guerre amoureuse.

Et non pourtant, j'ay esté advisé
20   Que Bel Acueil a fait grant aliance
Encontre moy, et qu'il est embuschié
Pour me prendre, s'il peut, par decevance.
Ung de ses gens, appelé Acointance,
M'assault tousjours, mais souvent je me taiz,
25   Monstrant semblant que je ne quier que paiz,
Sans me bouter en paine dangereuse,
Comme lassé de la guerre amoureuse.

L'envoy
Voisent faire jeunes gens leurs essaiz,
Car reposer je me vueil desormaiz.
30   Plus cure n'ay de pensee soingneuse,
Comme lassé de la guerre amoureuse.

B88   **Balade**   [p. 138]

Yeulx rougis, plains de piteux pleurs,
Fourcelle d'espoir reffroidie,
Teste enrumee de douleurs
Et troublee de frenesie,
5   Corps percus sans plaisance lie,*
Cueur du tout pausmé en rigueurs,

Ballade

Aha! God of Love, where have you lodged me?
Right in range of Desire and Pleasure,
Where Sweet Regard and Pleasant Attraction
Can easily wound me
5   To the point of death, which I greatly fear.
Lend me a shield so I can guard myself.
Unarmed now, not long ago I gave away
My harness on the advice of Idleness,
As one wearied by the lovers' war.

10   You know well I have kept myself
For a long time from lovers' worthy deeds,
With which I was so involved
While you held sway over me.
Now I am beyond that. God give me the strength
15   To refrain henceforth from such business,
For, coming to know the doings of lovers,
I have rejected a life so full of pain,
As one wearied by the lovers' war.

And yet I have been advised that
20   Fair Welcome has formed a grand alliance
Against me, laying an ambush
To take me prisoner, if he can, with some trick.
One of his own people, Acquaintance by name,
Assaults me daily, but often I hold my tongue,
25   Appearing to seek only peace,
Without exposing myself to dangerous suffering,
As one wearied by the lovers' war.

Envoy

Let young people go try their luck,
For henceforth I intend to rest.
30   No longer do worrisome thoughts concern me,
As one wearied by the lovers' war.

Ballade

Red eyes running with pitiful tears,
A breast where hope's grown cold,
A head painfully sick
And troubled by delirium,
5   A body paralyzed, no joy that pleases,
A heart weakened and numb,

Voy souvent avoir a plusieurs
Par le vent de Merencolie.

Migraine de plaingnans ardeurs,
10   Transe de sommeil mipartie,
Fievres frissonnans de maleurs,
Chault ardant fort en reverie,
Soif que Confort ne rassasie,
Dueil baigné en froides sueurs,
15   Begayant et changeant couleurs,
Par le vent de Merencolie.

Goute tourmentant en langueurs,
Colique de forcenerie,
Gravelle de soings assailleurs,
20   Rage de desirant folie,
Anuys enflans d'ydropisie,
Maulx ethiques, aussi ailleurs,
Assourdissent les escouteurs,
Par le vent de Merencolie.

L'envoy

25   Guerir ne se puet maladie
Par phisique ne cireurgie,
Astronomians n'enchanteurs,
Des maulx que seuffrent povres cueurs
Par le vent de Merencolie.

B89   **Balade**   [p. 139]

Ce que l'ueil despend en plaisir,
Le cuer l'achete chierement,
Et quant vient a compte tenir,
Raison, president sagement,
5   Demande pourquoy et comment
Est despendue la richesse
Dont Amours deppart largement,
Sans grant espargne de lïesse.

Lors respond Amoureux Desir :
10   «Amours me fist commandement
De Joyeuse Vie servir
Et obeir entierement,
Et, s'ay failly aucunement,
On n'en doit blasmer que Jeunesse
15   Qui m'a fait ouvrer sotement,
Sans grant espargne de lïesse.»

This is what I often see many suffer
Through the wind of Melancholy.

A burning, aching head that weeps,
10   A trance half mixed with sleep,
A fever shaking with unhappiness,
A burning heat dominated by reverie,
A thirst there's no satisfying,
A pain bathed in cold sweat,
15   Stuttering and changing color
Through the wind of Melancholy.

Gout that pains and torments,
Colic of furious madness,
Sickness that painfully assaults,
20   Rage of mad desire,
Swelling pains of dropsy,
And also a fever that withers,
Deafening those who listen
Through the wind of Melancholy.

Envoy

25   This malady cannot be healed
By treatment or surgery,
By astrologers or magicians,
Of the ills that unfortunate hearts suffer
Through the wind of Melancholy.

Ballade

What the eye spends in pleasure
The heart pays dearly for,
And when accounts must be rendered,
Reason, wisely presiding,
5   Asks why and how
Were spent the riches
Love distributes generously
Without much sparing of happiness.

Then Amorous Desire answers:
10   "Love issued me this command,
To serve Joyous Life
And obey her completely,
And, if I have failed in anything,
Youth alone should be blamed,
15   Who has made me act foolishly,
Without much sparing of happiness."

Pas ne mouray sans repentir,
Car je m'en repens grandement.
Trouvé m'y suis pis que martir,
20   Souffrant maint douloureux tourment.
Desormais en gouvernement
Me metz, et es mains de Vieillesse
Bien sçay qu'y vivray soubrement,
Sans grant espargne de lïesse.

L'envoy
25   Le temps passe comme le vent,
Il n'est si beau jeu qui ne cesse,
En tout fault avoir finement,
Sans grant espargne de lïesse.

B90   **Balade**   [p. 140]

Je qui suis Fortune nommee
Demande la raison pourquoy
On me donne la renommee
Qu'on ne se puet fïer en moy
5   Et n'ay ne fermeté ne foy,
Car, quant aucuns en mes mains prens,
D'en bas je les monte en haultesse,
Et d'en hault en bas les descens,
Monstrant que suis dame et maistresse.

10   En ce je suis a tort blasmee,
Tenant l'usage de ma loy
Que de long temps m'a ordonnee
Dieu, sur tous le souverain Roy,
Pour donner au monde chastoy,
15   Et se de mes biens je despens
Souventesfoiz a grant largesse,
Quant bon me semble les suspens,
Monstrant que suis dame et maistresse.

C'est ma maniere acoustumee,
20   Chascun le scet, comme je croy,
Et n'est pas nouvelle trouvee,
Mais fays ainsi comme je doy.
Me mocquant, je les monstre au doy
Tous ceulx qui en sont malcontens.
25   En gré prengnent joye ou destresse
Qu'ayent l'un des deux me conscens,
Monstrant que suis dame et maistresse.

I'll not die without repenting,
For I very much do repent,
And this makes me suffer worse than death itself,
20   As I endure many a painful torment.
Henceforth I put myself in the hands
And under the rule of Old Age.
I shall live there soberly, this I know,
Without much sparing of happiness.

Envoy

25   Time passes like the wind,
There's no sport so fine it has no end,
All things must have their conclusion,
Without much sparing of happiness.

Ballade

I whose name is Fortune
Demand to know why
I've got the reputation
That no one should put his trust in me,
5   And that I lack stability or faithfulness,
For, seizing someone in my grasp,
From below I raise him to the heights,
And from there on high I bring him low,
Showing I am lady and mistress.

10   For this I'm wrongly blamed,
Keeping to the customs of my law,
Just as for long ages God has
Commanded me, King and Sovereign over all,
So the world might be duly chastised,
15   And if I often bestow my goods
With great generosity,
I withhold them when I think it just,
Showing I am lady and mistress.

It is my wont to act this way,
20   As everyone knows, I believe,
And this is not thought something new,
But rather what I should be doing.
Mockingly, I point my finger
At everyone who feels displeased.
25   Let them good-heartedly accept joy or distress
For they'll have one or the other — this I agree to,
Showing I am lady and mistress.

L'envoy

Sur ce, s'advise qui a sens,
Soit en jeunesse ou en vieillesse,
30   Et qui ne m'entent, je m'entens,
Monstrant que suis dame et maistresse.

B91   **Balade**   [p. 141]

Fortune, je vous oy complaindre
Qu'on vous donne renom a tort
De savoir et aider et faindre,
Donnant plaisir et desconfort.
5   C'est vray, et encore plus fort
Souventesfoiz contre raison,
Boutez de hault plusieurs en bas,
Et de bas en hault. Telz debas
Vous usez en vostre maison.

10   Bien savez de Plaisance paindre
Et d'Espoir, quand prenez depport,
Aprés effacer et destaindre
Toute joye sans nul support,
Et mener a douloureux port,
15   Ne vous chault en quelle saison.
Jamais vous n'ouvrez par compas.
Beaucoup pis que je ne dy pas
Vous usez en vostre maison.

Pour Dieu, vueillez vous en reffraindre
20   Affin qu'on ne face rapport,
Qui vouldra vostre fait actaindre,
Que vous soyez digne de mort.
Vostre maniere chascun mort,
Plus qu'autre sans comparaison,
25   Qui regarde par tous estas.
Anuy et meschief a grans tas
Vous usez en vostre maison.

L'envoy

Ne jouez plus de vostre sort,
Car trop le passez oultre bort.
30   Se gens ne laissez en pais, on
Appellera les advocas
Qui plaideront que tresfaulx cas
Vous usez en vostre maison.

Envoy

The sensible man takes this into account,
Whether young or old.
30 And if he misunderstands, I understand myself,
Showing I am lady and mistress.

Ballade

Fortune, I hear you complaining
How you've been wrongly reputed
To possess the power both to help and to deceive,
To bestow pleasure and distress.
5 This is the truth. And, even worse,
Oftentimes against reason
You shove many from high to low,
And from low to high. These are the games
You play at in your house.

10 You know well how to paint with the colors
Of Pleasure and Hope, when amused,
After rubbing out and discoloring
All joy beyond any remedy,
And leading folks to the port of pain
15 In seasons of which you take no account.
Never do you follow any rule.
Even worse games than I report
You play at in your house.

For God's sake, please abstain,
20 So no report can be made
Accusing you of misdeeds
So you'd be judged worthy of death.
Your actions harm those
Of all estates, as is evident,
25 More than do others, beyond all comparison.
Pain and misfortune aplenty are what
You play at in your house.

Envoy

Toy no more with your destiny,
For you exceed your boundaries.
30 If you don't leave people in peace,
Lawyers will be summoned,
To plead against the practices so very false
You play at in your house.

B92 [Ballade] [p. 142]

Or ça, puisque il fault que responde,
Moy, Fortune, je parleray.
Sy grant n'est, ne puissant ou monde,
A qui bien parler n'oseray.
5   J'ay fait, faiz encore, et feray
Ainsi que bon me semblera
De ceulx qui sont soubz ma puissance.
Parle qui parler en vouldra,
Je n'en feray qu'a ma plaisance.

10   Quant les biens qui sont en la ronde
Sont miens, et je les donneray
Par grant largesse, dont j'abonde,
Et aprés je les reprandray.
Certes, a nul tort ne feray.
15   Qui esse qui m'en blamera?
Je l'ay ainsi d'acoustumance.
En gré le preigne qui poura,
Je n'en feray qu'a ma plaisance.

En raison jamais ne me fonde,
20   Mais mon vouloir acompliray.
Les aucuns convient que confonde,
Et les autres avanceray.
Mon propos souvent changeray
En plusieurs lieux, puis ça, puis la,
25   Sans regle ne sans ordonnance.
Ou est il qui m'en gardera?
Je n'en feray qu'a ma plaisance.

L'envoy

On escript : «Tant qu'il nous plaira»,
Es lettres des seigneurs de France.
30   Pareillement de moy sera :
Je n'en feray qu'a ma plaisance.

B93 [Ballade fragment] [p. 143]

Fortune, vray est vostre comte
Que, quant voz biens donné avez,
Vous les reprenés, mais c'est honte
Et don d'enfant, bien le savez.
Ainsi faire ne le devez.
5   Voz faiz vous mectez a l'enchiere,
Chascun ce qu'il en peut en a

Ballade

So be it, since I must answer,
I, Fortune, will indeed speak.
There's no man so high or mighty
To whom I dare not speak directly.
5   I have done, do still, and will do
Just as I think right
With those under my power.
Let that man speak who would.
I will do only as I please.

10   Since the goods around me
Are my own, I'll give them away
Through the great generosity that's abundantly mine,
And afterward I'll reclaim them.
Surely, I'll wrong no one.
15   Who can blame me for so doing?
I've acted according to custom.
Let whoever can, accept this with good grace.
I will do only as I please.

I'm never concerned about Reason,
20   But instead act according to my desire.
I needs must bring some to ruin
While advancing the cause of others.
Often my purpose changes,
One place or another, now here, now there,
25   There's no rule or order to it.
Where is the man to prevent me?
I will do only as I please.

Envoy
"As long as it pleases us" is written
In the letters of the great lords of France.
30   It will be the same with me.
I will do only as I please.

Ballade fragment

Fortune, what you say is true:
After bestowing your gifts,
You take them back. But that's shameful,
A gift worthy only of a child, as well you know.
You should not act this way.
5   You put your goods up for auction.
Everyone has of them what he can get,

Et ne vous chault comment tout va.
Pour Dieu, changez vostre maniere!

[Unfinished. The rest of the page is blank]

B94   **Balade***   [p. 144]

Escollier de Merencolie,*
A l'estude je suis venu,
Lettres de mondaine clergie
Espelant a tout ung festu,
5   Et moult fort m'y treuve esperdu.
Lire n'escripre ne sçay mye,
Dez verges de Soussy batu,
Es derreniers jours de ma vie.

Pieça, en jeunesse fleurie,
10   Quant de vif entendement fu,
J'eusse apris en heure et demye
Plus qu'a present. Tant ay vesqu
Que d'engin je me sens vaincu.
On me deust bien, sans flaterie,
15   Chastïer, despoillié tout nu,
Es derreniers jours de ma vie.

Que voulez vous que je vous die?
Je suis pour ung asnyer tenu,
Banny de Bonne Compaignie,
20   Et de Nonchaloir retenu
Pour le servir. Il est conclu!
Qui vouldra, pour moy estudie.
Trop tart je m'y suis entendu
Es derreniers jours de ma vie.

L'envoy
25   Se j'ay mon temps mal despendu,
Fait l'ay par conseil de Follye.
Je m'en sens et m'en suis sentu,
Es derreniers jours de ma vie.

B95   **Balade**   [p. 145]

L'autre jour tenoit son conseil,
En la chambre de ma pensee,
Mon cueur qui faisoit appareil
De deffence contre l'armee

And the result does not concern you.
For God's sake, change your ways!

Ballade

Scholar of Melancholy,
I've come to school,
Using a straw to help me spell out
The letters of worldly works,
5   And I find myself completely lost.
I cannot read or write at all,
Beaten by the rods of Care
In the final days of my life.

In times past, in the bloom of youth,
10   When my mind was sharp,
I would have learned more in an hour
And a half than I do now. I've lived so long
I find my wit overcome.
And, it's no joke, I should certainly
15   Be punished, stripped of my clothes,
In the final days of my life.

What do you want me to tell you?
I'm taken for an ass,
Banished from Good Company
20   And retained by Indifference
To serve him. That's the end of the matter!
Whoever wishes, let him study in my place.
I've taken this up too late
In the final days of my life.

Envoy

25   If I've wasted my time,
Folly advised me to do so.
I resent it, and have resented it
In the final days of my life.

Ballade

The other day my heart
Held council in the chamber
Of my thought, for he was preparing
His defenses against the army

5   De Fortune mal advisee,
        Qui guerryer vouloit Espoir,
        Se sagement n'est reboutee,
        Par Bon Eur et Loyal Vouloir.

        Il n'est chose soubz le souleil
10   Qui tant doit estre desiree
        Que Paix. C'est le don non pareil
        Dont Grace fait tousjours livree
        A sa gent qu'a recommandee.
        Fol est qui ne la veult avoir,
15   Quant elle est offerte et donnee
        Par Bon Eur et Loyal Vouloir.

        Pour Dieu, laissons dormir Traveil.
        Ce monde n'a gueres duree,
        Et Paine, tant qu'elle a sommeil,
20   Souffrons que prengne reposee.
        Qui une foiz l'a esprouvee
        La doit fuÿr de son povoir.
        Par tout doit estre deboutee
        Par Bon Eur et Loyal Vouloir.

                        L'envoy
25   Dieu nous doint bonne destinee
        Et chascun face son devoir.
        Ainsi ne sera redoubtee
        Par Bon Eur et Loyal Vouloir.

B96   **Balade**   [p. 146]

        En la chambre de ma pensee,
        Quant j'ay visité mes tresors,
        Mainteffoys la treuve estoffee
        Richement de plaisans confors.
5   A mon cueur je conseille lors
        Qu'i prenons nostre demouree,
        Et que par nous soit bien gardee
        Contre tous ennuyeux rappors,

        Car Desplaisance maleuree
10   Essaye souvent ses effors
        Pour la conquester par emblee
        Et nous bouter tous deux dehors.
        Se Dieu plaist, assez sommes fors
        Pour bien tost rompre son armee,

5   Of Fortune, full of evil intentions,
        Who intended to make war on Hope,
        That is, if not wisely repulsed
        By Happiness and Faithful Will.

        There's nothing under the sun
10   That should be desired as much
        As peace. It's the gift beyond compare
        Grace always presents as a livery
        To the people she's taken up.
        Only a fool would not desire it
15   When offered and bestowed
        By Happiness and Faithful Will.

        For God's sake, let Misery slumber.
        This world won't last much longer.
        And as long as Suffering sleeps on,
20   Let her take some rest.
        Whoever experiences Suffering
        Should flee with all his strength.
        She's to be repulsed everywhere
        By Happiness and Faithful Will.

Envoy
25   God grant us a fair destiny,
        And may every man do his duty.
        Then Suffering will never be feared
        By Happiness and Faithful Will.

Ballade

        In the chamber of my thought,
        After I have visited my treasure,
        I find it many times provisioned
        Richly with pleasant comfort.
5   Then I counsel my heart
        That we take up lodging there
        To offer the heart good protection
        Against all worrisome reports,

        For miserable Displeasure
10   Often essays its strength
        To conquer with tricks
        And force us both out.
        Please God, we're strong enough
        To destroy Displeasure's army utterly

15   Se d'Espoir banyere est portee
        Contre tous ennuyeux rappors.

        L'inventoire j'ay regardee
        De noz meubles en biens et corps.
        De legier ne sera gastee,
20   Et si ne ferons a nulz tors.
        Mieulx aymerïons estre mors,
        Mon cueur et moy, que courrocee
        Fust Raison sage et redoubtee,
        Contre tous ennuyeux rappors.

                    L'envoy
25   Demourons tous en bons accors
        Pour parvenir a joyeux pors.
        Ou monde, qui a peu duree,
        Soustenons Paix, la bien amee,
        Contre tous ennuyeux rappors.

B97   **[Ballade]**   [p. 147]

        Je n'ay plus soif, tairie est la fontaine;
        Bien eschauffé, sans le feu amoureux,
        Je voy bien cler, ja ne fault c'on me maine.
        Folie et Sens me gouvernent tous deux,
5   En Nonchaloir resveille sommeilleux.
        C'est de mon fait une chose meslee,
        Ne bien ne mal, d'aventure menee.

        Je gaingne et pers, m'escontant par sepmaine;
        Ris, Jeux, Deduiz, je ne tiens conte d'eulx.
10   Espoir et Dueil me mettent hors d'alaine;
        Eur, me flatent, si m'est trop rigoreux.
        Dont vient cela que je riz et me deulz?
        Esse par sens ou folie esprouvee?
        Ne bien ne mal, d'aventure menee.

15   Guerdonné suis de malleureuse estraine;
        En combatant, je me rens couraigeux;
        Joye et Soussy m'ont mis en leur demaine.
        Tout desconfit, me tiens au ranc des preux.
        Qui me saroit desnouer tous ses neux?
20   Teste d'assier y fauldroit, fort armee,
        Ne bien ne mal, d'aventure menee.

15   If the banner of Hope is carried forward
         Against all worrisome reports.

         I've looked over the inventory
         Of our movable goods and personnel.
         The chamber will not easily be pillaged,
20   And yet we'll do no one wrong.
         We'd prefer death itself,
         My heart and me, to Reason,
         Wise and respectable, being angered,
         Against all worrisome reports.

Envoy

25   Let's all remain on good terms
         In order to reach a joyful destination.
         In a world not long to last
         Let us uphold Peace, well loved,
         Against all worrisome reports.

Ballade

         I've no more thirst, dry is the fountain;
         Well-warmed, lacking the fire of love,
         I see clearly, no need for a guide.
         Folly and Good Sense both rule me.
5   In Indifference I awake, still full of sleep.
         My affairs are a tangle of contraries,
         Neither good nor bad, directed by chance.

         I gain and lose, sinking into debt as weeks pass.
         Laughter, Games, Delights—of these I take no account.
10   Hope and Suffering keep me out of breath.
         Happiness, taking my part, is too hard on me.
         Why do I laugh and lament?
         Is it from good sense or folly?
         Neither good nor bad, directed by chance.

15   My rewards are unfortunate gifts.
         Still fighting, I surrender, full of courage.
         Joy and Care have dominion over me.
         Utterly defeated, I think I'm one of the worthy.
         Who could untie all these knots for me?
20   What's needed is a head of steel, fully armed,
         Neither good nor bad, directed by chance.

Prince

Veillesse fait me jouer a telz jeux,
Perdre et gaingner, et tout par ses conseulx.
A la faille j'ay joué ceste annee,*
25   Ne bien ne mal, d'aventure menee.

B98   Balade · Orlians   [p. 148]

Pourquoy m'as tu vendu, Jennesse,
A grant marchié, comme pour rien,
Es mains de ma Dame Viellesse,
Qui ne me fait gueres de bien?
5   A elle peu tenu me tien,
Mais il convient que je l'endure,
Puis que c'est le cours de nature.

Son hostel de noir de Tristesse
Est tandu. Quant dedans je vien,
10   G'y voy l'istoire de Destresse,
Qui me fait changer mon maintien
Quant la ly, et maint mal soustien.
Espargnee n'est creature,
Puis que c'est le cours de nature.

15   Prenant en gré ceste rudesse,
Le mal d'aultruy conpare au myen.
Lors me tance Dame Sagesse,
Adoncques en moy je revien
Et croy de tout le conseil sien,
20   Qui est en ce plain de droiture,
Puis que c'est le cours de nature.

Prince

Dire ne saroye conbien
Dedans mon cueur mal je retien.
Serré d'une vielle sainture,
25   Puis que c'est le cours de nature.

B99   Balade · Orleans   [p. 149]

Mon cueur vous adjourne, Viellesse,
Par Droit, huissier de parlement,
Devant Raison qui est maistresse
Et juge de vray jugement.
5   Depuis que le gouvernement
Avez eu de luy et de moy,

Prince

Old age makes me play at such games,
Winning and losing, and by everything it counsels.
I've played the whole year through, but to no avail,
25   Neither good nor bad, directed by chance.

Ballade — Orleans

Why have you sold me, Youth,
At such a cheap price, in fact for nothing,
Into the hands of my lady Old Age,
Who provides me with scarcely a benefit?
5   I hardly think myself obligated,
Yet must endure her,
Since this is the course of nature.

Her mansion is all decorated in the black
Of Sadness. Entering, I see depicted
10   The history of Distress,
Which, as I read, makes me change
My way of life, enduring much suffering.
No creature at all is spared
Since this is the course of nature.

15   Cheerfully accepting this cruelty,
I compare others' pain to my own.
Lady Wisdom reproaches me.
Then I am myself again,
Trusting completely in her counsel,
20   Full of righteousness in the matter,
Since this is the course of nature.

Prince

I cannot say how much misery
I keep stored within my heart,
Bound with some old belt,
25   Since this is the course of nature.

Ballade — Orleans

My heart summons you, Old Age,
By Right, bailiff of the high court,
Before Reason, who is the mistress
And judge of true judgment.
5   Since it's you who hold sway
Over him and me as well,

Vous nous avez, par tirennye,
Mis es mains de Merencolie
Sans savoir la cause pourquoy.

10   Par avant nous tenoit Jennesse
Et nourrissoit si tendrement
En plaisir, confort et lïesse,
Et tout joyeulx esbastement.
Or faictez vous tout autrement.
15   Se vous est honte, sur ma foy,
Car en douleur et maladie
Nous faictez user nostre vie,
Sans savoir la cause pourquoy.

De quoy vous sert ceste destresse
20   A donner sans aleigement?
Cuidés vous pour telle rudesse
Avoir honneur aucunement?
Nennil, certez, car vrayement
Chascun vous moustrera au doy,
25   Disant : «La vielle rassoutie
Tient tous maulx en sa compaignie,
Sans savoir la cause pourquoy.»

Prince   [p. 150]
Ce saint Martin, presentement
Qu'avocas font commencement
30   De plaidier les faiz de la loy,
Prenez bon conseil, je vous prie.
Ne faictez desbat ne partie
Sans savoir la cause pourquoy.

B100   [Ballade] [Meschinot]*

Plus ne voy riens qui recomfort me donne,   [p. 151]
Plus dure ung jour que ne me souloit cent,
Plus n'est saeson qu'a nul bien m'abandonne,
Plus voy plaisir et mains mon cueur s'en scent,
5   Plus qu'oncques mais mon vouloir bas descent,
Plus me souvient de vous et plus m'enpire,
Plus quier esbas c'est lors que plus soupire,
Plus fait beau temps et plus me vient d'ennuys,
Plus ne m'atens fors tousjours d'avoir pire,
10   Puys que de vous approcher je ne puys.

Plus suis dolant que nul autre personne,
Plus n'ay espoir d'aucun alegement,

You have in your tyranny put us
Into the hands of Melancholy,
Without knowing why.

10   Formerly Youth had charge of us,
Giving us such tender care,
In pleasure, comfort, and happiness,
And in diversions full of joy.
Now you do just the opposite.
15   And it's to your shame, by my faith,
For in suffering and illness
You make us spend our lives,
Without knowing why.

How do you profit from giving us
20   This distress with no relief?
Do you think with such cruelty
To obtain some kind of honor?
Not at all, to be sure, for truly
Everyone will point their finger at you,
25   Saying: "The old fool's a companion
To suffering of every kind
Without knowing why."

Prince
Now on this St. Martin's day
The lawyers began
30   Pleading the facts of the law.
Take good counsel, I beg you.
Begin no quarrel or trial
Without knowing why.

Ballade

No more do I see anything that gives me comfort,
More does one day now last than a hundred once did,
No more is it a time when I abandon myself to any good,
The more pleasure I see, the less my heart feels it,
5   More than ever before my desire wanes,
The more I remember you, the worse it gets,
The more I seek diversion, the more I sigh,
The more lovely the weather, the more boredom comes to me,
The greater my experience, the worse things get
10   Ever since I have not been able to be by your side.

More sorrowful I am than any other person,
No more do I hope for any relief,

        Plus ay desir crainte d'autre part sonne,
        Plus vueill aller vers vous mains scey comment,
15   Plus suis espris et plus ay de tourment,
        Plus pleure et plains et plus pleurer desire,
        Plus chose n'est qui me saroyt suffire,
        Plus n'ay repos je hey les jours et nuys,
        Plus que jamés a douleur me fault duyre,
20   Puys que de vous approcher je ne puys.

        Plus vivre ainssi ne m'est pas chose bonne,
        Plus vueill mourir et raison s'y assent,
        Plus qu'a nully Amours de maulx m'ordonne,
        Plus n'a ma voix bon acort ne assent.
25   Plus fait on jeus mielx desire estre absent,
        Plus force n'ay d'endurer tel martire,
        Plus n'est vivant homme qui tel mal tire,
        Plus ne cognoes bonnement ou je suis,
        Plus ne scey brieff que pencer faire ou dire,   [p. 152]
30   Puys que de vous approcher je ne puys.

L'envoy

        Plus n'ay mestier de jouir ne de rire,
        Plus n'est le temps si non de tout despire,
        Plus cuide avoir de Douceur les apuys
        Plus suis adonc desplaisant et plain de ire,
35   Puis que de vous approcher je ne puis.

B101   Orleans · Balade

        Chascun s'ébat au myeulx mentir,
        Et voulentiers je l'aprendroye,
        Mais maint mal j'en voy advenir,
        Parquoy savoir ne le vouldroye.
5   De mantir par deduit ou joye
        Ou par passe temps ou plaisir,
        Ce n'est point mal fait, sans faillir,
        Se faulceté ne s'y employe.

        Faulx menteurs puisse l'en couvrir,
10   Sur les montaignes de Savoye, *
        De naige, tant que revenir
        Ne puissent par chemin ne voye,
        Jucques querir je les renvoye.
        Pour Dieu, laissez les la dormir :
15   Ilz ne scevent de riens servir
        Se faulceté ne s'i employe.

The more desire I feel, the more fear reveals itself,
The more I want to go to you, the less I know how,
15   The more inflamed with love, the more torment I feel,
The more I cry and weep, the more I want to weep,
The more there is nothing, the more can it satisfy me,
The more rest I miss, the more I hate days and nights,
More than ever must I take instruction from pain,
20   Ever since I have not been able to be by your side.

The more I live this way, the more I find nothing good,
More I wish to die and reason is in agreement,
More than to anyone else Love ordains evil for me,
The more my voice finds neither agreement nor assent,
25   The more games are played, the more I wish to be absent,
No more strength have I to endure such misery,
The more there's no living man who feels such ills,
The more I do not properly know where I am,
The more I know not, in short, what to think, to do, to say,
30   Ever since I have not been able to by your side.

Envoy

No more have I the need to sport or laugh,
No more is it the time save to despair of everything,
The more I think to have the assistance of Sweetness
The more I am then discontented and filled with anger,
35   Ever since I have not been able to be by your side.

Orleans — Ballade

Everyone plays at being the better liar,
And I'd willingly learn the craft,
But I've seen much misery then result
And so wouldn't like to learn the craft.
5   To tell false tales for fun and amusement,
Or to pass the time or for pleasure,
Is doubtless not a bad thing to do
Unless hypocrisy is involved.

Let false liars be covered up
10   With snow in the mountains of
Savoy, so much snow they cannot
Return by any path or road,
Until I send to have them searched out.
For God's sake, let them sleep there!
15   They're no good for anything
Unless hypocrisy is involved.

Pourquoy se font il tant haïr?   [p. 153]
Vueulent il que l'en les guerroye?
Cuident il du monde tenir
20   Tous les deulx boux de la courroye?
C'est folie, que vous diroye?
Leur prouffit puissent parfournir,
Et laissent les autres chevir,
Se faulceté ne s'y enploye.

[L'envoy]

25   Paix crie, Dieu la nous octroye!
C'est ung tresor qu'on doit cherir,
Tous biens s'en pevent ensuïr,
Se faulceté ne s'y enploye.

Jam nova progenies
celo demittitur alto [Villon]   [p. 154]

O louee concepcïon
Envoiee sa jus des cieulx,
Du noble lis digne syon,*
Don de Jhesus tresprecieulx,
5   Marie, nom tresgracieulx,
Fons de pitié, source de grace,
La joye, confort de mes yeulx,
Qui nostre paix batist et brasse.

La paix, c'est assavoir, des riches,
10   Des povres le substantament,
Le rebours des felons et chiches,
Tresnecessaire enfantement
Conceu, portee honnestement
Hors le pechié originel,
15   Que dire je puis sainctement
Souverain bien de Dieu Eternel.

Nom recouvré, joye de peuple,*
Confort des bons, de maulx retraicte,
Du doulx seigneur premiere et seule
20   Fille, de son cler sang extraicte,
Du dextre costé Clovis traicte,*
Glorieuse ymage en tous fais,
Ou hault ciel cree et pourtraicte
Pour esjouÿr et donner paix.

25   En l'amour et crainte de Dieu,
Es nobles flans Cesar conceue,

Why do they make themselves so hated?
Do they want someone to make war on them?
Do they think they're controlling
20   The whole world?
That's foolishness, what more should I say?
Let them realize their profit,
Allowing others to go about their business,
Unless hypocrisy is involved.

Envoy
25   Cry "Peace." God grant it to us!
That's a treasure to be cherished.
Every kind of benefit should flow
Unless hypocrisy is involved.

Just now a new progeny is sent down from the high heavens — Villon

O exalted conception,
Sent from the heavens down to this place,
Worthy scion of the noble lily,
Gift so precious from Jesus,
5   Mary, name so gracious,
Fountain of pity, source of grace,
The joy, the comfort of my eyes,
Who brings our peace and makes it strong.

The peace, that is to say, of the rich,
10   Sustenance of the poor,
Standing against felons and misers,
Childbirth so necessary,
Honestly conceived and carried,
Beyond original sin,
15   And so in reverence I can call this
A sovereign good of Eternal God.

Name recovered, the people's joy,
Consolation of the virtuous, shelter from the evil,
First and only daughter of the kindly
20   Lord, come from his pure blood,
Drawn from the right side of Clovis,
Image glorious in all things,
Created and shaped in Heaven on high
To bring us joy and peace.

25   Conceived in the love and fear
Of God, and from Caesar's noble loins,

Des petis et grans, en tout lieu,
A tresgrande joye receue,   [p. 155]
De l'amour Dieu traicte et issue
30   Pour les discordez ralïer
Et aux encloz donner yssue,
Leurs lïans et fers deslïer.

Aucunes gens qui bien peu sentent,
Nourriz en simplesse et confiz,
35   Contre le vouloir Dieu attentent,
Par ignorance desconfiz,
Desirans que feussiez ung filz,
Mais qu'ainsy soit, ainsy m'aist Dieux,
Je croy que ce soit grans proufiz.
40   Raison : Dieu fait tout pour le mieulx.

Du Psalmiste je prens les dictz :*
Delectasti me, Domine,
In factura tua, si diz :
Noble enfant, de bonne heure né,
45   A toute doulceur destiné,
Manna du ciel, celeste don,
De tout bien fait le guerdonné,
Et de noz maulx le vray pardon!

Combien que j'ay leu en ung dit :
50   *Inimicum putes,* y a,*
Qui te presentem laudabit,
Toutesfois, non obstant cela,
Oncques vray homme ne cela
En son courage aucun grant bien,
55   Qui ne le monstrast ça et la :   [p. 156]
On doit dire du bien le bien.

Saint Jehan Baptiste ainsy le fist,*
Quant l'aignel de Dieu descela.
En ce faisant pas ne mesfist,
60   Dont sa voix es tourbes vola,
De quoy saint Andry Dieu loua,
Qui de lui cy ne sçavoit rien,
Et au filz de Dieu s'aloua :
On doit dire du bien le bien.

65   Envoiee de Jhesucrist,
Rappeller sa jus par deça
Les povres que Rigueur proscript,
Et que Fortune betourna.

By those of low and high estate
Received with great joy everywhere,
Brought forth from the love of God, created
30   To beat down every discord
And bestow freedom on those imprisoned,
Breaking their chains and bonds.

Some people, understanding little,
Fed on thought naive and simple,
35   Struggle against the will of God,
Undone by ignorance,
Wishing you had been a son,
But be that as it may, so help me God,
I believe much good will come from it.
40   The reason: God does everything for the best.

I take these words from the Psalmist:
"For Thou, Lord, through Thy works
Have made me glad," so I say, too.
Noble child, born to good fortune,
45   Destined for every sweet thing,
Manna from heaven, celestial gift,
The reward for every good deed,
And true pardon for our trespasses!

Although I have read that it is said:
50   "Consider your enemy, those
Who praise you in your presence,"
Although, and in spite of these words,
No faithful man has ever kept secret
In his breast any great good thing
55   And does not show it here and there.
Good should be well spoken of.

So did St. John the Baptist,
When he made known the Lamb of God,
So doing, he did no wrong,
60   For his voice moved throngs of people,
And St. Andrew praised God,
Who had known nothing of Him,
And he devoted himself to the Son of God.
Good should be well spoken of.

65   O womanly child, sent by Jesus Christ
Here below from above to strengthen once again
The poor proscribed by Harshness
And done wrong by Fortune.

70 Cy sçay bien comment y m'en va :
De Dieu, de vous, vie je tien.
Benoist celle qui vous porta!*
On doit dire du bien le bien.

Cy, devant Dieu, fais congnoissance
Que creature feusse morte,
75 Ne feut vostre doulce naissance
En charité puissant et forte
Qui ressuscite et reconforte
Ce que Mort avoit prins pour sien.*
Vostre presence me conforte :
80 On doit dire du bien le bien.

Cy vous rans toute obeyssance,   [p. 157]
Ad ce faire Raison m'exorte
De toute ma povre puissance.
Plus n'est deul qui me desconforte,
85 N'aultre ennuy de quelconque sorte.
Vostre je suis et non plus mien.
Ad ce droit et devoir m'enhorte :
On doit dire du bien le bien.

O grace et pitié tresimmense,
90 L'entré de paix et la porte,
Some et benigne clemence,
Qui noz faultes toust et supporte,
Cy de vous louer me deporte,
Ingrat suis, et je le maintien,
95 Dont en ce refrain me transporte :
On doit dire du bien le bien.

Princesse, ce loz je vous porte,
Que sans vous je ne feusse rien.
A vous et a tous m'en rapporte :
100 On doit dire du bien le bien.

Euvre de Dieu, digne, louee
Autant que nulle creature,
De tous biens et vertus douee
Tant d'esperis que de nature,
105 Que de ceulx qu'on dit d'aventure
Plus que rubis noble ou balais,
Selon de Caton l'escripture :*
Patrem insequitur proles.   [p. 158]

I know well what will happen to me:
70   From God, from you I take my life.
Blessed be the woman who bore you!
Good should be well spoken of.

Here, in the presence of God, I acknowledge
I should have been dead as a creature
75   Had it not been for your gracious birth,
Firm and powerful in charity,
Which revives and consoles
Him whom Death has taken for his own.
Your presence gives me comfort.
80   Good should be well spoken of.

Here I render you complete obedience,
Reason exhorts me to do so,
With all the poor power I possess.
No longer will any pain trouble me,
85   Not other worries, no matter what kind.
I am yours, no longer my own.
Right and Duty demand this of me.
Good should be well spoken of.

O grace and pity so immense,
90   The entryway and gate to peace,
Pinnacle of benign mercy,
Who takes away and endures our faults,
If I abstain from magnifying you,
I am an ingrate and I maintain,
95   So much am I taken back to this refrain:
Good should be well spoken of.

Princess, I bring you this praise,
For without you I should be nothing.
And to you and everyone I affirm:
100   Good should be well spoken of.

Work of God, worthy, exalted
More than any other creature,
Endowed with every good and virtue,
As much in spirit as in nature
105   As of those things that chance brought you,
They are nobler, finer than any ruby,
Just as Cato has written:
"The son follows the father's path."

Port asseuré, maintien rassiz
110   Plus que ne peut nature humaine,
Et eussiez des ans trente six.
Enfance en rien ne vous demaine
Que jour ne le die et sepmaine,
Je ne sçay qui le me deffant.
115   Ad ce propoz ung dit ramaine :
De saige mere saige enfant.

Dont resume ce que j'ay dit :
Nova progenies celo,
Car c'est du poete le dit,
120   *Jamjam demittitur alto.*
Saige Cassandre, bel Echo,*
Digne Judich, caste Lucresse,
Je vous congnois, noble Dido
A ma seule dame et maistresse.

125   En priant Dieu, digne pucelle,
Qui vous doint longue et bonne vie,
Qui vous ayme, ma demoiselle,
Ja ne coure sur lui envie.
Entiere dame et assouvie,
130   J'espoir de vous servir ainçoys,
Certes, se Dieu plaist, que devie :
Vostre povre escolier Françoys.

B102   **[Ballade]**   [p. 160]

Je meurs de soif auprés de la fontaine;*
Suffisance ay, et si suis convoiteux.
Une heure m'est plus d'une quarantaine.
Droit et parfait, je chemine en boiteux.
5   Trespacient, plus que nul despiteux.
Je retiens tout, et ce que j'ay depars.
A moy cruel et aux aultres piteux,
Le neutre suis, et si tiens les deulx pars.

En doubte suis de chouse trescertaine.
10   Infortuné, je me repute eureux.
Vraye conclus une chouse incertaine.
Rien je ne fois, et suis avantureux.
Flebe me tiens, quant me sens vigoreux.
Plain de moisteur, tout tremblant au feu ars.
15   Doulx et begnin, de semblant rigoreux,
Le neutre suis, et si tiens les deulx pars.

Assured bearing, composed manner,
110   Of more than human nature,
Even as if your age were thirty-six.
Childhood rules you in nothing,
And so there's no day or week
Anyone I know would stop me saying so.
115   I quote a saying on this theme:
"From a wise mother comes a wise child."

So I shall sum up what I have said:
A new progeny from the heavens,
For this is the poet's saying,
120   Now sent down from on high.
Wise Cassandra, fair Echo,
Worthy Judith, chaste Lucretia,
I acknowledge you, noble Dido,
As my only lady and mistress.

125   Praying to God, worthy maiden,
To grant you a long and virtuous life,
That he who loves you, my young lady,
May never suffer the assault of envy.
Lady perfect and pure,
130   I hope to serve you,
If it please God, until I die:
Your poor scholar, Francis.

Ballade

I die of thirst beside the fountain.
I have enough, and yet am covetous.
To me an hour lasts longer than forty days.
Straight and perfect, I walk a crooked path.
5   Very patient, more arrogant than any other.
I keep everything, and give away all I have.
Cruel to myself, with pity for others.
I'm neutral and hold to both sides.

I doubt something very certain.
10   Unfortunate, I count myself lucky.
I consider true what is yet unproved.
I do nothing and try my luck.
I think myself weak, feeling vigorous.
Full of moisture, all trembling I burn in the fire.
15   Sweet and innocent, my manner unyielding,
I'm neutral and hold to both sides.

Quant dueil me prant, grant joye me demaine.
Par grant plaisir je deviens langoreux.
Indigent suis, possident grant demaine.
20   Qui n'a nul goust, je le tiens savoureux.
Qui m'est amer, de luy suis amoureux.
Ygnorant suis, et si sçay les sept ars.
En grant seurté, fort craintif et paoureux,
Le neutre suis, et si tiens les deulx pars.

[L'envoy]
25   Qui me loue, il m'est injurieux.
Je ne bouge, quant d'ung lieu je me pars.
Par bien ouvrer, en vain laborieux,
Le neutre suis, et si tiens les deulx pars.

B103   [Ballade]   [p. 161]

Je meurs de soif auprés de la fontaine.
Tant plus mengue, et tant plus je me affame.
Pouvre d'argent ou ma bourse en est plaine,
Marié suis et si n'ay point de fame.
5   Qui me honnore, grandement me diffame.
Quant je vois droit, lors est que me devoye.
Pour loz et pris, j'é tiltre de diffame.
Grief desplaisir m'est excessive joye.

Quant l'en me toult, richement on me estraine.
10   Dix mile onces ne me sont que une drame.
Sec et brahaing, je porte fleur et graine.
En reposant, sur mer tire a la rame.
Actainé suis en tous lieux ou n'a ame.
Acompaigné, je n'ay qui me convoye.
15   Toute entiere est la chose que je entame.
Grief desplaisir m'est excessive joye.

En aspirant, je retiens mon alaine.
Quant eur me vient, maleureux je me clame.
Fort et puissant, flexible comme laine,
20   Transsi d'amours sans avoir nulle dame,
Homme parfait, privé de corps et d'ame,
Paisible suis, et ung chascun guerroye.
Mes ennemis plus que tous autres ame.
Grief desplaisir m'est excessive joye.

[L'envoy]
25   Mauvaise odeur m'est plus fleurant que basme.
Pasmé de dueil, angoisseux me resjoye.

When grief seizes me, great joy takes me forward.
Through great pleasure I turn melancholic.
I'm poor, possessing a great estate.
20 What has no taste, I find flavorful.
Who shows me bitterness, I show him friendship.
I'm ignorant and know the seven arts.
In great security, terribly fearful and frightened,
I'm neutral and hold to both sides.

Envoy
25 Whoever praises me does me harm.
I do not budge when leaving a place.
Through doing good works, laboring in vain,
I'm neutral and hold to both sides.

Ballade

I die of thirst beside the fountain.
The more I eat, the hungrier I get.
Poor in the money of which my purse is full.
I'm married, yet have no wife.
5 The man who honors me defames me greatly.
Walking straight is when I wander.
For praise and esteem, I have an infamous title.
Grievous displeasure to me is excessive joy.

When you take something from me, you give me a rich gift.
10 Ten thousand ounces I think but a dram.
Dry and sterile, I bring forth flower and grain.
Resting, I row across the sea.
I'm accused everywhere there is no one.
Accompanied, I have no companion.
15 Quite whole is the thing I have bitten into.
Grievous displeasure to me is excessive joy.

Exhaling, I hold my breath.
Having good luck, I call myself unfortunate.
Strong and mighty, I'm as soft as wool,
20 Bashful with love but having no lady.
Perfect man, deprived of body and soul,
I'm peaceful and make war on everyone.
More than all others, I love my enemies.
Grievous displeasure to me is excessive joy.

Envoy
25 A terrible odor smells more pleasant than balm.
Faint from pain, I rejoice in my suffering.

En eaue plongié, je brule tout en flame.
Grief desplaisir m'est excessive joye.

B104   [Ballade]   [p. 162]

Je n'ay plus soif, tarie est la fontaine.
Repeu suis de competent viande.
J'ay pris treves affin que on ne me attaine,
Dissimulant, fault que le hurt attende.
5   Adjoint des deulx, sans que nul vilipende,
Je festie l'ung, a l'autre fois la moue.
En ce faisant, pour eviter escande,
Entre deulx eaus, comme le poisson, noue.*

En grant travail j'ai frapé la quintaine,
10   Jusquez ung temps fault que a repos entende.
Pour obvier a voie trop haultaine,
Le moien tiens, affin que ne descende.
J'ai eu delay de paier mon amende.
En courroux faint couvertement me joue.
15   En reculant pour mieulx saillir en lande,
Entre deulx eaus, comme le poisson, noue.

Ne vert, ne meur, mon blé mengue en graine,
Dueil et plaisir me tiennent en commande.
En divers lieux ça et la me pourmaine.
20   La moitié fois, quant tout l'en me commande.
A demy trait lors est que l'arc debande,
Pour abreger, ne l'ung ne l'autre loue,
Participant de l'une et l'autre bande,
Entre deulx eaus, comme le poisson, noue.

[L'envoy]
25   Par priere de affaitee demande,
Interrogé se l'ung ou l'autre avoue,
A ce respons, se aucun le me demande :
Entre deulx eaus, comme le poisson, noue.

B105   [Ballade] Villon   [p. 163]

Je meurs de seuf auprés de la fontaine.
Chault comme feu, et tremble dent a dent.
En mon pays, suis en terre loingtaine.
Lez ung brasier, frissonne tout ardent.
5   Nu comme ung ver, vestu en president.
Je riz en pleurs, et attens sans espoir.

Plunged into water, I burn, encompassed by flame.
Grievous displeasure to me is excessive joy.

Ballade

I thirst no more, the fountain has gone dry.
I have overfed on a reasonable diet.
I've signed a truce so as not to be attacked,
Hiding my feelings, I must await the blow.
5 Joined by two others, insulting neither,
I celebrate with one, spurn the other.
While doing this, to avoid a fuss,
I run with the hare and hunt with the hounds.

Laboring hard, I've struck at the quintain
10 Until the time came I had to rest.
To avoid the path that is too high,
I hold to the middle way, so go no lower.
I've delayed paying what I owe.
Pretending to be enraged, I secretly exult.
15 Falling back the better to leap forward,
I run with the hare and hunt with the hounds.

Neither green nor ripe, I eat my wheat in the husk.
Grief and pleasure hold me in their sway.
In various places to and fro I roam.
20 I just do half when ordered to do the whole.
It is at half pull that I release the arrow,
In short, I praise neither one nor the other,
A member of one gang and another, too,
I run with the hare and hunt with the hounds.

Envoy

25 Replying to a pointed request,
Asked if I pledge myself to one or the other,
I answer, since the question has been asked,
"I run with the hare and hunt with the hounds."

Ballade — Villon

I die of thirst beside the fountain.
Hot as if on fire, and my teeth chattering.
In my homeland, I'm in a far-off country.
Beside a fire I shiver, all ablaze.
5 Naked as a worm, dressed like a judge,
I laugh while weeping, am expectant without hope.

Confort reprens en triste desespoir.
Je m'esjouÿs, et n'ay plaisir aucun.
Puissant je suis, sans force et sans povoir,
10   Bien recueully, debouté de chascun.

Rien ne m'est seur que la chose incertaine,
Obscur, fors ce qui est tout evident.
Doubte ne fais, fors en chose certaine.
Science tiens a soudain accident.
15   Je gaigne tout, et demeure perdent.
Au point du jour diz : Dieu vous doint bon soir.
Gisant en vers, j'ai grant paeur de cheoir.
J'ay bien de quoy, et si n'en ay pas ung.
Echoicte actens, et d'omme ne suis hoir,
20   Bien recueully, debouté de chascun.

De riens n'ay soing, si mectz toute m'atayne
D'acquerir biens, et n'y suis pretendent.
Qui mieulx me dit, c'est cil qui plus m'actaine,
Et qui plus vray, lors plus me va bourdent.
25   Mon ami est qui me faict entendent
D'ung cigne blanc que c'est ung corbeau noir,
Et qui me nuyst, croy qui m'ayde a pourvoir.
Bourde, verité, au jourd'uy m'est tout ung.
Je retiens tout, riens ne sçay concepvoir,
30   Bien recueully, debouté de chascun.

L'envoy

Prince clement, or vous plaise sçavoir   [p. 164]
Que j'entens moult, et n'ay sens ne sçavoir.
Parcial suis, a toutes loys commun.
Que fais je plus? quoy? les gaiges ravoir,*
35   Bien recueully, debouté de chascun.

B106   Balade [Villon]

Parfont conseil, *eximium,*
En ce saint livre *exortatur,*
Que l'omme, *in matrimonium,*
Folement *non abutatur.*
5   Raison? le sens *hebetatur*
De omni viro, quel qui soit :
Fol *non credit* tant qui reçoit.

Et constat, par ceste leççon,
Pour conserver *vim et robur,*
10   *Prestat* ne faire mot ne son,

I find comfort in my sad despair.
I rejoice and feel no pleasure.
I'm powerful, lacking strength and might,
10   Nicely welcomed, rejected by everyone.

Nothing is sure for me but something uncertain.
Obscure, save that it is completely evident.
I doubt nothing but what I find proven.
I hold knowledge what is a sudden chance.
15   I gain everything and remain a loser.
As day begins, I say, "God give you good night!"
Lying on my back, I greatly fear falling.
I have much, yet possess nothing.
I expect an inheritance and am no man's heir,
20   Nicely welcomed, rejected by everyone.

I desire nothing, yet put all my energies
Into acquiring goods, but have no claim to them.
Who speaks the nicest to me annoys me most,
And who affirms the most truth, tells me the most lies.
25   That man's my friend who makes me understand
That a white swan is truly a black crow,
And the man who injures me does his best to help.
Falsehoods, truth—today they're all the same to me.
I retain everything, can get my mind around nothing,
30   Nicely welcomed, rejected by everyone.

Envoy
Merciful prince, now may it please you to know
I understand much and have no sense or knowledge.
I'm unique, yet subject to the laws that govern all.
What more do I know? What? Redeeming my pledges,
35   Nicely welcomed, rejected by everyone.

Ballade—Villon

A profound counsel, excellent,
Is exhorted in the Holy Book
That the man, in marriage,
Should not foolishly abuse his rights.
5   The reason? Good sense goes limp
In every man, no matter who he is.
A fool does not believe until he has proof.

And it consists, according to this teaching,
In maintaining vim and vigor.
10   It is better to utter no word or sound,

Souffrir et escouter *murmur,*
Si conjunx clamat ad ce mur.*
Fingat que pas ne le conçoit :
Fol *non credit* tant qui reçoit.

15   *Fortior multo* que Sanson
En cest assault *convincitur.*
Contra de Venus l'escusson
Le plus fort bourdon *plicatur*
. . . .
Sed quisquis pas ne le conçoit
20   Fol *non credit* tant qui reçoit.

[L'envoy]
Prince tressaige, *legitur*
Quod astucior si deçoit;
Le mieulx nagent y *mergitur :*
Fol *non credit* tant qui reçoit.

B107   [Ballade]   [p. 165]

Je meurs de soif auprés de la fontaine.
J'ai tresgrant fain, et si ne puis mengier.
Je suis au bas en la maison haultaine,
Et en chartre en ung tresbeau vergier,
5   En grant peril et hors de tout dangier.
Les biens que j'ay me font povre, indigent.
En beau logis ne me sçay ou logier.
Je gaigne assez, et si n'ay point d'argent.

Je fay grant deul, tristesse m'est loingtaine.
10   Dormir ne puis et ne fay que songier.
Je suis tout sain et ay fievre quartaine.
Tout esdenté, mon frain me fault rongier.
Verité dy, et si suis menssongier.
Je suis rencluz, hanté de toute gent,
15   Congneu de tous et a tous estrangier.
Je gaigne assez, et si n'ay point d'argent.

Grant doubte fay de chose bien certaine.
Incertain suy, et si en veul jugier.
Ou champ estroit je jouste a la quintaine.
20   Non offencé, je me cuide vengier.
Ung pesant faiz me semble treslegier.
Je suy paillart et contrefay du gent.
Par trop couart, hardy comme ung Ogier.*
Je gaigne assez, et si n'ay point d'argent.

To endure and listen to the grumbling.
If the spouse cries out: "Help!"
Let him pretend he does not understand.
A fool does not believe until he has proof.

15   Stronger by far than Samson was,
In this assault he is vanquished.
Against the shield of Venus
The stoutest club is bent.
. . . .
But whoever does not understand
20   A fool does not believe until he has proof.

Envoy

O prince most wise, one reads
That the more clever man comes to grief.
The strongest swimmer goes under.
A fool does not believe until he has proof.

Ballade

I die of thirst beside the fountain.
My hunger is very great, yet I cannot eat.
I'm at the bottom of a house so high,
Imprisoned in a very beautiful garden,
5   In great peril and beyond all danger.
The riches I possess make me poor, indigent.
In a handsome lodging I know not where to lodge.
I earn plenty, yet have no money.

I suffer great pain, sadness is far off.
10   I cannot sleep and do nothing but dream.
I'm completely healthy and have a quartan fever.
Toothless, I can't hold back from devouring.
I speak the truth, yet am a liar.
I'm a recluse, and everyone frequents me.
15   Known to all and a stranger to everyone.
I earn plenty, yet have no money.

I entertain great doubts about what is certain.
Uncertain I am, and so wish to render an opinion.
On a narrow field I tilt my lance at the target.
20   Not offended, I plan on taking vengeance.
A weighty matter seems very silly to me.
I'm a vagabond and play at being noble.
A thorough coward, as brave as any Ogier.
I earn plenty, yet have no money.

Prince

25   Prince, je suy siche, pour abregier,
      Prodigue aussi, nonchallant, diligent,
      Assez subtil, plus simple que bergier,
      Je gaigne assez, et si n'ay point d'argent.

B108   [Ballade]

      Je meurs de soif auprés de la fontaine.   [p. 166]
      Je treuve doulx ce qui doit estre amer.
      J'aime et tiens chier tous ceulx qui me font hayne,
      Je hé tous ceulx que fort je deusse amer.   Montbeton*
5   Je loue ceulx que je deusse blamer,
      Je prens en gré plus le mal que le bien,
      Je vois querant ce qu'a trouver je doubte.
      Croire ne puis cela que je sçay bien,
      Je me tiens seur de ce dont plus j'ay doubte.

10   Je prens plaisir en ce qui m'est atayne.
      Ung peu de chose m'est grant comme la mer.
      Je tiens de prés celle qui m'est loingtaine.
      Je garde entier ce que deusse entamer.
      Saoul suis de ce qui me fait affamer.   Robertet*
15   J'ay largement de tout, et si n'ay rien,
      J'oublie ce que plus a cuer je boute.
      Ce qui me lasche me tient en son lien.
      Je me tiens seur de ce dont plus j'ay doubte.

      Je tiens pour basse chose qui est haultaine,
20   Je fuy tous ceulx que deusse reclamer,
      Je croy plus tart le vray que une fredaine.
      Tant plus suis froit, plus me sens enflamer.
      Quant j'ay bon cuer, lors je prens a pasmer.
      Ce que j'aquiers je ne tiens pas pour mien.
25   Je prise peu ce qui bien chier me couste.
      Sote maniere m'est plus que beau maintien,
      Je me tiens seur de ce dont plus j'ay doubte.

[L'envoy]   [p. 167]
      Prince, j'ay tout, et si ne sçay combien.
      J'atire a moy ce qui plus me deboute.
30   Ce que j'esloigne m'est plus prés qu'autre rien,
      Je me tiens seur de ce dont plus j'ay doubte.

Prince

25   Prince, I am stingy, to cut it short,
A spendthrift too, careless, diligent,
Smart enough, simpler than a shepherd.
I earn plenty, yet have no money.

Ballade

I die of thirst beside the fountain.
I find sweet what should be bitter.
I love and hold dear all who hate me.
I hate all those I should love passionately.   Montbeton
5   I praise those I should blame.
I am gladder to have ill than good.
I go seeking what I fear to find.
I cannot believe what I know well.
I think myself safe with what I fear the most.

10   I take pleasure in what brings me vexation.
The smallest thing I think big as the sea.
I hold close what is far distant.
I keep whole what I should cut up.
I am satiated by what makes me hunger.   Robertet
15   I have all in abundance, yet have nothing.
I forget what I shove closest to my heart.
What delivers me holds me in bonds.
I think myself safe with what I fear the most.

I think low what is on high,
20   I flee all those I should call upon,
I believe the truth more slowly than foolishness.
The colder I am, the more I feel myself ablaze.
When I take good heart, I faint away.
What I obtain I do not think my own.
25   I prize little what costs me dear.
I value silly ways more than fine behavior.
I think myself safe with what I fear the most.

Envoy

Prince, I have everything, and do not know how much.
I draw toward what most repels me.
30   What I send from me is closer than all else,
I think myself safe with what I fear the most.

B109 [Ballade]

Je meurs de soif auprés de la fontaine.   [p. 168]
Verbe normal, sans conjugacïon,
Congruité de incongruité plaine.
Declinable, sans declinacïon,
5   Approprié par appellacïon.
Determiné, sans quelque terminance.
Ou brief ou long, sans variacïon,
C'est plus fort fait que ouvrer par nigromance.

Mat et vaincu, je frape la quintaine.
10   Sans violence je fois invasïon,
Affirmatif d'une chouse incertaine,
Sillogisant sans proposicïon,
Meuf figure ou n'a conclusïon.
Emptimeme sans quelque consequence,
15   Convertible ou n'a conversïon.
C'est plus fort fait que ouvrer par nigromance.

J'ame repos, et desire la paine,
Corruptible en generacïon.
Le vray au faulx je reduis et ramaine,
20   De maxime je fois opinïon.
Diffinient je fois descripcïon,
Et l'accident je mue en sustance.
Aveugle suis en clere visïon,
C'est plus fort fait que ouvrer par nigromance.

[L'envoy]
25   Incomplexif, avant complexïon.*
Irregulier, je suis de l'observance,
Je suis actif, designant passïon.
C'est plus fort fait que ouvrer par nigromance.

B110 [Ballade] · maistre Berthault   [p. 169]
de Villebresme*

Je meurs de soif auprés de la fontaine,
Tout affamé en mengier sumptueux,
Comblé de dueil, en lëesse haultaine,
Sec et brahaing en pays fructueux,
5   Loing de vertuz entre les vertueux,
Entre joieux plainctif et souspirant,
En lieu de bien, de mal affectueux,
Et va mon fait tousjours en empirant.

Ballade

I die of thirst beside the fountain.
A regular verb, lacking a conjugation.
Congruity full of incongruity.
Declinable, lacking a declension.
5   Appropriated without a court order.
Finite, without any ending,
Short or long, without variation,
Harder to do than practicing wizardry.

Defeated and overwhelmed, I strike at the target.
10   With no violence, I launch an invasion,
Positive about an uncertain thing,
Making a syllogism with no proposition,
A figure of speech with no conclusion,
Enthymeme without a consequence,
15   Convertible but lacking any conversion.
Harder to do than practicing wizardry.

I love rest, and desire trouble,
Corruptible right from birth.
I reduce and limit the true to false.
20   From a maxim I make an opinion.
I turn a definition into a description,
Into substance I transform accident.
My vision clear, I am blind,
Harder to do than practicing wizardry.

Envoy
25   Having an end, but no beginning,
Irregular, I am rule-abiding,
I am active, designating the passive.
Harder to do than practicing wizardry.

Ballade — Master Berthault
de Villebresme

I die of thirst beside the fountain,
Consumed by hunger at a sumptuous meal,
Overcome with sadness, in exalted happiness,
Dry and sterile in a fruitful countryside.
5   Far from virtue among the virtuous,
Plaintive among the joyful, and full of sighs,
In place of good, affected by ill,
And every day my situation grows worse.

Entre tous biens je suis de mal quintaine,
10   Alangoré entre les vigoreux,
Entre esbanoys, de regretz cappitaine,
Amertumé entre les doulcereux,
Tremblant de froit en manoir chalereux,
En grand santé tousjours mal endurant,
15   Entre courtois, despit et rigoreux,
Et va mon fait tousjours en empirant.

Forvoyé suis par hanter voye certaine
Et avouyé en lieu avantureux.
Ma nacïon m'est regïon loingtaine.
20   En lieu tresseur je suis fort paoreux,
Espris d'amour sans estre amoureux.
La lerme a l'ueil je me voiz deduisant.
Tout me desplaist, sans estre dangereux,
Et va mon fait tousjours en empirant.

25   Prince, cesser fay le mal qui m'attaine
Ou autrement je m'en iray mourant,
Car je suis prés d'avoir fievre quartaine,
Et va mon fait tousjours en empirant.

B111   Balade · de M. J. Caillau*   [p. 170]

Je meurs de soif auprés de la fontaine,
Tramblant de froit ou feu des amoureux.
Je suis tout sein en langueur et en paine,
Et suis asseur ou tout est dangereux.
5   Tout mal, tout grief m'est doulx et savoureux.
Plain de tourment mene joyeuse vie,
Et ce qui plaist a tous ne me plaist mie.
En povreté je suis trés richement.
En angoisse j'ay plaisance assovye.
10   Or jugez donc se je vis plaisanment.

Je suis joyeux sans plaisance mondaine.
Ou chascun rit, pensif et douloureux.
Sans nul travail si suis je hors d'alaine.
Pres de tout bien suis le treslangoreux.
15   Ce qui me plaist est aspre et rigoreux.
J'ayme estre seul et si vueil compagnie.
Je dors assez et suis en frenesie.
En desespoir j'ay grant allegement.
Ce qui est doulx m'est plus amer que suye.
20   Or jugez donc se je viz plaisanment.

Among the healthy I suffer quintan fever,
10   Feeble among the vigorous.
Amidst delights the captain of regrets,
Filled with bitterness among the sweet,
Trembling with cold in a warm manor,
In fine health always suffering illness,
15   Among the courtly, rough-edged and spiteful,
And every day my situation grows worse.

I get lost frequenting a sure path,
And find my way in the place chance provides.
My nation is a far distant region.
20   In a place very safe I am terribly fearful,
Smitten with love without being loving.
Tears in my eyes, I follow the path of delight.
Everything displeases, but does not oppress me,
And every day my situation grows worse.

25   Prince, make cease the misery assaulting me,
Otherwise I go to my death,
For I'm close to having a quartan fever,
And every day my situation grows worse.

Ballade by M. J. Caillau

I die of thirst beside the fountain.
Trembling with cold by the lovers' fire.
I enjoy fine health in languor and pain
And feel secure where everything threatens.
5   All ill, all grief is sweet and pleasant to me.
Full of torment I lead a joyful life,
And what pleases everyone pleases me not at all.
Impoverished, I'm very well off.
In anguish I have pleasure enough.
10   Judge now if I live pleasantly.

I am joyful without worldly pleasure.
Where everyone laughs, I am pensive and pained.
Doing no labor I am out of breath.
Among those doing well I'm the most languorous.
15   What pleases me is bitter and harsh.
I love being alone and yet yearn for company.
I sleep enough and am in a daze.
In despair I find great relief.
What is sweet I find more bitter than soot.
20   Judge now if I live pleasantly.

Je suis seigneur sans terre et sans demaine.
Tant plus ay biens et plus suis maleureux.
Je meurs de fain, et ay ma grange plaine.
Ou tout est seur si suis je trespeureux,
25   Des plus vaillans et moins chevalereux.
Qui mal me fait, je lui rens courtoysie.
S'il fait beau temps, je demande la pluye.
Se je meurs tost, si vis je longuement.
En grant repos plain de forsenerie.   [p. 171]
30   Or jugez donc se je viz plaisanment.

                    L'envoy
Prince, mon fait est droicte faerie.
Je hay travail, et le repos m'ennuye.
Maintenant d'ung et tantost autrement.
J'ay tous les jeux et quicte la partie.
35   Or jugez donc se je vis plaisanment.

B112   [Ballade] · Gilles des Ourmes *   [p. 172]

Je meurs de soif auprés de la fontaine,
Tremblant de froit ou feu des amoureux.
Je suis joieux s'aucun mal me demaine.
Plaintz et souspirs sont mes riz et mes jeux.
5   Je n'ay sancté sinon quant je me deulx.
Beau temps me plaist, et desire la pluye.
Qui bien me fait, je le tien mon hayneux.
Or regardez et jugiez s'il m'ennuye!

Je n'ay repos qu'en doleur et en paine.
10   J'ayme travail et si suis paresceux.
Ung mois ne m'est qu'a ung autre sepmaine,
Et m'est advis que le jour dure deux.
Se j'ay nul bien, je m'en tien maleureux.
Quant j'ayme aucun, force est que je le fuye.
15   Qui m'est courtois, je luy suis rigoreux.
Or regardez et jugiez s'il m'ennuye!

J'ay mille maulx, et ma personne est saine.
Plaisirs mondains me sont malencontreux.
Quant je suis seul, lors ung chascun m'ataine.
20   Rien n'ay asseur, si je n'en suis doubteux.
Gens bien en point me semblent soufreteux.
En plain midy j'ay la veue esbluye.
Je n'ayme rien et si suis convoiteux.
Or regardez et jugiez s'il m'ennuye!

I'm a lord with no land or domain.
The more goods I have, the unhappier I am.
I die of hunger, and my storehouse is full.
In the safest place, I'm the most fearful,
25   One of the most valiant and least chivalrous.
Who does me wrong, I treat with courtesy.
If the weather is fair, I ask for rain.
If I die soon, then I live long.
In great repose full of madness.
30   Judge now if I live pleasantly.

Envoy

Prince, my situation is truly marvelous.
I hate work, and rest annoys me.
Now one thing, and in a flash something else.
I win every game and leave the company.
35   Judge now if I live pleasantly.

Ballade — Gilles des Ourmes

I die of thirst beside the fountain,
Trembling with cold by the lovers' fire.
I'm joyful if any ill seizes me.
Moans and sighs are my laughter and sport.
5   I'm only healthy when I'm ill.
Fine weather pleases, yet I long for rain.
Whoever treats me well, I think my enemy.
Now look and judge if I am discomfited!

I have no rest save in pain and sorrow.
10   I love work and am lazy.
A month to me is a week for another.
And I think one day lasts two.
If I have any good, I think myself unfortunate.
If I love someone, I must flee him.
15   Whoever is courteous to me I treat harshly.
Now look and judge if I am discomfited!

I suffer a thousand ills, and my body is healthy.
Worldly pleasures I find disagreeable.
When I am alone, I am attacked by one and all.
20   I find nothing certain, and so am not doubtful.
People in fine fettle I think in terrible shape.
At high noon my view's obscured.
I like nothing and yet am covetous.
Now look and judge if I am discomfited!

L'envoy

25 Sans mot sonner, je dy mon cas piteux.
    Je n'ay regret qu'en ce que je ne veulx.
    Ce qui est doulx m'est plus amer que suye.
    Quant gens n'ont rien, je vueil mordre sur eulx.
    Or regardez et jugiez s'il m'ennuye!

B113   [Ballade] · Simonnet Caillau *   [p. 173]

    Je meurs de soif auprés de la fontaine.
    Coste plaisir, mon cueur plaint et souppire.
    Tout aresté, sens marchier, l'on me maine.
    Remply de dueil, vouloir me prent de rire.
5   En plaisans lieux je n'ay sinon martire.
    A nul ne suis, et si fault que m'avoue.
    Parler sçay bien, et ne puis mon cas dire.
    Or regardez se tel homme se joue!

    Croire ne vueil, et est chose certaine.
10 Sans me toucher, je sens que l'on me tire.
    En lit bien fait, la ne seuffre que paine.
    Le chois ay eu, et est ma part la pire.
    Sans avoir riens, j'ay tant qu'il deust souffire.
    Qui mal me fait, de cestui la me loue.
15 Pres des joyeux je ne me sçay deduire.
    Or regardez ce tel homme se joue!

    Esgaré suis, et voy la voye plaine.
    Ou tout est bien, assez treuve a redire.
    Sans grant chaleur sa et la me pourmaine.
20 Les yeulx bandez en mirouer me myre.
    Loing de chault feu, je ne cesse de frire.
    Tel me flate qui puis me fait la moue.
    Ce qui est mien, j'en voy ung aultre sire.
    Or regardez ce tel homme se joue!

25 J'ay piez et sens, et ne me sçay conduire.
    En beau chemin je suis cheust en la boue.
    J'ayme estre a part, et compaignie desire.
    Or regardez ce tel homme se joue!

Co3   Complainte de France   [p. 191]

    France, jadis on te souloit nommer,
    En tous pays, le tresor de noblesse,
    Car un chascun povoit en toy trouver

Envoy

25   Not saying a word, I speak about my pitiful case.
I only long for what I do not want.
What is sweet I find more bitter than soot.
When people have nothing, I wish to feed off them.
Now look and judge if I am discomfited!

Ballade — Simonnet Caillau

I die of thirst beside the fountain.
Close to pleasure, my heart weeps and sighs.
At a complete halt, not walking, I'm led off.
Filled with sorrow, I feel the desire to laugh.
5   In pleasant places I have only suffering.
I belong to no one, yet must acknowledge a master.
I can speak ably and cannot explain my situation.
Now see if such a man enjoys himself!

I will not believe, and the thing is beyond doubt.
10   Without being touched, I sense I'm being drawn along.
In a bed well made, I suffer only pain.
The choice was mine, and my share is the worst.
Having nothing, I have so much it should suffice.
Whoever does me wrong, with him I take my lodging,
15   When with the joyful I cannot take pleasure.
Now see if such a man enjoys himself!

I'm lost and see the clear path.
Where all is well, I find enough to reproach.
Not overheated, I walk here and there.
20   Blindfolded, I look at myself in a mirror.
Far from a hot fire, I do not stop shivering.
He who flatters me then makes a face.
What is mine, I see another as its master.
Now see if such a man enjoys himself!

25   I have feet and know not where to go,
On a fine road I fell into the mud.
I like to be alone and desire company.
Now see if such a man enjoys himself!

The complaint for France

France, in times past you were wont
To be called in every land the treasure of manners.
For every man could find in you

Bonté, honneur, loyauté, gentillesse,
5   Clergie, sens, courtoisie, proesse.
Tous estrangiers amoient te suïr.
Et maintenant voy, dont j'ay desplaisance
Qu'il te couvient maint grief mal soustenir,
Trescretïen, franc royaume de France!

10   Scez tu dont vient ton mal, a vray parler?
Congnois tu point pourquoy es en tristesse?
Conter le vueil, pour vers toy m'acquiter,
Escoutes moy et tu feras sagesse.
Ton grant ourgueil, glotonnie, peresse,
15   Couvoitise, sans justice tenir,
Et luxure, dont as eu abondance,
Ont pourchacié vers Dieu de te punir,
Trescretïen, franc royaume de France!

Ne te vueilles pour tant desesperer,
20   Car Dieu est plain de merci, a largesse.
Va t'en vers lui sa grace demander,
Car il t'a fait, de ja pieça, promesse,
Mais que faces ton advocat Humblesse,
Que tresjoyeux sera de toy guerir.
25   Entierement metz en lui ta fiance,
Pour toy et tous, voulu en crois mourir,
Trescretïen, franc royaume de France!

Souviengne toy comment voult ordonner
Que criasses Montjoye, par lïesse,*
30   Et qu'en escu d'azur deusses porter
Trois fleurs de lis d'or, et pour hardïesse   [p. 192]
Fermer en toy, t'envoya sa haultesse,
L'auriflamme, qui t'a fait seigneurir
Tes ennemis. Ne metz en oubliance
35   Telz dons haultains, dont lui pleut t'enrichir,
Trescrestïan, franc royaume de France!

En oultre plus, te voulu envoyer
Par un coulomb, qui est plain de simplesse,
La unctïon dont dois tes roys sacrer,
40   Afin qu'en eulx dignité plus encresse,
Et, plus qu'a nul, t'a voulu sa richesse
De reliques et corps sains departir.
Tout le monde en a la congnoissance.
Soyes certain qu'il ne te veult faillir,
45   Trescrestïan, franc royaume de France!

Virtue, honor, loyalty, nobility,
5   Learning, reason, courtliness, prowess.
Foreigners one and all hastened to your banner.
And now I see, to my dismay,
You enduring many a grievous ill,
Kingdom of France so Christian and noble!

10   Do you truly know whence comes this ill?
Do you see why you are in distress?
I intend to tell you, and so fulfill my duty toward you,
Listen to me and you do wisdom.
Your great arrogance, gluttony, sloth,
15   Greed, maintained without justice,
And desire for rich living, which you possess aplenty,
Have moved God to punish you,
Kingdom of France so Christian and noble!

Yet do not despair,
20   For God abounds with mercy.
Go to Him and beg His grace,
For long ago He made you a promise
That if you would but make Humility your spokesman,
He would be very happy to heal you.
25   Put all your trust in Him, who was
Eager to die on the cross for you and all others,
Kingdom of France so Christian and noble!

Remember how He ordained that you
Should cry out "Montjoy" in happiness,
30   And that on your shield of blue you should bear
Three lily flowers all of gold, and to strengthen
Your courage, He sent you what was exalted,
The oriflamme, which gave you the power to
Rule your enemies. Don't forget
35   These grand gifts it pleased Him to enrich you with,
Kingdom of France so Christian and noble!

And even more, it was His wish to send
By a dove, full of simplicity,
The unction with which you anoint your kings
40   So dignity might take root within them,
And He thought to share with you, more than
With others, His rich store of precious and holy relics.
All the world acknowledges this.
Be certain He does not intend to fail you,
45   Kingdom of France so Christian and noble!

Court de Romme si te fait appeller
Son bras dextre, car souvent de destresse
L'as mise hors, et pource approuver
Les papes font te seoir, seul sans presse,
50   A leur dextre, se droit jamais ne cesse,
Et pource dois fort pleurer et gemir,
Quant tu desplais a Dieu qui tant t'avance
En tous estas, lequel deusses cherir,
Trescrestïan, franc royaume de France!

55   Quelz champïons souloit en toy trouver
Crestïenté! Ja ne fault que l'expresse :
Charlemeine, Rolant et Olivier
En sont tesmoings. Pource, je m'en delaisse,
Et saint Loys Roy, qui fist la rudesse*
60   Des Sarrasins souvent aneantir
En son vivant, par travail et vaillance.   [p. 193]
Les croniques le moustrent, sans mentir,
Trescrestïen, franc royaume de France!

Pource, France, vueilles toy adviser,
65   Et tost reprens de bien vivre l'adresse.
Tous tes meffais metz paine d'amender,
Faisant chanter et dire mainte messe
Pour les ames de ceulx qui ont l'aspresse
De dure mort souffert, pour te servir.
70   Leurs loyautez ayes en souvenance,
Riens espargnié n'ont pour toy garantir,
Trescrestïen, franc royaume de France!

Dieu a les bras ouvers pour t'acoler,
Prest d'oublier ta vie pecheresse.
75   Requier pardon, bien te vendra aidier
Nostre Dame, la trespuissant princesse,
Qui est ton cry et que tiens pour maistresse.
Les sains aussi te vendront secourir,
Desquelz les corps font en toy demourance.
80   Ne vueilles plus en ton pechié dormir,
Trescrestïen, franc royaume de France!

Et je, Charles, duc d'Orlians, rimer
Voulu ces vers ou temps de ma jeunesse,
Devant chascun les vueil bien advouer,
85   Car prisonnier les fis, je le confesse,
Priant a Dieu, qu'avant qu'aye vieillesse,
Le temps de paix partout puist avenir,
Comme de cueur j'en ay la desirance,

The Court of Rome acknowledges you
As its right arm, for often you have delivered it
From distress, and to make this manifest
The popes have you sit, not among the crowd,
50   But at their right, so justice might never lack.
And so you should weep hard and moan
When you displease God, Who has furthered you
In every way, the One you should love,
Kingdom of France so Christian and noble!

55   What champions Christendom used to
Find in you! I have no need to spell it out:
Charlemagne, Roland, and Oliver
Are the proof. So I pass over such things.
And Louis, king and saint, who often
60   Beat down the violence of the Saracens
While he lived, showing prowess in hardship.
The chronicles make this clear and do not lie,
Kingdom of France so Christian and noble!

And so, France, please take counsel,
65   And regain the path of right living.
Take pains to amend all your misdeeds
By having sung and said many a mass
For the souls of those who suffered the bitterness
Of a hard death in order to serve you.
70   Be mindful of their faithfulness.
They spared nothing to keep you safe,
Kingdom of France so Christian and noble!

God's arms open to embrace you,
Ready to forget your sinful life.
75   Ask for pardon; Our Lady will surely come
To your aid, the princess so very powerful,
Whom you call upon and think your mistress.
The saints as well will come to your assistance,
Whose bodies find their resting place in you.
80   Slumber no longer in your sinfulness,
Kingdom of France so Christian and noble!

And I, Charles, duke of Orleans, was pleased
To compose these verses in the time of my youth;
Before one and all I acknowledge
85   That as a prisoner I wrote them, this I confess,
Praying to God, that before old age falls upon me,
A time of peace might everywhere come to pass,
As is the desire of my heart,

        Et que voye tous tes maulx brief finir,
90   Trescrestïan, franc royaume de France!

B114   Balade   [p. 194]

        En regardant vers le païs de France,
        Un jour m'avint, a Dovre sur la mer,
        Qu'il me souvint de la doulce plaisance
        Que souloye ou dit pays trouver,
5   Si commençay de cueur a souspirer,
        Combien certes que grant bien me faisoit
        De voir France que mon cueur amer doit.

        Je m'avisay que c'estoit non savance
        De telz souspirs dedens mon cueur garder,
10   Veu que je voy que la voye commence
        De bonne paix, qui tous biens peut donner.
        Pource, tournay en confort mon penser,
        Mais non pourtant mon cueur ne se lassoit
        De voir France que mon cueur amer doit.

15   Alors chargay en la nef d'Esperance
        Tous mes souhaitz, en leur priant d'aler
        Oultre la mer, sans faire demourance,
        Et a France de me recommander.
        Or nous doint Dieu bonne paix sans tarder!
20   Adonc auray loisir, mais qu'ainsi soit,
        De voir France que mon cueur amer doit.

                        L'envoy
        Paix est tresor qu'on ne peut trop loer.
        Je hé guerre, point ne la doy prisier.
        Destourbé m'a long temps, soit tort ou droit,
25   De voir France que mon cueur amer doit!

[82]

B115   Balade   [p. 195]

        Priés pour paix, doulce Vierge Marie,
        Royne des cieulx, et du monde maistresse,
        Faictes prier, par vostre courtoisie,
        Saints et saintes, et prenés vostre adresse
5   Vers vostre filz, requerant sa haultesse
        Qu'il lui plaise son peuple regarder,
        Que de son sang a voulu racheter
        En deboutant guerre qui tout desvoye.

And I see all your ills soon end,
90   Kingdom of France so Christian and noble!

Ballade

While gazing toward the country of France
One day at Dover by the sea
I recalled the sweet pleasure
I used to find in that country.
5   And so from the heart I began to sigh,
Even though it certainly did me much good
To look at France, which my heart should love.

I realized it was not wise
To keep such sighs within my heart,
10   For I saw the way lay open
Toward good peace, which can bestow all benefits.
So I turned my thoughts toward consolation,
Yet my heart never did cease
To look at France, which my heart should love.

15   Then I loaded all my desires into the ship
Of Hope, entreating them to make their way
Over the sea, not stopping,
And recommend me to France.
May God grant us a good peace without delay!
20   Then I'll have the chance—if it is so—
To look at France, which my heart should love.

Envoy

Peace is a treasure that cannot be overpraised,
I hate war, have no reason to esteem it.
War has, rightly or wrongly, long made it difficult for me
25   To look at France, which my heart should love!

Ballade

Pray for peace, sweet Virgin Mary,
Queen of the heavens and mistress of the earth.
In your courtesy, have all the saints
Say their prayers, and make your way
5   To your Son, begging His Highness
To please look upon His people,
Whom He wished to redeem with His blood,
Beating down the warfare that brings total devastation.

De prieres ne vous vueilliez lasser :
10   Priez pour paix, le vray tresor de joye!

Priez, prelas et gens de sainte vie,
Religieux ne dormez en peresse,
Priez, maistres et tous suivans clergie,
Car par guerre fault que l'estude cesse.
15   Moustiers destruis sont sans qu'on les redresse,
Le service de Dieu vous fault laissier.
Quant ne povez en repos demourer,
Priez si fort que briefment Dieu vous oye.
L'Eglise voult a ce vous ordonner :
20   Priez pour paix, le vray tresor de joye!

Priez, princes qui avez seigneurie,
Roys, ducs, contes, barons plains de noblesse,
Gentilz hommes avec chevalerie,
Car meschans gens surmontent gentillesse.
25   En leurs mains ont toute vostre richesse,
Debatz les font en hault estat monter,
Vous le povez chascun jour veoir au cler,
Et sont riches de voz biens et monnoye
Dont vous deussiez le peuple suporter :
30   Priez pour paix, le vray tresor de joye!

Priez, peuple qui souffrez tirannie,   [p. 196]
Car voz seigneurs sont en telle foiblesse
Qu'ilz ne peuent vous garder par maistrie,
Ne vous aidier en vostre grant destresse.
35   Loyaulx marchans, la selle si vous blesse*
Fort sur le dox. Chascun vous vient presser
Et ne povez marchandise mener,
Car vous n'avez seur passage ne voye,
Et maint peril vous couvient il passer :
40   Priez pour paix, le vray tresor de joye!

Priez, galans joyeux en compaignie,
Qui despendre desirez a largesse,
Guerre vous tient la bourse desgarnie.
Priez, amans, qui voulez en lïesse
45   Servir amours, car guerre, par rudesse,
Vous destourbe de voz dames hanter,
Qui maintesfoiz fait leurs vouloirs tourner,
Et quant tenez le bout de la couroye,
Un estrangier si le vous vient oster :
50   Priez pour paix, le vray tresor de joye!

Please do not turn a deaf ear to such prayers!
10   Pray for peace, the true treasure chest of joy!

Pray, you prelates and men of holy life,
You religious folk, do not sleep in sloth!
Pray, you masters and all who pursue knowledge,
For war makes an end of learning.
15   Churches have been destroyed and not rebuilt.
You are forced to abandon God's service.
Since you can find no place to rest,
Pray fervently so God hears you at once.
The church issues you this command:
20   Pray for peace, the true treasure chest of joy!

Pray, you princes who have dominion,
Kings, dukes, counts, barons of great nobility,
Well-born men of chivalry,
For scoundrels are bringing gentility low.
25   They have in their hands all your riches.
Disputes raise them to high estate
(You can clearly see this every day),
And they are enriched by your goods and money,
With which you should support the people.
30   Pray for peace, the true treasure chest of joy!

Pray, you people who are enduring tyranny,
For your lords find themselves so weak
They have not the mastery to keep you safe,
Or give you help in your great distress.
35   Honest merchants, you have a heavy burden
To bear; every man presses you,
And you cannot transport your goods,
For you have no safe passage or road,
And you must pass through many a danger.
40   Pray for peace, the true treasure chest of joy!

Pray, you gallant lovers in your companies,
Who think to spend liberally.
War keeps your purse empty.
Pray, you lovers who wish in happiness
45   To serve Love, for war, in its rudeness,
Prevents you from frequenting your ladies
And makes them often change their minds.
And when you hold the end of the strap,
A foreigner comes to take it from you.
50   Pray for peace, the true treasure chest of joy!

L'envoy

Dieu tout puissant nous vueille conforter!
Toutes choses en terre, ciel et mer,
Priez vers lui que brief en tout pourvoye,
En lui seul est de tous maulx amender :
55   Priez pour paix, le vray tresor de joye!

[83]

BALADES DE PLUSIEURS PROPOS*   [p. 203]

B116   Orlians · contre Garencieres*

Je, qui suis Dieu des amoureux,
Prince de joyeuse plaisance,
A toutes celles et a ceulx
Qui sont de mon obeissance,
5   Requier qu'a toute leur puissance
Me viengnent aidier et servir,
Pour l'outrecuidance punir
D'aucuns qui, par leur janglerie,
Veulent par force conquerir
10   Des grans biens de ma seigneurie,

Car Garencieres, l'un d'entr'eulx,
Si dit en sa folle vantance,
Pour faire le chevalereux,
Qu'avant yer, par sa grant vaillance,
15   Luy et son cueur, d'une aliance,
Furent devant Beauté courir.
Je ne luy vy pas, sans faillir,
Mais croy qu'il soit en resverie,
Car si pres n'oseroit venir
20   Des grans biens de ma seigneurie!

Il dit qu'il est tant douloureux
Et qu'il est mort sans recouvrance,
Mais bien seroit il maleureux
Qui donneroit en ce creance.
25   On peut veoir que celle penance
Qu'il lui a couvenu souffrir
N'a fait son visage pallir
Ne amaigrir de maladie.
Ainsi se moque, pour chevir
30   Des grans biens de ma seigneurie.

Envoy

May Almighty God be pleased to comfort you!
Everything on the earth, sky, and sea,
Pray Him that soon He sees to all that is needed.
He alone can alleviate all our ills.
55   Pray for peace, the true treasure chest of joy!

BALLADES ON MANY SUBJECTS

Ballade — Orleans in response to Garencières

I, who am the God of lovers,
Prince of joyful pleasure,
To all men and women
Who owe obedience to me
5   I demand that with all their strength
They come to help and serve me
In order to punish the presumption
Of some who, in their boastfulness,
Wish to acquire by force
10   The great benefits of my lordship.

For Garencières, one of that crew,
Has said with his foolish bragging
In order to act the chivalrous man
That the day before yesterday, very boldly,
15   He and his heart, making common cause,
Went to the lists against Beauty.
I did not see him, make no mistake,
But I believe he's somewhat deluded,
For he'd not dare go so close to
20   The great benefits of my lordship!

He says he suffers so much
He must die — beyond any recovery.
But he'd be pretty wretched
Whoever would credit this.
25   One could see that such pain
As he has had to suffer
Has not made his face pale,
Nor has disease made him lose weight.
And so, in order to prevail, he mocks
30   The great benefits of my lordship.

L'envoy   [p. 204]

Sur tous me plaist le retenir
Roy des heraulx pour bien mentir.
Cest office je luy ottrie.
C'est ce que lui vueil departir
35   Des grans biens de ma seigneurie!

[84]

B117   Balade · Responce de Garencieres

Cupido, Dieu des amoureux,
Prince de joyeuse plaisance,
Moy, Garencieres, tressoingneux
De vous servir de ma puissance,
5   Vien devers vous en obeissance,
Pour vous humblement requerir
Que vous vueilliez faire punir
Un homme de mauvaise vie,
Qui, contre raison, veult tenir
10   Le droit de vostre seigneurie.

C'est un enfant malicïeux,
Ou nul ne doit avoir fïance,
Car il en a ja plus de deux
Deceues, ou païs de France,
15   Dont vous deussiez prandre vengeance,
Pour faire les autres cremir.
C'est le prince de Bien Mentir,
Ainsné frere de Janglerie,
Qui, contre raison, veult tenir
20   Le droit de vostre seigneurie.

Onques Lucifer, l'orgueilleux,
Ne fist si grant oultrecuidance
Quant il emprist d'estre envïeux   [p. 205]
Sur le Dieu de toute puissance.
25   Il me semble que, par sentence,
Vous le deussiez faire bannir
De vostre court sans revenir,
Lui et sa faulse compaignie,
Qui, contre raison, veult tenir
30   Le droit de vostre seigneurie.

L'envoy

Prince, s'on doit avoir vaillance
Pour mentir a grant habondance

Envoy

Beyond all others I am pleased to retain him
As king of the heralds—he lies so well.
This is the office I grant him.
It's what I wish to give him of
35   The great benefits of my lordship!

Ballade—Response by Garencières

Cupid, God of lovers,
Prince of joyful pleasure,
I, Garencières, very eager
To serve you as best I can,
5   Obediently come before you
To humbly request
That you please have punished
A man of dissolute life,
Who, against reason, wishes to have
10   Rights in your lordship.

He's a mischievous child,
Whom no man should trust,
For he has deceived more than two
Women in the land of France,
15   And you should take vengeance therefore
And thus put fear in others.
He is the Prince of Skillful Lying,
Older brother of Boasting,
Who, against reason, wishes to have
20   Rights in your lordship.

Never did Lucifer, the arrogant one,
Do anything so outrageous
When he undertook to rival
God Almighty.
25   I think that with a sentence
You should have this man banished
From your court with no return,
That one, along with his false company,
Who, against reason, wishes to have
30   Rights in your lordship.

Envoy

Prince, if one must be daring
To lie extravagantly

Et pour faulseté maintenir,
Vous verrés icellui venir*
35   A grant honneur, n'en doubtez mie,
Qui, contre raison, veult tenir
Le droit de vostre seigneurie.

[85]

B118   **Balade**

En acquittant nostre temps vers Jeunesse
Le nouvel an et la saison jolie,
Plains de plaisir et de toute lïesse,
Qui chascun d'eulx chierement nous en prie,
5   Venuz sommes en ceste mommerie,
Belles, bonnes, plaisans et gracïeuses,
Prestz de dancer et faire chiere lie,
Pour resveillier voz pensees joieuses.

Or bannissiez de vous toute peresse,
10   Ennuy, soussy avec merencolie,   [p. 206]
Car froit yver, qui ne veult que rudesse,
Est desconfit et couvient qu'il s'en fuye.
Avril et May amainent doulce vie
Avecques eulx. Pource, soyez soingneuses
15   De recevoir leur plaisant compaignie
Pour resveillier voz pensees joieuses.

Venus aussi, la tresnoble Deesse,
Qui sur femmes doit avoir la maistrie,
Vous envoye de confort a largesse,
20   Et Plaisance de grans biens enrichie,
En vous chargeant que de vostre partie
Vous acquittiés sans estre dangereuses.
Aidier vous veult, sans que point vous oublie,
Pour resveillier voz pensees joyeuses!

[86]

B119   **Balade**

Bien moustrez, Printemps gracïeux,
De quel mestier savez servir,
Car Yver fait cueurs ennuieux
Et vous les faictes resjouïr.
5   Si tost comme il vous voit venir,

And perpetuate falseness,
You will see such a man come
35   With great honor, don't doubt at all,
Who, against reason, wishes to have
Rights in your lordship.

Ballade

In spending the time we owe to Youth,
During the New Year and merry season,
Full of pleasure and happiness of every kind
(All of them seeking our attention),
5   We men have come to this masked ball,
You ladies fair, kind, pleasant, and graceful,
Ready to dance and make merry,
And thus awaken your thoughts of happiness.

Now banish all sloth from you,
10   Worry, care, and also melancholy,
Since the cold winter, which knows only cruelty,
Has been vanquished and must flee.
April and May bring the good life
With them. And so, ladies, make ready
15   To receive their pleasant company
And thus awaken your thoughts of happiness.

Venus as well, the very noble Goddess,
Who should hold lordship over women,
Sends you bountiful comfort
20   And Pleasure, enriched with fine goods,
Charging you, for your part,
To do as you should without danger.
Not neglecting you, she wishes to help you
And thus awaken your thoughts of happiness!

Ballade

You show well, gracious Spring,
With what office you know to serve,
For Winter makes hearts wearisome,
And you give them back their joy.
5   As soon as he sees you coming,

Lui et sa meschant retenue
Sont contrains et prestz de fuïr
A vostre joyeuse venue.

Yver fait champs et arbres vieulx,
10   Leurs barbes de neige blanchir,
Et est si froit, ort et pluieux,
Qu'emprés le feu couvient croupir.
On ne peut hors des huis yssir,   [p. 207]
Comme un oisel qui est en mue,
15   Mais vous faittes tout rajeunir
A vostre joyeuse venue.

Yver fait le souleil es cieulx
Du mantel des nues couvrir.
Or maintenant, loué soit Dieux,
20   Vous estes venu esclersir
Toutes choses et embellir.
Yver a sa peine perdue,
Car l'an nouvel l'a fait bannir,
A vostre joyeuse venue!

[88]

B120   **Balade**

Je fu en fleur ou temps passé d'enfance,
Et puis aprés devins fruit en jeunesse.
Lors m'abaty de l'arbre de Plaisance,
Vert et non meur, Folie, ma maistresse,
5   Et pour cela, Raison qui tout redresse
A son plaisir, sans tort ou mesprison,
M'a a bon droit, par sa tresgrant sagesse,
Mis pour meurir ou feurre de prison.

En ce j'ay fait longue continuance,
10   Sans estre mis a l'essor de Largesse.
J'en suy contant et tiens que, sans doubtance,
C'est pour le mieulx, combien que par peresse
Deviens fletry et tire vers vieillesse.
Assez estaint est en moy le tison
15   De sot desir, puis qu'ay esté en presse
Mis pour meurir ou feurre de prison.   [p. 208]

Dieu nous doint paix, car c'est ma desirance.
Adonc seray en l'eaue de Lïesse

He and his evil crew
Are pressed hard and ready to take flight
With your joyful arrival.

Winter renders fields and trees old,
10   Makes white with snow their beards,
And it is so cold, miserable, and rainy,
You have to huddle around the fire.
No one can go out the door,
Like a bird that is in molt,
15   But you make everything young again
With your joyful arrival.

Winter covers the sun in the heavens
With a cloak of clouds.
But in this present season, praise God,
20   You have come to brighten
And beautify everything.
Winter has wasted his efforts,
For the New Year has had him banished
With your joyful arrival.

Ballade

Long ago I blossomed as a child,
And afterward in youth became a fruit.
Then my mistress Folly knocked me down,
Green and unripe, from the tree of Pleasure.
5   And for this, Reason, who corrects all
As she pleases, without wrong or mistake,
Rightfully, in her very great wisdom, had me
Put on prison straw to grow ripe.

For a long time I have remained thus,
10   Never enjoying the free air of Generosity.
I am satisfied and consider that, no doubt,
It's for the best, although through sloth
I grow slack and draw near to old age.
Dead within me are the embers
15   Of foolish desire since I have been by force
Put on prison straw to grow ripe.

God give us peace, for that's my desire.
Then I will be refreshed at once by the water

Tost refreschi, et au souleil de France
20   Bien nettié du moisy de Tristesse.
J'attens Bon Temps, endurant en humblesse,
Car j'ay espoir que Dieu ma guerison
Ordonnera. Pource, m'a sa haultesse
Mis pour meurir ou feurre de prison.

L'envoy
25   Fruit suis d'yver qui a meins de tendresse
Que fruit d'esté. Si suis en garnison,
Pour amolir ma trop verde duresse,
Mis pour meurir ou feurre de prison!

[89]

B121   Balade

Cueur, trop es plain de folie.
Cuides tu de t'eslongnier
Hors de nostre compaignie
Et en repos te logier?
5   Ton propos ferons changier :
Soing et Ennuy nous nommons.
Avecques toy demourrons,
Car c'est le commandement
De Fortune, qui en serre
10   T'a tenu moult longuement
Ou royaume d'Angleterre.

Dy nous, ne congnois tu mie
Que l'estat de prisonnier   [p. 209]
Est que souvent lui ennuye,
15   Et endure maint dangier
Dont il ne se peut vengier?
Pource, nous ne te faisons
Nul tort, se te gouvernons
Ainsi que communement
20   Sont prisonniers pris en guerre,
Dont es l'un presentement
Ou royaume d'Angleterre.

En lieu de Plaisance lye,
Au lever et au couschier,
25   Trouveras Merencolie.
Souvent te fera veillier,
La nuit et le jour songier.
Ainsi te guerdonnerons,

Of happiness and, in the sun of France,
20   Be well cleansed of the mold of Sadness.
I wait for Good Times, humbly enduring,
For I have hope that God will ordain
My cure; and that's why His Excellency had me
Put on prison straw to grow ripe.

Envoy

25   I am a winter fruit with less tenderness
Than fruit in summer; and thus I am in storage
So that the overgreen hardness might soften,
Put on prison straw to grow ripe!

Ballade

Heart, you are too full of madness.
Do you think to put distance between
Yourself and our company
And find someplace to rest?
5   We will have you change your mind.
We are called Worry and Care.
We shall make our home with you.
For it's the ordinance
Of Fortune who has kept you
10   In prison for a long time
In the kingdom of England.

Tell us, do you not acknowledge
That the state of being a prisoner
Is to be often tormented
15   And suffer much danger
For which one can take no vengeance?
And so we shall be doing you
No injury if we treat you
Just as prisoners by custom
20   Are treated when taken in war,
And of these you are one
In the kingdom of England.

In the place of merry Pleasure
When you rise and take your rest
25   You will encounter Melancholy.
Often she will make you stay awake
At night and dream during the day.
This is the reward we will bestow on you,

30   Et es fers te garderons
      De Soussy et Pensement.
      Se tu peuz, si te defferre!
      Par nous n'auras autrement
      Ou royaume d'Angleterre.

[90]

B122   **Balade**

      Nouvelles ont couru en France
      Par mains lieux que j'estoye mort,
      Dont avoient peu desplaisance
      Aucuns qui me hayent a tort.
5   Autres en ont eu desconfort,
      Qui m'ayment de loyal vouloir,
      Comme mes bons et vrais amis.   [p. 210]
      Si fais a toutes gens savoir
      Qu'encore est vive la souris!*

10   Je n'ay eu ne mal ne grevance,
      Dieu mercy, mais suis sain et fort,
      Et passe temps en esperance
      Que paix, qui trop longuement dort,
      S'esveillera, et par accort
15   A tous fera lïesse avoir.
      Pource, de Dieu soient maudis
      Ceulx qui sont dolens de veoir
      Qu'encore est vive la souris!

      Jeunesse sur moy a puissance,
20   Mais Vieillesse fait son effort
      De m'avoir en sa gouvernance.
      A present faillira son sort.
      Je suis assez loing de son port,
      De pleurer vueil garder mon hoir.
25   Loué soit Dieu de Paradis,
      Qui m'a donné force et povoir
      Qu'encore est vive la souris!

                    L'envoy
      Nul ne porte pour moy le noir,
      On vent meillieur marchié drap gris.
30   Or tiengne chascun pour tout voir,
      Qu'encore est vive la souris!

And we will keep you in the chains
30　　Of Worry and Deep Thought.
If you can, free yourself!
From us you will have nothing else
In the kingdom of England.

Ballade

The news ran through France
In many places that I was dead,
And this gave but little displeasure
To some who unjustly despise me.
5　　Some were distressed,
Those who love me with a faithful will,
Like my fine and true friends.
So I let everyone know
That the mouse is still alive!

10　　I've had neither ill nor pain,
Thank God, but am healthy and strong,
And I pass the time in hope
That peace, who has slept too long,
Will awaken and, through a treaty,
15　　Shall make everyone happy.
And so may God then curse
Those who are pained to see
That the mouse is still alive!

Youth has power over me,
20　　But Old Age makes an effort
To keep me under her power.
At present she has no chance.
I am very distant from her harbor.
I intend to keep my heir from weeping.
25　　May God in Paradise be praised,
Who has given me force and power so
That the mouse is still alive!

Envoy
Let no man wear black for me.
Gray cloth is sold at a better price.
30　　Let everyone consider it the whole truth
That the mouse is still alive!

B123   Balade   [p. 211]

Puis qu'ainsi est que vous alez en France,
Duc de Bourbon, mon compaignon treschier,*
Ou Dieu vous doint, selon la desirance
Que tous avons, bien povoir besongnier,
5   Mon fait vous vueil descouvrir et chargier
Du tout en tout, en sens et en folie.
Trouver ne puis nul meillieur messagier :
Il ne fault ja que plus je vous en die.

Premierement, se c'est vostre plaisance,
10   Recommandez moy, sans point l'oublier,
A ma dame. Ayez en souvenance,
Et lui dictes, je vous pry et requier,
Les maulx que j'ay, quant me fault eslongnier,
Maugré mon vueil, sa doulce compaignie.
15   Vous savez bien que c'est de tel mestier,
Il ne fault ja que plus je vous en dye.

Or y faictes comme j'ay la fiance,
Car un amy doit pour l'autre veillier.
Se vous dictes : «Je ne sçay, sans doubtance,
20   Qui est celle, vueilliez la ensaignier.»
Je vous respons qu'il ne vous fault serchier,
Fors que celle qui est la mieulx garnie
De tous les biens qu'on sauroit souhaidier :
Il ne fault ja que plus je vous en dye.

L'envoy
25   Sy ay chargié a Guillaume Cadier*
Que par dela bien souvent vous supplie :
«Souviengne vous du fait du prisonnier,
Il ne fault ja que plus je vous en dye.»

[91]

B124   Balade   [p. 212]

Mon gracïeux cousin, duc de Bourbon,
Je vous requier, quant vous aurez loisir,
Que me faittes, par ballade ou chançon,
De vostre estat aucunement sentir,
5   Car quant a moy, sachiez que, sans mentir,
Je sens mon cueur renouveller de joye,
En esperant le bon temps avenir
Par bonne paix que brief Dieu nous envoye.

Ballade

Since you are going to France,
Duke of Bourbon, my very dear companion,
Where may God grant you—just as we all
Desire it—that you can conduct your business well,
5   I want to tell you how I am and report everything
To you, whether this is sense or madness.
I can find no better messenger.
I need to tell you no more of this.

First, if it be your pleasure,
10   Don't neglect to commend me
To my lady. Remember this,
And speak to her, I beg and ask you,
About the ills I suffer when I must be distant,
Against my will, from her sweet company.
15   You know well what's called for.
I need to tell you no more of this.

Do now what I trust you will,
For one friend must watch out for another.
If you say: "I do not know beyond doubt
20   Who she is—please tell me."
I will answer that you need only seek
The lady who is most graced
With all the virtues one could desire.
I need to tell you no more of this.

Envoy

25   Just so have I charged Guillaume Cadier
Over there that he should many times beg you:
"Remember the situation of the prisoner.
I need to tell you no more of this."

Ballade

My gracious cousin, Duke of Bourbon,
I beg you, when you have the chance,
That you let me know something
About how you are, in a ballade or a song,
5   Since, for my part, know that with no lie
I feel my heart renew with joy,
As I hope for good times to come
With good peace—may God send it soon.

Tout Crestïan, qui est loyal et bon,
10   Du bien de paix se doit fort resjoïr,
Veu les grans maulx et la destruccïon
Que guerre fait par tous pays courir.
Dieu a voulu Crestïanté punir
Qui a laissié de bien vivre la voye,
15   Mais puis aprés, il la veult secourir
Par bonne paix que brief Dieu nous envoye.

Et pour cela, mon treschier compaignon,
Vueilliez de vous desplaisance bannir,
En oubliant vostre longue prison
20   Qui vous a fait mainte doleur souffrir.
Merciez Dieu, pensez de le servir,
Il vous garde de tous biens grant montjoye*
Et vous fera avoir vostre desir
Par bonne paix que brief Dieu nous envoye.

L'envoy
25   Resveilliez vous en joyeux souvenir,
Car j'ay espoir qu'encore je vous voye,
Et moy aussi, en confort et plaisir
Par bonne paix que brief Dieu nous envoye!

B125   **Balade**   [p. 213]

Mon chier cousin, de bon cueur vous mercie
Des blans connins que vous m'avez donnez,*
Et oultre plus, pour vray vous certiffie,
Quant aux connins que dittes qu'ay amez,
5   Ilz sont pour moy, plusieurs ans a passez,
Mis en oubly; aussi mon instrument
Qui les servoit a fait son testament
Et est retrait et devenu hermite.
Il dort tousjours, a parler vrayement,
10   Comme celui qui en riens ne prouffite.

Ne parlez plus de ce, je vous en prie,
Dieux ait l'ame de tous les trespassez!
Parler vault mieulx, pour faire chiere lie,
De bons morceaulx et de frians pastez,
15   Mais qu'ilz soient tout chaudement tastez!
Pour le present, c'est bon esbatement,
Et qu'on ait vin pour nettier la dent.
En char crue mon cueur ne se delitte.
Oublions tout le vieil gouvernement
20   Comme celui qui en riens ne prouffite!

Every Christian who is loyal and virtuous
10   Should rejoice mightily at the benefits of peace,
Seeing the great ills and the destruction
War has made through every land.
God did intend to punish Christendom,
Which has forsaken the path of right living,
15   But afterward has desired to save it
With good peace — may God send it soon.

And for this reason, my very dear companion,
Please banish sorrow from you,
Forgetting your long imprisonment,
20   Which has made you suffer many an ill.
Give thanks to God, think of serving Him.
For you He will keep an abundance of every good thing
And bring it about that you obtain your desire
With good peace — may God send it soon.

Envoy
25   Awaken yourself to joyful memory,
For I have hope to see you again,
And me as well, in comfort and pleasure,
With good peace — may God send it soon.

Ballade

My dear cousin, I thank you with a good heart
For the white rabbits you have given me.
And, moreover, I affirm to you as the truth,
In regard to the rabbits that you say I have loved,
5   I have now entirely forgotten them, for it has been
Several years. Also my instrument,
Which served them, has made out his testament,
And so he has retired and become a hermit.
He is always asleep, to speak the truth,
10   Like a man who finds profit in nothing.

Say no more about this to me, I beg you.
May God keep the soul of everyone who has gone!
So as to make merry, it were better to speak
Of tasty morsels and delicious cakes,
15   Provided they are tasted when well heated!
This is fine entertainment for the present,
And there should be wine to clean the palate.
My heart finds no pleasure in raw meat.
Let us forget the way we used to live,
20   Like a man who finds profit in nothing.

Quant Jeunesse tient gens en seigneurie,
Les jeux d'amours sont grandement prisez,
Mais Fortune, qui m'a en sa baillie,
Les a du tout de mon cueur deboutez,
25   Et desormais, vous et moi, excusez
De tels esbas serons legierement,
Car faiz avons noz devoirs grandement
Ou temps passé : vers Amours me tiens quicte.
Je n'en vueil plus, mon cueur si s'en repent,
30   Comme celui qui en riens ne prouffite.

L'envoy   [p. 214]

Vieulx soudoiers avecques jeune gent
Ne sont prisiez la valeur d'une mitte.
Mon office resine plainement
Comme celui qui en riens ne prouffite.

[93]

B126   Balade

Dame qui cuidiez trop savoir,
Mais vostre sens tourne en folie
Et cuidiez les gens decevoir
Par vostre cautelle jolie.
5   Qui croiroit vostre chiere lie
Tantost seroit pris en voz las :
Encore ne m'avez vous mie,
Encore ne m'avez vous pas!

Vous cuidiez bien qu'apercevoir
10   Ne sache vostre moquerie.
Si fais, pour vous dire le voir,
Et pource, chierement vous prie,
Alez jouer de l'escremie*
Autre part, car, quant en ce cas,
15   Encore ne m'avez vous mie,
Encore ne m'avez vous pas!

Vous ferez bien vostre devoir,
Se m'atrapés par tromperie,
Car trop ay congneu, main et soir
20   Les faulx tours dont estes garnie.
On vous appelle : foul s'i fie.
Deportez vous de telz esbas :
Encores ne m'avez vous mie,
Encore ne m'avez vous pas!

[94]

When Youth holds lordship over people,
The games of love are highly prized.
But Fortune, who has me in her dominion,
Has chased them right out of my heart.
25   And henceforth you and I will be
Readily excused from such delights,
For in grand style we have carried out our duties
In times past. I consider myself quit with Love.
I wish for nothing else, and my heart repents of it,
30   Like a man who finds profit in nothing.

Envoy

By the side of the young, old soldiers
Find no esteem at all.
I resign my office, there is no doubt,
Like a man who finds profit in nothing.

Ballade

Lady, you think to know a great deal
(But your wisdom turns to folly),
And you think you can deceive men
With your fine games.
5   Whoever trusts your smiling face
Would soon be caught in your bonds.
Still you do not have me at all.
Still you do not have me!

You certainly think me unable
10   To recognize how you mock.
Yet I do, to tell you the truth,
And for this I beg you dearly:
Go play your fancy tricks
Somewhere else, for in this case
15   Still you do not have me at all.
Still you do not have me!

You will do your job well
If you trap me with your deceptions,
For I've recognized clearly, morning and night,
20   The false tricks you have at your disposal.
Your game is up, untrustworthy one.
Have your fun with such pastimes.
Still you do not have me at all.
Still you do not have me!

B127   Balade · Orlians a Bourgogne*   [p. 215]

        Puis que je suis vostre voisin
        En ce païs presentement,
        Mon compaignon, frere et cousin,
        Je vous requier treschierement
5   Que de vostre gouvernement
        Et estat me faictes savoir,
        Car j'en orroye bien souvent,
        S'il en estoit a mon vouloir.

        Il n'est jour, ne soir, ne matin,
10   Que ne prie Dieu humblement
        Que la paix prengne telle fin
        Que je puisse joyeusement
        A mon desir prouchainement
        Parler a vous et vous veoir.
15   Ce seroit treshastivement,
        S'il en estoit a mon vouloir.

        Chascun doit estre bien enclin
        Vers la paix, car certainement
        Elle departira butin
20   De grans biens a tous largement.
        Guerre ne sert que de tourment.
        Je la hé, pour dire le voir!
        Bannie seroit plainement,
        S'il en estoit a mon vouloir.

              L'envoy
25   Va, ma ballade, prestement
        A Saint Omer, moustrant comment
        Tu vas pour moy ramentevoir
        Au duc a qui suis loyaument,
        Et tout a son commandement,
30   S'il en estoit a mon vouloir!

[95]

B128   Balade · Response de Bourgogne   [p. 216]
                     a Orlians

        S'il en estoit a mon vouloir,
        Mon maistre et amy sans changier,
        Je vous asseure, pour tout voir,
        Qu'en vo fait n'auroit nul dangier,
5   Mais par deça, sans attargier,

Ballade — Orleans to Burgundy

Since I'm your neighbor
In this country at the moment,
My companion, brother, and cousin,
I beg you with much affection
5   To inform me about
Your situation and state,
For I should often hear of these things,
If I had my wish.

There is no day, no evening, no morning
10   I do not pray God humbly
That peace might so come about
That I might to my joy,
As I desire, very soon
See you and speak to you.
15   This would be at once
If I had my wish.

Every man should highly favor
Peace, for certainly
It will distribute a booty
20   Of great benefits very generously.
War brings only torment.
I hate it, to tell the truth!
No doubt, it would be banished
If I had my wish.

Envoy

25   Go, my ballade, in haste
To St. Omer, making clear
You do this so the duke will remember me
For I am his man in good faith,
And entirely at his command,
30   If I had my wish!

Ballade — Response of Burgundy
to Orleans

If I had my wish,
My master and friend beyond any alteration,
I assure you, in all truth,
You would be facing no threat,
5   For on this side, with no delay,

Vous verroye hors de prison,
Quitte du tout, pour abregier
En ceste presente saison.

Se tel don povez recevoir
10   Par la grace Dieu, de legier
Pourrés tel a paix esmouvoir
Qui la desire eslongier.
Nul contre n'osera songier,
Car confort aurés bel et bon,
15   Se Dieu nous veult assoulagier,
En ceste presente saison.

Mettons nous en nostre devoir
Qu'en paix nous puissions herbergier.
Il n'est ou monde tel manoir,
20   Qui desir a de s'i logier.
Abregeons sans plus prolongier :
Il en est temps, ou jamais non,
Pour nous de guerre deslogier,
En ceste presente saison.

L'envoy
25   Or pensons de vous allegier
De prison, pour tout engagier,
Se n'avons paix et unïon,
Et du tout m'y vueil obligier,
En ceste presente saison.

[96]

B129   Balade · Orlians a Bourgogne   [p. 217]

Pour le haste de mon passage
Qu'il me couvient faire oultre mer,
Tout ce que j'ay en mon courage
A present ne vous puis mander,
5   Mais non pour tant, a brief parler,
De la ballade que m'avés
Envoyee, comme savés,
Touchant paix et ma delivrance,
Je vous mercie chierement,
10   Comme tout vostre entierement
De cueur, de corps et de puissance.

Je vous envoyeray message,
Se Dieu plaist, briefment sans tarder,

I should see you out of prison,
Quit of everything, in a word,
In this present season.

If you can receive such a gift
10 Through God's grace, you could easily
Move toward peace any man
Who wished to thrust it aside.
No one will dare be against it.
But instead you will find a fair and good comfort,
15 If God wishes to console us
In this present season.

Let us get on with our work
So we might be able to take refuge in peace.
There's no such manor in the world,
20 For anyone who desires to lodge there.
Let us cut it short, prolong it no more.
The time is now or never
For us to free ourselves from war,
In this present season.

Envoy

25 Now let us see about setting you free
From prison, giving this all our attention
If we do not conclude a peace and agreement.
And I'll commit myself to accomplishing all this
In this present season.

Ballade — Orleans to Burgundy

Because the time is short before
I must travel over the sea,
Everything that is in my heart
At present I cannot report to you.
5 Nevertheless, to put it in a few words,
For the ballade you have
Sent me, as you know,
Concerning peace and my deliverance,
I thank you affectionately,
10 As someone entirely yours,
With heart, body, and might.

I'll send a messenger to you,
Should God please, shortly, without delay,

Loyal, secret et assez sage,
15   Pour bien a plain vous infourmer
De tout ce que pourray trouver
Sur ce que savoir desirés.
Pareillement, fault que mettés
Et faictes, vers la part de France,
20   Diligence soingneusement.
Je vous en requier humblement,
De cueur, de corps et de puissance.

Et sans plus despendre langage,
A cours mots, plaise vous penser
25   Que vous laisse mon cueur en gage
Pour tousjours, sans jamais faulser.
Si me vucilliez recommander
A ma cousine, car croyés
Que en vous deux, tant que vivrés,
30   J'ay mise toute ma fiance,
Et vostre party loyaument   [p. 218]
Tendray, sans faire changement,
De cueur, de corps et de puissance.

L'envoy
Or y parra que vous ferés,
35   Et se point ne m'oublierés,
Ainsi que g'y ay esperance.
Adieu vous dy presentement.
Tout Bourgongnon sui vrayement.
De cueur, de corps et de puissance.

B130   Balade · Responce
de Bourgogne a Orlians

De cueur, de corps et de puissance
Vous mercie treshumblement
De vostre bonne souvenance
Qu'avez de moy soingneusement.
5   Or povez faire entierement
De moy, en tout bien et honneur
Comme vostre cueur le propose,
Et de mon vouloir soyez seur,
Quoy que nul die ne deppose.

10   Ne mectés point en oubliance
L'estat et le gouvernement
De la noble maison de France,
Qui se maintient piteusement.

A man faithful, discreet, and rather wise,
15   Who will fully inform you
About everything I might learn
Of the matters you wish to know.
You must do just the same
And carry this off, on behalf of France,
20   With care and diligence.
This I beg you humbly
With heart, body, and might.

And without spending more speech,
My words brief, may you be pleased to think
25   I leave my heart with you as a warrant
For always, never proving false.
So please commend me
To my cousin, for believe
That in you two, as long as I live,
30   I've placed all my trust.
And I'll faithfully take
Your part, never changing,
With heart, body, and might.

Envoy
Now we shall see what you can do and
35   Whether you do not forget me,
As I hope you won't.
I tell you good-bye for the present.
I am truly all Burgundian,
With heart, body, and might.

Ballade — Response
of Burgundy to Orleans

With heart, body, and might
I thank you in all humility
For having remembered me
In such a fine and gracious fashion.
5   You can find me entirely
At your disposal, in virtue and honor,
As your heart proposes,
And depend completely on my good will,
No matter what anyone says or affirms.

10   Do not forget in the least
The state and condition
Of the noble house of France,
Which is in a pitiful state.

Vous saurés tout, quoy et comment.
15   Je n'en dy plus pour le meilleur,
Mais on en dit tant et expose
Que c'est a oïr grant orreur,   [p. 219]
Quoy que nul dye ne depose.

Pensez a vostre delivrance,
20   Je vous en prie chierement,
Car, sans ce, je n'ay esperance
Que nous ayons paix nullement.
On la heit tant mortellement
Que trop peu treuve de faveur.
25   Ne sera, comme je suppose,
Se ce n'est par vostre labeur,
Quoy que nul dye ne deppose.

L'envoy
Or prions Dieu, par sa doulceur,
Qu'a vous delivrer se dispose,
30   Car trop avez souffert douleur
Quoy que nul dye ne deppose.

B131   Balade · Orlians a Bourgogne*

Des nouvelles d'Albion,
S'il vous en plaist escouter,
Mon frere et mon compaignon,
Sachez qu'a mon retourner
5   J'ay esté deça la mer
Receu a joyeuse chiere,
Et a fait le roy passer
En bons termes ma matiere.

Je doy estre une saison
10   Eslargi pour pourchasser
La paix, aussi ma raençon.   [p. 220]
Se je puis seurté trouver
Pour aler et retourner,
Il fault qu'en haste la quiere,
15   Se je vueil brief achever
En bons termes ma matiere.

Or, gentil duc Bourgongnon,
A ce cop vueilliez m'aydier,
Comme mon entencïon
20   Est vous servir et amer,

You'll know all, the how and why.
15   I say no more, it's for the best,
But so much has been said and made known
It's very horrible to listen,
No matter what anyone says or affirms.

Think about your deliverance,
20   I entreat you with affection,
For, without this, I've no hope
We will obtain peace at all;
Peace is mortally hated
And so finds too little favor.
25   There will be no peace, I believe,
Unless it is through your efforts,
No matter what anyone says or affirms.

Envoy

Now let us pray God that in His grace
He determines to deliver you,
30   For you have suffered too much grief,
No matter what anyone says or affirms.

Ballade — Orleans to Burgundy

Concerning news from England,
If it pleases you to hear it,
My brother and my companion,
Know that when I returned,
5   I was received on this side
Of the sea with much joy
And the king has brought
My mission to a happy conclusion.

I am to be at liberty
10   For a season in order to work for
Peace, and my ransom as well,
If I can find some warrant for
My going and returning.
I must make haste in seeking it,
15   If in a short time I wish to bring
My mission to a happy conclusion.

Now, noble duke of Burgundy,
Please help me at this time,
Since my intention is to serve and love you
20   As long as I live.

Tant que vif pourray durer.
En vous ay fiance entiere
Que m'ayderez a finer
En bons termes ma matiere.

L'envoy
25   Mes amis fault esprouver
S'ilz vouldront, a ma priere
Me secourir pour mener
En bons termes ma matiere.

[100]

B132   Balade

J'ay tant joué avecques Aage
A la paulme que maintenant
J'ay quarante cinq. Sur bon gage*
Nous jouons, non pas pour neant.
5   Assez me sens fort et puissant
De garder mon jeu jusqu'a cy,
Ne je ne crains riens que Soussy.

Car Soussy tant me descourage   [p. 221]
De jouer, et va estouppant
10   Les cops que fiers a l'avantage.
Trop seurement est rachassant.*
Fortune si lui est aidant,
Mais Espoir est mon bon amy,
Ne je ne crains riens que Soussy.

15   Vieillesse de douleur enrage
De ce que le jeu dure tant,
Et dit en son felon langage
Que les chasses dorenavaant*
Merchera, pour m'estre nuisant,
20   Mais ne m'en chault, je la deffy,
Ne je ne crains riens que Soussy.

L'envoy
Se Bon Eur me tient convenant,*
Je ne doubte ne tant ne quant
Tout mon adversaire party,
25   Ne je ne crains riens que Soussy.

I have complete trust in you,
That you will help me carry through
My mission to a happy conclusion.

Envoy
25 My friends must be put to the proof,
If they intend to help me,
As I have prayed, bring
My mission to a happy conclusion.

Ballade

I have played tennis so long
With Age that at this moment
I am forty-five. For a real prize
We play on, not for nothing.
5   I have felt strong and sprightly enough
To keep up my side until this moment,
Nor do I fear anyone save Care.

For Care discourages me mightily
From playing and goes around retrieving
10 The balls from the good strokes I've made,
These he chases down and returns too easily.
Fortune has helped him do so.
But Hope is my good friend,
Nor do I fear anyone save Care.

15 Old Age goes mad with pain
Because the game goes on so long,
And she says with her vile words
That from now on she will mark
Where the balls land and so do me harm.
20 But I do not care—I defy her —
Nor do I fear anyone save Care.

Envoy
If Good Fortune keeps her promise to me,
I am not in the least afraid of
The whole party that opposes me.
25 Nor do I fear anyone save Care.

B133   **Balade**   [p. 222]

Visage de baffe venu,
Confit en composte de vin,
Menton rongneux et peu barbu
Et dessiré comme un coquin,
5   Malade du mal Saint Martin*
Et aussi ront q'un tonnellet,
Dieu le me sauve ce varlet!

Il est enroué devenu,
Car une pouldre de raisin
10   L'a tellement en l'ueil feru
Qu'endormy l'a comme un touppin.
Il y pert un chascun matin,
Car il en a chault le touppet.
Dieu le me sauve ce varlet!

15   Rompre ne sauroit un festu,
Quant il a pincé un loppin*
Saint Poursain, qui l'a retenu
Son chier compaignon et cousin,
Combien qu'ayent souvent hutin,
20   Quant ou cellier sont en secret.
Dieu le me sauve ce varlet!

                    L'envoy
Prince, pour aler jusqu'au Rin,
D'un baril a fait son ronssin,
Et ses esperons d'un foret.
25   Dieu le me sauve ce varlet!

[101]

B134   **Balade**   [p. 223]

Amour, qui tant a de puissance
Qu'il fait vieilles gens rassoter
Et jeunes plains d'oultrecuidance,
De tout estas se scet meller.
5   Je l'ay congneu pieça au cler,
Il ne fault ja que je le nye,
Par quoy dis et puis advouer,
Ce n'est fors que plaisant folie.

A droit compter sans decevance,
10   Quant un amant vient demander

Ballade

Face dazed, as though by a blow,
Soaked with wine punch,
Chin all scabs, scraggly beard,
Dressed in rags like a rogue,
5   Ill with St. Martin's day sickness
And round as a small cask—
God save this servant for me!

He has gone hoarse,
For the taste of the grape
10   Has so affected him
He's sleeping like a top.
Every morning it's just the same,
For his head is still hot with it.
God save this servant for me!

15   He couldn't break a piece of straw
After he has swallowed a bit
Of St. Pourçain, which he has made
His dear companion and relation,
Even though they often quarrel
20   When alone in the cellar.
God save this servant for me!

Envoy

Prince, to travel as far as the Rhine
He makes a horse out of his cask,
His spurs from a barrel stave.
25   God save this servant for me!

Ballade

Love, who has so much power,
Makes the old go mad
And fills the young with arrogance,
Approaching those of all estates.
5   Some time ago I came to know him well.
I must never deny him,
And that's why I say and then affirm:
It is nothing but a pleasant madness.

To offer a true account, with no evasions,
10   When a lover comes to request

Confort de sa dure grevance,
Que vouldroit il faire ou trouver?
Cela, je ne l'ose nommer.
Au fort, il fault que je le dye :
15   Ce qui fait le ventre lever,*
Ce n'est fors que plaisant folie.

Bien sçay que je fais desplaisance
Aux amoureux d'ainsi parler
Et que j'acquier leur malvueillance,
20   Mais, s'il leur plaist me pardonner,
Je leur prometz qu'au par aler,
Quant leur chaleur est refroidie,
Ils trouveront que, sans doubter,
Ce n'est fors que plaisant folie.

L'envoy

25   Prince, quant un prie d'amer,
Se l'autre s'i veult accorder,
Il n'y a plus, sans moquerie.
Laissiez les ensemble jouer,
Ce n'est fors que plaisant folie!

[102]

B135   Balade · Orlians a Bourgogne   [p. 224]

Beau frere, je vous remercie,
Car aidié m'avez grandement,
Et oultre plus, vous certiffie
Que j'ay mon fait entierement.
5   Il ne me fault plus riens qu'argent
Pour avancer tost mon passage,
Et pour en avoir prestement
Mettroye corps et ame en gage!

Il n'a marchant en Lombardie,
10   S'il m'en prestoit presentement,
Que ne fusse toute ma vie
Du cueur a son commandement,
Et tant que l'eusse fait content,
Demourer vouldroie en servage
15   Sans espargnier aucunement
Pour mettre corps et ame en gage,

Car se je suis en ma partie
Et oultre la mer franchement,

Comfort for his harsh suffering,
What would he do at the encounter?
What indeed—this I dare not say.
However, I must tell him:
15   Something that makes the groin swell.
It is nothing but a pleasant madness.

I know well I give displeasure
To lovers when I speak this way,
And that I thereby earn their ill will.
20   But, if they're pleased to pardon me,
I promise that in the end
When their ardor has cooled again,
They will, without doubt, discover
It is nothing but a pleasant madness.

Envoy

25   Prince, when someone begs for love,
If the other wishes to agree,
There's nothing for it, and no joke.
Let them enjoy each other.
It is nothing but a pleasant madness!

Ballade—Orleans to Burgundy

Fair brother, I thank you,
For you have given me much help,
And, even more, I affirm to you
I'm managing my business with no fuss.
5   The only thing I need is money
To hasten my passage to France.
And to obtain this at once
I would leave my body and soul as a pledge.

There's no merchant in Lombardy,
10   Whose command, if he should so
Entreat, I would not follow
With my whole heart for all my life.
And as long as he was pleased thereby,
I should remain in his service,
15   And not spare a thing, so that
I would leave my body and soul as a pledge.

For if I'm in my own land
And across the sea in freedom,

20   Dieu mercy, point ne me soussie
      Que n'aye des biens largement,
      Et desserviray loyaument
      A ceulx qui m'ont de bon courage
      Aidié, sans faillir nullement
      Pour mettre corps et ame en gage.

L'envoy
25   Qui m'ostera de ce tourment,
      Il m'achetera plainement
      A tousjours mes, a heritage.
      Tout sien seray sans changement,
      Pour mettre corps et ame en gage.

[103]

B136   Balade · Orlians a Bourgogne   [p. 225]

      Pour ce que je suis a presant
      Avec la gent vostre ennemie,
      Il fault que je face semblant,
      Faignant que ne vous ayme mye.
5   Non pour tant, je vous certiffie
      Et vous pri que vueillez penser
      Que je seray toute ma vie
      Vostre loyaument, sans faulser.

      Tous maulx de vous je voiz disant
10   Pour aveugler leur faulse envye.
      Non pour tant, je vous ayme tant,
      Ainsi m'aid la Vierge Marie
      Que je pry Dieu qu'il me maudye
      Se ne trouvez au par aler
15   Que vueil estre, quoy que nul dye,
      Vostre loyaumant, sans faulser.

      Faignez envers moy mal talant
      A celle fin que nul n'espye
      Nostre amour, car par ce faisant,
20   Sauldray hors du mal qui me anuye.
      Mais faictes que Bonne Foy lye
      Noz cuers, qu'ilz ne puissent muer,
      Car mon vouloir vers vous se plye,
      Vostre loyaument, sans faulser.

25   Vous et moy avons maint servant
      Que Convoitise fort mestrie.

God be thanked, I'm not worried that
20   I should not obtain abundant benefit.
And I'll faithfully serve
Those who, with a good heart, have
Helped me, never failing them in anything, and so
I would leave my body and soul as a pledge.

Envoy
25   Whoever rescues me from this torture
Would get all of me for himself,
From this time forward, as a bequest.
I will be all his, never to change, therefore
I would leave my body and soul as a pledge.

Ballade — Orleans to Burgundy

Because at present I am
Among the people of your enemies,
I must pretend,
Feigning I love you not at all.
5   Nevertheless, I affirm to you,
And beg you please to so think,
That all my life I will be
Yours faithfully, never to prove false.

I go about only speaking ill of you
10   In order to blind their false envy.
Nevertheless, I love you so much,
So help me Virgin Mary,
That I pray God curse me
If you don't find in the end
15   I intend being, no matter who says what,
Yours faithfully, never to prove false.

Pretend you think ill of me
So that no man might sense
Our love, for by doing this,
20   I'll avoid the trouble that worries me.
Yet make certain that Good Faith binds
Our hearts so they cannot change,
For my desire brings me to be
Yours faithfully, never to prove false.

25   You and I have many servants
Whom Covetousness strictly rules.

Il ne fault pas, ne tant ne quant,
Qu'ilz saichent nostre compaignie.
Peu de nombre fault que manye
30   Noz fais secrez par bien celer,   [p. 226]
Tant qu'il soit temps qu'on me publie
Vostre loyaument, sans faulser.

Tout mon fait saurez plus avant
Par le porteur en qui me fye.
35   Il est leal et bien saichant,
Et se garde de janglerye.
Creez le de vostre partie,
En ce qu'il vous doit raconter,
Et me tenez, je vous en prie,
40   Vostre loyaument, sans faulser.

L'envoy
Dieu me fiere d'espidimie,
Et ma part es cieulx je renye,
Se jamais vous povez trouver
Que me faigne par tromperie,
45   Vostre loyaument, sans faulser.

[104]

B137   **Balade**   [p. 227]

Par les fenestres de mes yeulx,
Ou temps passé, quant regardoie,
Avis m'estoit, ainsi m'ait Dieux,
Que de trop plus belles veoye
5   Qu'a present ne fais, mais j'estoie
Ravy en plaisir et lÿesse,
Es mains de ma dame Jennesse.

Or, maintenant que deviens vieulx,
Quant je lys ou livre de Joie,
10   Les lunectes prens pour le mieulx,
Par quoy la lectre me grossoye,
Et n'y voy ce que je souloie.
Pas n'avoye ceste foiblesse
Es mains de ma dame Jennesse.

15   Jennes gens, vous deviendrez tieulx,
Se vivez et suivez ma voie,
Car au jourd'uy n'a soubz les cieulx
Qui en aucun temps ne fouloye.

It's not necessary, not in any way,
That they learn of our companionship.
Only a few need manage
30   Our secret doings in order to hide them well,
Until the time comes to make public how I am
Yours faithfully, never to prove false.

In a while you'll learn all about my affairs
By the messenger whom I trust.
35   He's faithful and very knowledgeable,
And keeps away from foolish talk.
For your part put trust into
What he is to tell you,
And consider me, this I beg you,
40   Yours faithfully, never to prove false.

Envoy

May God strike me down with sickness,
Even as I renounce my place in heaven,
If you're ever able to discover
That, intending to deceive, I'm pretending to be
45   Yours faithfully, never to prove false.

Ballade

Through the windows of my eyes,
In times past when I was looking,
It seemed to me, so help me God,
I saw many more belles
5   Than I do at present; instead I was
Carried away by pleasure and happiness,
In the hands of my lady Youth.

Yet, now that I grow old,
When I read in the book of Joy,
10   I need spectacles to see better,
For they make the letters bigger,
And there I don't see what I was wont to.
I did not have this weakness at all
In the hands of my lady Youth.

15   Young people, you'll become the same,
If you live on and follow my path,
For today there is under heaven
No one who at times does not act the fool.

Puis faut que Raison son compte oye
20   Du trop despendu en simplesse,
Es mains de ma dame Jennesse.

L'envoy
Dieu en tout, par grace, pourvoye,
Et ce qui nicement forvoye,
A son plaisir, en bien radresse
25   Es mains de ma dame Jennesse!

[105]

B138   Balade   [p. 228]

Par les fenestres de mes yeulx
Le chault d'Amours souloit passer,
Mais maintenant que deviens vieulx,
Pour la chambre de mon penser
5   En esté freschement garder,
Fermees les feray tenir,
Lessant le chault du jour aler
Avant que je les face ouvrir.

Aussi en yver le pluieux,
10   Qui vens et broillars fait lever,
L'air d'Amour epidimieux
Souvent par my se vient bouter.
Si fault les pertuiz estouper
Par ou pourroit mon cuer ferir.
15   Le temps verray plus net et cler,
Avant que je les face ouvrir.

Desormais en sains et seur lieux,
Ordonne mon cuer demourer,
Et par Nonchaloir pour le mieulx,
20   Mon medecin, soy gouverner.
S'Amour a mes huyz vient hurter,
Pour vouloir vers mon cuer venir,
Seurté lui fauldra me donner,
Avant que je les face ouvrir.

L'envoy
25   Amours, vous venistes frapper
Pieça mon cuer, sans menacer.
Or, ay fait mes logiz batir
Si fors que n'y pourrez entrer,
Avant que je les face ouvrir.

[106]

So Reason must listen to the tale
20 Of one who, in naiveté, has wasted too much time
In the hands of my lady Youth.

Envoy

May God in His mercy watch over everyone,
And may he who foolishly goes wrong
Get back on the right path, as he wishes,
25 In the hands of my lady Youth.

Ballade

Through the windows of my eyes,
The heat of Love was wont to pass,
But now that I grow old,
So as to keep in summer freshness
5 The chamber of my heart,
I'm going to keep them shut,
Letting the heat of the day pass by
Before I open them.

Also in rainy winter,
10 Which rouses up mist and wind,
The air full of Love's disease
Often makes its way among us.
So I must shut the gateways
Through which it could strike my heart.
15 I'll see weather finer and more beautiful
Before I open them.

Henceforth I'll have my heart make his home
In places healthier and more secure,
And Indifference — my physician —
20 Will govern him for the best.
If Love comes knocking on my door,
Desiring to draw near my heart,
He must guarantee my safety
Before I open them.

Envoy

25 Love, in times past you came to strike
My heart a blow, but with no threat.
Now I've had my residence built
So strongly you'll not be able to enter
Before I open them.

B139   **Balade**   [p. 229]

Ung jour a mon cuer devisoye,
Qui en secret a moy parloit,
Et en parlant lui demendoye
Se point d'espargne fait avoit
5   D'aucuns biens, quant Amours servoit.
Il me dit que tresvoulentiers
La verité m'en compteroit,
Mais qu'eust visité ses papiers.

Quant ce m'eust dit, il print sa voye
10   Et d'avecques moy se partoit.
Aprés entrer je le veoye
En ung comptouer qu'il avoit.
La deça et dela queroit,
En cherchant plusieurs vieulx cayers,
15   Car le vray monstrer me vouloit,
Mais qu'eust visité ses papiers.

Ainsi par un temps l'atendoye.
Tantost devers moy retournoit
Et me monstra, dont j'eux grant joye,
20   Ung livre qu'en sa main tenoit,
Ouquel dedens escript portoit
Ses faiz, au long et bien entiers,
Desquelz informer me feroit,
Mais qu'eust visité ses papiers.

25   Lors demenday se g'y liroye,
Ou se mieulx lire lui plaisoit.
Il dit que trop peine prendroye.
Pourtant a lire commançoit,   [p. 230]
Et puis getoit et assommoit*
30   Le conte des biens et dangiers
Tout a ung. Vy que revendroit,
Mais qu'eust visité ses papiers.

Lors dy : «Jamais je ne cuidoye,
Ne nul autre ne le croiroit,
35   Qu'en amer, ou chascun s'employe,
De prouffit n'eust plus grant exploit.
Amours ainsi les gens deçoit,
Plus ne m'aura en telz santiers.
Mon cuer bien efacier pourroit,
40   Mais qu'eust visité ses papiers.»

Ballade

One day I was talking to my heart,
Who then spoke to me in secret,
And while conversing I asked him
If he'd laid by any savings
5   While in Love's service.
Very willingly he affirmed
He'd recount to me the truth,
If he could first review his papers.

After telling me this, he went his way
10   And took his leave from me.
Then I saw him open up
A cabinet that was his.
Here and there he searched,
Looking for some ancient notebooks,
15   For he wished to show me the truth,
If he could first review his papers.

In this way I waited some time for him.
Soon enough he made his way back
And showed me—which gave me great joy—
20   A book he held in his hand
In which was written
A full account of all his doings,
Of which he would inform me,
If he could first review his papers.

25   Then I asked if he would have me read
Or if he would prefer to read himself.
He said it would pain me too much,
And that's why he began to read.
Then he figured out and calculated
30   The reckoning of benefit and hardship
All together. I saw he would return,
If he could first review his papers.

Then I said: "Never should I have believed,
Nor would any other man believe
35   That in loving, which everyone practices,
There should be no great accruing of profit.
Thus does Love fool people.
No longer will he keep me on such paths.
He might well strike my heart from his roll,
40   If he could first review his papers."

L'envoy
Amours savoir ne me devroit
Mal gré, se blasme ses mestiers.
Il verroit mon gaing bien estroit,
Mais qu'eust visité ses papiers.

[107 the duke's numbering of the ballades ends here]

B140   Balade   [p. 231]

En tirant d'Orleans a Blois
L'autre jour par eaue venoye,
Si rencontré par plusieurs foiz,
Vaisseaux, ainsi que je passoye,
5   Qui singloient leur droicte voye
Et aloient legierement,
Pour ce qu'eurent, comme veoye,
A plaisir et a gré le vent.

Mon cueur, Penser et moy, nous troys,
10   Les regardasmes a grant joye,
Et dit mon cueur a basse vois :
«Voulentiers en ce point feroye,
De Confort la voille tendroye
Se je cuidoye seurement
15   Avoir, ainsi que je vouldroye,
A plaisir et a gré le vent.

Mais je treuve le plus des mois,
L'eaue de Fortune si quoye,
Quant ou bateau du Monde vois,
20   Que, s'avirons d'Espoir n'avoye,
Souvent en chemin demouroye,
En trop grant ennuy longuement.
Pour neant en vain actendroye
A plaisir et a gré le vent!

L'envoy
25   Les nefz dont cy devant parloye
Montoient, et je descendoye
Contre les vagues de Tourment.
Quant il lui plaira, Dieu m'envoye
A plaisir et a gré le vent.»

Envoy

Love should not hold me in
Disfavor if I fault his doings.
He'd see my benefit is very small,
If he could first review his papers.

Ballade

In traveling from Orleans to Blois,
The other day I came by the water,
And so many times met up with
Vessels, as I passed along,
5   Setting sail upon the true path
And making their way with ease
Because they had, as I saw,
An agreeable, favoring wind.

My heart, Thought, and myself, we three
10   Did look upon these with great joy,
And my heart said with a quiet voice:
"Willingly I would do the same,
Deploying the sail of Comfort
If I believed for certain to possess
15   According to my desire
An agreeable, favoring wind.

"And yet most months I find
The waters of Fortune so becalmed
When I travel on the boat of the World
20   That, had I not the oars of Hope,
Often on the way I'd be becalmed
For a long time in great annoyance.
In vain and for nothing I'd await
An agreeable, favoring wind!

Envoy

25   "The ships I was speaking of before
Were going upstream and I down
Into the waves of Torment.
When He pleases, God will send me
An agreeable, favoring wind."

B141 **Balade** [p. 232]

L'autre jour je fis assembler
Le plus de conseil que povoye,
Et vins, bien au long, raconter
Comment deffié me tenoye,
5   Comme par lectres monstreroye
De Merencolie et Douleur,
Pourquoy conseiller me vouloye
Par les Trois Estas de mon cueur.

Mon advocat prist a parler,
10   Ainsi qu'anformé je l'avoye.
Lors vissiez mes amis pleurer,
Quant sceurent le point ou j'estoye.
Non pourtant je les confortoye,
Qu'a l'aide de Nostre Seigneur,
15   Bon remede je trouveroye
Par les Trois Estas de mon cueur.

Espoir, Confort, Loyal Penser,
Que mes chiefz conseillers nommoye,
Se firent fors, sens point doubter,
20   Se par eulx je me gouvernoye,
De me trouver chemin et voye
D'avoir brief secours de Doulceur
Avecques l'aide que j'aroye
Par les Trois Estas de mon cueur.

L'envoy

25   Prince, Fortune me guerroye
Souvent a tort et par rigueur.
Raison veult que je me pourvoye
Par les Trois Estas de mon cueur.

B142 **Balade · par le duc d'Orliens** [p. 233]

Bon regime *sanitatis*
Pro vobis, neuf en mariage.
Ne de vouloirs *effrenatis*
Abusez *nimis* en mesnage.
5   *Sagaciter* menez l'ouvrage,
Ainsi fait *homo sapiens*,
Testibus les phisiciens.

Ballade

The other day I had assemble
The grandest council I could manage
And I appeared there to recount in detail
How I considered myself defied
5   By Melancholy and Pain,
As I should show by documents,
And this is why I wished to be advised
By the Three Estates of my heart.

My lawyer began to speak,
10   Just as I'd advised him to do.
Then you would have seen my friends crying
After they realized the state I was in.
Nevertheless I comforted them,
So that with the help of Our Lord
15   I might be provided with a good remedy
By the Three Estates of my heart.

Hope, Comfort, Faithful Thought,
Whom I had appointed my chief counselors,
Gave strong assurances, beyond any doubt,
20   That if I should be ruled by them
They'd find the way and means
Quickly to obtain the help of Gentleness,
Along with the assistance provided me
By the Three Estates of my heart.

Envoy

25   Prince, Fortune wars upon me
Continuously, unjustly, harshly.
Reason wants me to be guided
By the Three Estates of my heart.

Ballade — by the duke of Orleans

A fine regime of good health
For you who are new to marriage.
Living together, do not abuse
The desire you feel, now unbridled.
5   Wisely carry out the work.
The wise man does so,
According to physicians.

Premierement, *caveatis*
De coitu trop a oultrage,
10   Car, se souvent *hoc agatis*,
Conjunx le vouldra par usage
Chalenger, *velud* heritaige,
Aut erit quasi hors du sens,
Testibus les phisiciens.

15   Oultre plus, non *faciatis*
Ut Philomena ou boucaige,*
Se voz amours *habeatis*,
Qui siffle *carens* de courage
Cantandi, mais monstrés visage
20   Joyeux et *sitis paciens*,
Testibus les phisiciens.

L'envoy

Prince, *miscui* en potage
Latinum et françois langage,
Docens loiaulx advisemens,
25   *Testibus* les phisiciens.

B143   [Ballade] [Fredet]*   [p. 234]

Du regime *quod dedistis*
Cognoscens que tressagement
Me, Monseigneur, *docuistis*,
Je vous remercie humblement,
5   Mais d'ainsi faire seurement
Nunquam uxor concordabit :
Hoc mains debas *generabit*.

Je ne sçay si bien *novistis*
L'infinie peine et torment
10   *In quibus me posuistis*,
Se je croy vostre enseignement,
Car tant congnoys s'aucunement
Fais du sourt *quando temptabit*,
Hoc mains debas *generabit*.

15   Je voy trop bien *quod dixistis*
Se qu'on doit dire bonnement
Et qu'aussi *me avertistis*
De ma santé entierement,
Mais quant je feray autrement,

More important, take care
Not to have intercourse too much,
10   For, if you do so often,
Your wife will either grow accustomed to it
And be eager to claim it as her right,
Or go out of her mind,
According to physicians.

15   At the same time, do not behave
As did Philomela in the bushes,
If you possess your love,
For the lady whistled, lacking the heart
To sing, but instead let your face show
20   The joy you feel, and exercise patience,
According to physicians.

Envoy

Prince, I have mixed up a stew
Of Latin and French,
Giving sound advice,
25   According to physicians.

Ballade—Fredet

For this regimen you gave me,
Acknowledging that you, my lord,
Have instructed me very wisely,
I thank you humbly,
5   But as to putting this idea into practice,
A wife would never agree.
This will give rise to many debates.

I don't know if you're well aware of
The endless pain and torment
10   To which you have condemned me
If I believe your teaching,
For I know for a fact, that if I turn
A deaf ear when she makes a pass,
This will give rise to many debates.

15   I see very well that the words you said
Were spoken out of kindness,
And that you've also issued me
A very clear warning about my health,
But when I do the opposite,

20   Le fait d'autres *recordabit* :
        Hoc mains debas *generabit*.

                        L'envoy
        Prince, selon mon sentement
        Il fault s'acquiter leaument,
        Quia qui non labourabit
25   *Hoc* mains debas *generabit*.

Co4   **Complainte**   [p. 306]

        L'autrier en ung lieu me trouvay,
        Triste, pensif et doloreux,
        Tout mon fait, bien au long, comptay
        Au hault prince des amoureux,
5   Lequel m'a esté rigoreux
        Ou temps que mon cueur le servoit,
        Et ainsy qu'il me respondoit,
        Souvenir, qui fut au plus pres,
        Ses ditz et les miens escripvoit
10   En la maniere cy aprés :

        Helas! Amours, de vous me plains,
        Mais les griefs maulx le me font faire,
        Dont mon cueur et moy sommes plains,
        Car trop estes de dur afaire.
15   S'un peu me feussiez debonnaire,   l'Amant
        Espoir que j'ay du tout perdu,
        Si me seroit tantost rendu,
        Mais pas n'avez tel vostre vueil,
        Ainçois par vous m'est deffendu
20   Plaisant Desir et Bel Acueil.

        Amours respond : A trop grant tort
        Vous complaignez et sans raison,
        Car envers chascun Reconfort
        N'est pas tousjours en sa saison,
25   Et si savez qu'en ma maison
        Une coustume se maintient,   Amours
        C'est assavoir que qui se tient
        Pour serviteur de mon hostel,
        Maintesfois souffrir luy convient :
30   L'usaige de mes gens est tel.

        Certes, Sire, vous dictes vray,   [p. 307]
        Mes l'ordonnance riens ne vault,
        Parler en puis, car bien le sçay,

20   She will think of what others have done.
        This will give rise to many debates.

Envoy
        Prince, according to my view,
        It is necessary that one act faithfully,
        For if one does not belabor the thing too much,
25   This will give rise to many debates.

Complaint

        The other day I found myself in a place,
        Where I was sad, contemplative, and filled with pain.
        All my case, from beginning to end, I recounted
        To the high prince of lovers,
5   The one who has been hard on me
        During the time my heart served him,
        And as he was answering me,
        Memory, who stood nearby,
        Transcribed what I said and his words as well,
10   In the manner that here follows:

        Alas! Love, you are the subject of my complaint,
        But these grievous ills are the cause
        That fills me and my heart,
        For your manner is too harsh.
15   If you showed me some kindness,   The Lover
        The hope I have completely lost
        Would return to me at once.
        But this is not your intention.
        Instead you have forbidden me
20   Pleasant Desire and Fair Welcome.

        Love answers: It's very wrong
        That you complain, not right at all.
        For Consolation does not attend to
        Everyone at the same time,
25   And you know that in my house
        A custom is upheld: Love
        Which is to say that whoever
        Holds the office of servant in my hostel
        Must many times endure suffering:
30   Such is the practice of my people.

        Surely, lord, you speak the truth,
        But this injunction is of no value,
        Familiar to me, I can speak to it,

Et ay dancié a ce court sault,
35   Par quoy je cognois le deffault   l'Amant
De doulx plaisir que l'en y a,
Car, quant mon cueur vous depria
Secours, il luy fut escondit,
Adoncques de dueil regnya
40   Vostre povoir et s'en partit.

Dea! beaulx amis, se dit Amours,
Celuy qui a servir se met,
S'il veult avoir tantost secours
Et le gardon qu'on luy promect,
45   Ou aultrememt, il se desmect   Amours
Du service qu'il a empris,
De Leaulté seroit repris,
Quant je tiendray mon jugement,
Et si perdroit tout los et pris,
50   Sans jamais nul recouvrement.

Voire, Sire, doit on servir
Sans prouffit ou guerdon avoir?
Nennil, ung cueur devroit mourir
Puis qu'il a fait leal devoir
55   Entierement a son povoir,   l'Amant
Et qu'il luy fault querir son pain.
A vous, qui estes souverain,
En est le plus de deshonneur,
Veu que par faulte meurt de fain
60   Vostre bon leal serviteur.

Qu'on meure de fain n'en vueil pas,   [p. 308]
Mes le trop hasté s'eschauda,
Il convient aller pas a pas,
Et puis aprés on cognoistra
65   Qui mieulx son devoir fait aura.   Amours
Alors doibt estre guerdonné.
Je suis assez abandonné
A grant largesse de mes biens,
Mais quant j'ay maintesfoiz donné
70   A plusieurs, semble qu'ilz n'ont riens.

De ceulz ne suis quant est a moy.
Sur ce, je respondz a briefs motz :
Je vous asseure, par ma foy,
Oncques ne fuz en ce propos,
75   J'ay tousjours porté sur mon dos   l'Amant
Paine, Travail a grant planté,

Having danced this quickstep at this court,
35   And so I recognize the absence   The Lover
Of sweet pleasure here,
For, when my heart begged you
For assistance, he was refused,
And then the pain made him renounce
40   Your power and depart the place.

Indeed! Fair friend, so says Love,
A man puts himself into this service
If he would be helped at once
And receive the promised reward,
45   Or, alternatively, if he withdraws   Love
From the service he has entered,
Loyalty will reprimand him
When I render my judgment,
And in this way he would lose praise and esteem
50   Beyond all hope of their recovery.

Truly, lord, should one serve
Without receiving any profit or reward?
No heart should ever die in this way
After completing his faithful duty
55   To the utmost of his ability   The Lover
And being forced to secure his own bread.
You, who are his lord, would merit
The greater part of this dishonor,
Seeing that it is by your fault
60   Your most faithful servant dies of hunger.

I do not intend that anyone die from hunger,
But the over-hasty man works himself into a lather.
He must proceed at a walking pace,
And afterward the man who has better
65   Performed his duty will receive due recognition.
Then will his reward come.   Love
I am rather prodigal
With the goods I have in abundance,
But many times after I've given them out to
70   One and all, they think they have nothing.

In my view, I am not one of that company.
Take these few words for my answer:
On my faith I assure you
That this was never my intention.
75   Always on my back have I borne   The Lover
Pain, Trouble aplenty,

Ne nulle chose n'ay hanté,
Dont on dye qu'aye failly,
Combien qu'en dueil m'aiez planté,
80   Come faint seigneur et amy.

Estre mon maistre vous voulez,
Par vostre parler, ce me semble,
Et grandement vous me foulez,
Mais l'estrif de nous deux ensemble,
85   Comme en puet cognoistre, ressemble   Amours
Au debat du verre et du pot.*
Fain avez qu'on vous tiengne a sot.
Devant Raison soit assigné,
Se j'ay tort, paier vueil l'escot,
90   Quant le debat sera finé.

Il fault que le plus foible doncques   [p. 309]
Soit tousjours gecté soubz le pié,
Ne je ne viz autrement oncques.
Rendre se fault, qui n'a traictié.
95   J'ay cogneu ou j'ay peu gaingnié,   l'Amant
Vostre court, a mont et a val,
Et, soit a pié ou a cheval,
On n'y scet trouver droit chemin,
Quoy qu'on y trouve bien ou mal,
100   Il fault tout partir a butin.

Pour le present, plus n'en parlons.
Puis que j'ay puissance sur tous,
Quelque chose que debatons,
A mon plaisir feray de vous.
105   Ne me chault de vostre courroux,   Amours
Ne de chose que l'on me dye.
Se je vous ay fait courtoisie,
Se vous voulez, prenez l'en gré,
Car le premier vous n'estez mie
110   Qu'ay courcié en plus grant degré.

Co5   **Lettre en complainte envoyee**   [p. 175]
        par Fredet au duc d'Orleans*

Monseigneur, pource que sçay bien
Que vous avez de vostre bien
Autresfois pris plaisir a lire
De mes fais qui ne vallent rien,
5   Dont trop a vous tenu me tien,

Nor have I ever concerned myself with
What it could be said I've failed at,
Even though you have loaded me down with misery,
80 Like a false lord and false friend.

Your words show, I think,
That you would be master over me,
And you press me hard,
But the argument between us two,
85 As is evident, resembles   Love
The debate between the glass and the pot.
You're eager to be considered a fool.
Let the case be presented to Reason.
If I'm in the wrong, I'll pay the penalty
90 When the debate concludes.

The weakest man must always
Be thrown beneath your feet,
And I never see it otherwise.
The man not making terms must surrender.
95 I see I've gained little   The Lover
At your court, up hill or down dale.
And, either afoot or mounted,
A man cannot find the right path.
It matters not if good or ill is found there!
100 The risks must be equally shared.

For the present, we'll speak no more of the matter.
Since I wield sovereignty over all,
No matter what we debate,
I will do as I like with you.
105 Your anger does not concern me,   Love
No more than any word you speak.
If I have treated you courteously,
Accept that gracefully if you're so inclined,
For you are by no means the first
110 Whom I've angered in the worst way.

Letter in complaint form sent by
Fredet to the duke of Orleans

My lord, because I know well
That you have in your goodness
Taken pleasure in former times to read about
My affairs, which are worth nothing,
5 For which I consider myself much indebted to you,

Vouloir m'est pris de vous escripre
Et mon aventure vous dire,
Laquelle conter vous desire,
Car c'est raison que je le face,
10   Esperant que de mon martire,
Tel conseil, qui devra suffire,
Me donnerez de vostre grace.

Il est vray que de par Amours,
Ung jour saint Valentin a Tours,
15   Fut une grant feste ordonnee,
Et fist assavoir par les cours,
Comme de coustume a tousjours,
Que chascun vint a la journee,
La eut grant joye demenee
20   Et mainte haulte loy donnee.
Qui fut sans per, choysit adoncques,
Si euz, comme par destinee,
A mon gré la meilleure nee
Qui en France se trouvast oncques.

25   Comme ma Dame, ma maistresse
Et ma terrienne deesse,
Tousjours la sers et l'ay servie,
Car il m'a, par deffense expresse,
Commandé lui faire promesse
30   D'estre sien pour toute ma vie,   [p. 176]
Et tant ma pensee a ravie
Et a la cherir asservie
Que je ne pourroye, sur m'ame,
D'autre jamais avoir envie,
35   Tant feust elle bien assouvye,
Si fort lui a pleu que je l'ame.

Mais ainsi m'en va que depuis
Qu'a elle donné je me suis,
Je ne peuz avoir bien ne joye,
40   Fors que tous maulx et tous ennuys
Qui a toute heure, jours et nuis,
Me tourmentent ou que je soye,
Tant que ne sçay que faire doye,
Et semble, se dire l'osoye,
45   Qu'ilz ayent tous ma mort juree.
Se vostre bonté n'y pourvoye,
Force sera que par eulx voye
Finer ma vie maleuree.

The desire has seized me to write you
And tell you about what has befallen me,
For I am eager to relate the matter to you.
Indeed it is right I do so,
10   In the hope that touching my suffering,
You should give me, in your generosity,
Such counsel as should suffice.

It is true that in honor of Love
One St. Valentine's Day at Tours
15   A great feast was ordained,
And this was made known throughout the courts,
As the custom has always been,
So that everyone traveled there that day,
Where there was great rejoicing
20   And many an exalted judgment rendered.
Whoever had no mate made his choice,
And I, as if by destiny,
Obtained the lady best born (in my view)
Whom France has ever known.

25   As my Lady, my mistress,
And my earthly goddess,
I always serve and have served her.
For Love had commanded me,
By express command, to make a promise
30   To be his all my life,
And he so dominated my thoughts,
Affirming that I was to cherish her,
I could not, upon my soul,
Ever desire another,
35   No matter how perfect she might be,
So mightily was he pleased that I love her.

But it happened that after
Giving myself to her
I have not been able to obtain benefit or joy,
40   Nothing but every sort of misery and agony,
And these at every hour, day and night,
Torment me wherever I am,
So much that I do not know what I should do,
And it seems, if I dare to say it,
45   They have all condemned me to death.
If your kindness does not make some provision,
They will force me to see
My unfortunate life come to its end.

Pource que souvent ne la voy,
50   Le plus que je puis, sur ma foy,
Je ne fais qu'en elle penser.
Savez vous la cause pourquoy?
En esperant que mon ennoy
Se deust aucunement cesser,
55   Mais il ne me veult delaissier
Car plus en elle est mon penser,
Et plus de douleur me court seure,
Qui m'est si tresdure a passer
Que je desire trespasser
60   Plus de mille foys en une heure!

Que je sceusse prendre plaisir,   [p. 177]
En riens qui soit, fors desplaisir,
Las! je ne pourroye loing d'elle,
Car c'est celle que mon desir
65   M'a fait pour maistresse choisir,
Comme s'il n'en feust point de telle.
Tout mon bien et mal vient de celle.
Ainsi, comme il plaist a la belle,
Il n'en est qu'a sa voulenté,
70   Et ne cuidez pas que vous celle
Que ce ne soit celle qu'appelle
Devant chascun : ma leauté.

Puis que je l'ame si tresfort,
N'a pas doncques Amours grant tort
75   De moy faire tant endurer?
Ou dire fault qu'il soit d'accort
Que pour trop amer prengne mort,
Ou moy faire desesperer,
Quant pour plaindre, pour souspirer,
80   Pour mal qu'il me voye tirer,
Il ne m'en a que pis donné!
En ce point me fault demourer,
Car mieulx vault ainsy qu'enpirer :
Veez la comment suis gouverné!

85   Helas! ce qui plus me tourmente
Et dont fault que plus de dueil sente,
C'est la grant doubte que je fais,
Que je deffaille a mon entente,
Et que du tout perde l'actente
90   De mes tant desirez souhais,
Car je suis seur, plus qu'oncques mais,   [p. 178]

Because I do not see her often,
50   Only as much as I can, upon my faith,
I do nothing but think of her.
Do you know why?
In the hope that my suffering
Will thus cease somewhat,
55   But suffering will not release me,
For the more I think of her,
The more pain torments me,
Which is so very difficult to bear
I feel a desire for death a thousand times and
60   More with every passing hour.

Would that I could find pleasure
In anything except displeasure,
Alas! I could not, far from her,
For she is the lady my desire
65   Led me to choose as mistress,
As one who had no peer.
From that lady comes all my good and ill,
And in so far as the belle is pleased,
There is nothing but what she wishes,
70   And do not think I would conceal from you
That she is the lady I call
Before one and all my loyalty.

Since I love her so passionately,
Is not Love then terribly wrong
75   To make me endure so much?
Either he should say he agrees
That I die for loving too much
Or he should make me fall into despair,
When, in regard to complaining and sighing,
80   Or to the ill that he sees me experience,
He has given me nothing but the very worst!
I must remain in this condition
For it is better than doing even worse.
Consider what it is I experience!

85   Alas! What torments me the most
And what gives me the most pain,
Is the great fear I feel
That I might fail in my aim,
And lose completely what might come
90   Of those wishes I am so intent on,
For I am certain, more than ever,

Que si par vous ne sont parfais,
User ma vie me fauldra
En languissant desoresmais,
95   Comme cil a qui, pour jamais,
Toute plaisance deffauldra.

Et quant devers Amours je viens
Luy compter les maulx que soustiens,
En lui requerant allegence,
100   Il me respond : «Je n'y puis riens,
Mais va t'en au duc d'Orliens,
Que fors lui n'en a la puissance.
Fay donc qu'ayes son accointance
Et te metz en sa bienveillance,
105   Car, si tu le puis faire ainsi,
Tu ne doibs faire doubtance
Que de ta dure desplaisance
Il n'en ait voulentiers merci.»

A vous doncques me fault venir
110   Et vostre du tout devenir,
Puis que vous avez ce povoir
Que de moy faire parvenir
Au plus hault bien qui avenir
Me peut jamais a dire veoir.
115   Pour quoy il vous plaise savoir
Que, se vous y faictes devoir
Et voulez a mon fait entendre
Tellement que je puisse avoir
Celle qui tant me plaist a voir,
120   Vostre a tousjours je m'iray rendre.

Or n'oubliez pas, Monseigneur,   [p. 179]
Vostre treshumble serviteur,
Mais escoutez mes dolans plains
Desquieulx je vous fais la clameur,
125   Et vueillez par vostre doulceur
Que par vous ilz soient estains,
Car croiez qu'ilz ne sont pas fains,
Ains pires avant plus que mains.
Puis me donnez de vostre grace,
130   Je vous en pry a jointes mains,
Tel responce qui soirs et mains
Tout mon vivant joyeux me face.

That if you do not make them come true,
I must spend my life
Henceforth in languishing,
95   Like a man who must always
Fail to gain everything that affords pleasure.

And when I appear before Love
To recount the ills I bear,
Asking him for relief,
100   He answers: "I can do nothing about this,
But seek out the duke of Orleans,
For, save him, no one has such power.
Make sure that you make his acquaintance
And commend yourself to his goodwill,
105   For, if you can manage this,
You will have no need to worry
That he won't gladly
Pity your deep unhappiness."

I must then make my way to you
110   And become your man completely
Since you possess the power
To have me accede
To the most exalted benefit that might ever
In truth come my way.
115   And may you be pleased to learn
That, if you do your duty
And willingly attend to my affair
In such a way that I come to possess
The lady I am so pleased to look upon,
120   I will then proclaim myself forever yours.

Now do not forget, my Lord,
Your ever-humble servant,
But, instead, attend to my painful complaints,
What I bemoan to you,
125   And please in your graciousness
See to it that they are ended,
But believe that they are not trifling,
Rather ever worsening, not diminishing.
Then in your graciousness render me
130   (This I beg you with my hands joined together)
An answer that will make me rejoice
Day and night for the rest of my life.

Co6   Autre lectre en complainte ·
         faisant responce audit Fredet*

Fredet, j'ay receu vostre lectre,
Dont vous mercie chierement,
Ou dedens avez voulu mectre
Vostre fait bien entierement.
5   Fïer vous povez seurement
En moy, tout, non pas a demi.
Au besoing congnoist on l'ami.

S'amour tient vostre cuer en serre,   [p. 180]
Ne vous esbahissez en rien.
10   Il n'est nulle si forte guerre
Qu'au derrain ne s'appaise bien.
Amour le fait, comme je tien,
Pour esprouver mieulx vostre vueil.
Grant joye vient aprés grant dueil.

15   Se vous dictes : «Las! je ne puis
Une telle doleur porter,»
Je vous respons : «Beau sire, et puis
Vous en voulez vous depporter
Ou au Dieu d'Amours rapporter?
20   L'un des deux fault, se m'aist Dieux, voire :
Puis qu'il est trait, il le fault boire.»

Cuidez vous par dueil et courrouz
Ainsi gangner vostre vouloir?
Nennyl, ce ne sont que coups rouz
25   Qu'Amours met tout en nonchaloir.
De riens ne vous peuent valoir,
Et se les couchez en despence.*
Trop remaint de ce que fol pense.

Voulez vous rompre vostre teste
30   Contre le mur? ce n'est pas sens.
Il fault denser, qui est en feste.
Certes, autre raison n'y sens,
Et pour cela je me consens
Que souffrez qu'Amours vous demaine :
35   Grant bien ne vient jamais sans paine.

Mais de voz doleurs raconter
Faictes bien, ainsi qu'il me semble,
Et les assommer et compter   [p. 181]
Devant Amours, car il ressemble

A second letter in complaint form
responding to the aforesaid Fredet

Fredet, I have received your letter,
And thank you warmly for it,
In which your intention was to recount
Everything of your affairs.
5   You can, to be sure, put your trust
In me, and completely, not halfway.
In times of need a friend makes himself known.

If love retains your heart in bonds,
Do not be dismayed in the least.
10   There is no war so fierce
That does not readily conclude with a peace.
Love does this, so I think,
In order to put your desire to the proof.
A great joy follows great suffering.

15   If you say: "Alas! I cannot
Bear up under such suffering,"
I answer you: "Fair sir, then
Do you intend either to abstain from it
Or to side with the God of Love?
20   So help me God, it must be one or the other, truly,
One must drain the glass that's poured."

Do you think by misery and anger
Thus to gain what you desire?
Not at all, these are only clumsy blows
25   About which Love is completely indifferent.
They can be worth nothing to you,
So accept them as inevitable.
Such thoughts are too foolish by far.

Do you want to crack your head
30   Against the wall? This is not sensible.
If you're at a feast, you have to dance.
Surely, any other course makes no sense,
And for this reason I conclude
That you are to suffer Love's control of you.
35   A great benefit never comes without pain.

But you do well to tell
Of your miseries, so it seems to me,
And tot them up and recount them
To Love, for he resembles

40   A l'ostellier qui met ensemble
        Et tout dedens son papier couche :
        Pour parler est faicte la bouche.

        De pieça je fuz en ce point,
        Encores pis, loing d'allegence.
45   Toutesfoiz ne vouluz je point
        De moy mesmes faire vengence,
        Mais chauldement par diligence
        Pourchassay et plaiday mon fait :
        Peu gangne celuy qui se tait.

50   Et pource que la lectre dit
        Qu'Amours veult que vers moy tirez,
        De moy ne serez escondit
        S'aucune chose desirez
        A vostre bien, quant l'escriprez.
55   Paine mectray, d'entente franche,
        Que l'ayez de croq ou de hanche.

        Combatez d'estoc et de taille,
        Vostre dure merencolie,
        Et reprenez, commant qu'il aille,
60   Espoir, confort et chiere lie.
        De ne vous oublier me lie,
        Autant en ce que puis et doy,
        Que se me teniez par le doy. *

        Or retournons a mon propos
65   Et ne parlons plus de cecy
        Vray est que je suis en repos
        D'Amours, mais non pas de Soussy,
        Et pource, je vous vueil aussy   [p. 182]
        De me conseillier travaillier :
70   L'amy doit pour l'autre veiller.

        Soussy maintient que c'est raison
        Qu'il ait sur tous vers moy puissance.
        Nonchaloir dit qu'en ma maison
        Vault mieulx qu'il ait la gouvernance,
75   Car il ramenera Plaisance
        Que Soussy a banye a tort,
        Sans reveiller le chat qui dort.*

        Soussy respond qu'estre ne peut,
        Tant qu'on est ou monde vivant,

40 The innkeeper who takes account
  Of everything and records it in his ledger:
  The mouth is made for speaking.

  I was in this situation a long time ago,
  Even worse off, far from consolation.
45 However it was not my intention at all
  To wreak vengeance on myself,
  But instead diligently, eagerly
  I proceeded with and pleaded my case.
  The man who stands silent gains little.

50 And because the letter says
  Love wishes you to come to me,
  I will not refuse
  Anything you wish that might
  Benefit you when you write it down.
55 I will take pains, my intent generous,
  That you obtain it by hook or crook.

  Fight with cut and stroke
  Against your bitter melancholy,
  And win back, however it turns out,
60 Hope, consolation, and a happy demeanor.
  I pledge not to forget you
  In this, as much as I can and should,
  Provided you hold on to me.

  Now let us turn to my situation
65 And speak no more of these matters.
  Truly I slumber in regard
  To Love, but not in regard to Care,
  And for this reason, I wish that you in turn
  Would advise me how to labor.
70 One friend should watch out for the other.

  Care maintains it's reasonable
  For him to have power over me in all things.
  Indifference says that in my house
  It's better he be the master.
75 For he'll bring back Pleasure,
  Whom Care has wrongly banished,
  Not waking the sleeping cat.

  Care answers that this cannot be,
  As long as this is the world of the living,

80   Car Fortune par tout s'esmeut
        Et est a chascun estrivant,
        En tous lieux va mal escrivant,
        Et toutes choses met en doubte.
        Elle a beaux yeulx et ne voyt goute.

85   Si ne sçay que je doye faire,
        Ne lequel d'eulx me laissera,
        Car veu que tousjours j'ay affaire,
        Soussy jamais ne cessera,
        Mais mon plaisir rabessera
90   En quelque place que je voyse.
        Bien est aise qui est sans noyse.

        Quant en Nonchaloir je m'esbas
        Et Desplaisir vueil debouter,
        Jamais ne sçay parler si bas
95   Que Soussy ne viengne escouter.
        Las! je le doy tant redoubter,
        Car a tort souvent me ravalle,
        Mais sans mascher fault que l'avalle.   [p. 183]

        Je ne sçay remede quelconques,
100   Quant ay mis ces choses en poys,*
        Pour tous deux contenter adoncques,
        Fors les faire servir par moys.
        Mandez moy sur ce quelque foys,
        Fredet, bon conseil, par vostre ame,
105   Foy que devez a vostre dame.

Co7 Responce de Fredet au duc d'Orleans*

        Monseigneur, j'ay de vous receu
        Et aussi de mot a mot leu
        Une lectre qu'il vous a pleu
        Moy rescripre touchant mon fait,
5   Par laquelle j'ay apperceu
        Le bon vouloir qu'avez eu
        Vers moy tousjours qui n'est pas peu,
        Dont tout mon dueil avez deffait,
        Et oultre plus, comme j'ay veu,
10   Avez voulu que j'aye sceu
        De quoy il ne m'a point despleu,
        Ce qui tant vous griefve ou refait.
        Sur quoy, de vous obeir meu,
        Non pas ainsi comme il est deu,

80   For Fortune holds sway everywhere,
        Battles with everyone,
        Everywhere she goes, authoring evil,
        And she renders everything uncertain.
        Her eyes are beautiful, and she sees nothing.

85   So I don't know what to do,
        Nor which of them will leave me be,
        For seeing I always have difficulties,
        Care will never cease,
        But rather beat down my pleasure
90   Wherever I might go.
        The man with no troubles is very much at ease.

        Since I find my sport in Indifference
        And intend kicking out Misery,
        I could never speak so softly
95   That Care would not come to listen.
        Alas! I must fear him greatly,
        For he often wrongly brings me down.
        But without chewing I must swallow this.

        I've come up with no solution whatsoever,
100   After weighing the matter in my mind,
        To how I might make both of them content,
        Save to remain in their service a long time.
        Fredet, some time send me useful advice
        About this, upon your soul,
105   By the faith you owe your lady.

Response of Fredet to the duke of Orleans

        My lord, I've received from you
        And also read, word by word,
        A letter you've been pleased to write
        In response concerning my situation,
5   And in it I've recognized
        The goodwill you have always
        Felt for me, which is hardly slight,
        And thus you've relieved all my pain;
        And, even more, I have seen
10   That you've wanted me to learn
        (And this has not displeased me in the least)
        What it is that grieves or improves you.
        And about this matter, since I'm inclined to comply,
        Not at all as if you'd issued me a command,

15   Mais du tout au mieulx que j'ay peu,
      Mon conseil tel quel vous ait fait :

      Vous plaignez de la rigueur
      Et aigreur   [p. 184]
      Que vous fait, par sa fureur
20   Et chaleur,
      Cellui que nommez Soucy,
      Qui sans cause et sans couleur
      Et langueur,
      Par son ennuyeux labeur
25   Et maleur,
      Vous tourmente sans mercy,
      Dont par force de douleur
      Vostre cueur
      Est noyé par grant longueur,
30   Tout en pleur,
      Et souvent devient transy,
      Puis racontez, Monseigneur,
      Quel doulceur,
      Nonchaloir, par son bon eur,
35   Et valeur,
      Se offre vous faire aussi.

      De Soussy vous vueil escripre :
      C'est ung tresmerveilleux sire
      Et fault dire
40   Que cellui n'a pas courage
      D'omme saige
      Qui veult qu'avec lui demeure,
      Car il ne sert que de nuyre,
      Et ne pense ne desire
45   Qu'a destruire
      Et fait a chascun dommaige
      Et oultraige.

      Ne lui chault qui vive ou meure,   [p. 185]
      Et fust il seigneur d'empire,
50   Ou qui que soit, tout fait frire
      Et martire.
      Tant qu'il est en son servaige.
      Avantage
      N'a nul, je le vous asseure.
55   Mille maulx, tous d'une tire,
      Ne lui peuent trop suffire.
      Il n'est pire,
      Tant fait de tourmenter rage,

15 But entirely in the best way I'm able,
  Here is the advice I have in mind for you.

  You complain of the harshness
  And bitterness
  That, in his furor
20 And heat and languor too,
  The one you name Care brings
  Upon you, who without cause
  And pretext,
  Through his worrisome travail
25 And misfortune,
  Torments you without mercy,
  And so through the force of pain,
  Your heart
  Drowns in great delay,
30 Full of tears,
  And often the heart becomes delirious;
  Then you report, my Lord,
  What sweetness
  Indifference, through his good graces
35 And worthiness,
  Offers to bring you.

  I wish to write you about Care:
  He is an incredible lord,
  And it must be said
40 That whoever wishes Care
  To remain by his side
  Has not the heart of a wise man,
  For serving Care only does him harm,
  And Care thinks and intends
45 But to destroy,
  And he harms everyone,
  Treating them outrageously.

  He does not care who lives or dies,
  And no matter if the lord of an empire,
50 Or anyone at all, he makes him tremble
  All over and suffer
  As long as he's in Care's service,
  No man
  Endures more, I assure you.
55 A thousand ills, and all at once,
  Do not suffice for Care.
  There's no one worse,
  He is so eager to torment,

        Et enraige
60   Qu'a son gré tout ne demeure.

        Soussy tolt d'estre joyeux
        Et fait merencolïeux
        Par tous lieux
        Et bien souvent furïeux
65   Tous ceulx ou il a puissance.
        Par lui les biens gracïeux
        Deviennent mal gracïeux.
        Jennes, vieulx,
        Tout fait trouver ennuyeux
70   A qui plaist son acointance,

        Puis, par sa grande savance,
        Il avance
        Autour d'eulx Desesperance
        Qui, par ses diz ennuyeux
75   Et ses fais malicïeux
        Et crueux,
        Les met en ceste creance
        Que jamais ilz n'auront mieulx.   [p. 186]
        Lors sont a tel desplaisance
80   Que plus seroit leur plaisance
        Sans doubtance
        Brief mourir qu'estre mais tieulx.

        Se les maulx compter vouloye,
        Et la puissance en avoye,
85   Que Soussy vous feroit bien!
        Mais a quoy l'entreprendroye?
        Car certes je ne sauroye
        D'un an vous dire combien,
        Et pource, atant je m'en tien,
90   Et maintenant je revien
        Pour faire vostre vouloir,
        A parler, se j'en sçay rien,
        Du grant aise, du hault bien,
        Lequel donne Nonchaloir.

95   Qui a Nonchaloir s'adresse,
        Et tout pour estre sien lesse
        Et delesse,
        En lëesse
        Sans que jamais mal le blesse,
100   Pourra sa vie passer.
        Dueil, Soussy, Couroux, Aspresse,

And enraged that nothing
60 Stays as he likes.

Care steals the joy from life
And renders melancholic
And entirely consumed by anger
All those in whatever
65 Place he holds sway.
Through him gracious goods
Are emptied of graciousness.
The young, the old,
Whoever gets to know him
70 Finds nothing but trouble,

And then, in his great craftiness,
He brings forward
Misery into their presence,
Who, by his troublesome speech
75 And his deeds both malicious
And cruel,
Makes them believe
They'll never have it better.
Then these people feel such misery
80 It would be more pleasurable for them
(Of this there is no doubt) to die at once
Than to remain any longer in such a state.

If I intended to recount these ills
And had the power to do so,
85 Would that Care might act to your benefit!
But why undertake such a thing?
For surely I'd not be able
In a year to tell you of so many;
And this is why I hold back now.
90 And at this time I return
To do what you wish,
Namely to speak, if I can manage it,
Of the great consolation, of the exalted reward
Indifference provides.

95 Whoever turns to Indifference
And becomes his man in every way,
Giving him everything,
That man proves able to spend his life
In happiness,
100 With no ill ever wounding him.
Pain, Worry, Anger, Bitterness,

Et tous ceulx de leur promesse,
Soit Tristesse
Ou Destresse
105   Ou Rudesse,
Qui de mains grever ne cesse,
Tous les fait avant passer.

Contre lui n'ont hardïesse.   [p. 187]
Il les vaint par sa sagesse
110   Et abesse
Leur duresse,
Leur haultesse,
Nul ose lui faire presse,
N'encontre lui s'amasser,
115   Car il maine Joye en lesse,
Qui le deffent d'eulx sans cesse
Par prouesse.
Or donc qu'esse?
Est il ou monde richesse
120   Qui sceust ung tel bien passer?
De lui vient Plaisante Vie
Qui desvie
Dueil, Soussy, de toute place.
De repos Aise assouvie,
125   Sans envie
De bien qu'a autruy se face,
Les autres bonnes efface
Et defface.
Tout est en Joye ravye,
130   Tout fait a joyeuse face,
Dont la grace
De vous a bien desservye.

Nonchaloir, de sa nature,
Lui soit Fortune ou non dure.
135   L'un et l'autre tout endure
Et prent en gré l'avanture,
Car il ne tient d'ame conte.
Joye, dueil, paix ou murmure,   [p. 188]
Gangner, perdre sans mesure,
140   Soit a tort ou par droiture,
Tout lui est ung, je vous jure.
Ne lui chault s'il besse ou monte,
Ou se maindre le surmonte.
D'un chascun a son gré compte.
145   De quanque lui vient n'a honte,

And all those of their alliance,
Be it Sadness,
Or Distress,
105   Or Harshness,
Who never ceases to grieve many,
Indifference makes them all go away.

They've not the boldness to oppose him.
With his cunning, he defeats them
110   And beats down
Their harshness,
Their arrogance.
No man dares lead a host against him,
Nor mass an army in opposition,
115   For he holds Joy on a leash,
Whom, with prowess,
He ceaselessly defends from them.
Now then what is Indifference?
Is there any precious object in the world
120   That could surpass it?
From Indifference comes Pleasant Living,
Who puts to flight
Pain and Worry from every place.
Ease, calmed with rest,
125   Not envious of
Any benefit done for another,
Does away with other good things,
Making them disappear.
All is carried off to Joy.
130   With a joyful face everything is done,
And so this well merits
Your favor.

Indifference, by his nature,
Whether Fortune proves harsh or not,
135   Endures all, one thing and the next,
And willingly accepts what comes,
For he pays no mind to anyone.
Joy, suffering, peace, or uproar,
Gain, loss without measure,
140   Whether any of these is right or wrong,
These things are all the same to him (I swear).
Indifference cares not if he rises or falls,
Or if something of minor importance prevails.
He's pleased either way.
145   He feels no shame for what comes his way.

Soit bien ou mal, rien n'en compte,
A tout faire s'avanture.
Autant lui est roy que conte,
La cause est comme il raconte,
150   Car a nulluy ne rent compte,
Et pource, la fin de conte,
Tousjours sa vie en paix dure.

Pour quoy servir je vous conseille
De nostre maistre Nonchaloir,
155   Et bannissez, vueille ou non vueille,
Soucy, sans plus vous en chaloir.
De lui mieulx ne povez valoir,
Mais soit hors de vostre memoire :
Qui demande conseil doit croire.

160   Je vous supply qu'il vous suffise,
Et aussi il ne vous desplaise
D'une questïon qu'ay cy mise,
D'un mien amy tres en malaise.
Dont, Monseigneur (mais qu'il vous plaise)
165   Vostre conseil avoir m'en fault :
L'adviz de deux mieulx que d'un vault.

Selui que diz est si espris
D'une tant belle, bonne dame,   [p. 189]
Qu'il ne pourroit estre pris
170   Tellement si tresfort il ame,
Mais espoir n'a point, sur son ame,
D'avoir jamais d'elle secours :
Pas n'est en paix qui sert Amours.

Que autre dame, se lui semble,
175   Qui n'a point de meilleur vivant,
Par le bien qu'en elle s'assemble,
Le vouldroit bien pour son servant.
Non pourtant il mourroit avant
Que son cueur se peust sien clamer :
180   Par force l'en ne peut amer.

Et pource, maintenant demande
Qui lui sera mains chose forte,
Celle amer qu'Amours lui commande,
Ou toute s'esperance est morte,
185   Ou l'autre, combien qu'il rapporte
Qu'amer ne la peut ne desire?
De deux maulx on prent le mains pire.

No matter if it's good or bad, he pays no heed.
He risks every deed.
To him a count is the same as a king;
The reason is just as he affirms,
150   For he renders accounts to no one.
And for this reason, to the very end,
His life remains always at peace.

And this is why I advise you to serve
Our master Indifference
155   And banish Worry whether he likes it
Or not, without caring more about it.
You can do no better
Than to banish all this from your memory.
Let him who asks for advice trust to it.

160   Be satisfied with this, I beg you,
And not displeased
By a question I've broached here
From one of my friends who is very badly off.
And so, my Lord (as long as you are pleased),
165   I must have your advice.
The counsel of two is better than that of one.

The man I mention is so smitten
With a lady very fine and virtuous
He could not yield to attraction again
170   In the same way, so very strongly does he love,
But he has no hope at all, upon his soul,
To ever gain her assistance;
No man who serves Love is at peace.

For another lady, better than whom,
175   In his view, there is none living
Because of the goodness in her,
Would certainly want him for her servant,
Notwithstanding he would die before
His heart could call itself hers.
180   One cannot be forced to love.

And so now he asks
What he would find less difficult,
To love the lady whom Love ordains,
For whom all his hope has expired,
185   Or the other, although he reports
He cannot love or desire her?
One chooses the lesser of two evils.

Veez la de mon amy le cas,
Auquel fauldroye bien envis,
190   Mais conseiller ne le puis pas,
Sans en avoir de vous l'adviz.
Fait en soit a vostre devis,
Monseigneur, car c'est bien raison,
Et a tant fine ma raison.

B144   **[Ballade]**   [p. 313]

O thou, Fortune, which hast the governnance
Of all thynges kyndely mevyng to se fro
Thaym to demene after thyn ordonnance,
Right as thou lyst to grante hem wele or wo.
5   Syth that thou lyst that I be on of tho
That must be rewlyd be thyn avisines,
Why wylt thou not wythstand myn hevynes?

Me thyng thou art unkynde as in thys case,
To suffre me so long a whylle endure
10   So grete a peyn, wehout mercy and grase,
Which grevyth me right sore, I the ensure.
And syth thou knawst I am that creature
That wolde be favour be thy gentilles,
Why whylt thou not wythstand myn hevynes?

15   What causyth the to be myn adversarie?
I have not done which that schuld the displese,
And yit thou art to myn entent contrarie,
Which makyth alwey my sorous to encrese,
And syth thou worst myn hert ys not in ese,
20   But ever in trouble wythout sykurenes,
Why wylt thou not wythstand myn hevynes?

To the allonly thys compleynt I make,
For thou art cause of myn adversite,
And yet y wote welle thou mayst undertake
25   For myn welfare if that thou lyst agre.
I have no cause to blame no wyght but the,
For this thou doste of verrey wylfulnes.
Why wylt thou not wythstand myn hevynes?

Here is the situation of my friend,
Whom I would regret to fail,
190   But I cannot advise him
Without consulting with you.
Let it be done as you say,
My lord, for that's certainly wise;
And now let my argument end.

Ballade

O, you, Fortune, who hold sway
Over all things as they shift here and there by Nature
In order to dispose them according to your purpose,
Just as you're pleased to grant good luck or ill.
5   Since you wish me to be one of those
Who must be ruled by your counsels,
Why will you not oppose my distress?

It seems in this case you are unnatural
To allow me to endure so long a time
10   Such a terrible pain, with no mercy or grace,
Which grieves me mightily, I assure you.
And since you know I am such a person
Who'd be favored by your graciousness,
Why will you not oppose my distress?

15   What makes you my enemy?
I've done nothing to displease you,
And yet you've opposed my desire,
And this always increases my sorrows,
And since you know my heart has no ease,
20   But is always in fear with no security,
Why will you not oppose my distress?

To you alone I make this complaint,
For you're the cause of my adversity,
And yet I know well you can undertake,
25   If it pleases you, providing for my well-being.
I've cause to blame no one but you,
For you do this from true willfulness.
Why will you not oppose my distress?

Ch1   **Chançon***   [p. 235i]

Ce may, qu'Amours pas ne sommeille
Mais fait amans eslïesser,
De riens ne me doy soussïer,
Car pas n'ay la pusse en l'oreille.*

5   Ce n'est mie doncques merveille
Se je vueil joye demener,
Ce may, *qu'Amours pas ne sommeille*
Mais fait *amans eslïesser.*

Quant je me dors, point ne m'esveille,
10   Pource que n'ay a quoy penser.
Sy ay vouloir de demourer
En ceste vie nompareille,
Ce may, *qu'Amours pas ne sommeille.*

[The poet begins a new numbering series here (in square brackets). Below each *chan-çon/roundel* the reader will find a reference to what is copied on the other half of the page (in this case nothing; the upper portion of the page is blank).]

[1] 235s: blank

Ch2   **Chançon**   [p. 236i]

Tiengne soy d'amer qui pourra,
Plus ne m'en pourroye tenir,
Amoureux me fault devenir,
Je ne sçay qu'il m'en avendra.

5   Combien que j'ay oÿ, pieça,
Qu'en amours fault mains maulx souffrir,
Tiengne soy *d'amer qui pourra,*
Plus ne *m'en pourroye tenir.*

Mon cueur devant yer accointa
10   Beauté qui tant le scet chierir
Que d'elle ne veult departir.
C'est fait, il est sien et sera!
Tiengne soy *d'amer qui pourra.*

[2] 236s: blank

Chanson

This May, when Love sleeps not
But makes those in love rejoice,
I should worry about nothing,
For I have no flea in my ear.

5   It is hardly then a marvel
If I wish to live in joy
This May, when Love sleeps not
But makes those in love rejoice.

When I'm asleep, I do not toss and turn
10   Because I've nothing to brood about.
So my wish is to continue
In this life that has no equal,
This May, when Love sleeps not.

Chanson

Let him keep from loving who can,
I can no longer refrain,
I must become a lover,
What will happen to me I know not.

5   Although I've heard, some time ago,
That those in love must suffer many an ill,
Let him keep from loving who can,
I can no longer refrain.

The other day my heart became acquainted
10   With Beauty, who can so enrapture him
He does not wish to leave her.
It's all over. He is hers and will so remain!
Let him keep from loving who can.

Ch3   **Chançon**   [p. 237i]

Quelque chose que je dye
D'Amour ne de son povoir,
Toutesfois, pour dire voir,
J'ay une dame choisie,

5   La mieulx en bien acomplie
Que l'en puist jamais veoir,
Quelque chose *que je dye*
D'Amour ne *de son povoir.*

Mais a elle ne puis mie
10   Parler, selon mon vouloir,
Combien que, sans decevoir,
Je suis sien toute ma vie,
Quelque chose *que je dye.*

[3] 237: blank

Ch4   **Chançon**   [p. 238i]

N'est elle de tous biens garnie
Celle que j'ayme loyaument?
Il m'est advis, par mon serement,
Que sa pareille n'a en vie.

5   Qu'en dittes vous? Je vous en prie,
Que vous en semble vrayement?
N'est elle *de tous biens garnie*
Celle que *j'ayme loyaument?*

Soit qu'elle dance, chante ou rie
10   Ou face quelque esbatement,
Faictes en loyal jugement,
Sans faveur ou sans flaterie.
N'est elle *de tous biens garnie?*

[4] 238s: blank

Ch5   **Chançon**   [p. 239i]

Quant j'ay nompareille maistresse
Qui a mon cueur entierement
Tenir me vueil joyeusement,
En servant sa gente jeunesse.

Chanson

Whatever I might say
About Love or his power,
It's no matter, truly,
I have chosen a lady.

5   The lady most perfect in virtue
One could ever lay eyes upon,
Whatever I might say
About Love or his power.

But to her I can in no way
10   Speak, as is my wish,
Although without deception
I am hers all my life,
Whatever I might say.

Chanson

Is she not replete with every good,
The lady I love faithfully?
It seems to me, upon my oath,
No lady alive is her equal.

5   What do you say about this? I beg you,
What do you truly think?
Is she not replete with every good,
The lady I love faithfully?

No matter if she dances, sings or laughs,
10   Or enjoys some game,
Judge faithfully in this matter
With no bias or flattery.
Is not she replete with every good?

Chanson

Since I have a mistress beyond compare
Who has all my heart,
I'll keep rejoicing,
Serving her noble youthfulness.

5 Car certes je suis en l'adresse
  D'avoir de tous biens largement,
  Quant j'ay *nompareille maistresse*
  Qui a mon *cueur entierement.*

  Or en ayent dueil ou tristesse
10 Envïeux, sans allegement,
  Il ne m'en chault, par mon serement,
  Car leur desplaisir m'est lïesse,
  Quant j'ay *nompareille maistresse.*

[5] 239s: blank

Ch6   Chançon   [p. 240i]

  Dieu qu'il l'a fait bon regarder,
  La gracïeuse, bonne et belle!
  Pour les grans biens qui sont en elle
  Chascun est prest de la louer.

5 Qui se pourroit d'elle lasser?
  Tousjours sa beauté renouvelle.
  Dieu qu'il *l'a fait bon regarder*
  La *gracïeuse, bonne et belle.*

  Par deça ne dela la mer
10 Ne sçay dame ne damoiselle
  Qui soit en tous biens parfais telle.
  C'est un songe que d'y penser.
  Dieu qu'*il l'a fait bon regarder.*

[6] 240: blank

Ch7   Chançon   [p. 241i]

  Par Dieu, mon plaisant bien joyeux,
  Mon cueur est si plain de lëesse,
  Quant je voy la doulce jeunesse
  De vostre gent corps gracïeux.

5 Pour le regard de voz beaulx yeux
  Qui me met tout hors de tristesse,
  Par Dieu, *mon plaisant bien joyeux,*
  Mon cueur *est si plain de lëesse.*

5   For surely I'm on the path
Of gaining an abundance of every good
Since I have a mistress beyond compare
Who has all my heart.

Now let the envious feel pain
10   Or sadness, with no relief,
I don't care at all, upon my oath,
For their distress makes me happy,
Since I have a mistress beyond compare.

Chanson

God, how fine He made her to look at,
The gracious lady, virtuous and fair!
Because of the great virtues that are hers
Every man is ready to praise her.

5   Who could tire of her?
Every day her beauty renews itself.
God, how He made her fine to look at,
The gracious lady, virtuous and fair.

On this side of the sea or the other
10   I know no lady or maiden
So perfect in every virtue.
It's a dream even to muse about her.
God, how fine He made her to look at.

Chanson

By God, my pleasant, joyous good,
My heart is so full of happiness
Whenever I look upon the sweet youth
Of your noble, gracious person.

5   Because of the look from your beautiful eyes
Which rid me completely of sadness,
By God, my pleasant, joyous benefactress,
My heart is so full of happiness.

Combien que parler envïeux
10   Souventesfois moult fort me blesse,
       Mais ne vous chaille, ma maistresse,
       Je n'en feray pourtant que mieulx,
       Par Dieu, *mon plaisant bien joyeux.*

[7] 241s: blank

Ch8   Chançon   [p. 242i]

       Que me conseilliez vous, mon cueur?
       Iray je pardevers la belle,
       Luy dire la peine mortelle
       Que souffrez pour elle en doleur?

5   Pour vostre bien et son honneur,
       C'est droit que vostre conseil celle.
       Que me *conseilliez vous, mon cueur,*
       Iray je *par devers la belle?*

       Si plaine la sçay de doulceur
10   Que trouveray mercy en elle,
       Tost en aurez bonne nouvelle.
       G'y vois, n'est ce pour le meilleur?
       Que me *conseilliez vous, mon cueur?*

[8] 242s: blank

Ch9   Chançon   [p. 243i]

       Ou regard de voz beaulx doulx yeulx,
       Dont loing suis par les envïeux,
       Me souhaide si tressouvent
       Que mon penser est seulement
5   En vostre gent corps gracïeux.

       Savez pourquoy, mon bien joyeux,
       Celle du monde qu'ayme mieulx
       De loyal cueur sans changement
       Ou regard *de voz beaulx doulx yeulx,*
10   Dont loing *suis par les envïeux*
       Me souhaide *si tressouvent?*

       Pource que vers moy en tous lieux
       J'ay trouvé plaisir ennuieux
       Trop fort, puis le departement

Although envious speech
10   Oftentimes wounds me deeply,
Do not concern yourself, my mistress,
I'll only do better as a result,
By God, my pleasant, joyous benefactress.

Chanson

How do you advise me, my heart?
Will I make my way to that belle,
To tell her the mortal pain
You miserably suffer for her sake?

5   For your good and her honor,
It's right I keep secret your advice.
How do you advise me, my heart,
Will I make my way to that belle?

I know she's so full of sweetness
10   I will find mercy in her.
Soon you'll have good news.
I'll go there, is it not for the best?
How do you advise me, my heart?

Chanson

In the glance of your sweet pretty eyes
(From which the envious have distanced me),
Is where I often wish myself to be,
For my thoughts are only
5   Of your noble, gracious person.

Do you know why, my joyous treasure,
The lady in the world I love best
With a faithful heart, never altering,
In the glance of your sweet pretty eyes
10   (From which the envious have distanced me),
Is where I often wish myself to be?

It is because everywhere I have found
The pleasure that comes to me annoying
In the extreme ever since I departed

15   Que de vous fis derrainnement,
      A regret merencolïeux,
      Ou regard *de voz beaulx doulx yeulx.*

[9] 243s: blank

Ch10   Chançon   [p. 244i]

      Qui la regarde de mes yeulx
      Ma dame, ma seule maistresse,
      En elle voit a grant largesse,
      Plaisirs croissans de bien en mieulx.

5   Son parler et maintien sont tieulx
      Qu'ilz mettent un cueur en lïesse,
      Qui la *regarde de mes yeulx*
      Ma dame, *ma seule maistresse.*

      Tous la suient, jeunes et vieulx,
10   Dieu scet qu'elle n'est pas sans presse.
      Chascun dit : «C'est une deesse
      Qui est descendue des cieulx!»
      Qui la *regarde de mes yeulx.*

[10] 244s: blank

Ch11   Chançon*   [p. 245i]

      Ce mois de may, nompareille princesse,
      Le seul plaisir de mon joyeulx espoir,
      Mon cueur avez et quanque puis avoir.
      Ordonnez en comme dame et maistresse.

5   Pource, requier vostre doulce jeunesse
      Qu'en gré vueille mon present recevoir,
      Ce mois *de may, nompareille princesse,*
      Le seul *plaisir de mon joyeux espoir.*

      Et vous supply, pour me tollir tristesse,
10   Treshumblement et de tout mon povair,
      Qu'a m'esmayer ayez vostre vouloir
      D'un reconfort bien garny de lïesse,
      Ce mois *de may, nompareille princesse.*

[11] 245s: blank

15   Not long ago from you,
Feeling melancholy regret for the one
In the glance of your sweet pretty eyes.

Chanson

Who looks upon her with my eyes,
My lady, my only mistress,
Sees in her a great abundance of
Pleasing qualities improving from good to better.

5   Her speech and manner are such
They make the heart happy,
Whoever looks upon her with my eyes,
My lady, my only mistress.

All chase after her, young and old,
10   God knows she does not lack for company.
Every man says: "She's a goddess
Descended from the heavens!"
Who looks upon her with my eyes.

Chanson

This month of May, princess beyond compare,
The sole pleasure of my joyous hope,
You have my heart and whatever is mine.
Give the order, like a lady and mistress.

5   And so, I ask you, in your sweet youthfulness,
To please graciously receive my present
This month of May, princess beyond compare,
The sole pleasure of my joyous hope.

And I beg you, in order to relieve my sadness,
10   Very humbly and with all my power,
To bestow on me, if you wish it,
Comfort well supplied with happiness
This month of May, princess beyond compare.

Ch12   Chançon   [p. 246i]

Commandez vostre bon vouloir
A vostre treshumble servant.
Il vous sera obeissant
D'entier cueur et loyal povair.

5   Prest est de faire son devoir,
Ne l'espargnez ne tant ne quant.
Commandez *vostre bon vouloir*
A vostre *treshumble servant.*

Mettez le tout a nonchaloir,
10   Sans lui estre jamais aydant,
S'en riens le trouvez refusant.
Essaiez se je vous dy voir :
Commandez *vostre bon vouloir.*

[12] 246s: blank

Ch13   Chançon   [p. 247i]

Belle, se c'est vostre plaisir
De me vouloir tant enrichir
De reconfort et de l'iesse,
Je vous requier, comme maistresse,
5   Ne me laissiez du tout mourir.

Car je n'ay vouloir ne desir
Fors de vous loyaument servir
Sans espargnier dueil ne tristesse,
Belle, *se c'est vostre plaisir*
10   De me *vouloir tant enrichir*
De reconfort *et de l'iesse.*

Et s'il vous plaist a l'acomplir,
Vueilliez tant seulement bannir
D'avec vostre doulce jeunesse
15   Dolent refus qui tant me blesse,
Dont bien vous me povez guerir,
Belle, *se c'est vostre plaisir.*

[13] 247s: R357

Chanson

Command your most humble servant
To do all you wish.
He will obey you in this
With his whole heart and faithful power.

5   He's ready to do his duty,
Do not spare him in any way.
Command your most humble servant
To do all you wish.

Be indifferent about everything,
10   Aiding him in nothing at all,
Should you find any refusal in him.
Put to the test the truth of my words:
Command your most humble servant.

Chanson

Belle, if you are pleased
To desire I be enriched
With consolation and joy,
I ask you, as my mistress,
5   Do not let me die.

For I've no intention or desire
Save serving you loyally
Without sparing pain or distress,
Belle, if you are pleased
10   To desire I be enriched
With consolation and joy.

And if you wish to carry this out,
Please do one thing: banish
From the society of your sweet youth
15   Painful refusal, who wounds me so,
And thus you can readily heal me,
Belle, if you are pleased.

Ch14   Chançon   [p. 248i]

Rafreschissez le chastel de mon cueur
D'aucuns vivres de Joyeuse Plaisance,
Car Faulx Dangier, avec son alïance,
L'a assegié tout entour de Doleur.

5   Se ne voulez le siege sans longueur
Tantost lever ou rompre par puissance,
Rafreschissiez *le chastel de mon cueur*
D'aucuns *vivres de Joyeuse Plaisance.*

Ne souffrez pas que Dangier soit seigneur
10   En conquestant soubz son obeissance
Ce que tenez en vostre gouvernance.
Avancez vous et gardez vostre honneur,
Rafreschissez *le chastel de mon cueur.*

[14] 248s: R356

Ch15   Chançon   [p. 249i]

Se ma doleur vous saviés,
Mon seul joyeux pensement,
Je sçay bien certainement
Que mercy de moy auriés.

5   Du tout Refus banniriés,
Qui me tient en ce tourment,
Se ma *doleur vous saviés*
Mon seul *joyeux pensement.*

Et le don me donneriés
10   Que vous ay requis souvent,
Pour avoir allegement.
Ja ne m'en escondiriés,
Se ma *doleur vous saviés.*

[15] 249s: R355

Ch16   Chançon   [p. 250i]

Ma seule, plaisant, doulce joye,
La maistresse de mon vouloir,
J'ay tel desir de vous veoir,
Que mander ne le vous sauroye.

Chanson

Re-provision the castle of my heart
With some victuals from Joyous Pleasure,
For False Danger, with his allies,
Has besieged it all around with Pain.

5   If you don't wish to raise the siege at once,
Or without delay break it with your might,
Re-provision the castle of my heart
With some victuals from Joyous Pleasure.

Do not permit Danger to become lord
10   By conquering and putting under his dominion
What you hold under your governance.
Move forward to protect your honor,
Re-provision the castle of my heart.

Chanson

If you knew of my pain,
My only joyous thought,
I'm certain
You would have mercy on me.

5   Once and for all you'd banish Refusal,
Who keeps me in such torment,
If you knew of my pain,
My only joyous thought.

And you would bestow on me the gift
10   I've often requested of you,
So as to have relief.
Never would you refuse me
If you knew of my pain.

Chanson

My only joy, sweet and pleasant,
Mistress of my desire,
I feel such an urge to see you
My message could not tell you.

5   Helas! pensez que ne pourroye
Aucun bien, sans vous, recevoir,
Ma seule, *plaisant, doulce joye,*
La maistresse *de mon vouloir.*

Car, quant Desplaisir me guerroye
10   Souventesfois de son povair,
Et je vueil reconfort avoir,
Esperance vers vous m'envoye,
Ma seule, *plaisant, doulce joye.*

[16] 250s: R354

Ch17   Chançon   [p. 251i]

Je ne vueil plus riens que la mort,
Pource que voy que Reconfort
Ne peut mon cueur eslÿesser.
Au meins pourray je vanter
5   Que je seuffre douleur a tort,

Car puis que n'ay d'Espoir le port,
D'Amours ne puis souffrir l'effort,
Ne doy je donc Joye laisser?
Je ne *vueil plus riens que la mort,*
10   Pource *que voy que Reconfort*
Ne peut *mon cueur eslÿesser.*

Au Dieu d'Amour je m'en rapport
Qu'en peine suis bouté si fort
Que povair n'ay plus d'endurer.
15   S'en ce point me fault demourer,
Quant est de moy, je m'y accort.
Je ne *vueil plus riens que la mort.*

[17] 251s: R353

Ch18   Chançon   [p. 252i]

Belle que je cheris et crains,
En cest estat suis ordonné
Que Dangier m'a emprisonné
De vostre grant beauté loingtains.

5   N'il ne m'a de tous biens mondains
Qu'un souvenir abandonné.

5   Alas! Remember I can
Receive no good save from you,
My only joy, sweet and pleasant,
Mistress of my desire.

For, when Discontentment wars against me
10   Often with all his might,
And I wish for consolation,
Hope sends me to you,
My only joy, sweet and pleasant.

Chanson

I wish no longer for anything save death
Because I see that Consolation
Cannot bring my heart joy.
At least I'll be able to boast
5   I suffer pain unjustly,

For since I have not the port of Hope,
And cannot endure the force of Love,
Should I not abandon Joy?
I wish no longer for anything save death
10   Because I see that Consolation
Cannot bring my heart joy.

I report to the God of Love
That I'm felled by such fierce pain
I have no longer the strength to endure.
15   If forced to continue in this way,
I accept that, as far as I'm concerned.
I wish no longer for anything save death.

Chanson

Belle, whom I love and fear,
I have been reduced to such a state
That Danger has imprisoned me
Far distant from your great beauty.

5   Of all earthly goods he has bestowed
But a single memory upon me,

Belle *que je cheris et crains,*
En cest *estat suis ordonné.*

Mais de nulle riens ne me plains
10   Fors qu'il ne m'a tost raençonné,
Car bien lui seroit guerdonné,
Se j'estoie hors de ses mains,
Belle *que je cheris et crains.*

[18] 252s: R352

Ch19   Chançon   [p. 253i]

Ma dame, tant qu'il vous plaira
De me faire mal endurer,
Mon cueur est prest de le porter.
Jamais ne le refusera.

5   En esperant qu'il guerira,
En cest estat veult demourer,
Ma dame, *tant qu'il vous plaira*
De me *faire mal endurer.*

Une fois Pitié vous prandra,
10   Quant seulement vouldrez penser
Que c'est pour loyaumant amer
Vostre beauté qu'il servira,
Ma dame, *tant qu'il vous plaira!*

[19] 253s: R351

Ch20   Chançon   [p. 254i]

De la regarder vous gardez,
La belle que sers ligement;
Car vous perdrés soudainement
Vostre cueur, se la regardez.

5   Se donner ne lui voulés,
Clignez les yeulx hastivement :
De la *regarder vous gardez*
La belle *que sers ligement.*

Les biens que Dieu lui a donnez
10   Emblent un cueur soubtilement.

Belle, whom I love and fear,
I have been reduced to such a state.

And yet I have lodged no complaint
10   Save that he has not demanded ransom for me at once,
And Danger would be well rewarded
Were I out of his hands,
Belle, whom I love and fear.

Chanson

My lady, to the degree you are pleased
To make me suffer ill,
My heart is ready to bear it;
Never will he refuse.

5   While hoping to be cured,
In this state he intends remaining,
My lady, to the degree you are pleased
To make me suffer ill.

At some point Pity will seize you
10   When you'll come to think
It's only to love your beauty
Faithfully that he performs service,
My lady, to the degree you are pleased!

Chanson

Do not dare to look at her,
The belle I serve faithfully,
For you'll lose your heart
At once if you gaze upon her.

5   If you do not wish to give it to her,
Close your eyes at once:
Do not dare to look at her,
That belle I serve faithfully.

The qualities God has bestowed upon her
10   Steal hearts craftily.

Sur ce prenez avisement,
Quant devant elle vous vendrés;
De la *regarder vous gardez!*

[20] 254s: R350

Ch21   Chançon   [p. 255i]

Puis que je ne puis eschapper
De vous, Courrous, Dueil et Tristesse,
Il me couvient suïr l'adresse
Telle que me vouldrés donner.

5   Povoir n'ay pas de l'amender,
Car Doleur est de moy maistresse,
Puis *que je ne puis eschapper*
De vous, *Courrous, Dueil et Tristesse.*

Si manderay par un penser
10   A mon las cueur vuit de lïesse,
Qu'il prangne en gré sa grant destresse,
Car il lui fault tout endurer,
Puis *que je ne puis eschapper!*

[21] 255s: R349

Ch22   Chançon   [p. 256i]

C'est fait, il n'en fault plus parler,
Mon cueur s'est de moy departy;
Pour tenir l'amoureux party,
Il m'a voulu abandonner.

5   Riens ne vault m'en desconforter
Ne d'estre dolent ou marry.
C'est fait, *il n'en fault plus parler,*
Mon cueur *s'est de moy departy.*

De moy ne se fait que mocquer;
10   Quant piteusement je lui dy
Que je ne puis vivre sans luy,
A peine me veult escouter.
C'est fait, il n'en fault plus parler.

[22] 256s: R348

Be on your guard against this
When you appear before her:
Do not dare to look at her!

Chanson

Since I'm unable to escape
From you, Anger, Pain, and Sadness,
I must follow the path
You're pleased to direct me upon.

5   I have no power to amend this,
For Pain is mistress over me,
Since I'm unable to escape
From you, Anger, Pain, and Sadness.

So in a thought I'll send a message
10   To my weary heart, empty of happiness,
That he willingly accept great distress,
For he must endure it all
Since I'm unable to escape!

Chanson

It's done. There's nothing more to say.
My heart has departed from me;
To join the lovers' party,
It was his wish to abandon me.

5   It's no use to make myself disconsolate,
Or sorrowful therefore, or downcast.
It's done. There's nothing more to say.
My heart has departed from me.

All he does is make fun of me;
10   When I tell him pitifully
I cannot live without him,
He'll hardly listen to me.
It's done. There's nothing more to say.

Ch23   Chançon   [p. 257i]

    Puis qu'Amour veult que banny soye
    De son hostel, sans revenir,
    Je voy bien qu'il m'en fault partir,
    Effacé du livre de Joye.

5   Plus demourer je n'y pourroye,
    Car pas ne doy ce mois servir.
    Puis *qu'Amour veult que banny soye*
    De son *hostel, sans revenir.*

    De confort ay perdu la voye,
10   Et ne me veult on plus ouvrir
    La barriere de Doulx Plaisir,
    Par Desespoir qui me guerroye,
    Puis *qu'Amour veult que banny soye.*

[23] 257s: R347

Ch24   Chançon   [p. 258i]

    Pour le don que m'avez donné,
    Dont tresgrant gré vous doy savoir,
    J'ay congneu vostre bon vouloir,
    Qui vous sera bien guerdonné.

5   Raison l'a ainsi ordonné;
    Bienfait doit plaisir recevoir,
    Pour *le don que m'avez donné,*
    Dont *tres grant gré vous doy savoir.*

    Mon cueur se tient emprisonné
10   Et obligié, pour dire voir,
    Jusqu'a tant qu'ait fait son devoir
    Vers vous et se soit raençonné
    Pour *le don que m'avez donné.*

[24] 258s: R346

Ch25   Chançon   [p. 259i]

    Se j'eusse ma part de tous biens
    Autant que j'ay de loyauté,
    J'en auroye si grant planté
    Qu'il ne me fauldroit jamais riens.

Chanson

Since Love wishes I be banished
From his mansion, never to return,
I see well that I must depart the place,
Erased from the book of Joy.

5   I can no longer remain,
For I'd do no service this month,
Since Love wishes I be banished
From his mansion, never to return.

I've lost the path toward consolation,
10   And there's no desire to open any longer
The gate to Sweet Pleasure,
Because of Despair, who wars upon me,
Since Love wishes I be banished.

Chanson

Because of the gift you've given me,
Which I must thank you warmly for,
I've recognized your good will,
For which you'll be well rewarded.

5   Reason has ordained it thus.
Good Deed should take pleasure
Because of the gift you've given me,
Which I must thank you warmly for.

My heart will keep himself a prisoner
10   And under obligation, to tell the truth,
Until he's fulfilled his duty
Toward you and can be redeemed
Because of the gift you've given me.

Chanson

If I possessed my share of all good things
As much as I have loyalty,
I should have them in such great store
I'd never lack for anything.

5   Et si gaingneroye des miens,
         Madame, vostre voulenté,
         Se j'eusse *ma part de tous biens*
         Autant *que j'ay de loyauté.*

         Car pour asseuré je me tiens
10   Que vostre tresplaisant beauté
         De s'amour me feroit renté
         Maugré Dangier et tous les siens,
         Se j'eusse *ma part de tous biens.*

[25] 259s: R345

Ch26   Chançon   [p. 260i]

         Pour les grans biens de vostre renommee,
         Dont j'oy parler a vostre grant honneur,
         Je desire que vous aiez mon cueur,
         Comme de moy tresloyaumaent amee.

5   Tresoriere je vous voy ordonnee
         A le garder en plaisance et doulceur,
         Pour les *grans biens de vostre renommee,*
         Dont j'oy *parler a vostre grant honneur.*

         Recevez le, s'il vous plaist et agree,
10   Du mien ne puis vous donner don mellieur,
         C'est mon vaillant, c'est mon tresor greigneur.
         A vous l'offre, de loyalle pensee,
         Pour *les grans biens de vostre renommee.*

[26] 260s: R344

Ch27   Chançon   [p. 261i]

         En songe, souhaid et pensee
         Vous voy chascun jour de sepmaine,
         Combien qu'estes de moy loingtaine,
         Belle, tresloyaument amee.

5   Pource qu'estes la mieulx paree
         De toute plaisance mondaine,
         En songe, *souhaid et pensee,*
         Vous voy *chascun jour de sepmaine.*

5   And so I'd acquire for mine,
My lady, your own good will,
If I possessed my share of all good things
As much as I have loyalty.

For I think what would surely happen
10   Is that your great beauty
Would endow me with its love
Despite Danger and all his company,
If I possessed my share of all good things.

Chanson

Because of the great virtues of your renown,
Which I have heard spoken of to your great honor,
I want you to possess my heart,
As the lady so loyally loved by me.

5   I see you designated as the treasurer
To guard it with pleasure and graciousness,
Because of the great virtues of your renown
Which I've heard spoken of to your great honor.

Receive it, if you are pleased and so agree.
10   I can give you no greater gift from what I have.
It is the sum of my worth, it is my greatest treasure.
I offer it to you, with faithful intentions,
Because of the great virtues of your renown.

Chanson

In dream, wish, and thought
I see you every day of the week,
Even though you're far from me,
Belle, so loyally loved.

5   Because you are the lady best endowed
With every earthly pleasure,
In dream, wish, and thought
I see you every day of the week.

   Du tout vous ay m'amour donnee,
10 Vous en povez estre certaine,
   Ma seule dame souveraine
   De mon las cueur moult desiree,
   En songe, *souhaid et pensee.*

[27] 261s: R343

Ch28   Chançon   [p. 262i]

   De leal cueur, content de joye,
   Ma maistresse, mon seul desir,
   Plus qu'oncques vous vueil servir
   En quelque place que je soye.

5 Tout prest en ce que je pourroye,
   Pour votre vouloir adcomplir,
   De leal *cueur, content de joye,*
   Ma maistresse, *mon seul desir.*

   En desirant que je vous voye,
10 A vostre honneur et mon plaisir,
   Qui seroit briefment, sans mentir,
   S'il fust ce que souhaideroye
   De leal *cueur, content de joye.*

[28] 262s: R342

Ch29   Chançon   [p. 263i]

   Se mon propos vient a contraire,
   Certes, je l'ay bien desservy,
   Car je congnois que j'ay failly
   Envers ce que devoye plaire.

5 Mais j'espoire que debonnaire
   Trouveray sa grace et mercy.
   Se mon *propos vient a contraire,*
   Certes, *je l'ay bien desservy.*

   Je vueil endurer et me taire,
10 Quant cause sui de mon soussy;
   Las! je me sens en tel party
   Que je ne sçay que pourray faire,
   Se mon *propos vient a contraire.*

[29] 263s: R341

I have given you all my love,
10   Of this you can be certain,
My only sovereign lady,
Whom my weary heart desires,
In dream, wish, and thought.

Chanson

With faithful heart, content in joy,
My mistress, my one desire,
More than ever I would serve you
Wherever I find myself.

5   I'm all ready to do what I might
To fulfill your wish,
With faithful heart, content in joy,
My mistress, my one desire,

While desiring to see you,
10   To your honor and for my pleasure,
Which would be soon, and this is no lie,
If it were according to my wish,
With faithful heart, content in joy.

Chanson

If my plans go awry,
I surely have well deserved it,
For I acknowledge I have failed
Where I should have pleased.

5   But I hope I find benevolent
Her grace and mercy,
If my plans go awry,
I surely have well deserved it.

I wish to endure and keep silent,
10   Since I'm the cause of my own misery;
Alas! I sense I'm in such a fix
I don't know what I can do
If my plans go awry.

Ch30   Chançon   [p. 264i]

Par le pourchas du regard de mes yeulx,
En vous servant, ma tresbelle maistresse,
J'ay essayé qu'est plaisir et tristesse,
Dont j'ay trouvé maint penser ennuieux.

5   Mais de cellui que j'amoye le mieulx
N'ay peu avoir qu'a petite largesse,
Par le pourchas *du regard de mes yeulx*,
En vous *servant, ma tresbelle maistresse.*

Car pour un jour qui m'a esté joyeux,
10   J'ay eu trois moys la fievre de destresse,
Mais Bon Espoir m'a guery de lïesse,
Qui m'a promis de ses biens gracïeux,
Par le pourchas *du regard de mes yeulx.*

[30] 264s: R340

Ch31   Chançon   [p. 265i]

Pour vous moustrer que point ne vous oublie,
Comme vostre que suis ou que je soye,
Presentement ma chançon vous envoye,
Or la prenés en gré, je vous en prie.

5   En passant temps plain de merencolie,
L'autrier la fis, ainsi que je pensoye,
Pour vous *moustrer que point ne vous oublie,*
Comme *vostre que suis ou que je soye.*

Mon cueur tousjours si vous tient compaignie,
10   Dieu doint que brief vous puisse veoir a joie!
Et, a briefz motz, en ce que je pourroye,
A vous m'offre du tout a chiere lye,
Pour vous *moustrer que point ne vous oublie.*

[31] 265s: R339

Ch32   Chançon   [p. 266i]

Loingtain de joyeuse sente
Ou l'en peut tous biens avoir,
Sans nul confort recevoir,
Mon cueur en tristesse s'ente.

Chanson

Through the searching look of my eyes,
While serving you, my very beautiful mistress,
I've experienced pleasure and sadness,
Which has given me many a worrisome thought.

5   But from the thought I love the best
I've been able to obtain only a slight bestowal,
Through the searching look of my eyes,
While serving you, my very beautiful mistress.

Indeed, for every day I've found joyous,
10   For three months I've suffered the fever of distress,
But Good Hope has cured me with happiness,
For he's promised me some of his gracious benefits,
Through the searching look of my eyes.

Chanson

To show I do not ever forget you,
As one who's yours wherever I may be,
I now send you my chanson.
Receive it willingly, I beg you.

5   While passing time filled with melancholy,
The other day I wrote it from the thoughts I had,
To show I do not ever forget you,
As one who is yours wherever I may be.

My heart always accompanies you;
10   God grant I see you soon, to my joy!
And, to be brief, in so far as I'm able,
I offer all of me to you with good cheer,
To show I do not ever forget you.

Chanson

Far from the path of joy,
Where all good things can be obtained,
Receiving no comfort,
My heart holds fast to sadness.

5   Par quoy couvient que je sente
       Mains griefz maulx, pour dire voir,
       Loingtain *de joyeuse sente*
       Ou l'en peut *tous biens avoir.*

       En dueil a fait sa descente
10   De tous poins, sans s'en mouvoir,
       Et s'il fault qu'a mon savoir
       Maugré mien je m'y consente,
       Loingtain *de joyeuse sente.*

[32] 266s: R338

Ch33   Chançon   [p. 273i]

       Dedens mon sein, pres de mon cueur,
       J'ay mussié un privé baisier
       Que j'ay emblé, maugré Dangier,
       Dont il meurt en peine et langueur.

5   Mais ne me chault de sa douleur,
       Et en deust il vif enragier,
       Dedens *mon sein, pres de mon cueur,*
       J'ay *mussié un privé baisier.*

       Se madame, par sa doulceur,
10   Le veult souffrir sans m'empeschier,
       Je pense d'en plus pourchassier
       Et en feray tresor greigneur
       Dedens *mon sein, pres de mon cueur.*

[33] 273s: R337

Ch34   Chançon   [p. 274i]

       De vostre beauté regarder,
       Ma tresbelle, gente maistresse,
       Ce m'est certes tant de lÿesse
       Que ne le sauriés penser.

5   Je ne m'en pourroye lasser,
       Car j'oublie toute tristesse
       De vostre *beauté regarder,*
       Ma tresbelle, *gente maistresse.*

5 That is why I must feel
 Many grievous ills, to tell the truth,
 Far from the path of joy,
 Where all good things can be obtained.

 My heart has sunk completely
10 Into grief, not budging at all,
 And so it's necessary in my view
 That I consent to this, against my will,
 Far from the path of joy.

Chanson

 Within my breast, near my heart,
 I've hidden a secret kiss
 I stole, despite Danger,
 Who makes my heart die in pain and distress.

5 But his misery does not concern me,
 Even should he go stark raving mad,
 Within my breast, near my heart,
 I've hidden a secret kiss.

 If my lady, through her sweetness,
10 Will allow, not hindering me,
 I think to get more of them,
 And thus amass a greater treasure
 Within my breast, near my heart.

Chanson

 Looking upon your beauty,
 Mistress mine, so lovely and gracious,
 Is for me so full of happiness
 You cannot imagine it.

5 I could never tire of this,
 For I've forgotten all my sadness
 Looking upon your beauty,
 Mistress mine, so lovely and gracious.

10   Mais, pour mesdisans destourber
De parler sus vostre jeunesse,
Il fault que souvent m'en delaisse,
Combien que ne m'en puis garder
De vostre *beauté regarder.*

[34] 274s: R336

Ch35   Chançon   [p. 271i]

Prenez tost ce baisier, mon cueur,
Que ma maistresse vous presente,
La belle, bonne, jeune et gente,
Par sa tresgrant grace et doulceur.

5   Bon guet feray, sus mon honneur,
A fin que Dangier riens n'en sente.
Prenez *tost ce baisier, mon cueur,*
Que ma *maistresse vous presente.*

Dangier toute nuit en labeur
10   A fait guet. Or gist en sa tente.
Acomplissez brief vostre entente
Tantdis qu'il dort—c'est le meillieur—
Prenez *tost ce baisier, mon cueur.*

[35] 271s: R335

Ch36   Chançon   [p. 272i]

Comment vous puis je tant amer
Et mon cueur si tresfort haïr
Qu'il ne me chault de desplaisir
Qu'il puisse pour vous endurer?

5   Son mal m'est joyeux a porter,
Mais qu'il vous puisse bien servir.
Comment *vous puis je tant amer*
Et mon cueur *si tresfort haïr?*

Las! Or ne deusse je penser
10   Qu'a le garder et chier tenir,
Et non pour tant, mon seul desir,
Pour vous le vueil abandonner.
Comment *vous puis je tant amer?*

[36] 272s: R334

But, to prevent gossips
10   From speaking of your youth,
I often must leave off doing so,
Although I cannot cease
Looking upon your beauty.

Chanson

Take this kiss quickly, my heart,
Which my mistress offers you,
Beautiful, virtuous, young, and noble,
Through her sweetness and so great kindness.

5   I'll mount a good watch, on my honor,
So Danger will sense nothing.
Take this kiss quick, my heart,
Which my mistress offers you.

Danger, all night at work,
10   Is watching. Now he's lying in his tent.
Hurry up and do what you intend
While he slumbers—it's for the best—
Take this kiss quick, my heart.

Chanson

How can I love you so much
And hate my heart with such vehemence
That I care not about the misery
It might endure for your sake?

5   Its ills are a joy for me to bear,
As long as it is able to serve you well.
How can I love you so much
And hate my heart with such vehemence?

Alas! Now I should only think about
10   Protecting and holding it dear,
And nonetheless, my one desire,
For you I am willing to abandon it.
How can I love you so much?

Ch37　　　　　　**Chançon**　　　　　　　　　　[p. 267i]

Je ne prise point telz baisiers
Qui sont donnez par contenance,
Ou par maniere d'acointance.
Trop de gens en sont parçonniers.

5　　On en peut avoir par milliers,
A bon marchié grant habondance.
Je ne *prise point telz baisiers*
Qui sont *donnez par contenance.*

Mais savez vous lesquelz sont chiers?
10　Les privez venans par plaisance.
Tous autres ne sont, sans doubtance,
Que pour festier estrangiers.
Je ne prise *point telz baisiers!*

[37] 267s: R333

Ch38　　　　　　**Chançon**　　　　　　　　　　[p. 268i]

Ma seule amour, ma joye et ma maistresse,
Puis qu'il me fault loing de vous demorer,
Je n'ay plus riens a me reconforter
Q'un souvenir pour retenir lÿesse.

5　　En allegant, par Espoir, ma destresse,
Me couvendra le temps ainsi passer,
Ma seule *amour, ma joye et ma maistresse,*
Puisqu'il *me fault loing de vous demorer.*

Car mon las cueur, bien garny de tristesse,
10　S'en est voulu avecques vous aler,
Ne je ne puis jamais le recouvrer,
Jusques verray vostre belle jeunesse,
Ma seule *amour, ma joye et ma maistresse.*

[38] 268s: R332

Ch39　　　　　　**Chançon**　　　　　　　　　　[p. 269i]

Se desplaire ne vous doubtoye,
Voulentiers je vous embleroye
Un doulx baisier priveement

Chanson

I don't prize in the least such kisses
As those bestowed only for show,
Or in some flighty fashion.
Too many men take their share of them.

5   They can be had in their thousands,
A great abundance at a cheap price.
I don't prize in the least such kisses
As those bestowed only for show.

But do you know which have value?
10   The private ones given in pleasure.
All others serve, and there is no doubt,
Only to honor strangers.
I don't prize in the least such kisses!

Chanson

My one love, my joy, and my mistress,
Since I must remain far distant from you,
I no longer have anything to console me
Save a memory to hold onto happiness.

5   Complaining about my distress to Hope
Is how I must pass the time,
My one love, my joy and my mistress,
Since I must remain far distant from you.

For my weary heart, well supplied with sadness,
10   Desired to go with you,
Nor can I ever have him back,
Until I gaze upon your beautiful youth,
My one love, my joy and my mistress.

Chanson

If I were not afraid of displeasing you,
I would willingly steal from you
A sweet kiss, discreetly,

      Et garderoye seurement
5   Dedens le tresor de ma joye.

      Mais que Dangier soit hors de voye,
      Et que sans presse je vous voye,
      Belle que j'ayme loyaument.
      Se desplaire *ne vous doubtoye,*
10   Voulentiers *je vous embleroye*
      Un doulx *baisier priveement.*

      Jamais ne m'en confesseroye,
      Ne pour larrecin le tendroye,
      Mais grant aumosne vrayement,
15   Car a mon cueur joyeusement
      De par vous le presenteroye,
      Se desplaire *ne vous doubtoye.*

[39] 269s: R331

Ch40   Chançon   [p. 270i]

      Malade de mal ennuieux,
      Faisant la peneuse sepmaine,*
      Vous envoye, ma souveraine,
      Un souspir merencolïeux.

5   Par lui saurez, mon bien joyeux,
      Comment desplaisir me demaine,
      Malade *de mal ennuieux,*
      Faisant *la peneuse sepmaine.*

      Car aler ne peuent mes yeulx
10   Vers la beauté dont estes plaine,
      Mais au fort, ma joye mondaine,
      J'endureray pour avoir mieulx,
      Malade *de mal ennuieux.*

[40] 270s: R330

Ch41   Chançon   [p. 279i]

      S'il vous plaist vendre voz baisiers,
      J'en achatteray voulentiers,
      Et en aurés mon cueur en gage
      Pour les prandre par heritage,
5   Par douzaines, cens ou milliers.

And guard it securely
5   Within the treasure chest of my joy.

If only Danger were far away,
And I could see you without a crowd,
Belle, whom I loyally love.
If I were not afraid of displeasing you,
10   I would willingly steal from you
A sweet kiss, discreetly.

Never would I confess this,
Or consider it thievery,
But truly an act of great charity,
15   For joyously to my heart
I'd present it on your behalf,
If I were not afraid of displeasing you.

Chanson

Sick with a troubling ill,
Enduring my torment,
I send you, my sovereign lady,
A melancholy sigh.

5   Through it you'll learn, my joyous help,
How misery rules me,
Sick with a troubling ill,
Passing a week in pain.

For my eyes cannot make their way
10   To the beauty that's yours in abundance,
Yet in the end, my joy in this world,
I'll endure this to obtain better,
Sick with a troubling ill.

Chanson

Were you pleased to sell your kisses,
I'd willingly purchase them,
And for them you'd have my heart on account
So I could claim them by right
5   In their dozens, hundreds, or thousands.

Ne les me vendez pas si chiers
Que vous feriés a estrangiers.
En me recevant en hommage,
S'il vous *plaist vendre voz baisiers*
10   J'en achatteray *voulentiers*,
Et en *aurés mon cueur en gage.*

Mon vueil et mon desir entiers
Sont vostres, maugré tous dangiers.
Faittes, comme loyalle et sage,
15   Que pour mon guerdon et partage
Je soye servy des premiers,
S'il vous *plaist vendre voz baisiers.*

[41] 279s: R329

Ch42   Chançon   [p. 280i]

Ma seule amour que tant desire,
Mon reconfort, mon doulx penser,
Belle, nompareille sans per,
Il me desplaist de vous escrire.

5   Car j'aymasse mieulx a le dire
De bouche sans le vous mander,
Ma seule *amour que tant desire,*
Mon reconfort, *mon doulx penser.*

Las! Or n'y puis je contredire,
10   Mais Espoir me fait endurer,
Qui m'a promis de retourner
En lïesse mon grief martire,
Ma seule *amour que tant desire.*

[42] 280s: R328

Ch43   Chançon   [p. 281i]

Logiés moy entre voz bras
Et m'envoiez doulx baisier
Qui me viengne festier
D'aucun amoureux soulas.

5   Tantdis que Dangier est las,
Et le voyez sommeillier,

Do not sell me them at so dear a price
As you would to a stranger.
Receiving my homage,
Were you pleased to sell your kisses,
10   I would willingly purchase them,
And for them you'd have my heart on account.

My will and all my desire
Are yours, despite every difficulty.
Make it happen, in a manner loyal and wise,
15   That, as my share and reward,
I might be served among the first,
Were you pleased to sell your kisses.

Chanson

My one love whom I desire so,
My consolation, my sweet thought,
Belle, unrivaled without equal,
I am sorry to have to write you.

5   For I would have preferred saying this
With my own mouth, not sending a message,
My one love whom I desire so,
My consolation, my sweet thought.

Alas! Now I cannot countermand this,
10   But rather Hope makes me endure,
Who has promised to transform
My grievous suffering into happiness,
My one love whom I desire so.

Chanson

Give me lodging in your arms
And send me a sweet kiss,
Which might come to raise my spirits
With some kind of lover's consolation.

5   While Danger is weary,
And you see him slumbering,

Logiés *moy entre voz bras*
Et m'envoiez *doulx baisier.*

Pour Dieu, ne l'esveilliez pas,
10   Ce faulx, envïeux Dangier.
Jamais ne puist s'esveillier!
Faittes tost et parlez bas :
Logiés *moy entre voz bras*!

[43] 281s: R327

Ch44   [Chançon]

Se Dangier me tolt le parler   [p. 282i]
A vous, mon bel amy sans per,
Par le pourchas des envïeux,
Non plus qu'on toucheroit aux cieulx
5   Ne me tendray de vous amer.

Car mon cueur m'a voulu laissier
Pour soy du tout a vous donner
Et pour estre vostre en tous lieux,
Se Dangier *me tolt le parler*
10   A vous, *mon bel amy sans per,*
Par le *pourchas des envïeux.*

Tout son povoir ne peut garder
Que, sur tous autres, n'aye chier
Vostre gent corps tresgracïeux,
15   Et se ne vous voy de mes yeulx,
Pour tant ne vous vueil je changier,
Se Dangier *me tolt le parler.*

[44] 282s: Blank

Ch45   Chançon

Va tost, mon amoureux desir,   [p. 277i]
Sur quanque me veulx obeir,
Tout droit vers le manoir de Joye,
Et pour plus abregier ta voye,
5   Prens ta guide Doulx Souvenir.

Metz peine de me bien servir
Et de ton message acomplir.
Tu congnois ce que je vouldroye :

Give me lodging in your arms
And send me a sweet kiss.

For God's sake, do not wake him,
10   That false, envious Danger.
May he never prove able to wake up!
Do it quickly, and speak softly:
Give me lodging in your arms.

Chanson

If Danger prevents me from speaking
To you, my handsome friend without rival,
Because of the power of the envious,
No more than one might touch the heavens
5   Would I refrain from loving you.

For my heart has wished to abandon me
To give itself entirely to you
And be yours everywhere,
If Danger prevents me from speaking
10   To you, my handsome friend without rival,
Because of the power of the envious.

All his power cannot prevent
My holding dear, above all others,
Your noble person so very gracious,
15   And if I do not lay eyes upon you,
I still don't want to have another in your place
If Danger prevents me from speaking.

Chanson

Go quickly, my lover's desire,
On whatever mount, obedient to me, you choose,
Straight toward the manor house of Joy,
And to make your path shorter
5   Bring Sweet Memory along as your guide.

Take pains to serve me well
And deliver your message.
You know what I'd like:

Va tost, *mon amoureux desir,*
10   Sur *quanque me veulx obeir,*
Tout *droit vers le manoir de Joye.*

Recommandes moy a Plaisir
Et se brief ne peuz revenir,
Fay que de toy nouvelles oye
15   Et par Bon Espoir les m'envoye.
Ne vueilles au besoing faillir.
Va tost, *mon amoureux desir!*

[45] 277s: Blank

Ch46   Chançon   [p. 278i]

Je me metz en vostre mercy,
Tresbelle, bonne, jeune et gente,
On m'a dit qu'estes mal contente
De moy, ne sçay s'il est ainsi.

5   De toute nuit je n'ay dormy,
Ne pensez pas que je vous mente.
Je me *metz en vostre mercy,*
Tresbelle, *bonne, jeune et gente.*

Pource, treshumblement vous pry
10   Que vous me dittes vostre entente,
Car d'une chose je me vante :
Qu'en loyauté n'ay point failly.
Je me metz *en vostre mercy.*

[46] 278s: R326

Ch47   Chançon   [p. 275i]

Trop estes vers moy endebtee,
Vous me devés plusieurs baisiers.
Je vouldroye moult voulentiers
Que la debte fust acquittee.

5   Quoy que vous soyez excusee
Que n'osez pour les faulx Dangiers,
Trop *estes vers moy endebtee,*
Vous *me devés plusieurs baisiers.*

Go quickly, my lover's desire,
10 On whatever mount will obey me,
Straight toward the manor house of Joy.

Commend me to Pleasure,
And if you cannot return quickly,
Make sure I hear news of you,
15 Sent through Good Hope.
Please don't fail at this task.
Go quickly, my lover's desire.

Chanson

I put myself at your mercy,
Lady so beautiful, virtuous, young, and noble.
I've been told you're discontented
With me; I don't know if this is true.

5 I haven't slept the whole night long.
Don't think I tell you lies.
I put myself at your mercy,
Lady so beautiful, virtuous, young, and noble.

And so, very humbly I beg you
10 To speak all your mind to me,
For of one thing I do boast:
I've never failed in loyalty.
I put myself at your mercy.

Chanson

You're deeply indebted to me,
You owe me many kisses.
I'd very much like
The debt to be settled.

5 Although you might be excused
For not daring because of false Danger,
You're deeply indebted to me,
You owe me many kisses.

J'en ay bonne lettre seellee,
10   Paiez les, sans tenir si chiers.
      Autrement, par les officiers
      D'Amours, vous serez arrestee.
      Trop estes *vers moy endebtee*!

[47] 275s: R325

Ch48   Chançon   [p. 276i]

      Vostre bouche dit : Baisiez moy,
      Se m'est avis quant la regarde,
      Mais Dangier de trop pres la garde,
      Dont mainte doleur je reçoy.

5   Laissiez m'avoir, par vostre foy,
      Un doulx baisier sans que plus tarde.
      Vostre *bouche dit : Baisiez moy,*
      Se m'est *avis quant la regarde.*

      Dangier me heit, ne sçay pourquoy,
10   Et tousjours Destourbier me darde.
      Je prie a Dieu que mal feu l'arde!
      Il fust temps qu'il se tenist coy.
      Vostre bouche *dit : Baisiez moy.*

[48] 276s: R324

Ch49   Chançon   [p. 289i]

      Je ne les prise pas deux blans
      Tous les biens qui sont en amer,
      Car il n'y a que tout amer
      Et grant foison de faulx semblans.

5   Pour les maulx qui y sont doublans,
      Pires que les perilz de mer,
      Je ne *les prise pas deux blans*
      Tous *les biens qui sont en amer.*

      Ilz ne sont a riens ressemblans,
10   Car un jour viennent entamer
      Le cueur et aprés embasmer.
      Ce sont amourettes tremblans,
      Je ne les *prise pas deux blans.*

[49] 289s: R323

I have a bill for them, a fine one with a seal.
10 Pay them, don't hold the kisses so precious.
Otherwise, by the officers
Of Love, you'll be arrested.
You're deeply indebted to me.

Chanson

Your mouth says: Kiss me,
So it seems when I look that way,
But Danger keeps too close a guard,
And this makes me feel much pain.

5   Let me have, upon your faith,
A sweet kiss with no more delay.
Your mouth says: Kiss me,
So it seems when I look that way.

Danger hates me, I don't know why,
10   And Trouble always stabs at me.
I pray God that the evil fire consume him!
It should be time he keeps silent.
Your mouth says: Kiss me.

Chanson

I don't care two cents for them,
For all the good things in love,
Since they, false in their appearance,
Contain only bitterness in abundance.

5   For the ills they contain multiply,
Worse than perils on the sea.
I don't care two cents for them,
For all the good things in love.

They resemble nothing else,
10   For one day they come and deal the heart
A wound, afterward putting it to sleep.
These are passing infatuations,
I don't care two cents for them.

Ch50   Chançon   [p. 290i]

    Au besoing congnoist on l'amy*
    Qui loyaument aidier desire,
    Pour vous je puis bien cecy dire,
    Car vous ne m'avez pas failly.

5   Mais avez, la vostre mercy,
    Tant fait qu'il me doit bien souffire.
    Au besoing congnoist on l'amy
    Qui loyaument aidier desire.

    Bien brief pense partir decy
10   Pour m'en aler vers vous de tire.
    Loisir n'ay plus de vous escrire
    Et pource plus avant ne dy :
    Au besoing congnoist on l'amy.

[50] 290s: R322

Ch51   Chançon   [p. 287i]

    Fuyés le trait de doulx regard,
    Cueur qui ne vous savez deffendre,
    Veu qu'estes desarmé et tendre,
    Nul ne vous doit tenir couard.

5   Vous serés pris ou tost ou tard,
    S'Amour le veult bien entreprandre.
    Fuyés le *trait de doulx regard,*
    Cueur *qui ne vous savez deffendre.*

    Retrayez vous soubz l'estandart
10   De Nonchaloir, sans plus attendre.
    S'a Plaisance vous laissiez rendre,
    Vous estes mort, Dieu vous en gard!
    Fuyés *le trait de doulx regard.*

[51] 287s: R321

Ch52   Chançon   [p. 288i]

    Mon seul amy, mon bien, ma joye,
    Cellui que sur tous amer veulx,
    Je vous pry que soiez joieux
    En esperant que brief vous voye.

Chanson

In need one finds out who one's friends are,
Who are eager out of loyalty to help.
I can certainly say this about you,
For you have not failed me.

5   Instead, you have, thanks be to you,
Done so much it should suffice me well.
In need one finds out who one's friends are,
Who are eager out of loyalty to help.

I surely think to leave here soon,
10   Making my way to you in haste.
I do not have the leisure to write
And so I shall say no more:
In need one finds out who one's friends are.

Chanson

Flee the bowshot of Sweet Regard,
Heart, you who cannot defend yourself,
Seeing you're disarmed and soft-skinned,
No man should think you a coward.

5   Soon or late, you'll be taken prisoner
If Love intends to get involved.
Flee the bowshot of Sweet Regard,
Heart, you who cannot defend yourself.

Retreat beneath the standard
10   Of Indifference without delay.
If you let yourself be taken by Pleasure,
You're a dead man, God preserve you!
Flee the bowshot of Sweet Regard.

Chanson

My only sweet friend, my good, my joy,
The man I intend to love above all others,
I beg you to be joyful,
Hoping I will see you soon.

5   Car je ne fais que querir voye
       De venir vers vous, se m'aist Dieux,
       Mon seul *amy, mon bien, ma joye*
       Cellui *que sur tous amer veulx.*

       Et se par souhaidier povoye
10   Estre emprés vous un jour ou deux,
       Pour quanqu'il a dessoubz les cieulx
       Autre rien ne souhaideroye,
       Mon seul *amy, mon bien, ma joye.*

[52] 288s: R320

Ch53   Chançon   [p. 283i]

       Fault il aveugle devenir?
       N'ose l'en plus les yeulz ouvrir
       Pour regarder ce qu'on desire?
       Dangier est bien estrange sire,
5   Qui tant veult amans asservir.

       Vous lerrez vous aneantir,
       Amours, sans remede querir?
       Ne peut nul Dangier contredire?
       Fault il *aveugle devenir?*
10   N'ose l'en *plus les yeulx ouvrir*
       Pour *regarder ce qu'on desire?*

       Les yeulz si sont fais pour servir
       Et pour raporter tout plaisir
       Aux cuers, quant ilz sont en martire.
15   A les en garder Dangier tire,
       Est ce bien fait de le souffrir?
       Fault il *aveugle devenir?*

[53] 283s: Blank

Ch54   Chançon   [p. 284i]

       Regardez moy sa contenance,
       Lui siet il bien a soy jouer?
       Certes, c'est le vray mirouer
       De toute joyeuse plaisance.

5   Entre les parfaictes de France
       Se peut elle l'une advouer?

5 For I do nothing but seek the path
 To go to you, so help me God.
 My only friend, my good, my joy,
 The man I intend to love above all others.

 And if by wishing I might be able
10 To remain with you a day or two,
 No matter what there is under heaven
 I'd not wish for anything else,
 My only sweet friend, my good, my joy.

Chanson

 Is it necessary to go blind?
 Dare a man no longer open his eyes
 To gaze upon his desire?
 Danger is a very strange lord,
5 So eager to turn lovers into slaves.

 You'll let yourself be destroyed,
 Love, without seeking any remedy?
 Can no man contradict Danger?
 Is it necessary to go blind?
10 Dare a man no longer open his eyes
 To gaze upon his desire?

 The eyes are made to serve
 And report every kind of pleasure
 To hearts when they are suffering.
15 Danger tries to prevent them doing so.
 Is it good to let him have his way?
 Is it necessary to go blind?

Chanson

 Look at her face for me,
 Is it well suited to having fun?
 Surely, it's the true mirror
 Of every joyful pleasure.

5 Among the perfect beauties of France
 Can she affirm she's one?

Regardez *moy sa contenance,*
Lui siet *il bien a soy jouer?*

Pour fel me tien, quant je m'avence
10   De vouloir les grans biens louer
Dont Dieu l'a voulue douer.
Ses fais en font la demoustrance :
Regardez *moy sa contenance!*

[54] 284s: R319

Ch55   Chançon   [p. 285i]

Reprenez ce larron souspir
Qui s'est emblé soudainement
Sans congié ou commandement
Hors de la prison de Desir.

5   Mesdisans l'ont ouÿ partir*
Dont ilz tiennent leur parlement.
Reprenez *ce larron souspir*
Qui s'est *emblé soudainement.*

Se le meschant eust sceu saillir
10   Sans noyse tout priveement,
N'en peust chaloir, mais sotement
L'a fait; pource l'en fault pugnir.
Reprenez *ce larron souspir.*

[55] 285s: R318

Ch56   Chançon   [p. 286i]

Et eussiez vous, Dangier, cent yeulx
Assis et derriere et devant,
Ja n'yrez si prez regardant
Que vostre propos en soit mieulx.

5   Estre ne povez en tous lieux,
Vous prenez peine pour neant,
Et eussiez *vous, Dangier, cent yeulx,*
Assis *et derriere et devant.*

Les fais des amoureux sont telz :
10   Tousjours vont en assoubtivant.

Look at her face for me,
Is it well suited to having fun?

I think badly of myself when I set about
10 Praising the great virtues with which
God has been pleased to endow her.
Her actions are the proof.
Look at her face for me!

Chanson

Recapture this furtive sigh
That suddenly stole away
Without leave or command
From the prison of Desire.

5   Evil tongues heard it depart
And are conferring about the matter.
Recapture this furtive sigh
That suddenly stole away.

If the knave could have sallied forth
10 Discreetly and making no noise,
It should not have mattered, but he has acted
Foolishly and so should be punished.
Recapture this furtive sigh.

Chanson

Even if you had a hundred eyes, Danger,
Mounted behind and in front as well,
You'd not prove able to look around so closely
As to manage your business better.

5   You cannot be everywhere.
You take pains for nothing,
Even if you had a hundred eyes, Danger,
Mounted behind and in front as well.

This is how lovers act:
10 Always they conduct themselves cunningly.

Jamais ne saurez faire tant
Qu'ilz ne vous trompent, se m'aist Dieux,
Et eussiez *vous, Dangier, cent yeulx*!

[56] 286s: R317

Ch57   Chançon   [p. 295i]

Dont vient ce soleil de Plaisance
Qui ainsi m'esbluyst les yeulz?
Beauté, Douceur, et encor mieulx
Y sont a trop grant abondance.

5   Soudainement luyst par semblance
Comme ung escler venant des cieulx.
Dont vient *ce soleil de Plaisance,*
Qui ainsi *m'esbluyst les yeulx?*

Il fait perdre la contenance
10   A toutes gens, jeunes et vielz.
N'il n'est eclipse, se m'aist Dieux,
Qui de l'obscurcir ait puissance.
Dont vient *ce soleil de Plaisance?*

[57] 295s: R316

Ch58   Chançon   [p. 296i]

Laissez moy penser a mon ayse,
Helas! Donnez m'en le loisir.
Je devise avecques Plaisir,
Combien que ma bouche se tayse.

5   Quant Merencolie mauvaise
Me vient maintes fois assaillir,
Laissez *moy penser a mon ayse,*
Helas! *Donnez m'en le loisir.*

Car affin que mon cuer rapaise,
10   J'appelle Plaisant Souvenir
Qui tantost me vient resjouïr.
Pource pour Dieu ne vous desplaise,
Laissez *moy penser a mon ayse.*

[58] 296s: R315

Never could you do enough
That they wouldn't fool you, so help me God,
Even if you had a hundred eyes, Danger!

Chanson

Whence comes this sun of Pleasure
Making it hard for my eyes to see?
Beauty, Sweetness, and even better
Are there in such great abundance.

5   The brightness comes as suddenly
As a lightning bolt from heaven.
Whence comes this sun of Pleasure
Making it hard for my eyes to see?

It makes one and all lose their wits,
10   Young and old alike.
There's no eclipse, so help me God,
Powerful enough to darken it.
Whence comes this sun of Pleasure?

Chanson

Give me time to think.
Alas! Allow me the leisure to do so.
I'm chatting with Pleasure,
Although my mouth falls silent.

5   When evil Melancholy
Comes again and again to assault me,
Give me time to think.
Alas! Allow me the leisure to do so.

For in order to soothe my heart,
10   I call on Pleasant Memory,
Who comes at once to cheer me.
So, for God's sake, do not be displeased,
Give me time to think.

Ch59   Chançon   [p. 297i]

Levez ces cuevrechiefs plus hault
Qui trop cuevrent ces beaulx visages.
De riens ne servent telz umbrages,
Quant il ne fait hale ne chault.

5   On fait a Beaulté, qui tant vault,
De la musser tort et oultraiges :
Levez *ces cuevrechiefs plus hault*
Qui trop *cuevrent ces beaulx visages.*

Je sçay bien qu'a Dangier n'en chault
10   Et pense qu'il ait donné gaiges
Pour entretenir telz usages,
Mais l'ordonnance rompre fault.
Levez *ces cuevrechiefs plus hault.*

[59] 297s: R314

Ch60   Chançon   [p. 298i]

Entre les amoureux fourrez,
Non pas entre les decoppez,
Suis, car le temps sans refroidy
Et le cueur de moy l'est aussy.
5   Tel me veez, tel me prenez.

Jeunes gens qui Amours servez,
Pour Dieu, de moy ne vous moquez,
Il est ainsi que je vous dy :
Entre *les amoureux fourrez,*
10   Non pas *entre les decoppez,*
Suys, *car le temps sans refroidy.*

Car, quant Amours servy aurez
Autant que j'ay, vous devendrez
Pareillement en mon party,
15   Et quant vous trouverez ainsy
Comme je sui, lors vous serez
Entre *les amoureux fourrez!*

[60] 298s: R313

Chanson

Lift up your kerchiefs higher,
Which cover too much of these lovely faces.
Such parasols serve no purpose
With no heat or sun to worry about.

5   To do this to Beauty, covering her,
Is a wrong and outrage to one so worthy.
Lift up your kerchiefs higher,
Which cover too much of these lovely faces.

I know Danger doesn't care,
10   And I think he's paid out advances
To support such practices.
Yet this custom must be broken.
Lift up your kerchiefs higher.

Chanson

Among lovers decked out in furs,
Not among the young dandies,
Am I, for the weather feels cold
And my heart is just the same.
5   Take me as you see I am.

Young people who serve Love,
For God's sake, do not mock me,
It's just as I say:
Among lovers decked out in furs,
10   Not among the young dandies,
Am I, for the weather feels cold.

For, when you've served Love
As much as I, you'll become
A member of the very same party.
15   And when you find yourselves
Just like me, you'll be
Among lovers decked out in furs.

Ch61 [Chançon] [p. 293i]

Dieu vous conduie, Doubz Penser
Et vous doint faire bon voyage,
Rapportez tost joyeux messaige
Vers le cuer pour le conforter.

5   Ne vueillez gueres demourer,
Exploictez comme bon et saige,
Dieu *vous conduie, Doubz Penser*
Et vous *doint faire bon voyage.*

Riens ne vous convient ordonner,
10   Les secrez savez du couraige,
Besongnez a son avantaige
Et pensez de brief retourner :
Dieu *vous conduie, Doubz Penser!*

[61] 293s: R312

Ch62 Chançon [p. 294i]

Les fourriers d'Amours m'ont logé
En un lieu bien a ma plaisance,
Dont les mercy de ma puissance
Et m'en tiens a eulx obligé.

5   Afin que tost soit abregé
Le mal qui me porte grevance,
Les fourriers *d'Amours m'ont logé*
En un lieu *bien a ma plaisance.*

Desja je me sens alegé,
10   Car acointié m'a Esperance,
Et croy qu'amoureux n'a en France
Qui soit mieulx de moy hebergé :
Les fourriers *d'Amours m'ont logé.*

[62] 294s: R311

Ch63 Chançon [p. 291i]

Que c'est estrange compaignie
De Penser joint avec Espoir!
Aidier scevent et decevoir
Ung cueur qui tout en eulx se fie.

Chanson

God be your guide, Sweet Thought,
And grant your voyage is good.
Deliver your joyous message at once
To the heart and thus console it.

5   Please don't delay a moment;
Make haste like someone virtuous and wise.
God be your guide, Sweet Thought,
And grant your voyage is good.

You have no arrangements to make,
10   Knowing the secrets of the heart.
Manage this to his advantage
And determine to return quickly:
God be your guide, Sweet Thought!

Chanson

The harbingers of Love have lodged me
In a place that pleases me well,
For which I give such thanks as I can,
Considering myself obliged to them.

5   In order to end soon
The grief that causes me such ill,
The harbingers of Love have lodged me
In a place that pleases me well.

Already I feel relieved,
10   For Hope has made my acquaintance,
And I believe no lover in France
Has better shelter than I:
The harbingers of Love have lodged me.

Chanson

What a strange company this is,
With Thought joined to Hope!
They can both aid and deceive
Any heart trusting entirely to them.

5   Il ne fault ja que je le dye,
       Chascun le peut en soy savoir
       Que c'est *estrange compaignie*
       De Penser *joint avec Espoir*!

       D'eulx me plains et ne m'en plains mye,
10   Car mal et bien m'ont fait avoir.
       Manty m'ont et aussi dit voir,
       Je l'aveu et si le renye.
       Que c'est *estrange compaignie*!

[63] 291s: R310

Ca1   Carole   [p. 315]

       Las! Merencolie,
       Me tendrés vous longuement
       Es maulx dont j'ay plus de cent,
       Sans pensee lie?

5   Je l'ay souffert main et soir,
       Loingtain de joyeulx confort,

       Mais nul bien n'en puis avoir
       Dont mon cueur est presque mort.

       Au meins, je vous en prie
10   Que me laissiez seulement
       Aucun peu d'alegement
       Sans m'oster la vie,
       Las! *Merencolie.*

       Esperance d'avoir mieulx
15   Dist qu'elle me veult aidier,

       Mais tousjours maugracïeux
       Je treuve le faulx Dangier

       Qui tant me guerrie.
       Si vous requier humblement
20   Qu'en ce douloureux tourment
       Ne me laissiez mie,
       Las! Merencolie.

5   There's no need for me to say so.
          Everyone can realize it himself.
          What a strange company this is,
          With Thought joined to Hope!

          I complain of them yet do not complain at all,
10   For they've invested me with ill and benefit.
          They've lied to me and also spoken truth.
          I affirm and also renounce this.
          What a strange company this is!

Carol

          Alas! Melancholy,
          Will I be kept long
          In miseries, of which I've more than a hundred,
          With no happy thought?

5   I suffered these morning and night,
          Far from joyful consolation.

          But I can obtain no good this way,
          And so my heart's near death.

          At the least, I beg you
10   Allow me
          A little relief
          Without taking my life,
          Alas! Melancholy.

          Hope-of-Obtaining-Better
15   Said she wished to help me,

          But always I find
          False Danger unfavoring,

          Who wars so much against me.
          So I humbly beg you,
20   Don't abandon me
          At all to this painful torment,
          Alas! Melancholy.

Ca2   Carole   [p. 316]

      Avancez vous, Esperance,
      Venez mon cueur conforter,
      Car il ne peut plus porter
      Sa tresgreveuse penance.

5   Pieça, Joyeuse Pensee
      S'esbatoit avecques lui,

      Mais elle s'en est alee,
      Tant a pourchassié Ennuy.

      Se vous n'avez la puissance
10   De tout son mal lui oster,
      Plaise vous a alegier
      Au meins un peu sa grevance.
      Avancez *vous, Esperance.*

      Vous lui avez fait promesse
15   De le venir secourir

      Et de lui tollir tristesse,
      Mais trop le faittes languir.

      Ayez de lui souvenance
      Et le venez deslogier
20   De la prison de Dangier
      Ou il meurt en desplaisance :
      Avancez *vous, Esperance.*

Ca3   Carole   [p. 317]

      M'avez vous point mis en oubly?
      Par Dieu, je doubte fort, oÿ,
      Ma seule maistresse et ma joye.
      Non pour tant, quelque part que soye,
5   Je m'atens a vostre mercy.

      Espoir m'a dit que Leauté
      Vous fera souvenir de moy,
      Car vostre bonne voulenté
      Ne peut faillir, comme je croy.

10   Quant est a moy, je vous supply,
      Pensez que l'amoureux party

Carol

Come forward, Hope,
Come comfort my heart,
For he can bear no longer
His very grievous affliction.

5   Some time ago, Joyful Thought
Disported with him,

But she has gone her way,
Worry has so much harassed her.

If you do not have the power
10   To cure his every ill,
Please relieve at least
His affliction somewhat.
Come forward, Hope.

You promised
15   To come to his aid

And take his sadness from him,
Yet you let him languish too long.

Do remember him
And obtain his release
20   From the prison of Danger,
Where he dies in misery:
Come forward, Hope.

Carol

Have you forgotten me altogether?
By God, I greatly fear it, yes,
My sole mistress and my joy.
Nevertheless, wherever I might be,
5   I await your mercy.

Hope has told me that Loyalty
Will make you remember me,
For your goodwill
Cannot fail, so I trust.

10   As for me, I beg you,
Bear in mind I could not change from

Que j'ay prins, changier ne pourroye.
Certes, avant mourir vouldroye.
Je vous prometz qu'il est ainsi.
15   M'avez *vous point mis en oubly*?

Amour a tort, se m'est avis,
Qu'il ne fait aux dames sentir
Les maulx ou leurs servans sont mis
Pour les tresleaument servir.

20   Pour vous, ma dame, je le dy,
Car se vous saviez le soussy
Qu'Amour, pour vous servir, m'envoye,
Vous diriés bien que j'auroye
De droit gaingnié le don d'amy.
25   M'avez vous *point mis en oubly*?

R1   Rondel d'Orleans · a Nevers*   [p. 318i]

Pour paier vostre belle chiere,
Laissez en gaige vostre cueur,
Nous le garderons en doulceur
Tant que vous retournez arriere.

5   Contentez, car c'est la maniere,
Vostre hostesse pour vostre honneur,
Pour paier *vostre belle chiere*.

Et se voiez nostre priere
Estre trop plaine de rigueur,
10   Changons de cuer, c'est le meilleur,
De voulenté bonne et entiere,
Pour paier vostre belle chiere.

[64] 318s: R108

R2   [Rondel] Responce de Nevers*   [p. 319i]

Mon tresbon hoste et ma tresdoulce hostesse,
Treshumblement et plus vous remercie
Des biens, honneurs, bonté et courtoisie
Que m'avez fais tous deux, par vostre humblesse.

5   Aussi fay je de vostre grant largesse
Et tres soingneuse et bonne compaignie,
Mon tresbon hoste *et ma tresdoulce hostesse*.

The lover's role I've chosen.
Surely, I'd rather die first.
This is true, I promise you.
15   Have you forgotten me altogether?

Love is wrong, I think,
Not to make ladies feel
The ills that afflict their servants
Because they faithfully love them.

20   It is for you, my lady, that I say this,
For if you knew of the cares
That Love sends me because I serve you,
You would certainly say I have
Rightfully earned the lover's gift.
25   Have you forgotten me altogether?

Rondel from Orleans to Nevers

To pay for your fair welcome,
Leave your heart in pledge.
We'll guard it gently
Until you come back here again.

5   Satisfy your hostess, for that's
The custom, to your honor,
To pay for your fair welcome.

And if you think our request
Too full of harshness,
10   Let's have a change of heart, for the best,
With a will good and unwavering,
To pay for your fair welcome.

Rondel — response of Nevers

My very good host and so gracious hostess,
I thank you with great humility
For the favors, honors, kindnesses, and courtesies
You both have graciously bestowed upon me.

5   My thanks also for your great generosity
And your company elegant and fine,
My very good host and so gracious hostess.

Mon povre cuer pour paiement vous lesse,
Prenez en gré, et je vous en supplie,
10   Et oultre plus, tant que je puis, vous prie
Que m'octroyez estre maistre et maistresse,
[Mon tresbon hoste et ma tresdoulce hostesse.]

[65] 319s: R109

R3   [Rondel] Par Orlians   [p. 320s]

A ce jour de Saint Valentin
Que chascun doit choisir son per,
Amours, demourray je non per,
Sans partir a vostre butin?

5   A mon resveillier au matin,
Je n'y ay cessé de penser,
A ce jour *de Saint Valentin.*

Mais Nonchaloir, mon medicin,
M'est venu le pouse taster,
10   Qui m'a conseillié reposer
Et rendormir sur mon coussin,
A ce jour *de Saint Valentin.*

[66] 320i: R4

R4   [Rondel]   [p. 320i]

J'ay esté poursuivant d'Amours,*
Mais maintenant je suis herault.
Monter me fault en l'eschaffault
Pour jugier des amoureux tours.

5   Quant je verray riens a rebours,
Dieu scet se je crieray bien hault :
J'ay esté *poursuivant d'Amours!*

Et s'amans vont faisans les lours,
Tantost congnoistray leur deffault.
10   Ja devant moy cloichier ne fault,
D'amer sçay par cuer le droit cours :
J'ay esté *poursuivant d'Amours.*

[67] 320s: R3

I leave you my poor heart as payment.
Kindly take it, I beg you,
10   Moreover, as much as I can, I ask
That you agree to be my master and mistress,
My very good host and so gracious hostess.

Rondel by Orleans

On this St. Valentine's Day
When every man is to choose his mate,
Love, will I remain without a mate,
Not sharing in your reward?

5   Since waking up this morning,
I have not stopped thinking of it
On this St. Valentine's Day.

But Indifference, my physician,
Has come to take my pulse,
10   And advised me to rest
And go back to sleep on my pillow,
On this St. Valentine's Day.

Rondel

I've been a follower of Love,
But now I'm his herald.
I must mount the platform
To judge how lovers joust.

5   If I see anything go wrong,
God knows I'll shout out loud:
I've been a follower of Love!

And if lovers go playing the clumsy oaf,
I'll soon enough recognize their failings.
10   They'd better not blunder in my presence.
The proper path of love—I know this full well.
I've been a follower of Love.

R5   **[Rondel] par Cecile***   [p. 321s]

     Aprez une seule exceptee
     Je vous serviray ceste annee,
     Ma doulce Valentine gente,
     Puis qu'Amours veult que m'y consente
5   Et que telle est ma destinee.

     De moy, pour autre habandonnee
     Ne serez, mais si forte amee
     Qu'en devrez bien estre contente
     Aprez une seule *exceptee*.

10   Or me soit par vous ordonnee,
     S'il vous plaist, a ceste journee,
     Vo volenté doulce et plaisente,
     Car a la faire me presente
     Plus que pour dame qui soit nee,
15   Aprez une seule *exceptee*.

[68] 321i: R6

R6   **[Rondel]***   [p. 321i]

     Je suis desja d'amour tanné
     Ma tresdoulce Valentinee,
     Car pour moy fustes trop tost nee,
     Et moy pour vous fus trop tart né.

5   Dieu lui pardoint qui estrené
     M'a de vous pour toute l'annee.
     Je suis desja *d'amour tanné*.

     Bien m'estoye suspeçonné
     Qu'aroye telle destinee,
10   Ains que passast ceste journee.
     Combien qu'Amours l'eust ordonné,
     Je suis desja *d'amour tanné*.

[69] 321s: R5

R7   **[Rondel] par Orlians**   [p. 322s]

     Soubz parler couvert
     D'estrange devise
     Monstrez qu'avez prise
     Douleur; il y pert.

Rondel by Sicily

With the exception of one lady,
This year I will serve you,
My Valentine sweet and noble,
Since Love wishes I consent to this
5   And it is my destiny.

I'll not abandon you
For another lady, but love you so fiercely
You'll find contentment,
With the exception of one lady.

10   Now let me follow your command,
If it pleases you, this day
And do your will, sweet and pleasant,
For I am eager to do so,
More than for any woman born,
15   With the exception of one lady.

Rondel

I'm already wearied by love,
My very sweet Valentine,
Since you were born too soon for me
And I too late for you.

5   May God pardon the man who made a present
Of you to me for all the year.
I'm already wearied by love.

I was very doubtful
I'd have such a destiny
10   Before this day ended,
Although Love has so ordained,
I'm already wearied by love.

Rondel by Orleans

With obscure words
Of a strange conversation,
You show you've taken Sadness
Prisoner; so much is evident.

5   Du tout en desert
       N'est pas vostre emprise,
       Soubz parler *couvert*.

       Se Confort ouvert
       N'est a vostre guise,
10   Tost, s'Amour s'avise,
       Sera recouvert
       Soubz parler *couvert*.

[70] 322i: R8

R8   [Rondel]   [p. 322i]

       Laissez aler ces gorgias,
       Chascun yver a la pippee.
       Vous verrez comme la gelee
       Reverdira leurs estomas.*

5   Dieu scet s'ilz auront froit aux bras
       Par leur manche deschiquetee.
       Laissez *aler ces gorgias*!

       Ilz portent petiz soulers gras
       A une poulaine embourree.*
10   Froidure fera son entree
       Par leurs talons nuz par embas.
       Laissez *ces gorgias*!

[71] 322s: R7

R9   Rondel   [p. 323i]

       Veu que j'ay tant Amour servy,
       Ne suis je pas mal guerdonné?
       Du plaisir qu'il m'avoit donné
       Sans cause m'a tost desservy. *

5   Mon cuer loyaulment son serf vy,
       Mais a tort l'a habandonné
       Veu que j'ay *tant Amour servy*.

       Plus ne lui sera asservy.
       Pour Dieu, qu'il me soit pardonné,
10   Je croy que suis a ce don né

Not a waste at all
Is your enterprise
With obscure words.

If an open Consolation
Is not to your taste,
10   At once, if Love so advises,
It will be kept secret
With obscure words.

Rondel

Let these dandies go out
Every winter hunting for birds.
You'll see how the frost
Numbs their stomachs.

5   God knows their arms will be cold
In dagged sleeves.
Let these dandies go out!

They wear poulaines,
Padded and stuffed;
10   Cold will find its way in
Through the naked heels below.
Let these dandies go out!

Rondel

Seeing I have served Love so much,
Have I not been badly rewarded?
The pleasure bestowed upon me,
He's deprived me of for no reason.

5   I saw my heart as Love's loyal servant,
But Love has wrongly abandoned it
Seeing I have served Love so much.

No longer will my heart be put in his service.
I should be pardoned for this, by God.
10   I've been born to this gift, I think,

D'avoir mal pour bien desservy,
Veu que j'ay *tant Amour servy.*

[72] 323s: R110

R10   [Rondel] Secile*   [p. 324s]

Pour tant se vous plaignez d'Amours,
Il n'est pas temps de vous retraire,
Car encor il vous pourra faire
Tel bien que perdrez voz dolours.

5   Vous congnoissez assez ses tours,
Je ne dy pas pour vous desplaire.
Pour tant *se vous plaignez d'Amours,*

Ayez fiance en lui tousjours
Et mectez paine de lui plaire,
10   Combien que mieulx me voulsist taire,
Car vous pensez tout le rebours
Pour tant *se vous plaignez d'Amours.*

[73] 324i: R11

R11   [Rondel]   [p. 324i]

Se vous estiez comme moy,
Las! vous vous devriez bien plaindre,
Car de tous mes maulx le meindre
Est plus grant que vostre ennoy.

5   Bien vous pourriez, sur ma foy,
D'Amours alors vous complaindre,
Se vous estiez *comme moy.*

Car si tresdolent me voy,
Que plus la mort ne vueil craindre.
10   Toutesfoiz, il me fault faindre.
Aussi feriez vous, se croy,
Se vous estiez *comme moy.*

[74] 324s: R10

Receiving ill rather than a reward well-merited,
Seeing I have served Love so much.

Rondel — Sicily

Even though you complain of Love,
It's not time for you to withdraw,
For he could still bestow upon you
Some good to relieve your sorrow.

5   You know his ways well enough.
I say this not to displease you,
Even though you complain of Love.

May you always trust in Love
And take pains to please him,
10   Although I'd rather be silent
Since you think just the opposite,
Even though you complain of Love.

Rondel

Were you like me,
Alas! You'd loudly bemoan your lot,
For the least of my woes
Is greater than all your trouble.

5   You surely could, upon my faith,
Complain of Love,
Were you like me.

For you see me so terribly sad
I no longer fear death.
10   However, I must pretend.
You'd do the same, I think,
Were you like me.

R12   **[Rondel] Response par Orlians**   [p. 325s]

Chascune vielle son dueil plaint.*
Vous cuidez que vostre mal passe
Tout aultre, mais ja ne parlasse
Du mien, se n'y feusse contraint.

5   Saichez, de voir, qu'il n'est pas faint
Le torment que mon cuer enlasse.
Chascune vielle *son dueil plaint.*

Ma paine pers, comme fait maint,
Et contre Fortune je chasse.
10   Desespoir de pis me menasse,
Je sens ou mon pourpoint m'estraint.*
Chascune vielle *son dueil plaint.*

[75] 325i: R13

R13   **[Rondel] Secile***   [p. 325i]

Bien deffendu, bien assailly,
Chascun dit qu'il a grant dolours,
Mais, au fort, je vueil croire Amours
Par qui le debat est sailly,

5   Affin que qui aura failly
N'aye jamais de lui secours.
Bien deffendu, *bien assailly.*

Car se j'ay en riens deffailly
De compter mon mal puis deux jours,
10   Banny vueil estre de ses cours
Com un homme lache et failly.
Bien deffendu, *bien assailly.*

[76] 325s: R12

R14   **[Rondel] Responce per Orlians**   [p. 326s]

Bien assailly, bien deffendu,
Quant assez aurons debatu,
Il fault assembler noz raisons,
Et que les fons vouler faisons*
5   Du debat nouvel advenu.

Rondel — Response by Orleans

Every old woman bemoans her pain.
You think your suffering
Surpasses every other, but I'd never
Speak of mine if not forced to do so.

5   Know this is the truth, that it's not negligible,
The torment that binds my heart.
Every old woman bemoans her pain.

I waste my effort, as do many,
And Fortune opposes my pursuit.
10   Despair menaces me with worse,
And I know where my shoes are pinching.
Every old woman bemoans her pain.

Rondel — Sicily

Well defended, well assaulted,
Every man says he feels great distress,
But, in the end, I'm intent on believing Love,
Who started the debate,

5   For whoever will have failed
May he never be helped by Love,
Well defended, well assaulted.

For if I've neglected in any way
To report my sufferings these last two days,
10   I wish his court to banish me
As a coward and an oaf,
Well defended, well assaulted.

Rondel — Response by Orleans

Well assaulted, well defended,
After we've disputed enough,
We must sum up our arguments
And get to the bottom
5   Of the debate recently concluded.

Tresfort vous avez combatu,
Et j'ay mon billart bien tenu.*
C'est beau debat que de deux bons :*
Bien assailly, *bien deffendu.*

10   Vray est qu'estes d'Amour feru
Et en ses fers estroit tenu,
Mais moy non ainsi l'entendons.
Il a passé maintes saisons
Que me suis aux armes rendu :
15   Bien assailly, *bien deffendu.*

[77] 326i: R15

R15   [Rondel] Secile   [p. 326i]

Si dolant je me treuve a part
De laisser ce dont mon bien part,
C'est celle en qui n'a que redire,
Que ne fus onques si plain d'yre,
5   Ou jamais Dieu n'ait en moy part,

Car, quant je pense en mon depart,
Et qu'aler me fault autre part,
Je ne sçay plus que je dois dire,
Si dolant *je me treuve a part.*

10   Fortune, qui les lotz depart,
M'a baillé ce dueil pour ma part,
Qu'est pis qu'on ne seroit redire,
Et si ne lui puis contredire,
Dont a peu que mon cuer n'en part,
15   Si dolant *je me treuve a part.*

[78] 326s: R14

R16   [Rondel] Per Orlians   [p. 327s]

Durant les trieves d'Angleterre
Qui ont esté faictes a Tours
Par bon conseil, avec Amours
J'ay prins abstinence de guerre.

5   S'autre que moy ne la desserre,
Content suis que tiengne tousjours,
Durant *les trieves d'Angleterre.*

You have struggled very valiantly,
And I have kept my end up very well.
It's a fine debate which contains two proofs,
Well assaulted, well defended.

10   True it is that Love struck you a blow
And holds you fast in his irons.
But that is not my case.
Many seasons have come and gone
Since I surrendered:
15   Well assaulted, well defended.

Rondel—Sicily

I find myself alone, so pained
To abandon the source of my happiness
—The lady beyond all reproach—
That never before has grief so filled me
5   Or (if that is untrue) may God have no part of me.

For thinking about my departure,
Since I must travel elsewhere,
No longer do I know what to say,
I find myself alone, so pained.

10   Fortune, who distributes fates,
Has allotted me this pain,
Worse beyond any description,
And unable to oppose her,
My heart nearly breaks,
15   I find myself alone, so pained.

Rondel by Orleans

During the truce with England,
Concluded at Tours,
Following good advice, I have abstained
From warring with Love.

5   If someone else does not break it,
I'd be pleased for it to last forever,
During the truce with England.

Il n'est pas bon de trop enquerre
Ne s'empeschier es fais des cours.
10   S'on m'assault pour avoir secours,
Vers Nonchaloir yray grant erre,
Durant les trieves *d'Angleterre.*

[79] 327i: R111

R17   [Rondel] Fredet*   [p. 328s]

Jusques Pasques soient passees,
Donnez trieves a mes pensees,
Je vous pri, tant que puis, Amours,
Car c'est bien droit qu'a ces bons jours
5   En paix de vous soient lessees.

Assez voz gens les ont lassees
Et pour ceste foiz courroussees.
Alez ailleurs faire voz tours,
Jusques Pasques *soient passees.*

10   Pour plus dont n'estre d'eulx pressees,
Qui tant les ont fort menassees,
Faictes les crier par voz cours
Et leur deffendez bien tousjours
Que par eulx ne soient cassees
15   Jusques Pasques *soient passees.*

[80] 328i: R18

R18   [Rondel] Responce par Orlians   [p. 328i]

Tant que Pasques soient passees,
Sans resveillier le chat qui dort,
Fredet, je suis de vostre accort
Que pensees soyent cassees

5   Et en aumaires entassees
Fermans a clef, tresbien et fort,
Tant que Pasques *soient passees.*

Quant aux miennes, ilz sont lassees,
Mais de les garder mon effort
10   Feray, par l'avis de Confort,

No good to ask too much
Or meddle in the affairs of court,
10   If anyone chases after me for help,
I'll hasten toward Indifference,
During the truce with England.

Rondel — Fredet

Until Eastertide has passed,
Let my thoughts enjoy a truce,
As long as possible, Love, this I ask,
For it's surely just that in these good days
5   My thoughts be left in peace by you.

Your people have wearied them enough
And at present stirred them up.
Go ply your trade elsewhere,
Until Eastertide has passed.

10   So that my thoughts are no longer oppressed
By those who've threatened them so much,
Have it proclaimed throughout your courts,
And enjoin your people at all times
Not to break this truce
15   Until Eastertide has passed.

Rondel — Response by Orleans

Until Eastertide has passed,
Without waking up the sleeping cat,
Fredet, I agree with you
That thoughts should be suppressed

5   And heaped up in armoires,
Locked up very tightly and safely with a key,
Until Eastertide has passed.

Concerning my own, they are weary,
But, following what Comfort advises,
10   I'll do my best to keep them safe,

En fardeaus d'espoir amassees,
Tant que Pasques *soient passees.*

[81] 328s: R17

Ch64   [Chançon]*   [p. 329i]

Beauté, gardez vous de mez yeulx,
Car il vous viennent assaillir.
S'il vous pouoient conquerir,*
Il ne demanderoyent mielx.

5   Vous estes seule soubz lez cieulx,
Le tresor de parfait plaisir,
Beauté, *gardez vous de mez yeulx,*
Car il *vous viennent assaillir.*

Congneus lez ay, jeunes et vieulx,
10   Qu'il ne leur chauldroit de morir
Mais qu'eussent de vous leur desir.
Je vous avise qu'il sont tieulx :
Beauté, *gardez vous de mez yeulx*!

[82] 329s: R112

Ch65   [Chançon]   [p. 330i]

Bien viengne Doulz Regard qui rit,
Quelque bonne nouvelle porte,
Dont Dangier fort se desconforte
Et de courrous en douleur frit.

5   Ne peut chaloir de son despit
Ne de ceulz qui sont de sa sorte.
Bien viengne *Doulz Regard qui rit,*
Quelque *bonne nouvelle porte.*

Dangier dist : «Baille par escript,
10   Et qu'il n'entre point en la porte.»
Mais Amour, comme la plus forte,
Veult qu'il entre sans contredit.
Bien viengne *Doulz Regard qui rit*!

[83] 330s: R113

Bundled up in parcels of hope,
Until Eastertide has passed.

Chanson

Beauty, protect yourself from my eyes,
For they come to assault you.
If they prove able to conquer,
They'd demand no better.

5   Under heaven there's no lady your peer,
A treasure of perfect pleasure,
Beauty, protect yourself from my eyes,
For they come to assault you.

I've come to know this about them, young and old,
10   That death would not concern them
If only they could get what they desire from you.
Such is their nature, I advise you:
Beauty, protect yourself from my eyes.

Chanson

Welcome to Sweet Look who laughs,
The bearer of some fine news,
That mightily discomfits Danger
Who trembles with the anger that pains him.

5   His turmoil cannot matter,
Nor that of those like him.
Welcome to Sweet Look who laughs,
The bearer of some fine news.

Danger said: "Send this written message
10   To make sure Sweet Look never enters the gate."
But Love, being mightier,
Intends that he enter unopposed.
Welcome to Sweet Look who laughs!

Ch66 [Chançon] [p. 331i]

En la promesse d'Esperance
Ou j'ay temps perdu et usé,
J'ay souvent conseil reffusé,
Qui me povoit donner Plaisance.

5   Las! Ne suis le premier de France
Qui sottement s'est abusé
En la promesse *d'Esperance*
Ou j'ay *temps perdu et usé.*

Et de ma nysse gouvernance
10   Devant Raison, j'ay accusé
Mon cuer, mais il s'est excusé
Disant que deceu l'a Fïance
En la promesse *d'Esperance.*

[84] 331s: R114

Ch67 [Chançon] [p. 332i]

Mon cuer, il me fault estre mestre
A ma fois, aussi bien que vous.
N'en ayés anuy ou courrous,
Certez il couvient ainsi estre.

5   Trop longuement m'avez fait pestre
Et tous jours tenu au dessous.
Mon cuer, *il me fault estre mestre*
A ma foiz, *aussi bien que vous.*

Alez a destre ou a senestre,
10   Priz serez, sans estre recous.
Passer vous fault, mon amis doulx,
Ou par la, ou par la fenestre :
Mon cuer, *il me fault estre mestre.*

[85] 332s: R115

Ch68 [Chançon] [p. 333i]

Mes yeulz trop sont bien reclamés
Quant ma dame si lez apelle,
Leur moustrant sa grant beauté belle,
Il reviennent comme afamés.

Chanson

In the promise of Hope,
Where I've spent and wasted time,
Often I've refused the advice
Pleasure was able to offer me.

5   Alas! I'm not the first from France
Who's stupidly deceived himself
In the promise of Hope,
Where I've spent and wasted time.

And about my foolish conduct,
10   I've accused my heart before
Reason, but the heart made excuses,
Saying Trust deceived him
In the promise of Hope.

Chanson

My heart, I must be master
In my turn, as much as you are.
Don't be annoyed or angry.
Surely, it must be so.

5   You've sent me packing for too long,
Always wielding the upper hand.
My heart, I must be master
In my turn, as much as you are.

Go right or left. You'll be
10   Captured, and there'll be no rescue.
My sweet friend, you must pass through,
Either over there, or through the window.
My heart, I must be master.

Chanson

My eyes are very well summoned
When my lady calls them in this way,
Showing them her beauty fine and great,
They come back famished with desire.

5 Maugré mesdisans, peu amés,
 Et Dangier qui tient leur querelle,
 Mes yeulz *trop sont bien reclamés*
 Quant *ma dame si lez apelle.*

 Estre devroyent diffamés
10 S'il ne voloyent de bonne elle
 Vers les grans biens qui sont en elle.
 De ce ne seront ja blasmés.
 Mes yeulz *trop sont bien reclamés.*

[86] 333s: R116

Ch69   [Chançon]   [p. 334i]

 Retraiez vous, regart mal avisé,
 Vous cuidez bien que nulluy ne vous voye?
 Certes, Aguet par tous lieux vous convoie
 Priveement, en habit desguisé.

5 De gens saichans en estes moins prisé
 D'ainsi tousjours trotter par my la voye.
 Retraiez vous, *regart mal avisé,*
 Vous cuidez *bien que nulluy ne vous voye?*

 Dangier avez contre vous atisé,
10 Quant Sot Maintien tellement vous forvoie.
 Au derrenier, fauldra qu'il y pourvoye.
 Il est ainsi que je l'ay devisé :
 Retraiez vous, *regart mal avisé.*

[87] 334s: R117

Ch70   [Chançon]   [p. 335i]

 Regart, vous prenez trop de paine,
 Tousjours courés et recourés,
 Il semble qu'aux barrez jouez.*
 Reprenez ung peu vostre alaine.

5 Cuers qu'Amours tient en son demaine
 Cuident qu'assaillir les voulez.
 Regart, vous *prenez trop de paine,*
 Tousjours *courés et recourés.*

5   Despite the evil tongues, who are little loved,
    And Danger, who takes their side,
    My eyes are very well summoned
    When my lady calls them in this way.

    They'd be marked by ill fame
10   Did they not fly with dispatch
    Toward her great goodness.
    They'll never be faulted for doing such a thing.
    My eyes are very well summoned.

Chanson

    Withdraw, you ill-advised glance,
    Do you really think no one sees you?
    Surely, Vigilance follows you everywhere
    Discreetly, disguised in a monk's habit.

5   Those in the know esteem you less
    For always ambling along the path.
    Withdraw, you ill-advised glance,
    Do you really think no one sees you?

    You've made Danger your foe
10   Because Foolish Behavior leads you astray.
    In the end, he's bound to take charge.
    It is just as I've reported.
    Withdraw, you ill-advised glance.

Chanson

    Glance, you exert yourself too much.
    You're always running to and fro.
    It seems that you've been playing at tag.
    Catch your breath a bit.

5   The hearts Love governs in his domain
    Think you're intent on assaulting them.
    Glance, you exert yourself too much.
    You're always running to and fro.

Au moins une foiz la sepmaine
10   C'est raison que vous reposez,
Et affin que ne morfondez,
Il fauldra que l'en vous pourmaine.
Regart, *vous prenez trop de paine.*

[88] 335s: R118

Ch71   [Chançon]   [p. 336i]

Le voulez vous
Que vostre soye?
Rendu m'octroye
Pris ou recours.

5   Ung mot pour tous,
Bas qu'on ne l'oye :
Le voulez vous
Que vostre soye?

Maugré jalous,
10   Foy vous tendroye.
Or sa, ma joye,
Accordons nous :
Le voulez *vous*?

[89] 336s: R119

Ch72   [Chançon]   [p. 337i]

Crevez moy les yeulx
Que ne voye goutte,
Car trop je redoubte
Beaulté en tous lieulx.

5   Ravir jusqu'aus cieulx
Veult ma joye toute.
Crevez *moy les yeulx*
Que ne *voye goutte.*

D'elle me gard Dieulx,
10   Affin qu'en sa route
Jamais ne me boute.
N'esse pour le mieulx?

At least once a week
10   It's reasonable that you rest.
But so you'll not catch a chill,
You'll be needing some exercise.
Glance, you exert yourself too much.

Chanson

Is it your wish
That I might be yours?
I give myself up,
Overcome or surrendered.

5   One word says it all.
Softly so it won't be heard:
Is it your wish
That I might be yours?

Despite the jealous,
10   I'll keep faith with you.
Now here, my joy,
Let's agree:
Is it your wish?

Chanson

Poke out my eyes
So I don't see a thing,
For I very much fear Beauty
Wherever I go.

5   She wishes to exalt
All my joy to the heavens.
Poke out my eyes
So I don't see a thing.

God protect me from her
10   So I never intrude myself
Into her company.
Isn't that for the best?

Crevez moy les yeulx
Que ne *voye goutte*!

[90] 337s: R120

[Four lines added in the lower margin in the duke's hand:]

Quant je la regarde
Elle vient ferir
Mon cueur de la darde
D'amoureus Desir

Ch73   [Roundel (English chanson)]*   [p. 346s]

Myn hert hath send Glad Hope in hys message
Unto Confort Plesans Joye and Sped.
I pray to God that grace may hym leed
Wythout lettyng or daunger of passage.

5   In tryst to fynd profit and avauntage
Wythyn short tym to the help of hys ned,
Myn hert *hath send Glad Hope in hys message*
Unto Confort *Plesans Joye and Sped.*

Till that he come, myn hert yn ermytage
10   Of thoght shall dwel alone (God gyve hym med!)
And of wysshyng of tymys shal hym fed.
Glad Hope folyw and sped well thys viage!
Myn hert *hath send Glad Hope in hys message.*

346i: Ch74

Ch74   [Roundel (English chanson)]*   [p. 346i]

Whan shal thow come, Glad Hope, fro the vyage?
Thow hast taryd to long many a day.
For all conford is put fro my away
Tyll that I her tythyng of thy message.

5   What that had be lettyng of thy passage
Or tariyng, alas! I can not say,
Whan shal *thow come, Glad Hope, fro the vyage?*
Thow hast *taryd to long many a day.*

Thow knows fulwel that I have gret damage
10   In abydyng of the, that is no nay,

Poke out my eyes
So I don't see a thing.

———————————

When I look at her
She comes to pierce
My heart with the dart
Of amorous Desire.

Roundel

My heart dispatched Glad Hope as messenger
To Comfort, Pleasure, Joy, and Success.
May grace be his guide, I pray God,
With no hindrance or peril on the way.

5   Trusting he'd discover profit and advantage
Very quickly to satisfy his need,
My heart dispatched Glad Hope as messenger
To Comfort, Pleasure, Joy, and Success.

Until he arrives, my heart must remain
10   Alone in the hermitage of thought (God reward him!)
And often he'll feed on what he wishes.
May Glad Hope follow and the journey be a fine success!
My heart dispatched Glad Hope as messenger.

Roundel

When shall you arrive, Glad Hope, from your journey?
Many a day you've too long delayed.
For all comfort flees me
Until your message brings me tidings.

5   What has hindered
Or delayed you, alas! I cannot say.
When shall you arrive, Glad Hope, from your journey?
Many a day you've too long delayed.

You know very well I've suffered greatly
10   Waiting for you, there's no denying,

And thof y syng and dauns or lagh and play
In blake mournyng is clothyd my corage.
Whan shal *thow come, Glad Hope, fro the vyage?*

346s: Ch73

R19   Rondel   [p. 338i]

Jennes amoureux nouveaulx
En la nouvelle saison
Par les rues, sans raison,
Chevauchent, faisans les saulx,

5   Et font saillir des carreaulx
Le feu, comme de cherbon,
Jennes *amoureux nouveaulx.*

Je ne sçay se leurs travaulx
Ilz emploient bien ou non,
10   Mais piqués de l'esperon
Sont autant que leurs chevaulx,
Jennes *amoureux nouveaulx!*

[91] 338s: R121

R20   [Rondel]   [p. 339i]

Gardez le trait de la fenestre,
Amans, qui par ruez passez,
Car plus tost en serez blessez
Que de trait d'arc ou d'arbalestre.

5   N'alez a destre ne a senestre
Regardant, mais les yeulx bessez,
Gardez *le trait de la fenestre.*

Se n'avez medecin, bon maistre,
Si tost que vous serez navrez,
10   A Dieu soyez recommandez.
Mors vous tiens, demandez le prestre.
Gardez *le trait de la fenestre!*

[92] 339s: R122

And though I sing and dance or laugh and sport
My heart wears mourning black.
When shall you arrive, Glad Hope, from your journey?

Rondel

Young people, new to love,
In the new season,
Ride, to no purpose,
Cavorting through the streets.

5   And they make sparks fly
From the cobblestones, as if from coals,
Young people, new to love.

I know not if they make
Good use of their labors or not,
10   But they're pricked by the spur
As much as their horses,
Young people, new to love.

Rondel

Watch out for a shot from the window,
Lovers, you who pass through the streets,
For you'll be wounded more readily that way
Than by some shaft from bow or arbalest.

5   Don't go along looking to the right
Or left, but keep your eyes lowered.
Watch out for a shot from the window.

If you have no physician, fair master,
The moment you're wounded
10   You should be commended to God.
I think you're dead—summon a priest!
Watch out for a shot from the window!

R21   [Rondel]

En gibessant toute l'aprés disnee
Par my les champs pour me desanuyer,
N'a pas long temps que faisoye l'autrier
Voler mon cueur aprés mainte pensee.

5   L'aquilote, Souvenance nommee,*
Sourdoit deduit et savoit remerchier,*
En gibessant *toute l'aprés disnee.*

Gibessiere, de Passe Temps ouvree,
Enpli toute d'assez plaisant gibier,
10   Et puis je peu mon cueur, au derrenier,*
Sur un faisant d'Esperance Celee,
En gibessant *toute l'aprés disnee.*

[93] 340s: R123

R22   Rondel

Que fault il plus a ung cuer amoureux
Quant assiegé l'a Dangier de Tristesse,
Qu'avitailler tantost sa forteresse
D'assez vivres de Bon Espoir eureux?

5   Cappitaine face Desir Songneux,
Qui, nuyt et jour, fera guet sans peresse.
Que fault il plus *a ung cuer amoureux?*

Artillié soit d'Avis Avantureux,
Coulevrines et canons a largesse,
10   Prestz, assortiz et chargiez de Sagesse,
Es boulevers et lieux avantageux.
Que fault il *plus a ung cuer amoureux?*

[94] 341s: R124

R23   Rondel

Des maleureux porte le pris,
Servant dame loyalle et belle,
Qui, pour mourir en la querelle,
N'ascheve ce qu'a antrepris.

Rondel

While birding the whole afternoon,
Through the fields for diversion,
The other day in no time I made
My heart fly off pursuing many a thought.

5   The kestrel, named Memory,
Started the hunt and could mark the prey
While birding the whole afternoon.

Huntress, fashioned by Pastime,
Filled to the top with pleasant game,
10   And then I fed my heart, at the last,
On a pheasant of Hidden Hope,
While birding the whole afternoon.

Rondel

What more does a heart in love require,
When Danger besieges it with sorrow,
Than for its fortress to be provisioned at once
With stores aplenty from Good Hope, the fortunate?

5   Make Careful Desire captain
Who'll keep watch night and day without fail,
What more does a heart in love require?

Let there be artillery from Adventurous Advice,
Small guns and cannons in profusion,
10   Readied, mounted, and charged with Wisdom,
On the ramparts and bastions.
What more does a heart in love require?

Rondel

Among the unfortunate he takes the prize,
Serving a dame faithful and fine,
He who, to die in this cause,
Does not finish what he's begun.

5   Diffamé de droit et repris
         Par devant dame et damoiselle,
         Des maleureux *porte le pris.*

         Pourquoy est d'amer si espris,
         Quant congnoist que son cuer chancelle
10   En soy donnent repreuve telle?
         Ou a il ce mestier apris?
         Des maleureux *porte le pris!*

[95] 342s: R125

R24   Rondel   [p. 343i]

         En amer n'a que martire,
         Nulluy ne le devroit dire
         Mieulx que moy.
         J'en sauroye, sur ma foy,
5   De ma main ung livre escripre.

         Ou amans pourroient lire,
         Des yeulx larmoyans sans rire,
         Je m'en croy :
         En amer *n'a que martire.*

10   Des maulx qu'on y peut eslire
         Cellui qui est le mains pire,
         C'est Anoy
         Qui n'est jamés apart soy.
         Plus n'en dy, bien doit souffire.
15   En amer *n'a que martire.*

[96] 343s: R126

R25   Rondel   [p. 344i]

         Me fauldrez vous a mon besoing,
         Mon reconfort et ma fiance?
         M'avez vous mis en obliance?
         Pour tant se de vous je suis loing,

5   N'avez vous pitié de mon soing?
         Sans vous, savez que n'ay puissance.
         Me fauldrez vous *a mon besoing*?

5   Justly defamed and scorned
In the company of lady and maiden,
Among the unfortunate he takes the prize.

Why is he so smitten with love
When he knows her heart is uncertain,
10   And reproaches itself as a result?
Where did he learn such behavior?
Among the unfortunate he takes the prize.

Rondel

In love there's only suffering,
No one has better cause
To say so than me.
Upon my faith, I could write
5   A book about it with my own hand,

In which lovers might be able to read,
Not laughing, their eyes full of tears.
Of this I'm certain:
In love there's only suffering.

10   Of the ills one might choose,
The least troublesome
Is Annoyance,
Who is never on her own.
I'll say no more, this should be enough.
15   In love there's only suffering.

Rondel

Will you fail me in my time of need,
My consolation and my trust?
Have you forgotten me?
Though I may be far from you,

5   Do you not feel pity for my plight?
Know that without you I have no strength.
Will you fail me in my time of need?

On feroit dez larmez ung baing,
Qu'ay pleurees de desplaisance,
10   Et crie, par desesperance,
Ferant ma poitrine du poing.
Me fauldrez vous *a mon besoing*?

[97] 344s: R127

R26   Rondel   [p. 345i]

Cueur endormy en pensee
En transes, moitié veillant,
S'on lui va riens demandant,
Il respont a la volee.*

5   Et parle de vois cassee
Sans pourpos, ne tant ne quant,
Cueur endormy *en pensee.*

Tout met en galimafree,
Lombart, Anglois, Alemant,
10   François, Picart et Normant.
C'est une chose faee,
Cueur endormy *en pensee*!

[98] 345s: R128

Ca4   Carole en Latin   [p. 347]

Laudes Deo sint atque gloria,
Hoc tempore, pre cordis gaudio,
Exultemus cum Dei Filio,
Misso nobis a Patris gracia.

5   Hunc prophete vere predixerant
Nasciturum de pura virgine
Ut salvaret hos qui perierant,
Pro parentum dampnati crimine.

Tunc natus est ex stirpe regia,
10   Flos ascendens de Jesse gremio.
Illi honor et benedictio
Qui nos replet tanta leticia.
Laudes *Deo sint atque gloria.*

One could fill a bath with the tears
I've cried in my misery,
10   And I weep, in desperation,
Striking my breast with my fist.
Will you fail me in my time of need?

Rondel

Heart slumbering in thought,
Entranced, half waking,
If anyone goes to ask him something,
He responds flippantly,

5   And speaks with halting tongue
To no purpose in the least,
Heart slumbering in thought.

Everything put into a mixed stew,
Lombard, English, German,
10   French, Picard, and Norman.
It's a crazy thing,
Heart slumbering in thought.

Carol in Latin

Praise and glory be to God,
At this time; with joy in our hearts,
Let us exult with the Son of God,
Sent us through the Father's grace.

5   The prophets truly predicted
He would be born from a pure virgin
To save those who had been lost,
Condemned because of their parents' sin.

Then He was born from the tree of kings,
10   A flower springing from the bosom of Jesse.
Honor and blessing to the man
Who fills us with such joy.
Praise and glory be to God.

Sic induit se carne hominis
15   Ut per carnem carnem redimeret,
Sic amorem demonstrans servulis,
Quos creavit ne ipsos perderet.

O miranda Regis clemencia!
Qui non parcens corpori proprio,
20   Se obtulit diro supplicio,
Nostra sanans cruore vicia.
Laudes *Deo sint atque gloria.*

R27   Rondel   [p. 349i]

Il vit en bonne esperance,
Puis qu'il est vestu de gris,
Qu'il aura, a son devis,
Encore sa desirance.

5   Combien qu'il soit hors de France,
Par deça le mont Senis,*
Il vit *en bonne esperance.*

Perdu a sa contenance
Et tous sez jeus et ses ris,
10   Gaigner lui fault Paradis
Par force de pacïance,
Il vit *en bonne esperance.*

[99] 349s: R131

R28   Rondel   [p. 350i]

Maistre Estienne Le Gout, nominatif,
Nouvellement, par maniere optative,
Si a voulu faire copulative,
Mais failli a en son cas genitif.

5   Il avoit mis .vi. ducatz en datif,
Pour mielx avoir s'amie vocative,
Maistre Estienne *Le Gout, nominatif.*

Quant rencontré a un acusatif
Qui sa robe lui a fait ablative,
10   De fenestre assez superlative
A fait un sault portant coups en passif,
Maistre Estienne *Le Gout, nominatif.*

[100] 350s: R132

He took on the flesh of man
15   So flesh should be redeemed by flesh,
In this way showing His servants love,
His own creation, so He should not lose them.

O marvelous mercy of the King!
He who did not spare His own body,
20   Opened Himself to terrible punishment,
Healing our sins with His blood.
Praise and glory be to God.

Rondel

He lives in good hope,
Since he's clothed in gray,
For he'll have, just as he wishes,
What he still desires.

5   Though outside France,
On this side of Mt. Cenis,
He lives in good hope.

He's lost his composure,
And all his sport and good humor;
10   He's sure to gain Paradise
Through the power of his patience,
He lives in good hope.

Rondel

Master Etienne Le Gout, nominative,
Recently, in mood optative
Has intended to create a copulative,
But has failed to do so in the genitive.

5   He paid out six ducats, dative,
The better to possess his beloved, vocative,
Master Etienne Le Gout, nominative.

When he encountered an accusative,
Who deprived him of his robe, ablative,
10   From the window rather superlative
He leapt, suffering some blows, passive,
Master Etienne Le Gout, nominative.

R29   Rondel · Responce de   [p. 351s]
           maistre Estienne Le Gout*

      Monseigneur, tres suppellatif,
      Pour respondre au narratif
      De vostre briefve expositive,
      Elle fut premier voquative,
5   Par le moien du genitif.

      Les six ducatz sont nombratif,
      Mais quant au fait du possessif
      La chose est un peu neutrative,
      Monseigneur, *tres suppellatif.*

10   Et quant au dangier du passif,
      J'ay saufconduit prerogatif,
      Per quoy mectray paine soultive
      D'acorder sus la negative,
      L'adjectif et le substantif,
15   Monseigneur, *tres suppellatif.*

[101] 351i: R133

R30   [Rondel] Orleans a Alençon   [p. 352i]

      En la vigne jusqu'au peschier*
      Estez bouté, mon filz treschier,
      Dont par ma foy suis tresjoieus
      Quant de rimer vous voy songnieus
5   Et vous en voulez empeschier.

      Soit au lever, ou au couchier,
      Ou quant vous devez chevauchier,
      Esbatés vous y pour le mieuls
      En la vigne *jusqu'au peschier.*

10   Se Desplaisir vous vient serchier,
      Pour de lui tost vous despeschier,
      Sans estre merencolïeus,
      Grant bien vous fera, se m'aid Dieus,
      Passez y temps sans plus preschier,
15   En la vigne *jusqu'au peschier.*

[102] 352s: R134

Rondel—Response from Master Etienne Le Gout

My lord, quite superlative,
To respond to the narrative
Of your brief expositive,
She was first vocative,
5   By means of the genitive.

The six ducats are numerative,
But in regard to the possessive,
The thing is rather neutrative,
My lord, quite superlative.

10   And as far as the power of the passive,
I have of a safe conduct the prerogative,
Through which I'll make an effort, active
To reach an agreement on negative,
Adjective and substantive,
15   My lord, quite superlative.

Rondel—Orleans to Alençon

A great deal to drink
You've had, dear boy.
'Pon my faith I laugh
To see you trying to write a poem
5   Yet wanting to get away from it.

At sunrise or sunset
Or any time you go riding,
Make merry to the best of your ability, with
A great deal to drink.

10   If some annoyance comes your way,
To get rid of it quickly,
And melancholy along with it,
You will benefit, so help me God,
Spending your time, without further ado, having
15   A great deal to drink.

R31   Rondel · Responce de Alençon   [p. 353s]

Le vigneron fut atrapé
Quant il fut trouvé en la vigne,
Trop mieulx que poison a la ligne,
Ne que rat au lardon hapé.

5   D'un trait d'ueil fut prins et frapé
Par celle qui pas ne forligne.
Le vigneron *fut atrapé.*

A peine lui fut eschapé
Le povre compaignon qui pigne,*
10   Tresmal pigné des dens d'un pigne,
Ainsi sourprins et agrapé,
Le vigneron *fut atrapé.*

353i: R32

R32   [Rondel]   [p. 353i]

Quant je fus prins ou pavillon
De ma dame, tresgente et belle,
Je me brulé a la chandelle,
Ainsi que fait le papillon.

5   Je rougiz comme vermillon,
Aussi flambant que une estincelle,
Quant je fuz *prins ou pavillon.*

Se j'eusse esté esmerillon
Ou que j'eusse eu aussi bonne aille,
10   Je me feusse gardé de celle
Qui me bailla de l'aguillon,
Quant je fuz *prins ou pavillon.*

[103] 353s: R31

R33   [Rondel]   [p. 354i]

Mon cueur plus ne volera,
Il est enchaperonné.
Nonchaloir l'a ordonné,
Qui ja pieça le m'osta.

Rondel — Response of Alençon

The wine grower was caught
When found in his cups,
Better than a fish on a line,
Or a rat caught by a bit of bacon.

5   At a single glance he was taken and beaten
By the lady who tells no lies.
The wine grower was caught.

He only just got away from her,
The poor howling fellow,
10   After a very sound thrashing,
Taken unawares and nabbed.
The wine grower was caught.

Rondel

When caught in the trap
Set by my lady, so noble and fine,
I burned myself on the candle,
Just as the butterfly does.

5   I turned red as scarlet,
Flaming just like an ember,
When caught in the trap.

Had I been a falcon
Or possessed wings as good,
10   I'd have protected myself from the one
Who stabbed me with her spur,
When caught in the trap.

Rondel

My heart will fly off no more.
He has been hooded.
Indifference has seen to it,
Some time ago taking the heart from me.

5   Confort depuis ne lui a
      Cure n'atirer donné.
      Mon cueur *plus ne volera.*

      Se sa gorge gettera
      Je ne sçay, car gouverné
10   Ne l'ay, mais abandonné.
      Soit com a venir pourra,
      Mon cueur *plus ne volera.*

[104] 354s: R135

R34   [Rondel]   [p. 355i]

      Chascun dit qu'estez bonne et belle,
      Mais mon euil jugier ne saura,
      Car Lignage m'avuglera,
      Qui maintendra vostre querelle.

5   Quant on parle de demoiselle
      Qui a largesse de biens a,
      Chascun dit *qu'estez bonne et belle.*

      A nostre assemblee nouvelle
      Verray ce qu'il m'en samblera,
10   Et s'ainsi est, bien me plaira.
      Or prenons que vous soyez telle :
      Chascun dit *qu'estez bonne et belle.*

[105] 355s: R136

R35   Rondel   [p. 356i]

      Encore lui fait il grant bien
      De voir celle qu'a tant amee
      A cellui qui cueur et pensee
      Avoit en elle, comme tien.

5   Combien qu'il n'y aye plus rien
      Et qu'aultre la lui ait ostee,
      Encore *lui fait il grant bien.*

      En regardant son doulz maintien
      Et son fait qui moult lui agree,
10   S'il la peut tenir embrassee

5   Ever since Comfort has given
Him no care or covering,
My heart will fly off no more.

Whether or not he rejects his food
I do not know, for I did not
10   Control him, but let him go.
Whatever might happen,
My heart will fly off no more.

Chanson

Every man says you're fine and virtuous,
But my eye's unable to judge,
For Lineage will blind me,
Who will take your side.

5   When someone speaks of a maiden
Who possesses qualities in abundance,
Every man says you're fine and virtuous.

At our new assembly
I'll see how this seems,
10   And if it's true enough, I'll be well pleased.
Now let's consider if you're such a lady,
Every man says you're fine and virtuous.

Rondel

It still does him much good
To see the lady so much loved
By the man who has bestowed heart
And thought on her, saying, "Take it."

5   Although he might have nothing more
And another has taken her from him,
It still does him much good.

Looking upon her gracious person
And her manner, which pleases him greatly,
10   If that man can hold her in his arms,

Il pense que une fois fut sien :
Encore *lui fait il grant bien.*

[106] 356s: R137

R36   Rondel   [p. 357i]

Avoglé et assourdy
De tous poins en nonchaloir,
Je ne puis ouïr ne voir
Chose dont soye esjouÿ.

5   De desplaisant ou marry
Tout m'est un, pour dire voir,
Avoglé *et assourdy.*

Es escolez fu nourry
D'Amours, pensant mielx valoir.
10   Quant plus y cuiday savoir,
Plus m'y trouvay rassoty,
Avoglé *et assourdy*!

[107] 357s: R138

R37   Rondel   [p. 358i]

J'estraine de bien loing m'amie,
De cueur, de corps et quanque j'ay,
En bon an lui souhaideray
Joye, santé et bonne vie.

5   Mais que ne m'estraine d'oblie*
Ne plus ne mains que la feray.
J'estraine *de bien loing m'amie.*

Mon cueur de chapel de soussie,
Ce jour de l'an, estreneray,
10   Et a elle presanteray
Dez fleurs de ne m'obliés mie.
J'estraine *de bien loing m'amie.*

[108] 358s: R139

He thinks that one time she was his.
It still does him much good.

Rondel

Blinded and deafened,
Wholly in indifference,
I can hear or see
Nothing in which I might rejoice.

5   Things unpleasant or troubled
Are all the same to me, to tell the truth,
Blinded and deafened.

In the schools of Love I was
Nourished, thinking to become worthier.
10   The more I think I know of it,
The more stupid I find myself,
Blinded and deafened.

Rondel

From far off I make my beloved a gift,
Of heart, of body, of whatever is mine,
In this good year I shall wish for her
Joy, health, and a pleasant life.

5   As long as she does not give me forgetfulness,
No more or less will I do for her,
From far off I make my beloved a gift.

To my heart I will offer on this first day
Of the year a chaplet of marigolds,
10   And to her I'll present
The flowers called forget-me-nots.
From far off I make my beloved a gift.

R38   Rondel   [p. 359i]

Parlant ouvertement
Des faiz du Dieu d'Amours,
N'a il d'estranges tours
En son commandement?

5   Ouïl, certainement.
Qui dira le rebours,
Parlant *ouvertement*?

S'on faisoit loyaulment
Enqueste par les cours,
10   On orroit tous les jours
Qu'on s'en plaint grandement,
Parlant *ouvertement*.

[109] 359s: R140

R39   Rondel   [p. 360i]

Tant sont les yeulx de mon cuer endormis
En Nonchaloir qu'ouvrir ne les pourroye.
Pource, parler de Beaulté n'ozeroye
Pour le present, comme j'ay fait jadiz.

5   Par cuer retiens ce que j'en ay apris,
Car plus ne sçay lire ou Livre de Joye
Tant sont *les yeulx de mon cuer endormis.*

Chascun diroit qu'entre les rassotiz,
Com avugle des couleurs jugeroye.
10   Taire m'en weil, rien n'y voy, Dieu y voye!
Plaisans Regars n'ont plus en moy logis,
Tant sont *les yeulx de mon cuer endormis.*

[110*] 360s: R141

R40   Rondel · de Maistre Jehan Caillau   [p. 361i]

Tant sont les yeulx de mon cuer endormis
En Nonchaloir qu'ouvrir ne les pourroye.
Pource, parler de Beaulté n'ozeroye
Pour le present, comme j'ay fait jadis.

Rondel

Speaking openly
Of the deeds of the God of Love,
Do not some strange things happen
Under his command?

5   Yes, certainly,
Who will say the opposite,
Speaking openly?

Were a faithful inquiry
To be made throughout the courts,
10   One would constantly hear
Loud complaints made of this,
Speaking openly.

Rondel

So long have the eyes of my heart slumbered
In Indifference I could not open them.
And so, I dare not speak about Beauty
For the present, as I did once.

5   I retain by heart what I've learned,
For I can no longer read in the Book of Joy
So long have the eyes of my heart slumbered.

Every man would say that among the love-crazed,
I would judge as a blind man judges colors.
10   I'll keep silent, seeing nothing, God be my witness!
Pleasant Look no longer resides in me,
So long have the eyes of my heart slumbered.

Rondel by Master Jean Caillau

So long have the eyes of my heart slumbered
In Indifference I could not open them.
And so, I dare not speak about Beauty
For the present, as once I did.

5   Joye et Soulas ne sont plus mes amis,
       Chose ne voy de quoy je me resjoye,
       Tant sont *les yeulx de mon cuer endormis.*

       Je suis moullié et retrait et remis,
       Morne et pensif trop plus que ne souloye,
10   J'y voy trouble, car es yeulx ay la taye,
       Et n'y congnois le blanc d'avec le bis,
       Tant sont *les yeulx de mon cuer endormis.*

[111] 361s: R142

R41   **[Rondel]**   [p. 362i]

       Helas! me tuerés vous?
       Pour Dieu retraiez cest euil
       Qui d'un amoureux acueil
       M'occit, se ne suis rescous.

5   Je tiens vostre cuer si douls
       Que me rendz tout a son vueil.
       Helas! *me tuerés vous?*

       De quoy vous peut mon courrous
       Valoir, ne servir mon deuil,
10   Quant humblement sans orgueil
       Je requier mercy a tous?
       Helas! *me tuerés vous?*

[112] 362s: R143

R42   **[Rondel]**   [p. 363i]

       Ung cueur, ung veuil, une plaisance,
       Ung desir, ung conscentement,
       Ung reconfort, ung pansement,
       Fermez en loyale fiance,

5   Dieu que bonne en est l'acointance!
       Tenir la doit on chierement.
       Ung cueur, *ung veuil, une plaisance.*

       Contre Dangier et sa puissance,
       Qui les het trop mortelement,
10   Guardons les bien et sagement.

5   Joy and Comfort are my friends no longer,
I see nothing to make me rejoice,
So long have the eyes of my heart slumbered.

I'm wet with tears, retreating and rejected,
Sadder and more pensive than my wont,
10   I see trouble here, but have specks in my eyes,
And do not distinguish white from brown,
So long have the eyes of my heart slumbered.

Rondel

Alas! Will you kill me?
For God's sake, take away the eye
That with an amorous welcome
Will kill me unless I am rescued.

5   I think your heart so sweet
I surrender completely to its wish.
Alas! Will you kill me?

What value can my sorrow have
For you, how can my pain serve?
10   When humbly, without arrogance
I ask everyone for mercy,
Alas! Will you kill me?

Rondel

One heart, one will, one pleasure,
One desire, one consent,
One consolation, one thought,
Made firm in faithful trust,

5   God, how good knowing her is!
One should with affection hold on to her.
One heart, one will, one pleasure.

Against Danger and his power,
Who bears them a mortal hatred,
10   Let us wisely keep them quite safe.

N'est ce toute nostre chevance,
Ung cueur, *ung veuil, une plaisance?*

[113] 363s: R144

R43   Rondel   [p. 364i]

Les fourriers d'Esté sont venus
Pour appareillier son logis
Et ont fait tendre ses tappis
De fleurs et verdure tissus.

5   En estandant tappis velus
De vert herbe par le païs,
Les fourriers *d'Esté sont venus.*

Cueurs d'ennuy pieça morfondus,
Dieu mercy, sont sains et jolis.
10   Alez vous ent, prenez païs,
Yver, vous ne demourrés plus :
Les fourriers *d'Esté sont venus!*

[114] 364s: R145

R44   Rondel   [p. 365i]

Le temps a laissié son manteau
De vent, de froidure et de pluye,
Et s'est vestu de brouderie,
De soleil luyant, cler et beau.

5   Il n'y a beste ne oyseau
Qu'en son jargon ne chante ou crie :
Le temps *a laissié son manteau!*

Riviere, fontaine et ruisseau
Portent, en livree jolie,
10   Gouttes d'argent d'orfaverie.
Chascun s'abille de nouveau :
Le temps *a laissié son manteau!*

[115] 365s: R146

Is this not the sum of our good fortune,
One heart, one will, one pleasure?

Rondel

The harbingers of Summer have come
To make his lodging ready,
And they've displayed his tapestries
Of ornamental flowers and greenery.

5   Spreading out velvet carpets
Of green grass throughout the country,
The harbingers of Summer have come.

Hearts once undone by worry
Are healthy and joyful, thanks be to God.
10   Go away! take to the country,
Winter, you'll stay no longer:
The harbingers of Summer have arrived!

Rondel

The season has abandoned its coat
Of wind, of frost, of rain,
Clothing itself in fabric embroidered
With a gleaming sun, clear and fine.

5   There's no creature or bird
That does not sing or cry out in its language:
The season has abandoned its coat!

Riverbank, spring, and stream
Bear along, with splendid livery,
10   Drops of silver crafted by the goldsmith.
Each one dons new clothes:
The season has abandoned its coat!

R45   Rondel   [p. 366i]

Cueur, a qui prendrez vous conseil?
A nul ne pouez descouvrir
Le tresangoisseus desplaisir
Qui vous tient en peinne et traveil.

5   Je tiens qu'il n'a soubz le soleil
De vous plus parfait vray martir.
Cueur, *a qui prendrez vous conseil?*

Au meins faitez vostre apareil
De bien vous faire ensevelir,
10   Ce n'est que mort d'ainsi languir
En tel martire nonpareil.
Cueur, *a qui prendrez vous conseil?*

[116] 366s: R147

R46   Rondel   [p. 367i]

Dedens mon Livre de Pensee
J'ay trouvé escripvant mon cueur,
La vraye histoire de douleur,
De larmes toute enluminee,

5   En deffassant la tresamee
Ymage de plaisant doulceur,
Dedens *mon Livre de Pensee.*

Helas! ou l'a mon cueur trouvee?
Lez grossez gouttez de sueur
10   Lui saillent, de peinne et labeur
Qu'il y prent et nuit et journee,
Dedens *mon Livre de Pensee.*

[117] 367s: R148

R47   Rondel   [p. 368i]

En regardant ces belles fleurs
Que le temps nouveau d'Amours prie,
Chascune d'elles s'ajolie
Et farde de plaisans couleurs.

Rondel

Heart, from whom do you take advice?
You can reveal to no man
The very painful displeasure
That keeps you in hurt and suffering.

5   I believe there's under the sun
No martyr more perfect than you.
Heart, from whom do you take advice?

At the least make your preparations
To be buried in a fine style,
10   For it's death itself to languish thus
In such unparalleled suffering.
Heart, from whom do you take advice?

Rondel

Within my Book of Thought
I found my heart writing
The true history of suffering,
Illuminated all with tears,

5   While defacing the very beloved
Image of pleasant sweetness,
Within my Book of Thought.

Alas! Where did my heart find it?
Huge drops of sweat
10   Fall off him, from the pain and labor
He expends on this night and day,
In my Book of Thought.

Rondel

While looking at these lovely flowers
That the new season begs from Love,
Each of them grows beautiful
And paints itself a pleasant color.

5   Tant enbasmees sont de odeurs
        Qu'il n'est cueur qui ne rajeunie
        En regardant *ces belles fleurs.*

        Les oyseaus deviennent danseurs
        Dessuz mainte branche flourie
10   Et font joyeuse chanterie,
        De contres, deschans et teneurs,
        En regardant *ces belles fleurs.*

[118] 368s: R149

R48   Rondel   [p. 369i]

        Onquez feu ne fut sans fumee,
        Ne doloreus cueur sans pensee,
        Ne reconfort sans esperance,
        Ne joyeus regart sans plaisance,
5   Ne beau soleil qu'aprez nuee.

        J'ay tost ma sentence donnee,
        De plus sachant soit amendee,
        J'en dy selonc ma congnoissance :
        Onquez *feu ne fut sans fumee.*

10   Esbatement n'est sans risee,
        Souspir sans chose regretee,
        Souhait sans ardant desirance,
        Doubte sans muer contenance,
        C'est chose de vray esprouvee :
15   Onques *feu ne fut sans fumee.*

[119] 369s: R150

R49   Rondel   [p. 370i]

        Chantez ce que vous pensés,
        Moustrant joyeuse maniere,
        Ne la vendez pas si chiere,
        Trop envis la despensés.

5   Or sus, tost vous avancés,
        Laissez coustume estrangiere,
        Chantez *ce que vous pensés.*

5   So perfumed are they with scent
There's no heart that does not grow young
While looking at these lovely flowers.

The birds become dancers
On many a flowering branch
10   And sing a joyful service,
With counter-tenors, descants, and tenors,
While looking at these lovely flowers.

Rondel

There's never fire without smoke,
No heart in pain without thought,
No consolation without hope,
No joyful glance without pleasure,
5   No lovely sun except after clouds.

I pronounced my sentence quickly:
May it be corrected by the wisest!
I've spoken according to my understanding.
There's never fire without smoke.

10   There's no sport without laughter,
No sigh without cause for regret,
No wish without ardent desire,
No doubt without a telltale look,
This is proven true by experience:
15   There's never fire without smoke.

Rondel

Sing what's on your mind,
Making a pleasant face.
Do not sell it so dear,
You dispense it too grudgingly.

5   Now up, get to it at once.
Abandon your diffident manner,
Sing what's on your mind.

Tous noz menus pourpensés
Descouvrons, a lye chiere,
10   L'un a l'autre sans priere.
J'acheveray : commencés.
Chantez *ce que vous pensés.*

[120] 370s: R151

R50   Rondel   [p. 371i]

Gens qui cuident estre si sages
Qu'il pensent plusieurs abestir,
Si bien ne se sauront couvrir
Qu'on n'aperçoive leurs courages.

5   Payer leur fauldra lez usages
De leurs becz jaunes sans faillir,*
Gens *qui cuident estre si sages.*

On scet par anciens ouvrages
De quel mestier scevent servir.
10   Melusine n'en peut mentir,*
Elle les congnoist aux visages,
Gens *qui cuident estre si sages.*

[121] 371s: R152

R51   Rondel*   [p. 372i]

Quant j'ay ouÿ le tabourin
Sonner pour s'en aler au may,
En mon lit fait n'en ay effray
Ne levé mon chef du coissin.

5   En disant : il est trop matin,
Ung peu je me rendormiray,
Quant j'ay ouÿ *le tabourin.*

Jeunes gens partent leur butin,
De Nonchaloir m'acointeray,
10   A lui je m'abutineray,*
Trouvé l'ay plus prochain voisin,
Quant j'ay ouÿ *le tabourin.*

[122] 372s: R153

Let us reveal our every small
Intention with good cheer,
10   One to the other without having to beg.
I'll make an end: you, begin.
Sing what's on your mind.

Rondel

The people who think they are so wise
That they can pull the wool over others' eyes
Cannot cover their tracks so well
No one sees what is in their hearts.

5   They must pay without fail
For what they've done in their stupidity,
The people who think they are so wise.

One learns from works long ago
What they can get up to.
10   Melusine understands the truth of this,
Having known the likes of
The people who think they are so wise.

Rondel

When I heard the tambourine
Sound the call for the May ceremony,
In my bed I made no fuss,
And didn't lift my head from the pillow.

5   Saying: it is too early,
I'll go back to sleep some more.
When I heard the tambourine.

Let the young distribute their booty.
I'll buddy up to Indifference.
10   From him I'll get a reward.
I found him my closest neighbor,
When I heard the tambourine.

R52   **Rondel**   [p. 373i]

Le premier jour du mois de may,
De tanné et de vert perdu,
Las! j'ay trouvé mon cuer vestu,
Dieu scet en quel piteux array!

5   Tantost demandé je lui ay
Dont estoit cest abit venu,
Le premier jour *du mois de may.*

Il m'a respondu : «Bien le sçay,
Mais par moy ne sera congneu.
10 Desplaisance m'en a pourveu,
Sa livree je porteray,
Le premier *jour du mois de may.*»

[123] 373s: R154

R53   **Rondel**   [p. 374i]

De riens ne sert a cueur en desplaisance
Chanter, danser, n'aucun esbatement,
Il lui souffit de povoir seulement
Tous jours penser a sa male meschance.

5   Quant il congnoit qu'en hazart gist sa chance,
Et desir n'est a son commandement,
De riens *ne sert a cueur en desplaisance.*

S'on rit, pleurer lui est d'acoustumance.
S'il peut, a part se met le plus souvent,
10 Afin qu'a nul ne tiengne parlement.
Pour le guerir ja mire ne s'avance.
De riens *ne sert a cueur en desplaisance.*

[124] 374s: R155

R54   **[Rondel]**   [p. 375i]

Fiés vous y!
A qui?
En quoy?
Comme je voy,
5   Riens n'est sans sy.

Rondel

The first day of the month of May,
In brown and darkest green,
I found, alas, my heart dressed,
God knows in what pitiful state!

5   At once I asked him
Whence had come his costume,
The first day of the month of May.

He answered: "I am well aware,
But will never acknowledge it.
10   Misery provided me with these things.
It's her livery I'll wear
The first day of the month of May."

Rondel

Nothing does a heart in misery any good,
Singing, dancing, not any sport.
All he can do every day
Is mull over his ill fortune.

5   Once he sees his good luck at risk
And desire not under his sway,
Nothing does a heart in misery any good.

If there's laughter, the heart's way is to weep.
If able to do so, he most times wanders off alone
10   So he must speak to no one.
No physician will ever come heal it.
Nothing does a heart in misery any good.

Rondel

Trust in it!
In whom?
In what?
As I see it,
5   Nothing lacks a "but."

Ce monde cy
A sy
Pou foy.
Fiés *vous y!*

10   Plus je n'en dy,
N'escry.
Pour quoy?
Chascun j'en croy
S'il est ainsy.
15   Fiés *vous y!*

[125] 375s: R156

R55   Rondel   [p. 376i]

De legier pleure a qui la lippe pent.*
Ne demandés jamais comment lui va,
Laissez l'en paix, il se confortera,
Ou en son fait mettra apointement.

5   A son umbre se combatra souvent,
Et puis son frein runger lui convendra.
De legier *pleure a qui la lippe pent.*

S'on parle a lui, il en est malcontent.
Cheminee au derrain trouvera
10   Par ou passer sa fumee pourra.
Ainsi avient le plus communement.
De legier *pleure a qui la lippe pent.*

[126] 376s: R157

R56   Rondel   [p. 377i]

Dont viens tu maintenant, Souspir?
Aportez tu nulles nouvelles?
Dieu doint que puissent estre telles
Que voulentiers lez doye ouïr.

5   S'il viennent de devers Desir,
Il ne sont que bonnes et belles.
Dont *viens tu maintenant, Souspir?*

Mais s'il sourdent de Desplaisir,
J'ayme mieulx que tu lez me celes,

This world here
Has so
Little faith.
Trust in it!

10   I say and write
No more of it.
Why?
I believe every man
If it is thus.
15   Trust in it!

Rondel

The moody one cries easily.
Never ask how he's doing.
Left in peace, he'll console himself
Or do something about his troubles.

5   He will often fight with his own shadow,
Champing at the bit.
The moody one cries easily.

If someone says a word, he's ill at ease.
In the end he'll find some chimney
10   Through which his smoke can pass.
Most often this is what happens.
The moody one cries easily.

Rondel

Where do you come from now, Sigh?
Do you bring tidings?
May God grant they're the sort
To which I'll happily listen.

5   If these come from Desire,
They'll be only good and fine,
Where do you come from now, Sigh?

But if they arise from Misery,
I'd rather you keep them from me.

10   Assez et trop j'en ay de celles.
        Ne dy riens que pour m'esjouïr.
        Dont *viens tu maintenant, Souspir?*

[127] 377s: R158

R57   Rondel   [p. 378i]

        Ou pis, ou mieulx,
        Mon cueur aura.
        Plus ne sera
        En soussis tieulx.

5   Par Dieu, dez cieulx
        Chemin prendra,
        Ou pis, *ou mieulx.*

        En aucuns lieux,
        Fortune, or ça,
10   On vous verra
        Plus cler aux yeulx,
        Ou pis, *ou mieulx.*

[128] 378s: R159

R58   Rondel   [p. 379i]

        S'en mez mains une fois vous tiens,
        Pas ne m'eschaperés, Plaisance,
        Ja Fortune n'aura puissance
        Que n'aye ma part de voz biens

5   En despit de Deuil et dez siens,
        Qui me tourmentent de penance,
        S'en mez *mains une fois vous tiens.*

        Doy je tous jours, sans avoir riens,
        Languir en ma dure grevance?
10   Nennil, promis m'a Esperance
        Que serez de tous poins dez miens,
        S'en mez *mains une fois vous tiens.*

[129] 379s: R160

10   I've enough of such things, too many.
    Say nothing but what will cheer me up.
    Where do you come from now, Sigh?

Rondel

Either better or worse
Will be my heart's destiny.
No longer will it suffer
Worries like these.

5   By God, from heaven
    It will find its path,
    Either better or worse.

In several places,
Now here, Fortune, now there
10   Eyes will see you
    More clearly,
    Either better or worse.

Rondel

If I hold you just once in my hands,
You'll not escape me, Pleasure,
Never will Fortune have the power
To stop me from getting my share of the good in you.

5   Despite Pain and those of his company,
    Who torment me with punishment,
    If I hold you just once in my hands.

Must I always, having nothing,
Languish in my terrible misery?
10   Not at all: Hope has promised
    You'll be mine completely
    If I hold you just once in my hands.

R59   **Rondel**

>   Plus penser que dire
>   Me couvient souvent,
>   Sans moustrer comment
>   N'a quoy mon cueur tire.
>
> 5 Faignant de sousrire
>   Quant suis tresdolent,
>   Plus *penser que dire*
>   [*Me couvient souvent.*]*
>
>   En toussant, souspire
> 10 Pour secrettement
>   Musser mon tourment.
>   C'est privé martire,
>   Plus *penser que dire!*

[130] 380s: R161

R60   **Rondel**

>   Je ne suis pas de sez gens la
>   A qui Fortune plaist et rit,
>   De reconfort trop m'escondit,
>   Veu que tant de mal donné m'a.
>
> 5 S'on demande comment me va,
>   Il est ainsi, comme j'ay dit :
>   Je ne *suis pas de sez gens la.*
>
>   Quant je dy que bon temps vendra,
>   Mon cueur me respont par despit :
> 10 Voire, s'Espoir ne vous mentit,
>   Plusieurs deçoit et decevra.
>   Je ne *suis pas de sez gens la.*

[131] 381s: R162

R61   **Rondel**

>   Remede comment
>   Porray je querir
>   Du mal qu'a souffrir
>   J'ay trop longuement?

Rondel

Thinking more than speaking
Is what I must often do,
Not revealing how
Nor toward whom my heart feels drawn.

5   Feigning a smile
When greatly saddened,
Thinking more than speaking
Is what I must often do.

Coughing, I sigh
10   To dissimulate
My secret torment.
This suffering is private,
Thinking more than speaking!

Rondel

I'm not one of those people
Whom Fortune pleases and smiles upon.
She has too often refused me consolation,
Having presented me with so many ills.

5   If someone asks how I'm doing,
It is just as I have said:
I'm not one of those people.

When I say good times will come,
My heart answers spitefully:
10   "Indeed, unless Hope is lying to you,
Who deceives and will deceive many."
I'm not one of those people.

Rondel

How can I
Seek out a remedy
For the ill I've had
To suffer too long?

5   Qu'en dit loyaument
        Conseil : sans mentir,
        Remede *comment*
        [*Porray je querir?*]*

        Pour abregement,
10   Guerir, ou morir!
        Plus ne puis fournir,
        Se Sens ne m'aprent
        Remede *comment*
        [*Porray je querir.*]

[132] 382s: R163

R62   Rondel   [p. 383i]

        Quant je voy ce que ne veuil mie,
        Et n'ay ce dont suis desirant,
        Pensant ce qui m'est desplaisant,
        Est ce merveille s'il m'anuye?

5   Nennil. Force est que me soussie
        De mon cueur qui est languissant,
        Quant *je voy ce que ne veuil mie.*

        En douleur et merencolie
        Suis, nuit et jour, estudiant.
10   Lors je me boute trop avant
        En une haulte theologie,
        Quant *je voy ce que ne veuil mie.*

[133] 383s: R164

R63   Rondel   [p. 384i]

        Sot euil, raporteur de nouvelles,
        Ou vas tu, et ne sces pour quoy,
        Ne sans prendre congié de moy
        En la compaignie dez belles?

5   Tu es trop tost acointé d'elles.
        Il te vaulzit mieulx tenir quoy,
        Sot euil, *raporteur de nouvelles.*

        Se ne changez manieres telles
        Par Rayson, ainsi que je doy,

5   Let someone render
Faithful counsel, with no lies:
How can I
[Seek out a remedy]?

To put it briefly,
10   A cure or death!
I can go on no longer
If Sense does not teach me
How can I
[Seek out a remedy]?

Rondel

When I see what I do not want,
And do not have what I desire,
Thinking thoughts I find unpleasant,
Is it any wonder I'm troubled?

5   Not at all, I'm forced to take care of
My heart, which languishes
When I see what I do not want.

In misery and melancholy
I make my studies night and day.
10   Then I push myself too far ahead
Into the higher realms of theology,
When I see what I do not want.

Rondel

Foolish eye, bearer of tidings,
Where are you going, not knowing why,
And without taking leave of me
Among the company of beautiful ladies?

5   You've made their acquaintance too quickly.
It would be better for you to keep silent,
Foolish eye, bearer of tidings.

If you don't intend changing your ways
As Reason advises, I'll punish you,

10   Chastïer te veuil, sur ma foy.
        Contre toy j'ay assez querelles,
        Sot euil, *raporteur de nouvelles.*

[134] 384s: R165

R64   Rondel   [p. 385i]

        Est ce vers moy qu'envoyez ce souspir?
        M'aporte il point quelque bonne nouvelle?
        Soit mal ou bien, pour Dieu, qu'il ne me celle
        Ce que lui veuil de mon fait enquerir.

5   Suis je jugié de vivre ou de morir?
        Soustendra ja Loyauté ma querelle?
        Est ce vers *moy qu'envoyez ce souspir?*

        Et nuit et jour j'escoute pour ouïr
        S'auray confort de ma peinne cruelle.
10   Pire ne peut estre se non mortelle.
        Ditez se riens y a pour m'esjouÿr?
        Est ce *vers moy qu'envoyez ce souspir?*

[135] 385s: R166

R65   Rondel   [p. 386i]

        Alons nous esbatre,
        Mon cueur, vous et moy,
        Laissons a par soy
        Soussi se combatre.

5   Tous jours veult debatre
        Et jamés n'est quoy.
        Alons *nous esbatre.*

        On vous devroit batre
        Et moustrer au doy,
10   Se dessous sa loy
        Vous laissez abatre.
        Alons *nous esbatre.*

[136] 386s: R167

10   As I should, upon my faith.
      I have quarrels aplenty with you,
      Foolish eye, bearer of tidings.

Rondel

Do you send me this sigh?
Does it bear some pleasant news?
Whether bad or good, for God's sake, let it not conceal
What I would learn about my affair.

5   Have I been judged to live or die?
      Will Loyalty ever take up my cause?
      Do you send me this sigh?

Night and day I listen to hear
If I'll find consolation for my cruel pain.
10   Unless mortal, it could not be worse.
      Tell me is there anything to cheer me up?
      Do you send me this sigh?

Rondel

Let us go make merry,
My heart, you and I.
Let's leave Care alone
To struggle by himself.

5   Every day he wants to argue
      And never keeps silent.
      Let us go make merry.

You should be beaten
And have fingers shaken at you
10   If you let yourself
      Be dominated by his rule.
      Let us go make merry.

R66 **Rondel**   [p. 387i]

Je vous areste de main mise,*
Mes yeulx, enprisonnés serés.
Plus mon cueur ne gouvernerés
Desormais, je vous en avise.

5   Trop avez fait a vostre guise,
Par ma foy plus ne le ferés.
Je vous *areste de main mise.*

En peut bien pour vous corner prise.*
Pris estes, point n'eschaperés.
10   Nul remede n'y trouverés,
Riens n'y vault apel ne franchise.
Je vous *areste de main mise.*

[137] 387s: R168

R67 **Rondel**   [p. 388i]

En mes païs, quant me treuve a repos,
Je m'esbaïs, et n'y sçay contenance,
Car j'ay apris traveil dez mon enfance,
Dont Fortune m'a bien chargié le dos.

5   Que voulez que vous die a briefs mos?
Ainsi m'est il, ce vient d'acoustumance
En mes *païs, quant me treuve a repos.*

Tout a part moy, en mon penser m'enclos,
Et fais chasteaulz en Espaigne et en France.*
10   Oultre lez montz forge mainte ordonnance.
Chascun jour j'ay plus de mille propos,
En mes *païs, quant me treuve a repos.*

[138] 388s: R169

R68 **Rondel**   [p. 389i]

Alez vous ant, allez, alés,
Soussy, Soing et Merencolie,
Me cuidez vous, toute ma vie,
Gouverner, comme fait avés?

Rondel

With my hands I arrest you,
Eyes of mine, you will be imprisoned.
You will govern my heart no more
From this time forward, this I warn you.

5   You have done too much as you wish,
This you'll do no longer, upon my faith.
With my hands I arrest you.

The hunting horn could well sound "captured."
You're taken and won't escape at all.
10   You'll find no remedy, nothing
Will help, not appeal, not privilege:
With my hands I arrest you.

Rondel

In my country, when I find myself at rest,
I'm astonished and don't know how to act,
For since childhood I've experienced troubles
Fortune has loaded on my back.

5   What, in short, do you want me to say?
This is how it is with me, it comes from habit
In my country, when I find myself at rest.

On my own, I'm wrapped up in my own thoughts,
Building castles in Spain or France.
10   I have many ideas about the land beyond the mountains.
Every day more than a thousand plans occur to me
In my country, when I find myself at rest.

Rondel

Go your way, go, go,
Care, Worry, and Melancholy,
Do you think you can rule me
All my life, just as you have done?

5   Je vous prometz que non ferés,
       Raison aura sur vous maistrie.
       Alez *vous ant, allez, alés.*

       Se jamais plus vous retournés
       Avecques vostre compaignie,
10   Je pri a Dieu qu'il vous maudie
       Et ce par qui vous revendrés.
       Alez *vous ant, allez, alés.*

[141 NB: 2 lyrics missing] 389s: R170

R69   Rondel   [p. 390i]

       Se vous voulés que tout vostre deviengne,
       En me moustrant quelque joyeus samblant,
       Ditez ce mot : «Je vous tiens mon servant,
       Servez si bien que contente m'en tiengne.»

5   Devoir feray, comment qu'il m'en aviengne,
       Tresloyalment, dez ores en avant,
       Se vous *voulés que tout vostre deviengne.*

       Sans que Merci ne Grace me soustiengne,
       S'en Loyalté je faulz ne tant ne quant,
10   Punissez moy tout a vostre talant,
       Et se bien sers, pour Dieu vous en souviengne,
       Se vous *voulés que tout vostre deviengne.*

[142] 390s: R171

R70   Rondel   [p. 391i]

       A l'autre huis
       Souvent m'envoye Esperance,
       Et me tense
       Quant en tristesse je suis.

5   Jours et nuys
       Ce lui demande alegence,
       A l'autre *huis*
       [*Souvent m'envoye Esperance.*]*

       Oncques puis
10   Que failli ma desirance,
       De plaisance

5 I promise you'll not.
 Reason will be master over you.
 Go your way, go, go.

 If you ever again return
 With your company,
10 I pray God curse you
 And whatever brings you back.
 Go your way, go, go.

Rondel

 If you want me to become all yours,
 By showing me a pleasant manner,
 Speak these words: "I consider you my servant,
 Make me satisfied with the service you offer."

5 I'll perform my duties, no matter what happens,
 Very faithfully, from this time forward,
 If you want me to become all yours.

 If Mercy and Grace do not sustain me
 And I fail somewhat in loyalty,
10 Punish me as you like,
 And if I serve well, for God's sake remember it,
 If you want me to become all yours.

Rondel

 To the other door
 Hope often sends me,
 Chastising me
 When I fall into sadness.

5 By day and night
 If I ask her for consolation,
 To the other door
 [Hope often sends me.]

 Ever since
10 I failed to obtain my desire,
 I've been empty

Mon cueur et moy sommes vuys.
A l'autre *huis*
[*Souvent m'envoye Esperance.*]

[143] 391s: R172

R71   [Rondel]   [p. 392i]

Comme j'oy que chascun devise,
On n'est pas tousjours a sa guise.
Beau chanter si ennuye bien.
Jeu qui trop dure ne vault rien.
5   Tant va le pot a l'eaue qu'i brise.*

Il couvient que trop parler nuyse,
Se dit on, et trop grater cuise.
Riens ne demeure en ung maintien,
Comme j'oy *que chascun devise.*

10   Aprés chault temps vient vent de bise.
Aprés hucques robbe de frise.
Le monde de passé revien.
A son vouloir joue du sien
Tant entre gens layz que d'Eglise,
15   Comme j'oy *que chascun devise.*

[144] 392s: R173

R72   [Rondel]   [p. 393i]

Ad ce premier jour de l'annee
De cueur, de corps et quanque j'ay
Priveement estreneray
Ce qui me gist en ma pensee.

5   C'est chose que tendray cellee
Et que point ne descouvreray
Ad ce premier *jour de l'annee.*

Avant que soit toute passee
L'annee, je l'aproucheray
10   Et puis a loisir conteray
L'ennuy qu'ay quant m'est eslongnee,
Ad ce premier *jour de l'annee.*

[145] 393s: R174

Of pleasure, and so has my heart.
To the other door
Hope often sends me.

Rondel

As I've heard every man affirm,
No one is always at ease.
Even a fine song is somewhat boring.
A game that goes on too long is worth nothing.
5   The pot goes to the water until it breaks.

Too much talk can only annoy,
As they say, and too much scratching makes you itch.
Nothing remains as it is,
As I have heard every man affirm.

10   After hot weather comes the north wind.
After a summer cloak, winter clothes of a thick woolen frisé.
The world of long ago returns.
And things go as they will,
For the laity and the clergy too,
15   As I have heard every man affirm.

Rondel

On this first day of the year,
My heart, my person, and all I possess
I bestow as a secret gift
On the one always in my thoughts.

5   This is something I'll keep secret,
Revealing nothing of it
On this first day of the year.

Before the year has run
Its full course, I'll approach her
10   And then, at my leisure, relate
The pain I feel when she's far distant,
On this first day of the year.

R73   Rondel double

Que voulez vous que plus vous die,
Jeunes assotez amoureux?
Par Dieu, j'ay esté l'un de ceulx
Qui ont eu vostre maladie.

5   Prenez exemple, je vous prie
A moy qui m'en complains et deulx.
Que voulez vous *que plus vous die?*

Et pource, de vostre partie,
Se voulez croire mes conseulx,
10   D'abregier conseiller vous veulx
Voz faiz en sens ou en folie.
Que voulez vous *que plus vous die?*

Plusieurs y treuvent chiere lie
Maintesfoiz et plaisans acueulx.
15   Que voulez vous *que plus vous die?*

Mais au derrain Merencolie
De ses huis fait passer les ceulx
En dueil et soussi, Dieu scet quieulx!
Lors ne chault de mort ou de vie.
20   Que voulez vous *que plus vous die?*

[146] Occupies entire page

R74   [Rondel]

A ce jour de saint Valentin,*
Que prandré je, per ou non per?
D'Amours ne quiers riens demander,
Pieça j'eus ma part du butin.

5   Veu que plus resveille matin
Ne vueil avoir, mais reposer,
A ce jour *de saint Valentin.*

Jennes gens voisent au hutin
Leurs sens ou folie esprouver.
10   Vieulx suis pour a l'escolle aller.
J'entans assés bien mon latin
A ce jour *de saint Valentin.*

[147] 395s: R175

Double Rondel

What more would you have me tell you,
Foolish young lovers?
By God, I have been one of that company,
Suffering the ill you suffer.

5   I beg you take me as an example,
I who complain and lament.
What more would you have me tell you?

And so, for your part,
If you credit my counsel,
10   I advise you to curtail
Your carrying on, be it sense or madness.
What more would you have me tell you?

Oftentimes many find in love
A joyful demeanor and pleasant welcome.
15   What more would you have me tell you?

But in the end Melancholy
Makes them pass over his threshold
Into pain and sorrow, God knows how!
Then whether you live or die no longer matters.
20   What more would you have me tell you?

Rondel

On this St. Valentine's Day,
Will I take a companion, or not?
I intend to ask nothing from Love,
Having taken my share of his booty long ago.

5   And that I no longer wish to have
An early morning rising, but rather rest,
On this St. Valentine's Day.

Let young people engage in a contest
To prove their folly or good sense.
10   I'm old to attend this school.
I know my Latin well enough
On this St. Valentine's Day.

R75   **Rondel**   [p. 396i]

Contre le trait de Faulceté,
Couvient harnoys de bonne espreuve,
Artillerie forgé neufve,
Chascun jour en soutiveté.

5   A! Jhesus, benedicite!
Nul n'est qui seurement se treuve
Contre le trait *de Faulceté.*

Au derrain fera Loyaulté
Faulseté de son penser veufve.
10   Pour Raison fault que Dieu s'esmeuve,
Monstrant sa puissance et bonté
Contre le trait *de Faulceté.*

[148] 396s: R176

R76   **Rondel**   [p. 397i]

En ne peut servir en deux lieux,
Choisir convient, ou ça, ou la.
Au festu tire qui pourra
Pour prandre le pis ou le mieulx.

5   Qu'en dictes vous, jeunes et vieulx?
Parle qui parler en vouldra.
En ne peut *servir en deux lieux.*

Les faiz de ce monde sont tieulx :
Qui bien fera, bien trouvera.
10   Chascun son paiement aura,
Tesmoing les Deesses et Dieux :
En ne peut *servir en deux lieux.*

[149] 397s: R177

R77   **[Rondel]**   [p. 398i]

Quant tu es courcé d'autres choses,
Cueur, mieulx te vault en paix laisser,
Car, s'on te vient araisonner,
Tost y treuves d'estranges gloses.

Rondel

Against the missiles of Falseness,
Armor of good proof is needed,
Artillery freshly forged
Every day in subtlety.

5   Ah, Jesus! Bless my soul!
There's no man who finds himself secure
Against the missiles of Falseness.

In the end Loyalty will take away
All the impoverished thoughts of Falseness.
10   For the sake of Reason, God must bestir Himself,
Showing His power and virtue
Against the missiles of Falseness.

Rondel

No one can serve in two places.
A choice must be made, here or there.
Let whoever can draw straws
Take the worse or the better.

5   What do you say of this, young and old?
Let whoever wishes speak his mind.
No one can serve in two places.

This is how things go in this world:
Whoever does good will find good.
10   Every man will have his reward,
So witness the Goddesses and Gods:
No one can serve in two places.

Rondel

When you're angry at other things,
Heart, better for you to hold your peace,
For, should someone come reason with you,
You'd soon find strange comments to make.

5   De ton desplaisir monstrer n'oses
       A aucun, pour te conforter
       Quant *tu* es *courcé d'autres choses.*

       De tes levres les portes closes
       Penses de saigement garder,
10   Que dehors n'eschappe Parler
       Qui descuevre le pot aux roses*
       Quant *tu* es *courcé d'autres choses.*

[150] 398s: R178

R78   [Rondel]   [p. 399i]

       J'ayme qui m'ayme, autrement non,
       Et non pour tant je ne hay rien,
       Mais vouldroye que tout fust bien,
       A l'ordonnance de Raison.

5   Je parle trop, las! se faiz mon!
       Au fort, en ce propos me tien :
       J'ayme qui *m'ayme, autrement non.*

       De pensees son chapperon
       A brodé le povre cueur mien.
10   Tout droit de devers lui je vien,
       Et m'a baillé ceste chançon :
       J'ayme qui *m'ayme, autrement non.*

[151] 399s: R179

R79   [Rondel]*   [p. 400i]

       Ce qui m'entre par une oreille
       Par l'autre sault com est venu,
       Quant d'y penser n'y suis tenu.
       Ainsi Raison le me conseille.

5   Se j'oy dire : vecy merveille,
       L'ung est long, l'autre court vestu.
       Ce qui m'entre *par une oreille*
       [*Par l'autre sault com est venu*].*

       Mais paine pert et se travaille
10   Qui devant moy trayne ung festu.*

5   You dare not reveal your misery
       To anyone in order to find consolation
       When you're angry at other things.

       Bear in mind wisely to keep shut
       The gateways of your lips
10   So speech does not escape
       And clear up the mystery,
       When you're angry at other things.

Rondel

       I love who loves me, otherwise not,
       And nonetheless there are none I hate,
       But rather I wish everything might be well,
       As Reason ordains.

5   I say too much, alas! It's a fact.
       In the end, I keep to this principle:
       I love who loves me, otherwise not.

       My poor heart has embroidered
       His hood with thoughts.
10   I make my way straight to him,
       And he has given me this song:
       I love who loves me, otherwise not.

Rondel

       What enters one of my ears
       Flies out the other, as it happens,
       When I don't have to give it a thought.
       Such is the counsel of Reason.

5   If I hear: "That's marvelous,
       One wears long clothes, the other short,"
       What enters one of my ears
       [Flies out the other, as it happens.]

       But whoever trails a straw before me
10   Wastes his time and trouble.

Comme ung chat, suis viel et chenu,
Legierement pas ne m'esveille
Ce qui m'entre *par une oreille*.

[152] 400s: R180

R80   Rondel   [p. 401i]

Quelque chose derriere
Couvient tousjours garder.
On ne peut pas monstrer
Sa voulenté entiere.

5   Quant on est en frontiere
De Dangereux Parler,
Quelque chose *derriere,*
[*Couvient tousjours garder.*]*

Ce pensee legiere
Veult mots trop despencer,
10   Raison doit espargnier,
Comme la tresoriere
Quelque chose *derriere*.

[153] 401s: R181

R81   Rondel   [p. 402i]

Que cuidez vous qu'on verra
Avant que passe l'annee?
Mainte chose demenee
Estrangement, ça et la.

5   Veu que des cy et des ja
Court merveilleuse brouee,
Que cuidez vous *qu'on verra?*

Viengne que advenir pourra!
Chascun a sa destinee,
10   Soit que desplaise ou agree.
Quant nouveau monde viendra,
Que cuidez vous *qu'on verra?*

[154] 402s: R182

Like a cat, I'm old and hoary,
It does not easily awaken me
What enters one of my ears.

Rondel

Something in reserve
Is what one should always keep.
One cannot reveal
All of one's desire.

5   When one is at the point
Of Dangerous Speech,
Something in reserve
One must always keep.

If flighty thought
10   Intends to spend too many words,
Reason must retain,
Acting as treasurer,
Something in reserve.

Rondel

What do you think we'll see
Before the year ends?
Many a strange thing
Taking place, here and there.

5   Seeing that a marvelous fog
Of "yes" and "never" now moves in,
What do you think we'll see?

Let what happens happen!
Every man to his own destiny,
10   Whether it displeases or suits.
When a new world arrives,
What do you think we'll see?

R82   **Rondel · pour Estampes**   [p. 403i]

Je suis mieulx pris que par le doy
Et fort enserré d'un anneau.
S'a fait ung visaige si beau,
Qui m'a tout conquesté a soy.

5   Je rougis et bien l'aparçoy,
Ainsi q'un amoureux nouveau.
Je suis mieulx *pris que par le doy.*

Et d'amourectes par ma foy,
J'ay assemblé ung grant fardeau
10   Qu'ay mussees soubz mon chappeau.
Pour Dieu! ne vous mocqués de moy.
Je suis mieulx *pris que par le doy.*

[155] 403s: R183

R83   **[Rondel]**   [p. 404i]

Marché nul autrement
Avecques vous, Beauté,
Se de vous Loyaulté
N'a le gouvernement.

5   Puis que mes jours despens
A vous vouloir amer,
Et aprés m'en repens,
Qui en doit on blasmer?

Riens fors vous seullement
10   A qui tiens féaulté.
Quant monstrés cruaulté,
Veu qu'Amour le deffent,
Marché nul *autrement.*

[156] 404s: R184

R84   **[Rondel]**   [p. 405i]

As tu ce jour ma mort juree,
Soussy? je te pry, tien te quoy,
Car a tort ma douleur par toy
Est trop souvent renouvellee.

Rondel for Estampes

I'm better captured than by the finger
And strongly encircled by a ring.
A face so fair has worked that trick,
Utterly conquering me.

5   I blush, and know it well,
In the manner of a new lover.
I'm better captured than by the finger.

And, upon my faith, I've gathered
A huge bouquet of wildflowers
10   I've hidden beneath my hat.
For God's sake, don't mock me.
I'm better captured than by the finger.

Rondel

No more business transacted
With you, Beauty,
If Faithfulness does not exercise
Dominion over you.

5   Since I spend my days
Desiring to love you,
And afterward repent,
Whose should be the blame?

To no one but you alone
10   Do I owe fealty.
Since you show cruelty,
Seeing that Love forbids it,
No more business transacted.

Rondel

Have you sworn my death today,
Care? I beg you, keep still,
For my pain is wrongly
And too often renewed by you.

5   A belle ensaigne desploiee,
        Me cours sus, et ne sçay pourquoy.
        As tu ce jour *ma mort juree?*

        La guerre sera tost finee,
        Se tu veulx, de toy et de moy,
10   Car je me rens, or me reçoy.
        Hola! paix, puis qu'elle est criee!
        As tu ce jour *ma mort juree?*

[157] 405s: R185

R85   Rondel   [p. 406i]

        Quant commanceray a voler
        Et sur elles me sentiray,
        En si grant aise je seray
        Que j'ay doubte de m'essorer.

5   Beau crier aura et leurrer,*
        Chemin de Plaisant Vent tendray,
        Quant *commanceray a voler.*

        La mue m'a fallu garder
        Par long temps. Plus ne le feray,
10   Puis que doulx temps et cler verray.
        On le me devra pardonner,
        Quant *commanceray a voler.*

[158] 406s: R186

R86   Rondel   [p. 407i]

        Je congnois assez telz debas
        Que l'ueil et le cueur ont entre eulx.
        L'un dit : Nous serons amoureux,
        L'autre dit : Je ne le vueil pas.

5   Raison s'en rit, disant tout bas :
        Escoutez moy ces malleureux!
        Je congnois *assez telz debas.*

        Lors m'en vois, plus tost que le pas,
        Et les tanse si bien tous deux
10   Que je les laisse treshonteux.

5   With a fine banner displayed
You attack me, and I know not why.
Have you sworn my death today?

The war will soon end,
If you wish, the one between you and me,
10   For I surrender, now take me.
Hey, truce, since it's been called!
Have you sworn my death today?

Rondel

When I take flight
And feel I'm on wings,
I'll be so much at ease
I fear I'll soar right away.

5   No point in shouting and tempting me back.
I'll follow the path of a Pleasant Wind
When I take flight.

I've had to be kept in the moulting cage
A long time; I'll be so no longer
10   Once I see the weather clear and fair.
I shall be pardoned
When I take flight.

Rondel

I know well enough the kind of debate
The eye and the heart engage in.
The one says: "We'll be in love."
The other says: "This isn't what I desire."

5   Reason laughs, saying with a hush:
"Listen to these miserable wretches!
I know well enough the kind of debate."

Then I get going, faster than at the walk,
And chastise those two so thoroughly
10   I leave them quite shamefaced.

Maintesfois ainsi me combas.
Je congnois *assez telz debas.*

[159] 407s: R187

R87   Rondel   [p. 408i]

Cueur, que fais tu? revenge toy
De Soussy et Merencolie.
C'est deshonneur et vilenie
De lachement se tenir coy.

5   Je t'aideray tant qu'est a moy
Voulentiers. Or ne te fains mie.
Cueur, *que fais tu? revenge toy.*

N'espergne riens, scez tu pourquoy?
Pource qu'abregeras ta vie
10   Se lez tiens en ta compaignie.
Desconfitz les et prens leur foy.
Cueur, *que fais tu? revenge toy.*

[160] 408s: R188

R88   Rondel   [p. 409i]

Par lez portes dez yeulx et dez oreilles,
Que chascun doit bien sagement garder,
Plaisir Mondain va et vient sans cesser
Et raporte de diverses merveilles.

5   Pource, mon cueur, s'a Raison te conseilles,
Ne le laissez point devers toy entrer
Par *lez portes dez yeulx et dez oreilles.*

A celle fin que par lui ne t'esveilles,
Veu qu'il te fault desormais reposer,
10   Dy lui : «Va t'en sans jamais retourner,
Ne revien plus, car en vain te traveilles
Par *lez portes dez yeulx et dez oreilles.*»

[161] 409s: R189

Many times I struggle thus.
I know well enough the kind of debate.

Rondel

Heart, what are you doing? Avenge yourself
On Care and Melancholy.
It's dishonorable and villainous
To do nothing like a coward.

5   I'll gladly help you with what
Concerns me. Now do not weaken.
Heart, what are you doing? Avenge yourself.

Spare nothing, do you know why?
Because you'll shorten your life
10   If you keep them among your company.
Defeat them and take their surrender.
Heart, what are you doing? Avenge yourself.

Rondel

Through the gateways of eyes and ears
That everyone should carefully guard
Worldly Pleasure comes and goes without ceasing,
Bringing many marvelous tidings.

5   And so, my heart, if you take Reason's advice,
Don't let him enter you in any way
Through the gateways of eyes and ears.

To the end that you don't wake up on his account,
Seeing that you should henceforth rest,
10   Tell him: "Go away and never come back,
Don't ever return, for you labor in vain
Through the gateways of eyes and ears."

R89   Rondel   [p. 410i]

    A qui les vent on
    Ces gueines dorees?*
    Sont il achetees
    De nouvel, ou non?

5   Par prest ou par don
    En fait on livrees?*
    A qui *les vent on?*

    Alant au pardon,*
    Je lez ay trouvees.
10   De telles denrees
    C'est petit guerdon.
    A qui *les vent on?*

[162] 410s: R190

R90   Rondel   [p. 411i]

    A qui vendez vous voz coquilles*
    Entre vous, amans pelerins?*
    Vous cuidez bien par voz engins
    A tous pertuis trouver chevilles.*

5   Sont ce coups d'esteufs ou de billes
    Que ferez, tesmoing voz voisins?
    A qui *vendez vous voz coquilles?*

    On congnoist tous voz tours d'estrilles
    Et bien clerement voz latins.
10   Trotés, reprenés voz patins
    Et troussés voz sacs et voz quilles.*
    A qui *vendez vous voz coquilles?*

[163] 411s: R191

R91   Rondel   [p. 412i]

    Envoyez nous un doulz regart
    Qui nous conduie jusqu'a Blois,
    Nous le vous rendrons quelque fois,
    Quoy que l'atente nous soit tart.

Rondel

To whom are these sold,
These golden chains?
Have they been recently
Bought or not?

5   Are these provisions meant
As loan or gift?
To whom are these sold?

Going to the festival of indulgence
I discovered them.
10   Such recompense
Is but a small reward.
To whom are these sold?

Rondel

Whom do you take me for?
Among your company, you unfaithful lovers?
You certainly think through your tricks
To find a solution for every problem.

5   Are these strokes for tennis or billiards
That you make, with your neighbors as witnesses?
Whom do you take me for?

All your tricks, your sweet talk
Are understood clearly and well.
10   Get on your way, put on your ragged clothes,
And clear off!
Whom do you take me for?

Rondel

Send a sweet look our way
To go with us as far as Blois.
Sometime we'll pay you back,
Though the wait might be long.

5   Puis qu'en emportés l'estandart
         De la Doulceur que bien congnois,
         Envoyez *nous un doulz regart.*

         Et pry Dieu que toutez vous gart,
         Et vous doint bons jours, ans et mois
10   A voz desirs, vouloirs et chois.
         Aquittez vous de vostre part :
         Envoyez *nous un doulz regart.*

[164 Here the duke's numbering ceases] 412s: R192

R92   **Rondel**   [p. 413i]

         Pource qu'on joute a la quintaine
         A Orleans, je tire a Blois.
         Je me sens foulé du harnois
         Et veulx reprandre mon alaine.

5   Raisonnable cause m'y maine,
         Excusé soye ceste fois,
         Pource *qu'on joute a la quintaine.*

         Je vous promet que c'est grant paine
         De tant faire «baille lui bois».*
10   Eslongner quelque part du mois
         Vault mieulx, pour avoir teste saine,
         Pource *qu'on joute a la quintaine.*

413s: R193

R93   **Rondel**   [p. 414i]

         Des arreraiges de Plaisance
         Dont trop endebté m'est Espoir,
         Se quelque part j'en peusse avoir,
         Du surplus donnasse quictance.

5   Mais au pois et a la balance
         N'en puis que bien peu recevoir
         Des arreraiges *de Plaisance.*

         Usure ou perte de chevance
         Mectroye tout a non chaloir,

5   Since you are bearing away the banner
Of the Sweetness well known to me,
Send a sweet look our way.

And I beg God to protect all of you
And make your days, years, and months good ones
10   Just as you desire, wish, and choose.
Acquit yourself for your part.
Send a sweet look our way.

Rondel

Because there's no jousting at the quintain
In Orleans, I make my way to Blois.
I feel wearied by this armor
And eager to catch my breath.

5   A good reason takes me there,
So let me be excused this time,
Because there's jousting at the quintain.

I promise you it's an effort to do as much
As to strike a blow with a lance.
10   To get away part of the month
Is better, if I'm to stay sane,
Because there's jousting at the quintain.

Rondel

Of the arrears of Pleasure,
For which Hope is deeply indebted to me,
If I might receive some part of them,
I should forgive the rest of the debt.

5   But measured by weight and the scales,
I receive but very little
Of the arrears of Pleasure.

Usury or loss of profit,
I'd be indifferent to all

10   Se je savoye a mon vouloir
        Recouvrer prestement finance
        Des arreraiges *de Plaisance.*

414s: R194

R94   **Rondel**   [p. 415i]

        Rescouez ces deux povres yeulx
        Qui tant ont nagé en Plaisance
        Qu'ilz se nayent sans recouvrance.
        Je les tiens mors ou presque tieulx.

5   Vidés les tost, se vous ait Dieulx
        En la sentine d'Alegeance.
        Rescouez *ces deux povres yeulx.*

        Courés y tous, jennes et vieulx
        Et a cros de bonne Esperance
10   De les tirer hors c'om s'avance!
        Chascun y face qui mieulx mieulx.
        Rescouez *ces deux povres yeulx.*

415s: R195

R95   **Rondel**   [p. 416i]

        A recommancer de plus belle
        J'en voy ja les adjournemens
        Que font vers vieulx et jennes gens
        Amours et la saison nouvelle.

5   Chascun d'eulx aussi bien lui qu'elle,
        Sont tous aprestés sur les rens
        A recommancer *de plus belle.*

        Comme toute la chose est telle,
        Je congnois telz esbatemens
10   Assez, de pieça m'y entens,
        Ce n'est que ancienne querelle
        A recommancer *de plus belle.*

416s: R196

10   Could I but at once recover
As I'd like the funds
Of the arrears of Pleasure.

Rondel

Rescue these two poor eyes
That have swum so much in Pleasure
They are drowning, beyond recovery.
I consider them dead or nearly so.

5   Send help quickly, so help you God,
Along the path of Relief.
Rescue these two poor eyes.

Run along, one and all, young and old,
And as you go, pull up
10   The anchor of good Hope!
Let every man do his best.
Rescue these two poor eyes.

Rondel

To begin again with even greater force,
I see already the summons
That in regard to young and old
Love and the new season are issuing.

5   Everyone, he as much as she,
Is wholly prepared in the lists
To begin again with even greater force.

Inasmuch as the whole affair is such,
I recognize these games
10   Well enough, long have I known them.
It's nothing but an ancient cause
To begin again with even greater force.

R96   **[Rondel]**   [p. 417i]

    Ainsi doint Dieux a mon cueur joye
    En ce que souhaidier vouldroye
    Et a mon penser reconfort
    Comme voulentiers prisse accort
5   A Soussy qui tant me guerroye.

    Mais remede n'y trouveroye
    Et qui pis est je n'oseroye
    Descouvrir les maulx qu'ay a tort.
    Ainsi *doint Dieux a mon cueur joye.*

10 Quant je lui dy : Dieu te convoye,
    Lesse m'en paix, va t'en ta voye.
    Par ton enchantement et sort
    Gueres mieulx ne vaulx vif que mort.
    Je languis quelque part que soye.
15 Ainsi *doint Dieux a mon cueur joye.*

417s: R197

R97   **Rondel**   [p. 418i]

    Maudit soit mon cueur se j'en mens,
    Quant a mon lesir estre puis
    Et avecques Pensee suis,
    En mez maulx prens alegemens,

5   Car Soussis, plains d'encombremens,
    Boutons hors et leur fermons l'uis!
    Maudit soit *mon cueur se j'en mens.*

    Assez y treuve esbatemens,
    Lors lui dy : «Ma maistresse, et puis
10 Serons nous ainsi jours et nuis?
    G'y donne mez consentemens.»
    Maudit *soit mon cueur se j'en mens.*

418s: R198

R98   **Rondel**   [p. 419i]

    En la querelle de Plaisance,
    J'ay veu le rencontre des yeulx
    Qui estoient, ainsi m'aid Dieux,
    Tous pres de combatre a oultrance.

Rondel

May God give my heart joy
In what I desire,
And consolation for my thoughts,
For I'd willingly make peace
5   With Care, who wars on me so much.

But I would find no remedy this way,
And, what is worse, I would not dare
Reveal the ills I unjustly bear.
May God give my heart joy.

10   When I tell Care, "Go with God,
Leave me in peace, take off.
Because of your enchantment and spell,
I'm hardly better off alive than dead,
Languishing no matter where I am."
15   May God give my heart joy.

Rondel

Cursed be my heart if I lie:
When I'm at ease
And in the company of Thought
I find relief in my suffering.

5   But let us expel Care, loaded with troubles,
And close the door against them
Cursed be my heart if I lie.

I find sport enough here,
Saying to Thought: "Mistress mine, and so
10   Is that how we'll find it, day and night?
I certainly agree."
Cursed be my heart if I lie.

Rondel

In the struggle against Pleasure
I've seen the encounter of the eyes
Which were, so help me God,
Prepared to fight to the bitter end.

5   Rangez par si belle ordonnance
        Qu'on ne sauroit deviser mieulx
        En la *querelle de Plaisance.*

        S'Amours n'y mectent pourveanse
        De pieça je les congnois tieulx
10   Qu'au derrenier jennes ou vieulx
        Mourront tous par leur grant vaillance
        En la *querelle de Plaisance.*

419s: R199

R99   Rondel   [p. 420i]

        De la maladie des yeulx
        Feruz de pouldre de Plaisir,
        Par le vent d'Amoureux Desir
        Est fort a guerir, se m'aid Dieux.

5   Toutes gens et jeunes et vieulx
        S'en scevent bien a quoy tenir
        De la *maladie des yeulx.*

        Je n'y congnois remedes tieulx
        Que hors de presse soy tenir
10   Et la compaignie fuïr.
        Qui plus en saura dye mieulx
        De la *maladie des yeulx.*

420s: R200

R100   Rondel   [p. 421i]

        Par m'ame, s'il en fust en moy,
        Soussi, Dieu scet que je feroye!
        Moy et tous de toy vengeroye.
        Il y a bien rayson pour quoy.

5   Riens ne dy qu'ainsi que je doy,
        Et telle est la voulenté moye.
        Par m'ame, *s'il en fust en moy!*

        Un chascun se complaint de toy,
        Pource, voulentiers fin prendroye
10   Avecques toy se je povoye.

5   Dispose your troops so expertly
That no one could do better
In the struggle against Pleasure.

If Love does not take precautions,
I've long known that the eyes
10   Will in the end with their great valor
Do everyone to death, young and old,
In the struggle against Pleasure.

Rondel

Concerning the diseases of the eyes
That are struck with Pleasure's dust
Borne along on the wind of Amorous Desire,
This is something hard to heal, so help me God.

5   All people, young and old,
Know very well what to make of it
Concerning the diseases of the eyes.

I know no remedy for it better
Than to keep myself far from the crowd
10   And flee such company.
Whoever knows more, let him say something better
Concerning the diseases of the eyes.

Rondel

By my soul, if I had it in me,
Care, God knows what I'd do!
Along with the rest, I'd take vengeance on you.
There's good reason to do so.

5   I say nothing but what I should,
And this is my desire,
By my soul, if I had it in me!

Everyone complains about you,
And so I'd willingly
10   Finish with you if I could.

Je n'y vois qu'a la bonne foy,
Par m'ame, *s'il en fust en moy!*

421s: R201

R101   **Rondel**   [p. 422i]

Mon cueur se plaint qu'il n'est payé
De sez despens pour son traveil
Qu'il a porté si nompareil
Qu'onquez tel ne fut essayé.

5   Son payement est delayé
Trop longtemps. Sur ce quel conseil?
Mon cueur *se plaint qu'il n'est payé.*

Puis qu'il n'est de gages rayé
Mais prest en loyal apareil
10   Autant que nul soubz le soleil,
Se mieulx ne peut, soit defrayé.
Mon cueur *se plaint qu'il n'est payé.*

422s: R202

R102   **Rondel**   [p. 423i]

Ou Loyaulté me payera
Dez servicez qu'ay fais sans faindre,
Ou j'auray cause de me plaindre,
Qui mon guerdon delayera.

5   Bon Droit pour moy tant criera
Qu'aux cieulz fera sa vois ataindre,
Ou Loyaulté *me payera.*

Quant Fortune s'effrayera,
Dieu a povoir de la reffraindre,
10   Et Rayson, qui ne doit riens craindre,
De moy aider s'essayera,
Ou Loyaulté *me payera.*

423s: R203

Only in good faith would I proceed,
By my soul, if I had it in me!

Rondel

My heart complains he's not been paid
For what he's expended in the troubles
He has endured, so beyond compare
No one ever experienced the like.

5   His payment has been too long
Delayed. What do you advise?
My heart complains he's not been paid.

Since he has not been paid his wages,
But is eager, more furnished with loyalty
10   Than any other man under the sun,
If it can't be better, let him be paid his expenses.
My heart complains he's not been paid.

Rondel

Unless Loyalty rewards me
For the services I've tirelessly performed,
I'll have reason to lodge a complaint
Against the one who is slow to pay me.

5   True Justice will cry out for my sake
So loudly her voice will reach the heavens,
Unless Loyalty rewards me

When Fortune goes berserk
God has the power to restrain her,
10   And Reason, who should fear no one,
Will strive to help me,
Unless Loyalty rewards me

R103   Rondel   [p. 424i]

Mon cuer, n'entrepren trop de choses,
Tu peus penser ce que tu veulz,
Et faire selon que tu peuz
Et dire ainsi comme tu oses.

5   Qui vouldront sur ce trouver gloses,
Je m'en rapporteray a eulz.
Mon cuer, *n'entrepren trop de choses.*

Se ces raisons garder proposes,
Tu feras bien par mes conseulz.
10   Laisse les embesoingnez seulz,
Il est temps que tu te reposes.
Mon cuer, *n'entrepren trop de choses.*

424s: R204

R104   Rondel   [p. 425i]

Comment ce peut il faire ainsy
En une seulle creature
Que tant ait des biens de nature?
Dont chascun en est esbahy.

5   Oncques tel chief d'euvre ne vy
Mieulx acomply oultre mesure.
Commant *ce peut il faire ainsy?*

Mes yeulx cuiday qu'eussent manty,
Quant apporterent sa figure
10   Devers mon cuer en pourtraiture,
Mais vray fut et plus que ne dy.
Commant *ce peut il faire ainsy?*

425s: R205

R105   Rondel   [p. 426i]

Ne m'en racontez plus, mes yeulx,
De Beaulté que vous prisez tant,
Car plus voys ou monde vivant
Et mains me plaist, ainsi m'aist Dieux.

Rondel

Heart of mine, do not attempt too much.
You can think whatever you like,
And do whatever you can,
And speak out as much as you dare.

5   Whoever wishes further comment,
I leave it up to them.
Heart of mine, do not attempt too much.

If you intend to follow reason,
You'll do well to act as I advise.
10   Don't bother about hard workers,
It's time you took a rest.
Heart of mine, do not attempt too much.

Rondel

How could it be
That in one lady alone
So many of nature's benefits are found?
It astonishes every man.

5   Never did I see such a masterpiece
Brought to such limitless perfection.
How could it be?

I thought my eyes deceived me
When they conveyed her image
10   And inscribed it within my heart,
But it was much truer than I can say.
How could it be?

Rondel

Eyes of mine, tell me no more
Of the beauty you esteem so highly,
For the more I live on this earth
The less pleased I am, so help me God.

5   Trouver je ne me sçay en lieux
         Qu'il m'en chaille ne tant ne quant.
         Ne m'en *racontez plus, mes yeulx.*

         Qu'est ce cy? deviens je des vieux?
         Ouÿ certes. D'or en avant
10   J'ay fait mon karesme prenant,*
         Et jeusne de tous plaisirs tieulx.
         Ne m'en *racontez plus, mes yeulx.*

426s: R206

R106   Rondel   [p. 427i]

         Si hardis, mez yeulx
         De riens regarder
         Qui me puest grever,
         Qu'en valés vous mieulx?

5   Estroit, se m'aid Dieux,
         Vous pense garder.
         Si hardis, *mez yeulx!*

         Vous devenés vieulx
         Et tous jours troter
10   Voulez, sans cesser.
         Ne soyez plus tieulx,
         Si hardis, *mez yeulx!*

427s: R207

R107   Rondel   [p. 428i]

         N'est ce pas grant trahison
         De mes yeulx en qui me fye,
         Qui me conseillent folye
         Maintes foys contre raison?

5   Que male part y ait on
         D'eulx et de leur tromperie!
         N'est ce pas *grant trahison?*

         Mieulx me fust en ma maison
         Estre seul a chiere lye,

5   I never find myself someplace
Where anything matters to me at all.
Eyes of mine, tell me no more.

What is this? Do I grow old?
Yes, indeed. Henceforth,
10   My days of indulgence are over,
And I abstain from all such pleasures.
Eyes of mine, tell me no more.

Rondel

You, my eyes, are so reckless
To look at something
That can do me harm.
Do you think thus to better yourselves?

5   So help me God, I think
To keep a strict watch over you.
You, my eyes, are so reckless!

You'll grow old and eager
To scurry about
10   Restlessly all the time.
Don't let this happen to you,
You, my eyes, are so reckless!

Rondel

Is this not a great betrayal,
That the eyes in which I trust
Give me a fool's advice,
Many times opposing reason?

5   May evil be the destiny
That overtakes them and their foolishness!
Is this not a great betrayal?

It would be better for me
To be alone and happy

10   Qu'avoir telle compaignie
        Qui me bat de mon baston.
        N'est ce pas *grant trahison?*

428s: R208

R108   **[Rondel]**   [p. 318s]

        Et ne cesserez vous jamais?
        Tousjours est a recommancer.
        C'est folie d'y plus penser,
        Ne s'en soussïer desormais.

5   Plus avant j'en diroye mais,
        Rien n'y vault flacter ne tanser,
        Et ne cesserez *vous jamais?*

        Passez a plusieurs mois des Mays
        Qu'Amour vous vouldrent avanser.
10   Mal les voulez recompanser
        En servant de telz entremais.
        Et ne cesserez *vous jamais?*

318i: R1

R109   **[Rondel]**   [p. 319s]

        Qu'il ne le me font
        Pour voir que feroye
        Et se je sauroye
        Leur donner le bont!*

5   Puisque telz ilz sont,
        Affin qu'on les voye,
        Qu'il ne *le me font!*

        Droit a droit respont
        Payer les vouldroye
10   De telle monnoye
        Qu'il desserviront.
        [Qu'il ne le me font!]

319i: R2

10 Than to have such companions
  Who beat me with my own stick.
  Is this not a great betrayal?

Rondel

  And will you never stop?
  Always there's a need to begin again.
  It's crazy to think more about it,
  Or to worry henceforth.

5 After this I'll have nothing more to say.
  Flattery and reproach are worth nothing.
  And will you never stop?

  Many Mays have come and gone
  Since Love was eager to advance you.
10 You wish to recompense them badly
  By providing them with such diversions.
  And will you never stop?

Rondel

  May they not do it to me,
  To see what I'd do
  And if I could manage
  To make fun of them!

5 Since this is how they are,
  In order that they be seen,
  May they not do it to me!

  Right answers right,
  I would pay them back
10 In the very same coin
  That they'll merit.
  May they not do it to me!

R110   [Rondel]   [p. 323s]

Les en voulez vous garder
Ces rivieres de courir
Et grues prendre et tenir
Quant hault les veez voler?

5   A telles choses muser
Voit on folz souvent servir.
Les *en voulez vous garder?*

Laissez le temps tel passer
Que Fortune veult souffrir
10   Et les choses avenir
Que l'en ne scet destourber.
Les *en voulez vous garder?*

323i: R9

R111   [Rondel]   [p. 327i]

Vous vistes que je le veoye
Ce que je ne vueil descouvrir,
Et congnustes a l'ueil ouvrir,
Plus avant que je ne vouloye.

5   L'ueil d'embusche saillit en voye,
De soy retraire n'eust lesir,
Vous *vistes que je le veoye.*

Trop est saige qui ne foloye,
Quant on est es mains de Plaisir,
10   Qui lors vint vostre cuer saisir
Et fist comme pieça souloye.
Vous *vistes que je le veoye.*

327s: R16

R112   [Rondel]   [p. 329s]

La veez vous la, la lyme sourde,
Qui pense plus qu'elle ne dit?
Souventesfoiz s'esbat et rit
A planter une gente bourde.

Rondel

Do you want to stop them,
These rivers, from flowing,
And grab hold of cranes
When you see them flying on high?

5   Musing about such things
Is what fools are often seen doing.
Do you want to stop them?

Let the time pass in just the way
That Fortune will allow,
10   And let things happen
That none can prevent.
Do you want to stop them?

Rondel

You saw I was looking at it,
What I did not wish to reveal,
And you understood, opening your eye,
Much more than I intended.

5   The eye rushes onto the path from ambush,
It had not the chance to retreat,
You saw I was looking at it.

The man is very wise who does not go mad
When in the hands of Pleasure,
10   Who then comes to seize your heart
And do what has long been his custom.
You saw I was looking at it.

Rondel

Do you see her there, that sly woman,
Who thinks more than she says?
Oftentimes she sports and laughs,
Making a pleasant jest.

5   Contrefaisant la coquelourde,
        Soubz ung malicïeux abit
        La veez vous *la, la lyme sourde?*

        Quelle part que malice sourde,
        Tost congnoist s'il y a prouffit.
10   Benoist en soit le Saint Esprit
        Qui de si finete me hourde!*
        La veez vous la, *la lyme sourde?*

329i: Ch64

R113   [Rondel]   [p. 330s]

        Helas! et qui ne l'aymeroit
        De Bourbon le droit heritier,*
        Qui a l'estomac de papier
        Et aura la goute de droit?

5   Se Lymosin ne lui aidoit,
        Il mourroit, tesmoing Villequier.
        Helas! *et qui ne l'aymeroit?*

        Jamais plus hault ne sailliroit,
        S'elle lui monstroit ung dangier,
10   Et pource, Fayete et Gouffier,*
        Aidiez chascun en vostre endroit.
        Helas! *et qui ne l'aymeroit?*

330i: Ch65

R114   [Rondel]   [p. 331s]

        Dieu vous envoye pascïence,
        Gentil conte Cleremondois,*
        Vous congnoissez a ceste fois
        Qu'est d'amoureuse penitance.

5   Puis qu'estes hors de la presance
        De celle que bien je congnois,
        Dieu vous *envoye pascïence.*

        Vouer vous povez alïance,
        A la riche, comme je croys
10   Ne vous trouverez de ce mois,

5   Playing her tricks,
Under a cloak of maliciousness,
Do you see her there, that sly woman?

Wherever malice makes an appearance,
She realizes at once if it's to her profit.
10   Blessed be the Holy Spirit
Who lands me with such a crafty creature.
Do you see her there, that sly woman?

Rondel

Alas! And who would not love him,
The true heir of Bourbon,
Whose stomach is so weak
And who rightly will suffer from gout?

5   If Limousin comes not to his aid,
He will die, so testifies Villequier.
Alas! And who would not love him?

Never would he leap so high
Were she to treat him with disdain,
10   And so, Fayete and Gouffier,
You help every man in your area.
Alas! And who would not love him?

Rondel

May God give you patience,
Noble count Cleremondois,
At present you know
What penance is for lovers.

5   Since you're not in the presence
Of the lady I know so well,
May God give you patience.

You can promise marriage
To the wealthy lady, so I believe,
10   But you'll not manage it this month,

Las! trop estes loing d'alegence.
Dieu vous *envoye pascïence.*

331i: Ch66

R115 [Rondel] [p. 332s]

Sauves toutes bonnes raisons,
Mieulx vault mentir pour paix avoir
Qu'estre batu pour dire voir.
Pource, mon cuer, ainsi faisons.

5   Riens ne perdons, se nous taisons
Et se jouons au plus savoir,*
Sauves *toutes bonnes raisons.*

Parler boute feu en maisons
Et destruit paix, ce riche avoir.
10   On aprent a taire et a veoir,
Selon les temps et les saisons,
Sauves *toutes bonnes raisons.*

332i: Ch67

R116 [Rondel] [p. 333s]

Il souffist bien que je le sache,
Sans en enquerir plus avant,
Car se tout aloye disant,
On vous pourroit bien dire : actache.

5   Nul de la langue ne m'arrache
Ce qu'en mon cuer je voys pensant.
Il souffist *bien que je le sache.*

Ainsi qu'en blanc pert noire tache,
Vostre fait est si apparant
10   Que m'y treuve trop congnoissant.
Qui est descouvert, mal se cache :
Il souffist *bien que je le sache.*

333i: Ch68

Alas! You're a long way from finding relief.
May God give you patience.

Rondel

Despite fine reasons of every kind,
Better to lie and have peace
Than be beaten for speaking the truth.
And so, my heart, let us do so.

5   We'll lose nothing by remaining silent,
And if we play a game of twenty questions,
Despite fine reasons of every kind,

Speaking sets fire to houses
And destroys the peace, that worthy good.
10   We learn to be silent and observe,
According to time and season,
Despite fine reasons of every kind.

Rondel

It's enough that I know it,
Without inquiring more about the matter,
For if I went around telling all,
Some could well say: post the notice.

5   No one could force my tongue to say
What I'm thinking in my heart.
It's enough that I know it.

Just as a black spot stands out against white,
Your carrying on is so obvious
10   I'm only too well aware of it.
Whoever is found out, hides himself badly.
It's enough that I know it.

R117   **[Rondel]**   [p. 334s]

    Pense de toy
    Dorenavant,
    Du demourant
    Te chaille poy.

5   Ce monde voy
    En enpirant.
    Pense *de toy.*

    Regarde et oy,
    Va peu parlant.
10   Dieu tout puissant
    Fera de soy.
    Pense *de toy.*

334i: Ch69

R118   **[Rondel]**   [p. 335s]

    Ce n'est riens qui ne puist estre,
    On voit de plus grans merveilles
    Que de baster aus corneilles*
    Lez maris et l'erbe pestre.

5   Car de jouer tours de maistre
    Femmes sont lez nonpareilles.
    Ce n'est *riens qui ne puist estre.*

    Tant aux huis comme aux fenestres,
    En champs, jardins ou en trailles,
10   Par tout ont yeulx et oreilles,
    Soit a destre ou a senestre.
    Ce n'est *riens qui ne puist estre.*

335i: Ch70

R119   **[Rondel]**   [p. 336s]

    Or est de dire : Laissez m'en paix,
    Et tout plain de : Rien ne m'est plus,
    Mes propos sont en ce conclus
    Qu'ainsi demourray desormais.

Rondel

Think of yourself.
Henceforth,
Let the rest
Concern you little.

5   I see this world
Grow worse.
Think of yourself.

Look and listen,
Say little as you go.
10   God Almighty
Will do as He pleases.
Think of yourself.

Rondel

There is nothing that might not be;
One sees even greater marvels
Than husbands given the gate
And sent packing.

5   For in playing masterly tricks
Women have no rivals.
There is nothing that might not be.

As much at doors as at windows,
In the fields, gardens, or trellises,
10   Their eyes and ears are everywhere,
Either to the right or the left.
There is nothing that might not be.

Rondel

Now it's time to say: leave me in peace,
And again: I care no more about anything,
My thoughts have come to this conclusion.
I'll remain in such a state henceforth.

5   De s'entremettre de mez fais,
       Je n'en requier nullez ne nuls,
       Or est *de dire: Laissez m'en paix.*

       Fortune par sez faulz atrais,
       En pipant a pris a la glus
10   Mon cueur, et en soussi reclus
       Se tient sans departir jamais.
       Or est *de dire: Laissez m'en paix.*

336i: Ch71

R120   [Rondel]   [p. 337s]

       C'est grant paine que de vivre en ce monde,
       Encore esse plus paine de mourir.
       Si convient il, en vivant, mal souffrir,
       Et au derrain, de mort passer la bonde.

5   S'aucune foiz joye ou plaisir abonde,
       On ne les peut longuement retenir,
       C'est grant *paine que de vivre en ce monde.*

       Pource, je vueil comme fol qu'on me tonde
       Se plus pense, quoy que voye a venir,
10   Qu'a vivre bien et bonne fin querir.
       Las! il n'est rien que Soussy ne confonde.
       C'est grant *paine que de vivre en ce monde.*

337i: Ch72 and quatrain in lower margin

R121   [Rondel]   [p. 338s]

       En vivant en bonne esperance
       Sans avoir desplaisance ou dueil,
       Vous aurez brief a votre vueil,
       Nouvelle plaine de plaisance.

5   De guerre n'avons plus doubtance,
       Mais tousjours gracïeux acueil,
       En vivant *en bonne esperance.*

       Tous nouveaulx revendrons en France,
       Et quant me reverrés a l'ueil,
10   Je suis tout autre que je sueil,

5   To get involved in my business
I ask no man and no lady.
Now it's time to say: leave me in peace.

As birds are trapped by call and lime,
Fortune has trapped my heart. It will
10   Remain closeted with care
Nevermore to depart.
Now it's time to say: leave me in peace.

Rondel

Living in this world is great torment;
Greater still is the torment of dying,
So it has to be: one suffers ills in life
And in the end crosses death's barrier.

5   If at any time joy or pleasure abounds,
No man can hold onto them for long,
Living in this world is great torment.

So I'd like to be tonsured like a fool
If I continue to think, no matter what I see coming,
10   About living a good life and seeking a fine end.
Alas! There's nothing that Care does not confound.
Living in this world is great torment.

Rondel

While living in good hope,
Feeling neither displeasure nor pain,
You'll soon have, as you wish,
News that will mightily please.

5   We have no more fear of war,
But always a gracious welcome,
While living in good hope.

All changed we'll return to France,
And when you see me again in person,
10   I'll be quite different from what I was,

Au mains j'en fais la contenance,
En vivant *en bonne esperance.*

338i: R19

R122   [Rondel] · Orlians a Cecille   [p. 339s]

Vostre esclave et serf ou que soye,
Qui trop ne vous puis mercier,
Quant vous a pleu de m'envoyer
Le don qu'ay receu a grant joye.

5   Tel que dy et plus, se povoye,
Me trouverés a l'essaier
Vostre esclave *et serf ou que je soye.*

Paine mectray que brief vous voye,
Et toust arez sans delaier
10   Chose qui est sus le mestier
Qui vous plaira; plus n'en diroye.
Vostre esclave *et serf ou que je soye.*

339i: R20

R123   [Rondel]   [p. 340s]

Tellement quellement
Me fault le temps passer
Et soucy amasser
Maintesfois mallement.

5   Quant ne puis nullement
Ma fortune casser,
Tellement *quellement*
[*Me fault le temps passer.*]

G'iray tout bellement
10   Pour paour de me lasser
Et sans trop m'enlasser
Ou monde follement,
Tellement *quellement.*

340i: R21

At least giving the appearance of being so,
While living in good hope.

Rondel—Orleans to Sicily

Your slave and serf wherever I might be,
Who cannot thank you enough,
When you were pleased to send me
The gift I received with great joy.

5   These are the words I say, and more were I able,
You'll find me, if you test me,
Your slave and serf wherever I might be.

I shall take pains to see you soon,
And soon you will possess without delay
10   Something that is ongoing
And will please; I'll say no more.
Your slave and serf wherever I might be.

Rondel

This way and that
I must pass the time
And amass cares
Often to my disadvantage.

5   Since I can in no way
Rid myself of my destiny,
This way and that,
[I must pass the time].

I will keep on in fine fashion
Fearful of wearying myself
10   And without getting involved
Too foolishly in the world,
This way and that.

R124   **[Rondel]**   [p. 341s]

A tout bon compte revenir
Couvendra, qui qu'en rie ou pleure,
Et ne scet on le jour ne l'eure.
Souvent en devroit souvenir.

5   Prenez qu'on ait dueil ou plaisir
En brief temps ou longue demeure,
A tout bon compte *revenir*
[*Couvendra, qui qu'en rie ou pleure.*]*

Las! on ne pense qu'a suÿr
10   Le monde qui tousjours labeure,
Et quant on cuide qu'il sequeure,
Au plus grant besoing vient faillir
A tout bon compte *revenir.*

341i: R22

R125   **[Rondel]**   [p. 342s]

Vous estes paié pour ce jour,
Puis qu'avez eu ung doulx regart.
Devant ung ancien regnart
Tost est apparceu ung tel tour.

5   Quant on a esté a sejour,
Ce sont les gaiges de musart.
Vous estes *paié pour ce jour.*

Il souffist pour vostre labour,
Et s'aprés on vous sert de l'art,
10   Prenez en gré, maistre coquart,
Ce n'est qu'un restraintif d'amour :
Vous estes *paié pour ce jour.*

342i: R23

R126   **[Rondel]**   [p. 343s]

Puis qu'estes en chaleur d'amours,
Pour Dieu, laissez voir vostre orine.
On vous trouvera medecine
Qui briefment vous fera secours.

Rondel

To render a good account
Will be necessary, whoever laughs or cries,
And no one knows either the day or the hour.
One should often remember this.

5   Accept that there might be pain or pleasure
For a brief time or quite long,
To render a good account
[Will be necessary, whoever cries or laughs].

Alas! He thinks only of following
10   The world, the man who labors ceaselessly,
And, though he believes the world will help
At his time of greatest need, he comes to fail3
To render a good account.

Rondel

You've been paid for this day,
Since you've had a pleasant look.
To an old fox here present
Such a trick is readily apparent.

5   When one has been at leisure,
These are the wages of a wastrel
You've been paid for this day.

This suffices for your labor,
And if you're then served with trickery,
10   Take it in good grace, you conceited rogue,
It's nothing but a lover's astringent:
You've been paid for this day.

Rondel

Since you are feeling love's fever,
For God's sake, let us examine your urine.
A medicine will be found
To quickly bring you help.

5   Trop tost oultre le commun cours
       Vous bat le cuer en la poitrine,
       Puis qu'estes *en chaleur d'amours.*

       La fievre blanche ses sejours
       A fait. Se voulez que termine
10   Et que plus ne vous soit voisine,
       Repousez vous pour aucuns jours,
       Puis qu'estes *en chaleur d'amours.*

343i: R24

R127   [Rondel]   [p. 344s]

       Saint Valentin, quant vous venez
       En Karesme au commancement,
       Receu ne serez vrayement
       Ainsi que acoustumé avez.

5   Soussy et Penance amenez.
       Qui vous recevroit lyement,
       Saint Valentin, *quant vous venez?*

       Une autresfoiz vous avancez
       Plus tost, et alors toute gent
10   Vous recuilleront autrement,
       Et pers a choysir amenez,
       Saint Valentin, *quant vous venez!*

344i: R25

R128   [Rondel]   [p. 345s]

       Saint Valentin dit : «Veez me ça
       Et apporte pers a choysir.
       Viengne qui y devra venir,
       C'est la coustume de pieça.»

5   Quant le jour des Cendres «hola!»
       Respond, auquel doit on faillir?
       Saint Valentin *dit : «Veez me ça.»*

       Au fort, au matin couvendra
       En devocïon se tenir,
10   Et aprés disner a loisir

5 Very quickly, far faster than normal pace,
  The heart beats within your chest,
  Since you are feeling love's fever.

  A white fever has taken up
  Residence. If you wish it to end
10 And no longer be your neighbor.
  Take to your bed for a few days
  Since you are feeling love's fever.

Rondel

  Saint Valentine, when you come
  At the beginning of Lent,
  You will not be received, truly,
  In the manner to which you're accustomed.

5 You bring Care and Penance along.
  So who would receive you joyfully,
  Saint Valentine, when you come?

  Another time you'll arrive
  Sooner, and then all the people
10 Will welcome you in another fashion
  And you'll lead off companions as you choose,
  Saint Valentine, when you come!

Rondel

  Saint Valentine says: "Look upon me
  And lead away the companion you choose.
  Let come here whosoever will,
  This has long been the custom."

5 When the first day of Lent answers
  "Hey there," which of these should one disappoint?
  Saint Valentine says: "Look upon me."

  In the end, one must in the morning
  Go to devotions,
10 And after dinner let him at his leisure

Choisisse qui choisir vouldra.
Saint Valentin *dit : «Veez me ça.»*

345i: R26

R129   Rondel   [p. 348s]

A trompeur trompeur et demi,
Tel qu'on seme couvient cuillir.
Se mestier voy partout courir,
Chascun y joue et moy aussi.

5   Dy je bien de ce que je dy?
De tel pain souppe fault servir,
A trompeur *trompeur et demi.*

Et qui n'a pas langaige en lui
Pour parler selon son desir,
10   Ung truchement lui fault querir.
Ainsi, ou par la ou par cy,
A trompeur *trompeur et demi.*

348i: R130

R130   Rondel   [p. 348i]

Baillez lui la massue*
A celui qui cuide estre
Plus soubtil que son maistre,
Et sans raison l'argue,

5   Ou il sera beste mue
Quant on l'envoira pestre.
Baillez *lui la massue.*

Quoy qu'il regibe ou rue
Si sault par la fenestre,
10   Comme s'il vint de nestre
Sera chose esperdue.
Baillez *lui la massue.*

348s: R129

Choose who wishes to choose.
Saint Valentine says: "Look upon me."

Rondel

Every rogue meets his match.
You reap just as you sow.
This is the art I see everywhere;
Every man plays at it, and so do I.

5   Do I speak well in what I said?
You must serve a soup from such bread,
Every rogue meets his match.

And whoever lacks the words
To speak what it is he wants,
10   That man must seek out an interpreter.
And so, either here or there,
Every rogue meets his match.

Rondel

Give him a fool's bauble,
The one who thinks he's
Craftier than his master,
And who claims that with no reason.

5   If not, he'll be a dumb beast
When sent out to pasture.
Give him a fool's bauble.

Even though he balks or kicks,
Then jumps through the window,
10   As if he were some suckling babe,
He'll be a lost cause.
Give him a fool's bauble.

R131   [Rondel]   [p. 349s]

Ubi supra . . .*
N'en parlons plus
Des tours cornulz
Et cetera.

5   *Non est cura*
De telz abuz.
Ubi [*supra*].

Malla jura
Sont suspendus
10   Ou deffendus,
Et reliqua
Ubi [*supra*].

349i: R27

R132   [Rondel]   [p. 350s]

Noli me tangere*
Faulte de serviteurs,
Car bonté de seigneurs
Ne les scet *frangere.*

5   Il vous fault *regere*
En craintes et rigueurs.
Noli me [*tangere*],

Ne hault *erigere*
Trop tost en grans faveurs,
10   Se ne sont que foleurs.
Bien m'en puis *plangere.*
Noli me [*tangere*].

350i: R28

R133   Rondel   [p. 351i]

Pres la, briquet aus pendantes oreilles,
Tu scez que c'est de deduit de gibier,
Au derrenier tu auras ton loyer,
Et puis seras viande pour corneilles.

Rondel

Sometime ago . . .
Let us say no more
About rotten tricks
And other such.

5   There's no problem
With such abuses.
Sometime ago . . .

Evil laws
Are suspended
10   Or defended,
And so forth,
Sometime ago . . .

Rondel

Touch me not,
Lacking servants,
The kindness of lords
Cannot break them down.

5   You must reign
In fear and cruelty.
Touch me not.

Don't raise them up high
Too quickly to favorable positions.
10   For that is only folly.
Well may I complain about this.
Touch me not.

Rondel

Come here, you droopy-eared hound,
You know the delights of the chase,
In the end you'll get your reward
And afterward be food for crows.

5   Tu ne fais pas miracles, mais merveilles,
        Et as ayde pour te bien ensaigner.
        Pres la, *briquet aus pendantes oreilles,*

        A toute heure diligemment traveilles
        Et en chasse vaulz autant qu'un limier.
10   Tu amaines au tiltre de levrier
        Toutez bestes et noires et vermeilles :
        Pres la, *briquet aus pendantes oreilles.*

351s: R29

R134   [Rondel]   [p. 352s]

        Or s'y joue qui vouldra :
        Qui me change, je le change.
        Nul ne tiengne chose estrange
        D'avoir selonc qu'il fera!

5   Quant par sa faulte sera,
        Gré ne dessert ne louange.
        Or s'y joue *qui vouldra.*

        Puis que advisé on l'en a
        Et a Raison ne se range,
10   S'aprés selle se revange,
        Le tort a qui demourra?
        Or s'y joue *qui vouldra.*

352i: R30

R135   [Rondel]   [p. 354s]

        Satis, satis, plus quam satis,
        N'en avez vous encor assés?
        Par Dieu, vous en serés lassés
        Dez folies *quas amatis.*

5   *Cum sensibus ebetatis,*
        Sottez gens, vous lez amassés.
        Satis, [*satis, plus quam satis.*]

        Et pource, *si me credatis,*
        Oubliés tous lez temps passés
10   Et voz meschans pensers cassés,

5   You do not work miracles, but rather marvels,
       And you've help to guide you well.
       Come here, you droopy-eared hound.

       At all hours you work diligently
       And in the hunt you're valuable as a fine dog.
10   You bring in, just like a greyhound,
       Beasts of all kind, the black as well as the red.
       Come here, you droopy-eared hound.

Rondel

       Now let whoever wishes play the game.
       I change the one who changes me.
       Let no one think it strange
       To receive in turn what he will do.

5   Whenever the fault is his,
       He deserves neither thanks nor praise.
       Now let whoever wishes play the game.

       Since he's been advised
       And makes no friend of Reason,
10   If she afterward takes her revenge,
       Whose should be the blame?
       Now let whoever wishes play the game.

Rondel

       Enough, enough, more than enough,
       Don't you have enough already?
       By God, you'll weary
       Of the mad things you love.

5   With feelings bewildered,
       Foolish people, you gather them up.
       Enough, enough, more than enough.

       And this is why, if you believe me,
       You'll forget all times past
10   And suppress your evil thoughts,

Dolendo de perpetratis :
Satis, [satis, plus quam satis!]

354i: R33

R136   [Rondel]   [p. 355s]

Non temptabis, tien te coy,
Regard plain d'atrayement,
Vade retro tellement
Que point n'aproches de moy.

5   *Probavi te, sur ma foy*,
Je crains ton assotement.
Non temptabis, [tien te coy,
Regard plain d'atrayement.]

Ecce la rayson pourquoy :
10   Tu resveillez trop souvent
Corda : bien congnois comment*
Presches l'amoureuse loy.
Non temptabis, [tien te coy!]

355i: R34

R137   [Rondel]   [p. 356s]

Gardez vous de *mergo*,
Trompeurs faulz et rusés,
Qui lez gens abusés
Maintesfois *a tergo*.

5   En tous lieus ou *pergo*,
Fort estes acusés,
Gardez [vous de *mergo*.]

Mercy dit : *abstergo*
Lez faultes dont usés,
10   Mais que lez refusés.
Avisez vous *ergo*.
Gardez [vous de *mergo*.]

356i: R35

Sorrowing over hardships:
Enough, enough, more than enough!

Rondel

You will not tempt, keep yourself still,
Glance, full of attraction,
Make your way back
So as not to come near me.

5   I've put you to the proof, on my faith,
I fear your madness.
You will not tempt, keep yourself still,
Glance, full of attraction.

And here's the reason why:
10   You'll too often awaken
Feelings; I readily acknowledge
You preach the lover's life,
You will not tempt, keep yourself still!

Rondel

Keep yourself from "I'm sinking,"
You betrayers false and full of tricks,
Who have many times
Done people in behind their backs.

5   Everywhere I've ever gone,
You have been harshly accused,
Keep yourself from "I'm sinking."

Mercy says "I will erase
All the sins you've committed,
10   Providing you renounce them."
So just think about it.
Keep yourself from "I'm sinking."

R138   [Rondel]   [p. 357s]

Quant n'ont assez fait dodo,
Cez petitz enfanchonnés,
Il portent soubz leurs bonnés
Visages plains de bobo.

5   C'est pitié s'il font jojo*
Trop matin, lez doulcinés,
Quant *n'ont assez fait dodo,*

Mieulx amassent a gogo
Gesir sur molz coissinés,
10   Car il sont tant poupinés!*
Helas! *che gnogno, gnogno,**
Quant *n'ont assez fait dodo.*

357i: R36

R139   [Rondel]   [p. 358s]

Procul a nobis
Soyent ces trompeurs,
Dentur aus flateurs
Verba pro verbis,

5   *Sicut «pax vobis»,*
Et tendent ailleurs
Procul [*a nobis.*]

Non semel sed bis
Et dez fois plusieurs
10   Sont loups ravisseurs
Soubz peauls de brebis.
Procul [*a nobis!*]

358i: R37

R140   Rondel   [p. 359s]

Faulcette confite
En plaisant parler,
Laissez la aler,
Car je la despite!

Rondel

When they've not slept enough,
These tiny infants,
They have, under their bonnets,
Faces splotched with red.

5   It's a shame if they play around
Too early, these sweet things,
When they've not slept enough.

They'd very much prefer
Lying on soft cushions,
10   For they're so chubby!
Alas, how they whine, whine
When they've not slept enough.

Rondel

Far from us
May these betrayers remain,
To flatterers are given
Words for words.

5   And let it be, "Peace to you,"
And may they head elsewhere
Far from us.

Not once but twice
And sometimes more often
10   They are ravening wolves
Beneath sheep's clothing.
Far from us!

Rondel

Hypocritical woman,
With her fair words,
Let her go her way,
For I despise her!

5   Se n'est que redite
         De tant l'esprouver,
         Faulcete *confite.*

         Et quant on s'aquitte
         Plus de l'amender,
10   Pis la voy ouvrer.
         C'est chose maudite,
         Faulcete *confite!*

359i: R38

R141   [Rondel]   [p. 360s]

         Il fauldroit faire l'arquemie,
         Qui vouldroit forger Fauceté
         Tant qu'elle devint Loyauté,
         Quant en malice est endurcie.

5   C'est rompre sa teste en folie
         Et temps perdre en oysiveté.
         Il fauldroit *faire l'arquemie.*

         Plus avant qu'on y estudie,
         Et meins y congnoit on seurté,
10   Car de faire de mal bonté
         L'un a l'autre trop contrarie.
         Il faudroit *faire l'arquemie.*

360i: R39

R142   Rondel   [p. 361s]

         En changeant mes appetiz
         Je suis tout saoul de blanc pain,
         Et de menger meurs de fain
         D'un fres et nouveau pain bis.

5   A mon gré, ce pain faitiz
         Est ung morceau souverain
         En changeant *mes appetiz.*

         S'il en fust a mon devis,
         Plus tost anuyt que demain

5   It's only saying the same old thing
To put such as her to proof,
Hypocritical woman.

And the more one takes the trouble
To correct her,
10   The worse she gets.
It's a dreadful business,
Hypocritical woman!

Rondel

Alchemy should be what you use
If you intend working on Falseness
Until she's transformed into Faithfulness,
So inured is she to her evil game.

5   It's foolish to crack one's head
And waste time on pointless measures.
Alchemy should be what you use.

The more one studies the matter,
The less one knows for sure,
10   Since for turning vice into virtue
Those two are much too different.
Alchemy should be what you use.

Rondel

In regard to changing my desire,
I'm stuffed full of white bread,
And, eating, die of hunger
For brown bread fresh baked.

5   To my taste, this coarse bread
Is quite a delicacy
In regard to changing my desire.

Were I to get my wish,
Sooner tonight than tomorrow

10   J'en eusse mon vouloir plain,
        Car grant desir m'en est pris
        En changeant *mes appetiz.*

361i: R40

R143   Rondel · de Fredet*   [p. 362s]

        Pour mectre a fin la grant doleur
        Que par trop amer je reçoy,
        Secourez moi.
        Las! ou autrement sur ma foy,
5   Mes jours n'auront pas grant longueur.

        Car si trestourmenté je suis
        De tant d'ennuys
        Qui sans cesser me courent seure

        Que je n'ay bons jours, bonnes nuys,
10   Et si ne puis
        Trouver, fors vous, qui me sequeure.

        Aydez a vostre serviteur,
        Qui est mieulx pris que par le doy,
        Ou mort me voy
15   Se ne montrez brief, savez quoy?
        Que vous ayez mon fait a cueur
        Pour mectre *a fin la grant doleur.*

362i: R41

R144   [Rondel] Responce de Orlians   [p. 363s]

        Pour mectre a fin vostre doleur
        Ou pour le present je vous voy,
        Descouvrez moy
        Tout vostre fait, car sur ma foy,
5   Je vous secourray de bon cueur.

        Plus avant offrir ne vous puis,
        Fors que je suis
        Prest de vous ayder a toute heure

        A vous bouter hors des ennuys
10   Que jours et nuys
        Dictes qu'avec vous font demeure.

I'd have as much of it as I want,
10   Filled as I am with eagerness
In regard to changing my desire.

Rondel by Fredet

To bring to an end the great pain
I suffer for loving too much,
Do come to my aid.
Alas! If not, upon my faith,
5   My life will not long continue,

For I'm terribly tormented
By so many miseries,
Which, never ceasing, attack me,

That I don't have good days, good nights
10   And cannot
Find anyone to help me, save you.

Help your servant,
Held tight by more than his finger.
Otherwise, I face death
15   Unless you soon show—do you know what?—
That you've taken my suit to heart
To bring to an end the great pain.

Rondel—Response of Orleans

To bring an end to your pain
That I see you now suffering,
Reveal to me everything
About your affair, for upon my faith
5   With a good heart I'll help you.

More than this I cannot offer,
Only that I am
Ready to assist you at every hour

To lift you out of the miseries
10   That day and night
You say lodge within.

Quant vous tenez mon serviteur,
Et vostre doleur apparçoy,
Monstrer au doy
15   On me devroit, se tenir quoy
Vouloye, comme faynt seigneur,
Pour mectre *a fin vostre doleur.*

363i: R42

R145   Rondel   [p. 364s]

Aprés l'escadre route,
Mectons a sacquement
Annuyeulx Pensement
Et sa brigade toute.

5   Il crye : «Volte route!
Ralïons nostre gent,
Aprés l'escadre *route.*»

Se Loyauté s'y boute,
Par advis saigement,
10   Crye gaillerdement :
«Da ly brusque sans doubte,
Aprés l'escadre *route.*»

364i: R43

R146   [Rondel]*   [p. 365s]

Se mois de may, ne joyeux ne dolent
Estre ne puis. Auffort, vaille que vaille,
C'est le meilleur que de riens ne me chaille,
Soit bien ou mal, tenir m'en fault content.

5   Je lesse tout courir a val le vent,
Sans regarder lequel bout devant aille,
Se mois de may, *ne joyeux ne dolent.*

Qui Soussy suyt, au derrain s'en repent.
C'est ung mestier qui ne vault une maille,
10   Avantureux comme le jeu de faille.
Que vous semble de mon gouvernement,
Se mois de may, *ne joyeux ne dolent?*

365i: R44

Since you consider yourself my servant
And I see your misery,
Someone should accuse me publicly
15   If I intended
Like some feeble lord to say nothing,
To bring an end to your pain.

Rondel

After the rout of the squadron,
Let us strip the booty
From annoying Thought
And all in his battalion.

5   He cries: "Back to the fight,
Let's rally our forces,
After the rout of the squadron."

If Faithfulness gets involved,
In wise fashion,
10   Shout out fiercely,
"Without fail strike that man a sharp blow,
After the rout of the squadron."

Rondel

This month of May, neither joyful nor sorrowing
Can I manage. In the end, one way
Or the other, it's best I don't care at all.
Whether things go well or badly, I must find contentment.

5   I let everything run with the wind,
Not looking which way it goes,
This month of May, neither joyful nor sorrowing.

Whoever follows Care repents in the end.
Such business isn't worth a penny,
10   Hazardous as a game of "loser pays."
What do you think of how I'm doing
This month of May, neither joyful nor sorrowing?

R147   Rondel*   [p. 366s]

Pource que Plaisance est morte,
Ce may, suis vestu de noir,
C'est grant pitié de veoir
Mon cueur qui s'en desconforte.

5   Je m'abille de la sorte
Que doy pour faire devoir,
Pource *que Plaisance est morte.*

Le temps cez nouvelles porte,
Qui ne veult deduit avoir,
10   Mais par force de plouvoir
Fait dez champs clorre la porte,
Pource *que Plaisance est morte.*

366i: R45

R148   [Rondel]   [p. 367s]

A Dieu! qu'il m'anuye,
Helas! qu'esse cy?
Demourray je ainsi
En merencolie?

5   Qui que chante ou rie,
J'ay tous jours soussi.
A Dieu! *qu'il m'anuye!*

Penser me guerrie,
Et Fortune aussi,
10   Tellement et si
Fort que hé ma vie.
A Dieu! *qu'il m'anuye!*

367i: R46

R149   Rondel   [p. 368s]

Ci pris, ci mis,
Trop fort me lie
Merencolie
De pis en pis.

Rondel

Since Pleasure is dead,
I'm dressed this May in black.
It's a great pity to see my heart,
Which is so desolated thereby.

5   I'm dressed in the manner
I should be to do my duty,
Since Pleasure is dead.

The season brings this news,
That it wishes no good sport,
10   But rather through mighty rain
Shuts the gateway to the fields,
Since Pleasure is dead.

Rondel

Oh God! How this troubles me!
Alas! What is this about?
Will I linger in such a state,
Full of melancholy?

5   No matter who sings or weeps,
I'm every day filled with cares.
Oh God! How this troubles me!

Thought makes war on me,
And Fortune as well,
10   In such a fashion and
So fiercely that I hate my life.
Oh God! How this troubles me!

Rondel

Taken here, put here,
Melancholy presses
Me fiercely,
Worse and worse.

5   Quant me tient pris
       En sa baillie,
       Ci pris, *ci mis,*

       Se hors Soussis
       Je ne m'alie
10   A Chiere Lie,
       Vivant languis,
       Ci pris, *ci mis.*

368i: R47

R150   **[Rondel]**   [p. 369s]

       Et de cela, quoy?
       Se Soussi m'assault,
       A mon cueur n'en chault,
       N'aussi peu a moy.

5   Comme j'aperçoy,
       Courrous riens n'y vault.
       Et de *cela, quoy?*

       Par luy je reçoy
       Souvent froid et chault,
10   Puis qu'estre ainsi fault,
       Remede n'y voy.
       Et de *cela, quoy?*

369i: R48

R151   **[Rondel]**   [p. 370s]

       Et de cela, quoy?
       En ce temps nouveau,
       Soit ou laid, ou beau,
       Il m'en chault bien poy.

5   Je demourray quoy
       En ma vielle peau.
       Et de *cela, quoy?*

       Plusieurs, comme voy,
       Ont des pois au veau.*
10   Je mettray mon seau

5   When she holds me prisoner
In her domain,
Taken here, put here.

If, beyond Care,
I make no alliance
10   With Pleasant Demeanor,
I languish then, still alive,
Taken here, put here.

Rondel

And so what?
If Care assaults me,
It matters not to my heart,
Nor to me either.

5   As I see,
Anger avails not at all.
And so what?

By him I often
Am made to feel hot and cold;
10   Since it cannot be otherwise,
I see no remedy.
And so what?

Rondel

And so what?
In this new season,
Whether it's ugly or pleasant,
It matters very little to me.

5   I'll remain at peace
In my old skin.
And so what?

Many, as I see,
Have the strength for lovemaking.
10   I'll put my seal thereupon,

Qu'ainsi je le croy.
Et de *cela, quoy?*

370i: R49

R152   Rondel   [p. 371s]

Le trouveray je ja mais
Un loyal cueur joint au mien,
A qui je soye tout sien
Sans departir desormais?

5   D'en deviser par souhais,
Souvent m'y esbas et bien.
Le *trouveray je ja mais?*

Autant vault se je m'en tais,
Car certainement je tien
10 Qu'il ne s'en fera ja rien.
En toute chose a un mais.
Le trouveray *je ja mais?*

371i: R50

R153   [Rondel]   [p. 372s]

Il me pleust bien*
—Se tour il a—
Quan me moustra
Que estoit tout mien.

5   Par son maintien
Tost me gaigna :
Il me *pleust bien.*

Sens dire rien,
Mon cueur pensa
10 Et ordonna
Qu'il seroit sien;
Il me pleust *bien.*

372i: R51

For I believe it's so.
And so what?

Rondel

Will I ever find it,
A faithful heart joined to mine,
Whose I might be completely,
Never to depart?

5   Conjuring this up as a wish
I often find pleasant and good sport.
Will I ever find it?

It's all the same if I keep silent,
For I'm certain
10   This will never come to anything.
Everything has its "but."
Will I ever find it?

Rondel

He pleased me well
—If this is a trick—
When he showed me
He was all mine.

5   Through his bearing
He won me over quickly:
He pleased me well.

Without saying a word
My heart deliberated
10   And determined
That it would be his;
He pleased me well.

R154   **Rondel**   [p. 373s]

    En mon cueur cheoit,
    Et la devinoye,
    Comme je pensoye
    Qu'ainsi avendroit.

5   Fol, tant qu'il reçoit,
    Ne croit rien qu'il voye.
    En mon *cueur cheoit,*

    Sotye seroit
    Se plus y musoye.
10   Ma teste romperoye.
    Soit ou tort ou droit,
    En mon *cueur cheoit.*

373i: R52

R155   **[Rondel]**   [p. 374s]

    Le monde est ennuyé de moy,
    Et moy pareillement de lui.
    Je ne congnois riens au jourd'uy
    Dont il me chaille que bien poy.

5   Dont quanque devant mes yeulx voy
    Puis nommer anuy sur anuy.
    Le monde *est ennuyé de moy.*

    Cherement se vent bonne foy,
    A bon marché n'en a nulluy,
10   Et pource, se je suis cellui
    Qui m'en plains, j'ay raison pour quoy :
    Le monde *est ennuyé de moy.*

374i: R53

R156   **Rondel**   [p. 375s]

    Vous y fiez vous*
    En Mondain Espoir?
    S'il scet decevoir,
    Demandez a tous.

Rondel

Into my heart she fell,
And I realized as much
Just at the moment I thought
This is what would happen.

5   A fool, though given much,
Believes nothing he sees.
Into my heart she fell.

It would be foolish
If I mused further on it.
10   I'd split open my head.
Whether wrong or right,
Into my heart she fell.

Rondel

The world is tired of me,
And I'm tired of it.
Today there's nothing I know
That I care more than a little about.

5   And so whatever my eyes see,
I rehearse one worry after another.
The world is tired of me.

Good faith sells at a high price,
No one gets it cheap,
10   And so if I'm the one
Who complains, I've good reason why:
The world is tired of me.

Rondel

Do you put your trust there
In Worldly Hope?
Is he able to deceive?
Ask everyone.

5   Son atrait est doulx
       Pour gens mieulx avoir.
       Vous *y fiez vous?*

       De joye ou courroux,
       Soing ou Nonchaloir,
10   Veult, a son vouloir,
       Tenir les deux boux :
       Vous *y fiez vous?*

375i: R54

R157   [Rondel]   [p. 376s]

       Vengence de mes yeulx
       Puisse mon cueur avoir.
       Ilz lui font recevoir
       Trop de maulx en mains lieux.
5   Amours, le roy des dieulx,
       Faictes vostre devoir :
       Vengence *de mes yeulx!*

       Se jamais plus sont tieulx
       Encontre mon vouloir,
10   Sur eulx et main et soir
       Crieray jusques aux cieulx :
       Vengence *de mes yeulx!*

376i: R55

R158   Rondel   [p. 377s]

       Espoir ne me fist oncques bien,
       Souvent me ment pour me complaire
       Et assez promet sans rien faire,
       Dont a lui peu tenu me tien.

5   En ses dis ne me fie en rien.
       Se Dieu m'aist, je ne m'en puis taire.
       Espoir ne *me fist oncques bien.*

       Quant Confort requerir lui vien
       Et cuide qu'il le doye faire,
10   Tousjours me respont au contraire,

5   His bearing is pleasant,
       The better to trap people.
       Do you put your trust there?

       Whether with joy or anger,
       Care or Indifference,
10   He wishes, according to his whim,
       To be the master of all:
       Do you put your trust there?

Rondel

       Vengeance on my eyes,
       May my heart be able to manage that.
       They made it suffer
       A multitude of ills in many a place.
5   Love, the king of sorrows,
       Do your duty here:
       Vengeance on my eyes!

       If henceforth there are those
       Who oppose my desire,
10   I'll raise a cry against them
       To the heavens day and night:
       Vengeance on my eyes!

Rondel

       Hope never did me any good,
       Often telling lies to please me.
       And promising much while doing nothing,
       So I think I owe him very little.

5   I trust to nothing he says.
       So God help me, I can keep silent no longer.
       Hope never did me any good.

       When Comfort comes to beseech Hope,
       Believing it's what he should do,
10   Always Hope turns me down

Et me hare Reffus son chien.
Espoir ne *me fist oncques bien.*

377i: R56

R159   [Rondel]   [p. 378s]

C'est par vous seullement, Fïance,
Qu'ainsi je me treuve deceu,
Car, se par avant l'eusse sceu,
Bien y eusse mis pourveance.

5   Auffort, quant je suis en la dance,
Puis qu'il est trait, il sera beu.
C'est par vous *seullement, Fïance.*

Je doy bien haïr l'acointance
Du premier jour que vous ay veu,
10   Car prins m'avez au despourveu.
Nul n'est trahy qu'en esperance.
C'est par vous *seullement, Fïance.*

378i: R57

R160   Rondel   [p. 379s]

Par vous, Regard, sergent d'Amours,
Sont arrestez les povres cueurs,
Souvent en plaisirs et doulceurs,
Et maintesfoiz tout au rebours,

5   Devant les amoureuses cours,
Les officiers et gouverneurs,
Par vous, *Regard, sergent d'Amours,*
[*Sont arrestez les povres cueurs,*]*

Et adjournez a trop briefz jours,
Pour leur porter plus de rigueurs,
10   Comme subgietz et serviteurs,
Endurent mains estranges tours,
Par vous, *Regard, sergent d'Amours.*

379i: R58

And sets his dog Refusal on me.
Hope never did me any good.

Rondel

It's by you alone, Trust,
That I find myself deceived,
For, had I known of this,
I'd certainly have taken precautions.

5   In the end, because I'm in the dance,
Since the drink is poured, I'll down it.
It's by you alone, Trust.

I strongly resented making your acquaintance
Right from the first day I laid eyes upon you,
10   For you took me by surprise.
No one is betrayed except in hope.
It's by you alone, Trust.

Rondel

By you, Glance, officer of Love,
Poor hearts are put under arrest,
Often in conditions pleasant and sweet,
And many times in just the opposite,

5   Before courts of love,
The officials and rulers there,
By you, Glance, officer of Love,
[Poor hearts are put under arrest].

And summoned on very short notice
10   So they suffer more miseries,
As subjects and servants,
They endure many a strange twist and turn,
By you, Glance, officer of Love.

R161　　　　　　　[Rondel]　　　　　　　　　[p. 380s]

Payés selonc vostre desserte
Puissés vous estre, faulz trompeurs!
Au derrenier dez cabuseurs
Sera la malice deserte.

5　　D'entre deux meurez une verte*
　　Vous fault servir pour voz labeurs.
　　Payez *selonc vostre desserte.*

　　Vostre besongne est trop ouverte,
　　Ce n'est pas jeu d'entrejetteurs.
10　　Aux eschés s'estes bons joueurs,
　　Gardés l'eschec a descouverte :
　　Payez *selonc vostre desserte.*

380i: R59

R162　　　　　　　Rondel　　　　　　　　　　[p. 381s]

Mort de moy! vous y jouez vous
Avec Dame Merencolye?
Mon cueur, vous faictes grant folye!
C'est la nourrice de Courroux.

5　　Un baston qui point a deux boutz
　　Porte, dont elle s'escremye.
　　Mort de moy! *vous y jouez vous?*

　　Je tiens saiges toutes et tous
　　Qui eslongnent sa compagnie.
10　　Saint Jehan! je ne m'y mectray mye,
　　Que je m'y boutasse a quans coups,
　　Mort de moy! *vous y jouez vous?*

381i: R60

R163　　　　　　　[Rondel]　　　　　　　　　[p. 382s]

Allez, allez, vielle nourice
De Courroux et de Malle Vie,
Rassoutée mere Ancolye,
Vous n'avez que deul et malice.

Rondel

Paid according to your merits
May you be, you false deceivers!
In the end, cheats
Will reap the reward of their malice.

5   A green one for two that are ripe,
You must accept this for your labors,
Paid according to your merits.

Your carrying on is too much in the open,
It's no game for tricksters.
10   If you play well at chess,
You'll take care not to expose your king:
Paid according to your merits.

Rondel

The death of me! You make a game of this
With Lady Melancholy?
My heart, you perpetrate great folly!
She's the wet-nurse of Anger.

5   A stick sharpened at both ends
Is what she wields, using it as a sword.
The death of me! You make a game of this?

I consider wise all men and women
Who distance themselves from her company.
10   Saint John! I'll not mix with them,
For then I'd bring many blows down upon me.
The death of me! You make a game of this?

Rondel

Go on, go on, you old wet-nurse
Of Anger and Evil Life,
Demented mother Melancholy,
There's nothing to you but pain and malice.

5   Desormés plus n'aurez office
        Avec mon cueur, je vous regnye :
        Allez, alez, *vielle nourice!*

        Pour vous n'y a point lieu propice,
        Confort l'a prins, n'en doubtez mye,
10   Fuyez hors de la compaignie
        D'Espoir. Faiz nouvel ediffice :
        Allez, allez, *vielle nourice!*

382i: R61

R164   Rondel   [p. 383s]

        Vous ne tenez compte de moy,
        Beau sire, mais qui estez vous?
        Voulez vous estre seul seur tous
        Et qu'on vous laisse tenir quoy?

5   Merencolye suiz et doy,
        En tous faiz, tenir l'un des boutz.
        Vous ne tenez *compte de moy.*

        Si je vous pinsse par le doy,
        Ne me chault de vostre courroux,
10   On verra ce serez rescours
        De mes mains, par qui, et pourquoy.
        Vous ne tenez *compte de moy!*

383i: R62

R165   [Rondel]   [p. 384s]

        Ainsi que chassoye aux sangliers,
        Mon cueur chassoit aprés Dangiers
        En la forest de ma Pensee,
        Dont rencontra grant assemblee
5   Trespassans par divers sentiers.

        Deux ou trois saillirent premiers,
        Comme fors, orguilleux et fiers.
        N'estoit pas chose effroyee
        Ainsi *que chassoye aux sangliers?*

5   Henceforth you'll conduct no more business
With my heart—I refuse you:
Go on, go on, you old wet-nurse!

There's no proper place for you.
Comfort has taken it, do not doubt it.
10   Take flight from the company
Of Hope. Fashion some new edifice:
Go on, go on, you old wet-nurse!

Rondel

You take no account of me,
Fair sir, but who are you?
Do you wish to be alone, more than the rest,
And left in peace?

5   I am Melancholy and should,
In all things, be master of the game.
You take no account of me.

If I pinch your finger,
I don't care that you're annoyed,
10   We'll see if you will be delivered
From my hands, by whom and for what reason.
You take no account of me!

Rondel

While I was hunting boars,
My heart pursued Danger
In the forest of my Thought,
Where it met up with a great crowd
5   Making its way along various paths.

Two or three attacked at first,
In the manner of the proud, strong, and fierce.
Was this not a frightful thing
While I was hunting boars?

10   Lors mon cueur lascha sus levriers,
        Lesquelz sont nommez Desiriers.
        Puis Esperance, l'asseuree,
        L'espieu au poing, sainte l'espee,
        Vint pour combatre voulentiers,
15   Ainsi *que chassoye aux sangliers.*

384i: R63

R166   Rondel   [p. 385s]

        Mort de moy! vous y jouez vous?
        —En quoy? —Es fais de tromperie.
        —Ce n'est que coustume jolie
        Dont un peu ont toutez et tous!

5   —Renversés sen dessus dessous,
        Est ce bien fait, je vous en prie?
        Mort de moy! *vous y jouez vous?*

        —Laissez moy taster vostre pous,
        Vous tient point celle maladie?
10   —Parlez bas, qu'on ne l'oye mie,
        Il samble que criés aus lous :
        Mort de moy! *vous y jouez vous?*

385i: R64

R167   Rondel   [p. 386s]

        M'apelez vous cela jeu
        D'estre tousjours en ennuy?
        Certes, je ne voy nulluy
        Qui n'en ait plus trop que peu.

5   Nul ne desnoue ce neu,
        S'il n'a de Fortune apuy.
        M'apelez vous *cela jeu?*

        On s'art qui est pres du feu,
        Et pource je suis celuy
10   Qui a mon povoir le fuy,
        Quant je n'y congnois mon preu.
        M'apelez vous *cela jeu?*

386i: R65

10   Then my heart unleashed its hounds,
       The ones that are named Desires.
       Afterward Hope, the confident one,
       Lance in his hand, girded with a sword,
       Came forward eagerly to fight,
15   While I was hunting boars.

Rondel

       The death of me! You make a game of this?
       —How so? —With deeds of trickery.
       —This is no more than a pleasant custom
       Upheld by all men and women to some degree.

5   —You turn everything upside down.
       Is this well done? This is what I ask you:
       The death of me! You make a game of this?

       —Let me examine your pulse,
       Does this illness affect you at all?
10   —Speak softly so no one hears,
       It seems you're crying wolf:
       The death of me! You make a game of this?

Rondel

       Are you telling me it's some game
       To always suffer anxiety?
       Surely, no one I see doesn't
       Suffer more than a little from it.

5   No one unties this knot
       Unless he has Fortune's help.
       Are you telling me it's some game?

       The one close to the fire gets burned,
       And this is why I'm the one
10   Who flees from it as fast as I can,
       Seeing no profit for me there.
       Are you telling me it's some game?

R168 Rondel [p. 387s]

Aussi bien laides que belles
Contreffont les dangereuses,
Et souvent les precieuses,
Il ont les manieres telles.

5   Pareillement les pucelles
Deviennent tantost honteuses,
Aussi bien *laides que belles.*

Les veilles font les nouvelles
En paroles gracïeuses
10   Et actointanses joyeuses.
C'est la condicïon d'elles,
Aussi bien *laides que belles.*

387i: R66

R169 Rondel* [p. 388s]

Qui a toutes ses hontes beues,
Il ne lui chault que l'en lui die,
Il laisse passer mocquerie
Devant ses yeulx, comme les nues.

5   S'on le hue par my les rues,
La teste hoche a chiere lie.
Qui a toutes *ses hontes beues,*

Truffes sont vers lui bien venues.
Quant gens rient, il fault qu'il rie.
10   Rougir on ne le feroit mie.
Contenances n'a point perdues,
Qui a toutes *ses hontes beues.*

388i: R67

R170 Rondel [p. 389s]

Repaïssez vous en parler gracïeux
Avec dames qui menguent poisson,
Vous qui jeusnez par grant devocïon :
Ce venredi ne povez faire mieux.

Rondel

The ugly as much as the fair of womankind
Make a show that they're disdainful
And often that they're very worthy.
This is how they carry on.

5   Similarly maidens
Become cautious at once of being shamed,
The ugly as much as the fair of womankind.

Old women tell their news
With words of kindness
10   And joyful greetings.
That's their condition,
The ugly as much as the fair of womankind.

Rondel

Whoever has drunk down all his shame,
Does not care what's said to him;
He lets mockery go right by,
Before his eyes, just like a passing cloud.

5   If shouted at on the street,
He shakes his head with a merry grin,
Whoever has drunk down all his shame.

Mocking jests he finds welcome.
When people laugh, he's forced to giggle.
10   No one can make him blush.
In no way has he lost face,
Whoever has drunk down all his shame.

Rondel

Feast on gracious speech
Among ladies who are eating fish,
You who fast with great devotion.
On this Friday you can do no better.

5   Se vous voulez de deesses ou dieux
      Avoir confort ou consolacïon,
      Repaïssez vous *en parler gracïeux.*

      Lire vous voy fais merencolïeux
      De Troïlus, plains de compassïon.
10   D'Amour martir fu en sa nascïon :
      Laissez l'en paix, il n'en est plus de tieux!
      Repaïssez vous *en parler gracïeux.*

389i: R68

R171   Rondel   [p. 390s]

      Hau! guette, mon euil! —Et puis quoy?
      —Voyez vous riens? —Ouyl, assés.
      —Qu'est ce? —Cela que vous savés.
      Cler le vous puis moustrer au doy.

5   —Regardez plus avant un poy,
      Vos regars ne soyent lassés.
      Hau! guette, *mon euil! —Et puis quoy?*

      Acquitté me suis, comme doy,
      Il a ja plusieurs ans passés,
10   Sans avoir mez gagez cassés.
      —Bien avez servi, sur ma foy.
      Hau! guette, *mon euil! —Et puis quoy?*

390i: R69

R172   Rondel   [p. 391s]

      Que nous en faisons*
      De telles manieres
      Et doulces et fieres
      Selon les saisons !

5   En champs ou maisons
      Par bois et rivieres,
      Que nous *en faisons!*

      Ung temps nous taisons,
      Tenans assez chieres
10   Noz joyeuses chieres,

5   If you wish to obtain consolation
From either goddesses or gods,
Feast on gracious speech.

I see you reading about the melancholy deeds
Of Troilus, and you're filled with compassion.
10   Among his nation he was a martyr to Love.
Leave him in peace, there are no more like him!
Feast on gracious speech.

Rondel

Ha, take notice, my eye! —And then what?
—Do you see anything? —Indeed, quite a bit.
—What is it? —What you know.
I can clearly point it out.

5   —Look again a little further on,
May your gazing not grow tired.
Ha, take notice, my eye! —And then what?

I acquitted myself as I should,
Many years have passed since then,
10   And my pledges were not declared null.
—You've served well, upon my faith.
Ha, take notice, my eye! —And then what?

Rondel

What fun we have
With such goings-on,
Both quiet and active,
According to the seasons!

5   In fields or houses,
Woods and rivers,
What fun we have!

Quiet for a time,
Staying happy,
10   Our faces joyful,

Puis nous rapaisons.
Que nous *en faisons!*

391i: R70

R173   Rondel · Clermondois*   [p. 393s]

Qui veulst acheter de mon dueil?
D'en avoir trop, las! je me vante,
Car ma povre vie doulante
N'en peut plus, non fait pas mon vueil.

5   Partout ou je vois, mon requeil
Est si piteus, et mon atante!
[*Qui veulst acheter de mon dueil?*]

Que j'aye ung petit bon aqueil
Au commancement de ma vante,
10   Et puis aprés, se jamais hante
Amours, c'on me cresve ce hueil!
Qui veulst *acheter de mon dueil?*

393i: R72

R174   Rondel   [p. 392s]

Vendez autre part vostre dueil,
Quant est a moy, je n'en ay cure.
A grant marché, oultre mesure,
J'en ay assez contre mon vueil.

5   Ja n'entrera dedens le sueil
De mon penser, je le vous jure.
Vendez *autre part vostre dueil.*

Desconforté, la lerme a l'ueil,
Ailleurs quiere son avanture,
10   Plus ne vous mene vie dure.
Puis que mal vous fait son acueil,
Vendez *autre part vostre dueil!*

392i: R71

Then we take a rest.
What fun we have!

Rondel — Clermondois

Who wants to buy some of my sorrow?
Having too much, alas, that's my boast,
For my poor life full of pain
Can last no longer, and neither can my will.

5   Everywhere I go, my reception
Is pitiful, so too are my expectations!
Who wants to buy some of my sorrow?

What a barely decent welcome I received
At the outset of my sale,
10   So then afterward, if I ever become a familiar of
Love, may someone poke out my eye!
Who wants to buy some of my sorrow?

Rondel

Sell your sorrow somewhere else —
For my part, I don't want it.
I've acquired plenty, a huge amount,
And cheaply too, never eager for it.

5   Never will it pass beyond the threshold
Of my mind, I swear to you.
Sell your sorrow somewhere else.

Disconsolate, tears in its eyes,
Let it seek its fortune elsewhere,
10   May it no longer make your life difficult.
Since her welcome distresses you,
Sell your sorrow somewhere else!

R175   Rondel   [p. 395s]

Mais que vostre cuer soit mien,
Ne doit le mien estre vostre?
—Ouïl, certes, plus que sien.

—Que vous semble? diz je bien?
5   —Vray comme la Patenostre,
Mais que *vostre cuer soit mien.*

Content et joyeux m'en tien,
Foy que doy saint Pol l'apostre,
Je ne desire autre rien,
10   Mais que *vostre cuer soit mien.*

395i: R74

R176   Rondel   [p. 396s]

Pour Dieu! boutons la hors,
Ceste Merencolie
Qui si fort nous guerrie
Et fait tant de grans tors.

5   Monstrons nous les plus fors,
Mon cuer, je vous en prie.
Pour Dieu! *boutons la hors!*

Trop lui avons amors
D'estre en sa compagnie,
10   Ne nous amusons mie
A croire ses rappors,
Pour Dieu! *boutons la hors.*

396i: R75

R177   Rondel   [p. 397s]

Aquitez vostre conscience
Et gardez aussi vostre honneur,
Ne laissez mourir en douleur
Ce qui avoir vostre aide pense.

5   Puis que avez le povoir en ce
De l'ayder par grace et doulceur,
Aquictez *vostre conscience.*

Rondel

Provided your heart is mine,
Shouldn't mine then belong to you?
—Yes, indeed, more than to itself.

  —What do you think? Do I speak well?
5   —As true as the Our Father,
Provided your heart is mine.

It makes me happy and content,
By the faith I owe Saint Paul the Apostle,
I desire nothing else,
10   Provided your heart is mine.

Rondel

For God's sake, toss her out,
This Melancholy
That wars upon us so fiercely
And does so many terrible wrongs.

5   Let us show ourselves at our bravest,
My heart, this I beg of you.
For God's sake, toss her out!

We show ourselves too pleased
To remain in her company,
10   So let's not waste our time
Crediting her reports,
For God's sake, toss her out!

Rondel

Assuage your conscience
And protect your honor,
Do not allow to die in pain
The man who thinks to have your help.

5   Since yours is the power in this matter
To aid him in your grace and kindness,
Assuage your conscience.

On criera sur vous vengence,
Se souffrez murdrir en rigueur
10   Ainsi a tort ung povre cueur.
Assez porte pascïence :
Aquictez *vostre conscience.*

397i: R76

R178   Rondel   [p. 398s]

Le trucheman de ma pensee
Qui est venu devers mon cueur,
De par Reconfort, son seigneur,
Lui a une lectre aportee.

5   Puis a sa creance contee
En langaige plain de doulceur,
Le trucheman *de ma pensee.*

Responce ne lui est donnee
Pour le present, c'est le meilleur.
10   Il aura, par conseil greigneur,
Son ambassade despeschee,
Le trucheman *de ma pensee.*

398i: R77

R179   Rondel   [p. 399s]

Le trucheman de ma pensee,
Qui parle maint divers langaige,
M'a rapporté chose sauvaige
Que je n'ay point acoustumee.

5   En françoys la m'a translatee,
Comme tressouffisant et saige,
Le trucheman *de ma pensee.*

Quant mon cueur l'a bien escoutee,
Il lui a dit : Vous faittes raige,
10   Oncques mais n'ouÿ tel messaige.
Venez vous d'estrange contree,
Le trucheman *de ma pensee?*

399i: R78

Vengeance will be cried against you,
If you allow a poor heart
10   To be murdered by your harshness.
He's already endured enough:
Assuage your conscience.

Rondel

The interpreter of my thought,
Who has come before my heart,
On behalf of Reconciliation, his lord,
Has brought a letter.

5   Then he read out his credentials
With words full of kindness,
The interpreter of my thought.

No answer was given him
For the present, that's for the best.
10   By a more important council,
He'll be dispatched on his mission,
The interpreter of my thought.

Rondel

The interpreter of my thought,
Who speaks many a language,
Has reported something wild to me
I am not accustomed to receive.

5   He translated it into French for me,
Like someone very competent and wise,
The interpreter of my thought.

After my heart heard him well out,
He told him: "You've lost your mind.
10   Never have I heard such a message.
Do you come from some strange land,
The interpreter of my thought?"

R180   Rondel   [p. 400s]

Comme le subgiet de Fortune
Que j'ay esté en ma jennesse,
Encores le suis en viellesse.
Vers moy la treuve tousjours une.

5   Je suis ung de seulx soubz la lune
Qu'elle plus a son vouloir dresse,
Comme le *subgiet de Fortune.*

Ce ne m'est que chose commune,
Obeir fault a ma maistresse.
10   Sans machier, soit joye ou tristesse,
Avaler me fault ceste prune,*
Comme le *subgiet de Fortune.*

400i: R79

R181   Rondel du Conte de Clermont*   [p. 401s]

Le trucheman de ma pensee,
Qui de long temps est commancee,
Va devers vous pour exposer
Ce que de bouche proposer
5   N'oze, craingnant d'estre tancee.

Combien que chose n'a pensee,
Dont deust estre desavancee,
Comme au long vous pourra gloser
Le trucheman *de ma pensee.*

10   Si soit par vous recompensee
Et selon son cas avancee,
Pour mieulx se povoir disposer,
Car plus ne pourra reposer,
Jusques sa joye ait prononcee
15   Le trucheman *de ma pensee.*

401i: R80

R182   Rondel du Conte de Clermont*   [p. 402s]

De bien ou mal, le bien faire l'emporte,
N'est il pas vray, ainsi que dist chascun?
Elas, ouÿ, car je n'en voy pas ung
Qui a la fin d'un jeu ne se depporte.

Rondel

Like the subject of Fortune,
Which once I was in youth,
I am still in old age.
She's the same to me—this I find.

5   I'm one of those few under the moon
Whom she directs according to her will,
Like the subject of Fortune.

It's a common enough rule
That I must obey my mistress.
10   Without chewing it, in joy or misery,
This is an annoyance I must swallow,
Like the subject of Fortune.

Rondel of the count of Clermont

The interpreter of my thought
Is he who has long assumed the task
Of going to you and reporting
What I dare not utter with
5   My own mouth, fearing a scolding,

Though he has no idea or thought
For which he should be blamed,
As he can tell you at length,
The interpreter of my thought,

10   So let it be that you reward
And, as he deserves, advance him,
So that he can better acquit himself,
For he will not be able to rest
Until his joy has been pronounced,
15   The interpreter of my thought.

Rondel of the count of Clermont

Of good and evil, doing good carries the day,
Is that not true, as every man avers?
Alas, indeed, but I see no one at all
Who does not abstain at the end of the game.

5   Je vous diray, quant la personne est morte
         Et a bien fait : il n'a esté commun.
         De bien ou mal, *le bien faire l'emporte.*

         Faisons le donc, nous trouverons la porte
         De Paradis ou il n'entre nesung,
10   Que peu ne soit, s'il n'est trop importun
         De prier Dieu, et a vous m'en rapporte.
         De bien ou mal, *le bien faire l'emporte.*

402i: R81

R183   Rondel par le duc d'Orlians   [p. 403s]

         Quant oyez prescher le renart,
         Pensez de voz oyes garder
         Sans a son parler regarder,
         Car souvent scet servir de l'art,

5   Contrefaisant le papelart,
         Qui scet ses parolles farder,
         Quant oyez *prescher le renart.*

         Lez faiz de Dieu je metz a part
         Ne je ne les vueil retarder,
10   Ne contre le monde darder.
         Chascun garde son estandart,
         Quant oyez *prescher le renart.*

403i: R82

R184   Rondel par Maistre   [p. 404s]
                  Jehan Cailleau*

         Las! le fault il? esse ton vueil,
         Fortune, dont me plains et dueil,
         Que tout mon temps en douleur passe?
         Seuffre que j'aye quelque espasse
5   De repos, entre tant de dueil.

         N'aray je de toy autre accueil
         Fors desdaing, reprouche et orgueil?
         Veulx tu qu'en ce point je trespasse?
         Las! le fault il? *esse ton vueil?*

5   I tell you, when the person is dead
And has done good, it's no ordinary thing.
Of good and evil, doing good carries the day.

Let's do so then, and we'll find the gate
Of Paradise where no one enters,
10   However lowly, unless he's not been too irritated
By offering prayers to God, and this is what I say:
Of good and evil, doing good carries the day.

Rondel by the duke of Orleans

When you hear the fox sermonize,
Be sure to protect your geese
And pay no mind to his talk,
For he often is given to trickery,

5   Pretending to be a religious fanatic
Who can dissemble with his speech,
When you hear the fox sermonize.

I put to one side the affairs of God,
And my wish is neither to disregard
10   Nor use them as a weapon against the world.
Let every man protect his own flag,
When you hear the fox sermonize.

Rondel by Master
Jehan Cailleau

Alas! Is this necessary? Is it your wish,
Fortune, you who make me sorrow and moan,
That I spend all my days in misery?
Permit me some time to rest
5   In the midst of so much unhappiness.

Will I not have from you some greeting
Other than disdain, reproach, and arrogance?
Do you wish me to die in such a state?
Alas! Is this necessary? Is it your wish?

10   Je ris de bouche et pleure d'ueil
       Et foys et dy ce que ne vueil.
       Ainsi ma vie se compasse,
       Maleureuse, chetifve et lasse,
       En paine et maulx dont trop recueil.
15   Las! le fault il? *esse ton vueil?*

404i: R83

R185   Rondel par le duc d'Orlians   [p. 405s]

       Las! le fault il? esse ton vueil,
       Fortune, qu'aye douleur mainte?
       De l'ueil me soubzris, mais c'est fainte
       Et soubz decepte, doulx accueil.

5   Ay je tort, quant reçoy tel dueil,
       S'ainsy je dy en ma complainte :
       Las! le fault il? *esse ton vueil?*

       Tue moy, puis en mon sercueil
       Me boute, c'est chose contrainte.
10   Lors n'y aura Dieu saint ne sainte,
       Qui n'apparçoive ton orgueil.
       Las! le faut il? *esse ton vueil?*

405i: R84

R186   Rondel   [p. 406s]

       Ne fais je bien ma besoingne?
       Quant mon fait cuide avancer,
       Je suis a recommancer
       Et ne sçay commant m'esloingne.

5   Fortune tousjours me groingne
       Et ne fait riens que tanser.
       Ne fais je bien *ma besoingne?*

       Certes tant je la ressoingne,
       Car mon temps fait despenser
10   Trop en ennuyeux penser,
       Dont en roingeant mon frein, froingne.
       Ne fais je bien *ma besoingne?*

406i: R85

10 My mouth smiles and my eyes weep,
And I do and say what I don't intend.
And so my life finds its form,
Ill-fortuned, wretched and miserable,
In the pain and suffering I endure too long.
15 Alas! Is this necessary? Is it your wish?

Rondel by the duke of Orleans

Alas! Is this necessary? Is it your wish,
Fortune, that I suffer great pain?
Your eyes smile, but it's a sham
And deceit hides within a sweet welcome.

5 Am I wrong, when I receive such pain,
If I say the following in my complaint:
Alas! Is this necessary? Is it your wish?

Kill me, then put me in
My coffin, this is what has to be.
10 Then God will have no saints, men
And women alike, who won't see your arrogance.
Alas! Is this necessary? Is it your wish?

Rondel

Do I not do my duty well?
When I think I'm advancing my suit,
I find myself beginning again
And do not know how to get away from it.

5 Fortune always smirks at me
And does nothing but scold.
Do I not do my duty well?

Surely I resent her so much,
For she makes me spend too much
10 Of my time in unpleasant thought,
And so I scowl, champing at the bit.
Do I not do my duty well?

R187   Rondel   [p. 407s]

Je ne hanis pour autre avaine*
Que de m'en retourner a Blois.
Trouvé me suis, pour une fois,
Assez longuement en Touraine.

5   J'ay galé a largesse plaine
Mes grans poissons et vins des Grois.*
Je ne hanis *pour autre avaine.*

A la court plus ne prendray paine
Pour generaulx et Millenois.*
10   Confesser a present m'en vois
Contre la peneuse sepmaine,
Je ne hanis *pour autre avaine.*

407i: R86

R188   Rondel   [p. 408s]

Que pensé je? dictes le moy,
Adevinez, je vous en prye,
Autrement ne le saurez mye,
Il y a bien raison pourquoy.

5   A parler a la bonne foy,
Je vous en foiz juge et partye.
Que pensé je? *dictes le moy.*

Vous ne saurez, comme je croy,
Car heure ne suiz ne demye
10   Qu'en diverse merencolye.
Devisez, je me tairay quoy.
Que pensé je? *dictes le moy!*

408i: R87

R189   Rondel   [p. 409s]

Plaindre ne s'en doit Leal Cueur,
S'Amours a servy longuement,
Recevant des biens largement
Et pareillement de douleur.

Rondel

I whinny for no other oats
Than to make my return to Blois.
This time I've found myself
Rather a long time in Touraine.

5   I've regaled myself very generously
With huge fish and the wines of Grois.
I whinny for no other oats.

At the court I'll no longer suffer pain
Because of tax collectors and men from Milan.
10   Right now I'm going to confess myself
In expectation of Holy Week,
I whinny for no other oats.

Rondel

What am I thinking? Tell me,
Have a guess—go on.
Otherwise you won't know.
There's a good reason why.

5   About speaking in good faith,
I appoint you judge and interested party.
What am I thinking? Tell me.

You do not know this, I believe,
But there's no hour or half
10   I do not suffer terrible melancholy.
Speak your mind, I'll keep quiet.
What am I thinking? Tell me.

Rondel

Faithful Heart should not bemoan it
If he has long served Love,
Receiving a generous portion of benefits
And pain in the same measure.

5   N'est ce raison que le seigneur
       Ait tout a son commandement?
       Plaindre ne s'en doit *Leal Cueur.*

       Se plus a deservi Doulceur
       Que ne trouve a son jugement,
10   En gré prengne pour payement
       Mains de proufit et plus de honneur :
       Plaindre ne s'en doit *Leal Cueur.*

409i: R88

R190   Rondel   [p. 410s]

       En faictes vous doubte?
       Point ne le devez,
       Veu que vous savez
       Ma pensee toute.

5   Quant mon cueur s'i boute,
       Et vostre l'avez,
       En faictes *vous doubte?*

       Dangier nous escoute,
       Sus, tost achevez,
10   Ma foy recevez,
       Ja ne sera route.
       En faictes *vous doubte?*

410i: R89

R191   Rondel   [p. 411s]

       En faictes vous doubte
       Que vostre ne soye?
       Se Dieu me doint joye
       Au cueur, si suis toute.

5   Rien ne m'en deboute
       Pour chose que j'oye.
       En faictes *vous doubte?*

       Dangier et sa route
       S'en voisent leur voye,
10   Sans que plus les voye,

5　　Is it not just that the lord
　　　Should have everything at his command?
　　　Faithful Heart should not bemoan it.

　　　If he has deserved more sweetness
　　　Than she's received,
10　　In good grace let him take for payment
　　　Less profit and more honor:
　　　Faithful Heart should not bemoan it.

Rondel

　　　Are you in doubt about this?
　　　You should not be in the least,
　　　Seeing that you know
　　　All my thoughts.

5　　When my heart makes its way there
　　　And you possess it as your own,
　　　Are you in doubt about this?

　　　Danger overhears us,
　　　Get up, bring this to a quick end,
10　　Receive my homage,
　　　Never will it be violated.
　　　Are you in doubt about this?

Rondel

　　　Are you in doubt about this,
　　　That I am yours?
　　　May God grant my heart
　　　Joy, so I am completely.

5　　Nothing at all, not anything
　　　That I hear repels me.
　　　Are you in doubt about this?

　　　Danger and his company,
　　　Let them make their way hence,
10　　Never again to lay eyes upon me.

Tousjours il m'escoute.
En faictes *vous doubte?*

411i: R90

R192   Rondel   [p. 412s]

Avez vous dit? — laissez me dire —
Amans, qui devisez d'Amours :
«Saincte Marie! que de jours
J'ay despenduz en martire! »?

5   Vous mocquez vous? je vous voy rire,
Cuidez vous qu'il soit le rebours?
Avez vous dit? — *laissez me dire!*

Parler n'en puis que ne souppire.
Raconter vous y sçay cent tours
10   Qu'on y a, sans joyeux secours,
S'au vray m'en voulez ouÿr lire,
Avez vous dit? — *laissez me dire!*

412i: R91

R193   Rondel de Nevers*   [p. 413s]

En la Forest de Longue Actente,
Mainte personne bien joyeuse
S'est trouvee moult doloreuse,
Triste, marrie et bien dolente.

5   D'y estre nul ne s'en talente,
La demeure est trop ennuyeuse
En la Forest *de Longue Actente.*

Chascun qui pourra s'en abscente,
Car l'entree en est perilleuse
10   Et l'issue fort dangereuse.
Pas de cent ung ne se contente
En la Forest *de Longue Actente.*

413i: R92

He's always listening out for me.
Are you in doubt about this?

Rondel

Have you spoken? —Let me say—
Lovers, you who speak of love:
"Blessed Mary! How many days
Have I spent in torment?"

5   Are you making fun? I see you laughing.
Do you think it might be the opposite?
Have you spoken? —Let me say!

I can only speak of this with a sigh.
I could tell you about a hundred tricks
10   That are involved in love, no joyous help there,
If you'll listen to me read the truth of the matter.
Have you spoken? —Let me say!

Rondel by Nevers

In the Forest of Long Awaiting,
Many a person of good cheer
Finds himself deeply saddened,
Miserable, disconsolate, and quite pained.

5   No man wants to remain in the place,
A sojourn is very distressing
In the Forest of Long Awaiting.

Every man who can absents himself,
For the way in is full of danger
10   And the way out very perilous.
Not one among a hundred is content
In the Forest of Long Awaiting.

R194   Rondel par Mgr*   [p. 414s]

En la Forest de Longue Actente,
Par vent de Fortune Dolente
Tant y voy abatu de bois
Que, sur ma foy, je n'y congnois
5   A present ne voye ne sente.

Pieça y pris joyeuse rente,
Jeunesse la payoit contente,
Or n'y ay qui vaille une nois
En la Forest *de Longue Actente.*

10   Vieillesse dit, qui me tourmente :
Pour toy n'y a pesson ne vente
Comme tu as eu autresfois.
Passez sont tes jours, ans et mois.
Souffize toy et te contente
15   En la Forest *de Longue Actente.*

414i: R93

R195   Rondel par Madame d'Orlians   [p. 415s]

En la Forest de Longue Actente
Entree suis en une sente,
Dont oster je ne puis mon cueur.
Pourquoy je viz en grant langueur
5   Par Fortune qui me tourmente.

Souvent Espoir chascun contente,
Excepté moy, povre dolente,
Qui nuyt et jour suis en doleur
En la Forest *de Longue Actente.*

10   Ay je donc tort se me garmente
Plus que nulle qui soit vivente?
Par Dieu, nennyl, veu mon maleur,
Car, ainsi m'aist mon Createur
Qu'il n'est paine que je ne sente
15   En la Forest *de Longue Actente.*

415i: R94

Rondel by my lord

In the Forest of Long Awaiting,
I see so many trees beaten down
By the wind of Sorrowful Fortune
That, upon my faith, at the moment
5   I see no path or road through the place.

Long ago the wages I received were pleasant.
Youth paid them in cash.
Now I haven't anything of value
In the Forest of Long Awaiting.

10   Old age, who tortures me, says this:
For you not a penny or pay-out
Like you once enjoyed.
Your time has done, the months and years.
Let that be enough and so content yourself
15   In the Forest of Long Awaiting.

Rondel by my lady of Orleans

In the Forest of Long Awaiting
I entered, following a path
From which I could not divert my heart.
And so I live on in great languor
5   Because of Fortune, who torments me.

Often Hope satisfies everyone,
Me excepted, poor and sorrowful me,
For night and day I suffer pain
In the Forest of Long Awaiting.

10   Am I wrong then to complain
More than any lady now living?
By God, not at all, considering my malady,
For, so help me my Creator,
There's no sort of pain I do not feel
15   In the Forest of Long Awaiting.

R196   Rondel · Fredet*   [p. 416s]

En la Forest de Longue Actente
Des brigans de Soussy bien trente
Helas! ont pris mon povre cueur,
Et Dieu scet se c'est grant orreur
5   De veoir commant on le tourmente.

Priant vostre ayde, lamente
Pource que chascun d'eulx se vente
Qu'ilz le merront a leur seigneur
En la Forest *de Longue Actente,*

10   Et pource, a vous il s'en garmente,
Car il voit bien qu'ilz ont entente
De lui faire tant de rigueur
Qu'il ne sera mal ne doleur,
Se n'y pourvoyez, qu'il ne sente
15   En la Forest *de Longue Actente.*

416i: R95

R197   Rondel · Orlians*   [p. 417s]

En la Forest de Longue Actente,
Forvoyé de joyeuse sente
Par la guide Dure Rigueur,
A esté robbé vostre cueur,
5   Comme j'entens, dont se lamente.

Par Dieu! j'en cognois plus de trente
Qui, chascun d'eulx, sans que s'en vente,
Est vestu de vostre couleur
En la Forest *de Longue Actente.*

10   Et en briefz motz, sans que vous mente,
Soiez seur que je me contente,
Pour allegier vostre doleur,
De traictier avec le seigneur
Qui les brigans soustient et hente
15   En la Forest *de Longue Actente.*

417i: R96

Rondel—Fredet

In the Forest of Long Awaiting
More than thirty brigands of Care's band,
Alas, have taken my poor heart prisoner,
And God knows it's a great horror
5   To see how tormented the heart is.

Begging for your aid, I lament
Because they all boast they'll bear away
The heart to their lord
In the Forest of Long Awaiting.

10   And here is why the heart complains to you:
He sees clearly that they're intent on
Making him suffer such harshness
That, should you not see to this,
There's no sort of ill or pain he will not feel
15   In the Forest of Long Awaiting.

Rondel—Orleans

In the Forest of Long Awaiting,
Turned away from the path of joy
By the guide Harsh Rigor,
Your heart has been abducted,
5   I understand, and this gives him cause to lament.

By God! I recognize more than thirty men there
Who, each and every one, hardly boasting,
Wearin your livery
In the Forest of Long Awaiting.

10   And, in short, I tell you no lies:
You may be sure I am happy
To assuage your suffering,
By treating with the lord
Who supports and is a friend to brigands
15   In the Forest of Long Awaiting.

R198   **Rondel**   [p. 418s]

Se vous voulez m'amour avoir
A tousjours mais sans departir,
Pensez de faire mon plaisir
Et jamais ne me decevoir.

5   Bien tost sauray apercevoir,
Au paraler, vostre desir,
Se vous voulez *m'amour avoir.*

Assez biens povez recevoir,
S'en vous ne tient. Sans y faillir,
10   Vous estez pres d'y avenir,
Faisant vers moy leal devoir,
Se vous voulez *m'amour avoir.*

418i: R97

R199   **Rondel · Fredet***   [p. 419s]

J'actens l'aumosne de Doulceur
Par l'aumosnier de Doulx Regart.
Espoir m'a promis de sa part
Qu'i me fera toute faveur.

5   En esperant que ma langueur
Cessera, qui tant mon cueur art,
J'actens *l'aumosne de Doulceur,*

Car comme leal serviteur,
J'ay servy tousjours main et tart.
10   Pensant qu'Amours aura regart
Quelquefoys a ma grant doleur,
J'actens *l'aumosne de Doulceur.*

419i: R98

R200   **Rondel**   [p. 420s]

Par l'aumosnier Plaisant Regart
Donnez l'aumosne de Doulceur
A ce povre malade cueur
Du feu d'Amours, dont Dieu nous gart.

Rondel

If you intend to gain my love,
Forever more never to depart,
Set about doing what pleases me
And never practice deception.

5   At last, I'll soon see
What you desire after all,
If you intend to gain my love.

You'll be able to receive good things aplenty,
And this depends only on you. Not failing,
10   You are close to getting what you want,
As you do your faithful duty to me,
If you intend to gain my love.

Rondel—Fredet

I await the alms of Sweetness
From the hands of Sweet Look, the almoner.
Hope has promised on his part
To show me every favor.

5   Hoping that my languor
Will cease, which so inflames my heart,
I await the alms of Sweetness.

For like a faithful servant,
I have always served, both morning and late,
10   Expecting that Love would show concern
Sometime for my terrible pain,
I await the alms of Sweetness.

Rondel

Through Pleasant Look, the almoner,
May you bestow the alms of Sweetness
Upon this poor heart afflicted
By the fire of Love, God save us from it.

5   Nuit et jour sans cesser il art.
         Secourez le pour vostre honneur
         Par l'ausmonier *Plaisant Regart.*

         S'il vous plaisoit de vostre part
         Prier Amours qu'en sa langueur
10   Pourvoyent a vostre faveur,
         Aydié sera plus tost que tart
         Par l'ausmonier *Plaisant Regart.*

420i: R99

R201   Rondel [?Fredet]*   [p. 421s]

         Ce n'est que chose acoustumee,
         Quant Soussy voy vers moy venir,
         Se tost ne lui venoye ouvrir,
         Il romproit l'uis de ma Pensee.

5   Lors fait d'escremie levee
         Et puis vient mon cueur assaillir.
         Ce n'est *que chose acoustumee.*

         Adonc prent d'espoir son espee,
         Mon cueur, pour dez coups soy couvrir
10   Et se deffendre et garentir.
         Ainsi je passe la journee.
         Ce n'est *que chose acoustumee.*

421i: R100

R202   Rondel   [p. 422s]

         Chascun devise a son propos.
         Quant a moy, je suis loing du mien,
         Mais mon cueur en espoir je tien
         Qu'il aura une fois repos.

5   Souvent dit, me tournant le dos :
         Je doubte que n'en sera rien.
         Chascun *devise a son propos.*

         Tenez l'uys de Pensee clos,
         Faitez ainsi pour vostre bien.

5   Night and day, never ceasing, it burns.
     Rescue it for the sake of your honor
     Through Pleasant Look, the almoner.

     If you were pleased for your part
     To beg Love that in its languor
10   The heart might be provided with your favor,
     Then soon rather than late it would find help
     Through Pleasant Look, the almoner.

Rondel — ?Fredet

     It's only an everyday occurrence
     When I see Care coming to visit me,
     If I didn't open up for him at once,
     He would break down the door of my Thought.

5   Then he strikes blows with his sword
     And afterward assaults my heart.
     It's only an everyday occurrence.

     Then my heart seizes his blade,
     Hoping to deflect these blows,
10   Defending and guarding himself.
     This is the way I pass the day.
     It's only an everyday occurrence.

Rondel

     Everyone speaks of his desire.
     As for me, I am far from mine,
     But I keep my heart in hope
     He'll find respite sometime.

5   Often he says, turning his back to me:
     "I fear there'll be nothing of the sort."
     Everyone speaks of his desire.

     Keep shut the door of Thought.
     Do so for your own good.

10   Soussi vous vouldroit avoir sien,
        Ne créés, n'escoutez sez mos.
        Chascun *devise a son propos.*

422i: R101

R203   Rondel   [p. 423s]

        Ennemy, je te conjure,
        Regard, qui aus gens cours sus.
        Viellars aux mentons chanus,
        Dont suis, n'avons de toy cure.

5   Jeune, navré de blesseure
        Fu par toy, n'y revien plus,
        Ennemy, *je te conjure.*

        Va querir ton avanture
        Sus amans nouveaulx venus.
10   Nous vieulz avons obtenus
        Saufconduitz de par Nature.
        Ennemy, *je te conjure!*

423i: R102

R204   Rondel   [p. 424s]

        Des amoureux de l'observance,*
        Dont j'ay esté ou temps passé,
        A present m'en treuve lassé
        Du tout, sy non de souvenance.

5   Ou je prens d'en parler plaisance,
        Quoy que suis de l'ordre cassé
        Des amoureux *de l'observance.*

        Souvent y ay porté penance
        Et sy pou de biens amassé
10   Que, quant je seray trespassé,
        A mes hoirs lairray peu chevance
        Des amoureux *de l'observance.*

424i: R103

10   Care would like to have you as his own,
         Do not believe, do not listen to his words.
         Everyone speaks of his desire.

Rondel

Enemy, I implore you,
You, Glance, who attack
Graybeards, of whom
I'm one, we take no interest in you.

5   When young I suffered a wound
      At your hands. Don't come back,
      Enemy, I implore you.

Go seek your fortune
Among lovers newly arrived.
10   We old men have obtained
      Safe-conduct passes from Nature.
      Enemy, I implore you.

Rondel

Of the Order of Love,
To which I once belonged,
I find myself now all wearied,
Except in my memory.

5   Yet I'm pleased to speak about love,
      Even though I'm dismissed from the ranks
      Of the Order of Love.

Often I there endured penance,
Amassing so few benefits
10   That, when I pass away,
      I'll leave my heirs but a small bequest
      Of the Order of Love.

R205   Rondel   [p. 425s]

Ostez vous de devant moy,
Beaulté, par vostre serment,
Car trop me temptez souvent.
Tort avez, tenez vous quoy.

5   Toutes les foys que vous voy
Je suis je ne sçay comment.
Ostez vous *de devant moy.*

Tant de plaisirs j'apparçoy
En vous, a mon jugement,
10   Qu'il troublent mon pensement.
Vous me grevez sur ma foy,
Ostez vous *de devant moy.*

425i: R104

R206   Rondel   [p. 426s]

Plaisant Regard, mussez vous,
Ne vous moustrez plus en place,
Mon cueur craint vostre menace,
Dont maintes fois l'ay rescous.

5   Vostre attrait, soubtil et douls,
Blesse sans qu'on lui mefface.
Plaisant *Regard, mussez vous!*

Se ditez : «Je fais a tous
Ainsi, car je m'y solace,»
10   A tort, sauve vostre grace,
Ne devez donner courrous.
Plaisant *Regard, mussez vous!*

426i: R105

R207   Rondel   [p. 427s]

Je ne vous voy pas a demy,
Tant ay mis en vous ma plaisance,
Tous jours m'estes en souvenance,
Puis le temps que premier vous vy.

Rondel

Remove yourself from my presence,
Beauty, in accord with your oath,
For you tempt me too often.
You're in the wrong, keep silent.

5   Every time I lay eyes upon you,
I don't know up from down.
Remove yourself from my presence.

Seeing you gives me so much
Pleasure, such is my view,
10   My thoughts become disturbed.
By my faith, you oppress me.
Remove yourself from my presence.

Rondel

Pleasant Look, hide yourself,
Show yourself no more,
My heart quakes at your threats,
I've rescued it many a time from them.

5   Your demeanor, subtle and sweet,
Deals a wound, though it's not been harmed.
Pleasant Look, hide yourself!

If you say: "This is what I do to one
And all, for it's there I take solace,"
10   Saving your grace, you should not
Wrongly make trouble.
Pleasant Look, hide yourself!

Rondel

I do not see you half enough,
So much does my pleasure depend on you,
You've been constantly on my mind
Since I first laid eyes upon you.

5   Assez ne puis estre esbahy
Dont vient si ardant desirance.
Je ne *vous voy pas a demy.*

Fin de compte, puisqu'est ainsy,
Fermons noz cueurs en alïance.
10   Quant plus ay de vous acointance,
Plus suis, ne sçay comment, ravy.
Je ne *vous voy pas a demy.*

427i: R106

R208   Rondel   [p. 428s]

Mon cueur, pour vous en garder
De mez yeulx qui tant vous temptent
Afin que devers vous n'entrent,
Faitez lez portes fermer.

5   S'il vous viennent raporter
Nouvellez, pensez qu'il mentent,
Mon cueur, *pour vous en garder.*

Mensongez scevent conter
Et trop de plaisir se vantent,
10   Folz sont qui en eulx s'atendent,
Ne les veuillez escouter,
Mon cuer, *pour vous en garder.*

428i: R107

R209   Rondel   [p. 429s]

Rendez compte, Viellesse
Du temps mal despendu
Et soctement perdu
Es mains Dame Jeunesse.

5   Trop vous court sus Foiblesse.
Qu'est Povair devenu?
Rendez compte, *Viellesse!*

Mon bras en l'arc se blesse
Quant je l'ay estandu,
10   Par quoy j'ay entendu
Qu'il couvient que jeu cesse.
Rendez compte, *Viellesse!*

5   My astonishment knows no bounds
About the source of such burning desire.
I do not see you half enough.

In the end, since things are thus,
Let's make allies of our hearts.
10   The more I know you,
The more I'm swept away—how, I know not.
I do not see you half enough.

Rondel

Heart of mine, so as to protect yourself
From my eyes, which sorely tempt you,
Close the gates against them
So they don't enter you.

5   If they come to bring you
Tidings, think them liars,
Heart of mine, so as to protect yourself.

They can tell lies
And boast too much of pleasure,
10   Those who take their part are fools,
Please do not listen to them,
Heart of mine, so as to protect yourself.

Rondel

Render an account, Old Age,
Of the time misspent
And foolishly wasted
In the hands of Lady Youth.

5   Feebleness attacks you fiercely.
What has become of strength?
Render an account, Old Age!

My arm hurts
When I draw the bow,
10   And this makes me understand
The game must come to an end.
Render an account, Old Age!

Tout vous est en destresse
Desormais chier vendu.
15   Rendez compte, *Viellesse!*

Des tresors de Lïesse
Vous sera peu rendu,
Riens qui vaille ung festu.
N'avez plus que Sagesse.
20   Rendez compte, *Viellesse!*

R429i: blank

R210   Rondel · du seigneur de Torsy*   [p. 430s]

Mais que mon mal si ne m'empire,
Je suis en bon point, Dieu mercy,
Ne n'ay ne douleur ne soucy
De chose que on me puisse dire.

5   Plus ne me plains, plus ne souspire,
Je mengue et dors bien aussi,
Mais *que mon mal si ne m'empire.*

Pleurer souloye en lieu de rire
En requerant grace et mercy.
10   Maintenant ne fais plus ainsi,
Car je ne crains point l'escondire,
Mais que mon *mal si ne m'empire.*

430i: R211

R211   Rondel du duc d'Orleans   [p. 430i]

Mais que mon propos ne m'enpire,
Il ne me chault des faiz d'Amours.
Voisent a droit, ou a rebours,
Certes je ne m'en fais que rire.

5   En ne peut de riens m'escondire,
Aide ne requiers ne secours,
Mais que *mon propos ne m'empire.*

Quant j'oy ung amant qui souspire,
A, ha! dis je, vela des tours
10   Dont usay en mes jennes jours.

Everything's painful for you,
Henceforth a high price you'll pay.
15   Render an account, Old Age!

From the treasure house of Happiness
Little will be paid you,
Nothing worth more than a straw.
You've nothing left but Wisdom.
20   Render an account, Old Age!

Rondel of the Lord of Torsy

Provided my illness does not worsen,
I'm in fine shape, thank God,
Nor am I pained or worried
By anything anyone might say.

5   I lament no more, no more do I sigh,
And, too, I eat and sleep very well,
Provided my illness does not worsen.

It was my wont to weep, not laugh,
Even as I begged grace and mercy.
10   Now I do nothing of the sort,
Not fearing refusal in the least,
Provided my illness does not worsen.

Rondel of the duke of Orleans

Provided my affair doesn't worsen,
The doings of Love are of no concern.
Let them advance or retreat,
Truly, I do nothing but laugh.

5   No one can refuse me,
I beg no help or assistance,
Provided my affair doesn't worsen.

When I hear a lover sigh,
Oh my, I say, that's what
10   I did in my younger days.

Plus n'en vueil, bien me doit souffire,
Mais que *mon propos ne m'empire.*

430s: R210

R212   Rondel du conte de Cleremont*   [p. 431s]

J'amasse ung tresor de regrés
Que ma tant amee m'envoie,
Mais jusqu'a ce que je la voye
Ne partiront de mes segrés.

5   La cause pourquoy je les celle,
Ses griefz maulx qui me font mourir?
C'est pour garder l'onneur de celle
Qui ne me daigne secourir.

Plus l'eslongne, plus d'elle est prés
10   Mon cuer, dont mon povre oeil lermoye.
Il n'est point douleur que la moye,
Car quant j'ay assez plaint, aprés
J'amasse ung tresor *de regrés.*

431i: R213

R213   [Rondel] Responce d'Orleans   [p. 431i]

C'est une dangereuse espergne
D'amasser tresor de regrés.
Qui de son cueur les tient trop prés
Il couvient que mal lui en preigne.

5   Veu qu'ilz sont si oultre l'enseigne,
Non pas assez nuysans, mais trés,
C'est une *dangereuse espergne.*

Se je mens, que l'en m'en repreigne.
Soient essaiez, puis aprés
10   On saura leurs tourmens segrés.
Qui ne m'en croira, si l'apreigne:
C'est une *dangereuse espergne.*

431s: R212

Not eager now for more of the same, I must make do,
Provided my affair doesn't worsen.

Rondel by the count of Cleremont

I amass a treasure trove of regrets
Sent me by the lady I love so much,
But until I lay eyes upon her
They shall remain secret.

5   The reason I keep them hidden,
These grievous ills that mean my death?
It's to keep safe the honor of the lady
Who does not deign to help me.

The more distant she is, the closer my heart
10   To her, and so my poor eyes weep.
There's no pain at all save my own,
For after I've lamented enough,
I amass a treasure trove of regrets.

Rondel — Response of Orleans

It's a perilous form of economy
To amass a treasure trove of regrets.
Whoever keeps them too near his heart
Will find they cause him distress.

5   Seeing that they are beyond what one can say,
Not somewhat harmful, but extremely so,
It's a perilous form of economy.

If I lie, let me be reproved.
Let them be put to the proof, then afterward
10   The torment they work in secret will be revealed.
Whoever does not believe me let him learn:
It's a perilous form of economy.

R214   Rondel a Fredet*   [p. 432s]

Le fer est chault, il le fault batre,*
Vostre fait que savez va bien.
Tout le saurez, sans celer rien,
Se venez vers moy vous esbatre.

5   Il a convenu fort combatre,
Mais, s'il vous plaist, parfait le tien.
Le fer est chault, *il le fault batre.*

Convoitise vouloit rabatre
Escharsement et trop du sien,
10   Mais ung peu j'ay aidié du mien
Qui l'a fait cesser de debatre.
Le fer est chault, *il le fault batre.*

432i: R215

R215   Rondel de Fredet*   [p. 432i]

Je regrette mez dolans jours
Comme cellui la qui tousjours
Ne fait que desirer sa mort,
Car plus vois avant et plus fort
5   Acroissent mez dures doulours.

Quant on me fait d'estranges tours,
Que mille fois le jour en plours
Me fault dire par desconfort :
Je regrette *mez dolans jours.*

10   En vous seul est tout mon recours,
Faitez dont plus tost que le cours
Cesser le mal que souffre a tort,
Ou autrement je me voy mort,
Et tout pour bien servir Amours.*
15   Je regrette *mez dolans jours.*

432s: R214

R216   [Rondel] Responce audit Fredet   [p. 433s]

Se regrettez voz dolens jours,
Et je regrette mon argent
Que j'ay delivré franchement,
Cuidant de vous donner secours.

Rondel to Fredet

The iron is hot, you must strike.
You know your affair goes well.
You'll learn all, nothing will stay secret
If you come and disport yourself with me.

5   A great struggle has been necessary,
Yet, if you please, hold on, it's at an end,
The iron is hot, you must strike.

Covetousness avariciously and excessively,
Wished to lower the price of what she owed,
10   But I added some of my own money to the pot,
Which made Covetousness stop her wrangling.
The iron is hot, you must strike.

Rondel of Fredet

I lament my days full of pain
Like someone who has never
Done anything but wish for death.
For the longer I live, the stronger
5   Grow the grievous pains I feel,

When terrible things are done to me,
So that, weeping, a thousand times a day
I must say, in my misery:
I lament my days full of pain.

10   All my recourse is to you alone.
With all haste now make sure
The pain I unjustly suffer ends,
Otherwise, I see myself dead,
And all for ably serving Love,
15   I lament my days full of pain.

Rondel—Answer to the said Fredet

If you lament your days filled with pain,
I for my part regret the money
I generously sent along,
Thinking to afford you help.

5   Se ne sont pas lez premiers tours
       Dont Convoitise sert souvent,
       Se regrettés *voz dolens jours.*

       Mais se vous n'avez voz amours,
       Puis que Convoitise vous ment,
10   Le mien recouvreray briefment,
       Ou mettray le fait en droit cours,
       Se regrettés *voz dolens jours.*

433i: R217

R217   Rondel a Daniel*   [p. 433i]

       Vous dictes que j'en ayme deulx,
       Mais vous parlez contre raison.
       Je n'ayme fors ung chapperon
       Et ung couvrechef; plus n'en veulx.

5   C'est assez pour ung amoureux.
       Mal me louez, ce faictes mon.
       Vous dictes *que j'en ayme deulx!*

       Certez je ne suis pas de ceulx
       Qui par tout veulent a foison
10   Eulx fournir en toute saison.
       N'en parlez plus, j'en suis honteux :
       Vous dictes que *j'en ayme deulx!*

433s: R216

R218   Rondel du Olivier de la Marche*   [p. 434s]

       Pour amours des dames de France
       Je suis entré en l'observance*
       Du tresrenommé saint François,
       Pour cuidier trouver une fois
5   La doulce voye d'alegence.

       Saint suis de corde de Souffrance
       Soubz haire d'Aigre Desirance,
       Plus qu'en mon Dieu ne me congnoiz,
       Pour amours *des dames de France.*

10   Soubrement vis de ma Plaisance
       Et june ce que Desir pense,

5   And these are not the first tricks
Covetousness has used,
If you lament your days filled with pain.

But if you do not possess your love
Because of the lies Covetousness tells,
10   I'll either shortly recover my money
Or set things on the right course,
If you lament your days filled with pain.

Rondel of Daniel

You say I'm in love with two,
But what you say is not right.
I love nothing but a hood and kerchief,
Nothing more do I wish.

5   That suffices a man in love.
You praise me badly, you do indeed.
You say I'm in love with two!

Indeed I'm not one of those
Who everywhere intend to seek
10   Abundance in every season.
Speak not another word; I'm ashamed.
You say I am in love with two.

Rondel of Olivier de La Marche

Out of love for the ladies of France,
I've begun following the Order
Of the renowned St. Francis,
Attempting one time to find
5   The sweet path of relief.

I'm girdled with the cord of Suffering
Over the hairshirt of Miserable Longing,
More intensely than I tell my God,
Out of love for the ladies of France.

10   I live soberly in regard to my Pleasure
And fast in the manner Desire wishes,

Mandiant par tout ou je vois,
Je veille a conter par mes dois,
Les maulx que m'a fait Esperance,
15   Pour amours *des dames de France!*

434i: R219

R219   [Rondel] Vaillant*   [p. 434i]

Des amoureux de l'observance,*
Je suis le plus subgiet de France,
Car je sers d'estre mandien
Et cherche le coctidien,
5   Mais nul en mon sac rien ne lance.

«Aux freres l'aumosne, pour Dieu,»
Tousjours voys criant d'uys en huis.
Las! Charité ne trouve en lieu,
Ne Pitié ne scet qui je suis.

10   Retourner m'en fault sans pitence,
Desir, le proveheur, me tance,
Puis le beau pere gardien.
Pis suis que Boesme n'Yndien.
L'ordre veil lesser sans doubtance
15   Des amoureux *de l'observance.*

434s: R218

R220   Rondel de George*   [p. 435s]

Les serviteurs submis a l'observance,*
Quoy que souvent il leur tourne a grevance
De non avoir leur plaisir a toute heure,
Toutevois, Dieu, soubz qui rien ne demeure,
5   A telz servans ne fit onc decevance.

Mains il convient, par contrainte eslevance,
Qu'Onneur, Fortune, ou Amour les avance
En quelque endroit, et au besoing secoeure
Les serviteurs *submis a l'observance.*

10   De long souffrir en penible estrivance
N'aist aux souffrans haulte et riche chevance,
Finablement, qui les paye et honneure.

Begging everywhere I go,
I stay awake counting on my fingers
The troubles Hope has inflicted upon me,

15   Out of love for the ladies of France!

Rondel—Vaillant

Of the Order of Love
I am the greatest practitioner in France,
Because I serve in the guise of a mendicant
And seek my daily bread,

5   But no one puts anything in my sack.

"Alms for the friars, for God's sake,"
That's what I cry from door to door.
Alas! I find charity nowhere,
And Pity does not know my name.

10   I must return without a pittance,
Desire, the purveyor, reproves me,
And afterward so does the good father superior.
I'm worse off than any Bohemian or Indian.
Certainly I no longer wish to be in the ranks

15   Of the Order of Love.

Rondel of George

These servants are submissive to the Order,
Though it often turns out badly
For they don't gain their objects of pleasure all the time.
However God, beneath Whom nothing is stable,

5   Never deceives such servants in the least.

For it's necessary, the highest kind of ordinance,
That Honor, Fortune, and Love advance them
Everywhere, and, in their time of need, assist
These servants submissive to the Order.

10   To suffer long in miserable striving
Is nothing less than an exalted and worthy destiny
In the end, whoever rewards and honors them,

Aprés l'aigret treuve on la doulce meure
Qui radoulcist en leur propre savance
15   Les serviteurs *submis a l'observance.*

435i: R221

R221   [Rondel] Vaillant*   [p. 435i]

Quant a moy, je crains le filé*
Que d'autres ne craignent mye,
C'est d'avoir dame sans amye,
Qui est ung cas mal compilé.

5   Le fait d'amour est avilé,
Car Pitié y est endormye.
Quant a moy, *je crains le filé.*

Puis voy par maint bec affilé*
Faire plus fort que l'arcquemie,
10   Dont, sur mon ame, je fremie
Et de paour d'estre aux piez pilé.
Quant a *moy, je crains le filé.*

435s: R220

R222   Rondel   [p. 436s]

Celle que je ne sçay nommer
Com a mon gré desireroye,
Ce jour de l'an, de biens et joye
Plaise a Dieu de vous estrener.

5   S'amie vous veuil apeller,
Trop simple nom vous bailleroye,
Celle *que je ne sçay nommer.*

De ma dame nom vous donner,
Orguilleuse je vous feroye.
10   Maistresse point ne vous vouldroye.
Comment dont doy je a vous parler,
Celle *que je ne sçay nommer?*

436i: R223

After the bitter fruit finds a good one,
Which lends sweetness to the wisdom of
15   These servants submissive to the Order.

Rondel — Vaillant

As for me, I fear the trap
Others do not fear at all,
That's to have a wife but no lover,
An ill-considered circumstance.

5   The doings of love are debased,
For Pity's fallen asleep.
As for me, I fear the trap.

Then I see many a sharp-tongued woman
Do more harm than alchemy,
10   And so, by my soul, I shake with fright,
And dread being crushed underfoot.
As for me, I fear the trap.

Rondel

Lady, whom I cannot name
As would be my preference,
This New Year's Day, may it please God
To bestow goods and joy aplenty on you.

5   If I wanted to call you lover,
I'd provide you with a very simple name,
Lady, whom I cannot name.

If I gave you the title "my lady"
I would make you arrogant.
10   I would not want you as my governess.
How then must I address you,
Lady, whom I cannot name?

R223   Rondel   [p. 436i]

 A ce jour de saint Valentin,
 Que l'en prent per par destinee,
 J'ay choisy, qui tresmal m'agree,
 Pluye, vent et mauvais chemin.

5 Il n'est de l'amoureux butin
 Nouvelle ne chançon chantee,
 A ce jour *de saint Valentin*.

 Bourges me donne ce tatin,
 Et a plusieurs de ma livree.
10 Mieulx vauldroit en chambre natee
 Dormir, sans lever sy matin,
 A ce jour *de saint Valentin*.

436s: R222

R224   Rondel de Bouciquault*   [p. 437s]

 Assez ne m'en peuz merveiller
 Qu'aucuns amoureux ont creance*
 D'estre de ceulx de l'observance,*
 Mes plus n'y vuelent travailler.

5 Je dy que leur vaulsist trop mieulx
 Plus large regle avoir choisie,
 Car servir jeunes et puis vieulx
 Lesser tout, c'est ypocrisie.

 Autre nom leur couvient bailler,
10 C'est apostaz, qui pour doubtance
 D'avoir ung pou de penitance
 Ont voulu Loyauté soiller.
 Assez ne m'en *peuz merveiller*.

437i: R225

R225   Rondel d'Orlians   [p. 437i]

 Ce n'est pas par ypocrisie,
 Ne je ne suis point apostat
 Pour tant se change mon estat
 Es derreniers jours de ma vie.

Rondel

On this Saint Valentine's Day
When mates are picked, as fortune directs,
My choice suits me very badly, for it's
Rain, wind, and a treacherous road.

5   For those in love there's no new
Reward or song to be sung,
On this Saint Valentine's Day.

Bourges strikes me this blow,
And several others who wear my livery.
10   Better to sleep inside a well-curtained
Room and not rise in the morning
On this Saint Valentine's Day.

Rondel by Bouciquault

I can hardly marvel enough
How some lovers have the authorization
To belong to the Order of Love
But are reluctant to work at it any more.

5   Much better it would have been, I say,
If they'd chosen an easier rule, .
For serving in youth and afterward in age
Then abandoning all is hypocrisy.

They must be given another name,
10   That of apostates, who out of fear
Of suffering a little penance
Have chosen to besmirch Loyalty.
I can hardly marvel enough.

Rondel by Orleans

It's not because of hypocrisy,
And I'm no apostate at all,
Even though I've changed my ways
In these last days of my life.

5   J'ay gardé ou temps de jeunesse,
         L'observance des amoureux.*
         Or m'en a bouté hors Viellesse,
         Et mis en l'ordre douloureux

         Des chartreux de Merencolie,
10   Solitaire sans nul esbat.
         A briefz motz, mon fait va de plat,
         Et pource, ne m'en blasmés mye,
         Ce n'est pas *par ypocrisie.*

437s: R224

R226   Rondel · Bousiquault*   [p. 438s]

         Monstrer on doit qu'il en desplaise
         Du meffait, a qui n'a povoir*
         De servir, car si cru, pour voir,
         En parler, il semble qu'il plaise.

5   Qui ne puet pour le mains se taise,
         Et face en dueil lermes plouvoir.
         Monstrer on doit *qu'il en desplaise.*

         Mais dire qu'on n'a temps ne aise,
         Pour aage, d'y faire devoir,
10   Chascun scet bien apparcevoir
         Que pou courcé tost se rappaise.
         Monstrer *on doit qu'il en desplaise.*

438i: R227

R227   [Rondel] de Mgr d'Orlians   [p. 438i]

         A quiconque plaise ou desplaise,
         Quant Vieillesse vient les gens prendre,
         Il couvient a elle se rendre
         Et endurer tout son malaise.

5   Nul ne puet faire son devoir
         De garder d'Amours l'observance,*
         Quant, avecques son bon vouloir,
         Il a povreté de puissance.

         Plus n'en dy, mieulx vault que me taise,
10   Car j'en ay a vendre et revendre.

5 In the time of youth I was faithful to
  The Order of Love.
  Then Old Age drove me out,
  Enrolling me in the Order of Misery

  In the prison house of Melancholy,
10 Solitary and with no delights at all.
  My prospects, in short, dwindle to nothing,
  And so assign me no blame,
  It's not because of hypocrisy.

Rondel — Bouciquault

  It must be shown that hypocrisy displeases
  A man who cannot serve Love, for, to believe him,
  You'd think he takes pleasure in
  Talking about it.

5 If he cannot serve, at least
  Let him remain silent and shed tears,
  It must be shown that hypocrisy displeases.

  But to say one hasn't the time or leisure
  Because of age to do one's duty,
10 Everyone knows well enough
  How a little bit of anger is quickly appeased.
  It must be shown that hypocrisy displeases.

Rondel by the lord of Orleans

  No matter who is pleased or displeased,
  When Old Age comes and takes hold of people,
  They're forced to surrender
  And endure all the ills she brings.

5 No man can do his duty
  And keep to the Order of Love,
  When, despite his good intent,
  His powers are diminished.

  I say no more, better to keep silent,
10 But I've plenty to sell and re-sell.

Ung chascun doit son fait entendre.
Qui ne puet ne puet, si s'appaise,
A quiconque *plaise ou desplaise.*

438s: R226

R228   Rondel de Fredet*   [p. 439s]

Le truchement de ma pensee,
Ceste saint Valentin passee,
J'ay envoyé devers Amours
Pour lui compter les grans dolours
5   Que seuffre pour ma tant amee,

Requerant ma peine alegee,
Autrement ma vie est finee,
Comme scet bien il a mains jours,
Le truchement *de ma pensee.*

10   Et quant sa raison eut contee,
Lui dist «Ta requeste m'agree,
Car trop leal l'ay veu tousjours.»
Lors fut commandé mon secours,
Et le m'apporta, la journee,
15   Le truchement *de ma pensee.*

439i: R229

R229   [Rondel] Simonnet Caillau*   [p. 439i]

Pour bref tels maulx d'Amours guerir,
Esgrun de Dueil te fault fuyr,
Les poix au veau te sont contraires*
Quant les fleurs de plaisans viaires
5   Sont dedans mises au boillir.

D'oubliete te peut servir,
Et l'erbe de Non Souvenir,
A faire bons electuaires
Pour bref *tels maulx guerir.*

10   Du triacle de Repentir,
Pour tes accez faire faillir,
Prendras sur les appoticaires.
Avecques siropz necessaires

Everyone should attend to his own affairs.
Whoever cannot, cannot, and should hold his peace,
No matter who is pleased or displeased.

Rondel of Fredet

The interpreter of my thought,
This past Saint Valentine's Day,
I sent along to Love
To recount the great pains
5   I suffer for the lady so much loved,

Begging for the relief of my pain,
Otherwise my life would end,
As he's known well for many a day,
The interpreter of my thought.

10   And when the interpreter spoke his thoughts,
Love responded: "Your request pleases me,
For I've always considered that man very loyal."
And so an order for my relief was then issued,
Which he brought to me that day,
15   The interpreter of my thought.

Rondel—Simonnet Caillau

To quickly heal the ills of Love,
You must abandon the bitter herb of Misery,
Peas with veal aren't right for you
When the flowers with pretty faces
5   Are put therein to boil.

Serve yourself with forgetfulness
And the herbs of Memory Lost,
In order to make useful purgatives
To quickly heal the ills of Love.

10   Some potions of Repentance
So that you can fend off coughing fits,
That's what you'll take from the pharmacy,
Along with the syrups required,

Faiz en sucrez de Deppartir,
15   Pour bref *tels maulx guerir.*

439s: R228

R230   [Rondel] Orleans   [p. 440s]

Recepte
      Les malades cueurs amoureux
      Qui ont perdu leurs appetis,
      Et leurs estomacs refroidis
      Par soussis et maulx douloureux,

5   Diete gardent sobrement
      Sans faire exces de Trop Douloir.
      Chaulx electuaires souvent
      Usent de Conforté Vouloir.

      Sucres de Penser Savoureux
10   Pour renforser leurs esperiz
      Ainsi peuent estre gueriz
      Et hors de Danger langoureux,
      Les malades cueurs *amoureux.*

440i: R231

R231   Rondel de Jehan de Lorraine   [p. 440i]

      Pour brief du mal d'amer guerir,
      Esloingner l'air de Souvenir
      Couvient, sans grant merencolie,
      Aprés tous mes, mengier l'oublie
5   Pres du couchier pour mieulx dormir.

      De Non Chaloir, pour adoulcir
      La medecine de Desir,
      Prendre fault la plus grant partie
      Pour brief *du mal d'amer guerir.*

10   Puis ung beau regime a l'issir
      De vostre accez pourrez choisir,
      D'une Leaulté my partie.
      Affin que ne rencheez mye,
      Faictes Reffuz d'Amour banir
15   Pour brief *du mal d'amer guerir.*

440s: R230

Made with the sugar of Leave-Taking,
15   To quickly heal the ills of Love.

Rondel — Orleans

Prescription

The hearts sick with the ills of love
Who've lost their appetites,
Their stomachs turned cold
By cares and painful torment,

5   Let them follow a strict diet
With no large portions of Too Much Pain.
Hot infusions of Consoled Will
Are what they often treat themselves with,

Sweet syrups of Appetizing Thought
10   To strengthen their spirits at the end.
This way they'll find a cure
To lift them out of languishing Danger,
The hearts sick with the ills of love.

Rondel of Jean, lord of Lorraine

To quickly cure the disease of loving,
You must put some distance between yourself
And Memory, far beyond great Melancholy,
And after every meal, eat of Forgetfulness
5   Just before bedtime in order to sleep better.

Of Indifference, in order to sweeten
The infusions of Desire,
You must consume the greater part,
To quickly cure the disease of loving.

10   Thus you can choose at the outset
A fine course of treatment for your attacks,
Some small portion of Loyalty.
So that you do not suffer a relapse,
Make sure Refusal of Love endures banishment
15   To quickly cure the disease of loving.

R232   [Rondel]   [p. 441s]

Recepte
    Pour tous voz maulx d'amours guerir,
    Prenez la fleur de Souvenir
    Avec le just d'une Ancollie,*
    Et n'obliés pas la Soussie,
5   Et meslez tout en Desplaisir.

    L'erbe de Loing de son desir,
    Poire d'angoisse pour refreschir,*
    Vous envoye Dieu, de vostre amye.

    Pouldre de Plains pour adoucir,
10   Feille d'Aultre que vous choisir
    Et racine de Jalousie,
    Et de tretout la plus partie
    Mectés au cuer avant dormir
    Pour tous *voz maulx d'amours guerir.*

441i: R233

R233   [Rondel]   [p. 441i]

    Puis que tu t'en vas,
    Penser, en message,
    Se tu fais que sage,
    Ne t'esgare pas.

5   Au mieulx que pourras,
    Pren le seur passage,
    Puis que *tu t'en vas.*

    Tout beau, pas a pas,
    Reffrain ton courage,
10   Qu'en si long voyage
    Ne deviengnes las,
    Puis que *tu t'en vas.*

441s: R232

R234   [Rondel]   [p. 442s]

    L'ueil et le cuer soient mis en tutelle
    Sitost qu'ilz sont rassotez en amours.
    Combien qu'il a plusieurs qui font les lours
    Et ont trouvé contenance nouvelle,

Rondel

Prescription
> So as to cure all your lover's ills,
> Take the flower of Memory
> With the juice of Aquilegia
> And don't neglect the Marigold,
5   And mix all this in Displeasure.

> The herb of Far-from-his-desire,
> The pear of anguish for refreshment,
> May God send you for your beloved.

> A powder of Laments for sweetening,
10   A leaf of Choosing-some-other-but-you,
> And some root of Jealousy,
> Now put the greater part of all this
> In the heart before going to sleep
> So as to cure all your lover's ills.

Rondel

> Since you are going away,
> Thought, my messenger,
> If you are to act wisely
> Do not lose your way.

5   As best you can,
> Take the surest path,
> Since you are going away.

> In fine fashion, step by step,
> Restrain the heart within you,
10   So that on such a long journey
> You may not weary,
> Since you are going away.

Rondel

> Let the eye and the heart be counseled
> As soon as they're driven mad by love,
> Even though there are some who act ill-advisedly
> Finding a new way to act,

5   Pour mieulx embler priveement Plaisance,
         Mommerie, sans Parler de la bouche,
         En beaux abiz d'or cliquant d'Acointance,
         Soubz visieres de Semblant qu'on n'y touche,

         Faignent souvant l'amoureuse querelle.
10   Ainsi l'ay veu faire en mes jennes jours.
         Vestu m'y suis a droit et a rebours.
         Je jangle trop, au fort, je me rapelle.
         L'euil et le cuer *soient mis en tutelle*!

442i: R235

R235   [Rondel] Mgr Jehan de Lorraine   [p. 442i]

         Pour eschiver plus grant dangier,
         Certes, mon cueur, il est mestier,
         Puis que nous alons veoir la belle,
         Que tenez mon euil en tutelle,
5   Qu'i ne vous donne a besongnier.

         Commandez lui bien sans prier
         Qu'i ne croie riens de legier,
         Dont il vous rapporte nouvelle.

         Et s'il ne s'i veult obligier,
10   Mettez Raison pour espïer
         A part sa couverte cautelle,
         Car c'est cellui seul qui se mesle
         De tieulx defaultes corrigier,
         Pour eschiver *plus grant dangier*.

442s: R234

R236   [Rondel]   [p. 443s]

         Chose qui plaist est a demi vendue,*
         Quelque cherté qui coure par païs.
         Jamais ne sont bons marchans esbaÿz,
         Tousjours gaignent a l'alee ou venue.

5   Car, quant les yeulx qui sont facteurs du cueur
         Voyent Plaisir a bon marchié en vente,
         Qui les tiendroit d'achatter leur bon eur,
         Et deussent ilz engagier biens et rente,

5   The better to keep Pleasure hidden and private,
By playing the mime, their mouths silent,
Wearing lovely clothes of gold clinking with Friendship,
Behind masks of Seeming no one touches,

Often pretending to endure the struggles of a lover.
10   As a youth, I saw it done so.
The demeanor I affected, conventional but also wild.
I chat too much, but, after all, I recall:
Let the eye and the heart be counseled!

Rondel — Jean, lord of Lorraine

So as to avoid greater danger,
There is certainly a need, my heart,
Since we are going to see the belle,
For you to act as counselor to my eye,
5   Provided it's no problem for you.

Command him firmly, without begging,
Not to believe readily
Those tidings he brings you.

And if he'll not agree,
10   Make sure Reason from a distance spies on
Those tricks he plays in secret,
For Reason alone undertakes
To correct this kind of misdeed,
So as to avoid greater danger.

Rondel

Something that pleases is half sold,
No matter what rising price runs through the land.
Able merchants are never dismayed,
Always turning a profit as they come and go.

5   For, when the eyes, agents of the heart,
Spy Pleasure for sale at a favorable price,
Who will keep them from buying their happiness,
Even if they should commit their goods and earnings,

Et a rachact toute leur revenue?
10   De lascheté seroient bien traÿs,
Et devroient d'Amours estre haÿs!
Marchandise doit estre maintenue :
Chose qui plaist *est a demi vendue.*

443i: R237

R237   [Rondel]

Chose qui plaist est a demi vendue,
A bon compte souvent, ou chierement.
Qui du marchié le denier a Dieu prent,
Il n'y peut plus mectre rabat ne creue.

5   D'en debatre n'est que paine perdue.
Prenez ore qu'aprés on s'en repent,
Chose qui plaist *est a demi vendue.*

S'aucun aussi monstre sa retenue*
Et au bureau va faire le serment,
10   Les officiers n'y font empeschement,
Mais demandent tantost la bien venue :
Chose qui plaist *est a demi vendue.*

443s: R236

R238   Rondel de Jehan Mgr de Lorraine

L'abit le moine ne fait pas.*
Pourtant, se je me veis de dueil,
J'ay la lerme assez loing de l'ueil,
Passant mes ennuiz au gros sas.

5   Je fains d'assembler a grans tas
Douleurs a part, mais quant je vueil,
L'abit le moine *ne fait pas.*

Conclusïon, vecy mon cas :
De nulle rien je ne me dueil,
10   En gré prens d'Amours le recueil,
Soit beau ou lait. Puis je diz bas :
L'abit le moine *ne fait pas.*

444i: R239

So they can recover their investment?
10   Cowardice would betray them
And they ought to be hated by Love!
Commerce should continue:
Something that pleases is half sold.

Rondel

Something that pleases is half sold,
Often at a good price, or dearly.
Whoever accepts the down payment
Cannot lower the price or raise it.

5   To debate this point is only wasted effort.
Take it now, for afterward you might repent,
Something that pleases is half sold.

If someone shows his letter of contract
And goes to the table to swear his oath,
10   The officers will not prevent him,
But ask at once for a gift of welcome:
Something that pleases is half sold.

Rondel of Jean, lord of Lorraine

The habit does not make the monk.
Even though I live in grief,
Tears are far from my eyes,
As I bear my huge burden of miseries.

5   I look as though I'm assembling great heaps
Of sorrows, but if I so wish,
The habit does not make the monk.

In conclusion, look at my situation:
Nothing makes me sorrow.
10   I accept with good will what Love sends,
Whether fine or unpleasant. Then I whisper:
The habit does not make the monk.

R239   Rondel de Mgr d'Orlians   [p. 444i]

L'abit le moyne ne fait pas,*
L'ouvrier se congnoist a l'ouvrage,
Et plaisant maintien de visage
Ne monstre pas tousjours le cas.

5   Aler tout soubrement le pas,
N'est que contrefaire le sage.
L'abit le moyne *ne fait pas.*

Soubtil sens couchié par compas,
Enveloppé en beau langage,
10   Musse le vouloir du courage.
Cuidier deçoit en mains estas :
L'abit le moyne *ne fait pas.*

444s: R238

R240 Rondel de Jehan Mgr de Lorraine   [p. 445s]

De fol juge briefve sentence.*
Certes bon cuer ne puet mentir,
Et si ne scet du sac yssir
Que ce qui est d'acoustumence.

5   La ou Raison pert pascïence,
On voit bien souvent avenir
De fol juge *briefve sentence.*

Envie atout sa double lance
Blesse en mains lieux sans cop ferir,
10   Dont il se couvient repentir
Aucune foiz, qui bien y pense.
De fol juge *briefve sentence.*

445i: R241

R241   [Rondel] de Mgr d'Orlians   [p. 445i]

De fol juge brefve sentence.
On n'y saroit remedyer
Quant l'advocat Oultrecuidyer,
Sans raison maintesfoiz sentence.

Rondel of my lord of Orleans

The habit does not make the monk.
The workman is known by his work,
And a pleasant look on someone's face
Doesn't always tell what's going on.

5   To proceed at a very cautious pace
Is only to imitate the wise man.
The habit does not make the monk.

A subtle sensibility carefully deployed,
Wrapped in fine language,
10   Conceals what the heart intends.
Thought misleads many a time.
The habit does not make the monk.

Rondel of Jean, lord of Lorraine

A short sentence from a foolish judge.
Surely a good heart cannot lie,
And so can only take from the sack
What is normally there.

5   Wherever Reason loses patience,
The consequence often seems to be
A short sentence from a foolish judge.

Envy with her double lance
Deals out wounds though striking no blow,
10   And so it should be regretted sometimes
By anyone who thinks aright:
A short sentence from a foolish judge.

Rondel by the lord of Orleans

A short sentence from a foolish judge.
There's no chance for remedy
When Overconfidence, as lawyer,
Often and without reason pronounces sentence.

5　　Aprés s'en repent et s'en tence.
　　C'est tart et ne se puet widyer.
　　De fol juge *brefve sentence.*

　　Fleurs portent odeur, et sentence
　　Et savoir vient d'estudyer,*
10　　Ce n'est pas ne d'anuyt ne d'yer.
　　J'en dy ce que mon cuer sent en ce :
　　De fol juge *brefve sentence.*

445s: R240

R242　　[Rondel] Madame d'Orlians*　　　　[p. 446s]

　　L'abit le moine ne fait pas,
　　Car quelque chiere que je face,
　　Mon mal seul tous les autres pace
　　De ceulx qui tant plaignent leur cas.

5　　Souvent en densant fais mains pas
　　Que mon cuer pres en dueil trespace.
　　L'abit le moine *ne fait pas.*

　　Las! mes yeulx gectent sans compas
　　Des lermes tant parmy ma face,
10　　Dont plusieurs foiz je change place,
　　Alant a part pour crier : las!
　　L'abit le moine *ne fait pas.*

446i: R243

R243　　　　[Rondel] Guiot Pot　　　　[p. 446i]

　　L'abit le moine ne fait pas,
　　Car tel n'est pas vestu de noir
　　Qui a cause de se douloir.
　　Par Dieu, qui cognoistroit son cas?

5　　S'on lui fait changer ses esbas
　　Contre raison et son vouloir,
　　L'abit le moine *ne fait pas.*

　　Quant Fortune charge le bas
　　Au compaignon, s'il a povoir
10　　Et il joue ung tour de savoir,

5   Afterward he scolds himself and holds back.
     It's late and he cannot disengage himself.
     A short sentence from a foolish judge.

     Flowers giving off fragrance, discernment
     And knowledge coming from study,
10   That's not today's news or yesterday's.
     I say only what's in my heart:
     A short sentence from a foolish judge.

Rondel my lady of Orleans

The habit does not make the monk,
But no matter what manner I affect,
My one ill surpasses all the others
Of those who so heartily lament their destinies.

5   Dancing, I often take many a step
     When my heart is near to dying of grief.
     The habit does not make the monk.

     Alas! My eyes weep everywhere,
     Tears streaming down my face,
10   And many times I change my seat,
     Wandering off alone to cry "alas."
     The habit does not make the monk.

Rondel — Guiot Pot

The habit does not make the monk,
For not all are dressed in black
Who have good cause to lament.
By God, who could understand his troubles?

5   If someone makes him change his distractions
     Against reason and against his will,
     The habit does not make the monk.

     When Fortune piles up the burden
     On her companion, if he is able
10   And plays a clever game,

Disant que de souffrir est las,
L'abit le moine *ne fait pas.*

446s: R242

R244 [Rondel] de Messire Philippe Pot*   [p. 447s]

En la Forest de Longue Actente
Ou mainte personne est dolente,
Espoir me promist de donner,
Se bien vouloie cheminer,
5   Ce qui tous amoureux contente.

J'ay tout mis, cuer, corps et entente
A traverser chemin et sente
Pour cuider ce grant bien trouver
En la Forest *de Longue Actente,*

10   Mais d'une chose je me vente
Que j'ay eu tous les jours de rente,
Pour ma queste parachever,
Paine et Ennuy, sans conquester
Riens, si non Dueil qui me tourmente
15   En la Forest *de Longue Actente.*

447i: R245

R245   [Rondel] Anthoyne de Lussay*   [p. 447i]

En la Forest de Longue Actente
Ou les contentés Dieu contente,
Je vous asseure sur ma foy,
Que je n'y ay eu, tant soit poy,
5   Joye ne bien dont je me sente.

Pensez se ma vie est dolente,
Veu qu'ainsi soit, je me garmente
Et que nul bien n'y a pour moi
En la Forest *de Longue Actente.*

10   Au fort, d'une chose me vente,
Se je ne faulx en mon entente,
Ou se la mort brief ne reçoy,
Que g'y auray, savez vous quoy?
Aucun plaisir qui vauldra rente
15   En la Forest *de Longue Actente.*

447s: R244

Saying that it's suffering that has wearied him,
The habit does not make the monk.

Rondel by my lord Philippe Pot

In the Forest of Long Awaiting
Where many a person is sorrowful,
Hope promised to give me
—If I'd go my way in fine fashion—
5   What contents all lovers.

I have devoted everything, heart, person, and will
To traversing this path and road,
Believing I would find great benefit
In the Forest of Long Awaiting.

10   But I do boast of one thing
I've gained in all this time,
To bring my quest to an end:
Pain and trouble, achieving
Nothing but the sorrow that torments me
15   In the Forest of Long Awaiting.

Rondel—Antoine de Lussay

In the Forest of Long Awaiting
Where those consoled are so by God,
Upon my faith I assure you
That I've not received any joy or benefit
5   I'm aware of, however small.

Consider if my life is filled with sorrow,
Seeing that this is how it is, I lament
And receive no benefit at all
In the Forest of Long Awaiting.

10   Indeed, I boast of one thing:
If my intention does not waver
Or death doesn't soon find me,
I'll have—do you know what?
No pleasure worth anything at all
15   In the Forest of Long Awaiting.

R246   [Rondel] Guiot Pot*   [p. 448s]

En la Forest de Longue Actente
Ja pieça fus en une sente,
La ou j'ay esgaré mon cueur,
Mais y soufrit tant de douleur
5   Que tousjours convient que s'en sente.

Depuis tousjours tant fort lamente
Par Fortune qui le tourmente,
Qu'il fault qu'il vive en grant langueur
En la Forest *de Longue Actente.*

10   Mais, s'il eschappe, bien se vente
Qu'il gardera c'on ne le tente
Par Beau Parler ne par Rigueur,
Car chascun se doit tenir seur
Que l'on fault bien a son entente
15   En la Forest de Longue Actente.

448i: Gilles: R247

R247   [Rondel] Gilles*   [p. 448i]

En la Forest de Longue Actente
Mon povre cuer tant se garmente
D'en saillir par aucune voye,
Qu'il ne lui semble pas qu'il voye
5   Jamais la fin de son entente.

Deconfort le tient en sa tente,
Qui par telle façon le tente
Que j'ay paour qu'il ne le forvoye
En la Forest *de Longue Actente.*

10   Espoir en riens ne le contente,
Comme il souloit, pour quoy dolente
Sera ma vie ou que je soye,
Et si auray en lieu de joye,
Dueil et Soussy tousjours de rente
15   En la Forest *de Longue Actente.*

448s: R246

Rondel — Guiot Pot

In the Forest of Long Awaiting
Not long ago I followed a path
Where I'd lost my heart,
Which there suffered so much
5   The pain was felt ever after.

He always laments fiercely
Because of Fortune, which so tortures him
He must live on in great misery
In the Forest of Long Awaiting.

10   But, should he escape, he'll boast loudly
How he'll take care not to be tempted
By Fine Speech or Force,
But everyone should be very certain
That all fail in their intentions
15   In the Forest of Long Awaiting.

Rondel — Gilles

In the Forest of Long Awaiting,
My poor heart's very desperate
To escape that place by any path,
For he thinks to never see
5   His endeavor brought to a conclusion.

Desolation traps the heart in his snare,
Gripping the heart in such a fashion
I fear he'll lead it astray
In the Forest of Long Awaiting.

10   Hope brings the heart no comfort,
As once he did, and so my life
Will be miserable wherever I am,
And instead of joy my wages
Will always be Suffering and Care
15   In the Forest of Long Awaiting.

R248   Rondel de Monseigneur   [p. 449s]

    Crié soit a la clochete
    Par les rues sus et jus :
    «Fredet! On ne le voit plus.
    Est il mis en oubliete?

5   Jadis il tenoit bien conte
    De visiter ses amis.
    Est il roy, ou duc, ou conte
    Quant en oubly les a mis?

    Banny a son de trompete
10   Comme marié confus,
    Entre chartreurs ou reclus,
    A il point fait sa retrete?»
    Crié soit *a la clochete!*

449i: R249

R249   [Rondel] Fredet*   [p. 449i]

    Se veoir ne vous voys plus,
    Helas! ce fait mariage,
    Qui me fait avoir courage
    D'estre desormais reclus.

5   Puis que si fort m'a confus,
    Ne le tenez a oultrage,
    Se veoir *ne vous voys plus.*

    Mais non pourtant je conclus
    Que ce n'est pas fait que sage,
10   Car j'en puis a brief langage
    Pour le moins perdre le plus,
    Se veoir *ne vous voys plus.*

449s: R248

R250   [Rondel] Orlians   [p. 450s]

    En l'ordre de mariage
    A il desduit ou courrous?
    Commant vous gouvernez vous?
    Y devient on fol, ou sage?

Rondel of my lord

Let the bells proclaim this
Up and down, through all the streets:
"Fredet! No one sees him any more.
Has he been sent to prison?

5   "Formerly he was very diligent
In visiting his friends.
Was he a king, duke, or count
At the moment he forgot them?

"Banished with a trumpet blast,
10   Like some confused husband,
To be among the Carthusians or hermits,
Has he beaten a retreat?
Let the bells proclaim this."

Rondel — Fredet

If I go no more to see you,
Alas, this is what marriage has done,
Giving me the courage
Henceforth to live as a recluse.

5   Since this has so confounded me,
Do not think it an outrage
If I go no more to see you.

Notwithstanding I conclude
That doing so was not wise,
10   For, to be brief, I will
Lose the greater for the lesser,
If I go no more to see you.

Rondel — Orleans

In the Order of matrimony,
Is there pleasure or annoyance?
How do you manage it?
Does one turn fool or sage?

5 Soit aux vielx ou jeunes d'age,
  Rapporter m'en vueil a tous
  En l'ordre *de mariage.*

  Le premier an c'est la rage,
  Tant y fait plaisant et douls.
10 Après . . . j'ay la tous,*
  Cesser me fait de langage
  En l'ordre *de mariage.*

450i: R251

R251   Rondel de Jacques,   [p. 450i]
bastart de la Trimoille*

  En la Forest de Longue Actente
  J'ay couru l'annee presente,
  Tant que la saison a duré,
  Mais j'ay esté plus maleuré
5 Que homme qui vive, je m'en vente.

  La haye fut garnie de tente,*
  Et fis ma queste belle et gente,
  Suivant les chiens je m'esgaré
  En la Forest *de Longue Actente.*

10 Je cours, je corne, je tourmente.
  En traversant sans trouver sente
  Me trouvay tresfort enserré.
  Tout seul, presque desesperé
  Cuiday mourir des foiz soixante
15 En la Forest *de Longue Actente.*

450s: R250

R252 [Rondel] Le cadet d'Alebret*   [p. 451s]

  Dedans l'abisme de douleur
  Ou tant a d'amere saveur,
  Aussi d'angoisseuse destresse,
  Se trouve tourmenté sans cesse,
5 Pour vous amer, mon povre cueur.

  Ma Dame, par vostre doulceur,
  Secourez ce bon serviteur

5   Whether old or young,
       I'll take counsel from everyone
       In the Order of matrimony.

       The first year, things are wonderful,
       So pleasant and so sweet.
10   Afterward, well . . . There's a frog in my throat,
       Words fail me
       In the Order of matrimony.

Rondel by Jacques, bastard of La Trimoille

       In the Forest of Long Awaiting
       I've wandered all this year,
       As long as the season lasted,
       But I've been more burdened with ills
5   Than any man alive, I dare say.

       The woods was provided with tents,
       And I went off on my hunt, fair and fine,
       Followed the dogs, but lost my way
       In the Forest of Long Awaiting.

10   I give chase, I sound my horn, I rage on.
       While crisscrossing, not finding a path,
       I find myself neatly stymied,
       All alone, nearly desperate.
       Sixty times I thought death close
15   In the Forest of Long Awaiting.

Rondel—the cadet of Alebret

       Deep within the abyss of despair,
       Where the taste is very bitter,
       And there's much painful distress,
       My poor heart finds himself ceaselessly
5   Tormented because of loving you.

       My Lady, through your sweetness,
       Succor this good servant

A qui l'on fait tant de rudesse
Dedans l'abisme *de douleur.*

10   Las! ostez de lui tout maleur,
      Ou autrement il se tient seur
      De jamais n'avoir que tristesse,
      Dont fauldra que sa vie cesse
      Piteusement en grant langueur,
15   Dedans l'abisme *de douleur.*

451i: R253

R253   [Rondel] Mgr d'Orlians   [p. 451i]

Dedens l'abisme de douleur
Sont tourmentees povres ames
Des amans, et, par Dieu, mes dames,
Vous leur portez trop de rigueur.

5   Ostez les de ceste langueur
      Ou ilz sont en maulx et diffames
      Dedens *l'abisme de douleur.*

      Se n'y monstrez vostre doulceur,
      Vous en pourrez recevoir blasmes.
10   Tost orra prieres de fames
      Dangier, des dyables le greigneur,
      Dedens *l'abisme de douleur.*

451s: R252

R254   [Rondel] Gilles des Ormes*   [p. 452s]

Dedens l'abisme de douleur
Sont tourmentez par grant fouleur
Maints cuers par faulte de secours,
Qui n'ont a personne recours
5   Qu'a Pitié, qui detient le leur.

      Car, quant ilz ont servy, on leur
      Taille la broche sans couleur.*
      Lors ilz s'en vont languir le cours
      Dedens *l'abisme de douleur.*

10   Par Dieu! c'est faulte de valeur
      A ceulx qui le font par chaleur,

Who has had much ill done him
Deep within the abyss of despair.

10   Alas! Alleviate all the heart's ills,
Otherwise he'll be certain that sadness
Will be the sum of his experience,
And his life must come to a pitiable
End, in great distress,
15   Deep within the abyss of despair.

Rondel—my lord of Orleans

Deep within the abyss of despair
The poor souls of lovers
Suffer torment, and, by God, my ladies,
You treat them too harshly.

5   Deliver them from this languor
Where they suffer misery and scorn
Deep within the abyss of despair.

If you do not show them kindness,
You could be blamed.
10   Danger, the greatest devil,
Will readily listen to the prayers of ladies
Deep within the abyss of despair.

Rondel—Gilles des Ormes

Deep within the abyss of despair
Many hearts, unconsoled,
Endure the pain of great madness,
And they have no recourse to anyone
5   Save Pity, who keeps them from consolation.

For, once they've served,
They are cast aside without any excuse.
Then they proceed to languish,
Deep within the abyss of despair.

10   By God! It's a failure of worthiness
For them to carry on with such ardor

Et de fait les tiennent si cours
Qu'i leur fault user tout le cours
De leur vie en paine et maleur
15   Dedens l'abisme *de douleur.*

452i: R255

R255   [Rondel] Philippe de Boulainvilliers*   [p. 452i]

Tirez vous la, Regart trop convoiteux,
Renon avez d'estre de nul piteux,
Vostre semblant demonstre, pour tout voir,
Qu'estez venu pour mon cueur decevoir,
5   Dont me desplaist, j'en suis trestout honteux.

Pour me tromper faictes le marmiteux,
Il ne fault point clocher devant boiteux.*
Allez, allez, je ne vous vueil plus voir.
Tirez vous la, *Regart trop convoiteux.*

10   Point ne vous fault faire le despiteux,
Car, quant vous voy, je suis toujours douteux
De quelque mal plus que de bien avoir.
Je vous congnois sans plus rien en savoir,
Ou que soiez, vous estes rioteux.
15   Tirez vous la, *Regart trop convoiteux.*

452s: R254

R256   Rondel de Cleremont*   [p. 453s]

Rendre vous fault de toutes choses conte,
Qu'avés vous fait, madame, de mon cueur?
N'en mentons point, est il plus serviteur
Vostre tenu, dont je tien sy grant conte?

5   A celle fin que l'en ne me mesconte,
Je vous diray, mais par mon createur,
Rendre vous fault *de toutes choses conte.*

Entendez vous ce que je vous raconte,
Dictes moy vray, hay avant, rigueur
10   Sera elle en vous? lui donrrez vous faveur?
Fy, Fy, nanyl, car ce vous seroit honte.
Rendre *vous fault de toutes choses conte.*

453i: R257

And restrain so tightly their hearts
That they must spend all the days
Of their lives suffering pain and ill fortune
15   Deep within the abyss of despair.

Rondel — Philippe de Boulainvilliers

Clear off, Glance, so full of desire!
You are reputed to take pity on no man.
Your manner makes it clear, to tell the whole truth,
You've come to deceive my heart,
5   And this displeases and shames me completely.

To trick me, you make a pretence of shame,
No need to remind the lame of their handicap.
Away with you, away! I wish to see no more of you.
Clear off, Glance, so full of desire.

10   There's no reason for you to be disdainful,
For, whenever I see you, I always worry
It's going to be bad, not something to profit me.
I know you so well there's not need to learn more,
Wherever you go, trouble follows.
15   Clear off, Glance, so full of desire.

Rondel of Cleremont

You must render an account for everything;
What have you done, my lady, to my heart?
Let us tell no lies, is he still to be considered
Your servant, something I value greatly?

5   In order that no one misreport my words,
I'll tell you, for the sake of my Creator,
You must render an account for everything.

Pay attention to what I'm telling you,
Tell me true, oh, go on, will you be stable
10   In your affections? Will you grant him your favor?
Fie, fie, not at all, for this would shame you.
You must render an account for everything.

R257   **Rondel · Orlians**   [p. 453i]

Que je vous aime maintenant,
Quant je congnois vostre maniere
Venant de voulenté legiere
Enveloppee en faulx samblant!

5   Je ne m'y fie tant ne quant,
Veu qu'en estes bien coustumiere.
Que je vous *aime maintenant,*

N'en peut chaloir, tirez avant,
Parfaictez comme mesnagiere,
10   De haulte lisse bonne ouvriere.*
Plus vous voy, plus vous prise tant.
Que je vous aime *maintenant!*

453s: R256

R258   **Rondel · Orlians**   [p. 454s]

Cuer, qu'esse la? —Ce sommes nous, voz yeux.
—Qu'aportez vous? —Grand foison de nouvelles.
—Quelles sont ilz? —Amoureuses et belles.
—Je n'en vueil point.—Voire? —Non, se m'aist Dieux.

5   —D'ou venez vous? —De plusieurs plaisans lieux.
—Et qu'i a il? —Bon marchié de querelles.
—Cuer, *qu'esse la? —Ce sommes nous, voz yeux.*

—C'est pour jeunes? —Aussi esse pour vieux.
—Trop sont vieulx soulz! —Pieça, n'en eustes telles.
10   —Si ay, si ay. —Au moins escoutez d'elles?
—Paix, je m'endors. —Non ferez pour le mieux.
—Cuer, *qu'esse la? —Ce sommes nous, voz yeux.*

454i: R259

R259   **Rondel · Orlians**   [p. 454i]

Soussy, beau sire, je vous prie . . .   Le Cueur
De quoy? que me demandez vous?   Soussy
Ostez moy d'anuy et courrous.   Le Cueur
Ou vous estes? Non feray mie.   Soussy

Rondel—Orleans

Oh, how I love you now,
When I realize that your manner,
The sign of a flippant mind,
Is enveloped in false seeming!

5   I don't trust it at all,
For this has been your custom.
Oh, how I love you now,

It cannot matter, come forward,
Carry on as the head of the household,
10   Only the best craftswoman can manage the hardest tapestry.
The more I see you, the greater my esteem.
Oh, how I love you now!

Rondel—Orleans

Heart, who's there? —It's us, your eyes.
—What do you bring? —A great abundance of news.
—Of what kind? —Delightful and romantic.
—I wish none of it. —Truly?—No, so help me God.

5   —Whence do you come? —From several pleasant spots.
—And what is there? —All manner of things.
—Heart, who's there? —It's us, your eyes.

—Is it for the young? —And for the old as well.
—The old had their fill! —It's some time since you had any.
10   —Yes, I have, I have. —Will you at least listen to some?
—Quiet, I'm sleeping. —You don't do what's for the best.
—Heart, who's there? —It's us, your eyes.

Rondel—Orleans

Care, fair sir, I beg you . . .   The Heart
—For what? What do you ask of me?   Care
—Take me from worry and anger.   The Heart
—Where you are? I'll not do so at all.   Care

5   Tenir je vous vueil compagnie.   Soussy
        Las! non faictes, soyez moy douls,   Le Cueur
        Soussy, *beau sire, je vous prie.*

        Parlez en a Merencolie.   Soussy
        Conseil[liez] premier entre vous.*   Le Cueur
10   Espoir y pourroit plus que nous.   Soussy
        Faictes dont qu'il y remedie,   Le Cueur
        Soussy, *beau sire, je vous prie.*

454s: R258

R260   Rondel · Orlians   [p. 455s]

        Quant Leauté et Amour sont ensamble
        Et on les scet a deu entretenir
        En tems et lyeu et pour lui retenir,
        Il font, par Dieu, feu grejois, ce me semble.

5   J'en congnois deus qui portent grant atour,
        Qui contre droyt en emportent le bruit,

        Helaz! voire, et ne font pas se tour,
        Car traïson en leurs cuers tousjours bruit.

        Garder se fault que nul ne les resemble,
10   Ne nulle aucy qu'il veulst a bien venir.
        Pour ce, conclus, pour au point revenir,
        Que jamais mal entre amoureux n'assemble,
        Quant Leauté *et Amour sont ensamble.*

455i: R261

R261   Rondel · Orlians   [p. 455i]

        Plus tost accointé que cogneu,
        Plus tost esprouvé que nourry,
        Plus tost plaisant que bien choisy,
        Est souvent en grace receu.

5   Mains tost que riche, despourveu
        Se treuve, garny de soussy.
        Plus tost *accointé que cogneu,*

        Assez tost meschant est recreu,
        Assez tost entreprent hardy,

5	—I wish to bear you company.	Care
	—Alas! Don't do so. Be kind to me,	The Heart
	Care, fair sir, I beg you.	
	—Speak of this to Melancholy.	Care
	—First take counsel among yourselves.	The Heart
10	—Perhaps there could be more than us two.	Care
	—Then have some remedy come of it,	The Heart
	Care, fair sir, I beg you.	

Rondel—Orleans

Whenever Faithfulness and Love assemble
And someone can keep them together
In time and place, retaining them for himself,
By God, those two concoct Greek fire, I think.

5   I recognize two lovers of grand bearing
Who, contrary to what is right, win renown.

Alas! This is true, and their tricks do not work,
For the treason in their hearts is forever rumbling.

Care must be taken so that no man does the same,
10   No lady either, if she aims at a good end.
So I conclude, returning to the point,
That ills never arise among lovers
Whenever Faithfulness and Love assemble.

Rondel—Orleans

Rather acquainted with than known well,
Rather tested than taught,
Rather pleasant than well chosen,
Such a man often finds favor.

5   Slower than a rich man, he finds himself
Impoverished, well supplied with care.
Rather acquainted with than known well!

Quite quickly the unfortunate one tires,
Quite quickly the brave man gets going,

10   Assez tost senti qui s'ardy,
        Tout ce mal est de chascun sceu.
        Plus tost *accointé que cogneu!*

455s: R260

R262   Rondel · Le cadet*   [p. 456s]

        Tu vas trop avant, retray toy,
        Mon cuer, ou tu te feras prendre,
        Pas n'est bon de tant entreprendre.
        Arreste et te tiens tout coy.

5   Le feras tu? or le dy coy,
        Affin qu'on ne te puist reprendre.
        Tu vas *trop avant, retray toy.*

        Seit toy quelque part en requoy,
        Pour mieulx te garder de surprendre,
10   Et de la tu pourras comprendre
        Ton fait bien au long, or m'en croy.
        Tu vas *trop avant, retray toy.*

456i: R263

R263   Rondel de Monseigneur   [p. 456i]

        A ce jour de Saint Valentin,
        Bien et beau Karesme s'en va.*
        Je ne sçay qui ce jeu trouva,
        Penser m'y a pris au matin.

5   Et puis pour jouer a tintin*
        Avecques moy tost se leva,
        A ce jour *de Saint Valentin.*

        Soussy m'a cuidé ung tatin
        Donner, mais pas ne l'acheva,
10   Bien garday que ne me greva.
        Maledicatur en latin,
        A ce jour *de Saint Valentin.*

456s: R262

10   Quite quickly the man on fire senses it,
All these miseries are known to everyone.
Rather acquainted with than known well!

Rondel — the cadet

You go too far, beat a retreat,
My heart, or you'll get yourself taken prisoner.
It's no good to undertake too much.
Stop and keep still.

5   Will you do it? Now I tell you why,
So no one can admonish you.
You go too far, beat a retreat.

Take a seat somewhere in private,
The better to guard against surprise,
10   And there you'll prove able to understand
Your situation, at length, I believe.
You go too far, beat a retreat.

Rondel by my lord

On this Saint Valentine's day,
Well and good, Lenten fasting is on its way out.
I know not who invented this game,
Thought trapped me in it this morning.

5   And then to play "loser pays"
She got up early with me,
On this Saint Valentine's day.

Care thought to give me
A tap, but did not bring it off,
10   I made sure she did me no harm.
Let her be cursed in Latin,
On this Saint Valentine's day.

R264   Rondel de Mgr d'Orlians   [p. 457s]

A ce jour de Saint Valentin,
Venez avant, nouveaux faiseurs,
Faictes de plaisirs ou douleurs
Rymes en françoys ou latin.

5   Ne dormez pas trop au matin,
Pensez a garder voz honneurs
A ce jour *de Saint Valentin.*

Heur et Maleur sont en hutin
Pour donner pers cy et ailleurs.
10   Autant aux maindres qu'aux greigneurs
Veullent deppartir leur butin,
A ce jour *de Saint Valentin.*

457i: R265

R265   Rondel · Orlians   [p. 457i]

A ce jour de Saint Valentin
Qu'il me couvient choisir ung per
Et que je n'y puis eschapper,
Pensee prens pour mon butin.

5   Elle m'a resveillé matin,
En venant a mon huis frapper,
A ce jour *de Saint Valentin.*

Ensemble nous arons hutin,
S'elle veult trop mon cueur happer,
10   Mais, s'Espoir je peusse atrapper,
Je parlasse d'autre latin,
A ce jour *de Saint Valentin.*

457s: R264

R266   Rondel par Benoit Damien*   [p. 458s]

Au plus fort de ma maladie
M'a abandonné Esperance,
Laquelle sans point decevance
Me devoit tenir compaignie.

Rondel by my lord of Orleans

On this Saint Valentine's Day,
Come forward, you poets newly minted,
Compose from pleasure or sorrow
Rhymes in French or Latin.

5   Don't sleep too long this morning,
Think to keep safe your honor
On this Saint Valentine's Day.

Happiness and Misery debate
The bestowing of mates here and there.
10   As much to the lowly as to the high-born,
They're intent on distributing their booty,
On this Saint Valentine's Day.

Rondel — Orleans

On this Saint Valentine's Day
When I must select a mate,
Not being able to avoid it,
I take Thought for my prize.

5   She awakened me in the morning,
Coming to rap upon my door,
On this Saint Valentine's Day.

We'll have a row
If she's bent on gripping my heart too firmly,
10   But if I could capture Hope,
I would be speaking another kind of Latin,
On this Saint Valentine's Day.

Rondel by Benoit Damien

At the crisis point of my malady
Hope abandoned me,
The one who with no deception
Was to bear me company.

5   Helas! se n'est pas mocquerie
        D'avoir perdu telle alliance,
        Au plus *fort de ma maladie.*

        Car certes, qui que chante ou rie,
        J'ay a tout heure desplaisance
10   Plus que nesung qui soit en France,
        Par quoy je ne sçay que je die
        Au plus fort *de ma maladie.*

458i: R267

R267   Rondel par Monseigneur   [p. 458i]

        Au plus fort de ma maladie
        Des fievres de Merencolie,
        Quant d'Anuy j'ay frissonné fort,
        J'entre en chaleur de Desconfort
5   Qui me met tout en Resverie.

        Lors je jangle mainte folie,
        Et meurs de soif de chiere lie.
        De mourir seroye d'accort,
        Au plus *fort de ma maladie.*

10   Adoncques me tient compaignie
        Espoir, dont je le remercie,
        Qui de me guerir se fait fort,
        Disant que n'ay garde de mort,
        Et qu'en riens je ne m'en soussie,
15   Au plus *fort de ma maladie.*

458s: R266

R268   Rondel par ledit Damien*   [p. 459s]

        Pour les maulx dont je suis sy plains,
        Fortune, ay je tort se me plains
        De ta grant fierté et rudesse
        Qui nuyt et jour sans point de cesse,
5   Me tient en douleur et en plains?

        Las! pense qu'ilz ne sont pas fains,
        Mais avant tresplus grans que mains,
        Veu que suis en telle foiblesse,
        Pour les *maulx dont je suis sy plains.*

5 Alas! If this isn't folly
   To have lost such an alliance
   At the crisis point of my malady.

   For, to be sure, no matter who sings or laughs,
   I suffer misery at every hour
10 More than any man in France,
   And this is why I know not what I say
   At the crisis point of my malady.

Rondel by my lord

   At the crisis point of my malady
   With the fevers of Melancholy,
   I shivered terribly because of Worry,
   And grew hot with Distress
5 Which has wholly delivered me to Delusion.

   Then I babble many a foolish thing,
   And die of thirst with a happy face.
   I wouldn't mind dying at all,
   At the crisis point of my malady.

10 And then Hope bears me
   Company, for which I thank him,
   Who did his best to heal me,
   Saying I should pay no heed to death,
   And that I should not worry about a thing,
15 At the crisis point of my malady.

Rondel by the said Damien

   Because of the ills that overwhelm me,
   Fortune, am I wrong to complain
   About the great arrogance and harsh treatment
   That, night and day, never ceasing,
5 Keep me in sorrow and misery?

   Alas! I think that these things are not imagined,
   But more terribly great rather than less so,
   Seeing that I suffer such weakness,
   Because of the ills that overwhelm me.

10   Or te requier a jointes mains
      Que tu vueillez a tout le mains
      Me tollir le mal qui me blesse,
      Car je suis en telle destresse,
      Que languir me fault soirs et mains,
15   Pour les *maulx dont je suis sy plains.*

459i: R269

R269   Rondel par ledit Damien*   [p. 459i]

      Pour parvenir a vostre grace,
      Esperant que mon dueil efface,
      Vous vueil servir jusqu'a la mort.
      De ce vous povez tenir fort
5   Que nul autre bien ne pourchace.

      Par quelque semblant que je face,
      Ne quelque chemin que je trace,
      N'est que pour arriver au port
      Pour parvenir *a vostre grace.*

10   Quant des yeulx ne vous voy en place,
      Pour rien qui soit ne me soulace,
      Dont Soussy me tient si tresfort.
      Non pour tant, mon seul reconfort,
      Ne me chault quoy qu'on me mefface,
15   Pour parvenir *a vostre grace.*

459s: R268

R270   Rondel de Mgr
a madame d'Angoulesme*   [p. 460s]

      A ce jour de saint Valentin,
      Puis qu'estes mon per ceste annee,
      De bien eureuse destinee
      Puissions nous partir le butin.

5   Menez a beau frere hutin
      Tant qu'ayez la pense levee,
      A ce jour *de saint Valentin.*

      Je dors tousjours sur mon coissin
      Et ne foys chose qui agree
10   Gueres a ma malassenee,

10   Now I ask, my hands joined,
     That you be willing at the very least
     To alleviate the ill that wounds me,
     For I'm in such distress
     I'm forced to languish night and day,
15   Because of the ills that overwhelm me.

Rondel by the said Damien

     In order to win your favor,
     Hoping to efface my sorrow,
     I intend serving you till death.
     You can be very certain
5   I seek no other benefit.

     Whatever expression I wear,
     Whatever road I must pass down,
     It's only to bring my ship to port
     In order to win your favor.

10   When I'm somewhere I can't see you,
     Nothing in the world brings solace,
     And Care grievously oppresses me.
     Yet even so, my sole consolation,
     I don't care if I have done wrong
15   In order to win your favor.

Rondel from my lord
to my lady of Angoulême

     On this Saint Valentine's Day,
     Since you are my valentine for this year,
     You and I might share the prize
     Of a very happy destiny.

5   Make love to my brother-in-law
     Until your belly swells up,
     On this Saint Valentine's Day.

     I remain sleeping on my pillow
     And do nothing at all that suits
10   My discontented lady,

Dont me fait les groings au matin,
A ce jour *de saint Valentin.*

460i: R271

R271   Rondel de Tignonville*   [p. 460i]

Pour la coustume maintenir
Ceste saint Valentin nouvelle,
Mon cuer a choisy damoiselle
Moyennant l'amoureux desir.

5   Par ung regart fait a loysir,
Se voult logier es mains de celle,
Pour la coustume *maintenir.*

S'on lui fait trop de mal souffrir,
Je m'accorde qu'il se rapelle
10   Et puis se tiengne a la plus belle
Que ses yeulx lui pourront choisir,
Pour la *coustume maintenir.*

460s: R270

R272   Rondel · Orlians*   [p. 461s]

Contre *fenoches* et *nox buze*
Peut servir ung «tantost» de France.
Da ly parolles de plaisance,
Au plus *sapere* l'en cabuze.

5   *Fa cossy* maintes foiz s'abuze,
Grandissime fault pourveance
Contre *fenoches* [et *nox buze*].

Sta fermo toutes choses uze,
Aspecte ung *poco* par savance,
10   *La Rasone* fa l'ordonnance
De quella medicine on uze
Contre *fenoches* [et *nox buze*].

461i: R273

Who grumbles in the morning
On this Saint Valentine's Day.

Rondel by Thignonville

So as to maintain the custom
This new Saint Valentine's day,
My heart has chosen a young lady,
Moved by a lover's desire.

5   Because of a look casually given,
He wishes to lodge within her hands,
So as to maintain the custom.

If he's made to suffer too much ill,
I agree that he can change his mind
10   And latch onto the most beautiful lady
His eyes can choose,
So as to maintain the custom.

Rondel — Orleans

Faced with useless Italian prattle
A French "get on with it!" will do.
Speak pleasant words to him,
Pretending to know more than you do.

5   Acting in this way puts him off,
One must take precautions on the grandest scale
Faced with useless Italian prattle.

Sit tight, he'll witter on endlessly,
Wait a little bit, that's wise.
10   Reason takes care to devise
What potion should be used
Faced with useless Italian prattle.

R273   Rondel · Orlians*   [p. 461i]

    Ce premier jour du mois de may,
    Quant de mon lit hors me levay,
    Environ vers la matinee,
    Dedans mon jardin de Pensee,
5   Avecques mon cueur seul entray.

    Dieu scet s'entrepris fu d'esmay,
    Car en pleurant tout regarday
    Destruit d'ennuyeuse gelee,
    Ce premier *jour du mois de may.*

10 En gast fleurs et arbres trouvay.
    Lors au jardinier demanday
    Se Desplaisance maleuree,
    Par tempeste, vent ou nuee,
    Avoit fait tel piteux array,
15 Ce premier *jour du mois de may.*

461s: R272

R274   Rondel · Orlians   [p. 462s]

    Qui est celluy qui s'en tendroit
    De bouter hors Merancolie,
    Quant toute chose reverdie
    Par les champs devant ses yeulx, voit?

5   Ung malade s'en gueriroit
    Et ung mort revendroit en vye.
    Qui est celluy *qui s'en tendroit?*

    En tous lieux on le nommeroit
    Meschant, endormy en follie.
10 Chasser de bonne compaignie
    Par raison, chascun le devroit.
    Qui est celluy *qui s'en tendroit?*

462i: R275

R275   Rondel · Orlians   [p. 462i]

    Allez vous musser maintenant,
    Ennuyeuse Merencolye,
    Regardez la saison jolye
    Qui par tout vous va reboutant.

Rondel—Orleans

This first day of the month of May
When I got up from my bed,
A bit towards morning,
I entered my garden of Thought
5   With just my heart.

God knows the enterprise was terrifying,
For, weeping, I saw everything
Had been destroyed by an unsettling frost,
This first day of the month of May.

10   Blasted flowers and trees I found there,
Then asked this question of the gardener,
If wretched Misery,
Through a tempest, wind, or clouds,
Had caused such a pathetic scene,
15   This first day of the month of May.

Rondel—Orleans

Who is the man who would hold back
From chasing Melancholy off
When he sees everything before
His eyes throughout the fields turned green?

5   A sick man would be healed thereby
And a dead man brought back to life.
Who is the man who would hold back?

In every place he'd be called
Wicked, sleepy, or a fool.
10   It's right that every one
Dismiss him from respectable company.
Who is the man who would hold back?

Rondel—Orleans

Now go hide yourself,
Annoying Melancholy,
Look at the pretty season
That everywhere chases you away.

5   Elle se rit en vous mocquant,
       De tous bons lieux estes bannye.
       Allez *vous musser maintenant.*

       Jusques vers Karesme prenant,
       Que jeusne les gens amaigrye
10   Et la saison est admortye,
       Ne vous monstrez ne tant ne quant.
       Alez *vous musser maintenant!*

462s: R274

R276   Rondel · Orlians   [p. 463s]

       Qui est celluy qui d'amer se tendroit,
       Quant Beaulté fait de morisque l'entree,
       De Plaisance si richement paree
       Qu'a l'amender jamés nul ne vendroit?

5   Cueur demy mort les yeulx en ouvreroit,
       Disant : «C'est cy raige desesperee.
       Qui est cellui *qui d'amer se tendroit?*»

       Lors quant Raison enseigner le vendroit,
       Il lui diroit : «A! vielle rassottee,
10   Lessés m'en paix, vous troublez ma pensee,
       Pour riens en ce nulluy ne vous croiroit.»
       Qui est cellui *qui d'amer se tendroit?*

463i: R277

R277   Rondel · Orlians   [p. 463i]

       Bon fait avoir cueur a commandement,
       Quant il est temps, qui scet laisser ou prendre
       Sans trop vouloir sotement entreprendre
       Chose ou ne gist gueres d'amendement.

5   Quel besoing est, quant on est a son aise,
       De se bouter en soussy et meschief?
       Je tiens amans pour folx, ne leur desplaise,
       De travailler sans riens mener a chief.

       C'est par Espoir ou par son mandement,
10   Qui tel mestier leur conseille d'aprendre.
       Il fait pechié, on l'en devroit reprendre.

5   She laughs while mocking you,
From all fine places you're banished.
Now go hide yourself.

Until Shrove Tuesday comes
While fasting makes folks grow thin
10   And the season's at death's door,
Don't show yourself here or there.
Now go hide yourself!

Rondel — Orleans

Who is the man who'd refrain from love
When Beauty begins a Morris dance,
So richly adorned with Pleasure
No man could improve upon her?

5   The heart half dead would open his eyes
And say: "This is absolute madness.
Who is the man who'd refrain from love?"

And then as Reason advances to tutor him,
He'd say: "Oh, you foolish old woman,
10   Leave me in peace, you trouble my thoughts,
There's no reason for any man to believe you."
Who is the man who'd refrain from love?

Rondel — Orleans

It's good to have your heart under command,
For when it's time the man can go ahead or leave off,
Unwilling to undertake some foolishness
That stands no chance of bettering his lot.

5   What need is there, when a man's at ease,
To get involved with worry and misfortune?
I consider lovers fools (may they not take offense),
For their labor brings them no fruits.

It's Hope who does this, or it's his command,
10   Counseling them to learn this way of life.
He commits a crime, he should be reprimanded.

J'en parle au vray, a mon entendement :
Bon fait avoir *cueur a commandement.*

463s: R276

R278   Rondel · Orlians   [p. 464s]

Je vous entens a regarder,
Et part de voz penser congnoys,
Essayé vous ay trop de foys,
De moy ne vous povez garder.

5   Cuidez vous par voz motz farder,
Mener les gens de deux en troys?
Je vous *entens a regarder.*

Vous savez tirer et tarder,
Rage faictes et feu gregoys.
10   Bien gangnez voz gages par moys,
Parachevez sans retarder :
Je vous *entens a regarder.*

464i: R279

R279   Rondel · Orlians   [p. 464i]

Plus de desplaisir que de joye,
Assez d'ennuy souvent a tort,
Beaucoup de soucy sans confort,
Oultraige de peine, ou que soye.

5   Trop de douleur a grant monjoye,
Foison de trespiteux rapport,
Plus de desplaisir *que de joye.*

Tant de grief que je ne diroye,
Mains amant ma vie que mort,
10   Pis que mourir, n'esse pas fort?
Telz beaux dons Fortune m'envoye,
Plus de desplaisir *que de joye.*

464s: R278

I speak the truth, according to my lights:
It's good to have your heart under command.

Rondel—Orleans

I understand you just by looking,
And see something of your thoughts,
Too many times I've tested you,
You cannot protect yourself from me.

5   Do you think that with tricky words
You can push men around from pillar to post?
I understand you just by looking.

You know how to advance and delay,
You live it up and make Greek fire.
10   Every month you ably earn your wages,
Delay no more and make an end:
I understand you just by looking.

Rondel—Orleans

More misery than joyfulness,
Plenty of worry, often unjust,
Much care and no consolation,
Painful outrage, wherever I am,

5   Too much sorrow in great abundance,
An overflowing of miserable news,
More misery than joyfulness.

Too much grief for me to express,
Loving life less than death,
10   Worse than dying, is this not a hard thing?
Such fine gifts are these that Fortune sends,
More misery than joyfulness.

R280   Rondel · Orlians   [p. 465s]

    Pour mon cueur qui est en prison,
    Mes yeulx vont l'aumosne querir.
    Guerez n'y peuent acquerir,
    Tant petitement les prise on.

5   Reconfort, qui est l'aumosnier,
    Et Espoir sont allez dehors.
    On ne donna point l'aumosne hier,
    Refuz estoit portier alors,
    Pour mon cuer *qui est en prison.*

10   Il est si plain de mesprison,
    De rien ne le fault requerir,
    N'essaier de le conquerir,
    Tousjours tient sa vielle aprison,
    Pour mon cuer *qui est en prison.*

465i: R281

R281   Rondel · Orlians   [p. 465i]

    Fortune! sont ce de voz dons,
    Engoisses que vous aportés?
    A present vous en deportés,
    Ce sont trop douloureux guerdons.

5   D'entrer ceans vous deffendons,
    Dures nouvelles rapportés.
    Fortune! *sont ce de voz dons?*

    Et oultre plus vous commandons
    Que les cueurs ung peu supportés.
10   Jouez vous et vous deportés
    Autre part, baillant telz pardons.
    Fortune! *sont ce de voz dons?*

465s: R280

R282   Rondel · Orlians   [p. 466s]

    Et commant l'entendez vous,
    Annuy et Merencolie?
    Voulez vous toute ma vie
    Me tourmenter en courrous?

Rondel — Orleans

For my heart which is in prison,
My eyes go seeking alms.
Achieving little doing so,
Such small value is placed on them.

5   Comfort, who is the almoner,
And Hope have made their way out.
Yesterday no alms were given me,
Refusal was the porter then,
For my heart which is in prison.

10   He is so full of injustice
There's no point asking him for anything
Or trying to foil him,
He clings to his old rancor
For my heart which is in prison.

Rondel — Orleans

Fortune! Are these your gifts,
These miseries you bring?
At this moment you rejoice in them.
Very painful rewards, that's what they are.

5   We forbid you entry here,
You bring bitter news.
Fortune! Are these your gifts?

And, even more, we command you
To lend hearts some support.
10   Take your sport and play your game
Somewhere else, offering such indulgences there.
Fortune! Are these your gifts?

Rondel — Orleans

And what is your understanding,
Worry and Melancholy?
Do you intend to torture me
All my life with your spiteful ways?

5   Le plus maleureux de tous
       Doy je estre? je le vous nye.
       Et commant *l'entendez vous?*

       De tous poins accordons nous,
       Ou, par la vierge Marie,
10   Se Raison n'y remedie,
       Tout va sen dessus dessous.
       Et commant *l'entendez vous?*

466i: R283

R283   Rondel · Orlians   [p. 466i]

       Voire, dea! je vous ameray,
       Anuyeuse Merencolie,
       Et servant de Plaisance lie,
       Par vous plus ne me nommeray.

5   Foy que doy a Dieu, si seray
       Tout sien, soit ou sens ou folie.
       Voire, dea! *je vous ameray.*

       Jamais ne m'y rebouteray
       En voz lactz se je m'en deslie,
10   Et se Bon Eur a moy s'alie,
       Je fais a vous . . . mais non feray.
       Voire, dea! *je vous ameray.*

466s: R24

R284   Rondel · Orlians   [p. 467s]

       Fortune, passez ma requeste,
       Quant assez m'aurez tort porté,
       Ung peu je soye deporté,
       Que Desespoir ne me conqueste.

5   Veu que je me suis en la queste
       D'Amours loyaument deporté,
       Fortune, *passez ma requeste.*

       Mon droit, sans que plus y acqueste,
       Aux jeunes gens j'ay transporté.
10   Se riens est de moy rapporté,

5   The most unfortunate of men,
Is that what I should be? I deny it.
And what is your understanding?

Let us find agreement on all points,
Or, by the Virgin Mary,
10   If Reason provides no remedy,
Everything will go topsy-turvy.
And what is your understanding?

Rondel — Orleans

Yes, it's true. I will love you,
Worrisome Melancholy,
And for your sake I'll no longer
Call myself a servant of merry Pleasure.

5   By the faith I owe God, I will be
All his, be this reason or madness.
Yes, it's true. I will love you.

Never will I let myself be trapped again
By your snares, once I free myself,
10   And should Good Fortune ally with me,
I make to you — but no, I won't.
Yes, it's true. I will love you.

Rondel — Orleans

Fortune, agree to my request,
Since you've done me so many wrongs,
May I have a little pleasure
So Despair does not overwhelm me.

5   Seeing that I've in good faith
Behaved loyally in the quest for Love,
Fortune, agree to my request.

Not taking further profit, I've
Surrendered my right to the young.
10   If you hear some report about me,

Je vous prie qu'on en face enqueste.
Fortune, *passez ma requeste.*

467i: R285

R285   Rondel · Orlians   [p. 467i]

De quoy vous sert cela, Fourtune?
Voz propos sont puis longs, puis cours,
Une foiz estes en decours,
L'autre plaine comme la lune.

5   On ne vous treuve jamais une,
Nouveltez sont en voz cours.
De quoy *vous sert cela, Fourtune?*

S'est vostre maniere commune,
Car, quant je vous requier secours,
10   Vous fuyez, aprés vous je cours
Et pitié n'a en vous aucune.
De quoy *vous sert cela, Fourtune?*

467s: R284

R286   Rondel · Orlians   [p. 468s]

Serviteur plus de vous, Merancolie,
Je ne seray, car trop fort y traveille.
Raison le veult, et ainsi me conseille
Que le face pour l'aise de ma vie.

5   A Nonchaloir vueil tenir compaignie
Par qui j'auray repos sans que m'esveille
Serviteur plus *de vous, Merancolie.*

Se de vous puis faire la departie,
Et il seurvient quelque estrange merveille,
10   Legierement passera par l'oreille.
Au contraire jamais nul ne me die
Serviteur plus *de vous, Merancolie.*

468i: R287

I beg you to make inquiries.
Fortune, agree to my request.

Rondel—Orleans

How does this serve you, Fortune?
Your plans are sometimes long, but then short,
One time you wane, the next
You've waxed full, just like the moon.

5   You're never found just the same.
Your court's full of novelty.
How does this serve you, Fortune?

This is your customary demeanor:
When I beg you for help,
10   You flee, then I chase after you,
And you feel no pity at all.
How does this serve you, Fortune?

Rondel—Orleans

No longer your servant, Melancholy,
Will I be, for I suffer too much.
This is Reason's advice and counsel too,
That I do this to live more at ease.

5   I wish to bear Indifference company,
Who'll provide me rest with no wakefulness,
No longer your servant, Melancholy.

If I manage to leave you,
And some strange thing occurs,
10   It will pass easily through my ear.
On the contrary, let no one ever say to me:
No longer your servant, Melancholy.

R287   Rondel · Orlians   [p. 468i]

Pourquoy moy, plus que les autres ne font,
Doy je porter de Fortune l'effort?
Par tout je vois criant : «Confort, Confort!»
C'est pour nyent, jamais ne me respont.

5   Me couvient il tousjours ou plus parfont
De Dueil nager sans venir a bon port?
Pourquoy moy *plus que les autres ne font?*

J'appelle aussi, et en bas et amont,
Loyal Espoir, mais je pense qu'il dort,
10   Ou je cuide qu'il contrefait le mort.
Confort, n'Espoir, je ne sçay ou ilz sont.
Pourquoy moy, *plus que les autres ne font?*

468s: R288

R288   Rondel · Orlians   [p. 469s]

Pourquoy moy, mains que nulluy
Que je congnoisse aujourd'uy,
Auray je part en Lïesse,
Veu qu'ay despendu Jennesse
5   Longement en grant anuy?

Doy je dont estre celluy
Qui ne trouvera en luy
Bon Eur qu'a peu de largesse?
Pourquoy moy, *mains que nulluy?*

10   J'ay Leal Desir süy
A mon povoir, et füy
Tout ce qui a tort le blesse.
Desormais, en ma veillesse,
Demouray je sans apuy?
15   Pourquoy moy, *mains que nulluy?*

469i: R289

R289   Rondel · Orlians   [p. 469i]

C'est pour rompre sa teste
De Fortune tanser
Qui a riens ne s'areste.

Rondel — Orleans

Why me, more than others,
Why should I bear the brunt of Fortune?
I go everywhere crying: "Comfort, Comfort."
All for nothing; I never get an answer.

5 Must I always swim in deepest
Sorrow, never coming to safe harbor?
Why me, more than others?

I call upon Faithful Hope
High and low, but I think he sleeps,
10 Or, it seems, he feigns death.
I know not where to find Comfort or Hope.
Why me, more than others?

Rondel — Orleans

Why do I, less than anyone
I know nowadays,
Share in Happiness,
Since I've spent long years
5 Of my youth in great suffering?

Should I then not be the one
Who'll find in his life
Even a modicum of good fortune?
Why do I, less than anyone?

10 I've followed Faithful Desire
As I could, fleeing
Everything that wrongfully hurts him.
Henceforth, in my old age,
Will I live on with no help?
15 Why do I, less than anyone?

Rondel — Orleans

It splits your skull
To dispute with Fortune,
Who stops at nothing.

        Trop seroit fait en beste.
5   C'est pour *rompre sa teste.*

        Quant elle tient sa feste,
        Lez aucuns fait danser,
        Et les autres tempeste,
        C'est pour *rompre sa teste.*

469s: R288

R290   Rondel   [p. 470s]

        Du tout retrait en hermitage
        De Nonchaloir, laissant Folie,
        Desormais veult user sa vie
        Mon cueur que j'ay veu trop volage.

5   Et savez vous qui son courage
        A changié? s'a fait maladie,
        Du tout *retrait en hermitage.*

        Fera il que fol ou que sage?
        Qu'en dictes vous, je vous en prie?
10   Il fera bien, quoy que nul die,
        Moult y trouvera d'avantage,
        Du tout *retrait en hermitage.*

470i: R291

R291   Rondel   [p. 470i]

        Sans faire mise ne recepte
        Du monde, dont compte ne tien,
        Mon cueur en propos je maintien
        Que mal et bien en gré accepte.

5   Se Fortune est mauvaise ou bonne,
        A chascun la fault endurer.
        Quant Raison y mectra la bonne,
        Elle ne pourra plus durer.

        Rien n'y vault engin ne decepte,
10   Au derrain on congnoistra bien
        Qui fera le mal ou le bien,
        Grans ne petiz je n'en excepte,
        Sans faire *mise ne recepte.*

470s: R290

It would be too stupid.
5   It splits your skull.

When she holds her feast,
She makes some dance
And torments others.
It splits your skull!

Rondel

Withdrawn completely to the hermitage
Of Indifference, leaving Folly behind,
My heart, whom I've known to be so fickle,
Intends henceforth there to pass his days.

5   And do you know what has made his feelings
Change? Illness has done it,
Withdrawn completely to the hermitage.

Will he act the sage or fool?
What, I ask, do you have to say about it?
10   Despite what anyone says, he'll do well,
Finding much to his advantage,
Withdrawn completely to the hermitage.

Rondel

Not paying any heed or attention
To the world, which I count as nothing,
I maintain my heart in such a state
That with grace it accepts both good and ill.

5   Whether Fortune is evil or favoring,
Every man must endure it.
When Reason sets limits,
Fortune no longer holds sway.

Nothing avails, trick or deceit,
10   In the end we'll know well
Who will do good, who ill,
I except neither high born nor humble,
Not paying any heed or attention.

R292   Rondel   [p. 471s]

Esse tout ce que m'apportez
A vostre jour, Saint Valentin?
N'auray je que d'Espoir butin,
L'actente des desconfortez?

5   Petitement vous m'enhortez
D'estre joyeulx ad ce matin.
Esse tout *ce que m'apportez?*

Nulle rien ne me rapportez
Fors *bona dies* en latin,
10   Vielle relique en viel satin.
De telz presens vous deportez.
Esse tout *ce que m'apportez?*

471i: R293

R293   Rondel · S. Cailleau*   [p. 471i]

Ou millieu d'espoir et de doubte,
Helas! je pense jours et nuys,
Mais, par Dieu! bien bref, se je puis,
J'auray pis, ou mieulx, quoy qu'il couste.

5   Mes yeulx ouvers, je n'y voy goute,
Si non que maintenant j'en suis
Ou millieu *d'espoir et de doubte.*

J'ay tant fait le guet et l'escoute
A la fenestre et a l'uys
10   Et n'ay pas se que g'y poursuys,
Ainçoys m'est force que j'escoute
Ou millieu *d'espoir et de doubte.*

471s: R292

R294   Rondel · Orlians   [p. 472s]

Quant Pleur ne pleut, Souspir ne vente,
Et que cessee est la tourmente
De Dueil, par le doulx temps d'Espoir,
La nef de Desireux Vouloir
5   A Port Eureux fait sa dessente.

Rondel

Is this all you bring me
On your day, Saint Valentine?
Will my sole reward be Hope,
The expectation of the malcontented?

5   You offer me scant cause
For celebration this morning.
Is this all you bring me?

You offer me nothing
Save "good day" in Latin,
10   An ancient relic in old satin.
You amuse yourself with such presents.
Is this all you bring me?

Rondel—S. Cailleau

Betwixt hope and doubt,
Alas, run my thoughts both day and night,
But, by God, very soon, if I prove able,
I'll have worse, or better, whatever the cost.

5   My eyes open, I see nothing,
Save that at present I am
Betwixt hope and doubt.

I've often watched and listened
At the window and door,
10   And do not find my quarry.
I must instead keep my ears open,
Betwixt hope and doubt.

Rondel—Orleans

When no Tears rain down, no Sighs burst forth,
And the torment of Suffering
Ceases because of Hope's fine weather,
The ship of Willing Desire
5   Ties up at the wharf of Fortunate Haven.

Sa marchandise met en vente
Et a bon marché la presente
A ceulx qui ont fait leur devoir.
Quant Pleur *ne pleut, Souspir ne vente.*

10   Lors les marchans de Longue Actente,
Pour engaiger et corps et rente
En ont ce qu'en peuent avoir,
D'en acheter font leur povoir
Tant que chascun cueur s'en contente.
15   Quant Pleur *ne pleut, Souspir ne vente.*

472i: R295

R295   Rondel · Faret*   [p. 472i]

Ou millieu d'espoir et de doubte,
Une foiz mal, autre foiz bien,
Je m'y treuve, mais je voy bien
Que c'est Fortune qui m'y boute.

5   Et pour vous dire, somme toute,
C'est une chose ou n'entens rien,
Ou millieu *d'espoir et de doubte.*

Mais quelque chose qui me coute,
Si esse bien le vouloir mien
10   De m'ouster hors de ce lieu
Aucunesfoiz, tant me reboute
Ou millieu *d'espoir et de doubte.*

472s: R294

R296   Rondel par Benoist Damien*   [p. 473s]

En la grant mer de Desplaisance,
Sans avoir espoir d'Alegence
De trouver port, fors de Douleur,
Nage tousjours mon povre cueur
5   En bateau bany d'Esperance.

Voille n'a que de Decevance,
Ne soutte que de Pacïence,
Jamais n'y vente que Maleur,
En la grant mer *de Desplaisance.*

It offers its goods for sale
And at favorable prices presents them
To those who've done their duty,
When no Tears rain down, no Sighs burst forth.

10   Then the merchants of Long Awaiting,
With their bodies and fortunes as collateral,
Obtain such goods as they can,
Do all in their power to buy as many
As will satisfy every heart,
15   When no Tears rain down, no Sighs burst forth.

Rondel—Faret

Betwixt hope and doubt,
One time ill, the next well,
I find myself, but I see clearly
It's Fortune who puts me there.

5   And to tell you the long and short,
I don't understand a thing,
Betwixt hope and doubt.

But whatever the cost to me,
It is certainly my wish
10   To get out of this plight.
At times, it is so repellent
Betwixt hope and doubt.

Rondel of Benoist Damien

On the great sea of Misery,
Without any hope that Relief
Might find a port, save that of Pain,
My poor heart sails ever on
5   In a boat banished from Hope.

This boat has no sail save one from Deceit,
No hold except one from Patience,
Never does any wind blow but Misfortune,
On the great sea of Misery.

10   Dueil, Soussy ont la gouvernance
      Qui ne luy donnent pour pitance
      Que bescuit durcy de Langueur,
      Avecques eaue de Rigueur.
      Ainsi languist, faisant penance,
15   En la grant mer *de Desplaisance.*

473i: R366

R297   Rondel Pour Mgr de Beaujeu*   [p. 475s]

      Puis qu'estes de la confrarie
      D'Amours, comme moustrent voz yeulx,
      Vous y trouvez vous pis, ou mieux?
      Qu'en dictes vous de telle vie?
5   Souffler vous y fault l'alquemye
      Ainsi que font jennes et vieux,
      Puis qu'estes *de la confrarie.*

      Ne cuidez par nygromancye
      Estre invisible. Se m'aist Dieux,
10   On cognoistra en temps et lieux
      Commant jourez de l'escremye,
      Puis *qu'estes de la confrarie.*

475i: R298

R298   Rondel · Orlians   [p. 475i]

      Dedans l'amoureuse cuisine,
      Ou sont les bons, frians morceaux,
      Avaler les convient tous chaux
      Pour reconforter la poitrine.

5   Saulce ne fault ne cameline
      Pour jennes appetiz nouveaux,
      Dedans *l'amoureuse cuisine.*

      Il souffist de tendre geline
      Qui soit sans octz, ne veilles peaux,
10   Mainssee de plaisans cousteaux.
      C'est au cueur vraye medecine
      Dedans *l'amoureuse cuisine.*

475s: R297

10   Sorrow, Care are in command,
         Who give it nothing nourishing
         Save the hard biscuit of Languor,
         Along with the water of Hard Times.
         Thus it languishes, doing penance,
15   On the great sea of Misery.

Rondel of my lord of Beaujeu

         Since you belong to the fellowship
         Of Love, as your eyes bear witness,
         Do you find yourself better off—or worse?
         What do you have to say about such a life?
5   You'll be needing alchemy,
         As do both young and old,
         Since you belong to the fellowship.

         Don't think that some sort of necromancy
         Will render you invisible. So help me God,
10   We'll know, the time and place will come,
         How you fare in the skirmishing,
         Since you belong to the fellowship.

Rondel—Orleans

         In the kitchen of love,
         Where appetizing morsels are found,
         You have to down them when they're hot
         To keep your belly satisfied.

5   No need of mustard sauce
         For these fresh, young appetites
         In the kitchen of love.

         A tender, young chicken fits the bill,
         Boneless and with skin not yet old,
10   Minced fine by pleasant knives.
         That's the heart's true remedy
         In the kitchen of love.

R299   Rondel · Orlians   [p. 476s]

Ou le trouvez vous en escript,
Se dient a mon cueur mes yeulx,
Que nous ne soions vers vous tieulx
Que devons de jours et de nuyt?

5   Se ne vous conseillon prouffit,
Nous en croirés vous? nennyl, Dieux!
Ou le trouvez *vous en escript?*

Quant rapportons quelque deduit
Que nous avons veu en mains lieux,
10   Prenez en ce qui vous plaist mieux,
L'autre lessez, esse mau dit?
Ou le trouvez *vous en escript?*

476i: R300

R300   Rondel · Orlians   [p. 476i]

L'eaue de Pleur, de Joye ou de Douleur,
Qui fait mouldre le molin de Pensee,
Dessus lequel la rente est ordonnee,
Qui doit fournir la despense du cueur,

5   Despartir fait farine de Doulceur
D'avecques son de Dure Destinee,
L'eaue de Pleur, *de Joye ou de Douleur.*

Lors le mosnier, nommé Bon, ou Mal Eur,
En prant prouffit ainsi que luy agree,
10   Mais Fortune souvent desmesuree
Lui destourbe maintesfoiz par rigueur,
L'eaue de Pleur, *de Joye ou de Douleur.*

476s: R299

R301   Rondel · Orlians   [p. 477s]

En verrai ge jamais la fin
De voz euvres, Merancolie?
Quant au soir de vous me deslie,
Vous me ratachez au matin.

Rondel — Orleans

Where do you find it written,
My eyes ask my heart,
That we haven't treated you
As we should both night and day?

5   If we counsel you not to your advantage,
Do you believe us? Not at all, by God.
Where do you find it written?

When we report on some delightful thing
That we've seen in many places,
10   Take what pleases you most,
Forget the rest, is that badly said?
Where do you find it written?

Rondel — Orleans

The waters of Weeping, Joy, or Sorrow,
Which make grind on the mill of Thought,
On which is fixed the rent
That is to provide for the heart's expenses,

5   Separate the flour of Sweetness
From the chaff of Bitter Destiny,
The waters of Weeping, Joy, or Sorrow.

Then the miller, named Good or Bad Luck,
Takes such profit as pleases him,
10   But Fortune, often immoderate,
Many times cruelly troubles
The waters of Weeping, Joy, or Sorrow.

Rondel — Orleans

Will I ever see the end,
Melancholy, of your works?
If I rid myself of you at night,
In the morning you're again stuck tight to me.

5   J'amasse mieulx autre voisin
         Que vous, que sy fort me guerrie.
         En verrai ge *jamais la fin?*

         Vers moy venez en larrecin
         Et me robez Plaisance Lie.
10   Suis je destiné en ma vie
         D'estre tousjours en tel hutin?
         En verrai ge *jamais la fin?*

477i: R369

R302   Rondel · Orlians   [p. 478s]

         Qu'est cela? — C'est Merencolye.
         — Vous n'entrerez ja. — Pourquoy? — Pource
         Que vostre compaignie acourse
         Mes jours, dont je foys grant folie.

5   — Se me chassez par Chiere Lye,
         Brief revendray de plaine cource.
         — Qu'est cela? — *C'est Merencolye.*

         — Il fault que Raison amolye
         Vostre cueur, et plus ne se cource,
10   Ainsi pourrez avoir ressource,
         Mais que vostre mal sens deslye.
         — Qu'est cela? — *C'est Merencolye.*

478i: R370

R303   Rondel · Orlians   [p. 479s]

         Ne cessés de tenser, mon cueur,
         Et fort combatre ces faulx yeulx
         Que nous trouvons, vous et moy, tieulx
         Qu'ilz nous font trop souffrir douleur.

5   Estrectement commandez leur
         Qu'ilz ne troctent en tant de lieulx.
         Ne cessés *de tenser, mon cueur,*

         Et leur monstrer telle rigueur
         Qu'ilz vous craignent, car c'est le mieulx
10   Qu'ilz obeissance, se m'aist Dieux,

5   I'd prefer any neighbor at all
       To you, warring on me so fiercely.
       Will I ever see the end?

       You come at me like a thief
       And rob me of merry Pleasure.
10   Am I fated all my life
       To remain forever in such turmoil?
       Will I ever see the end?

Rondel — Orleans

Who's there? — It's Melancholy.
— You won't get in. — Why? — Because
Your company shortens
My days, causing me to act the utter fool.

5   — If you chase me off with Pleasant Look,
       I'll return at once and in a hurry.
       Who's there? — It's Melancholy.

       — Reason must find a way to soften
       Your heart so as to be vexed,
10   In this way you'll find help,
       Provided Reason relieves you of your folly.
       — Who's there? — It's Melancholy.

Rondel — Orleans

Do not cease struggling, my heart,
And battle mightily against these false eyes
That you and I find are the sort
To make us suffer too much pain.

5   Strictly command them not
       To frequent so many places.
       Do not cease struggling, my heart.

       And show them such severity
       That they'll fear you — it's best
10   They obey you, God help me,

A vous, vous monstrant leur seigneur.
Ne cessés *de tenser, mon cueur.*

479i: R304

R304   Rondel · Orlians   [p. 479i]

Je ne voy rien qui ne m'anuye,
Et ne sçay chose qui me plaise.
Au fort, de mon mal me rapaise,
Quant nul n'a sur mon fait envye.

5   D'en tant parler ce m'est follie,
Il vault trop mieulx que je me taise.
Je ne voy *rien qui ne m'anuye.*

Vouldroit aucun changer sa vie
A moy, pour essaier mon aise?
10   Je croy que non, car plus mauvaise
Ne trouveroit, je l'en deffye.
Je ne voy *rien qui ne m'anuye.*

479s: R303

R305   Rondel · Orlians   [p. 480s]

Ne bien ne mal, mais entre deulx,
J'ay trouvé aujourd'ui mon cueur,
Qui, parmi Confort et Douleur,
Se seioit ou meillieu d'entre eulx.

5   Il me dit : «Qu'esse que tu veulx?»
Peu respondy pour le meilleur,
Ne bien ne mal, *mais entre deulx.*

Aux dames et aus paons faiz veulx,*
Se Fortune me tient rigueur,
10   De sa foy requerray Bon Eur.
Qu'il s'aquicte quant je me deulx,
Ne bien ne mal, *mais entre deulx.*

480i: R306

So make clear you are their lord.
Do not cease struggling, my heart.

Rondel — Orleans

I see nothing that does not trouble me,
And I know nothing that pleases.
Indeed, my pain diminishes
When no one envies my lot.

5   To say too much about this is folly,
It would be much better if I kept silent.
I see nothing that does not trouble me.

Would any man want to exchange his life
For mine, to taste the comfort I enjoy?
10   I think not, for he'd find nothing
Worse, that's my challenge to him.
I see nothing that does not trouble me.

Rondel — Orleans

Neither good nor bad, but between the two
I find my heart this day,
Who, between Comfort and Pain,
Finds himself in their very midst.

5   He says to me: "What is it that you wish?"
I say little in response, hoping for the best.
Neither good nor bad, but between the two.

I vow the peacock vow.
If Fortune provides me the resolve,
10   I'll ask Happiness, on his faith,
To keep his pledge whenever I complain,
Neither good nor bad, but between the two.

R306   Rondel · Orlians   [p. 480i]

Fermez luy l'uis au visaige,
Mon cueur, a Merancolye,
Gardez qu'elle n'entre mye,
Pour gaster nostre mesnaige.

5   Comme le chien plain de raige,
Chassez la, je vous en prye.
Fermez *luy l'uis au visaige.*

C'est trop plus nostre aventaige
D'estre sans sa compaignye,
10   Car tousjours nous tanse et crye,
Et nous porte grant dommaige.
Fermez *luy l'uis au visaige.*

480s: R305

R307   Rondel · Orlians   [p. 481s]

Ou milleu d'espoir et de doubte
Les cueurs se mussent plusieurs jours
Pour regarder les divers tours
Dont Dangier souvent les deboute.

5   L'oreille je tens et escoute
Savoir que, sur ce, dit Secours
Ou milleu *d'Espoir et de Doubte.*

Eslongnié de mondaine route
Me tiens, comme né en decours,
10   Entre les aveugles et sours.
Dieu y voye, je n'y voy goute
Ou milleu *d'Espoir et de Doubte.*

481i: R308

R308   Rondel · Orlians   [p. 481i]

Devenons saiges, desormais,
Mon cueur, vous et moy, pour le mieulx.
Noz oreilles, aussi noz yeulx,
Ne croyons de legier jamais.

Rondel — Orleans

Shut the door in his face,
That of Melancholy; make sure,
My heart, that he does not get in
To devastate our household.

5   As you would a dog that's gone mad,
Chase him off, I beg you.
Shut the door in his face.

It profits us much more
To be free of his company,
10   For every day he shouts and argues with us,
And he does us much hurt.
Shut the door in his face.

Rondel — Orleans

Betwixt Hope and Doubt
Hearts take refuge many a day
To observe the different ruses
Danger employs to rout them.

5   I perk up my ears and listen
To learn what Help has to say
Betwixt Hope and Doubt.

Far from the everyday crowd
I keep myself, as if born in an evil hour,
10   Among the blind and the deaf.
May God be my witness, I see nothing clearly
Betwixt Hope and Doubt.

Rondel — Orleans

Let us grow wise henceforth,
My heart, you and I, for the best.
Let us never lightly trust
Our ears or eyes.

5   Passer fault nostre temps en paix,
       Veu que sommes du renc des vieulx.
       Devenons *saiges, desormais.*

       Se nous povoions par souhaiz
       Rasjeunir, ainsi m'aide Dieulx,
10   Feu grejoix ferions en mains lieux,
       Mais les plus grans coups en sont faiz.
       Devenons *saiges, desormais.*

481s: R307

R309   Rondel   [p. 482s]

       Qui le vous a commandé,
       Soussy, de me mener guerre?
       Avant qu'on vous aille querre,
       Venez sans estre mandé.

5   M'ordonnez vous almandé,*
       Quant Mort de son dart m'enferre?
       Qui le vous *a commandé?*

       Pour Dieu, tost soit amendé
       Le mal qui tant fort me serre.
10   Aprés que seray en terre,
       Vous en sera demandé,
       Qui le vous *a commandé?*

482i: R371

R310   [Rondel]   [p. 291s]

       O tresdevotes creatures
       En ypocrisies d'amours,
       Que vous querez d'estranges tours
       Pour venir a voz aventures!

5   Vous cuidez bien par voz paintures
       Faire sotz, aveugles et sours.
       O tresdevotes *creatures!*

       On ne peut desservir deux cures,
       Ne prendre gaiges en deux cours.
10   Prenez les champs ou les faulbourgs,

5   We must pass our days in peace,
Now among the ranks of old men.
Let us grow wise henceforth.

If we had the power through some wish
To turn young again, so help me God,
10   We'd carry Greek fire to many a place,
But the heaviest blows have already been struck.
Let us grow wise henceforth.

Rondel

Who has given you the order,
Care, to war upon me?
Before anyone sought you out,
You come here unsummoned.

5   Do you command me like a conscript
When Death has pierced me with his iron point?
Who has given you the order?

For God's sake, let me be healed at once
Of the ill that so fiercely grieves me.
10   After I'm put in the ground,
You'll be asked the question:
Who has given you the order?

Rondel

O you creatures too devoted
To the hypocrisies of love,
How you seek out strange tricks
To bring your intrigues to conclusion!

5   You trust mightily in your deceptive words
To make others deaf, dumb, and blind.
O you creatures too devoted!

No one can serve two women,
Or take wages in two courts.
10   Consider the fields and the houses in town,

Ilz sont de diverses natures,
O tresdevotes *creatures!*

291i: Ch63

R311   [Rondel]   [p. 294s]

Puis que par deça demourons,
Nous, Saulongnois et Beausserons,
En la maison de Savonnieres,*
Souhaidez nous des bonnes cheres
5   Des Bourbonnois et Bourguignons.

Aux champs, par hayes et buissons,
Perdriz et lyevres nous prendrons,
Et yrons pescher sur rivieres,
Puis que par deça *demourons.*

10   Vivres, tabliers, cartes aurons
Ou souvent estudirons
Vins, mangers de plusieurs manieres.
Galerons, sans faire prieres,
Et de dormir ne nous faindrons,
15   Puis que par deça *demourons.*

294i: Ch62

R312   [Rondel]   [p. 293s]

Puis ça, puis la,
Et sus et jus,
De plus en plus,
Tout vient et va.

5   Tous on verra,
Grans et menus,
Puis ça, *puis la.*

Vieuls temps desja
S'en sont courus
10   Et neufs venus,
Que dea! que dea!
Puis ça, *puis la.*

293i: Ch61

These things have different natures,
O you creatures too devoted!

Rondel

   While we're staying over here,
   We residents of Sologne and Beauce,
   In this house in Savonnieres,
   Here's wishing very good cheer for us
5   From those of Bourbon and Burgundy.

   In the fields, through the hedges and brush,
   We'll take hares and partridge,
   And go fishing on the riverbanks,
   While we're staying over here.

10   We'll have provisions, table games, cards,
   To which we'll often devote ourselves,
   Wine, many different treats to eat.
   We'll have a high time and say no prayers,
   And never hesitate to take a nap,
15   While we're staying over here.

Rondel

   First here, then there,
   Up and down,
   More and more
   Everything comes and goes.

5   Everyone will see it,
   The great and low-born,
   First here, then there.

   Old times of yesterday
   Have sped away
10   And new times are upon us.
   Oh my! Oh my!
   First here, then there.

R313   **[Rondel]**   [p. 298s]

    Deux ou trois couples d'Ennuys
    J'ay tousjours en ma maison.
    Desencombrer ne m'en puis,

    Quoy qu'a mon povoir les fuis,
5   Par le conseil de Raison,
    Deux ou trois *couples d'Ennuys*
    [*J'ay tousjours en ma maison.*]*

    Je les chasse d'ou je suis,
    Mais en chascune saison
10   Ilz rentrent par ung autre huis,
    Deux ou trois *couples d'Ennuys.*

298i: Ch60

R314   **[Rondel]**   [p. 297s]

    As tu ja fait, Petit Souspir?
    Est il sur son trespassement
    Le cuer qu'as mis a sacquement?
    N'a il remede de guerir?

5   Tu as mal fait de le ferir
    En haste si piteusement.
    As tu *ja fait, Petit Souspir?*

    Amours, qui t'en doit bien pugnir,
    A fait de toy son jugement.
10   Pren franchise hastivement,
    Saufve toy, quant tu as loisir.
    As tu *ja fait, Petit Souspir?*

297i: Ch59

R315   **[Rondel] Fraigne***   [p. 296s]

    Et ou vas tu, Petit Soupir,
    Que j'ay ouÿ si doulcement?
    T'en vas tu mectre a saquement
    Quelque povre amoureux martir?

5   Vien ça, dy moy tost, sans mentir,
    Ce que tu as en pensement,
    Et ou vas tu, *Petit Soupir?*

Rondel

Two or three pairs of Worries
I keep always in my house.
I cannot free myself from them,

Although I flee them as I can,
5   Following Reason's counsel,
Two or three pairs of Worries
[I keep always in my house.]

I chase them off from where I am,
But every season
10   They enter again by some other door,
Two or three pairs of Worries.

Rondel

Have you done, Little Sigh?
Is he at the brink of death,
That heart you put in torment?
Is there no remedy?

5   You've done wrong to strike him
So piteously and in such haste.
Have you done, Little Sigh?

Love, who surely should punish you,
Has passed judgment on you.
10   Embrace generosity at once,
Save yourself while the going's good.
Have you done, Little Sigh?

R315   Rondel — Fraigne

And where are you going, little Sigh,
Which I heard so softly?
Are you going to torment
Some ill-fortuned martyr of love?

5   Come here, tell me quick, and don't lie,
Just what you have in mind,
And where are you going, little Sigh?

Dieu te conduye a ton desir,
Et te remaine a sauvement,
10   Mais je te requier humblement
Que ne faces ame mourir!
Et ou vas tu, *Petit Soupir?*

296i: Ch58

R316   [Rondel]   [p. 295s]

Penser, qui te fait si hardy,
De mectre en ton hostellerie
La tresdiverse compaignie
D'Anuy, Desplaisir et Soussy?

5   Se congié en as, si le dy,
Ou se le fais par ta folie,
Penser, *qui te fait si hardy?*

Nul ne repose pour leur cry,
Boute les hors, et je t'en prie,
10   Ou il fault qu'on y remedie.
Veulx tu estre a tous ennemy?
Penser, *qui te fait si hardy?*

295i: Ch57

R317   [Rondel]   [p. 286s]

L'ostellerie de Pensee,
Plaine de venans et alans
Soussis, soient petis ou grans,
A chascun est habandonnee.

5   Elle n'est a nul reffusee,
Mais preste pour tous les passans,
L'ostellerie *de Pensee.*

Plaisance chierement amee
S'i loge souvent, mais nuisans
10   Lui sont anuis, gros et puissans,
Quant ilz la tiennent empeschee,
L'ostellerie *de Pensee.*

286i: Ch56

May God guide you as you'd wish,
And bring you back in safety,
But I humbly ask you
Not to slaughter a single soul!
And where are you going, little Sigh?

10

Rondel

Thought, who has made you so bold,
To lodge in your place of residence
The very diverse company
Of Worry, Misery, and Care?

5

If you had permission, then say so,
Or if you did this in your madness,
Thought, who has made you so bold?

No one can rest with the noise they make,
Kick them out, I beg you,
Or we'll have to find some fix for this.
Do you want to be an enemy to all?
Thought, who has made you so bold?

Rondel

The Inn of Thought,
Full of cares that come
And go, some grave, some petty,
Lies open to every man.

5

No one is refused entrance,
For it is available to every passerby,
The Inn of Thought.

Pleasure, who is dearly loved,
Often lodges there, but finds
Worries harmful, imposing and mighty,
When they take possession of
The Inn of Thought.

10

R318   [Rondel]   [p. 285s]

Petit mercier, petit pannier!
Pour tant se je n'ay marchandise
Qui soit du tout a vostre guise,
Ne blasmez pource mon mestier.

5   Je gangne denier a denier,
C'est loings du tresor de Venise,
Petit mercier, *petit pannier.*

Et tandiz qu'il est jour ouvrier,
Le temps pers quant a vous devise.
10   Je voys parfaire mon emprise
Et par my les rues crier :
Petit mercier, *petit pannier.*

285i: Ch55

R319   [Rondel]   [p. 284s]

Riens ne valent ces mirlifiques
Et ses menues oberliques.
D'ou venez vous, petit mercier?
Gueres ne vault vostre mestier,
5   Se me semble, ne voz pratiques.

Chier les tenez comme reliques,
Les voulez vous mectre en croniques ?
Vous n'y gangnerez ja denier.
Riens ne valent *ces mirlifiques.*

10   En plusieurs lieux sont trop publiques,
Et pource, sans faire repliques,
Desploiés tout vostre pannier
Affin qu'on y puisse serchier
Quelques bagues plus autentiques.
15   Riens ne valent *ses mirlifiques.*

284i: Ch54

R320   [Rondel]*   [p. 288s]

Yver, vous n'estes q'un villain,
Esté est plaisant et gentil,
En tesmoing de May et d'Avril
Qui l'acompaignent soir et main.

Rondel

Petty tradesman, little basket!
Even though I have no goods for sale
That might suit your taste,
Don't put the blame on my profession.

5   Penny by penny my earnings come,
Far from being Venice's treasure trove,
Petty tradesman, little basket.

And since this is a working day,
Talking to you wastes my time.
10   I'll go finish my rounds,
Shouting through the streets:
Petty tradesman, little basket.

Rondel

These baubles are worth nothing,
The same for these small trinkets.
Where do you hail from, petty vendor?
Your goods are worth nothing,
5   And so are your deeds, I believe.

You think them dear as relics,
Do you want to set them down in some chronicle?
Nary a penny will this profit you.
These baubles are worth nothing.

10   They are well known in many places,
So make no protest,
But display all that your basket contains
So we can search therein
For some more genuine jewels.
15   These baubles are worth nothing.

Rondel

Winter, you're nothing but a low-life.
Summer is pleasant and high-born,
So testify May and April,
Who are his companions night and day.

5   Esté revest champs, bois et fleurs
       De sa livree de verdure
       Et de maintes autres couleurs
       Par l'ordonnance de Nature.

       Mais vous, Yver, trop estes plain
10   De nege, vent, pluye et grezil.
       On vous deust banir en essil.
       Sans point flater, je parle plain,
       Yver, *vous n'estes q'un villain!*

288i: Ch52

R321   [Rondel]   [p. 287s]

       Patron vous fays de ma galee,
       Toute chargee de pensee,
       Confort, en qui j'ay ma fiance,
       Droit ou pays de Desirance,
5   Briefment puissiez faire arrivee.

       Affin que par vous soit gardee
       De la tempeste fortunee
       Qui vient du vent de Desplaisance,
       Patron *vous fays de ma galee.*

10   Au port de Bonne Destinee
       Descharger tost sans demoree
       La marchandise d'Esperance,
       Et m'aportez quelque finance
       Pour paier ma joye empruntee.
15   Patron *vous fays de ma galee.*

287i: Ch51

R322   [Rondel]   [p. 290s]

       Hors du propos si baille gaige,
       Ce n'est que du jeu la maniere,
       Nulle excusacïon n'y quiere,
       Quoy que soit prouffit ou domage.

5   Tousjours parle plus fol que sage,
       C'est une chose coustumiere,
       Hors du propos *si baille gaige.*

5   Summer reclothes the fields, woods, and flowers
       With her livery all of green,
       And of many other colors too,
       Just as Nature commands.

       But you, Winter, are too much
10   Snow, wind, rain, and sleet.
       We should send you off to exile.
       No flattery this, my words are frank,
       Winter, you're nothing but a low-life.

Rondel

       I make you master of my galley,
       Fully loaded up with thought,
       Comfort, in whom I put my trust.
       May you prove able to make landfall
5   Right in the country of Desire.

       So you can keep the vessel safe
       In that tempest hazard-full,
       Blown up by Misery's wind,
       I make you master of my galley.

10   In the port of Good Fate,
       Discharge at once without delay
       The merchandise of Hope,
       And bring me some of the proceeds
       So I can pay the note on my borrowed joy.
15   I make you master of my galley.

Rondel

       If I make pledges without thinking,
       That's how the game is played,
       I offer no excuses for this,
       Be it to my profit or harm.

5   The fool always speaks more than the sage,
       That's the way things are,
       If I make pledges without thinking.

Se l'en me dit : «Vous contez rage,»
Blamez ma langue trop legere.
10   Raison, de Secret tresoriere,
La tance, quant despent lengage,
Hors du propos *si baille gaige!*

290i: Ch50

R323   [Rondel]   [p. 289s]

Je le retiens pour ma plaisance,
Espoir, mais que leal me soit,
Et se jamais il me deçoit,
Je renie son acointance.

5   Nous deus avons fait alïance
Tant que mon cueur tel l'aparçoit.
Je le retiens *pour ma plaisance.*

Monstrer me puisse bienvueillance,
Ainsi que mon penser conçoit,
10   Dont mainte lïesse reçoit.
Quant a moy, j'ay en luy fiance,
Je le retiens *pour ma plaisance.*

289i: Ch49

R324   [Rondel]   [p. 276s]

Ma plus chier tenue richesse
Ou parfont tresor de Pensee
Est soubz clef, seurement gardee
Par Esperance, ma Deesse.

5   Se vous me demandez : et qu'esse?
N'enquerez plus, elle est mussee,
Ma plus *chier tenue richesse.*

Avecques elle, seul sans presse,
Je m'esbas soir et matinee.
10   Ainsi passe temps et journee.
Au partir dy : «Adieu, maistresse,
Ma plus *chier tenue richesse!*»

276i: Ch48

If someone says: "You talk nonsense,"
You'd be blaming my too fickle tongue.
10　Reason, the treasurer of Secrets,
Faults it for wasting words,
If I make pledges without thinking.

Rondel

I retain Hope at my pleasure,
As long as he proves loyal,
And if he ever deceives me,
I will renounce his acquaintance.

5　We two have forged an alliance
To last as long as my heart sees him stay loyal.
I retain Hope at my pleasure.

Let him show me goodwill,
So that I can see it as such
10　And I come to know joy as a result.
For my part, I put my trust in him,
I retain Hope at my pleasure.

Rondel

The paragon I hold most dear
In the deep treasure chest of Thought
Is locked away, securely guarded
By Hope, my Goddess.

5　And if you ask: "Now what is it?"
Make no more inquiries, she's hidden away,
The paragon I hold most dear.

Alone, far from the crowd, I find
Pleasure morning and night in her.
10　Thus I pass my time and days.
Here are my parting words: "Good-bye, my lady,
The paragon I hold most dear."

R325   [Rondel]   [p. 275s]

Passez oultre, Decevant Vueil,
Ou portez vous cest estandart
De plaisant Actrayant Regart,
Soubz l'emprise de Bel Acueil?

5   De ma maison n'entrez le sueil
Plus avant, tirez autre part,
Passez oultre, *Decevant Vueil.*

Vous taschez a croistre mon dueil
Et gens engigner par vostre art.
10   A! a! maistre sebelin regnart,*
On vous congnoist tout cler a l'ueil.
Passez oultre, *Decevant Vueil!*

275i: Ch47

R326   [Rondel]   [p. 278s]

Ou puis parfont de ma merencolie
L'eaue d'Espoir que ne cesse tirer,
Soif de Confort la me fait desirer,
Quoy que souvent je la treuve tarie.

5   Necte la voy ung temps et esclercie,
Et puis aprés troubler et empirer
Ou puis *parfont de ma merencolie.*

D'elle trempe mon ancre d'estudie,
Quant j'en escrips, mais pour mon cueur irer
10   Fortune vient mon pappier dessirer
Et tout gecte par sa grant felonnie
Ou puis *parfont de ma merencolie.*

278i: Ch46

R327   [Rondel]   [p. 281s]

Anuy, Soussy, Soing et Merancolye,
Se vous prenez desplaisir a ma vie
Et desirez tost avancer ma mort,
Tourmentés moy de plus fort en plus fort,
5   Pour en passer tout a coup vostre envye.

Rondel

Pass on, Deceptive Urge,
Where are you bearing the standard
Of pleasant Attractive Look,
Under the emblem of Fair Welcome?

5   You'll not cross further the threshold
Of my dwelling, go somewhere else,
Pass on, Deceptive Urge.

You think to increase my pain
And trick people with your cunning.
10   Aha, aha! Master sable fox,
Our eyes see clearly what you are.
Pass on, Deceptive Urge.

Rondel

In the greatest depth of my melancholy,
A thirst for Comfort makes me long for
The waters of Hope, which I never stop drawing,
Though I often find them dried up.

5   I see them one time clear and clean,
And then the next troubled and foul
In the greatest depth of my melancholy.

With these waters I dilute the ink of my meditation
As I write, but to fill my heart with rage
10   Fortune comes and rips up the leaf,
And, an act of serious felony, throws it down
In the greatest depth of my melancholy.

Rondel

Worry, Care, Anguish and Melancholy,
If you take a dislike to my life
And are eager to quickly bring about my death,
Torment me even more cruelly
5   And have done with your hatred once and for all.

Ay je bien dit? Nennil, je le renye,
Et, par conseil de Bon Espoir, vous prye
Que m'espargnez, ou vous me ferez tort,
Anuy, Soussy, *Soing et Merancolye.*

10   Et qu'esse cy? je suis en resverie,
Il semble bien que ne sçay que je dye.
Je dy puis l'un, puis l'autre, sans accort.
Suis je enchanté? veille mon cueur ou dort?
Vuidez, vuidez de moy telle folye,
15   Anuy, Soussy, *Soing et Merancolye.*

281i: Ch43

R328   [Rondel]   [p. 280s]

Traytre regart, et que fais tu
Quant tu vas souvent *in questu?*
Tu fiers sans dire : garde toy,
Et ne sces la raison pourquoy,
5   N'il ne t'en chault pas ung festu.

Tu es de courage testu
Et de fureur trop *in estu,*
Change ton propos et me croy,
Traytre *regart, et que fais tu?*

10   On te deust batre devestu
Par my les rues *cum mestu,*
Par l'ordonnance de la loy,
Car tu n'as leaulté ne foy,
On le voit *in tuo gestu.*
15   Traytre *regart, et que fais tu?*

280i: Ch42

R329   [Rondel]   [p. 279s]

Monstrez les moy, ces povres yeulx,
Tous batuz et deffigurez.
Certes, ilz sont fort empirez
Depuis hier qu'ilz valloient mieulx.

5   Ne se congnoissent ilz pas tieulx?
Mal se sont au matin mirez.
Monstrez les moy, *ces povres yeulx.*

Have I spoken well? Not at all, I take it back,
And, on the advice of Good Hope, beg you
To spare me—if not, you do me wrong,
Worry, Care, Anguish and Melancholy.

10   What is this? I must have lost my mind.
It certainly seems I don't know what I'm saying.
I say one thing, then another, that contradict.
Am I under a spell? Does my heart wake or sleep?
Empty, empty me of this madness,
15   Worry, Care, Anguish and Melancholy.

Rondel

Traitorous look, what are you doing
Striking out so often on a quest?
You attack without saying, "Watch out!"
And you don't know why,
5   Nor does it matter to you a single bit.

You're big-headed in your boldness
And in your intensity too enraged,
Change your ways and trust me,
Traitorous look, what are you doing?

10   You should be beaten naked
Through the streets, and regretfully,
In the name of the law,
For you're neither faithful nor loyal.
We see it in the way you act.
15   Traitorous look, what are you doing?

Rondel

Show them to me, those poor eyes,
All bruised and disfigured.
Surely, their condition has worsened
Since yesterday, when they were better.

5   Don't they understand as much?
This morning they were looking bad.
Show them to me, those poor eyes.

Ont ilz pleuré devant leurs Dieux
Comme de leur grace inspirez?
10   Ou s'ilz ont mains travaulx tirez
Priveement en aucuns lieux?
Monstrez *les moy, ces povres yeulx.*

279i: Ch41

R330   [Rondel]   [p. 270s]

Pour nous contenter, vous et moy,
De bon cueur et entier povoir,
Ne s'espargne Leal Vouloir,
Viengne avant sans se tenir quoy.

5   Comandez moy je ne sçay quoy,
Vous verrez se feray devoir
Pour nous *contenter, vous et moy.*

Se faulz, par l'amoureuse loy,
Mis en fossé de Nonchaloir
10   Soye, sans grace recevoir.
Baillez la main, prenez ma foy,
Pour nous *contenter, vous et moy.*

270i: Ch40

R331   [Rondel]   [p. 269s]

Trop entré en la haulte game,
Mon cuer, d'ut, ré, mi, fa, sol, la,
Fut ja pieça, quant l'afola
Le trait du regart de ma dame.

5   Fors lui, on n'en doit blasmer ame,
Puis qu'ainsi fait comme fol l'a,
Trop entré *en la haulte game.*

Mieulx l'eust valu estre soubz lame,
Car sottement s'en afola.
10   Si lui dis je : «Mon cuer, hola!»
Mais conte n'en tint, sur mon ame,
Trop entré *en la haulte game.*

269i: Ch39

Have they wept before their gods
As if inspired by their favor?
10   Or perhaps they've suffered many hardships
Alone in one place or another?
Show them to me, those poor eyes.

Rondel

In order to satisfy us, you and me,
With a willing heart and all his strength,
May Faithful Desire hold back nothing;
Let him come forward and not hold his tongue.

5   Order me to do I don't know what,
You'll see if I carry out this duty
In order to satisfy us, you and me.

If I fail, according to the law of lovers,
Let me be dumped into the ditch
10   Of Indifference, receiving no mercy.
Give me your hand on it, trust my words,
In order to satisfy us, you and me.

Rondel

Too far into the high notes
Of do, re, mi, fa, so, and la, did my heart
Go long ago, when it was brought low
By the arrow of my lady's look.

5   Except for my heart, none should suffer blame,
Since in doing so he acted the fool,
Too far into the high notes.

Better for him to have died and been buried,
For foolishly he's gone mad.
10   Even now I tell him: "Heart of mine, hold on!"
But upon my soul he pays this no heed,
Too far into the high notes.

R332   [Rondel]   [p. 268s]

    Pourtant, s'avale soussiz mains,
    Sans macher, en peine confis,
    Si ne seront ja desconfis
    Les pensees qui m'ont en leurs mains.

5   En ce propos seurement mains
    Qu'il vendront a aucuns proffis,
    Pourtant, *s'avale soussiz mains.*

    Travail mectray, et soirs et mains,
    Autant ou plus qu'onques je fis,
10   S'a les achever ne souffis
    D'en faire quelque chose au mains,
    Pourtant, s'avale *soussiz mains.*

268i: Ch38

R333   [Rondel]   [p. 267s]

    Vivre et mourir soubz son danger
    Me veult faire Merancolye.
    Jamais vers moy ne s'amolye,
    Mais Plaisir me fait estranger.

5   D'ainsi demourer sans changer,
    Se me seroit trop grant folye
    Vivre *et mourir soubz son danger.*

    Pour d'elle plus tost me venger,
    Force m'est qu'a Confort m'alye,
10   Acompaigné de Chere Lye.
    A le suÿr me vueil ranger,
    Vivre et mourir *soubz son danger.*

267i: Ch37

R334   [Rondel]   [p. 272s]

    Resjouïssez plus ung peu ma pensee,
    Leal Espoir, et me donnez secours.
    Tousjours fuyez et aprés vous je cours,
    Ou j'ay assez de peine despensee.

Rondel

Even if I choked down many a care
Soaked in pain without chewing,
Never would the thoughts be defeated
That have me so much in hand.

5   I remain completely convinced
That they will afford some profit
Even if I choked down many a care.

I'll expose myself to suffering, day and night,
As much or even more than I've ever done,
10   And if this is not enough to finish them,
At least I will have done something,
Even if I choked down many a care.

Rondel

To live and die under his dominion,
That is what Melancholy intends for me.
Never does he soften in his attitude,
But instead makes me a stranger to Pleasure.

5   To remain thus without alteration
Would be too great a folly,
To live and die under his dominion.

To take the swiftest vengeance on her,
I am forced to ally myself with Comfort,
10   Whose companion is Fair Welcome.
He's the one I intend following,
To live and die under his dominion.

Rondel

Make my thoughts a bit more joyful,
Faithful Hope, and give me assistance.
You're always in flight as I chase after you,
Expending much effort.

5   La verray je jamais recompensee?
     Quelque office luy donnent en voz cours.
     Resjouïssez *plus ung peu ma pensee.*

     La penance soit par vous dispensee,
     Car desormais mes temps deviennent cours.
10   Ne souffrez plus son plaisir en decours.
     Veu que vers vous n'a faulte pourpensee,
     Resjouïssez *plus ung peu ma pensee.*

272i: Ch36

R335   [Rondel]   [p. 271s]

     Tousjours dictes : «Actendez, actendez».
     Pas ne payez vos reconfors contens,
     Joyeux Espoir, dont maints sont malcontens,
     Qui ne scevent comment vous l'entendez.

5   De Fortune, pour Dieu, l'arc destendez,
     Ne souffrez plus qu'elle face contens.
     Tousjours *dictes : «Actendez, actendez».*

     Vostre grace tost sur moy estandez,
     Vous cognoissez assez a quoy contens.
10   Plus ne perdray ung tel tresor com temps
     Ainsi que fait qui son eur met en dez.*
     Tousjours *dictes : «Actendez, actendez».*

271i: Ch35

R336   [Rondel]   [p. 274s]

     D'Espoir, et que vous en diroye?
     C'est ung beau bailleur de parolles,
     Il ne parle qu'en parabolles,
     Dont ung grant livre j'escriroye.

5   En le lisant je me riroye,
     Tant auroit de choses frivolles.
     D'Espoir, *et que vous en diroye?*

     Par tout ung an ne le liroye,
     Ce ne sont que promesses folles
10   Dont il tient chascun jour escolles.

5   Will I ever see them rewarded?
May they be granted some office in your court,
Make my thoughts a bit more joyful.

Assign me some penance
For I've little time left.
10   Do not allow my thoughts' pleasure to diminish.
Seeing they've intended you no disrespect,
Make my thoughts a bit more joyful.

Rondel

You always say: "Be patient, be patient."
You don't pay for your comforts in a hurry,
Joyful Hope, and many are dissatisfied,
Not understanding your intentions.

5   For God's sake, unstring Fortune's bow.
Don't let that one make more trouble.
You always say: "Be patient, be patient."

Bestow your favor on me now.
You know very well what my desire is.
10   No longer will I lose such a treasure as time
Like some man who gambles away his good fortune.
You always say: "Be patient, be patient."

Rondel

Of Hope? What should I say about him?
He's quite the chatterbox,
He speaks only in circumlocutions,
Of which I could compose a long book.

5   Reading it, I'd burst out laughing,
Finding so many frivolous things therein.
Of Hope? What should I say about him?

I couldn't finish reading it even in a year.
These are only foolish promises,
10   The sum of his daily instruction.

Telles estudes n'esliroye.
D'Espoir, *et que vous en diroye?*

274i: Ch34

R337   [Rondel]   [p. 273s]

M'amye Esperance,
Pour quoy ne s'avance
Joyeux Reconfort?
Ay je droit ou tort,
5   S'en lui j'ay fiance?

Peu de desplaisance
Prent en ma grevance.
Il semble qu'il dort,
M'amye *Esperance.*

10   Quoy qu'a lui je tence
Pour sa bien vueillance
Acquerir, au fort
Je suis bien d'accort
D'actendre allegence,
15   M'amye *Esperance.*

273i: Ch33

R338   [Rondel]   [p. 266s]

Tousjours dictes : «Je vien, je vien,»
Espoir, je vous congnois assez,
De voz promesses me lassez,
Dont peu a vous tenu me tien.

5   Se vous requier au besoing mien,
Legierement vous en passez.
Tousjours *dictes : «Je vien, je vien.»*

Vous ne vous acquictez pas bien
Vers moy, quant ung peu ne cassez
10   Les soussis que j'ay amassez.
En me contentant d'un beau rien,
Tousjours *dictes : «Je vien, je vien.»*

266i: Ch32

I would choose no such course of study.
Of Hope? What should I say about him?

Rondel

My friend Hope,
Why does Joyous Comfort
Not make his way forward?
Do I do wrong or right
5   Putting my trust in him?

He feels but little unease
In what I suffer.
He seems to slumber on,
My friend Hope.

10   Even though I carp at him
So as to gain
His good will, in essence
I am much disposed
To wait for relief,
15   My friend Hope.

Rondel

You always say: "I'm coming, I'm coming,"
Hope, I know well what you're about;
You weary me with promises,
So I put little stock in you.

5   If I summon you in a time of need,
You lightly pass the matter off.
You always say: "I'm coming, I'm coming."

You really don't do right
By me, when you fail to get rid of
10   A little of that heap of cares I've laid by.
Contenting me with some sweet nothing,
You always say: "I'm coming, I'm coming."

R339   [Rondel]   [p. 265s]

Armez vous de Joyeux Confort,
Je vous en pry, mon pouvre cueur,
Que Destresse, par sa rigueur,
Ne vous navre jusqu'a la mort.

5   Vous couvrant d'un paveis, au fort,
Tant qu'arez passé sa chaleur,
Armez *vous de Joyeux Confort.*

Faictes bon guet tant qu'elle dort.
Espoir dit qu'il sera seigneur
10   Et fera vostre fait meilleur.
Contre Dangier, qui vous fait tort,
Armez vous *de Joyeux Confort.*

265i: Ch31

R340   [Rondel]   [p. 264s]

Et bien, de par Dieu, Esperance,
Esse doncques vostre plaisir?
Me voulez vous ainsi tenir
Hors et ens tousjours en balance?

5   Ung jour j'ay vostre bienveillance,
L'autre ne la sçay ou querir.
Et bien, *de par Dieu, Esperance,*
[*Esse doncques vostre plaisir?*]*

Au fort, puis que suis en la dance,
Bon gré maugré m'y fault fournir,
10   Et n'y sçay de quel pié saillir.
Je reculle puis je m'avance.
Et bien, *de par Dieu, Esperance!*

264i: Ch30

R341   [Rondel]   [p. 263s]

En faulte du logeis de Joye,
L'ostellerie de Pensee
M'est par les fourriers ordonnee,
Ne sçay combien fault que je y soye.

Rondel

Arm yourself with Joyful Comfort,
I beg you, my poor heart,
So that Distress, with her violence,
Deals you not some mortal wound.

5   Moreover, take cover behind some large shield
Until you escape her ardor,
Arm yourself with Joyful Comfort.

Keep a good watch while she sleeps.
Hope says he'll take the upper hand
10   And improve your lot.
Against Danger, who has wronged you,
Arm yourself with Joyful Comfort.

Rondel

Now then, for God's sake, Hope,
Is this your pleasure?
Do you intend keeping me
Outside, then in, always on the scales?

5   One day I enjoy your good will,
The next I don't know where to find it.
Now then, for God's sake, Hope.
[Is this your pleasure?]

In any case, since I am at the dance,
10   Willy-nilly I must take part,
And I don't know what foot to stand on.
I fall back, then step forward,
Now then, for God's sake, Hope.

Rondel

Lacking the lodging of Joy,
The hostel of Thought
Has been assigned me by the harbingers,
I know not how long I must there remain.

5   Autre part ne me bouteroye,
       Content m'en tien et bien m'agree,
       En faulte *du logeis de Joye.*

       Je parle tout bas, qu'on ne l'oye,
       Pensant de veoir quelque annee
10   Quelle sera ma destinee,
       Et en quel lieu demourer doye,
       En faulte *du logeis de Joye.*

263i: Ch29

R342   [Rondel]   [p. 262s]

       Aidez ce povre caÿment,
       Souspir, je le vous recommende.
       De vous, quant aumosne demende,
       Ne se parte meschantement.

5   Son cas monstre piteusement,
       Il semble que la mort actende.
       Aidez *ce povre caÿment.*

       Donnez lui assez largement
       Qu'il ne meure, Dieu l'en deffende.
10   Affin que n'en faictes amende,
       Au jour d'amoureux jugement,
       Aidez *ce povre caÿment.*

262i: Ch28

R343   [Rondel] de Gilles des Ormes*   [p. 261s]

       Hola! hola! Souspir, on vous oyt bien.
       C'est a ung sourt a qui il le fault faire.
       Retrayez vous et pensez de vous taire,
       Car Dangier oit si cler qu'il n'y fault rien.

5   Se d'avanture il vous oyt, je vous tien
       Pour rué jus, car c'est vostre adversaire.
       Hola! hola! *Souspir, on vous oyt bien.*

       Ne saillez plus, actendez aucun bien.
       Vous voulez vous de vous mesmes deffaire?
10   Prenez conseil, quant c'est pour vostre affaire,

5   I would not take shelter elsewhere,
Here I am content, the place suits me well,
Lacking the lodging of Joy.

I speak very softly so no one hears,
Thinking some year to find out
10   What my fate will be,
And where I must make my dwelling,
Lacking the lodging of Joy.

Rondel

Help this poor beggar,
Sigh, I commend him to you.
Give him something when he begs alms,
Let him not depart malcontented.

5   He pleads his case piteously,
It seems he waits for death.
Help this poor beggar.

Give him a gift large enough
So he does not expire, God forbid,
10   And you'll have no amends to make
On lovers' judgment day,
Help this poor beggar.

Rondel of Gilles des Ormes

Stop! Stop! Sigh, you've been well heard.
Only the deaf need you to carry on so.
Withdraw and take care to keep silent,
For Danger hears clearly, missing nothing.

5   If by chance he hears you, I'll consider you
Cast down, for he's your enemy.
Stop! Stop! Sigh, you've been well heard.

Go out no more, wait for something good.
Are you bent on your own destruction?
10   Take counsel because this is your business,

Et pour le mieulx, croyez, sans plus, le mien.
Hola! hola! *Souspir, on vous oyt bien.*

261i: Ch27

R344 [Rondel] Philippe de Boulainvillier*   [p. 260s]

Hola! hola! Soupir, on vous hoit bien,
Vous vous cuidez embler trop coiaement,
Contrefaisant ung peu le cayement,
Grant fain avez qu'on vous die : tien!

5   Vous ne querez que d'ung cueur le soustien,
C'est de tieulx gens tousjours l'esbatement.
Hola! hola! *Soupir, on vous hoit bien.*

Trop vous hastez, de vray, comme je tien,
Car l'on congnoist vostre fait clerement,
10   Ung autresfoiz faictes plus sagement,
Car maintenant vous n'y gangnerez rien.
Hola! hola! *Soupir, on vous hoit bien.*

260i: Ch26

R345   [Rondel]   [p. 259s]

Mon cuer, estouppe tes oreilles
Pour le vent de Merencolie.
S'il y entre, ne doubte mye,
Il est dangereux a merveilles.

5   Soit que tu dormes ou tu veilles,
Fais ainsi que dy, je t'en prie :
Mon cuer, *estouppe tes oreilles.*

Il cause doleurs nompareilles,
Dont s'engendre la maladie
10   Qui n'est pas de legier guerie.
Croy moy, s'a Raison te conseilles,
Mon cuer, *estouppe tes oreilles.*

259i: Ch25

And, in short, it's best you trust what I advise.
Stop! Stop! Sigh, you've been well heard.

Rondel — Philippe de Boulainvillier

Stop! Stop! Sigh, you've been well heard,
You are too coy in your attempts to hide,
Pretending a bit to be a beggar,
You're very eager to hear someone say: hold on!

5   You seek nothing but sustenance for a heart.
That is always the game such folks play.
Stop! Stop! Sigh, you've been well heard.

You hurry off too quickly, it's true I say,
But what you do is carefully noted.
10   Next time act more circumspectly,
For right now you'll gain nothing here.
Stop! Stop! Sigh, you've been well heard.

Rondel

My heart, stop up your ears
Because of Melancholy's gusting.
If he enters, do not doubt
That he's a terrible threat.

5   Whether you slumber or wake,
Do just what I say, I beg you:
My heart, stop up your ears.

He causes pain beyond compare,
And so brings on an illness
10   That is not easily cured.
Believe me, if you credit Reason's advice,
My heart, stop up your ears.

R346   [Rondel]   [p. 258s]

Ça, venez avant, Esperance!
Or y perra que respondrez
Et comment vous vous deffendrez.
On se plaint de vous a oultrance.

5   L'un dit que promectez de loing,
Et qu'en estes bonne maistresse.

L'autre que faillez au besoing,
En ne tenant gueres promesse.

Quoy que tardez, c'est la fiance
10   Qu'aux faiz de chascun entendrez,
Et au derrain guerdon rendrez.
Dy je bien, ou se trop m'avance?
Ça, venez *avant, Esperance.*

258i: Ch24

R347   [Rondel]   [p. 257s]

Assez pourveu, pour decy a grant piece,
Et plus qu'assez, de penser et anuy,
Je me treuve sans cognoistre nulluy
Qui se vente d'en avoir telle piece.

5   Fortune dit, qui tout mon fait despiece,
Que j'endure comme maint aujourd'uy,
Assez pourveu, *pour decy a grant piece.*

Pourquoy souvent je metz soubz mon pié ce,
Prenant confort d'Espoir, comme celluy
10   Qui me fye parfaictement en luy,
Ainsi remains—qui le croiroit?—empiece,
Assez pourveu, *pour decy a grant piece.*

257i: Ch23

R348   [Rondel]   [p. 256s]

Sans ce, le demourant n'est rien.
—Qu'esse?—Je le vous ay a dire?
N'enquerez plus, il doit souffire,
C'est conseil que tressegret tien.

Rondel

Hey, Hope, come over here!
Now we'll see what answer you have
And how you'll defend yourself.
Serious complaints have been lodged.

5   One man says that what you promise is far-off
And that you're a trusty mistress in such matters.

The other that you fail in times of need,
And hardly keep to what you've pledged.

However slow you are, opinion holds
10   That you're attentive to the affairs of every man,
And in the end render a reward.
Do I say right, or have I gone too far?
Hey, Hope, come over here.

Rondel

Well provided for a long time now
With more than enough thoughts and worry,
I find I know no one myself
Who could boast he's endured so many.

5   Fortune, who wrecks all my plans, says
I suffer the same these days as do many,
Well provided for a long time now.

And that's why I pay this no mind sometimes
And take comfort in Hope, like a man
10   Who trusts in him completely.
I so remain—who would think it?—a while longer.
Well provided for a long time now.

Rondel

Without it, the rest is nothing.
—What is it?—I have to tell you?
Ask no more, this should suffice.
It's the counsel I keep most secret.

5   Pour tant n'y entendez que bien,
       Autrement je ne le desire;
       Sans ce, *le demourant n'est rien.*

       Ainsy m'esbas ou penser myen,
       Et mainte chose faiz escripre
10   En mon cueur pour le faire rire,
       Tout ung est mon fait et le sien,
       Sans ce, *le demourant n'est rien.*

256i: Ch22

R349   [Rondel]   [p. 255s]

       Tant que Pasques soient passees,
       Se nous avons riens trespassé,
       Prions mercy du temps passé,
       Et pour les ames trespassees.

5   Chascun, pas a pas, ses passees
       Face, avant que soit trespassé,
       Tant que Pasques *soient passees.*

       Foleur a fait grandes passees,
       Mains cueurs ont tout oultre passé;
10   Pource, par nous soit compassé
       D'eschever faultes compassees,
       Tant que Pasques *soient passees.*

255i: Ch21

R350   [Rondel]   [p. 254s]

       Mon cuer se combat a mon eueil,
       Jamais ne les treuve d'acort.
       Le cuer dit que l'oeil fait rapport
       Que touzjours lui acroist son dueil.

5   La verité savoir j'en veil :
       Que semble il qui en ait le tort?
       Mon cuer *se combat a mon eueil.*

       Se je treuve que Bel Acueil
       Ayt gecté entre eulx aucun sort,
10   Je la condampneray a mort.

5 Nevertheless, see only the good in this,
I would not have it otherwise:
Without it, the rest is nothing.

And so I take pleasure in the thoughts I have
And have inscribed many things
10 Within my heart to make it laugh,
My affairs and his own, it's all the same.
Without it, the rest is nothing.

Rondel

Until Eastertide passes by,
If we have committed any trespasses,
We'll beg mercy for times past,
And for those souls who have passed on.

5 Let everyone think on his past deeds,
One by one, before it's too late,
Until Eastertide passes by.

Foolishness has taken great strides,
Many hearts have passed beyond moderation;
10 And so, let us prepare
To right the wrongs we brought to pass,
Until Eastertide passes by.

Rondel

My heart struggles against my eye,
Never do I find them in accord.
The heart says that the eye brings news
That day by day increases the pain it feels.

5 I want to know the truth of the matter:
Who does it seem is in the wrong?
My heart struggles against my eye.

If I find that Fair Welcome
Has cast some spell upon them,
10 I will condemn that one to death.

Doiz je souffrir ung tel orgueil?
Mon cuer *se combat a mon eueil.*

254i: Ch20

R351   [Rondel]   [p. 253s]

Je prens en mes mains voz debas
Desormais, mon cueur et mes yeulx.
Se longuement vous seufre tieuls,
Moy mesmes de mon tour m'abas.

5   Pour vostre prouffit me combas,
Le desirant de bien en mieuls.
Je prens en mes mains *voz debas.*

Quant voz desirs souvent rabas
Desordonnés, en aucuns lieus,
10   Mon devoir fais, ainsi m'aid Dieus!
Passons temps en plus beaus esbas.
Je prens *en mes mains voz debas.*

253i: Ch19

R352   [Rondel]   [p. 252s]

Qui? quoy? comment? a qui? pourquoy?
Passez, presens ou avenir,
Quant me viennent en souvenir,
Mon cueur en penser n'est pas coy.

5   Au fort, plus avant que ne doy,
Ja mais je ne pense enquerir
Qui? quoy? *comment? a qui? pourquoy?*

On s'en puet rapporter a moy
Qui de vivre ay eu beau loisir
10   Pour bien aprendre et retenir,
Assez ay congneu, je m'en croy,
Qui? quoy? *comment? a qui? pourquoy?*

252i: Ch18

Should I permit such arrogance?
My heart struggles against my eye.

Rondel

I will take charge of your differences,
Heart and eyes of mine, from this day forward.
Permitting such goings-on for long
Would bring about my own destruction.

5   I will fight for what might profit you both,
Hoping to change the good to better.
I will take charge of your differences.

When I suppress your desires, unbridled as they are,
At different times and in several places,
10   I do my duty, so help me God!
Let's spend our time with more pleasant diversions.
I will take charge of your differences.

Rondel

Who? What? How? To whom? Why?
Past, present, or future,
When they come to mind
My heart is not silent about its thoughts.

Indeed, I never think to push my inquiry
Any further than I should,
Who? What? How? To whom? Why?

You can take my word for it:
In my life I've enjoyed considerable leisure
10   To learn things well and commit them to memory.
I have understood much, I think,
Who? What? How? To whom? Why?

R353   [Rondel]   [p. 251s]

L'un ou l'autre desconfira,
De mon Cueur et Merencolye.
Auquel que Fortune s'alye,
L'autre «je me rens» lui dira.

5   D'estre juge me suffira.
Pour mettre fin en leur folye,
L'un ou l'autre *desconfira*.

Dieu scet comment mon cueur rira,
Se gangne, menant chiere lye
10   Contre ceste saison jolye,
On verra comment en yra :
L'un ou l'autre *desconfira*.

251i: Ch17

R354   [Rondel]   [p. 250s]

Ne hurtez plus a l'uis de ma pensee,
Soing et Soussi, sans tant vous traveiller,
Car elle dort et ne veult s'esveiller,
Toute la nuyt en paine a despensee.

5   En dangier est, s'elle n'est bien pensee.
Cessez, cessez, laissez la sommeiller,
Ne hurtez plus *a l'uis de ma pensee*.

Pour la guerir Bon Espoir a pensee
Medecine qu'a fait apareiller.
10   Lever ne peut son chief de l'oreiller,
Tant qu'en repos se soit recompensee.
Ne hurtez plus *a l'uis de ma pensee*.

250i: Ch16

R355   [Rondel]   [p. 249s]

Se je fois lealle requeste,
Soing et Soucy, et bon vous semble,
Pour Dieu, acordons nous ensemble.
Qui a tort soit mis en enqueste.

Rondel

One or the other will prove the victor
In the contest between my Heart and Melancholy.
If one gains Fortune as an ally,
The other will say, "Accept my surrender."

5   I'll be content to play the judge
And so put an end to their madness.
One or the other will prove the victor.

God knows how my heart will burst out laughing
If he wins, putting on a show of good cheer
10   In this joyous season;
We'll see what happens:
One or the other will prove the victor.

Rondel

Bang no more at the door of my thought,
Care and Worry; do not tire yourselves out,
For thought sleeps and has no wish to wake up
After passing a long and painful night.

5   Thought is in danger, if not well guarded.
Stop, stop, let him go on sleeping,
Bang no more at the door of my thought.

To cure him Good Hope has come up with
A medicine it has prepared.
10   From the pillow, thought cannot raise its head
Before reaping the reward of proper rest.
Bang no more at the door of my thought.

Rondel

If I advance a request in good faith,
Care and Worry, and you find it worthwhile,
For God's sake, let us come to an agreement.
Let the one in the wrong be brought to the bar.

5   Quant vous ne moy bien n'y aqueste,
       Pour juger droit conseil asemble,
       Se je fois *lealle requeste.*

       Je ne requier autre conqueste
       Que d'Espoir, qui larron resemble
10   Et sans cause de mon cueur s'emble.
       Dieu me secoure en cette queste,
       Se je fois *lealle requeste.*

249i: Ch15

R356   [Rondel]   [p. 248s]

       Paix ou treves je requier, Desplaisance.
       S'en toy ne tient, pas ne tendra a moy
       Que ne soyons desormais en requoy.
       Acordon nous, chargeons en Esperance.

5   Que gaingne tu a me fere grevence?
       Assez me mectz en devoir, sur ma foy.
       Paix ou *treves je requier, Desplaisance.*

       Ou combatons tellement a oultrance
       Que l'ung die : Je me rens ou ren toy.
10   Mieulx estre mort je veil, s'estre le doy,
       Qu'ainsi languir. D'offrir premier m'avance.
       Paix ou *treves je requier, Desplaisance.*

248i: Ch14

R357   [Rondel]   [p. 247s]

       Espoir, confort des maleureux,
       Tu m'estourdis trop les oreilles
       De tes promesses non pareilles,
       Dont trompes les cueurs doloreux.

5   En amusant les amoureux,
       Et faisent baster aux corneilles,*
       Espoir, confort *des maleureux,*

       Ne soiez plus si rigoreux,
       Mieux vault qu'a Raison te conseilles,
10   Car chascun se donne merveilles

5   Since neither you nor I gain thereby,
       I will assemble an able court to pass judgment,
       If I advance a request in good faith.

       I ask for no victory
       Except over Hope, who's like a thief,
10   Having made off with my heart for no reason.
       May God further me in this suit,
       If I advance a request in good faith.

Rondel

Peace or truce is what I seek, Misery.
If it doesn't depend on you, it won't on me either
That we live henceforth in harmony.
So let's come to an agreement and get on board Hope.

5   What do you gain by hurting me?
       You're making it very much my duty, upon my faith.
       Peace or truce is what I seek, Misery.

       Otherwise we can fight it out to the end
       And one of us says: I give up or surrender.
10   I would rather die, if it must be so,
       Than languish in this way. I make the first offer.
       Peace or truce is what I seek, Misery.

Rondel

Hope, comfort of the unfortunate,
You stop my ears too full
Of promises unlike all others,
With which you deceive sorrowful hearts,

5   While amusing those in love,
       And leaving them all with their mouths agape,
       Hope, comfort of the unfortunate.

       You should not be so severe.
       Better to have Reason advise you,
10   For everyone is amazed

Que n'as pitié des langoreux,
Espoir, confort *des maleureux.*

247i: Ch13

R358   [Rondel] Le duc d'Orleans   [p. 292s]

Sera elle point jamais trouvee
Celle qui ayme loyauté
Et qui a ferme voulenté
Sans avoir legiere pensee?

5   Il convient qu'elle soit criee
Pour en savoir la verité.
Sera elle point *jamais trouvee?*

Je croy bien qu'elle est deffiee
Des aliez de Faulceté
10   Dont il y a si grant planté,
Que de paour elle s'est mussiee.
Sera elle point *jamais trouvee?*

292i: R359

R359   [Rondel] Le duc Jehan
            de Bourbon*   [p. 292i]

Duc d'Orleans, je l'ay trouvee
Celle qui ayme loyauté,
Et qui a ferme voulenté
Sans avoir legiere pensee.

5   Ja ne fault qu'elle soit criee,
J'en sçay assez la verité.
Duc d'Orleans, *je l'ay trouvee.*

C'est ma dame tresbien amee,
Qui a de biens si grant planté
10   Qu'el ne craint vostre Faulceté,
Ne de ceulx de vostre livree.
Duc d'Orleans, *je l'ay trouvee!*

Ll. 1, 5, 8. Initial letters omitted.

292s: R358

That you do not pity those who languish,
Hope, comfort of the unfortunate.

Rondel — the duke of Orleans

Will that lady ever be found,
The one who loves faithfully
And whose will is strong,
Untroubled by inconstant thoughts?

5 Her name should be loudly proclaimed
So the truth of the matter be made known.
Will that lady ever be found?

I firmly believe she has been challenged
By the allies of Falseness,
10 Whose company is so many,
And, fearful, she has taken to hiding.
Will that lady ever be found?

Rondel — the duke, John of Bourbon

Duke of Orleans, I've found the lady
Who loves faithfully,
And whose will is strong,
Untroubled by inconstant thoughts.

5 No need to loudly proclaim her name,
I know enough of the truth.
Duke of Orleans, I've found the lady.

She's my lady, who is very dearly loved,
And so overflows with virtues
10 That she fears not your Falsity,
Nor any who wear your livery.
Duke of Orleans, I've found the lady.

R360   [Rondel]*   [p. 310s]

Ayens the comyng of May
That is ful of lustynes,
Let us leve al hevynes
As fer as we can or may.

5   Now is tym of myrth and play.
Wynter weth hys ydylnes
Is dyscomfet as y ges
And redy to fle a way,
Ayens *the comyng of may.*

10   Wherfore, ladys, I yow pray
That ye take in yow gladnes
And do all your besynes
To be mery nyght and day,
Ayens *the comyng of may.*

310i: R361

R361   [Rondel]   [p. 310i]

Go forth myn hert wyth my lady.
Loke that ye spar no besynes
To serve hyr wyth seche lowlynes
That ye get hyr grace and mercy.

5   Pray hyr of tymes pryvely
That sche quippe trewly hyr promes.
Go forth *myn hert wyth my lady.*

I most as a hertles body
Abyde alone in hevynes,
10   And ye schal dwel wyth your maistres
In plesans glad and mery.
Go forth *myn hert wyth my lady.*

310s: R360

R362   [Rondel]   [p. 311s]

For the reward of half a yere
Tow trewe louys upon the brest,
Hyt ys ynow to brynge yn rest
A hert that love hold yn dangere.

Rondel

With the coming of May,
Which is full of youthful vigor,
Let us abandon all distress,
As much as we are able or allowed.

5   Now's the time for happiness and sport.
Winter with its idleness
Has been undone, I think,
And is ready to take flight
With the coming of May.

10   And so, ladies, I pray you
To be receptive to joy
And put all your energies
Into making merry night and day,
With the coming of May.

Rondel

Go forth, my heart, with my lady.
Take care you spare no effort
In serving her with such humility
That you obtain her grace and favor.

5   Ask her often in private
To be true to her promise.
Go forth, my heart, with my lady.

As a body without a heart, I must
Bide my time alone in distress,
10   While you dwell with your mistress
In joyful and riotous pleasure.
Go forth, my heart, with my lady.

Rondel

As a reward for half a year,
A couple of genuine coins in my lap
Are enough to quiet a heart
That love arrogantly imprisons.

5   Whene he hath be sume wat strangere
       To hym ys holyday and fest
       For the *reward of half a yere.*

       Thou seche hyt be a juel ful dere
       And a charme for the tempest,
10   Yet y conseille hym to be prest
       And fore ayens the warderere
       For the *reward of half a yere.*

311i: R363

R363   [Rondel]   [p. 311i]

       Alas mercy, wher shal myn hert yow fynd?
       Never had he wyth yow ful aqwaintans.
       Now com to hym and put of hys grevans,
       Ellys ye be unto yowr frend unkynd.

5   Mercy, he hath ever yow in hys mynd.
       Ons let hym have sum conforth of plesans!
       Alas mercy, *wher shal myn hert yow fynd?*

       Let hym not dey, but mak at ons a nende,
       In al hys woo an right hevy penans,
10   Noght is the help that whyl not hym avans,
       Slauth hys to me and ever com be hynde.
       Alas mercy, *wher shal myn hert yow fynd?*

311s: R362

R364   [Rondel]   [p. 312s]

       Ye shal be payd after your whylfulnes
       And blame nothyng but your mysgovernans,
       For when good love wold fayn had yow avans,
       Then went ye bak wyth wyly frauhyednes.

5   I knew anon your sotyl wylenes
       And your danger, that was mad for a scans.
       Ye schal be *payd after your whylfulnes.*

       Ye might have been my lady and maistres
       For ever mor withouthyn varians,
10   But now my hert yn Yngland or in France

5   When the heart has been somewhat the stranger,
       He thinks this a holiday and feast
       As a reward for half a year.

       You call it a very precious jewel
       And a charm against the tempest,
10   Yet I advise him to prepare
       To move against the warder
       As a reward for half a year.

Rondel

       Alas, Mercy, where shall my heart find you?
       He has never made your full acquaintance.
       Now come and alleviate his suffering,
       Otherwise you'll prove unkind to your friend.

5   Mercy, he always has you in mind.
       Let him take some comfort just once from pleasure!
       Alas, Mercy, where shall my heart find you?

       Don't let him die, but make an end of this at once.
       All his woe and grievous suffering
10   Do nothing to advance his cause.
       In my case, he delays and always follows behind.
       Alas, Mercy, where shall my heart find you?

Rondel

       You shall be repaid for your willfulness,
       And nothing merits blame but your recklessness,
       For when good love was eager to advance you,
       In your deceitfulness you retreated.

5   At once I recognized your subtle craftiness
       And your arrogance, made to deceive.
       You shall be repaid for your willfulness.

       You might have been my lady,
       Nevermore to change,
10   But now my heart in England or in France

Ys go to seke other nyw besynes.
Ye schal be *payd after your whylfulnes.*

312i: R365

R365   [Rondel]   [p. 312i]

So fayre, so freshe, so goodely on to se,
So welle dymeynet in al your governans,
That to my hert it is a grete plesans
Of your godenes when y remembre me,

5   And trustyth fully, wher that ever y be,
I wylle abyde undyr your obeyssance,
So fayre, *so freshe, so goodely un to se.*

For in my thought, ther is no mo but ye
Whom y have servid wythout repentance.
10   Wherfore y pray yow sethe to my grevance
And put osyde all myn adversite.
So fayre, *so freshe, so goodely un to se.*

312s: R364

R366   [Rondel] Orlians   [p. 473i]

Quant Pleur ne pleut, Souspir ne vente,
Le bruit sourt de Jeux et Risee,
Et Joye vient appareillee
De recevoir d'Espoir sa rente.

5   Assignee sur Longue Actente,
Mais aprés loyaument paiee,
Quant Pleur *ne pleut, Souspir ne vente.*

La, Reconfort est mis en vente,
Et Plaisance fait sa livree
10   De biens si richement ouvree
Que Dueil fuyt et s'en malcontente,
Quant Pleur *ne pleut, Souspir ne vente.*

473s: R296

Has gone to seek out some new affair.
You shall be repaid for your willfulness.

Rondel

So fair, so beautiful, so lovely to look upon,
Your demeanor, under your control, so pleasing,
It gives my heart great pleasure
When in your goodness you remember me,

5   And trust completely, wherever I may be,
That I will remain obedient to you,
So fair, so beautiful, so lovely to look upon.

For I think of no lady but you,
Whom I have served without regret,
10   And so, I beg you, attend to my distress
And alleviate all that troubles me.
So fair, so beautiful, so lovely to look upon.

Rondel—Orleans

When no Tear falls and no Sigh bursts forth,
The noise of Games and Laughter rises up,
And Joy arrives properly attired
To receive her dues from Hope,

5   Assigned to the time of Long Awaiting,
But afterward faithfully paid out,
When no Tear falls and no Sigh bursts forth.

There Good Cheer goes on sale,
And Pleasure dons his livery
10   So richly worked with goods
That Sorrow, disappointed, takes flight,
When no Tear falls and no Sigh bursts forth.

R367 [Rondel] Jehan Mgr de Lorraine* [p. 474s]

Chose qui plait est a demy vendue
En quelconque marchandise que se soit,
Mais l'eul prise tel chose qui desoit
Le plus souvent, quant elle est bien connue.

5 Car, quant Amour se vendoit a priere,
Peu de marchant y conquestoit proufit.
Desir survient qui met la fole enchere,
A qui marchié de raison ne suffit.

Adonc vela qui apouvrit et tue
10 Le maleureux que chascun monstre au doit,
Disant : C'est sil qui plus fait qui ne doit,
Dont s'ordre n'est a son droit maintenue.
Chose qui plait *est a demy vendue.*

474i: R368

R368 [Rondel] Orlians [p. 474i]

Quant je congnois que vous estes tant mien,
Et que m'aymez de cueur si loyaument,
Je feroye vers vous tropt faulcement
Se, sans faindre, ne vous aymoie bien.

5 Essaiez moy se vous fauldray en rien,
Gardant tousjours mon honneur seulement,
Quant *je congnois que vous estes tant mien.*

Se me dictes : «Las! je ne sçay combien
Vostre vouloir durera longuement,»
10 Je vous respons, sans aucun changement,
Qu'en ce propos me tendray et me tien,
Quant je congnois *que vous estes tant mien.*

474s: R367

R369 Rondel · Orlians [p. 477i]

Souper ou baing et disner ou bateau,
En ce monde n'a telle compaignie,
L'un parle ou dort, et l'autre chante ou crie,
Les autres font ballades ou rondeau.

Rondel—John, lord of Lorraine

The thing that pleases is already half-sold
No matter what the trade goods are,
But the eye prizes something that most often
Disappoints, when it is fully known,

5   For, when Love is sold at auction,
Few merchants find profit there.
Desire intervenes, her bids too high,
Since a reasonable bargain's not good enough.

So consider the woman who impoverishes and destroys
10   An unfortunate man, whom everyone points out,
Saying: "That man does more than he ought,
And so acts in ways that do not suit his station."
The thing that pleases is already half-sold.

Rondel—Orleans

Since I realize you are so much mine,
And love me from the heart so faithfully,
I would act too falsely toward you
If I did not love you well, without dissembling.

5   Put me to the test should I somehow fail you,
Guarding only my honor at every turn,
Since I realize you are so much mine.

If you tell me: "Alas! I don't know how
Long your good graces will last,"
10   I'll respond that, without changing at all,
I'll keep on and hold fast to this course,
Since I realize you are so much mine.

Rondel—Orleans

Supper in the bath, dinner on the boat,
In all the world there's no company like this one,
One talks or dozes, the other sings or shouts,
The rest compose ballades or rondels.

5   Et y boit on du viel et du nouveau,
       On l'appelle le desduit de la pie,*
       Souper ou baing *et disner ou bateau.*

       Il ne me chault ne de chien ne d'oyseau.
       Quant tout est fait, il fault passer sa vie
10   Le plus aise qu'on peut, en chiere lie.
       A mon advis, c'est mestier bon et beau,
       Souper ou baing et disner ou bateau.

477s: R301

R370   Rondel · Orlians   [p. 478i]

       En yver, du feu, du feu,
       Et en esté boire, boire,
       C'est de quoy on fait memoire,
       Quant on vient en aucun lieu.

5   Ce n'est ne bourde ne jeu,
       Qui mon conseil vouldra croire :
       En yver, *du feu, du feu.*

       Chaulx morceaulx faiz de bon queu
       Fault en froit temps, voire, voire.
10   En chault, froide pomme ou poire.
       C'est l'ordonnance de Dieu :
       En yver, *du feu, du feu!*

478s: R302

R371   [Rondel] Orlians   [p. 482i]

       Ces beaux mignons a vendre et a revendre,
       Regardez les, sont ilz pas a louer?
       Au service sont tous pres d'eulx louer
       Du Dieu d'Amours, s'il lui plaist a les prendre.

5   Son escolle saront bien tost aprandre,
       Bons escolliers, je les vueil avouer,
       Ces beaux *mignons a vendre et a revendre.*

       Et s'ilz faillent, il les pourra reprandre,
       Quant ilz vouldront trop nycement jouer,
10   Et sus leurs bras la chemise nouer,

5   There we down old wine and new,
That's what they call the delight of drinking,
Supper in the bath, dinner on the boat.

I care nothing about hounds or birds.
When all is said and done, you should spend
10   Your life as comfortably as you can, with a smile.
In my view, that's a fine and wonderful pastime.
Supper in the bath, dinner on the boat.

Rondel—Orleans

In winter, it's fire, fire,
And in summer, drinking, drinking,
That's what we recall
Whenever we go anywhere.

5   This is no game or laughing matter,
Whoever wishes to take my word for it:
In winter, it's fire, fire.

Steamy morsels whipped up by a fine chef
Are what's needed in cold weather, truly, truly.
10   In hot weather, cold apples or pears.
This is how God has arranged things:
In winter, it's fire, fire!

Rondel—Orleans

These pretty dandies for sale and re-sale,
Look them over, are they not for rent?
The whole crowd is ready to serve
The God of Love, if he wishes to take them on.

5   They will quickly and fully absorb his lesson,
Fine pupils they are, I am quick to affirm,
These pretty dandies for sale and re-sale.

And if they disappoint, he can discipline them
When they're bent on foolish amusements,
10   Knotting their shirts over their arms

Tant qu'au batre ne se puissent deffendre,
Ces beaux *mignons a vendre et a revendre.*

482s: R309

R372   Rondel · Maistre Jehan Cailleau*   [p. 483s]

Quant Pleur ne pleut, Souspir ne vente,
Si fait, dea! des fois plus de trente,
Maint se tourmente,
Souffrant le revers de son vueil,
5   Et toutesfois lerme de l'ueil
Ne ist hors du sueil
Pour paier du Courrouz la rente.

Du dolent ou de la dolente,
Qui sueffrent doleur non pas lente
10   Sans nulle attente
D'assouagement de leur dueil,
Quant Pleur *ne pleut, Souspir ne vente.*

Tant y en a en ceste sente,
Souffrans de corps, de cueur, d'entente,
15   Loing de la tente
Ou sont Plaisance et Doulx Acueil!
Quant a moy, des maulx que recueil,
Dont tant me dueil,
Seulet, a part moy, me guermente,
20   Quant Pleur *ne pleut, Souspir ne vente.*

483i: Blank

R373   [Rondel] Orlians   [p. 484s]

D'Espoir? Il n'en est nouvelles.
—Qui le dit?—Merencolie.
—Elle ment.—Je le vous nye.
A! A! vous tenez ses querelles.

5   —Non faiz, mais parolles telles
Courent, je vous certiffie.
D'Espoir? *Il n'en est nouvelles.*

—Parlons doncques d'aultres.—Quelles?
—De celles dont je me rie.
10   —Peu j'en sçay.—Or je vous prie

So they are helpless in combat,
These pretty dandies for sale and re-sale.

Rondel — Master Jean Cailleau

When no Tears rain down, no Sighs burst forth,
Yes, they do! More than thirty times,
Many torment themselves,
Suffering the opposite of what they wish,
5   And yet the tears from their eyes
Do not issue past their thresholds
In order to pay Sorrow's rent.

From sorrowful men and women,
Who suffer pains that are not slow
10   To come, who do not expect
Their misery to be assuaged,
When no Tears rain down, no Sighs burst forth.

Many follow this path,
Their bodies, hearts, and minds
15   Overwhelmed with suffering, far distant from the tent
Where Pleasure and Fair Welcome make their residence!
In my case, I lament alone
And by myself the miseries I experience
That pain me so grievously,
20   When no Tears rain down, no Sighs burst forth.

Rondel — Orleans

What about Hope? There is no news.
Who says so? — Melancholy.
She lies. — I deny that.
Oh, Oh! You take her side in this quarrel.

5   — No, I don't, but such an opinion
Makes the rounds, I promise you.
What about Hope? There is no news.

Let's speak then of other things. — Which?
— Those that bring a smile to my lips.
10   — I know few such. — Now I beg you

Que m'en contez des plus belles.
D'Espoir? *Il n'en est nouvelles.*

484i: R374

R374　　　　[Rondel] Orlians　　　　　　　　[p. 484i]

Une povre ame tourmentee
Ou Purgatoire de Soussy,
Est en mon corps : qu'il soit ainsy,
Il y pert et nuyt et journee.

5　　Piteusement est detiree,
Sans point cesser, puis la, puis cy,
Une povre *ame tourmentee.*

Mon cueur en a paine portee,
Tant qu'il en est presque transy,
10　　Mais esperance j'ay aussy
Qu'au derrenier sera sauvee
Une povre *ame tourmentee.*

484s: R373

R375　[Rondel] Maistre Jehan Caillau*　　　　　[p. 485s]

Espoir ou est—En chambre close.
—Et la que fait?—Il se repose.
—Sera il empiece esveillié?
—Il dit que il a trop veillié
5　　Et que dormir veult une pose.

—Que pour quelque pris je compose
A vous, et l'esveilliez.—Je n'ose,
Car il est las et traveillié.
—Espoir ou *est?—En chambre close.*

10　　—Par Dieu, ainsi que je suppose,
Il fait quelque rommant ou glose.
—Moy mesmes suis esmerveillié
De le voir si ensommeillié.
—Ne m'en direz vous autre chose?
15　　Espoir ou *est? En chambre close.*

485i: R376

Report to me the most pleasant.
What about Hope? There is no news.

Rondel — Orleans

A poor soul tormented
In the Purgatory of Care
Resides within my body: that this is so
Is apparent night and day.

5   He is piteously batted about
With never a halt, first there, then here,
A poor soul tormented.

My heart has suffered so much pain
That he is nearly dead,
10   But I also have hope
That in the end will be saved
A poor soul tormented.

Rondel — Master Jean Caillau

Hope, where is he? — Behind closed doors.
— What does he there? — He takes his rest.
— Will he wake any time soon?
— He says he spent too long awake
5   And thinks to sleep a while.

— No matter the consequences, let us agree
You must wake him up. — I dare not,
For he is tired and worn out.
— Hope, where is he? Behind closed doors.

10   — For God's sake, as I suppose,
He's writing a tale or some commentary.
— I marvel very much myself
To see him so very deeply asleep.
— Don't you have something else to say to me?
15   Hope, where is he? Behind closed doors.

R376   [Rondel] Orlians   [p. 485i]

Pour empescher le chemin,
Il ne fault qu'un amoureux
Qui, en penser desireux
Va songant soir et matin.

5   Donnez lui ung bon tatin,
Il s'endort le maleureux
Pour empescher *le chemin.*

D'eaue tout plain ung bassin
Eust il dessus ses cheveux?
10   D'un cop d'esperon ou deux
Ne veult chasser son roussin,
Pour empescher *le chemin.*

485s: R375

R377   [Rondel] Orlians   [p. 486s]

Qu'esse la? Qui vient si matin?
— Se suis je. — Vous, saint Valentin!
Qui vous amaine maintenant?
Ce jour de Karesme prenant*
5   Venez vous departir butin?

A present nulluy ne demande
Fors bon vin et bonne viende,
Banquetz et faire bonne chiere.

Car Karesme vient et commande
10   A Charnaige, tant qu'on le mande,
Que pour ung temps se tire arriere.

Ce nous est ung mauvais tatin,
Je n'y entens nul bon latin.
Il nous fauldra dorenavant
15   Confesser, penance faisant.
Fermons lui l'uys a tel hutin.
Qu'esse la? *Qui vient si matin?*

486i: R378

Rondel — Orleans

To obstruct the path,
All that's needed is that a man in love,
His thoughts on desire,
Go around dreaming night and day.

5   Give that man a good knock,
He's asleep, the wretch,
To obstruct the path.

Even if he had a basin
Full of water on his head?
10   With a prick or two from his spurs
He would not hurry on his nag,
To obstruct the path.

Rondel — Orleans

Who's there? Who comes so early?
—It's me.—You, Saint Valentine?
Who brings you here at this time?
This day just before Lent
5   Have you come to distribute your bounty?

At the moment no one asks for anything
Save tasty wine and good meat,
Banquets and merrymaking.

For Fasting comes and demands
10   That Feasting, until summoned again,
Makes himself scarce for some time.

What a terrible blow for us.
I see no good sense here.
Henceforth we are obligated
15   To confess and do penance.
Let's close the door to this unpleasantness.
Who's there? Who comes so early?

R378 [Rondel]

Commandez qu'elle s'en voise,
Mon cueur, a Merencolie,
Hors de vostre compaignie,
Vous laissent en paix sans noise.

5   Tropt a esté, dont me poise,
Avecques vous, c'est folie.
Commandez *qu'elle s'en voise.*

Oncques ne vous fut courtoise,
Mais les jours de vostre vie
10   A traictez en tirannie.
Sang de moy, quelle bourgoise!
Commandez *qu'elle s'en voise!*

486s: R377

R379 [Rondel] Bourbon jadis Clermont*

Je gis au lit d'amertume et doulleur,
Livré a mort par faulte de secours,
Et si ne sçay quant finera le cours
De mon aspre et inmortel malheur.

5   Priez pour moy, car je m'en voy mourir,
Mes bons amis aiez en souvenance.
On ne me veult au besoing secourir,
Requerez en, aprés mes jours, vangeance

Si vous m'amez, car c'est pour la valleur
10   D'une sans per, qu'ainsi mest au decours
Ma povre vie, sans respit ne recours.
Pour estre tant son loyal serviteur,
Je gis au lit *d'amertume et doulleur.*

487i: Blank

R380 [Rondel] Responce d'Orlians a Bourbon*

Comme parent et alyé
Du duc Bourbonnois a present,
Par ung rondeau nouvellement
Me tiens pour requis et payé.

Rondel

Order her to go away,
My heart, Melancholy
Should be far from your side,
Leaving you in peace without a fuss.

5   I'm grieved that she's been too long
With you, that's madness.
Order her to go away.

Never did she treat you courteously,
But rather all the days of your life,
10   Governed you like a tyrant.
Blood of mine, what a tradeswoman she is!
Order her to go away.

Rondel — Bourbon, formerly Clermont

I lie upon the bed of bitterness and pain,
Given over to death because I've had no help.
And I don't know when my miserable
And never-ending misfortune will run its course.

5   Pray for me, for I'm about to die,
Remember me to my good friends.
No one would help me in my time of need,
So, once my days come to an end, take vengeance

If you love me; but it is because of the worthiness
10   Of a peerless lady, who has brought to misfortune
My poor life, without respite or recourse.
For being very much her loyal servant,
I lie upon the bed of bitterness and pain.

Rondel — Response of Orleans to Bourbon

As the kinsman and relation
Now of the duke of Bourbon,
I consider myself recently paid back
With a rondel for a rondel requested of me.

5   Par une, gist malade, mis
       Ou lit d'amertume et grevance,

       Requerant tous ses bons amis,
       S'il meurt, qu'on demande vengeance.

       Quant a moy, j'ay ja deffié
10   Celle qui le tient en tourment,
       Et aprés son trespassement
       Par moy sera bien hault cryé
       Comme parent *et alyé*.

488i: R381

R381   [Rondel] Orlians   [p. 488i]

       Quant ung cueur se rent a beaux yeulx,
       Criant mercy piteusement,
       S'ilz le chastient rudement
       Et il meurt, qu'en valent ilz mieulx?

5   Batu de verges de Beaulté,
       De lui font sang partout courir,

       Mais qu'il n'ait fait desleaulté,
       Pitié le devroit secourir.

       S'il n'a point hanté entre tieulx
10   Qui ne s'acquittent loyaument,
       Doit estre tel pugnissement,
       A mon advis, en autres lieux,
       Quant *ung cueur se rent a beaux yeulx*.

488s: R380

R382   Rondel du senechal*   [p. 489s]

       Ma fille de confessïon,
       Vueillez avoir compassïon
       De cellui qui sert loyaument,
       Et qui est vostre entierement,
5   Sans point faire de fictïon.

       Selon raison et conscïence,
       Tort lui tiendrez, c'est ma creance,
       S'il n'a bien brief ce que tant vault.

5 Because of a lady he lies sick,
Confined to a bed of bitterness and grief,

And there calls out to all his good friends,
That should he die vengeance might be taken.

For my part, before this I have challenged
10 The lady who keeps him in torment,
And after he passes on,
I'll shout this challenge out loud and high
As the kinsman and relation.

Rondel—Orleans

When a heart surrenders to beautiful eyes,
Crying for mercy in a pitiable way,
If they punish him rudely
And he dies, how are they the better for it?

5 Beaten by the switches of Beauty,
They make his blood flow all over,

But unless he has been disloyal,
Pity should run to help him.

If he has not been the companion
10 Of those men whose deeds lack loyalty,
Then this kind of punishment,
I think, should be meted out elsewhere,
When a heart surrenders to Beautiful Eyes.

Rondel of the seneschal

My young girl at confession.
Please take pity
On the man who faithfully serves you,
And is yours completely,
5 With no pretense at all.

According to reason and conscience
You will do this man wrong, I think,
Should he not soon possess what is worth so much.

Je vous charge par penitence
10   Qu'ayez en lui toute fïance,
Sans plus respondre : Ne m'en chault.

Cellui qui souffrit Passïon
Vous doint bonne contriccïon,
Au chois de mon entendement.
15   Plus eureux soubz le firmament
N'auroit, dont il soit mencïon,
Ma fille *de confessïon.*

489i: Blank

R383   [Rondel] Responce
d'Orlians au senechal   [p. 490s]

Beau Pere! *benedicite,*
Je vous requier confessïon,
Et en humble contriccïon
Mon pechié sera recité.

5   En moy n'a eu mercy ne grace
Prenant de ma beaulté orgueil.

Amours me pardoint! ainsi face.
Desormais repentir m'en vueil.

Reffus a mon cueur delité.
10   J'en feray satisfacïon,
Donnez m'en absolucïon
En penance, par charité,
Beau Pere! *benedicite.*

490i: R384

R384   [Rondel] de Blosseville*   [p. 490i]

Ma tresbelle, plaisante seur,
Confiteor du bon du cueur
Dittes, par grant devocïon,
Sans plus avoir intencïon
5   De maintenir vostre folleur.

Car tost aprés de ma puissance
Vous absouldray, en esperance
Que doulce serez envers tous.

I charge you upon pain of punishment
10 To put all your faith in this man,
And answer him no more with "I don't care."

May He who suffered Passion
Grant you a proper contrition,
At least that is how I see things.
15 No man of those remembered
Would be more fortunate under heaven,
My young girl at confession.

Rondel—Response of Orleans to the seneschal

Good Father! Blessings upon you,
I wish to make my confession to you,
And with humble contrition
Recount my sins.

5 In me there's been neither grace nor mercy,
For I've taken pride in my beauty.

May Love pardon me! May he grant this request.
Henceforth I intend to repent.

My heart has delighted in refusing.
10 I'll make amends for everything,
Grant me absolution
Through penance and out of love,
Good Father! Blessings upon you.

Rondel of Blosseville

My most beautiful, graceful sister,
You utter your confession
With a good heart, with great devotion,
Not harboring any intention
5 To continue in your folly.

But as soon as I absolve you
Through my power my hope is
That you will be kind to every man.

10   Et vous enjoings, par penitance,
     De donner demain allegence
     A cellui qui se meurt par vous.

     Lequel par vostre grant rigueur
     Seuffre, comme j'entens, doleur,
     Et sans cause pugniciön,
15   Dont ja n'arés remissïon,
     Tant qu'il en soit hors, j'en suis seur,
     Ma tresbelle, *plaisante seur.*

490s: R383

R385   [Rondel] Bourbon*   [p. 491s]

     Je sens le mal qu'il me convient porter
     Non advenu, mais je crains qu'il aviengne
     Et qu'en la fin maleureux je deviengne
     Sans m'asservir ailleurs, ne transporter.

5   S'ainsi advient qu'a tort on m'abandonne,
     —Que Dieu ne vueille!—que feray je sans per?

     Las! je ne sçay! si ce mal on me donne,
     Des maleureux je seray le non per.

     Pour le meilleur, il me fault deporter
10   Jusques a tant que ce maleur me viengne,
     Mais a madame hardiement en souviengne,
     Car pour tousjours sa rigueur supporter,
     Je sens le mal *qu'il me convient porter.*

491i: Blank

R386 [Rondel] responce d'Orlians a Bourbon   [p. 492s]

     A voz amours hardyement en souviengne,
     Duc de Bourbon. Se mourez par rigueur
     Jamais n'auront ung si bon serviteur
     Ne qui vers eulz tant loyaument se tiengne.

5   Dieu ne vueille que tel meschief adviengne,
     Ilz perdroient leur regnon de doulceur.
     A voz amours *hardyement en souviengne.*

And I enjoin you as penance
10 To pledge your faith tomorrow
To the man who dies because of you.

And because of your great stubbornness
He suffers pain, I understand,
And punishment, though he is innocent,
15 And so you will never find remission
Until he is free of this, I'm sure,
My most beautiful, graceful sister.

Rondel — Bourbon

I sense the pain I must bear,
Not yet come, yet I fear it will
And that in the end I'll be miserable
But neither enslaved nor yielding.

5 If it happens I am wrongfully abandoned,
— May God not so wish! — what will I do alone?

Alas, I know not! If this ill comes upon me,
I will become the paragon of unfortunate men.

It is best that I make merry
10 Until this ill befalls me,
But bravely keep my lady in my thoughts;
For always enduring her domination,
I sense the pain that I must bear.

Rondel — Response of Orleans to Bourbon

May your loves keep this firmly in mind,
Duke of Bourbon: if you die through their harshness
Never again will they have so good a servant,
Nor any man to bear them such loyalty.

5 May, God willing, such misfortune not come to pass,
They will forfeit their reputation for graciousness.
May your loves keep this firmly in mind.

S'il est jangleur qui soctement me tiengne
Que Bourbonnois ont souvent legier cueur,
10   Je ne respons, fors que pour vostre honneur :
Esperance convient que vous soustiengne.
A voz amours *hardyement en souviengne!*

492i: R387

R387   [Rondel] Orlians   [p. 492i]

Descouvreur d'ambusche, sot oeil,
Pourquoy as tu passé le sueil
De ton logis sans mandement,
Et par oultrageux hardement
5   As entrepris contre mon vueil?

Demourer en repos je vueil
Et en paix faire mon recueil,
Sans guerre avoir aucunement,
Descouvreur *d'ambusche, sot oeil.*

10   En aguet se tient Bel Acueil,
Et se par puissance ou orgueil
Une foiz en ses mains te prent,
Tu fineras piteusement
Tes jours en la prison de Dueil,
15   Descouvreur *d'ambusche, sot oeil!*

492s: R386

R388   [Rondel] Me Berthault
             de Villebresme*   [p. 493s]

Puis que Atropos a ravy Dyopee*
Contre humain cours, prinse et anticipee,
Cupido, plus ne vous serviray!
Car tel doleur que pour vous servir ay,
5   Pour Demophon n'eut Phillis Rodopee.*

Plaisance s'est de moy emancipee,
Dueil m'est acquis, ma joie est dicipee.
En Boreas, Zephirus s'est viray,*
Puis *que Atropos a ravy Dyopee.*

10   Adieu vous dy, toute nymphe attrapee
Aux laqs Venus, com oyseau a pipee,

If some fool should stupidly inform me
That those of Bourbon are often fickle,
10   I'll say nothing unless your honor's at stake:
Hope must be the one to sustain you.
May your loves keep this firmly in mind!

Rondel — Orleans

Discoverer of ambushes, foolish eye,
Why have you passed over the threshhold
Of your dwelling uncommanded,
And through your outrageous boldness
5   Undertaken something against my will?

I wish you to remain at rest
And reflect in peace
Without the slightest conflict,
Discoverer of ambushes, foolish eye.

10   Fair Welcome lies in wait,
And if through his power or pride
He should one time get you in his hands,
You will end your days
Miserably and in the prison of Pain,
15   Discoverer of ambushes, foolish eye!

Rondel — Master Berthault
de Villebresme

Since Atropos carried off Dyopia
Against human custom, captured, her fate foretold,
Cupid, I no longer will serve you!
For in serving you I've borne much more pain
5   Than Rodopian Phyllis suffered for Demophon.

Pleasure has cut herself loose from me,
Misery has taken her place, my joy has fled.
Zephyrus has turned into Boreas,
Since Atropos carried off Dyopia.

10   I tell you farewell, every nymph caught
In the snares of Venus, like birds drawn to the trap,

Plus avec vous je ne me deduiray,
Mais a gemir du tout me reduiray,
Ou m'occiray, com Piramus, d'espee,*
15   Puis *que Atropos a ravy Dyopee.*

493i: Blank

R389   Rondel · d'Orlians   [p. 494s]

Amours, a vous ne chault de moy,
N'a moy de vous, c'est quicte et quicte.
Ung vieillart jamais ne proffitte
Avecques vous, comme je croy.

5   Puis que suis absolz de ma foy
Et Jeunesse m'est interditte,
Amours, *a vous ne chault de moy.*

Jeune, sceu vostre vieille loy;
Vieil, la nouvelle je deppitte,
10   Ne je ne crains la mort subitte
De Regard. Qu'en dictes vous? Quoy?
Amours, *a vous ne chault de moy.*

494i: R390

R390   [Rondel] Orlians   [p. 494i]

J'ay pris le logis de bonne heure
D'Espoir, pour mon cueur, aujourd'uy,
Affin que les fourriers d'Annuy
Ne le preignent pour sa demeure.

5   Veu que nuyt et jour il labeure
De me gaster, et je le fuy,
J'ay pris *le logis de bonne heure.*

Bon Eur, avant que mon cueur meure,
L'aidera, il se fye en luy.
10   Autrepart ne quiers mon apuy.
En actendant qu'il me sequeure,
J'ay pris *le logis de bonne heure.*

494s: R389

No longer will I delight in you,
But restrict myself to lamenting,
Or I'll kill myself, like Pyramus, with a sword,
15   Since Atropos carried off Dyopia.

Rondel by Orleans

Love, you care no more about me,
Nor I about you, we are both quits.
An old man never finds profit
In you, or so I believe.

5   Since I am absolved of my oath
And Youth is forbidden to me,
Love, you care no more about me.

Young, I knew your old law;
Old, I scorn the new,
10   Nor do I fear the sudden death
Of Look. What do you have to say? What?
Love, you care no more about me.

Rondel — Orleans

In good time I've taken lodging
With Hope, for the sake of my heart, this day,
So that the harbingers of Worry
Do not take it for his dwelling.

5   Seeing that night and day he labors
To ruin me, and I flee from him,
In good time I've taken lodging.

Happiness will come rescue my heart
Before it expires, it trusts in him.
10   I seek no other support.
Waiting for him to come and help me,
In good time I've taken lodging.

R391   Rondel de Fraigne   [p. 495s]

    Mon oeil m'a dit qu'il me deffie
    A tousjours mais, sans repentir,
    Se je ne luy foys ce plaisir
    D'amer une qu'il a choysie.

5   Se c'estoit pour sauver sa vie,
    Plus ne m'en pourroit requerir.
    Mon oeil m'a dit qu'il me deffie.

    Je lui ay dit : «Tu fais folye,
    Je te prie, laisse moy dormir,
10   Je n'ay pas a present loisir
    De penser a ta reverie.»
    Mon oeil m'a dit qu'il me deffie.

495i: R392

R392   [Rondel] Orlians   [p. 495i]

    Escoutez et laissés dire,
    Et en voz mains point n'enpire
    Le mal. Retournés le en bien,
    Tout yra, n'en doubtez rien,
5   Si bien qu'il devra souffire.

    Dieu comme souverain mire
    Fera mieulx qu'on ne desire,
    Et pourverra : tout est sien.
    Escoutez et laissés dire.

10   Chascun a son propos tire,
    Mais on ne peut pas eslire.
    Je l'ay trouvé, ou fait mien.
    Au fort, content je m'en tien,
    Car aprés pleurer vient rire.
15   *Escoutez et laissés dire.*

495s: R391

R393   Rondel par B. Damien*   [p. 496s]

    Contre fenouches et *nox buze*
    Convient l'un faire, l'*aultro* dire,
    Plourer d'un oeil, de l'*aultro* rire,
    Questo modo les gens abuze.

Rondel of Fraigne

My eye says he'll defy me
From now on, never repenting,
If I do not allow him the pleasure
Of loving the lady he's chosen.

5   Even were it to save his life,
He couldn't ask for more.
My eye says he'll defy me.

I said to him: "You play the fool,
I beg you, let me sleep,
10   I don't have the time now
To mull over your imaginings."
My eye says he'll defy me.

Rondel — Orleans

Listen and let it be said:
Don't let your own hands make a bad thing
Worse. Turn it into something good.
All this will go so well, you should not doubt
5   You'll be satisfied in the end.

God as supreme healer
Will do better than can be hoped for,
And He will provide: all things are His.
Listen and let it be said.

10   Everyone follows his own path,
But no one can choose it.
I've found this in my own experience.
In fact, I am contented it is so,
For laughter follows weeping.
15   Listen and let it be said.

Rondel by B. Damien

Faced with pointless chatter in Italian,
A man can say one thing and do another,
Weep from one eye and laugh with the other;
Acting this way puts people off.

5   Or *dapoy* que *lo mondo* en use,
     Non est *dy besoingno dormire*
     Contre [fenouches et *nox buze.*]

     Tanto principo comme *duze,*
     Veullent le lour *fato* conduire,
10   Et li soy servitor instruire
     A *sapere jouar* la ruze
     Contre [fenouches et *nox buze.*]

496i: R394

R394 Rondel par Me B. de Villebresme*   [p. 496i]

     Puis que chascun sert de fenouches
     Et de mentir, neiz que de mouches,
     Aucun aujourd'ui ne tient conte,
     Mais a chascun d'avoir son compte
5   Souffist, soit honneur, ou repproches.

     Retraire je me vueil es touches
     Des bois, ainsi que les farouches,
     Car d'estre au monde j'ay grant honte
     Puis que *chascun sert de fenouches.*

10   Je y congnois tant de males bouches,
     De clers voyans faisans les louches,*
     De bons et simples que l'on donte.
     Veu donc que mal bien y surmonte,
     Plus me plaist vivre entre les souches,*
15   Puis que *chascun sert de fenouches.*

496s: R393

R395   Rondel du duc de Bourbon*   [p. 497s]

     Prenez l'ommage de mon cueur
     En recevant sa feaulté,
     Et il gardera loyaulté
     Comme doit leal serviteur.

5   S'il se forfait en vous servant
     Et qu'il soit clerement cognu,
     Ne le tenez plus pour servant,
     Banny soit comme descogneu.

5   Since this is now the fashion,
       Better not let your guard down
       Faced with pointless chatter in Italian.

       Princes as well as dukes
       Intend to conduct their affairs
10   And teach their servants
       How to play this tricky game
       Faced with pointless chatter in Italian.

Rondel by Master B. de Villebresme

       Since everyone is given to deceitful talk
       And lying too, such things trouble
       People less these days than flies do;
       Rather all are satisfied with their situation,
5   Whether it be full of honor or reproach.

       I'd like to withdraw to the groves
       In the woods, just like wild things,
       For I am very ashamed to stay in the world
       Since everyone is given to deceitful talk.

10   There I come across so many evil tongues,
       Clear thinkers seeing wrongdoing but looking the other way,
       Good, simple folks being cowed.
       Seeing that evil holds sway over good in that place
       I'd rather live among nincompoops,
15   Since everyone is given to deceitful talk.

Rondel by the duke of Bourbon

       Take the homage of my heart
       While receiving its fealty,
       And he will keep loyalty safe
       As a faithful servant should do.

5   Should he go astray in serving you,
       And this be clearly recognized,
       Do not retain him as your servant,
       Let him be banished like one unknown.

　　　　Mais ce pendant toute doulceur
10　　Lui soit faicte, sans cruaulté,
　　　　Attendant que vostre beaulté
　　　　Ait pourveu a sa grant douleur.
　　　　Prenez *l'ommage de mon cueur.*

497i: R396

R396　　　　Rondel d'Orlians　　　　　　　　[p. 497i]

　　　　En arrierefief sobz mes yeulx,
　　　　Amours, qui vous ont fait hommage,
　　　　Je tiens de mon cueur l'eritage.
　　　　A vous sommes et serons tieulx.

5　　　Voz vrais subgez, voire des vieulx,
　　　　Soit nostre prouffit, ou dommage,
　　　　En arrierefief *sobz mes yeulx.*

　　　　J'appelle Deesses et Dieux
　　　　Sur ce, vers vous, en tesmoingnage,
10　　Se voulez, j'en tiendray ostage,
　　　　Vous puis je dire ou faire mieulx
　　　　En arrierefief *sobz mes yeulx?*

497s: R395

R397　　　　Rondel d'Orlians　　　　　　　　[p. 498s]

　　　　J'en baille le denombrement
　　　　Que je tiens soubz vous loyaument,
　　　　Loyal Desir et Bon Vouloir,
　　　　Mais j'ay trop engagié Povoir,
5　　　Se je n'en ay relievement.

　　　　Je vous ay servy longuement
　　　　En y despendant largement
　　　　Des biens que j'ay peu recevoir :
　　　　J'en baille *le denombrement.*

10　　Vieillesse m'assault fellement,
　　　　Et me veult a destruisement
　　　　Mener, maiz veu qu'ay fait devoir
　　　　Que m'aiderez, j'ay ferme espoir,
　　　　A mes droiz , voiez les comment :
15　　J'en baille *le denombrement.*

498i: R398

Yet at the same time let every kindness
10   Be done for him, without cruelty
And in the expectation that your beauty
Should provide for his great suffering.
Take the homage of my heart.

Rondel by Orleans

In a vassal's fief beneath my eyes,
Which have rendered you homage, Love,
I preserve the heritage of my heart.
We are yours and will so remain,

5   Your true subjects, in truth the oldest,
Whether to our profit or loss,
In a vassal's fief beneath my eyes.

I call on goddesses and gods
To bear witness to you about this matter.
10   If you wish, I'll offer a hostage.
Could I say or do better,
In a vassal's fief beneath my eyes?

Rondel by Orleans

I entrust to you an accounting
Of what I hold in loyalty from you,
Loyal Desire and Good Will;
But I have taken on too much Power
5   Unless some relief comes my way.

I have served you a long time,
Spending generously all the while
The favors I have been able to receive.
I entrust to you an accounting.

10   Old age cruelly assaults me,
And thinks to lead me off
To destruction, but, seeing I've done
My duty, it is my firm hope you'll help me
Get my due. See to how this should be done.
15   I entrust to you an accounting.

R398   [Rondel] Orlians   [p. 498i]

Je suis a cela
Que Merancolie
Me gouvernera.

     Qui m'en gardera?
5   Je suis *a cela.*

     Puis qu'ainsi me va,
     Je croy qu'a ma vie
     Autre ne sera.
     Je suis *a cela.*

498s: R397

R399   [Rondel] Orlians   [p. 499s]

On ne peut chastïer les yeux,
N'en chevir, quoy que l'en leur dye,
Dont le cueur se complaint et crye,
Quant s'esgarent en trop de lieux.

5   Seront il tousjours ainsi, Dieux?
     Rien n'y vault s'on les tanse ou prye :
     On ne peut *chastïer les yeux.*

     Quant aux miens, ilz sont desja vieux
     Et assez lassez de follye.
10 Les yeux jeunes, fault qu'on les lye
     Comme enragiez. N'est ce le mieux?
     On ne peut *chastïer les yeux.*

499i: R400

R400   [Rondel] Orlians   [p. 499i]

Sont les oreilles estouppees?
Rapportent il au cueur plus rien?
Ouyl, plus tost le mal que bien,
Quant on ne les tient gouvernees.

5   Se leurs portes ne sont fermees,
     Tout y court, de va et de vien.
     Sont les oreilles *estouppees?*

Rondel—Orleans

I'm in a spot
Where Melancholy
Will rule over me.

Who will protect me from it?
5   I'm in a spot.

Since this is how it goes,
I believe that in my life
There'll be nothing else.
I'm in a spot.

Rondel—Orleans

You cannot reprimand the eyes,
Or get the better of them, whatever you say;
And so the heart complains and cries out
When they go off in too many directions.

5   God, will they always do so?
Nothing avails, not angry words or pleas.
You cannot reprimand the eyes.

As for my own, they're old already
And foolishness has wearied them.
10   The young must be blindfolded
Like madmen. Isn't that for the best?
You cannot reprimand the eyes.

Rondel—Orleans

Are the ears stopped up?
Do they now convey nothing to the heart?
Indeed much more the bad than the good,
When they're not kept under control.

5   If their openings are not closed,
There's an incessant coming and going of everything.
Are the ears stopped up?

     Les miennes seront bien gardees
     De Non Challoir, que portier tien,
10   Dont se plaint et dit le cueur mien :
     «On ne me sert plus de pensees,
     Sont les oreilles *estouppees?*»

499s: R399

R401   [Rondel] Orlians   [p. 500s]

     Tel est le partement des yeulx,
     Quant congié prenent doulcement,
     D'eulx retraire piteusement
     En regretz privez pour le mieulx.

5   Lors divers se dient adieux,
     Esperans revenir briefment.
     Tel est *le partement des yeulx.*

     Et si laissent, en plusieurs lieux,
     Des lermes par engagement,
10   Pour payer leur deffrayement,
     En gectant souspirs, Dieu scet quieulx!
     Tel est *le partement des yeulx.*

500i: R402

R402   [Rondel] Orlians*   [p. 500i]

     Pour moustrer que j'en ay esté
     Des amoureux aucunesfoiz,
     Se may, le plus plaisant des moys,
     Vueil servir, ce present Esté.

5   Quoy que Soucy m'ait arresté,
     Sans son congié je m'y envoiz
     Pour moustrer *que j'en ay esté.*

     Pour ce, je me tiens apresté
     A deduiz, en champs et en bois.
10   S'Amours y prent nulz de ses droiz,
     Quelque bien m'y sera presté,
     Pour moustrer *que j'en ay esté.*

500s: R401

My own will be well looked after
By Indifference, whom I retain as porter.
10   So my heart complains and says:
"No more thoughts come my way,
Are the ears stopped up?"

Rondel — Orleans

Such is the departure of the eyes,
When sweetly taking their leave,
That they withdraw piteously
And for the best into their private sorrows.

5   And then several utter their good-byes,
Hoping for a quick return:
Such is the departure of the eyes.

And they leave behind, in many places,
Tears as promissory notes
10   To pay their expenses
While letting out sighs, God knows which ones!
Such is the departure of the eyes.

Rondel — Orleans

To show I have been one of them,
The company of lovers,
I intend this May, most pleasant of months,
To do service, this Summer.

5   Although Care has stopped me in my tracks,
Without his leave, I here present myself
To show I have been one of them.

That's why I've readied myself
For frolicking in the fields and woods;
10   If Love asserts some of his rights there,
Some good thing will come my way
To show I have been one of them.

R403   [Rondel] Orlians   [p. 501s]

Tant ay largement despendu
Des biens d'amoureuse richesse,
Ou temps passé de ma jennesse,
Que trop chier m'a esté rendu.

5   Car lors a rien je n'ay tendu
Qu'a conquester foison Lÿesse,
Tant ay *largement despendu.*

Commandé m'est et deffendu
Desormais par Dame Vieillesse,
10   Qu'aux jennes gens laisse prouesse.
Tout leur ay remiz et vendu,
Tant ay *largement despendu.*

501i: R404

R404   [Rondel] Orlians   [p. 501i]

Fyez vous y, se vous voulez,
En Espoir qui tant promet bien,
Mais souventesfoiz n'en fait rien,
Dont mains cueurs se sentent foulez.

5   Quant Desir les a affollez,
Au grant besoing leur fault du sien.
Fyez vous y, *se vous voulez.*

Lors sont de destresse affollez.
J'aymeroye, pour le cueur mien,
10   Mieulx que deux tu l'aras, ung tien.
Quant les oiseaulx s'en sont vollez,
Fyez vous y, *se vous voulez!*

501s: R403

R405   [Rondel] Orlians   [p. 502s]

Jaulier des prisons de Pensee,
Soussy, laissez mon cueur yssir.
Pasmé l'ay veu esvanouïr
En la fosse desconfortee.

Rondel—Orleans

So very generously have I spent
The goods of amorous wealth
In the times past of my youth
That I've paid too high a price.

5 For at the time I aimed at nothing
Save acquiring Happiness in abundance,
So very generously have I spent.

But Lady Old Age denies me
Henceforth, ordering me
10 To leave such exertions to the young.
I've given over and passed on everything to them,
So very generously have I spent.

Rondel—Orleans

Put your trust there, if you wish,
In Hope, who promises so much good,
But often delivers nothing at all,
Which makes many a heart feel betrayed.

5 After Desire has driven them mad,
Hope fails them in their greatest need.
Put your trust there, if you wish.

Then distress made them lose their minds.
For the sake of my heart, I would prefer
10 A bird in hand to two in the bush.
But when the birds have flown off,
Put your trust there, if you wish.

Rondel—Orleans

Jailor of the prisoners of Thought,
Care, let my heart escape.
I've seen it faint dead away
In the ditch of distress.

5   Mais que seurté vous soit donnee
       De tenir foy et revenir,
       Jaulier *des prisons de Pensee.*

       S'il mouroit en prison fermee,
       Honneur n'y povez acquerir.
10   Vueillez au moins tant l'eslargir
       Qu'ait sa finance pourchassee,
       Jaulier *des prisons de Pensee.*

502i: R406

R406   [Rondel] S. Cailleau*   [p. 502i]

       Jaulier des prisons de Pensee,
       Mon pouvre cueur aux fers tenez,
       Et dit on que vous luy donnez,
       Chascun jour, une bastonnee.

5   Est ce par sentence ordonnee
       Qu'en ce point le me gouvernez,
       Jaulier *des prisons de Pensee?*

       Se sa cause estoit bien menee,
       On jugeroit que mesprenez
10   Et qu'a grant tort le retenez,
       Sans plainte de personne nee,
       Jaulier *des prisons de Pensee*

502s: R405

R407   [Rondel] Thignonville*   [p. 503s]

       Jaulier des prisons de Pensee
       Avez vous le commandement
       De traictier ainsi rudement
       Les povres cueurs en ceste annee?

5   Vous est la puissance donnee
       De par Soussy, ou autrement,
       Jaulier *des prisons de Pensee?*

       Dedans la chartre adoulee,
       Tenir les deussiez doulcement.

5 But on the condition you are assured
 He will keep his word and return,
 Jailor of the prisoners of Thought.

 If he should die locked up in prison,
 You would find no honor there.
10 Please at least allow him freedom enough
 Until he's raised his ransom,
 Jailor of the prisoners of Thought.

Rondel—S. Cailleau

 Jailor of the prisoners of Thought,
 You keep my poor heart in irons,
 And it is reported you give him
 A beating every day.

5 Does some sentence ordain
 That you rule him this way for me,
 Jailor of the prisoners of Thought?

 If his suit had been well managed,
 You would be judged as doing wrong,
10 Holding him prisoner unjustly,
 With no complaint lodged by any creature born,
 Jailor of the prisoners of Thought.

Rondel—Thigonville

 Jailor of the prisoners of Thought,
 Are you following some command
 When you treat pitiful hearts
 So roughly this year?

5 Has the power to do so been granted you
 By Care, or has it been otherwise,
 Jailor of the prisoners of Thought?

 Within that distressing jail,
 You should treat them mercifully.

10   Batre ne devez nullement
        Prisonniers en fosse fermee,
        Jaulier *des prisons de Pensee.*

503i: R408

R408   [Rondel] Gilles des Ourmes*   [p. 503i]

        Jaulier des prisons de Pensee,
        Qui tenez tant de gens de bien,
        Ouvrez leur, il paieront bien,
        Le droit de l'yssue et l'entree.

5   Il m'ont commissïon baillee
        D'appointer : dictez moy combien,
        Jaulier *des prisons de Pensee,*

        Car j'ay cy finance apportee
        Assez, que du leur, que du mien,
10   Tant qu'on ne vous devra rien,
        Jusqu'a la derraine journee,
        Jaulier *des prisons de Pensee.*

503s: R407

R409   [Rondel] Orlians   [p. 504s]

        Donnez l'aumosne aux prisonniers,
        Reconfort et Espoir aussy.
        Tant feray au jaulier Soussy
        Qu'il leur portera voulentiers.

5   Ilz n'ont ne vivres ne deniers,
        Crians de fain : il est ainsy.
        Donnez *l'aumosne aux prisonniers.*

        Meschans ont esté mesnagiers
        Tenuz pour debte jusques cy :
10   Faictes les euvres de mercy,
        Comme vous estes coustumiers :
        Donnez *l'aumosne aux prisonniers.*

504i: R410

10   You ought never beat
Captives confined to a dungeon,
Jailor of the prisoners of Thought.

Rondel—Gilles des Ourmes

Jailor of the prisoners of Thought,
Who hold captive many of the well-born,
They'll pay handsomely if you offer them
The right to come and go.

5   They've charged me with the task
Of arranging terms, tell me how much,
Jailor of the prisoners of Thought.

For I believe I've brought along enough
Money, some of theirs, some of my own,
10   So much that you'll be owed nothing
Right up to the very last day,
Jailor of the prisoners of Thought.

Rondel—Orleans

Give the prisoners alms,
Consolation, Hope too.
I'll treat the jailor Care so nicely
He'll willingly deliver them these things.

5   They have neither food nor small change,
Weeping with hunger; so matters stand.
Give the prisoners alms.

They've had no luck with their finances,
Forced by debts to such a pass:
10   Show them some mercy,
As is your wont:
Give the prisoners alms.

R410   [Rondel] Benoist Damien*   [p. 504i]

N'oubliez pas les prisonniers,
Bonnes gens : aiez en mercy!
Il sont en la tour de Soucy
Et n'ont ne mailles ne deniers.

5   Larrons ne sont point ne murtriés,
Par Envie on les tient aincy :
N'oubliez pas *les prisonniers.*

Faictes comme bons aumosniers
Pour la grant pitié que vées cy,
10   Et pour vous priront Dieu aucy
De tresbon cueur et voulentiers.
N'oubliez pas *les prisonnier*s!

504s: R409

R411   [Rondel] H. le Voys*   [p. 505s]

Jaulier des prisons de Pensee,
Ouvrez a Reconfort la porte,
Car a mon cueur l'aumosne porte
Que mes yeulx lui ont pourchacee.

5   Tenu l'avez mainte journee
Ou cep d'Anuy et prison forte,
Jaulier *des prisons de Pensee.*

Tant a fain et soif enduree
Qu'il a perdu couleur et sorte.
10   Helas! pour Dieu, qu'on le supporte,
Autrement sa vie est finee,
Jaulier *des prisons de Pensee.*

505i: R412

R412   [Rondel] Orleans   [p. 505i]

Banissons Soussy, ce ribault,
Batu de verges par la ville.
C'est ung crocheteur trop habille
Pour embler Joye qui tant vault.

Rondel — Benoit Damien

Don't forget the prisoners,
My fine people. Have mercy on them!
They are locked in the tower of Care.
They have no pennies or small coins.

5   They are neither thieves nor murderers
And are locked up because of Envy:
Don't forget the prisoners.

Do as generous almsgivers do
Because of the piteous sight you see here.
10   And they'll pray to God for you,
Willingly and with a very good heart.
Don't forget the prisoners!

Rondel — H. de Voys

Jailor of the prisoners of Thought,
Open the door to Consolation,
For he brings my heart the alms
My eyes have sought from him.

5   You hold him locked up many a day
In the stocks and the stout prison of Worry,
Jailor of the prisoners of Thought.

He's suffered so much thirst and hunger
His color and bearing have fled.
10   Alas! For God's sake, help him!
Otherwise his life has come to its end,
Jailor of the prisoners of Thought.

Rondel — Orleans

Let's banish Care, that wretch,
And beat him with sticks through the town.
He's too cunning a sneak thief,
Stealing the joy you prize so highly.

5   Copper une oreille lui fault,
       Il est fort larron entre mille.
       Banissons *Soussy, ce ribault.*

       Se plus ne revient, ne m'en chault.
       Laissez le aller sans croix ne pille,
10   Le Deable l'ait ou trou Sebille!*
       Point n'en saille, pour frait ne chault :
       Banissons *Soussy, ce ribault!*

505s: R411

R413   [Rondel] Orlians   [p. 506s]

       Des vieilles defferres d'Amours
       Je suis a present, Dieu mercy!
       Vieillesse me gouverne ainsy,
       Qui m'a condempné en ses cours.

5   Je m'esbahys quant a rebours
       Voy mon fait, disant : Qu'est ce cy?
       Des vieilles *defferres d'Amours?*

       Mon vieulx temps couvient qu'ait son cours,
       Qui en tutelle me tient sy
10   Du jaullier appellé Soussy,
       Que rendu me tiens, pour tousjours,
       Des vieilles *defferres d'Amours.*

506i: R414

R414   [Rondel] Orlians   [p. 506i]

       Comme monnoye descriee,
       Amours ne tient conte de moy.
       Jeunesse m'a laissié, pour quoy
       Je ne suis plus de sa livree.

5   Puis que telle est ma destinee,
       Desormais me fault tenir coy,
       Comme *monnoye descriee.*

       Plus ne prens plaisir qu'en pensee
       Du temps passé, car, sur ma foy,

5   One of his ears should be lopped off,
He's the wiliest thief among a thousand.
Let's banish Care, that wretch.

If he does not return, I don't care.
Let him depart without a penny,
10   Let the Devil take him, or the Sibyl's cave!
Let him not escape, not for heat or cold.
Let's banish Care, that wretch!

Rondel—Orleans

Among the cast-offs of Love,
I now find myself, God be thanked!
In this, Old Age rules me,
Who has passed sentence on me in his court.

5   I marvel at how my life
Has changed so much, saying: What is this?
Among the cast-offs of Love?

The days of my old age must run their course,
Restraining me here under the tutelage
10   Of the jailor named Care,
So I surrender myself for the rest of my days
Among the cast-offs of Love.

Rondel—Orleans

Like coin of no value,
Love takes no account of me.
Youth has abandoned me and so
I no longer sport his livery.

5   Since this is to be my destiny,
Henceforth I must hold my tongue,
Like coin of no value.

I find no pleasure save in thoughts
Of days gone by, for, upon my faith,

10   Ne me chault du present que voy,
        Car Vieillesse m'est delivree,
        Comme *monnoye descriee.*

506s: R413

R415   [Rondel] Orlians   [p. 507s]

        Laissez baude buissonner,*
        Le vieil briquet se repose,
        Desormais travailler n'ose,
        Abayer, ne mot sonner.

5   On luy doit bien pardonner.
        Ung vieillart peult peu de chose!
        Laissez *baude buissonner.*

        Et Vieillesse emprisonner
        L'a voulu, en chambre close.
10   Par quoy, j'entens que propose
        Plus peine ne luy donner :
        Laissez *baude buissonner!*

507i: R416

R416   [Rondel] H. Le Voys*   [p. 507i]

        Comme monnoye descriee,
        Loyaulté je voy abriee
        Dessoubz le pavillon de Honte,
        Par Faulceté qui la surmonte,
5   Et l'a d'oultrance deffyée.

        De Bonne Foy s'est alyee
        Et de son ayde l'a priee,
        Mais on n'en tient que peu de conte,
        Comme monnoye *descriee.*

10   Du tout la tiens pour ravallee,
        Par montaigne et par vallee.
        Est notoire ce que raconte :
        En maison de duc ne de conte,
        Ne se treuve qu'a l'eschappee,
15   Comme monnoye *descriee.*

507s: R415

10   I care nothing for the present here before me,
For Old Age has thrust it upon me
Like coin of no value.

Rondel — Orleans

Leave the hound to his hunting,
This old dog is taking a rest,
Henceforth he dares not exert himself,
Bark, or speak a single word.

5   He should be forgiven for this.
An old man can do but little!
Leave the hound to his hunting.

And Old Age intends
To keep him imprisoned in a locked room.
10   I understand she thinks thereby
To make him suffer no more:
Leave the hound to his hunting.

Rondel — H. Le Voys

Like coin of no value,
I see Loyalty has taken refuge
Within the tent of Shame
Through Falseness, who has overwhelmed her
5   And issued an outrageous challenge.

She's allied with Good Faith
And has begged for assistance,
But that's considered of no importance,
Like coin of no value.

10   I think she's despised completely,
Here, there, and everywhere.
What I tell you is notorious:
In the house of any duke or count
Loyalty is only fleetingly found,
15   Like coin of no value.

R417   [Rondel] Orleans   [p. 508s]

Quant me treuve seul, a par moy,
Et n'ay gueres de compaignye,
Ne demandez pas si m'enuye,
Car ainsi est il, sur ma foy.

5   En riens plaisance n'apersoy,
Fors comme une chose endormye,
Quant *me treuve seul, a par moy.*

Mais s'entour moy pluseurs je voy,
Et qu'on rit, parle, chante ou crye,
10   Je chasse hors Merencolye
Que tant haÿr et craindre doy
Quant *me treuve seul, a par moy.*

508i: R418

R418   Rondel d'Orleans   [p. 508i]

Trop ennuyez la compaignie,
Douloureuse Merancolie
Et troublez la feste de Joye.
Foy que doy a Dieu, je vouldroie
5   Que fussiez du païs banye!

Vous venez sans que l'on vous prie,
Bon gré maulgré, a l'estourdie.
Alez! que plus on ne vous voye :
Trop ennuyez *la compaignie.*

10   Soucy avecques vous s'alye,
Si lui dy ge que c'est folie.
Quel mesnage! Dieu vous convoye
Si loings tant que je vous renvoye
Querir! — Quant? — Jamaiz en ma vie :
15   Trop ennuyez *la compaignie!*

508s: R417

R419   [Rondel] Orlians*   [p. 509s]

Escollier de Merencolye,
Des verges de Soussy batu,
Je suis a l'estude tenu,
Es derreniers jours de ma vye.

Rondel — Orleans

When I am all alone
And have no companions at all,
Don't ask if I find it troubling,
For so it is, upon my faith.

5   I find pleasure in nothing at all,
Except, like a thing gone to sleep,
When I am all alone.

But if I see others around me,
Who laugh, talk, sing, or cry,
10   I put Melancholy to flight,
Whom I should so much hate and fear
When I am all alone.

Rondel by Orleans

You annoy this company too much,
Sorrowful Melancholy,
And trouble the feasting of Joy.
By the faith I owe God, I want you
5   Banished from this country!

You come with no invitation,
Willy-nilly, any old way.
Take off! Let no one set eyes on you again.
You annoy this company too much.

10   Care allies herself with you,
And I tell her this is madness.
What a pair! May God escort you
Far away until I have you
Sought out! When? Not as long as I live.
15   You annoy this company too much!

Rondel — Orleans

Scholar of Melancholy,
Beaten by the rod of Care,
I'm bound to this course of study
In the very last days of my life.

5   Se j'ay ennuy, n'en doubtez mye,
        Quant me sens vieillart devenu,
        Escollier *de Merencolye.*

        Pitié couvient que pour moy prie,
        Qui me treuve tout esperdu
10   Mon temps je pers et ay perdu
        Comme rassoté en follye :
        Escollier *de Merencolye.*

509i: R420

R420   [Rondel] H. Le Voys*   [p. 509i]

        Escollier de Merencolye,
        Par Soussy qui est le recteur,
        A l'estude est tenu mon cueur,
        Et Dieu scet comme on le chastye!

5   De s'i mectre fist grant follye,
        Car on le tient a la rigueur
        Escollier *de Merencolye.*

        Bon temps n'aura jour de sa vye,
        Puis qu'il y est. De son maleur,
10   Dedans le livre de Douleur
        Luy est force qu'il estudye,
        Escollier *de Merencolye.*

509s: R419

R421   [Rondel] Orlians   [p. 510s]

        Et fust ce ma mort ou ma vie,
        Je ne puis de mon cueur chevir
        Qu'i ne vueille conseil tenir
        Souvent, avec Merencolie.

5   Si luy dy je que c'est folie,
        Mais comme sourt ne veult oïr,
        Et fust ce *ma mort ou ma vie.*

        A Grace, pource, je supplie
        Qu'i lui plaise me secourir.

5   Don't doubt at all that I am bored,
For I feel I've become an old man,
Scholar of Melancholy.

Pity requires me to pray for myself,
I who find myself completely distraught.
10   I waste and have wasted my time,
Like a man demented and mad:
Scholar of Melancholy.

Rondel—H. Le Voys

Scholar of Melancholy,
Because of Care, the rector here,
My heart is compelled to this study,
And God knows how he's punished!

5   For my heart to get involved was very foolish
Because restrained by force is he,
Scholar of Melancholy.

On no day of his life will he enjoy himself,
Stuck in such a plight. His heart is forced
10   To study, within the book of Sadness,
All about his misfortune,
Scholar of Melancholy.

Rondel—Orleans

Whether this means my life or death,
I cannot prevent my heart
From intending to counsel
Frequently with Melancholy.

5   So I tell him it's madness,
But, like a deaf man, he will not hear,
Whether this means my life or death.

And so I appeal to Favor
To please assist me.

10   Au paraller, ne puis fournir,
        Se ne m'aide par Courtoisie,
        Et fust ce *ma mort ou ma vie.*

510i: R422

R422   [Rondel] Orlians   [p. 510i]

▪Allez vous en dont vous venez,
Annuyeuse Merencolie!
Certes, on ne vous mande mie,
Trop privee vous devenez.

5   Soussi avecques vous menez,
        Mon huys ne vous ovreray mie :
        Allez vous en *dont vous venez.*

        Car mon cueur en tourment tenez,
        Quant estes en sa compaignie.
10   Prenez congié, je vous en prie,
        Et jamais plus ne retournez.
        Allez vous en *dont vous venez.*

510s: R421

R423   [Rondel] Orlians   [p. 511s]

A qui en donne l'en le tort,
Puis que le cueur en est d'acort,
Se les yeulx vont hors en voyage
Et rapportent aucun messaige
5   De Beaulté plaine de confort?

        Ilz crient : «Reveille qui dort!»
        Lors le cueur ne dort pas si fort
        Qu'i ne die : «J'oy compter rage.»
        A qui *en donne l'en le tort ?*

10   Adoncques Desir picque et mort,
        Savez commant? Jusqu'a la mort,
        Mais le cueur, s'il est bon et saige,
        Remede y treuve et avantaige,
        Bien ou mal en vient oultre bort.
15   A qui en donne *l'en le tort?*

511i: R424

10   In the end, I cannot bring it off
If Courtesy does not help,
Whether this means my life or death.

Rondel — Orleans

Go back where you came from,
Boring old Melancholy!
Surely, no one sent for you.
You become too familiar.

5   You bring Care along,
I'll not open the door even a crack:
Go back where you came from.

For you keep my heart in torment
When you're with him.
10   Take your leave, I beg you,
And never make your way here again.
Go back where you came from.

Rondel — Orleans

Who should be blamed
Since the heart agrees
To the eyes wandering off
And bringing back some message
5   From Beauty that's full of comfort?

They cry out: "Let the one who sleeps awake!"
Then the heart slumbers not so deeply
He does not say: "I hear folly spoken here."
Who should be blamed?

10   Then Desire stabs and bites him,
Do you know how? To the very death,
But the heart, if he is worthy and wise,
Will find a remedy there and advantage as well,
Good or evil beyond measure will come of it.
15   Who should be blamed?

R424 [Rondel] Orlians [p. 511i]

Doyvent ilz estre prisonniers,
Les yeulx, quant ilz vont assaillir
L'ambusche de Plaisant Desir,
Comme hardis avanturiers?

5 Veu qu'i sont d'Amours souldoyers
Et leurs gaiges fault desservir,
Doyvent ilz *estre prisonniers?*

Ilz se tiennent siens, si entiers,
Qu'au besoing ne peuent faillir,
10 Jusques a vivre ou a mourir,
Ilz le font bien et voulentiers.
Doyvent ilz *estre prisonniers?*

511s: R423

R425 [Rondel] Orlians [p. 512s]

N'oubliez pas vostre maniere!
Non ferez vous, je m'en fays fort,
Ennuy, armé de Desconfort,
Qui tousjours me tenez frontiere.

5 Venez combatre a la barriere,*
Et fetes acoup vostre effort :
N'oubliez pas *vostre maniere!*

Quant mectez sus vostre banyere,
Cueurs loyaulx, guerriez si fort
10 Que les faictes retraire ou fort
De Douleur, a piteuse chiere.
N'oubliez pas *vostre maniere!*

512i: Blank

R426 [Rondel] Orlians [513s]

Chiere contrefaicte de cueur,
De vert perdu et tanné painte,
Musique notee par Fainte,
Avec faulx bourdon de Maleur!*

Rondel — Orleans

Must they remain prisoners,
The eyes, when they go to attack
The ambush Pleasant Desire has laid,
Like courageous adventurers?

5   Seeing that they are the soldiers of Love
And must earn their wages,
Must they remain prisoners?

To Love they belong so completely
They cannot fail in times of need.
10   When life and death hang in the balance,
They act ably and with a good will.
Must they remain prisoners?

Rondel — Orleans

Do not forget yourself!
I swear you won't, Boredom,
Armed with Distress,
Forever opposing me.

5   Come fight it out in the lists
And expend your strength at once:
Do not forget yourself!

When you raise your banner high
Loyal hearts, you make such fierce war
10   You make them retreat to the stronghold
Of Suffering, their faces saddened.
Do not forget yourself!

Rondel — Orleans

A face counterfeiting what the heart feels,
Painted with drab green and washed-out brown,
Music whose notes are Deception,
With a faburden of unhappiness!

5   Qui est il, ce nouveau chanteur,
       Qui si mal vient a son actainte,
       Chiere *contrefaicte de cueur?*

       Je ne tiens contre ne teneur,
       Enroué, faisant faulte mainte,
10   Et mal entonné par Contraincte.
       C'est la chappelle de Douleur,
       Chiere *contrefaicte de cueur!*

513i: R427

R427   Rondel du grant senechal*   [p. 513i]

       Qui trop embrasse pou estraint :
       Je le dy pour maintes et maint
       Qui scevent servir de telz tours,
       Mectans loyaulté en decours,
5   Dont leur bon lous peut estre estaint.

       Qui a choysy et pris party,
       Puis que son cueur y a party,
       Esse bien fait de le laissier?

       Posé qu'on fust trop mieulx party,
10   Si seroit ce mal depparty,
       Et son honneur trop fort blessier.

       Qui varie, sans bien remaint,
       Par fermeté souvent on vaint,
       Les bons treuvent tousjours secours,
15   Ceulx qui changent l'ont a rebours.
       Il est pieça escript et paint :
       Qui trop *embrasse pou estraint.*

513s: R426

R428   [Rondel] Orlians   [p. 514s]

       Il n'est nul si beau passe temps
       Que se jouer a sa Pensee,
       Mais qu'elle soit bien despensee
       Par Raison, ainsi je l'entens.

5   Who is he, this new singer,
Failing so badly to achieve his aims,
A face counterfeiting what the heart feels?

I can't hold to tenor or countertenor,
My voice hoarse, missing many a note,
10   Out of tune because of Constraint.
It's the chapel of Pain,
A face counterfeiting what the heart feels!

Rondel by the Grand Seneschal

Whoever reaches for too much retains but little.
I say this for many men and women
Who knowingly practice such tricks,
Thereby debasing constancy
5   And forfeiting their good repute.

If a man has chosen and decided,
His heart now set on a course of action,
Is it good to abandon him?

Supposing he has chosen well,
10   Forsaking that choice would be bad
And should damage too much his honor.

Whoever keeps changing comes to no good.
Through steadfastness one often prevails;
The virtuous always find help,
15   Those who keep changing find the opposite.
For ages it has been written down and illustrated:
Whoever reaches for too much retains but little.

Rondel—Orleans

There is no finer pastime
Than to take pleasure in one's Thoughts,
Provided they have been well dispensed
By Reason, such is my understanding.

5   S'elle a fait nulz despens contens,
       Par Espoir soit recompensee :
       Il n'est *nul si beau passe temps.*

       Elle dit : «A ce je m'actens,
       Veu qu'ay Leaulté pourpensee,
10   Que de mes soussiz dispensee
       Seray, malgré les malcontens.»
       Il n'est nul *si beau passe temps.*

514i: Blank

R429   [Rondel] Fraigne*   [p. 515s]

       Le cueur dont vous avez la foy
       Se recommande a vous, madame,
       Vous faisant savoir qu'il vous ame,
       Mais pensez que ce n'est pas poy!

5   Il parle nuyt et jour a moy
       En vous louant, belle, plus que ame,
       Le cueur *dont vous avez la foy.*

       Il m'a juré—et je l'en croy—,
       Qu'a son vivant n'aura tant femme
10   —Et Dieu set commant il me blasme—
       Que plus souvent je ne vous voy,
       Le ♥ *dont vous avez la foy!*

515i: R430

R430   [Rondel]*   [p. 515i]

       Prophetizant de vostre advenement,
       Voyant venir voz haulx biens clerement
       Acompagnez de vostre grant beaulté,
       A vous amer si fort me suis bouté
5   Qu'au monde n'ay nul autre pensement.

       Tresque mon oueil vous vit premierement,
       Il ordonna mon cueur entierement
       Pour vous servir en toute feaulté,
       Prophetizant *de vostre advenement.*

10   Lor je jugé, a mon entendement,
       Que quelquefoiz j'aroye advencement,

5   If Thoughts have made cash expenditures,
May they be recompensed by Hope:
There is no finer pastime.

They say: "I expect,
Having intended to follow Loyalty,
10   That we will be relieved of the cares
We suffer, despite malcontents."
There is no finer pastime.

Rondel—Fraigne

The heart whose faith you possess
Commends himself to you, my lady,
Reporting that he loves you,
Provided you think this no triviality!

5   Night and day he speaks to me,
Praising you, belle, above any other,
The heart whose faith you possess.

He has sworn to me—and I believe him—
That while he lives there will be no lady
10   —And God knows how he corrects me—
I lay eyes upon more than I do you,
The heart whose faith you possess.

Rondel

Prophesying your arrival,
Seeing clearly your great charms come
Accompanied by your great beauty,
I am struck so mightily with love for you
5   I have no other thought in all the world.

Ever since my eye first spied you,
He completely disposed my heart
To serve you in all fealty,
Prophesying your arrival.

10   Then I considered, such was my understanding,
That sometimes I would advance my suit,

Vous remoustrant ma tresgrant loyaulté,
Et que de biens j'aroye a grant planté.
Cela je creu, des le commancement,
15   Prophetizant *de vostre advenement.*

515s: R429

R431   [Rondel] Fraigne*   [p. 516s]

Mon oueil, je te prie et requier
Que tu n'ayes plus en pensee
D'aler veoir ma tant desiree,
Ou tu me maiz en grant dangier.

5   Et si te dy, pour habergier
Que c'est ma mort toute juree,
Mon oueil, *je te prie et requier!*

Quant tu la verras au moutier,
Ou quelque part a la passee,
10   Ne te mez pas en sa visee,
Car perilleux est tel archier,
Mon oueil, *je te prie et requier!*

516i: Blank

R432   [Rondel] Orlians   [p. 517s]

Pour Dieu, faictez moy quelque bien,
Veu que m'a desrobé Veillesse,
Plaisance, car en ma jeunesse,
Savez que vous amoye bien.

5   Pour vous n'ay espargnay du myen,
Or suis pouvre, plain de foiblesse :
Pour Dieu, *faictez moy quelque bien!*

Devoir ferez, comme je tien,
Car j'ay despendu a largesse,
10   Pieça, mon tresor de lÿesse,
Et maintenant je n'ay plus rien.
Pour Dieu, *faictez moy quelque bien!*

517i: R433

Showing you the very great loyalty I possess,
And that I would gain favors in abundance.
I believed this from the beginning,
15   Prophesying your arrival.

Rondel—Fraigne

My eye, I ask and beg you
To entertain the thought no more
Of going to see the lady I desire so much,
Or you will put me in great danger.

5   And so I say that if you take lodging there,
A sentence of death will be passed upon me,
My eye, I ask and beg you!

When you spy her at church,
Or somewhere in passing,
10   Don't let her catch sight of you,
For that archer is deadly.
My eye, I ask and beg you.

Rondel—Orleans

For God's sake, do me some favor,
Pleasure, now that Old Age has
Robbed me blind, for in my youth
You know I loved you well.

5   I never spared anything for your sake,
Now I am impoverished, terribly weakened:
For God's sake, do me some favor!

Do what I think you should,
For I have paid out generously
10   In days past from my reserves of happiness,
And now I've nothing left.
For God's sake, do me some favor!

R433   [Rondel] Orlians

[p. 517i]

C'est la prison Dedalus*
Que de ma merencollie,
Quant je la cuide fallie,
G'i rentre de plus en plus.

5   Aucunes foiz, je conclus
D'i bouter Plaisance lie :
C'est la prison *Dedalus!*

Oncques ne fut Tantalus*
En si tres peneuse vie,
10   Ne, quelque chose qu'on die,
Chartreux, hermite ou reclus :
C'est la prison *Dedalus!*

517s: R432

R434   [Rondel] Anthoine de Cuise*

[p. 518s]

Ha! mort, helas!
Veu que je suis de vivre las,
Que ne tens tu vers moy tes las,
Pour abreger mon infortune,
5   Ausy pour montrer a Fortune,
Qui me fortune,
La puissance que sur elle as!

Fay ton effort et sy t'avance,
Mais, pour Dieu, que ce soit avant ce
10   Que je m'ocys de mes mains!

Montre ton povoir et savance,
Puis que je vueul faire l'avance,
Car certes tu ne pues a mains.

Pren tes esbas
15   A faire cesser nos debas,
Ausy bien sont se tes cabas
Que de tousjours trouver rancune.
Tu es seule, celle et chascune,
Sans aultre aucune
20   Par qui tout cesse hault et bas.
Ha! mort, helas!

518i: Blank*

Rondel — Orleans

It's the prison of Daedalus itself,
This melancholy I feel;
When I think to have escaped it,
Deeper and deeper I tumble back in.

5   Sometimes I come to the view
That merry Pleasure should be shoved in:
It's the prison of Daedalus itself!

Never did Tantalus
Find himself in such misery,
10   Nor did, no matter what anyone might say,
A Carthusian, monk, or recluse:
It's the prison of Daedalus itself!

Rondel — Antoine de Cuise

Aha, Death! Alas!
Now that I am tired of living,
Why shouldn't you seek to entrap me,
And so end my misfortune,
5   And also show Fortune,
Who treats me harshly,
The power you wield over her!

Make some effort and get going on this,
And for God's sake let it be before
10   I kill myself with my own hands!

Make known your strength and knowledge,
Because I wish this thing to proceed,
For surely you can do no less.

Make it your pleasure
15   To end our disagreement,
Your trickery is very much
What always leads to wrangling.
It's you alone, just you,
And no one else,
20   Who finishes everyone, high and low.
Aha, Death! Alas!

R435 [Rondel] Anthoine de Cuise*

[p. 519s]

Par bien celer mains tours divers,
Montrant de son vueil le revers,
Soubz ung peu de maniere fainte,
Avec abstinance contrainte,
5   Sont les segrés d'Amours ouvers.
Refuz les deffent a travers,
Et ne sont a nulz descouvers,
Que ce ne soit en tresgrant crainte,
Par bien celer mains tours *divers*.

10   Honte les tient clos et couvers
Pour les faulx dangers et pervers,
Dont elle a eu reprouche mainte,
Mais pour venir a nostre atincte,
Loyauté nous baille ces vers,
15   Par bien celer *mains tours divers*.

519i: Blank

R436 [Rondel] Anthoine de Cuise*

[p. 520s]

Ou val oscur, aventureux,
Ou les loyaulx cueurs doloreux
Des amoureux
Sont condempnez d'user leurs jours,
5   En piteux plains et grans clamours,
Me tient Amours,
Comme le chef des langoureux,

Et fault qu'avec les maleureux
Par son faulx refuz rigoureux,
10   Plus que poureux,
J'atende la mort a secours,
Ou val oscur, aventureux.

C'est le hault gardon dengereux,
Ordonné pour moy et pour eulx,
15   Peu savoureux,
Sans autre part avoir recours,
Et la voyant, nostre decours,
De crys et plours,
Faisons ung tresor plaintureux,
20   Ou val oscur, aventureux.

520i: Blank

Rondel—Antoine de Cuise

Through carefully concealing many different tricks,
Showing the opposite of one's intention
Beneath a somewhat deceptive manner,
With forced abstinence,
5   In this way are the secrets of Love revealed.
Refusal thoroughly protects them
And they are revealed to no one,
Unless it be with great fear
Through carefully concealing many different tricks.

10   Shame keeps them hidden and secret
Because of the false and perverse haughtiness
For which many have reproached her,
But to come to our meaning,
Loyalty provides us with these verses,
15   Through carefully concealing many different tricks.

Rondel—Antoine de Cuise

In that valley dark and dangerous
Where the loyal and suffering hearts
Of those in love
Are condemned to pass their days
5   In pitiable complaining and loud clamor,
Love makes me take my dwelling,
As chief of those who languish,

And it's necessary that with the unfortunate,
Through his false and firm refusal,
10   I wait for death to rescue me,
More than merely fearful,
In that valley dark and dangerous.

It's an exalted and perilous reward,
Ordained for me and them,
15   Not very appealing,
Lacking any recourse,
And seeing our misfortune,
With cries and laments
Let's make an abundant treasure,
20   In that valley dark and dangerous.

R437   [Rondel] Orleans   [p. 521s]

    A! que vous m'anuyés, Viellesse,
    Que me grevez plus que oncques mes!
    Me voulés vous a tousjours mes
    Tenir en courroux et rudesse?

5   Je vous faiz loyalle promesse
    Que ne vous aimeray jamés :
    A! que vous m'anuyés, Viellesse!

    Vous m'avez banny de Jennesse,
    Rendre me convient desormais.
10   Et faites vous bien? Nennil, mais
    De tous maulx on vous tient maistresse.
    A! que vous m'anuyés, Viellesse!

521i: Blank

R438   [Rondel] [?Meschinot]*   [p. 522s]

    Les biens de vous, honneur et pris,
    M'ont tant espris
    De vous amer, ma gente damme,
    Qu'il n'est pas en puissance d'amme
5   De tourner ailleurs mes espris.

    C'est a moy trop hault entrepris,
    Com mal apris,
    Mes blamez en, s'il y a blame,
    Les biens de vous, *honneur et pris.*

10   Donc, puis qu'Amour ainssi m'a pris
    En son pourpris,
    Et que tant loyaument vous ame,
    Amez moy, je prans sus mon ame
    Que jamés n'en seront repris
15   Les biens de vous, *honneur et pris.*

522i: R439

R439   [Rondel] [?Meschinot]*   [p. 522i]

    M'amerez vous bien,
    Dites par vostre ame,
    Mes que je vous ame
    Plus que nule rien?

Rondel — Orleans

Oh, how you pain me, Old Age,
Grieving me more than ever before!
Do you intend henceforth to hold me
Always fast in sorrow and bitterness?

5   I promise you faithfully
I will never hold you dear:
Oh, how you pain me, Old Age!

You've banished me from Youth,
I must surrender myself henceforth.
10   And is what you do right? Not at all, but
You are thought the mistress of every ill.
Oh, how you pain me, Old Age!

Rondel

Your good qualities, your honor and repute
Have so inflamed me with
Love for you, my noble lady,
That no one possesses the power
5   To turn my soul elsewhere.

For me this is quite a grand undertaking,
Who am so ill taught,
But put the blame, if blame there is, on
Your good qualities, your honor and repute.

10   And so, since Love has made me a prisoner
In his enclosure,
And I love you so faithfully,
Do love me; I swear on my soul
That never because of this will be sullied
15   Your good qualities, your honor and repute.

Rondel

Will you love me well?
Tell me upon your soul,
Seeing that I love you
More than anyone else.

5   Le vostre me tien,
       Sanz faire autre damme.
       M'amerez vous bien?

       Dieu mist tant de bien
       En vous que c'est bamme.
10   Pource, je me clame
       Vostre, mes combien
       M'amerez vous bien?

522s: R438

R440   [Rondel] [?Meschinot]*   [p. 523s]

       C'est par vous que tant fort soupire,
       Tousjours m'enpire.
       A vostre avis, faites vous bien
       Que tant plus je vous vieulx de bien
5   Et, sus ma foy, vous m'estes pire?

       Ha! ma damme, si grieff martire,
       Amme ne tire
       Que moy, dont ne puis maiz en rien.
       C'est par vous *que tant fort soupire.*

10   Vostre beauté vint de grant tire
       A mon oeill dire
       Que feist mon cueur devenir sien.
       Il le voulut. S'il meurt, et bien,
       Je ne luy puis ayder ou nuyre!
15   C'est par vous *que tant fort soupire.*

523i: Blank

R441   [Rondel] [?Meschinot]*   [p. 524s]

       Pour mettre fin a mes douloureux plains
       Et aux ennuys dont je me scens si plains,
       Fort me complains
       A tout heure, mes remyde n'y treuve,
5   Fors qu'il me fault de mort faire l'espreuve
       Ou dame neuve,
       Car la mienne se rit, tant plus me plains.

       Souvent m'a veu pleurant par baus et plains,
       A triste cueur, de dueill palez et tains,

5 I hold myself yours,
  With no other lady.
  Will you love me well?

  God has bestowed so much goodness
  On you that it is a balm,
10 And so I proclaim myself
  Yours, but to what degree
  Will you love me well?

Rondel

  It's you who make me sigh so deeply
  That I continually grow worse.
  Do you think you do right
  When the more I intend your benefit,
5 The worse you treat me, upon my faith?

  Aha, my lady, such grievous suffering
  Afflicts no one but me,
  And so there's nothing I can do.
  It's you who make me sigh so deeply.

10 Your beauty came up in great haste
  To tell my eye it should
  Make my heart be hers.
  This is what he wished. If he dies, oh well,
  I can do nothing, neither help nor hurt.
15 It's you who make me sigh so deeply.

Rondel

  To put an end to my painful complaints
  And the miseries of which I feel so full,
  I bemoan my fate loudly
  At every hour, but find no relief
5 Save that I must run the risk of death
  Or find some new lady, for the more
  I cry out the more amused my lady is.

  Often she spies me weeping through woods and fields,
  My heart saddened, marked and discolored by pain,

10   Pres que m'estains,
        Mes pensez vous que de riens el se meuve
        Pour mettre fin *a mes douloureux plains?*

        Nenny, ains dit par sa foy, qu'autres mains
        Seuffrent de maulx plus que moy, soirs et mains,
15   Et qu'en ay mains
        Que je ne dy. Ainssi mon fait repreuve.
        Bien luy plairoyt qu'elle fust de moy veufve,
        Son cas le preuve.
        Ne suy ge pas doncques en bonnes mains,
20   Pour mettre fin *a mes douloureux plains?*

524i: Blank

R442   [Rondel] Orleans   [p. 525s]

        Temps et temps m'ont emblé Jennesse
        Et laissé es mains de Viellesse
        Ou vois mon pouvre pain querant.
        Aage ne me veult tant ne quant
5   Donner l'aumosne de Lïesse.

        Puis qu'elle se tient ma maistresse,
        Demander ne luy puis promesse;
        Pource n'enquerons plus avant :
        Temps *et temps m'ont emblé Jennesse.*

10   Je n'ay repast que de Foiblesse,
        Couchant sur paille de Destresse.
        Suy je bien payé maintenant
        De mes jennes jours cy devant?
        Nennil, nul n'est qui le redresse :
15   Temps et temps *m'ont emblé Jennesse!*

525i: R443

R443   [Rondel] Orleans   [p. 525i]

        Asourdy de Non Chaloir,
        Aveuglé de Desplaisance,
        Pris de goute de Grevance,
        Ne sçay a quoy puis valoir.

10   Almost in a dead faint. But do you think
She was moved to do anything at all
To put an end to my painful complaints?

Not at all, in fact, but she swore that many others
Suffer harsher ills by night and day than I,
15   And that mine are less than what
I say they are. In this way she faults me.
She'd be well pleased to be my widow.
Her behavior proves it's so.
Am I not then in good hands
20   To put an end to my painful complaints?

Rondel — Orleans

Time and tide have stolen my Youth,
Abandoning me to the hands of Old Age,
Where I go begging for my pitiful bread.
Age has no intention in the least
5   Of giving me the alms of Happiness.

Since she thinks herself my mistress,
I can ask her for no assurances;
And so we'll ask no further questions:
Time and tide have stolen my Youth.

10   Feebleness has been my only nourishment,
As I lie on the straw pallet of Distress.
Am I well rewarded for
My younger days long past?
Not at all, no one can remedy this:
15   Time and tide have stolen my Youth.

Rondel — Orleans

Made deaf by Indifference,
Blinded by Distress,
Afflicted by the gout of Misery,
I don't know what I'm good for.

5   Voullez vous mon fait savoir?
       Je suis pres que mis en trance,
       Asourdy *de Non Chaloir.*

       Se le Medecin Espoir,
       Qui est le meilleur de France,
10   N'y met briefment pourveance,
       Viellesse estainct mon povoir,
       Assourdy *de Non Chaloir.*

525s: R442

R444   [Rondel] Orleans   [p. 526s]

       Dedens la maison de Doleur,
       Ou estoit trespiteuse dance,
       Soussy, Viellesse et Desplaisance
       Je vis dancer comme par cueur.

5   Le tabourin nommé Maleur
       Ne jouoit point par ordonnance
       Dedens la maison *de Doleur.*

       Puis chantoient chançons de Pleur,
       Sans musicque ne accordance.
10   D'ennuy, comme ravy en trance,
       M'andormy lors, pour le meilleur,
       Dedens la maison *de Doleur.*

526i: R445

R445   [Rondel] Simonnet Cailleau*   [p. 526i]

       Dedens la maison de Douleur,
       Ou n'a lëesse ne musique,
       Mon laz cuer gist merencolique,
       Malade ou piteulx lit de Pleur.

5   E Dieux! n'esse pas grand maleur?
       Il est piz que paralitique,
       Dedens la maison *de Douleur.*

       Par racine, fueille ne fleur,
       Ne par medicine autentique,
10   Remedier n'y scet phisique.

5   Do you want to know how I'm doing?
I'm almost delirious,
Made deaf by Indifference.

If that physician Hope,
Who is the finest in France,
10   Does not quickly treat me,
Old Age will steal away all my strength,
Made deaf by Indifference.

Rondel—Orleans

Within the house of Pain,
Where the dancing was quite pathetic,
I spied Care, Old Age, and Misery
Dancing as though they knew the steps.

5   The drummer named Misfortune
Did not play well at all
Within the house of Pain.

They then sang songs of Weeping,
With no music or accompaniment.
10   As if put in a trance by Misery,
I then fell asleep, and that was for the best,
Within the house of Pain.

Rondel—Simonnet Cailleau

Within the house of Pain,
Where there's no music or happiness,
My weary heart lies full of melancholy,
A sick man on the pitiful bed of Weeping.

5   Oh God! Is this not a great misfortune?
He is worse than paralytic,
Within the house of Pain.

Not through root, leaf, or flower,
Nor by proper potion
10   Can a physician contrive some remedy.

Confesse soy, s'est le meilleur,
Dedens *la maison de Douleur.*

526s: R444

R446   [Rondel] Orlians   [p. 527s]

Je vous sans et congnois venir,
Anuyeuze Merencolie.
Maintez fois, quant je ne vueil mye,
L'uys de mon cueur vous fault ovrir.

5   Point ne vous envoye querir,
Assez hay vostre compaignie :
Je vous sans *et congnois venir.*

Jennes peuent paine souffrir,
Plus que viellars. Pource, vous prie
10   Que n'ayez plus sur nous envie.
Ne nous vueilliez plus assaillir,
Je vous sans *et congnois venir.*

527i: Blank

R447   [Rondel] Orleans   [p. 528s]

Mentez, menteurs a carterons,*
Certes point ne vous redoubtons,
Ne vous ne voustre baverye.
Loyaulté dit, de sens garnye :
5   «Fy de vous et de voz raisons!»

On ne vous prise deux boutons,
Et pource, nous vous deboutons,
Esloignant nostre compaignie :
Mentez, menteurs *a carterons.*

10   Voz parlez, pires que poizons,
Boutent par tout feu en maisons.
Que voulés vous que l'en vous die?
Dieu tout puissant si vous mauldie,
Vous donnant de maulx jours foisons!
15   Mentés, menteurs *a carterons!*

528i: Blank

Let him make his confession, it's for the best,
Within the house of Pain.

Rondel — Orleans

I know and sense when you are coming,
Annoying old Melancholy.
Many times, and though I don't wish it so,
The door of my heart must open to you.

5   I never have you sent for,
I loathe your companionship:
I know and sense when you are coming.

The young can stand pain
Better than the old. And so I ask you
10   To entertain no more designs upon us.
Please assault us no more,
I know and sense when you are coming.

Rondel — Orleans

Lie, all you liars,
Surely we do not fear you in the least,
Neither you nor your useless talk.
Loyalty says, with good sense:
5   "Fie on you and your blatherings!"

People care nothing for you,
And so we put you to flight,
Driving you from our company:
Lie, all you liars.

10   You speak, it's worse than poison,
Setting fire to houses everywhere.
What would you have us say about it?
May Almighty God curse you,
Giving you many a miserable day!
15   Lie, all you liars!

R448   [Rondel] Gilles des Ourmez*   [p. 529s]

Pour bien mentir souvent et plaisemment,
Mais qu'il ne tourne a aucun prejudice,
Il m'est adviz que ce n'est point de vice,
Mais est vertu et bon entendement.

5   On en voit maint eslevé haultement,
Bien recueilly et requis en service,
Pour bien mentir *souvent et plaisemment.*

Mais controuveurs qui mentent faulcement
Pour diffamer quelc'un par leur malice,
10   Soient pugnis par droit, selon justice.
Pource, chascun s'avise saigement
Pour bien mentir *souvent et plaisemment.*

529i: Blank

R449   Rondel

Des soucies de la court*   [p. 530s]
J'ay acheté au jourd'uy.
De deulx bien garny j'en suy,
Quoy que mon argent soit court.

5   A les avoir chacung court,
Mais quant a moy, je m'enfuy
Des soucies *de la court.*

Je deviens viel, sourt et lourt,
Et quant me treuve en ennuy,
10   Non Chaloir est mon apuy,
Qui maintesfoiz me secourt
Des soucies de la court.

530i: R450

R450   [Rondel] Orleans   [p. 530i]

Tout plain ung sac de Joyeuse Promesse,
Soubz clef fermé, en ung coffin d'Oublie,
Qui ne poursuit, certes c'est grant folie,
Tant qu'on en ayt par Raison, a largesse.

Rondel—Gilles des Ourmez

Lying well often and amusingly,
Provided it harms no one,
Is no vice at all, this is what I think,
But rather a virtue, something well-considered.

5   As one sees, many are raised to high rank,
Well received and accepted in service,
Lying well often and amusingly.

But those fabricators who faithlessly lie
So as to defame someone through their malice,
10   Let them be rightly punished, as justice demands.
And so let every man wisely consider
Lying well often and amusingly.

Rondel

Marigolds from the court,
I've bought some of them today.
Well-supplied I am with two such,
Though my funds are limited.

5   Every man runs to get them,
But as for me, I flee
Marigolds from the court.

I grow old, I grow deaf and heavy,
And, finding myself in pain,
10   My support is Indifference,
Who many times comes to rescue me from
Marigolds from the court.

Rondel—Orleans

A sack chock-full of Joyful Promises,
Locked within the chest of Forgetfulness,
It's great folly for any man not to seek
Possessing such through Reason.

5   Craindre ne fault Fortune la diverse
         Qui Passe temps avecques elle alie,
         Tout plain ung sac *de Joyeuse Promesse.*

         Conseil requier a gens plains de sagesse,
         Qui mieulx sera, si leur plaist, c'om le die,
10   Car Bon Espoir, quoy c'on le contrarie,
         A droit vendra et trouvera richesse
         Tout plain *ung sac de Joyeuse Promesse.*

530s: R449

R451   Rondel de Benoist Damien*   [p. 531s]

         Nagent en angoisse parfonde,
         Ou joye ne plaisir n'abite,
         Mon dolent cueur en nef mauldite,
         D'Ercules a passé la bonde.

5   D'y avoir bien nul ne s'i fonde.
         La voye si est interdite,
         Nagent *en angoisse parfonde.*

         L'aider, nul ne peut en ce monde,
         Fors Thetis, qui Deesse est dite*
10   De la mer, car sans contredite
         En elle tout povoir habonde,
         Nagent *en angoisse parfonde.*

531i: R452

R452   [Rondel] par ledit Benoist*   [p. 531i]

         Tant plus regarde, moins y voy,
         Et plus y voy, moins y congnoys.
         Le monde va de deux en trois,
         Sans savoir comment ne pourquoy.

5   Faulseté regne, et tient sa loy
         En tretouz les lieux ou je vois :
         Tant plus regarde, *moins y voy.*

         Loyaulté si est en recoy,
         Deboutee on l'a tant de fois,
10   Que passez sont mains jours et moys,

5   No need to fear unstable Fortune,
       Who allies herself with Pastime,
       A sack chock-full of Joyful Promises.

       I ask men of great wisdom for advice,
       Please say who will be better off,
10   For Good Hope, no matter how opposed,
       Will rightly come forward to find riches,
       A sack chock-full of Joyful Promises.

Rondel of Benoit Damien

Sailing through the deep waters of misery,
Where no joy or pleasure can be found,
My anguished heart in an accursed ship
Has passed beyond the pillars of Hercules.

5   Let no one attempt finding any good in this.
       The way there is forbidden,
       Sailing through the deep waters of misery.

No one in this world can make a difference
Save Thetis, who is called Goddess
10   Of the sea, for all power
       Beyond any dispute is found abundantly in her,
       Sailing through the deep waters of misery.

Rondel by the aforesaid Benoit

The more I look, the less I see,
And the more I see, the less I understand.
The world goes its way without rhyme or reason,
And no one knows how or why.

5   Hypocrisy reigns, and upholds her law
       Everywhere I see:
       The more I look, the less I see.

Loyalty has taken to hiding,
Having been rebuffed so often
10   That many a day and month has passed

Qu'on ne la vit, comme je croy :
Tant plus regarde, *moins y voy.*

531s: R451

R453   [Rondel]   [p. 532s]

Dieu les en puisse guerdonner
Tous ceulx qui ainsi tourmenter
Font, de vent, de naige et de pluye,
Et nous et nostre compaignye,
5   Dont peu nous en devons louer.

Mais il fauldra qu'au paraller,
Commant qu'il en doye tarder,
Que nous, ou eulx, en pleure ou rie :
Dieu les *en puisse guerdonner!*

10   Or ça, il fault parachever
Et puis qu'il est trait, avaler!
On congnoistra qu'est de clergie,
D'Orleans, trait de Lombardie :
Tous biens faiz convendra trouver,
15   Dieu les *en puisse guerdonner!*

532i: R530

R454   [Rondel]   [p. 532i]

Prenons congié du plaisir de noz yeulx,
Puis qu'a present ne povons mieulx avoir,
De revenir faisons nostre devoir,
Quant Dieu plaira, et sera pour le mieulx.

5   Il fault changer aucunefoiz les lieux,
Et essayer, pour plus ou moins savoir :
Prenons congié *du plaisir de nos yeulx.*

Ainsi parlent les jennes et les vieulx.
Pource, chascun en face son povoir.
10   Nul ne mecte sa seurté en Espoir,
Car aujourd'uy courent les eurs tieulx quieulx.
Prenons congié du plaisir de nos yeulx.

532s: R529

When she is spied by no one, I think.
The more I look, the less I see.

Rondel

May God find the power to reward them
With wind, snow, and rain,
All those who bring torment
Upon us and our company,
5   For which we have scant cause to be pleased.

But in the end it must come to pass,
Whatever delay arises, that we
Or they find cause to weep or laugh:
May God find the power to reward them!

10   Come now, we must make an end
And drain the glass that has been poured!
We'll know if wisdom is to be found
In Orleans, whose line is Lombard:
All good deeds must be made public,
15   May God find the power to reward them!

Rondel

Let's take leave of the pleasure of our eyes,
For at present we can have no better,
Let's think about returning to our senses,
Whenever God pleases. It will be for the best.

5   Sometimes you must have a change of scene
And give it a go, learning something more or less.
Let's take leave of the pleasure of our eyes.

Both young and old say so.
Let everyone then do his best.
10   Let no one put his trust in Hope,
For these days luck runs willy-nilly.
Let's take leave of the pleasure of our eyes.

R455   **[Rondel]**   [p. 533s]

M'apelez vous cela jeu,
En froit d'aler par pays?
Or pleust a Dieu qu'a Paris
Nous feussions enprés le feu!

5   Nostre prouffit veullent peu,
Qui en ce point nous ont mis!
M'apelez vous *cela jeu?*

Deslyer nous fault ce neu
Et desployer fais et dis,
10   Tant qu'aviengne mieulx ou pis,
Passer convient par ce treu :
M'apelez vous *cela jeu?*

533i: Blank

R456   **[Rondel]**   [p. 534s]

De Veillesse porte livree
Qu'elle m'a puis ung temps donnee,
Quoy que soit contre mon desir,
Mais maulgré myen le faut souffrir,
5   Quant par Nature est ordonnee.

Elle est d'annuy si fort brodee,
Dieu scet que l'ay cheire achaptee
Sans gueires d'argent de plesir :
De Veillesse *porte livree.*

10   Par moy puist estre bien usee
En eur et bonne destinee,
Et a mon soubhet parvenir,
Tant que vivre puisse et mourir
Selon l'escript de ma penssee :
15   De Veillesse *porte livree.*

534i: Blank

R457   **[Rondel] Orleans**   [p. 535s]

Salués moy toute la compaignie
Ou a present estez a chiere lye
Et leur dites que voulentiés seroye

Rondel

Are you telling me this is a game,
Traveling through the countryside in such cold?
Please God that in Paris
We could be close by the fire!

5   They care little for our well-being,
Those who've put us on such a route!
Are you telling me this is a game?

We must untie this knot,
Devoting ourselves to words and deeds
10 Until matters improve or worsen,
Passing through this difficulty:
Are you telling me this is a game?

Rondel

I wear the livery of Old Age,
Who gave it to me some time ago,
Though it was in no way my wish;
And so she's brought me unwilling to this pass,
5   For Nature has ordained it must be so.

This livery is heavily brocaded with boredom,
God knows I've bought it at a heavy price
With hardly a bit of pleasure's coin:
I wear the livery of Old Age.

10 May I use it well
To find happiness and a fitting fate,
Achieving my desire
To be able to live and die
In the way my thoughts have written:
15 I wear the livery of Old Age.

Rondel—Orleans

Give my greetings to all the company
You're among at present with good cheer
And tell them I would willingly

        Avecques eulx, mais estre n'y pourroye
5   Pour Viellesse qui m'a en sa ballie.

        Au temps passé, Jennesse sy jolie
        Me gouvernoit. Las! or n'y suy ge mye,
        Et pour cela, pour Dieu, que escuzé soye:
        Salués moy *toute la compaignie!*

10   Amoureus fus, or ne le suy ge mye,
        Et en Paris menoye bonne vie.
        Adieu bon temps, ravoir ne vous saroye!
        Bien sanglé fus d'une estrete courroye,
        Que, par Age, convient que la deslie :
15   Salués moy *toute la compaignie!*

535i : Blank

R458   [Rondel] Bourbon*   [p. 536s]

        Gardez vous bien du cayement,
        Ung chascun, tendez y l'oreille :
        Pour vous decevoir tousjours veille.
        Escoutez s'il dit vray ou mant,

5   Il vous trompera, mes comment?
        Pource que sans cesser traveille.
        Gardez *vous bien du cayement.*

        Dieu met en mal an le Flament!
        Vous direz qu'il dort et sommeille
10   Quant il va, mais il se reveille
        En temps et lieu. Incessament
        Gardez vous bien *du cayement.*

536i : R459

R459   [Rondel] ung autre de luy*   [p. 536i]

        Des droiz de la porte Baudet,
        Pour toute recompense et paine,
        Tout au beau long de la sepmaine,
        Suis servy comme ung grant cadet.

5   Si doulx ne sont que muscadet,
        Rien n'en vault le fruit ne la graine
        Des droiz *de la porte Baudet.*

Be with them, but I cannot
5 Because of Old Age, who rules me.

In times past, Youth so merry
Governed me. Alas! Now I am no longer with her.
So for God's sake accept my excuses.
Give my greetings to all the company!

10 I was given to romance, but now not at all,
And in Paris I led a pleasant life.
Farewell to good times, I cannot have you back!
Well-girded I was with a tight belt,
Which Age makes me loosen:
15 Give my greetings to all the company.

Rondel — Bourbon

Keep a close eye on the beggar,
Each and every one, lend him your ear:
He's always looking to deceive you.
Listen if he's speaking true or false.

5 He will fool you, but how?
Because he never stops trying.
Keep a close eye on the beggar.

May God send that Fleming hard times!
You say he sleeps and naps
10 As he travels about, but he rouses
When it suits him. Never stopping,
Keep a close eye on the beggar.

Rondel — someone other than him

With payments from the Baudet toll,
As recompense for all my woes,
Right through the entire week
I am served like a gentleman officer.

5 They are not as sweet as muscadet,
Nothing's worth as much as the fruit or grain,
With payments from the Baudet toll.

C'est bien joué du soubz condet,*
Puisqu'il le fault, ribon ribayne,
10   Endurer, comme a la quintayne,
On en deust servir Mistodet*
Des droiz *de la porte Baudet!*

536s: R458

R460   [Rondel] P. Danche*   [p. 537s]

Gardez vous bien de ce fauveau,
C'est une dangereuse beste.
Arsoir me donna par la teste
Tant qu'il me rompit le cerveau.

5   Il est ferré tout de nouveau
Et rue comme la tempeste :
Gardez vous bien *de ce fauveau!*

Et combien qu'il soit bon et beau,
Doulx au brider et faisant feste
10   A ung chascun, vous amoneste
Que vous ne le peignez sans eau :
Gardez vous bien *de ce fauveau!*

537i: Blank

It is a good game, sort of,
Since it has to be endured, willy-nilly,
10   Just as the quintain is,
Mistodet should be served
With payments from the Baudet toll!

Rondel — P. Danche

Keep a close eye on this fawn horse,
It's a dangerous beast.
Recently it gave my head a knock
And almost spilled my brains.

5   Its hooves are newly iron-shod
And like a storm it bucks:
Keep a close eye on this fawn horse.

And although it's fair and handsome,
Easy to rein in and shows a pleasant manner
10   To everyone, I warn you
Not to curry it without water.
Keep a close eye on this fawn horse.

Textual Notes

NB: Many of the spaces various scribes left for larger decorative initials have not been filled. As this is a palaeographical matter rather than a textual one, we have omitted reference to these (though we have noted limning errors). For more detail on such matters, see Arn, *The Poet's Notebook*.

B1:   The heading "Balade" is missing from the first three poems, but is used regularly thereafter in the work of the first scribe. Of the 71 poems between the Introduction and *Le Songe en Complainte*, 20 have no envoy, but all others have, along with the heading *L'envoy*.

B6:   L. 5 is a syllable short. Champion prints *[il] me dist.*

B7:   "Lenvoy" is written in the margin to the right of l. 28, and l. 31, *Mon cueur etc.*, to the right of l. 30 in order to get the entire poem on to one page.

B22:   L. 24 *Dieu scet etc.* written alongside l. 23 to avoid carrying the last line of the stanza over to the following page.

B31:   Ll. 16, 24, 28 read *le don damy.*

B33:   In the MS., *L'amant*, *Le cueur*, etc. are placed to the right of the text. The number of such displaced headings suggests they were added after the poem was copied.

B37:   L. 27 *Tresor Lenvoy* written alongside l. 26 to enable the whole poem to fit the page.

B41:   l. 17 MS. reads *Le* for *Se.*

B45:   L. 1 MS. reads *Le* for *Se.*

B53:   L. 24 *Ou temps* is written alongside l. 23 to avoid carrying the one line over to the next page.

B56:   L. 32 MS. reads *lamoure chappelle.*

B57:   L. 10 MS. reads *Eas*, presumably for *Las.*

B59:   L. 16 is shortened to *Je pry a Dieu* and written alongside l. 15 in order to get the whole poem on to one page.

B62:   L. 24 has *doit* for *doint.*

B67:   The last stanza appears to be missing a couplet rhyming in *-ee* after l. 27, but it makes perfectly good sense as it stands. Either this couplet was never written, or it was omitted by the copyist because it interrupted the natural flow of the meaning from line 27 to line 28.

B70: L. 13 MS. reads *Lu* for *Lui*. L. 18 *Devant tous* is written alongside l. 17 to get the whole poem on to one page.

B73: The top of the page has been cropped, leaving the bottom of the letters *Balade* just visible. L. 9 *par* appears to have been *parmy* originally. The last two letters have been erased. The line reads well, and has the correct number of syllables without them.

B84: L. 9 MS. reads *Ie* for *Le*. L. 17 MS. reads *Doibles*; *Foibles* added in margin.

B86: Heading: "de Jacques" follows the word *Balade* on the same line. L. 17 MS. reads *Deulx*.

B88: L. 17 MS. reads *Tout*. *Goute* is the reading of MS. 375 of the Bibliothèque de Carpentras. Ll. 24, 29 MS. reads *Par le vent etc.* Hitherto the refrains have been complete.

B89: L. 1 MS. reads *Le*. L. 16, 28 MS. reads *Sans grant espargne etc.* L. 24 MS. reads *Sans grant etc.*

B91: L. 33 MS. reads *Vous usez etc.*

B93: The rest of the page is blank.

B100: L. 17 MS. reads *ma* for *me*.

B101: L. 2 MS. reads *aprendoye*. Rhyme and sense justify the correction.

Jam nova: L. 29 MS. reads *traicte tissue*. L. 47 *fait* omitted and added over *bien le*.

B102: No headings here and for the following nine "*fontaine*" *ballades*, except where indicated.

B105: *Lenvoy* has been added at the bottom of the page. L. 22 MS. reads *prttendent*.

B106: L. 13 omitted, and added at foot of page. L. 18 The rhyme pattern, and the number of lines in each stanza, show there is a line missing after l. 18, but the MS. leaves no space.

B108: The names *Montbeton* and *Robertet* are added in the MS. in the places indicated. Attributions are generally added in a hand other than that of the copyist (sometimes separated from the heading by a centered dot). Most are certainly fifteenth-century, though a few are more modern.

B110: The heading has been cropped; the name *Berthault de Villebresme* has been added in a later (post-medieval) hand, probably by whoever cropped the page, since only the very bottom of the letters survived.

B113: L. 1 MS. reads *o pres*.

B114: L. 17 Whole line omitted and added by Charles in the left margin.

B120: L. 5 MS. reads *Et pource la raison*.

B127: Heading has been cropped then rewritten in a later (post-medieval) hand. *Lenvoy* is added in the margin, there being no space between ll. 24 and 25.

B128: L. 9 Initial illuminated *L* for *S*. *Envoy* written in right margin.

B129:   *Lenvoy:* MS. has illuminated *B* for *L.*

B133:   L. 12 *un* omitted.

B134:   L. 24 Omitted, *ce nest* added in margin.

B138:   L. 16 MS. reads *jes face.*

B139:   L. 31 MS. reads *revendroye.* Rhyme and sense justify the correction.

Co5:   L. 50 After *le plus, souvent* struck out

Co7:   L. 22 MS. reads *sa couleur.* L. 145 MS. reads *quanquel.* L. 160 *il* after *Je* struck out. L. 169 Line is a syllable short. Champion prints *(re)pris.*

Ch1:   Heading "Chançon" at top. Next 17 lines left blank. Unlike most of the *ballades*, the *chançons* and *rondels* do not have the refrains written out in full, but just the first few (usually 1 to 3) words, followed by *etc.* Illuminated initial letters are often wrong, as here, l. 8 has *R* for *M.* (See Note on the *Chançons* and *Rondels.*)

Ch2–Ch8: Heading "Chançon" at top. Next 18 lines left blank.

Ch9:   Heading "Chançon" at top. Next 14 lines left blank.

Ch10:   Heading "Chançon" at top. Next 17 lines left blank. L. 5 MS. reads *Lon* for *Son.*

Ch11:   Heading "Chançon" at top. Next 18 lines left blank. L. 4 *en* omitted and inserted above *Ordonnez comme.*

Ch12:   Heading "Chançon" at top. Next 18 lines left blank.

Ch13:   Heading "Chançon" at top. L. 17 *Belle* written alongside l. 16 to get the whole poem on to the page.

Ch14:   Heading "Chançon" at top. L. 5 MS. reads *He* for *Se.*

Ch15:   Heading "Chançon" at top.

Ch16:   Heading "Chançon" at top.

Ch17:   Heading "Chançon" at top.

Ch18:   Heading "Chançon" at top. Ll. 7, 8 *Belle etc En cest etc* written alongside each other. L. 13 *Belle* written alongside l. 12 to get the whole poem on to one page, the first line having been written two lines lower down the page than usual.

Ch19:   Heading "Chançon" at top.

Ch20:   Heading "Chançon" at top.

Ch21:   Heading "Chançon" at top.

Ch22:   Heading "Chançon" at top.

Ch23:   Heading "Chançon" at top. New heading, "Rondel," added above the original "Chançon."

Ch24:   Heading "Chançon" at top. New heading, "Rondel," added above original *chançon.* L. 6 MS. reads *Bien fait.*

Ch25:   Heading "Chançon" at top.

Ch26:   Heading "Chançon" at top. L. 5 MS. reads *Hresoriere.*

Ch27:   Heading "Chançon" at top.

Ch28:   Heading "Chançon" at top. L. 5 MS. reads *Rout.*

Ch29:   Heading "Chançon" at top. New heading, "Rondel," added mid-page.

Ch30:   Heading "Chançon" at top. New heading, "Rondel," added mid-page.

Ch31:   Heading "Chançon" at top.

Ch32:   Heading "Chançon" at top.

Ch33:   Heading "Chançon" at top.

Ch34:   Heading "Chançon" at top. New heading, "Rondel," added mid-page.

Ch35:   Heading "Chançon" at top. New heading, "Rondel," added mid-page.

Ch36:   Heading "Chançon" at top.

Ch37:   Heading "Chançon" at top.

Ch38:   Heading "Chançon" at top.

Ch39:   Heading "Chançon" at top.

Ch40:   Heading "Chançon" at top.

Ch41:   Heading "Chançon" at top.

Ch42:   Heading "Chançon" at top.

Ch43:   Heading "Chançon" at top.

Ch44:   First 13 lines left blank.

Ch45:   Heading "Chançon" at top.

Ch46:   Heading "Chançon" at top.

Ch47:   Heading "Chançon" at top.

Ch48:   Heading "Chançon" at top.

Ch49:   Heading "Chançon" at top.

Ch50:   Heading "Chançon" at top.

Ch51:   Heading "Chançon" at top.

Ch52:   Heading "Chançon" at top.

Ch53:   Heading "Chançon" at top.

Ch54:   Heading "Chançon" at top.

Ch55:   Heading "Chançon" at top.

Ch56:   Heading "Chançon" at top.

Ch57:   Heading "Chançon" at top. L. 1 The first word, which is also that of the refrain, appears to read *Donc*, rendered by Champion (ed., I:238) as *D'onc*, which is untenable. The Carpentras MS., that of Charles's wife Marie de Clèves, reads very clearly *Dont*, which was certainly Charles's intention. Rather than an actual error, it is more likely to be a carelessly written *–t*, similar to that ending *esbluyst* in the following line.

Ch58:   Heading "Chançon" at top.

Ch59:   Heading "Chançon" at top.

Ch60:   Heading "Chançon" at top.

Ch61:   Heading "Chançon" at top.

Ch62: Heading "Chançon" at top. L. 6 *porte* written twice, second one struck out.

Ch63: Heading "Chançon" at top.

R1: Heading: *Rondel dorlians*, followed by what appears to be "etc etc" seems to be all in the same hand; *a Nevers* added in a later hand, perhaps that of the duke. From this point forward a centered dot (·) will separate the heading to the poem from any attribution, usually in another fifteenth-century hand. Some scribes actually insert such a dot at this point.

R3: L. 3 *pet* crossed out, replaced with *per.*

Ch64: Heading "Chançon" at top. New heading, "Rondel," added mid-page.

Ch65: Heading "Chançon" at top. New heading, "Rondel," added mid-page.

Ch66: Heading "Chançon" at top. New heading, "Rondel," added mid-page.

Ch67: Heading "Chançon" at top. New heading, "Rondel," added mid-page.

Ch68: Heading "Chançon" at top. New heading, "Rondel," added mid-page.

Ch69: Heading "Chançon" at top. New heading, "Rondel," added mid-page.

Ch70: Heading "Chançon" at top. New heading, "Rondel," added mid-page.

Ch71: Heading "Chançon" at top. New heading, "Rondel," added mid-page. Ll. 7, 8 *Le voulez etc, Que vostre etc* on one line to get the whole poem on to the page, the first line having been written too low down.

C72: Heading "Chançon" at top. New heading, "Rondel," added mid-page. Ll. 7, 8 *Crevez moy etc, Que ne etc* on one line, to get the whole poem on to the page, the first line having been written too low down.

R19: Heading "Chançon" at top an error for *Rondel.* New heading, "Rondel," added mid-page. This heading error is carried through R26.

R20: Heading "Chançon" at top.

R21: Heading "Chançon" at top. L. 11 MS. reads *despance.*

R22: Heading "Chançon" at top. New heading, "Rondel," added mid-page.

R23: Heading "Chançon" at top. New heading, "Rondel" (lacking initial R) added mid-page.

R24: Heading "Chançon" at top. New heading, "Rondel," added mid-page. L. 9 added alongside l. 8 to get the whole poem on to the page.

R25: Heading "Chançon" at top. New heading, "Rondel," added mid-page.

R26: Heading "Chançon" at top. New heading, "Rondel," added mid-page.

Ch74: Ll. 7, 8 *Whan shal etc how hast etc* on one line. Ll. 5, 9 Initial *W, T* omitted.

R27: The heading "Chançon" at top has been struck out and replaced with "Rondel" in a post-medieval hand. New heading, "Rondel," added mid-page.

R33: Heading "Chançon."

R34: Heading "Chançon."

R35: Heading "Chançon." New heading, "Rondel," added above the poem in a later hand.

R36:   Heading "Chançon" at top in a later hand. New heading, "Rondel,"
            added above the poem.
R42:   L. 5 MS. reads *Qant.*
R72:   L. 6 MS. reads *descouvray.*
R73:   No other poem on this page. 11 lines left blank between heading and
            text.
R74:   L. 3 MS. reads *rens.* L. 5 MS. reads *Neu.* Ll. 7, 12 The usual sign for
            etc. is missing. *A ce jour* is obviously adequate on its own.
R76:   L. 8 MS. reads *Des.*
R77:   Ll. 7, 12 *Quant es etc. tu* omitted.
R79:   L. 13 MS. reads *Ce qui m'entre.*
R80:   L. 12 *Quelque chose* lacks the usual sign for *etc.*
R83:   L. 1, 13 MS. reads *Parche, Marché* added in left margin opposite l. 1.
R84:   L. 9 MS. reads *vieulx; veulx* added in right margin.
R94:   L. 10 *c'om* corrected in right margin to *qu'on.*
R98:   L. 5 MS. reads *Langez,* R added in left margin.
R100:   L. 5 MS. reads *Viens.*
R101:   L. 5 MS. reads *Con.*
R102:   L. 1 MS. reads *Eu.* L. 5 MS. reads *Ton.* L. 6 MS. reads *au.*
R108:   Beginning with this *rondel,* headings are provided in brackets in cas-
            es in which no heading was written *above* the lyric that apply to it
            (i.e., the heading was generally intended to identify the lyric on the
            lower half of the page). The heading mid-page has been disregarded
            because it was not written by the scribe of the lyric on the lower half
            of the page, intending to identify his or her (earlier) lyric, but added
            later, sometimes by the scribe who copied the *rondel* above it.
R109:   L. 12 Scribe has written entire refrain line.
R111:   L. 6. Line partially erased.
R118:   L. 8 MS. reads *Sant. Tant* is written in the left margin.
R120:   L. 3 MS. reads *Sil.* Four lines have been added at the foot of this page.
R122:   L. 5 MS. reads *Sel,* corrected in the left margin to *Tel.*
R131:   Ll. 7 and 12 MS. reads *Ubi etc.*
R132:   Ll. 7 and 12 MS. reads *Noli me etc.* L. 8 MS. reads *Ne.* Champion
            corrects to *De.*
R134:   L. 5 MS. reads *Euant. Quant* is written in the margin.
R135:   Heading "Chançon" at top. This poem added directly beneath in a
            later hand. Ll. 7 and 12 MS. reads *Satis etc.*
R136:   Heading at top "Chançon." This poem directly beneath in the later
            hand.
R137:   Heading "Chançon" at top. Ll. 7 and 12 MS. reads *Gardez etc.*
R138:   Heading "Chançon" at top. L. 8 MS. reads *Dieulx. m* is written in
            the left margin.
R139:   Ll. 7 and 12 read *Procul etc.*

R144:   Heading: *R* omitted. Small *r* added.

R145:   L. 8 MS. reads *De.*

R156:   Ll. 1, 7, 12 MS. reads *Hous*, which Mühlethaler (468) reads as *Hons.* Nowhere else in Charles's poetry is this archaic form found. Accordingly, and in view of the very large number of mistakes in initial lettering, Champion's correction to *Vous* (ed., 2:398) has been adopted here. The Carpentras manuscript, usually a slavish copy of Charles's manuscript, has a very distinct initial *V.* L. 4 MS. reads *Demander.* L. 5 MS. reads *Mon atrait. Son* added in margin.

R166:   L. 5 MS. reads *Venverses. R* added in left margin.

R167:   L. 8 MS. reads *Mn.* Mühlethaler (490) reads *Musart. M* is corrected to *O* in the margin, and the second letter is an *n*, not a *u.* Accordingly, the corrected reading in the MS., which is also that of Champion (ed., 2:404), is followed here. L. 11 *preu* badly written. Corrected in left margin.

R168:   L. 8 MS. reads *Des.* L. 11 MS. reads *condicon.* The leaf that follows this leaf is missing from the MS.

R173:   L. 2 *trop* added above *avoir.* L. 7 Missing in MS. L. 9 *Au commancement* badly written, rewritten in right margin.

R181:   L. 7 MS. reads *eust.*

R186:   L. 7 MS. reads *Ie fais je bien.*

R189:   L. 5 MS. reads *Cest*, corrected to *Nest ce* in margin. L. 8 MS. reads *Ne.*

R210:   L. 5 MS. reads *Alus.* L. 7 omitted, *Mais* added in right margin. L. 8 MS. reads *Aleurer.*

R212:   L. 13 MS. reads *Mamasse.*

R213:   L. 5 MS. reads *Neu.*

R216:   L. 6 An *s* has been written over the *t* of *Convoitise.*

R220:   L. 10 MS. reads *Ce long.*

R221:   L. 8 Badly written word corrected to *larcquemie* in right margin. L. 8 MS. reads *Sourges.*

R229:   L. 6 MS. reads *Coubliete.* L. 8 MS. reads *eletuaires*, corrected in right margin to *electuaires.*

R230:   L. 1 MS. reads *Des.*

R232:   Champion inserts the refrain after l. 8. It is not there in the MS.

R233:   L. 7 Initial *P* omitted.

R234:   L. 9 MS. reads *Laignent.*

R235:   L. 4 MS. reads *eul*, corrected in left margin to *euil.* L. 8 Champion inserts a two-line refrain after this line, not in the MS.

R241:   L. 10 *pas* is written in the right margin, with a cross indicating it is to be placed after *est.* Mühlethaler (719) suggests *pas* was intended to replace *ne*, but *hier* usually makes one syllable, not two.

R245:   L. 10 MS. reads *Ou fort.*

R248:   L. 9 MS. reads *Ianny.*

R249:   L. 5 MS. reads *Suis que.*

R250:   L. 10 *foiz toussir* is written in the margin, probably indicating three
          coughs, which would give the line its correct length of eight syllables.
          Mühlethaler (719) assumes that *foiz toussir* was to be added to the
          line. Not only would this make the line too long, as he says, but it
          would also make no sense.

R252:   L. 10 MS. reads *oster.*

R265:   L. 5 MS. reads *Ille.*

R270:   Heading: MS. reads *ondel de mosr amadae dang.* Marie de Clèves's
          MS. (Carpentras 375) reads *Rondel de monsr a madame dangoulesme.*

R272:   L. 5 MS. reads *Ia.* L. 7 MS. reads *Contre fenoches etc.* L. 12 MS. reads
          Contre etc.

R273:   L. 10 MS. reads *arbes.*

R277:   The second stanza has no refrain.

R283:   L. 11 MS. reads *fait.*

R287:   L. 5 MS. reads *De* for *Me*, *ilz* for *il.* L. 8 MS. reads *Lappelle.*

R293:   L. 5 MS. reads *Mais* for *Mes.*

R296:   In this case the entire heading is in the same large hand, perhaps that
          of the author. L. 8 MS. reads *Me.*

R307:   L. 5 MS. reads *Soreille.*

R312:   L. 5 MS. reads *Fous.* L. 8 MS. reads *Sieuls.*

R313:   Ll. 2, 3 Champion (ed., 2:487) believes that a line has been omit-
          ted after l. 2. There is, however, no break in sense. L. 7. Initial letter
          erased. *Je* written in left margin.

R320:   L. 1. Initial letter partially erased. *Yver* written in left margin.

R324:   L. 9 *et* omitted and written in over *matinee.*

R329:   L. 7 MS. reads *Monstrez moy etc.*

R334:   L. 8 The second word has been rubbed out and *penance* inserted in
          the margin.

R335:   L. 5 MS. reads initial *V* for *D.*

R338:   L. 9 *peu* omitted and inserted over *ung ne.*

R343:   Heading: "Chançon" is a scribal error for "Rondel."

R348:   L. 5 MS. reads initial *S* for *P.*

R350:   L. 4 MS. reads *deueil*, the first *e* is crossed out.

R367:   L. 4 *est* is omitted in the MS.

R371:   L. 8 MS. reads *ilz* for *il.*

R393:   Ll. 7 and 12 MS. reads *Contre etc.*

R402:   L. 3 *Ce* written in left margin for *Se.*

R407:   L. 12 MS. reads *Jaullier*, first *l* erased. *S. Cailleau* written to the right
          on same line.

R425:   L. 6 *faites* added in left margin.

R429:   L. 12 Heart drawn in place of "cueur."

R430:   Probably by Fraigne, though his name is not given here in the MS. Ll. 1, 6, 10 Initial letters omitted. *Par bien celer* first 3 words of R437 only written here, remainder of page blank. L. 21 refrain written out in full.

R435:   L. 9 Refrain written out in full. R437, R438, and R439 are all in the same hand. Part of the first line is written at the end of R434 (*Par bien celer m*). Not enough room on the page for the whole *rondel*.

R436:   Ll. 12 and 20 Refrain written out in full.

R437:   L. 7 *vous* omitted. Ll. 7 and 12 Refrain written out in full. Ll. 7, 12 Refrain written out in full.

R441:   L. 10 This line was omitted, then added vertically to the left of ll. 9–15.

R449:   L. 12 Refrain written out in full.

R454:   L. 12 The refrain at the end is omitted.

R460   L. 7 The shortened refrain (*Gardez vous bien*) is not followed by *etc.* L. 12 The refrain line is written out in full.

Description of BnF MS. fr. 25458[1]

Charles d'Orléans, French poems c. 1439–c. 1465. fols 1r–300v. Ou temps passe quant nature me fist /. . . / Gardez vousbien de ce fauveau. A collection of fixed-form and narrative verse by Charles of Valois, duc d'Orléans, interspersed with lyrics by poets known to him, on the subject of secular love and several other matters.[2]

299 leaves, ff. iv + 295; pp. viij + 1–159 + xxxviij + 160–537 + xv. Modern pagination, with most blank leaves unnumbered, predates the eighteenth-century binding. Vellum.[3] 31 lines per page. Collation: π^4 A–K^8 L–N^6 O–P^8 Q^6 R–PP^8 (-EE6). Binding threads are visible in all quires except G. 165 × 120 mm; written space c. 125 × 82 mm.[4]

Pricking and ruling: Pricking has generally fallen under the binder's knife, but it is found in two parts of the manuscript, in the first leaf of the inserted (second) ruling batch (quire I, p. 129) and in the last batch of vellum (in the last leaf of MM, pp. 503–504 [but not 489–490] and in the two outer bifolia of NN, pp. 505–508 and 517–520). The pricking in I is within the bounding line, about 26mm. from the present outer edge of the leaf; that in NN is at the very outer edge of the leaves.[5]

The ruling standard throughout is thirty-one lines (thirty in π), the top line not written on. Ruling is in shades of red ink. The manuscript shows four different systems of ruling: in all four the vertical bounding rules go right down the

---

[1] For a fuller account of the manuscript see Arn, *The Poet's Notebook*, chapter 1.

[2] This may be item 65 in the inventory of books brought back from England: "Plusieurs kaieres de parchemin, nouvellement escripts et enluminez, apportez d'Angleterre, qui ne sont point reliez," identified by Patricia Stirnemann ("Français 25458," 180).

[3] Vellum is of good quality throughout, though that of the last four quires (MM through PP) is stiffer and thicker than the rest (though just as white).

[4] The lower margin seems to have been trimmed (if at all) much less than the outer and top margins. If we imagine a leaf with nearly identical margins on all three sides (which, judging from the decoration, would be adequate), the original manscript might have measured something like 195 × 130 mm.

[5] Quire N, pp. 505–506, 507–508, 517–518, 519–520.

page, and the top horizontal rule goes right across the page.[6] In all four systems the line initials have a space reserved by further vertical ruling.

Scribes and hands: Written in various (mostly cursive) French hands of the fifteenth century, usually in black ink. The entire manuscript is virtually unpunctuated and abbreviations are rare, consisting mainly of a straight or curved bar above a letter or letters to indicate contraction (Orls for Orleans) and a sign for etc. after shortened refrain lines. The first hand is a very regular cursive gothic book script (see frontispiece). The second most frequent hand is that of the duke himself. Champion lists eighty-three entire lyrics in his hand, and there are numerous corrections, headings, and numberings in his hand as well.[7] The remainder of the leaves are filled with work of a variety of French scribes (or scribal authors), often working in very short stints (often writing only a single lyric) and in no apparent pattern. Virtually all are French and of the period of the duke's life post-1440. Only a few are truly distinctive, most sharing letter forms and shapes common to northern French hands of the period. Comments on the hands of individual scribes will be taken up in the course of the exposition.

The duke numbered many of his poems, in two series.[8] Each number is placed between centered dots: ballades [·1·]–·107·; chançons and rondels in a single series, [·1·]–[·164·] (as much of this numbering as has survived is reproduced at the end of each lyric in this edition). No quire signatures are visible. Catchwords in quires B–G, R, T, X centered at the bottom of the page in pale ink were clearly meant to be trimmed; they are all the work of Scribe 1. Final sides of a number of quires left blank.[9] Leaves in quires X and Y are currently disordered and misbound.

It is more difficult than would be expected to trace the manuscript from the court at Blois to the eighteenth-century library of La Vallière. It is not to be identified in any of the inventories of the royal library. Most books in the duke's collection bore the sign of the ducal chancery: *De camera compotor. Bles.*, but fr. 25458 does not and seems not to have followed the same trajectory into the French royal collection as did the bulk of his books. It is unclear where La Vallière, who was a voracious purchaser of books from all quarters, bought (or "borrowed") it. The manuscript was sold in the post-mortem La Vallière sale of

---

[6] It was Johan Gerritsen who first noticed the differences in ruling pattern in different parts of the manuscript (on film!) and brought the fact to my attention. That discovery has had a profound impact on the amount we can learn from the physical manuscript about the history of its composition.

[7] Corrections are sometimes extensive, as in ll. 8–11 of the *rondel* on p. 365 (see frontispiece).

[8] See Champion, *Autographe*, pp. 11 and 31.

[9] These include the entirely blank quires L, M, and N. At the end of the first stint of copying, the final leaves of H–S and Y–BB were probably blank.

1783, whereupon it was purchased by the Bibliotheque du Roi.[10] The La Vallière manuscripts purchased at that sale were kept as a separate "La Vallière" collection and numbered sequentially (this manuscript receiving the number 193). It was not until the end of the nineteenth century, with the compilation of a new catalogue, that the collection was incorporated into the sequence of *fonds français* and given its present numbers in the Bibliothèque Nationale catalogue.

As the wear on the outsides of some quires and especially of the first written page shows, the work lay unbound for some time after it was written. Spine from eighteenth-century binding reused in the modern restoration; olive green morocco elaborately stamped in gold; spine reads: "Ballades du duc d'Orlean / m[ssen] vers sur velin." The manuscript was apparently trimmed at least twice, once in the eighteenth-century binding process and once thereafter (probably in the most recent rebinding, when the edges of the pages were also gilded).

Written in England (London) and France between 1439/40 and c. 1465. Marks of ownership: On f. 9r, "La Vall. 193."[11] Modern Bibliothèque Nationale stamp on page 1 (quire A1), on the recto of the preceding leaf (π7) and the verso of page 537 (PP2); Bibliothèque Impériale stamp on page 158 +1 (L16), page 160–1 (P1), and page 190 (Q16).

[10] Guillaume de Bure, *Catalogue des livres de la bibliothèque de feu M. le duc de la Vallière*, 3 vols. (Paris: G. de Bure, 1783), 2:264.

[11] Listed and described in the catalogue of the sale of La Valliere's library in 1783 as lot no. 2788 (La Valliere 193; not, as in Avril and Stirnemann, *Manuscrits*, 181, 'La Vallière 14'). It does not contain the stamp of the books owned by the house of Orléans, which formed the basis of the Chambre des Comptes de Blois before becoming part of the Bibliothèque Royale (Champion, *Autographe*, 86).

Appendices

1. Lyrics in the Duke's Hand

(headings and incidental additions and corrections in his hand are not included, for which see Champion, *Autographe*)

Mon cueur m'a fait commandement	B74
Beauté, gardez vous de mez yeulx	Ch64
Bien viengne Doulz Regard qui rit	Ch65
Mon cuer, il me fault estre mestre	Ch67
Mes yeulz trop sont bien reclamés	Ch68
Quant je la regarde	[Ch72a] quatrain in lower margin
En gibessant toute l'aprés disnee	R21
Me fauldrez vous a mon besoing	R25
Cueur endormy en pensee	R26
Laudes Deo sint atque gloria	Carole 4
Il vit en bonne esperance	R27
Maistre Estienne le Gout nominatif	R28*
En la vigne jusqu'au peschier	R30
Mon cueur plus ne volera	R33
Chascun dit qu'estez bonne et belle	R34
Encore lui fait il grant bien	R35
Avoglé et assourdy	R36
J'estraine de bien loing m'amie	R37
Cueur, a qui prendrez vous conseil	R45
Dedens mon Livre de Pensee	R46
En regardant ces belles fleurs	R47
Onquez feu ne fut sans fumee	R48
Chantez ce que vous pensés	R49
De riens ne sert a cueur en desplaisance	R53
Fiés vous y	R54

De legier pleure a qui la lippe pent	R55
Dont viens tu maintenant, Souspir	R56
Ou pis, ou mieulx	R57
S'en mez mains une fois vous tiens	R58
Plus penser que dire	R59
Je ne suis pas de sez gens la	R60
Remede comment	R61
Quant je voy ce que ne veuil mie	R62
Sot euil, raporteur de nouvelles	R63
Est ce vers moy qu'envoyez ce souspir	R64*
Alons nous esbatre	R65
Je vous areste de main mise	R66
En mes païs quant me treuve a repos	R67
Alez vous ant, allez, alés	R68
Se vous voulés que tout vostre deviengne	R69
Cueur, que fais tu? revenge toy	R87
Par lez portes dez yeulx et dez oreilles	R88
A qui les vent on	R89
A qui vendez vous voz coquilles	R90
Envoyez nous un doulz regart	R91
Maudit soit mon cueur se j'en mens	R97*
Par m'ame, s'il en fust en moy	R100
Mon cueur se plaint qu'il n'est payé	R101
Ou Loyaulté me payera	R102
Si hardis, mez yeulx	R106
Pense de toy	R117
Ce n'est riens qui ne puist estre	R118
Or est de dire: Laissez m'en paix	R119
Pres la, briquet aus pendantes oreilles	R133
Satis, satis, plus quam satis	R135
Non temptabis, tien te coy	R136
Gardez vous de *mergo*	R137
Quant n'ont assez fait dodo	R138
Procul a nobis	R139
Faulcette confite	R140
Il fauldroit faire l'arquemie	R141
Pource que Plaisance est morte	R147
A Dieu! qu'il m'anuye	R148

Ci pris, ci mis	R149
Et de cela, quoy	R150
Et de cela, quoy	R151
Le trouveray je ja mais	R152
Payés selonc vostre desserte	R161
Mort de moy! vous y jouez vous	R166
Se vous voulez m'amour avoir	R198
Par l'aumosnier Plaisant Regart	R200*
Ce n'est que chose acoustumee	R201
Chascun devise a son propos	R202
Ennemy, je te conjure	R203
Plaisant Regard, mussez vous	R206
Je ne vous voy pas a demy	R207
Mon cueur, pour vous en garder	R208
Je regrette mez dolans jours	R215*
Se regrettez voz dolens jours	R216*
Celle que je ne sçay nommer	R222

* Not in Pierre Champion's list (*Le manuscrit autographe,* 8–11).

2. Medieval Manuscripts and Early Printed Editions Containing All or a Significant Part of the Duke's French Poetry

All or significant parts of the collection of Charles d'Orleáns's French poetry survives in 9 manuscripts.[1]

A = Paris, Bibliothèque de l'Arsenal, MS. 2070, fols. 1–53v
Paper, second half of the fifteenth century, French
Contents: a selection of lyrics by Charles d'Orléans on fols. 1–53 (incl. the opening narrative, 27 *ballades*, *Songe en complainte*, 2 further *complaintes*, 1 *chançon*, and 2 *rondels*).

B = Paris, BnF MS. fr. 19139, fols. 1–117
Paper, mid-fifteenth century, French
Contents: 69 poems by the duke on pages 1–117 and imitations of his work, incl. work by Garencières and Chartier (incl. *La belle dame sans mercy*).

C = London, BL MS. Royal 16.F.ii, fols. 1–136v[2]
Vellum, c. 1480, 1500–1502, French (MS. copied in England)
Contents: 44 of the duke's lyrics, plus *Les Epistres de l'abesse Heloys* (137v–187v); *Les Demandes d'Amour* (188r–210r); and *Grace entiere* (210v–248v). Also contains the well-known illumination of Charles in the Tower of London.[3]

G = Grenoble, Bibliothèque de Grenoble MS. 873[4]
Vellum, before 1461 (bound in 1463), French and Latin

---

[1] This list is not intended to be exhaustive. Other work by the duke includes *Le livre contre tout péché*, written when he was ten (for which see Champion, ed., 604–5) and the *Canticum amoris*, written later in life (for which see Gilbert Ouy, "Un poème mystique de Charles d'Orléans: le *Canticum amoris*," *Studi francesi* 7 (1959): 64–84. See also Sergio Cigada, *L'opera poetica di Charles d'Orléans* (Milan: Società Editrice Vita e Pensiero, 1960), 1–16.

[2] Charles d'Orleans, *Choix de poésies: Editées d'après le MS. Royal 16 F II du British Museum*, ed. John Fox, Textes Littéraires 9 (Exeter: University of Exeter Press, 1973). It was long thought to have been made for Henry VII (see Janet Backhouse's analysis, in "Charles of Orléans Illuminated," in *Charles d'Orléans in England*, ed. Arn, 157–63).

[3] Often reproduced, it can be found, among other places, in *Charles d'Orléans in England*, frontispiece; Coldiron, *Canon, Period*, Fig. 1; Fox, *Lyric Poetry*, frontispiece. Fox reproduces a number of the text pages and one other illumination from this manuscript as well.

[4] Aimé Champollion-Figeac, ed., *Les Poésies du duc Charles d'Orléans publiées sur le manuscrit original de la Bibliothèque de Grenoble conféré avec ceux de Paris et de Londres* (Paris: J. Belin-Leprieur and C. de Batines, 1842). N.B.: This manuscript contains none of the Latin text and none of the duke's English poetry (on this misinformation corrected,

Contents: (1) a selection and reorganization of the material in the duke's manuscript, including a number of the "political" poems; (2) a Latin translation, presented in parallel columns, by Antonio Astisano (the duke inherited land from his mother in Asti), the duke's Italian secretary, made, with the duke's cooperation and (probable) oversight, from his personal manuscript beginning in ?1453 (the text was copied by Nicolas Astesano, Antonio's brother); and (3) various historical texts.[5]

H = London, BL MS. Harley 6916
Paper, second half of the fifteenth century (soon after the completion of O), French
Contents: a nearly complete copy of O.

L = London, BL MS. Lansdowne 380
Paper, end of the fifteenth century, French
Contents: the duke's poetry occupies folios 147 to 218. The manuscript, copied in many hands, also contains work by various fifteenth-century poets, as well as prayers, pious verse, and the "Vigiles des morts" by Pierre de Nesson.

M = Carpentras, Bibliothèque Inguimbertine, Carpentras MS. 375
Vellum, probably 1455–58, French and Latin
Made for Marie de Clèves, the duke's third wife
Contents: 77 folios (pre-1456) are a copy of part of O, followed by work by various fifteenth-century poets not ordered by verse form including some of the duke's later work.

O = Paris, BnF MS. fr. 25458[6]
Vellum, written over the years between c. 1439–c. 1464
French, English, Latin, some Italian words
Charles d'Orléans' personal copy

---

see J. P. M. Jansen, "The French Manuscripts of the English Poems of Charles of Orleans," *Notes and Queries* 35 [1988]: 439–40).

[5] Philippe Contamine, *Pages d'histoire militaire médiévale (XIVe–XVe siècles)*, Mémoires de l'Académie des Inscriptions et Belles-Lettres 32 (Paris: De Boccard, 2005), 221–32 (repr. from "Prodige et propagande. Vendredi 20 août 1451, de 7 h à h du matin: Le ciel de Bayonne," in B. Ribémont, ed., *Observer, lire, écrire le ciel au moyen âge* [Paris: Klincksieck, 1991], 63–86). For reproductions of manuscript pages, see Coldiron, *Canon, Period*, 112–44 and figs. 2–8.

[6] J.-Marie Guichard, ed., *Poésies de Charles d'Orléans publiées avec l'autorisation de M. le ministre de l'instruction publique, d'après les mss des Bibl. du Roi et de l'Arsenal* (Paris: Gosselin, 1842). Pierre Champion, *Poesies*.

O² = Paris, BnF MS. fr. 1104, 49 ff.
    Vellum, after 1458–65, French
    arms of Charles d'Orléans; owned by Catherine de Medici; in Colbert's library
    Contents: virtual copy of O (lacks the 3 final lyrics), as well as two rondels
    by Robertet and Cadier in praise of the duke; including the statement the duke
    pronounced at the trial of the duc d'Alençon in 1458.

In addition, a few manuscripts providing a rich context for the duke's literary
milieu have been published, including Raynaud, ed., *Rondeaux et autres poésies du
XVe siècle*; Inglis, *Le manuscrit B.N. Nouv. Acq. fr. 15771* (based on work by An-
gremy, "Un nouveau recueil de poésies françaises du XVe siècle"); and Françoise
Fery-Hue, ed., *Au grey d'amours...* (Fery-Hue complements and extends Marcel
Schwob's *Le Parnasse satyrique*).

Early printed editions (selection)

J = *Le Jardin de Plaisance et fleur de Rethoricque nouvellement imprime a Paris* (Antoine Vérard, c. 1501)[7]
    at least 7 lyrics by Charles, as well as lyrics by other authors represented in O

Ch = *La Chasse et le depart d'amours faict et compose par reverend pere en Dieu messire Octovien de Sainct Gelais evesque d'Angoulesme et par noble homme Blaise d'Auriol
bachelier en chascun droit demourant a Thoulouze* (Paris: Antoine Vérard, 1509).[8]
    Numerous unascribed *ballades* and *rondels* from the duke's hand

T = Jehan Lemaire de Belges, *Le Triomphe de l'amant vert/// comprins en deux
epistres fort joyeuses envoyees a madame Marguerite auguste composees/// par Jehan le
Maire de Belges... avecques plusieurs balades et rondeaux nouveaux...* (Paris: Denys
and Simon Janot, 1535)[9]
    7 *rondels* from the duke's hand, most unascribed

---

[7] Facsimile reprint in 2 vols. (Paris: Firmin-Didot, 1910).
[8] Mary Beth Winn, ed., *La Chasse d'Amours attribuée à Octovien de Saint-Gelais* (Paris and Geneva: Droz, 1984). Jean-Claude Mühlethaler, "Charles d'Orléans, une prison
en porte-à-faux. Co-texte courtois et ancrage référentiel: Les ballades de la captivité dans
l'édition d'Antoine Vérard (1509)," in *Charles d'Orléans in England*, ed. Arn, 165–82.
[9] Jean Stecher, ed., *Œuvres de Jean Lemaire de Belges*, 4 vols. (Louvain: J. Lefever,
1882; repr. Geneva: Slatkine, 1969).

3. Index of Medieval Authors Represented in BnF MS. fr. 25458

These entries are alphabetized under the form of the name found in the text. For sources, refer to the bibliography.

Albret, *see* cadet

Alençon, R30

In 1423, Jean (II), duc d'Alençon married Jeanne d'Orléans (d. c. 1432), daughter of the duc d'Orléans and his first wife, Jeanne de France; thereafter he married Marie d'Armagnac, daughter of Jean IV d'Armagnac and Isabelle de Navarre. He seems to have been of unstable personality. He made alliances with the English (he had also become a *chevalier de la Toison d'Or*), and in 1456 he was arrested by Dunois on the king's orders. Two years later he was brought to trial before the king in Vendôme. In his defence, Jean Juvénal des Ursins spoke of his service with *la Pucelle* and called on the king to be merciful. This was followed by a long plea from Charles d'Orléans for the same mercy on his son-in-law, but the king responded by confiscating all his earthly goods and sentencing him to death. (This was Charles's last public act; he died at Amboise, on his return trip to Blois.) Alençon was known to have composed other works, both *ballades* and *rondels* and a certain "livre de la best" which is described as "un livre de farces et de moralités," but none of this work seems to have survived. Champion describes this *rondel* as *bizarre* (*Vie*, 616–17).

Beaujeu, Monseigneur de, R297

Monseigneur Pierre de Beaujeu (1438–?) was the fourth son of Charles, duc de Bourbon, and Agnès de Bourgogne. Adopted by Charles and Marie de Clèves, the young child's aunt, he later had his own household in Blois (Champion, *Vie*, 393–95).

Blosseville, R384

Blosseville was a prominent poet of the period, but attempts to identify him have remained inconclusive. Raynaud's identification of him as *Hugues de Saint-Maard, vicomte de Blosseville, écuyer* (viii), is refuted by Inglis (and by Pierre Champion, in "Remarques sur un recueil de poésies du milieu du XVe siècle," *Romania* 48 (1922), 109–11, who suggests he was of the family Blosset de Blosseville (the Nivernaise branch), son of Jean Blosset seigneur du Plessis-Pâté et de la Mote, and Jossine d'Estouteville, the niece of Jean d'Estouteville, seigneur de Torcy (for whom, see below). According to Hasenohr and Zink (s.v. Blosseville), he was at the court of Blois at the same time as Pierre de Brézé, *grand sénéchal de Normandie*. Raynaud counts 30 *rondels* and *bergerettes* in BnF MS. fr. 2993 (viii–ix). He also composed a *ballade* on the occasion of the death, in 1445, of the dauphine Marguerite d'Écosse, herself a poet and a patron of poets. Between 1454 and 1456 Blosseville collected 27 of his poems along with 25 by his contemporaries in what is now BnF MS. nouv. acq. fr. 15771 (Inglis, 235). He also included his *Débat du vieil et du jeune* (also in nouv. acq. fr. 15771) in which he names as arbiters Pierre de Brézé and Jean d'Estouteville, seigneur de Torcy (see Raynaud, viii, and Inglis, 19–24, and passim). On the macaronic lyrics, see note to B106.

Bouciquault (Bousiquault), R224, R226

Bouciquault is believed to have been one of two nephews of maréchal de Boucicaut (one of the authors of the *Cent ballades*, along with Charles's father, Louis), who was captured with Charles at Agincourt and died in England in 1421. One of the two sons of Geoffroi Boucicaut, Jean and Louis, became seigneur de Breuildoré and is so identified in BnF nouv. acq. fr. 15771, but historians have yet to determine which of the two brothers possessed the seigneurie. Both died between 1484 and 1490. (See Inglis, 24–25, Hasenohr and Zink, s.v. Boucicaut; Champion, *Vie*, 626–27.) These two lyrics (R226 and R228) are the only ones known from this poet's hand. They also appear in BnF MS. nouv. aq. fr. 15771, where one bears the name "Boucicaut" and the other "seigneur du Breuildoré" (*Monsr du Bridoré* in BnF MS. fr. 9223); one of them also appears in BnF MS. fr. 1719) (see Hasenohr and Zink, s.v. Boucicaut; Raynaud, x–xi; Inglis, 24–25; see also Champion, *Vie*, 626–27).

Boulainvillier, Philippe de, R255, R344

Philippe de Boulainvillier was a page in the household of Charles de Bourbon and in 1447 became *écuyer tranchant* (the squire who served at table) to his son Pierre. In 1456 became *maître d'hotel* to Pierre de Beaujeu. He later held the office of *capitaine* of the *château* Pierrefonds. On his betrothal to Claude de Seurre, *dame de Villiers Adam*, Charles granted him in return for his service a year's income from the land of Villiers Adam of 90 *livres* (see Champion, ed., 2:612, also *Vie*, 394, 410–11, 608).

Bourbon, Jean (II), duc de, R173, R181, R182, R256, R359, R379, R385, R395, R458, R459 (see also Cleremont)

Clermondois is Jean (II), comte de Clermont (1426/7–1488), who took the title of *duc de Bourbon* on the death of his father Charles de Bourbon in 1456 (the duke named in B123 and B124 was his grandfather), and the lyrics from his pen are labelled accordingly in this collection. He is referred to in R113, and is the author of 10 *rondels* in the manuscript (see Champion, ed., 2:612–13; *Vie*, 617–20, who writes that those signed *Clermondois* are autograph). It is clear that he was on familiar terms with Charles d'Orléans. Charles was fond of his nephew, which is evident from the banter in their exchanges. Villon addressed a *ballade* to him. One (unique) *rondel* appears in BnF MS. fr. 9223 (see Raynaud, xii–xiii).

His seat was at Moulins, where he drew around him writers who served him in various ways: Jean Robertet (s.v.) was one of his secretaries, as was Guillaume Cadier (s.v.), and Fraigne (s.v.) frequented his court, according to Champion. He was by all accounts a lover of literature and a collector of books, among which were a number he inherited from his grandmother Marie, wife of Jean I, duc de Bourbon and daughter of Jean, duc de Berry. He married in turn Jeanne de France, daughter of Charles VII, Catherine d'Armagnac, and Jeanne de Bourbon-Vendôme (Champion, *Vie*, 617–20). See also note to R114.

Bourgogne, Philippe le Bon, duc de, B128, B130
    Philippe was not otherwise known as a poet.

cadet, d'Alebret, R252, R262
    Le cadet d'Al(e)bret, fourth son of Charles II d'Alebret and Anne, daughter of Bernard VII, comte d'Armagnac, was seigneur de Sainte-Bazille and a prominent army captain. In 1473 he opposed the king, Louis XI, and was executed (Champion, *Vie*, 627–28). He is the author of 5 *rondels*, 2 in fr. 25458 and 3 others in nouv. acq. fr. 15771 (see Hasenohr and Zink, s.v. Cadet d'Albret; Inglis, 25–26; see also Poirion, *Le poète*, 186).

Caill(e)au, Jehan, B80, B111, R40, R184, R372, R375
    Maistre Jehan Caillau was Charles's physician, friend, and counsellor and author of 6 lyrics in this collection. He was also a chess opponent and fellow book lover (a number of his manuscripts are housed in the Bibliothèque nationale). The duke was generous to him. He became *prévôt* of the church of Saint-Sauveur in Blois until he was made dean of Saint-Aignan in Orléans, and later canon of Saint-Martin in Tours (1454). He attended Marie during her pregnancies in 1458 and 1460 (Champion, *Vie*, 604–6; de Croÿ, "Notices biographiques," 422–24; *Dictionnaire de biographie française*, Paris: Letouzey et Ané, 1929–, s.v. Caillau).

Caill(e)au, Simonnet, B113, R229, R293, R406, R445
    Simonnet Caillau, a squire in the duke's household, was a member of a noble family from Picardy, apparently unrelated to Jean Caillau. See Champion, ed., 2:614–15, and *Vie*, 606–7; on Simon and Simonet Caillau, see de Croÿ, "Notices biographiques," 422.

Calabre, see Lorraine.

Cleremont, Clermondois, comte de, R173, R212, R256
    See Bourbon.

Cuise, Anthoine de, R434, R435, R436

Anthoine de Cuise (1425–1501/2), son of the Picard Adam II de Cuise, seigneur de la Mote, and Marguerite de Villers, was a member of the lesser nobility.
He was part of the entourage of Jacques de Luxembourg, brother-in-law and
compagnon d'armes of Arthur of Brittany (himself an amateur poet), and he accompanied Arthur on a visit to France in 1458. He inherited the lands of la Mote
and Hautevesnes on the death of his father in 1462 and the seigneurie of Neuf-
moustiers after the death of his mother. In 1492, he was *panetier ordinaire* to the
king. Nine of his poems have survived in BnF MS. nouv. acq. fr.15771 (see Inglis, 29–33). He seems to been at Blois in 1458 and to have had some poetic relations with Blosseville (see s.v.). One of his *rondels* ("Les douleurs dont me sens
tel somme") was set to music by Guillaume Dufay. If we accept the identification
of Antoine de Cuise with the poet designated by the first name "Antoine" in the
second part of Paris, BnF MS. fr. 9223, as Champion and Inglis propose, we can
add 15 poems to his œuvre, in which we can see the influence of Jean Meschinot.
(See Hasenohr and Zink, s.v. Antoine de Cuise; see also Raynaud; Inglis, 29–33,
and Champion, "Remarques," 108.)

Damien, Benoi(s)t, R266, R268, R269, R296, R393, R410, R451, R452
     Benoit Damien (or Damiano) was an Italian well established at the court in
Blois, as his eight contributions to Charles's manuscripts testify. A young *huissier
d'armes* (usher) of the duke, he was familiarly known as *le petit Benoit Damien*. He
seems to have been a favorite, who was rewarded for his *bons et agréables services.*
He was *échanson* (cup bearer) to the duke in 1456 (see Champion, *Vie*, 602–3)
and recorded his device (*Du surplus*) and signature in the duchess's copy of the
works of Alain Chartier (Pierre Champion, "Un 'liber amicorum' du XVe siècle."
Revue des bibliothèques 10–12 (1910): 332–33 and pl. 3). His lyrics in this collection are marked by references to mythology and raillery against certain Italians.
Other works from his hand are not known. See notes to R393 and R394. (See
also Champion, ed., 2:616–17.)

Danche, Pierre, R460
     Little is known about Pierre Danche, although this particular poem appears
in BnF MS. fr. 1719 (Fery-Hue, *Au grey d'amours*, 109, see p. 47) and in *Chasse et
Depart d'Amours* (Vérard, 1509; see Mühlethaler, 701).Daniel du Solier, R217
     Champion identifies the author as Daniel du Solier, a domestic of the duke's
household. He appears in the records in 1449 and again in 1455. His device (*En
atendant*) and signature appear in a copy of works by Alain Chartier belonging
to Marie de Clèves (Champion, "Un 'liber amicorum'," 325 and plate 2; see also
idem, *Vie*, 656).

Des O(u)rmes, Gilles, B112, R247, R254, R343, R408, R448
     Gilles des O(u)rmes (1438–after 1498) was a member of Charles's house-
hold, a good chess player, and a favourite of the duke's (in 1455 he was *bien-aimé*

écuyer tranchant to the duke at the age of 19). After Charles's death in 1465, he remained in the service of the house of Orléans, as *capitaine de Chambord* and *premier maître d'hôtel* to Charles's son Louis. In 1471 he married Jacquette de Perche, one of little Marie d'Orléans's ladies-in-waiting. Marie de Clèves was apparently favorably disposed toward the couple, for a gift to them of 500 livres is recorded, as well as a further gift of 50 livres' worth of cloth for their wedding. In 1483 Gilles became *seigneur de Saint-Germain*, in the diocese of Chartres, and was called to be a witness in the divorce proceedings of Louis XII in 1498 (see Champion, *Vie*, 600–2).

Author of six lyrics in this collection, he took part in a number of the *ballade* series on the same first line. In 1467 he composed a *ballade* on the occasion of the revolt of the Liegeois against Charles le Téméraire (*Changez propos, cer volant*), in response to a *ballade* by Georges Chastelain (*Souffle, Triton, en ta buse argentine*). Champion prints another of his lyrics from the Carpentras MS. (*Se j'eusse vostre fait congneu*, ed., 2:583; see Hasenohr and Zink, *Dictionnaire*, s.v. Gilles Des Ormes; Raynaud, xvii–xviii; Inglis, 34–35).

Estampes, R82

Jean de Bourgogne (1415–1491), *comte d'Étampes* (1416–1421, though he continued to use the title throughout his life), was the son of Philippe de Bourgogne (*comte de Nevers et de Rethel*, the youngest son of Philippe le Hardi, who died at Agincourt in the same year his son was born) and Bonne d'Artois, daughter of Philippe d'Artois, comte d'Eu. A knight of the Toison d'Or, he fought in the army of his cousin Philippe le Bon. At the death of his brother Charles in 1464, he inherited the title of *comte de Nevers* (for whom see note to R2).

Faret, François, R295

François Faret was *écuyer* and *bien amé échanson* of the duke. He was a part of the household by 1449 and undertook a number of missions for the duke. He recorded his device in the copy of the works of Alain Chartier owned by Marie de Clèves: *Ailleurs James Faret* (Champion, "Un 'liber amicorum,'" 325 and plate 2; idem, *Vie*, 603–4. Champion does not explain the name "James").

Fraigne, R315, R391, R429, R431

The identity of Fraigne is uncertain. He was a member of a noble family in the service of the duke of Bourbon (see Champion, *Vie*, 623–24). The quality of these lyrics suggests that he was a man of talent, but no other work from his hand is known.

Fredet, B143, Co5, Co7, R17, R143, R196, R199 [R201], R214, R215, R228, R249

Fredet (or Fradet) is a person about whom very little historical informa-tion is available—not even his full name, though Raynaud associates him with a Guillaume Fredet, *licencié es lois et garde des sceaux de la prévôte de Bourges* (xvi). Champion extends this brief claim with further archival material (*Vie*, 616). Inglis, however, remains doubtful that we have a firm identification (37–39). What we know about him we learn from his lyrics: above all that he was an amicable man and on very warm and friendly terms with the duke. He seems to have begun exchanging poems with the duke after 1444 and appears to have been a frequent visitor (if indeed he was not part of the household) during the years 1453–1454, near the end of which he was married.

Fredet contributes 12 lyrics to this collection, and he is also represented in parallel collections. In spite of his apparent obscurity, lyrics from his hand appear in both BnF MS. fr. 9223 (ed. Raynaud, 8 lyrics) and BnF MS. nouv. acq. fr. 15771 (ed. Inglis, 6 lyrics). Inglis analyzes the three manuscript collections and concludes that six of the lyrics appear outside the duke's manuscript, two of which are common to the two other collections (38–39). One lyric in the fr. 9223 collection (*A quoy tient que le cuer me volle*) was set to music and copied into the *Chansonnier Nivelle de la Chausée* (BnF Rés. Vinc. MS. 57, fols. 21v–22r). Taken together, this suggests (as Inglis concludes) that Fredet had some reputation as a poet beyond the court of Blois. One lyric that occurs in fr. 9223 is identified as Fredet's (*Ce n'est que chose acoustumee*, R203), whereas in the duke's manuscript the lyric has no attribution. (See Hasenohr and Zink, s.v. Frédet; Raynaud, xvi–xvii; Inglis, 37–39.)

Garencières, B117

Jean de Garencières (1370–1415) was an important person who went on crusade with Louis II, duc de Bourgogne, accompanied the king in a war against the duke of Brittany, and was charged by Charles VI to accompany his daughter Isabelle de France to England to marry Richard II. In 1403 he was named *chambellan* to Charles's father Louis. Later he sided with the Orléanists against the duc de Bourgogne and fought on Charles's behalf, dying by his side at Agincourt. While in captivity in Guyenne, he had occupied himself with writing poetry, lamenting his ill treatment in his "Lai de la prison," one of his best works.

He was a poet of some reputation whose work was well known to Charles (Neal, ed., *Poésies complètes de Jean de Garencières*). Some of his fixed-form verse survives in BnF MS. fr. 19139, and there are isolated lyrics in other collections, which total near 50 (see Hasenohr and Zink, *Dictionnaire*, s.v. Jean de Garencières).

George, Georges Chastellain, R220

George Chastellain (1405 or 1415–1475), from Louvain, was in the service of Philippe le Bon at the age of 18. After the Treaty of Arras in 1435, he went to France in the service of Charles VII, where he met Pierre de Brézé (see note to R427), for whom he undertook two diplomatic missions, returning to Burgundy's service in 1445, under whom he held various offices, including official chronicler. In 1473, Charles le Téméraire created him knight of the Toison d'Or and made him its chronicler.

Identified as simply 'George' in the manuscript, Chastellain was known as *le grand Georges*. His *Chronique* is one of the most important of the fifteenth century. He is perhaps best known today for *Les Douze dames de rhétorique*, which includes an epistolary exchange among Robertet, Chastelain, and a certain Jean de Montferrant. In 1463–1464 he composed the prose *Temple de Boccace* (*Livre de l'inconstance de fortune*) for Marguerite d'Anjou, daughter of René d'Anjou and wife of England's Henry VI, as well as other lyric, political, didactic, and moral works in both prose and verse. Though not primarily a poet in the courtly vein, he did compose *l'Oultré d'amour*, a love debate *à clef*, in which the hero is Pierre de Brézé (see s.v. Blosseville, above). See Hasenohr and Zink, s.v. Georges Chastellain; Fox, *The Middle Ages*, 317–19; *Dictionnaire de biographie française*, 8: cols. 739–40.

Gilles, see Des O(u)rmes

La Marche, Olivier de, R218

Olivier de La Marche (c. 1425–1502) was a distinguished Burgundian courtier, diplomat, chronicler, and poet, who served the ducs de Bourgogne. Beginning as a page at the court of Philippe le Bon, he afterwards served his son, Charles le Téméraire.

Although most of his works are in verse, among which are "Le Chevalier Délibéré," "Le Parement et la Triomphe des Dames d'Honneur" (in prose and verse), and "La Source d'Honneur pour maintenir la corporelle élégance des Dames," he is perhaps best known for his "Memoirs," which cover the years 1435–1488. He also composed *L'État de la maison du duc Charles de Bourgogne*, a poem on the death of Marie, and a work of advice for Maximilian. He is responsible for only one lyric in this collection, which may have been written when both he and Charles were at Mâcon in 1448 or at Nevers in 1454 (Hasenohr and Zink, *Dictionnaire*, s.v. Olivier de La Marche; H. Stein, *Olivier de La Marche* (Brussels: F. Hayez; Paris: A. Picand, 1888); and Champion, *Vie*, 632–33).

La Tremoille, Jacques, bâtard de, B86, R251

La Tremoille had been a soldier, described as a *vaillant chevalier en armes* before frequenting Charles's court at Blois. Champion identifies him as a son of Georges La Tremoille, but this seems unlikely (*Vie*, 627). He apparently signed Marie de Clèves's copy of the work of Alain Chartier twice, once with his device (*Serai vostre*) and his signature, once with the (large) letters M and C tied with a tasselled cord and beneath it his signature (Champion, "Un 'liber amicorum'," 328, 335, and plates 3 and 6). He contributed 2 lyrics to the duke's collection, this one and R251.

Le Gout, maistre Estienne, R29

Estienne Le Gout, Charles's secretary and friend, undertook a number of voyages on the duke's behalf. He appears to have had an amorous adventure which ended suddenly with his having to jump out of a window. No doubt he was a learned man, hence Charles's teasing him with terms borrowed from Latin grammar: nominative, optative, copulative (in grammar a conjunction, but one of a different kind here), genitive, etc. A rare example of humour from Charles. In the next poem the secretary responds in kind. We know of no other work from his hand.

Le Voys, H. (Hugues or Huguet), R411, R416, R420

H. le Voys was secretary to the duke, and a favorite of his (Champion, *Vie*, 599–600). His only known verse is that found in this manuscript.

Lorraine, Jehan, Monseigneur de, R231, R235, R238, R240, R367

Jehan de Calabre became Monseigneur de Lorraine after the death of his mother Isabelle of Lorraine in 1453. He was the son of René d'Anjou (see note to R5). A poet and man-of-letters like his father. A brief account of his life and literary activity is given by Inglis, 44–46. He recorded his device (*Ce mieulx ne puis*) and signature in the duchess's copy of the works of Alain Chartier (Champion, "Un 'liber amicorum'," 330–31 and pl. 3). He contributed 5 lyrics to Charles's collection, and R367; 5 more are to be found in Marie de Clèves's manuscript (Champion prints these on 597–601).

Lussay, Anthoyne de, R245

Anthoyne de Lussay was another *échanson* to the duke, who often played at tables with the duchess. We know of no other work from his hand (Champion, *Vie*, 604).

Meschinot [B100], [R441], [R438], [R439]

Jean Meschinot (c. 1420–1491), seigneur de Mortiers (near Nantes), served under five ducs de Bretagne: Jean V, François I, Pierre II, Arthur III, and François II. He later became the *maître d'hôtel* to Anne de Bretagne. One of the *grands rhétoriqueurs*, Meschinot is known above all for his didactic and moralising treatise, *Les Lunettes des Princes* (1493), a mixed-form poetic tour de force modelled on Boethius's *De Consolatione Philosophiae* (ed. Martineau-Genieys). This is followed in three manuscripts by a collection of *ballades*. Three of his lyrics appear in BnF MS. fr. 9332 and two in BnF MS. nouv. acq. 15771; 1 (*De tous plaisirs*) is common to both (see Hasenohr and Zink, *Dictionnaire*, s.v. Jean Meschinot; Raynaud, xxvi–xxvii; Champion, "Remarques sur un recueil de poésies du milieu du XV e siècle (B.N. Fr. 9223)," *Romania* 48 [1922]: 106–14, at 112; Inglis, 46–47).

Montbeton, B106

Montbeton (dates, and even his full name are unknown; Raynaud's "correction" to Montbreton is unsupported in any of the lyric collections, xxviii), was an associate of Robertet's, otherwise unknown (though Inglis makes a few suggestions [48]).

Nevers, R2

Charles de Nevers (1414–1464) was the cousin of Philippe le Bon. Nevers's father, Philippe de Bourgogne, comte de Nevers, who died at Agincourt, was the fourth son of Philippe le Hardi, duc de Bourgogne, and Marguerite de Dampierre, comtesse de Flandre, de Bourgogne, de Nevers, et de Rethel. Charles was the elder brother of "Estampes" (see note to R84); he married Marie d'Albret (1456), daughter of Charles d'Albret, comte de Dreux, and the niece of Charles's second wife, Bonne d'Armagnac. No other work is known from his hand see Champion, *Vie*, 445–46 and 611).

Orlians, Madame d', R195 and R242

Marie de Clèves was Charles's third wife (1426–1487), who married the duke on his return to France in 1440 when she was 14 years old. She was the daughter of Adolf de Clèves (b. 1373) and Marie de Bourgogne (b. 1394, herself the daughter of Jean sans Peur). Together Charles and Marie had three children: Marie d'Orléans, born 1457 (see *Jam nova*); Louis, born 1462, who became Louis XII; and Anne, born 1464, who became Abbess of Fontevrault. The duchess had a library of her own (see Champion, *La librairie*, 115–17) and evidently took pleasure in the literary life of the court at Blois. Carpentras, Bibliothèque Inguimbertine, Carpentras MS. 375, was copied for her from her husband's manuscript. See Champion, "Un 'Liber amicorum,'" pp. 320–36 plus figures 2–7. She is the author of two lyrics in this collection, one of which (one of the series *En la forest*) also appears in BnF Ms. fr. 9223 (Raynaud, xxix) and in nouv. acq. fr. 15771. She recorded her own device (*Rien ne m'est plus*, borrowed from Valentina books (Champion, "Un 'liber amoicorum'," 327 and pl. 3). Her device also appears on a number of pages of the Carpentras MS, e.g., 19.

Pot, Guiot, R243, R246

Like Berthault de Villebresme, Guyot Pot, comte de Saint-Pol and *bailli* de Blois, was *chambellan* and close confidant of the duke (whom he represented on various missions), and a trusted household member of both the duke and the duchess. His Italian mother, Catherine d'Angossoli, accompanied Valentine Visconti from Italy when she married Charles's father Louis. Guyot's father was Renier Pot, *chambellan* to Louis I. Champion terms Guyot "un puissant personnage" (*Vie*, 597) and Joseph de Croÿ calls him "l'une des figures les plus originales et les plus marquants du Blésois, au milieu du XVe siècle" ("Notices biographiques," xxix, 412–16; see also Gonzalez, *Un prince*, 105). He played at tables with the duchess on occasion and recorded his device (*Autrement non*) and his signature in her volume of the works of Alain Chartier (Champion, "Un 'liber amicorum'," 325 and pl. 2). After Charles's death, he became *gouverneur* to the young duke, Louis II (Gonzalez, *Un prince*, 88n, 231; see also 202, 290). In 1494 he founded at Blois "la chapelle de Notre-Dame de Pitié"; he was buried in the royal monastery of Saint-Lomer at Blois. He contributed only 2 lyrics to the duke's collection: R243 and R246, both written on first lines suggested by the duke.

Pot, Philippe, R244

Philippe Pot was the son of Guiot Pot (see previous note) and a young page in the duke's court. He later became abbot of Saint-Euverte in Orléans, canon of the Sainte Chapelle in Paris, and counsellor in the Parlement. This Pot family is related to the Pot family of Rhodes (see *Vie*, 597–98). This is the only lyric known from his hand.

Robertet, Jean, B108

Jean Robertet (d. 1502/3) was secretary to the duke of Bourbon and a prominent poet of the period. He appears in a poem by George Chastellain (see note to R220). One of the *grands rhétoriqueurs*, Robertet was born in the Auvergne of an ancient family established at Montbrison. His grandfather was a notary; his father a lawyer who became secretary to Jean II, duc de Bourbon. Following in his father's footsteps, he was among Jean II's closest counsellors, *plus ancien auditeur et familier secretaire* to the duke. In 1469 Louis XI founded the Order of Saint-Michel, and Robertet became its first *greffier* and collaborated with Jean Fouquet in drawing up the statutes of the Order. In 1469–1470 he became secretary to the king, and in 1471 he was named *en outre greffier du Parlement du Dauphiné*. He was raised to the nobility and married well.

Perhaps best known in our time for his part in *Les douze dames de rhétorique*, Robertet apparently initiated the purported correspondence it contains, which was ended by Georges Chastelain (see note to R220), historiographer of Philippe le Bon. In this work they represent the two ducal houses, and defend the *honneur* of each house. His most important work is the *Complaincte de la mort de Chastelain*, written in 1476. In the context of the duke's collection, Robertet is the author of a eloquent poem of praise of Charles d'Orléans, which survives only in Marie de Clèves's manuscript (see Champion, ed., 603). His earliest known verse is the *ballade* he wrote together with Montbeton in this manuscript. He was the first to translate into French the six *Triomphes* of Petrarch. See Hasenohr and Zink, *Dictionnaire*, s.v. Jean et François Robertet; Fox, *Middle Ages*, 317; Raynaud, xxx–xxxi; Inglis, 53–55. His work was edited by Margaret Zsuppan in 1970; see also eadem, "Jean Robertet's Life and Career."

Senechal, le (grant senechal) R382, R427

Le Senechal may not have been the same person as Le grant seneschal. Champion identifies both as Pierre de Brezé, *d'une ancienne famille noble d'Anjou* and *grand sénéchal de Normandie* (patron of Chastellain, Villon, and de Blosseville, great bibliophile and poet; see Champion, ed., 2:628 and *Vie*, 632–33). Two different *rondels* labelled R. Le Senescal are found in BnF fr. 9223, and Raynaud identifies this poet as a certain Robert or Robin Le Sénéchal who served the house of Orléans between 1383 and 1403 (xxiv). Inglis, whose collection contains a fifth and sixth *rondel* headed Robinet Le Senescal, disputes both Champion's and Raynaud's attributions. She follows Angremy in opting for a family of that name in Normandy, lords of Aumosne and Auberville, and she associates a Robert Le Sénéchal with the milieu of Torcy and Blosseville (see Inglis, 41–43). Robin (or Robinet) Le Senechal contributed 4 lyrics to BnF MS. fr. 9223, 2 to BnF MS. nouv.acq. 15771, and 1 to this collection, all of them unique.

Secile (Cecile), René d'Anjou, roi de, R5, R10, R13, R15

René, *duc d'Anjou, comte de Provence, roi de Naples et de Sicile* (1409–1480), often called *le Roi René*. With Bourbon and Bourgogne, the most eminent of the contributors to Charles's manuscript, a close friend, himself a poet, author of several works, in one of which he refers to Charles's love for a lady in England. See Champion, ed., 2:628 and *Vie*, 342–43 and 611–12. He recorded his device (*FVT*) and his signature in Marie de Clèves's copy of the works of Alain Chartier (Champion, "Un 'liber amicorum'," 329–30 and pl. 3).

T(h)ignonville, Guillaume de Monceau, R271, R407

T(h)ignonville, *chambellan* to the king and to Louis d'Orléans, was *écuyer panetier* to Marie de Clèves beginning in 1449 and was still recorded as *panetier* in 1466. In 1485 he was serving Louis II as *maître d'hôtel* (Champion, *Vie*, 607). He recorded his device (*Fors vous seulle* and ·*ae*·) and signature in the duchess's copy of the works of Alain Chartier (Champion, "Un 'liber amicorum'," 326–27 and pl. 2). Two other lyrics from his hand are found (uniquely) in her manuscript, Carpentras 375 (see Champion, ed., 582 and 587). His father, according to Gaston Raynaud a friend of Deschamps and Christine de Pizan, contributed to *Les Cent Ballades* (lxii).

Torsy, Jean d'Estouteville, seigneur de, R210

Jean d'Estouteville, le seigneur de Torsy (1405/9?–1494), son of Guillaume d'Estouteville, *grand maître des eaux et forêts de France*, seigneur de Torcy et de Blainville, had a long military and political career in royal service under Charles VII and Louis XI. In 1446 he was named *prévôt de Paris*, with a pension of 1,200 *livres*. He assisted in the trial of the duc d'Alençon, the duke's son-in-law, and was a member of the council of regency after the death of Louis XI.

Little of his work seems to have survived, despite his literary reputation in the fifteenth century: besides this lyric, only a *ballade* and a *rondel* in BnF MS. fr. 9223, of which the latter also appears in nouv. acq. fr. 15771, along with 4 other *rondels*, all unique to that MS. Inglis writes that he was known for his gallantry and his *courtoisie* and suggests that nouv. acq. fr. 15771 may have been made for him (58–59; see also Raynaud, xxxi–xxxii; *Dictionnaire de biographie française*, 13:col. 128).

Vaillant, B78, R219, R221

Vaillant (fl. 1445–1470) was for many years mistakenly thought to be Pierre Chastellain (see Inglis, 60–61, who lays the blame at Champion's door for trusting the work of J. Pasini [1749] and A. Piaget [1894] on Vaillant's identity: "Pierre Chastellain dit Vaillant," in Pierre Champion, *Histoire poétique*, Paris: Edouard Champion, 1923, 1:339–89) and lays out the critical history of the error. Daniel Poirion (*Le poète*, 159) has identified him with Jehan Vaillant, *écuyer* to Gaston IV, comte de Foix.

Vaillant addressed a *ballade* to Jacques Coeur before the latter's disgrace in 1450. In 1457 a Jehan Vaillant presented a *petit traicté d'amors* to René d'Anjou; this was probably his *Embusche Vaillant*, a work that was celebrated in his day. In all, some 48 of his works survive, among which his collection titled *Cornerie des anges* and nearly 50 lyrics in fixed forms. In all, 14 of his lyrics are to be found in BnF MS. fr. 9332 (ed. Raynaud, xxxiii–xxxiv) and 13 in BnF MS. nouv. acq. fr. 15771 (ed. Inglis, 60–62). (See Hasenohr and Zink, *Dictionnaire*, s.v. Vaillant; Champion, *Vie*, 625–26. His work is edited in Robert Deschaux's *Œuvres de Pierre Chastellain*.)

Villebresme, maistre Berthault de, B110, R388, R394

Berthault de Villebresme (d. ca. 1499) was a *bourgeois*, a native of of the Blois region, a diplomat, a lawyer, a *prévôt* de Blois (1461), and a counsellor and treasurer of the duke. He travelled twice to Asti in northern Italy representing Charles's interests there (see note to R394 and R395, and Champion, *Vie*, 395, 598 and note). In addition to composing the lyrics in this collection (in a style described by Champion as heavy and erudite), he is the author of *La geste du Chevalier au Cygne*, a prose translation of the first of three branches of the Old French Crusade Cycle, composed sometime between 1465 and 1473 at the request of Marie de Clèves (ed. E. A. Emplaincourt). Champion prints a *ballade* found in Marie de Clèves' manuscript beginning *Tost fut Priant puissant roy couronne*, as well as a companion poem by Pierre Chevalier, *auditeur des comptes* to the duchess (d. 1478; ed., 562–63, 615); see also *Vie*, 598, 395; de Croÿ, "Notices biographiques," xxix–xxx, 281–83.

Villon, François, [*Jam nova*], B105, [B106]

François Villon is the most famous poet of medieval France. Born François de Montcorbier in Paris in 1431, he was adopted at an early age by Guillaume de Villon, chaplain of a church in the old Latin Quarter from whom he took his name. He is the only poet represented in this collection with ties to the non-courtly world, to the university (he studied at the university of Paris), and to the Paris underworld. The city records tell us that he was found guilty of murder and of robbery, was pardoned, and was then banished from Paris for ten years in 1463. How his life ended is not known.

He visited the court at Blois, writing his contributions to Charles's manuscript specially for the occasion. The bulk of his poetry is contained in two mock testaments, *Le Lais*, which makes a series of joking bequests to friends and acquaintances before his first flight from Paris, and *Le Testament*, a later, much longer and more serious work, the preamble to which contains his best known verse before a final series of satirical legacies. In it he reflects sadly on his past and sets down his thoughts as they crowd untidily through his mind: regrets for his way of life; his sufferings and ill fortune; sorrow over the loss of his friends; the empty fickleness of love; the fear of death; the ephemeral nature of life; the vanity of all human things. (See Hasenohr and Zink, Dictionnaire, s.v. François Villon; Gert Pinkernell, *François Villon et Charles d'Orléans [1457 à 1461]: d'après les Poésies diverses, de Villon* Heidelberg: C. Winter, 1992.)

J.F.

Bibliography

This bibliography consists in general of works cited more than once, together with some entries for work on Charles d'Orléans that do not bear directly on this edition but are nonetheless important.

de Angulo, Lucy. "Charles and Jean d'Orléans: An Attempt to Trace the Contacts between Them during Their Captivity in England." In *Miscellanea di studi e ricerche sul quattrocento francese*, 59–92. Turin: Giappichelli, 1967.

Armstrong, Adrian. "François Villon: Rhétoriqueur?" In *Villon at Oxford: The Drama of the Text*, ed. Michael Freeman and Jane H. M. Taylor, 51–84. Études de langue et littérature françaises 65. Amsterdam: Rodopi, 1999.

Arn, Mary-Jo, ed. *Charles d'Orléans in England, 1415–1440*. Woodbridge, Eng., and Rochester, NY: Boydell and Brewer, 2000.

———, ed. *Fortunes Stabilnes: Charles of Orleans' English Book of Love*. MRTS 138. Binghamton, NY: Medieval and Renaissance Texts and Studies, 1994.

———. "A Need for Books: Charles d'Orléans and His Travelling Libraries in England and France," *Journal of the Early Book Society* 12 (2009), 77–98.

———. "Poetic Form as a Mirror of Meaning in the English Poems of Charles of Orleans." *Philological Quarterly* 69 (1990): 13–29.

———. *The Poet's Notebook: The Personal Manuscript of Charles d'Orléans (Paris, BnF MS fr. 25458)*. Texts and Transitions 3. Turnhout: Brepols, 2008.

Askins, William. "The Brothers Orléans and Their Keepers." In *Charles d'Orléans in England*, ed. Arn, 27–45.

Backhouse, Janet. "Charles of Orléans Illuminated." In *Charles d'Orléans in England*, ed. Arn, 157–63.

Badel, Pierre-Yves. *Le "Roman de la rose" au XIVe siècle: étude de la réception de l'oeuvre*. Publications Romanes et Françaises 153. Geneva: Droz, 1980.

Bagnoly, Suzanne. "Christine de Pizan et l'art de 'dictier' ballades." *Moyen Âge* 92 (1986): 41–67.

Bec, Pierre. *La lyrique française au moyen âge (XIIe–XIIIe siècles). Contribution à une typologie des genres poétiques médiévaux: études et textes*. 2 vols. Paris: A. & J. Picard, 1977–1978.

Boffey, Julia. *Manuscripts of English Courtly Love Lyrics in the Later Middle Ages*. Manuscript Studies 1. Woodbridge, Eng., and Rochester N.Y.,: Boydell and Brewer, 1985.

Boulton, Maureen. *The Song in the Story: Lyric Insertions in French Narrative Fiction, 1200–1400*. Philadelphia: University of Pennsylvania Press, 1993.

Brant, Sebastian. *Das Narrenschiff*, ed. Manfred Lemmer. 4th ed. Neudrucke deutscher Literaturwerke, n.s. 5. Tübingen: Max Niemeyer, 2004.

———. *The Ship of Fools*, trans. Edwin H. Zeydel. New York: Columbia University Press, 1944; repr. New York: Dover, 1962.

Brownlee, Kevin. *Poetic Identity in Guillaume de Machaut*. Madison: University of Wisconsin Press, 1989.

Butterfield, Ardis. *Poetry and Music in Medieval France: From Jean Renart to Guillaume de Machaut*. Cambridge: Cambridge University Press, 2002.

Camargo, Martin. *The Middle English Verse Love Epistle*. Tübingen: Max Niemeyer, 1991.

Catherine of Cleves, The Hours of. Facsimile, intro. and comm. John Plummer. New York: George Braziller, n.d.

Les cent ballades, poème du XIVe siècle composé par Jean le Seneschal avec la collaboration de Philippe d'Artois, comte d'Eu, de Boucicaut le jeune et de Jean de Crésecque, ed. Gaston Raynaud. SATF. Paris: Firmin-Didot, 1905.

Chalvet, Vincent. *Poésies de Charles d'Orléans, père de Louis XII et oncle de François Ier, rois de France*. Grenoble: Giroud, 1803.

Champion, Pierre. *Charles d'Orléans: poésies*, I. *La retenue d'Amours; ballades, chançons, complaintes et caroles*. II. *Rondeaux*. CFMA 34 and 56. Paris: Honoré Champion, 1923, 1927.

———. *Histoire poétique du quinzième siècle*. Vol. 2. Bibliothèque du XVe Siècle 28. Paris: Édouard Champion, 1923.

———. *Un inventaire des papiers de Charles d'Orléans (1444)*. Paris: Honoré Champion, 1912.

———. "Un 'liber amicorum' du XVe siècle: notice d'un manuscrit d'Alain Chartier ayant appartenu à Marie de Clèves, femme de Charles d'Orléans (Bibl. Nat., ms. français, 20026)." *Revue des bibliothèques* 10–12 (1910): 322–36.

———. *La librairie de Charles d'Orléans avec un album de fac-similés*. 2 vols. often bound as 1. Bibliothèque du XVe Siècle 11. Paris: Honoré Champion, 1910; repr. Geneva: Slatkine, 1975.

———. *Le manuscrit autographe des poésies de Charles d'Orléans*. Bibliothèque du XVe Siècle 3. Paris: Honoré Champion, 1907; repr. Geneva: Slatkine, 1975.

———. "Remarques sur un recueil de poésies du milieu du XVe siècle (B.N. fr. 9223)." *Romania* 48 (1922): 106–14.

———. *Vie de Charles d'Orléans (1394–1465)*. Bibliothèque du XVe Siècle 13. Paris: Honoré Champion, 1911.

Champollion-Figeac, Aimé. *Les poésies du duc Charles d'Orléans publiées sur le manuscrit original de la Bibliothèque de Grenoble [G] conféré avec ceux de Paris et de Londres*. Paris: J. Belin-Leprieur et Colomb de Batines, 1842.

Charpentreau, Jacques. *Dictionnaire de la poésie*. [Paris]: Fayard, 2006.

Chartier, Alain. *The Poetical Works of Alain Chartier*, ed. James C. Laidlaw. London: Cambridge University Press, 1974.

Chaucer, Geoffrey. *Troilus and Criseyde: A Facsimile of Corpus Christi College Cambridge MS 61*, with introductions by M. B. Parkes and Elizabeth Salter. Cambridge: D. S. Brewer, 1978.

Christine de Pizan. *Oeuvres poétiques*, ed. Maurice Roy. 3 vols. SATF 24. Paris: Firmin-Didot, 1886–1896; repr. New York: Johnson Reprint, 1965.

The Chronicles of Enguerrand de Monstrelet; Containing an Account of the Cruel Civil Wars between the Houses of Orleans and Burgundy . . ., trans. Thomas Johnes. 2 vols. London: J. Henderson, 1809; repr. London: W. Smith, 1840.

La chronique d'Enguerran de Monstrelet, ed. L. Douet-D'Arcq. 6 vols. Société de l'Histoire de France. Paris: Renouard, 1857–1862.

Chronique de Jean le Févre, seigneur de Saint-Remy, ed. François Morand. 2 vols. Paris: Renouard, 1877.

Les chroniques du roi Charles VII par Gilles le Bouvier dit le héraut Berry, ed. Henri Couteault and Léonce Celier, with Marie-Henriette Jullien de Pommerol. Sociéte de l'Histoire de France. Paris: C. Klincksieck, 1979.

Cigada, Sergio. *L'opera poetica di Charles d'Orléans*. Milan: Vita Pensiero, 1960.

Cocco, Mia. "The Italian Inspiration in the Poetry of Charles d'Orléans." *Mid-Hudson Language Studies* 2 (1979): 46–60.

Coldiron, A. E. B. *Canon, Period, and the Poetry of Charles of Orléans: Found in Translation*. Ann Arbor: University of Michigan Press, 2000.

Crane, Susan. "Anglo-Norman Cultures in England, 1066-1460." In *Cambridge History of Medieval English Literature*, ed. D. Wallace, 35-61. Cambridge: Cambridge University Press, 1999, 35–61.

Cropp, Glynnis M. "Fortune and the Poet in Ballades of Eustache Deschamps, Charles d'Orléans, and François Villon." *Medium Aevum* 58 (1989): 125–32.

de Croÿ, Joseph. "Notices biographiques." In *Cartulaire de la ville de Blois (1196–1493): recueil manuscrit du XVe siècle conservé à la Bibliothèque nationale*, ed. Jacques Soyer and Guy Trouillard, 281–432. Extrait des *Mémoires de la Sociéte des Sciences et Lettres de Loir-et-Cher* 17 (1903–1907). Paris: C. Migault, 1907.

Curry, Anne. *Agincourt: A New History*. Stroud, Eng.: Tempus, 2005.

———. *The Battle of Agincourt: Sources and Interpretations*. Woodbridge, Eng., and Rochester, NY: Boydell and Brewer, 2000.

Defaux, Gérard. "Charles d'Orléans ou la poétique du secret." *Romania* 93 (1972): 194–293.

Delisle, Léopold. *Le cabinet des manuscrits de la Bibliothèque impériale*. Paris: Imprimerie impériale, 1868–1881.

Deschamps, Eustache. *L'art de dictier*, ed. and trans. D. Sinnreich-Levi. East Lansing, Mich.: Colleagues Press, 1994.

————. *Oeuvres complètes*, ed. Gaston Raynaud. 11 vols. SATF. Paris: Firmin Didot, 1878–1903.

Deschaux, Robert. *Les œuvres de Pierre Chastellain et de Vaillant: poètes du XVe siècle.* Textes Littéraires Français 300. Geneva: Droz, 1982.

Dictionnaire de biographie française. Various editors. Paris: Letouzey et Ané, 1929–.

Fallows, David. "Words and Music in Two English Songs of the Mid-Fifteenth Century: Charles d'Orléans and John Lydgate." *Early Music* 5 (1977): 38–43.

Fery-Hue, Françoise, ed. *Au grey d'amours . . . (pièces inédites du manuscrit Paris, Bibl. nat., fr. 1719): étude et édition.* Special issue of *Le moyen français* 27–28 (1991).

Figg, Kristen Mossler. *The Short Lyric Poems of Jean Froissart: Fixed Forms and the Expression of the Courtly Ideal.* New York: Garland, 1994.

Fox, John. "Charles d'Orléans, poète anglais?" *Romania* 86 (1965): 433–62.

————. "Glanures." In *Charles d'Orléans in England*, ed. Arn, 89–98.

————. *The Lyric Poetry of Charles d'Orléans.* Oxford: Clarendon Press, 1969; *La poésie lyrique de Charles d'Orléans*, trans. D. Baye. Paris: Nizet, 1971.

————. *The Middle Ages.* A Literary History of France, vol. 1. London: Ernest Benn; New York: Barnes and Noble, 1974.

————, ed. *The Poetry of Villon.* London and New York: T. Nelson, 1962.

————, ed. *Robert de Blois, son oeuvre didactique et narrative.* Paris: Nizet, 1950.

Galderisi, Claudio. "Charles d'Orléans et l'"autre' langue: ce *français* que son 'cuer amer doit'." In *Charles d'Orléans in England*, ed. Arn, 79–87.

————. *Charles d'Orléans, "Plus dire que penser": une lecture bibliographique.* Biblioteca di Filologia Romanza 37. Bari: Adriatica, 1994.

————. *Le lexique de Charles d'Orléans dans les "rondeaux."* PRF 206. Geneva: Droz, 1993.

Garencières, Jean de, see Neal.

Gibbs, Stephanie Viereck, and Kathryn Karczewska, trans. *The Book of the Love-Smitten Heart, by René of Anjou.* New York and London: Garland, 2001.

Godefroy, Frédéric. *Dictionnaire de l'ancienne langue française.* 10 vols. Paris: F. Vieweg, 1881–1902; repr. Vaduz: Scientific Periodicals and Kraus Reprint, 1961.

Gonzalez, Elizabeth. *Un prince en son hôtel: les serviteurs des ducs d'Orléans au XVe siècle.* Histoire Ancienne et Médiévale 74. Paris: Publications de la Sorbonne, 2004.

Grand Larousse de la langue française. 6 vols. Paris: Librairie Larousse, 1971–1978.

Graves, Frances Marjorie. *Deux inventaires de la maison d'Orléans (1389 et 1408).* Bibliothèque du XVe Siècle 31. Paris: Honoré Champion, 1926.

Greimas, Algirdas Julien, and Teresa Mary Keane. *Dictionnaire du moyen français: la Renaissance.* Trésors du Français. Paris: Larousse, 1992.

Gros, Gérard, ed. and trans. *Charles d'Orléans: "En la forêt de longue attente" et autres poèmes*. Postface by Jean Tardieu [1962]. Poésie 365. Paris: Gallimard, 2001.

———. "Le livre du prince et le clerc: édition, diffusion et réception d'une œuvre (Martin le Franc lecteur de Charles d'Orléans)." In *L'écrivain éditeur*, 1: *Du moyen âge à la fin du XVIIIe siècle*, ed. François Bessire, 43–58. Travaux de littérature 14. Geneva: Droz, 2001.

Guichard, J. Marie. *Poésies de Charles d'Orléans publiées avec l'autorisation de M. le ministre de l'instruction publique, d'après les manuscrits des bibliothèques du Roi et de l'Arsenal*. Paris: Charles Gosselin, 1842.

Hall, Edward. *Hall's Chronicle Containing the History of England during the Reign of Henry the Fourth . . .* London: J. Johnson et al., 1809 (a reprint of *The Union of the Two Noble and Illustre Famelies of Lancastre & Yorke*, by Edward Halle. [London]: J. Johnson, 1548).

Hammond, Eleanor Prescott, "Charles of Orléans and Anne Molyneux," *Modern Philology* 22 (1924–25), 215–16.

Hasenohr, Geneviève. "L'essor des bibliothèques privées aux XIVe et XVe siècles." In *Les Bibliothèques médiévales: du VIe siècle à 1530*, ed. André Vernet, 214–63 Histoire des bibliothèques françaises. [Paris]: Promodis, 1989.

———, and Michel Zink, eds. *Dictionnaire des lettres françaises: le moyen age*. Encyclopédies d'Aujourd'hui. Paris: Fayard, 1964.

Henwood, Philippe, ed. *Les collections du trésor royal sous le règne de Charles VI (1380–1422): l'inventaire de 1400*. Histoire 18. Paris: CTHS, 2004.

d'Héricault, Charles, ed. *Poésies complètes de Charles d'Orléans*. 2 vols. Paris: Alphonse Lemerre, 1874; repr. Paris: Flammarion, 1896.

Huguet, Edmond. *Dictionnaire de la langue française du seizième siècle*. 7 vols. Paris: Édouard Champion, 1925–1932 (vols. 1–2); Editions Didier, 1946–1967 (vols. 3–7).

Huot, Sylvia. "'Ci parle l'aucteur': The Rubrication of Voice and Authorship in the *Roman de la Rose* Manuscripts." *SubStance* 56 (1988): 42–48.

———. *From Song to Book: The Poetics of Writing in Old French Lyric and Lyrical Narrative*. Ithaca, N.Y.: Cornell University Press, 1987.

———. *The "Romance of the Rose" and its Medieval Readers*. Cambridge: Cambridge University Press, 1993.

Inglis, Barbara L. S., ed. *Le manuscrit B. N. nouv. acq. fr. 15771: une nouvelle collection de poésies lyriques et courtoises du XVe siècle*. Bibliothèque du XVe Siècle 48. Paris: Honoré Champion, 1985.

Jarry, L. *Le châtelet d'Orléans au XVe siècle et la librairie de Charles d'Orléans en 1455*. Orléans: H. Herluison, 1873.

Jones, Michael K. "'Gardez mon corps, sauvez ma terre'—Immunity from War and the Lands of a Captive Knight: The Siege of Orléans (1428–29) Revisited." In *Charles d'Orléans in England*, ed. Arn, 9–26.

Joursanvault, M. le baron de. *Catalogue analytique des archives de M. le baron de Joursanvault, contenant une précieuse collection de manuscrits, chartes et documens originaux.* Vol. 1. Paris: J. Techener, 1838.

Kamath, Stephanie A. V. G., see Gibbs

Kay, Sarah. *The Place of Thought: The Complexity of One in Late Medieval French Didactic Poetry.* Philadelphia: University of Pennsylvania Press, 2007.

de Laborde, Le comte [Léon-E.-S.-J.]. *Les ducs de Bourgogne: études sur les lettres, les arts et l'industrie pendant le XVe siècle.* Part 2, vol. 3. Paris: Plon frères, 1852.

Laidlaw, James C. "The *Cent balades:* The Marriage of Content and Form." In *Christine de Pizan and the Medieval French Lyric,* ed. Earl Jeffrey Richards, 53–82. Gainesville: University Press of Florida, 1998.

Laurie, I. S. "Deschamps and the Lyric as Natural Music." *Modern Language Review* 59 (1964): 561–70.

———. "Eustache Deschamps: 1340(?)–1404." In *Eustache Deschamps, French Courtier-Poet: His Work and His World,* ed. Deborah M. Sinnreich-Levi, 1–72. AMS Studies in the Middle Ages 22. New York: AMS Press, 1998.

Le Franc, Martin. *Les Champion des Dames,* ed. Robert Deschaux. 5 vols. CFMA 127–131. Paris: Honoré Champion, 1999.

Le Roux de Lincy, A.-J.-V. *La bibliothèque de Charles d'Orléans à Blois en 1427.* Paris: Firmin-Didot, 1843.

Lecoy, Félix, ed. *Roman de la Rose.* 2 vols. CFMA 92 and 95. Paris: Honoré Champion, 1968, 1979.

Littré, Emile. *Dictionnaire de la langue française.* 5 vols. Paris: Hachette, 1873–1886; repr. Monte Carlo: Editions du Cap, 1970.

Lote, G. *Histoire du vers français.* 2 vols. Paris: Boivin, 1949.

de Machaut, Guillaume. *Guillaume de Machaut: The Fountain of Love (La fonteinne amoureuse) and Two Other Love Vision Poems,* ed. and trans. R. Barton Palmer. Garland Library of Medieval Literature 54A. New York: Garland, 1993.

———. *Le livre dou Voir Dit (The Book of the True Poem),* ed. Daniel Leech-Wilkinson; trans. R. Barton Palmer. Garland Library of Medieval Literature 106A; Garland Reference Library of the Humanities 1732. New York and London: Garland, 1998.

———. *Livre du voir-dit,* ed. Paul Imbs. Paris: Livre de Poche, 1999.

———. *La Louange des Dames,* ed. Nigel Wilkins. Edinburgh: Scottish Academic Press, 1972.

———. *Poésies lyriques,* ed. V. Chichmaref. Paris: Honoré Champion, 1909.

———. *La prise d'Alixandre (The Taking of Alexandria),* ed. and trans. R. Barton Palmer. New York and London: Routledge, 2002.

Mallet, Gilles. *Inventaire ou catalogue des livres de l'ancienne bibliothéque du Louvre, fait en l'année 1373.* Paris: Chez de Bure Frères, 1836.

McLeod, Enid. *Charles d'Orléans, Prince and Poet.* London: Viking Press, 1969.

Mera Cisternino, Concetta. *Charles d'Orléans, il Petrarca francese.* Bari: Resta, 1969.

Meschinot, Jean. *Les lunettes des princes*, ed. Christine Martineau-Genieys. Geneva: Droz, 1972.

Middle English Dictionary, T.1, ed. Robert E. Lewis. Ann Arbor: University of Michigan Press, 1993.

Morawski, Joseph. *Proverbes français antérieurs au XVe siècle*. CFMA 47. Paris: Édouard Champion, 1925.

Mühlethaler, Jean-Claude, ed. *Charles d'Orléans: ballades et rondeaux*. Lettres Gothiques 4531. Paris: Librairie Générale Française, 1992.

———. *Poétiques du quinzième siècle*. Paris: Nizet, 1983.

———. "Récrire *Le roman de la rose* au XVe siècle: Les commandements d'amour chez Charles d'Orléans et ses lecteurs." In *'Riens ne m'est seur que la chose incertaine'*: études sur l'art d'écrire au Moyen Âge offertes à Eric Hicks par ses élèves, collègues, amies et amis, ed. Jean-Claude Mühlethaler and Denis billotte. 105–19. Geneva: Slatkine, 2001.

Neal, Young Abernathy. *Le chevalier poète, Jean de Garencières, sa vie et sa poesies complètes, 1372–1415*. 2 vols. Paris: Nizet, 1953.

Nelson, Deborah Hubbard. *Charles d'Orléans: An Analytical Bibliography*. Research Bibliographies and Checklists 49. London: Grant and Cutler, 1990.

Niermeyer, J. F. *Mediae Latinitatis lexicon minus*. Leiden: Brill, 1976.

Oton de Grandson. *Oton de Grandson: sa vie et ses poésies*, ed. Arthur Piaget. Mémoires et Documents Publiés par la Société d'Histoire de la Suisse Romande, 3rd ser., vol. 1. Lausanne: Librairie Payot, 1941.

Ouy, Gilbert. "A propos des manuscrits autographes de Charles d'Orléans identifiés en 1955 à la Bibliothèque nationale," *Bibliothèque de l'Ecole des Chartes* 118 (1961): 179–88.

———. "A propos des manuscrits autographes de Charles d'Orléans identifiés en 1955 à la Bibliothèque nationale: hypothèse 'ingénieuse' on certitude scientifique?" *Bibliothèque de l'Ecole des Chartes* 118 (1961): 179-88.

———. *La librairie des frères captifs: les manuscrits de Charles d'Orléans et Jean d'Angoulême*. Texte, Codex & Contexte 4. Turnhout: Brepols, 2007.

———. "Recherches sur la librairie de Charles d'Orléans et de Jean d'Angoulême pendant leur captivité en Angleterre et étude de deux manuscrits autographes de Charles d'Orléans récemment identifiés" *Académie des inscriptions et belles-lettres* (1955): 273–88.

———. "Un poème mystique de Charles d'Orléans: le *Canticum amoris*." *Studi francesi* 7 (1959): 64–84.

Paden, William D. "Christine de Pizan and the Transformation of Late Medieval Lyric Genres." In *Christine de Pizan and the Medieval French Lyric*, ed. Richards, 27–49.

Page, Christopher. *The Owl and the Nightingale: Musical Life and Ideas in France, 1100–1300*. London: Dent, 1989.

Pearsall, Derek. "The Literary Milieu of Charles of Orléans and the Duke of Suffolk, and the Authorship of the Fairfax Sequence." In *Charles d'Orléans in England*, ed. Arn, 145–56.

———, ed. *"The Floure and the Leafe" and "The Assembly of Ladies."* Old and Middle English Texts. Manchester: Manchester University Press, 1980.

Pinkernell, Gert. *François Villon et Charles d'Orléans (1457 à 1461): d'après les Poésies diverses, de Villon.* Studia Romanica 79. Heidelberg: Winter, 1992.

Planche, Alice. *Charles d'Orléans ou la recherche d'un langage.* Bibliothèque du XVe Siècle 38. Paris: Honoré Champion, 1975.

Poirion, Daniel. *Le lexique de Charles d'Orléans dans les "ballades."* PRF 91. Geneva: Droz, 1967.

———. *Le poète et le prince: l'évolution du lyrisme courtois de Guillaume de Machaut à Charles d'Orléans.* Université de Grenoble, Publications de la Faculté des Lettres et Sciences Humaines 35. Paris: Presses Universitaires de France, 1965.

Procès de condamnation de Jeanne d'Arc, ed. Pierre Tisset. 3 vols. Paris: C. Klincksieck, 1960.

Quicherat, L[ouis]. *Thesaurus poeticus linguae latinae; ou, Dictionnaire prosodique et poétique de la langue latine.* Paris: Hachette, 1878.

Raynaud, Gaston, ed. *Les cent ballades: poème du XIVe siècle composé par Jean le Seneschal.* SATF. Paris: Firmin-Didot, 1905.

———, ed. *Rondeaux et autres poésies du XVe siècle publiés d'après le manuscrit de la Bibliothèque nationale.* [BnF MS fr. 9223 (R)] SATF 30. Paris: Firmin Didot, 1889; repr. New York and London: Johnson Reprint Company, 1968.

Regalado, Nancy Freeman. *"En ce saint livre:* mise en page et identité lyrique dans les poèmes autographes de Villon dans l'album de Blois (Bibl. Nat. ms. fr. 25458)." In *L'Hôtellerie de Pensée: études sur l'art littéraire au moyen âge offertes à Daniel Poirion par ses anciens élèves*, ed. Michel Zink and Daniele Regnier-Bohler, 355–72. Paris: Presses de l'Université de Paris-Sorbonne, 1995.

Le Religieux de Saint-Denis. *Chronique du religieux de Saint-Denys, contenant le règne de Charles VI de 1380 à 1422.* Latin text with facing-page French trans. by L[ouis] Bellaguet. Collection de Documents Inédits sur l'Histoire de France. 6 vols. Paris: Crapelet, 1839–1852; repr. Éditions du CTHS, 1994.

René d'Anjou. *The Book of the Love-Smitten Heart/Le livre du coeur d'amours épris*, ed. and trans. Stephanie Viereck Gibbs (Stephanie A. V. G. Kamath) and Kathryn Karczewska. New York: Routledge, 2001.

———. *Le livre de coeur d'amour épris*, ed. Florence Bouchet. Le Livre de Poche, 4567. Lettres Gothiques. Paris: Librairie générale française, 2003.

Robin, Françoise. "Le luxe des collections aux XIVe et XVe siècles." In *Les bibliothèques médiévales: du VIe siècle à 1530*, ed. André Vernet, 1:193–214. Histoire des bibliothèques françaises. 4 vols. [Paris]: Promodis, 1989.

Rothwell, William, ed. *Anglo-Norman Dictionary.* London: Modern Humanities Research Association in conjunction wih The Anglo-Norman Text Society, 1988. 2 vols.

Le Roux de Lincy, A. J. V. *Les quatre livres des rois traduits en français du XIIe siècle.* Paris: Imprimerie royale, 1841.

Rychner, Jean, and Albert Henry, eds. *Le lais Villon et Les poèms variés.* 1: *Texte.* 2. *Commentaire*, Textes Littéraires Français 239–240. Geneva: Droz, 1977.

———, eds. *Le testament Villon.* 2 vols. Textes littéraires Français 207–208. Geneva: Droz, 1974.

Rymer, Thomas. *Foedera, conventiones, literæ, et cujuscunque generis Acta Publica, inter Reges Angliæ*, ed. George Holmes. London: Joannes Neaulme, 1841.

de Sainte-Palaye, M. de La Curne. *Dictionnaire historique de l'ancien langage français.* 10 vols. Niort-Paris: L. Farre, 1875–1882.

Scott, Kathleen L. *Later Gothic Manuscripts, 1390–1490.* 2 vols. A Survey of Manuscripts Illuminated in the British Isles 6. London: Harvey Miller, 1996.

———. "Limner-Power: A Book Artist in England c. 1420." In *Prestige, Authority and Power in Late Medieval Manuscripts and Texts*, ed. Felicity Riddy, 55–75. York: York Medieval Press, 2000.

Steele, Robert, and Mabel Day. *The English Poems of Charles of Orleans.* EETS o.s. 215, 220. Oxford: Oxford University Press, 1941, 1946; repr. in one vol. London: Oxford University Press, 1970.

Stein, H[enri]. *Olivier de La Marche, historien, poète et diplomate bourguignon.* Brussels: F. Hayez; Paris: A. Picard, 1888.

Stevenson, Joseph, ed. *Letters and Papers Illustrative of the Wars of the English in France during the Reign of Henry the Sixth, King of England.* London: Longman, Green, Longman, Roberts, and Green, 1864.

Stirnemann, Patricia Danz. "Français 15458." In *Manuscrits enluminés d'origine insulaire, VIIe–XXe siècle*, ed. François Avril and eadem, 180–81. Paris: Bibliothèque nationale, 1987.

Stratford, Jenny. *The Bedford Inventories: The Worldly Goods of John, Duke of Bedford, Regent of France, 1389–1435.* Reports of the Research Committee of the Society of Antiquaries of London 49. [London]: Society of Antiquaries of London, 1993.

Taylor, Jane H. M. *The Making of Poetry: Late-Medieval French Poetic Anthologies.* Texts and Transitions 1. Turnhout: Brepols, 2007

———. *The Poetry of François Villon: Text and Context.* Cambridge: Cambridge University Press, 2001.

Thibault, Pascale. *La bibliothèque de Charles d'Orléans et de Louis XII au château de Blois.* Le Cahiers de la Bibliothèque Municipale de Blois 4. Blois: Les Amis de la Bibliothèque de Blois, Bibliothèque Municipale, 1989.

Thomas, Antoine. "Les premiers vers de Charles d'Orléans." *Romania* 85 (1893): 128–33.

Tobler-Lommatzsch, Adolph. *Altfranzösisches Wörterbuch.* 10 vols. Berlin: Weidmann, 1925–1976.

Trésor de la langue française: dictionnaire de la langue du XIXe et du XXe siècle (1789–1960). 16 vols. Paris: Éditions du CNRS, 1971–1994.

des Ursins, Jean Juvenal. *Histoire de Charles VI, roy de France.* In *Nouvelle collection des mémoires pour servir à l'histoire de France,* ed. J. Fr. Michaud. Paris: Editeur du commentaire analytique du code civil, 1836–.

de Villebresme, Berthault. *La geste du Chevalier au Cygne,* ed. Edmond A. Emplaincourt. Tuscaloosa: University of Alabama Press, 1989.

Villon François. *Complete Poems,* ed. and trans. Barbara N. Sargent Baur. Toronto, Buffalo, and London: University of Toronto Press, 1994.

Yeager, R. F. "John Gower's Audience: The Ballades." *Chaucer Review* 40 (2005): 81–105.

Wetherbee, Winthrop. "The *Consolation* and Medieval Literature." In *The Cambridge Companion to Boethius,* ed. J. Marenbon, 279–302. Cambridge: Cambridge University Press, 2009.

Willard, Charity Cannon. *Christine de Pizan: Her Life and Works.* New York: Persea Books, 1984.

Zsuppán, C. M[argaret] "Jean Robertet's Life and Career: A Reassessment." *Bibliothèque d'Humanisme et Renaissance* 31 (1969): 333–42.

———, ed. *Jean Robertet: oeuvres.* TLF 159. Geneva: Droz; Paris: Minard, 1970.

Index of First Lines

B = *ballade*
Bal = narrative *ballade*, part of the *Songe en complainte: Departie d'Amours*
Ca = *carole*
Ch = *chançon*
Co = *complainte*
R = *rondel*
Line-end punctuation is omitted.

	Poem #	Champion #	MS. Pg #	Page #
Aprés le jour qui est fait pour traveil [*Songe en complainte*]	no #	71a	100	144
Aprez une seule exceptee (*Cecile*)	R5	R5	321s	400
A! que vous m'enuyés, Viellesse	R437	R415	521s	786
A quiconque plaise ou desplaise	R227	R114	438i	602
A qui en donne l'en le tort	R423	R401	511s	772
A qui les vent on	R89	R76	410i	484
Aquitez vostre conscience	R177	R209	397s	558
A qui vendez vous vos coquilles	R90	R77	411i	484
Ardant desir de veoir ma maistresse	B27	B26	46	68
A recommancer de plus belle	R95	R82	416i	488
Armez vous de Joyeux Confort	R339	R313	265s	700
Asourdy de Non Chaloir	R443	R421	525i	790
Assez ne m'en peuz merveiller (*Bouciquault*)	R224	R111	437s	600
Assez pourveu, pour decy a grant piece	R347	R305	257s	706
As tu ce jour ma mort juree	R84	R71	405i	478
As tu ja fait, Petit Souspir	R314	R341	297s	678
A tout bon compte revenir	R124	R158	341s	514
A tresnoble, hault et puissant seigneur [*Songe,* letter]	no #	p. 116	117	168
A trompeur trompeur et demi	R129	R163	348s	518
Au besoing congnoist on l'amy	Ch50	Ch50	290i	380
Au court jeu de tables jouer	B46	B46	69	100
Au plus fort de ma maladie:				
Des fievres de Merencolie	R267	R251	458i	638
M'a abandonné Esperance (*Benoit Damien*)	R266	R250	458s	636
Aussi bien laides que belles	R168	R200	387s	552
Aux excellens et puissans en noblesse [*Songe,* La requeste]	no #	p. 105	105	152
Avancez vous, Esperance	Ca2	Ca2	316	394
Avez vous dit—laissez me dire	R192	R224	412s	572
Avoglé et assourdy	R36	Ch85	357i	438
A voz amours hardyement en souviengne	R386	R364	492s	740
Ayens the coming of may	R360	p. 569	310s	718
Baillez lui la massue	R130	R164	348i	518
Balades, chançons et complaintes	B72	B72	119	172
Banissons Soussy, ce ribault	R412	R390	505i	762
Beau frere, je vous remercie	B135	B93	224	292
Beau Pere! *benedicite*	R383	R361	490s	738
Beauté, gardez vous de mez yeulx	Ch64	Ch64	329i	412
Belle, bien avez souvenance	B30	B30	49	72
Belle, bonne, nompareille, plaisant	B1	B1	17	24
Belle, combien que de mon fait	B22	B22	40	60
Belle que je cheris et crains	Ch18	Ch18	252i	350
Belle que je tiens pour amye	B15	B15	32	48

	Poem #	Champion #	MS. Pg #	Page #
Encore lui fait il grant bien	R35	Ch84	356i	436
En faictes vous doubte:				
Point ne le devez	R190	R222	410s	570
Que vostre ne soye	R191	R223	411s	570
En faulte du logeis de Joye	R341	R311	263s	700
En gibessant toute l'aprés disnee	R21	Ch75	340i	424
En la chambre de ma pensee	B96	B119	146	218
En la forest d'ennuyeuse Tristesse	B63	B63	89	130
En la forest de Longue Actente:				
Chevauchant par divers sentiers	B81	B105	131	196
Des brigans de Soussy bien trente (*Fredet*)	R196	R227	416s	576
Entree suis en une sente (*Madame d'Orleans*)	R195	R226	415s	574
Forvoyé de joyeuse sente	R197	R228	417s	576
Ja pieça fus en une sente (*Guiot Pot*)	R246	R133	448s	620
J'ay couru l'annee presente (*Jacques bastard de la Trimoille*)	R251	R138	450i	624
Mainte personne bien joyeuse (*Nevers*)	R193	omitted	413s	572
Mon povre cueur tant se garmente (*Gilles*)	R247	R134	448i	620
Ou les contentés Dieu contente (*Anthoyne de Lussay*)	R245	R132	447i	618
Ou mainte personne est dolente (*Philippe Pot*)	R244	R131	447s	618
Par vent de Fortune Dolente	R194	R225	414s	574
En la grant mer de Desplaisance (*Benoist Damien*)	R296	R279	473s	662
En la nef de Bonne Nouvelle	B28	B28	47	68
En la promesse d'Esperance	Ch66	Ch66	331i	414
En la querelle de Plaisance	R98	R85	419i	490
En la vigne jusqu'au peschier	R30	R21	352i	432
En l'ordre de mariage	R250	R137	450s	622
En mes païs, quant me treuve a repos	R67	R54	388i	464
En mon cueur cheoit	R154	R186	373s	540
En ne peut servir en deux lieux	R76	R63	397i	472
Ennemy, je te conjure	R203	R234	423s	582
En regardant ces belles fleurs	R47	R34	368i	446
En regardant vers le païs de France	B114	B75	194	258
En songe, souhaid et pensee	Ch27	Ch27	261i	358
En tirant d'Orleans a Blois	B140	B98	231	302
Entre les amoureux fourrez	Ch60	Ch60	298i	388
En verrai ge jamais la fin	R301	R286	477s	666
En vivant en bonne esperance	R121	R155	338s	510
Envoyez nous un doulz regart	R91	R78	412i	484
En yver, du feu, du feu	R370	R348	478i	726
Escollier de Merancolie:				
A l'estude je suis venu	B94	B117	144	216
Des verges de Soussy batu	R419	R397	509s	768
Par Soussy qui est le recteur (*H. le Voys*)	R420	R398	509i	770

	Poem #	Champion #	MS. Pg #	Page #
Escoutez et laissés dire	R392	R370	495i	746
Espargniez vostre doulx actrait	B5	B5	21	30
Espoir, confort des maleureux	R357	R295	247s	714
Espoir m'a apporté nouvelle	B41	B41	62	90
Espoir ne me fist oncques bien	R158	R190	377s	542
Espoir ou est? En chambre close (*Jehan Caillau*)	R375	R353	485s	730
Esse tout ce que m'apportez	R292	R276	471s	660
Est ce vers moy qu'envoyez ce souspir	R64	R51	385i	462
Et bien, de par Dieu, Esperance	R340	R312	264s	700
Et commant l'entendez vous	R282	R266	466s	650
Et de cela, quoy:				
En ce temps nouveau	R151	R183	370s	536
Se Soussi m'assault	R150	R182	369s	536
Et eussiez vous, Dangier, cent yeulx	Ch56	Ch56	286i	384
Et fust ce ma mort ou ma vie	R421	R399	510s	770
Et ne cesserez vous jamais	R108	R142	318s	500
Et ou vas tu, Petit Soupir (*Fraigne*)	R315	R340	296s	678
Faulcette confite	R140	R172	359s	526
Fault il aveugle devenir	Ch53	Ch53	283i	382
Fermez luy l'uis au visaige	R306	R291	480i	672
Fiés vous y	R54	R41	375i	452
For the reward of half a yere	R362	p. 570	311s	718
Fortune, je vous oy complaindre	B91	B114	141	212
Fortune, passez ma requeste	R284	R268	467s	652
Fortune! sont ce de voz dons	R281	R265	465i	650
Fortune, vray est vostre comte	B93	B116	143	214
Fortune, vueilliez moy laissier	B40	B40	60	88
France, jadis on te souloit nommer	Co3	Co1	191	252
Fredet, j'ay receu vostre lectre	Co6	CoIVa	179	320
Fresche beauté, tresriche de jeunesse	B9	B9	25	38
Fuyés le trait de doulx regard	Ch51	Ch51	287i	380
Fyez vous y, se vous voulez	R404	R382	501i	756
Gardez le trait de la fenestre	R20	Ch74	339i	422
Gardez vous bien de ce fauveau (*P. Danche*)	R460	p. 595	537s	806
Gardez vous bien du cayement (*Bourbon*)	R458	p. 595	536s	803
Gardez vous de *mergo*	R137	R169	356s	524
Gens qui cuident estre si sages	R50	R37	371i	450
Go forth myn hert wyth my lady	R361	p. 570	310i	718
Ha! Dieu d'Amours, ou m'avez vous logié	B87	B110	137	206
Ha! Mort, helas (*Antoine de Cuise*)	R434	R412	518s	782
Haa, Doulx Penser, jamais je ne pourroye	B38	B38	58	84

Explanatory Notes

Abbreviations:

B	*ballade*
Bal	one of the seven narrative *ballades*
Ca	*carole*
Ch	*chançon*
Co	*complainte*
R	*rondel*
Intro.	the opening narrative section of the collection
Introduction	the introduction to the edition
Champion	P. Champion, *Poésies*
Galderisi	C. Galderisi, *Le Lexique de Charles d'Orléans dans les rondeaux*
Godefroy	F. Godefroy, *Dictionnaire de l'ancienne langue française*
Greimas	A. Greimas and T. M. Keane, *Dictionnaire du moyen français*
Hasenohr and Zink	G. Hasenohr and M. Zink, *Dictionnaire des lettres françaises*
Huguet	E. Huguet, *Dictionnaire de la langue française*
Inglis	B. Inglis, *Le manuscrit B.N. nouv. acq. fr. 15771*
Littré	E. Littré, *Dictionnaire de la langue française*
Morawski	J. Morawski, *Proverbes français*
Raynaud	G. Raynaud, *Rondeaux et autres poésies*
Rothwell	W. Rothwell, *Anglo-Norman Dictionary*
Tobler	Tobler-Lommatzsch, *Altfranzösisches Wörterbuch*

Notes

On the introductory narrative, see Introduction, §6, The introductory narrative and the Valentine poems. Pierre Champion's title for the opening narrative (*La retenue d'Amours*) does not appear in the manuscript and has not been retained here.

Introductory narrative, 13 The messenger Age, who conducts the youth from one stage in life to another appears again in the *Songe en complainte*, where, at first not recognized, he counsels him to leave the service of Love while still in his prime. He might be thought of as the aging process. It is another character, *Vieillesse, la mere de Courrous,* who represents Old Age.

24 See Introduction, §6.

114 "Orlians" is the usual spelling of the name at this time, though some scribes spelled it "Orleans."

164 Champion and others have been followed in transcribing this word as *povair,* though in the MS. it really appears as *pouair,* corresponding to the original pronunciation, cf. English "power," and spellings in other contemporary MSS such as *pooir, poons, poez,* etc., -v- being added in the course of the century on analogy with *avoir, devoir, savoir,* etc. *Pouair* may simply have been an archaic spelling, *povoir* appearing more frequently. Both spellings rhyme with *devoir, recevoir,* etc.

167 The fleur-de-lis was the emblem of royalty in France since the time of Louis VII in the twelfth century.

172 On Charles's father Louis d'Orléans, see Introduction, §6.

207–208 Solomon and Samson were often named as victims of love, cf. Villon:
> Folles amours font les gens bestes:
> Salmon en ydolatria,
> Sanson en perdit ses lunectes . . .
> (*Le Testament,* ll. 629–631; R-H, 1:63.)

272 *de main mise t'arreste.* Regular expression in Medieval French: "I arrest you (with hand placed on your collar)." The modern equivalent is: "mettre la main au collet de quelqu'un" (ModE "to collar someone"), cf. R66, 1, 7, 12.

280 This same line appears in B38, 34.

326–327 Association of *servir* and *volee* in the same line has led Mühlethaler (705) to explain the line as a metaphor from tennis, without revealing how he would translate it. This is quite wrong. In Charles's day as now you could not "serve a volley," or "at" or "to" a volley. An excellent commentary on *volee* as a tennis term, and on the quite separate expression *a la volee,* is provided by R-H (2:88–90). They show that *a la volee* was found in Charles's day with the meaning "abundantly." *Servir* was frequently used in medieval allegorical texts referring to Love (cf. R217, 14). The meaning is, therefore, ". . . although some hearts (i.e., in the context, "some men") ask for nothing better than to serve love abundantly (i.e., indiscriminately, not remaining faithful to one lady)." The situation is reversed in Villon's *Testament* (R-H 1:605–8), where one "lady" ends up loving any number of men. Needless to say, the two poets moved in very different circles. Champion (ed., 2:661) makes the same mistake as Mühlethaler above with R26 (l. 4): "Il respont a la volee." He sees it as a tennis term, but R-H show that expressions such as "respondre a la volee" were common at the time, meaning to reply without taking the time to reflect, i.e., flippantly, carelessly.

388 See Introduction §6, The introductory narrative and the Valentine poems.

426 *Danger* is an important allegorical figure in Charles's poetry. From Latin *dominiarium* (< *dominus*) it meant "dominion," more especially "someone else's dominion, power," hence to be at the mercy of opposing forces of any kind. During his captivity in England it often appears to refer to the English. See also Translator's Preface.

B1, 1 *Belle* is a frequent form of address in Charles's poetry, occurring in 21 poems. It was also used by contemporary poets. We have opted to translate it with the perhaps somewhat archaic but brief and accurate English word "belle." *Bonne*, very common as an adjective, was comparatively rare as a form of address, there being only 8 instances, 2 of which are plurals. Champion conjectures (*Vie*, 265) that the latter (Bonne) was a veiled reference to his second wife, Bonne d'Armagnac. See also Translator's Preface.

B7, 11 This is the first reference to *Nonchaloir*, later to become one of Charles's most frequent personifications, occurring in no fewer than 30 poems. In Charles's own English version of this poem he renders it as No Care (*Fortunes Stabilnes*, ed. Arn). The word implies indifference or resignation, a feeling which years of imprisonment might well give. Along with *Soussy, Soing, Merencolie*, it was to become a permanent feature of his mentality in his declining years.

B9 Like B54 (below), this *ballade* of 5 stanzas instead of the usual 3 was known as a "double ballade" or "chant royal." See Mühlethaler, 707, note to 71.

B10 A dramatic change of tone occurs in this poem, the first of many lamenting his being so far away from his lady. Love's joy has become Love's sorrow. Admittedly a conventional courtly theme (already used by the twelfth-century troubadour Jaufré Rudel), none the less it is likely that this was the first *ballade* composed during his long imprisonment in England, the Intro. and the first 9 *ballades* having been written while still in France, before Agincourt (see Introduction, §6).

B13, 1 *se souvent ne vous voy* (cf. "je ne vous voy souvent," B20, 13) implies that he does see her occasionally, in which case the reference cannot be to his wife Bonne. If she had been allowed to visit Charles in England there would be a record of it. B28 and B33 suggest that there had been an intention to send his *maistresse* in France (presumably his wife) across the sea to visit him in England, but it evidently came to nothing.

B14, 10 For the meanings of *Danger*, see note to Intro. 426.

B15, 2 *quelque part que je soye*. cf. B36, 18 *ou que je soye* refer, possibly, to his frequently being moved from place to place while in England. See Champion, *Vie*, 668–72.

> 7–8 *Qui a trouvé peu de mercy / En vous . . ."* This rebuttal can hardly refer to his wife. The poem may be a reference to some lady encountered in England.

B16, 9–16 Again a possible reference to a lady met in England.

B17 This is the first of eighteen poems concerning May, most of them presented as written on the first of the month. Those composed while a prisoner contrast the happiness of May with the sadness of his plight, expressed mainly in conventional courtly terms of separation from his lady, and later in terms of her death (B17, B42, B48, B53, B61, and B62), while those composed after his return to France at the age of 46 contrast the gaiety of springtime with the sadness of his later years (R51, R52, R108, R146, and R273; cf. R147, l. 2: "Ce may, suis vestu de noir . . ."). Six of the eighteen (B119, Ch1, Ch11, R320, R360, and R402, like the well-known R44: "Le temps a laissié son manteau / De vent, de froidure et de pluie...," celebrate the coming of spring. R360 is written in English: "Now is the tym of mirth and play . . ." (l. 5).

B20, 13 See note to B13.

B24, 5–7, 13–15, 25–27 *deux:crueulx, deulx:angoisseux, piteux:ceulx, eureux:seulx*. All appear to be assonance dressed up as rhyme by the addition of x after l. That there is just one -lx in each stanza suggests a little amusement on Charles's part or that of the scribe.

B25, 11 *pastis*. Pasture land of poor quality.

> 30 *nompareille de France* may be his wife Bonne d'Armagnac, who died in the early 1430s, cf. B35, 7; B44, 8; and B50, 2.

B27, 12 *feu gregeois*. Greek Fire was a combustible material for setting fire to enemy ships, first used by the Byzantines at Constantinople.

B28, 35 *escumeurs*. "Pirates," a word also used by Villon in *Le Testament*, 134 (R-H, 1:31).

B33, 13 *elle vient par deça la mer.* See note to B13, 1.

B36, 5–8 It is possible that the poet might actually be quoting from a real letter received. If he is, it would be tempting to think that the *chançon* was from his wife Bonne and that this is his reply. For another *chançon* written from a lady's point of view, see Ch44.

   18, see note to B15, 2.

B38, 34 See note to Intro., 280.

B40 That his misfortune had driven him to thoughts of death was not just poetic hyperbole is shown by this extract from Charles's speech in defence of the duke of Alençon: "en ma prison en Angleterre, pour les ennuis, desplaisances et dangiers en quoy je me trouvoye, j'ay maintefois souhaidié que j'eusse esté mort à la bataille ou je fus pris, pour estre hors des paines ou j'estoye" [in my prison in England, because of the troubles, displeasure, and dangers in which I found myself, I many a time wished I had been killed in the battle in which I was captured to be rid of the torments in which I was] (Champion, *Vie*, p. 547). The words *ennui, desplaisances, dangiers, paines* occur time and time again throughout his later verse, in and after his years of imprisonment.

B42 On May poems, see note to B17.

B44, 29 Champion (ed., 2:653) translates "appeler en combat singulier après avoir jeté son gage," so referring back to the poem's first line: "Dangier je vous giette mon gant." Mühlethaler (143) translates quite differently: ". . . je vous cite en tribunal pour vous demander un gage." Reference to Charles's own translation shows Champion's to be the correct one (see Arn, ed., *Fortunes Stabilnes*, 193): ". . . that you will not leave [here] without [taking up] my glove with which I challenge you here."

B46, 1 On backgammon in Charles's time see Arn, ed., *Fortunes Stabilnes*, 60. See also note to B75, 24.

4 *le point d'atentte*. Charles's own (English) term for this expression is "enter point" (Arn, l. 1632), which, Arn explains (*Fortunes Stabilnes*, 563), is "the point on a backgammon board where a taken piece may be entered."

6 *point lyé*, happy (i.e., lucky, good) point in the game (cf. Intro., 32 *de lyé cueur*). Mühlethaler, evidently associating *lyé* with the verb *lier*, translates "Si je sais tenir fermement ce point" (145).

27 *J'asseray les dez*. Lit. I shall "sit," i.e., place the dice, with implication of cheating: tell me how to throw the dice in such a way that I cannot lose. Tobler comments: "Trug beim Würfelspiel" (1:col. 584).

B48 On May poems, see note to B17.

B53 On May poems, see note to B17.

B54 This is a "double ballade" or "chant royal." See note to B9.

B57 28–32 The reference is to purgatory.

B61 On May poems, see note to B17. The same theme appears in the English poem *The Flower and the Leaf*, which Derek Pearsall has dated to the third quarter of the fifteenth century (placing it later than this poem); of course the two authors might have borrowed the idea from the same source (see "*The Floure and the Leafe*" and "*The Assembly of Ladies*." Old and Middle English Texts. Manchester: Manchester University Press, 1980, 13–20). Here he chooses the leaf because his "flower"—the lady he is mourning—has died. See Arn, *Fortunes Stabilnes*, 55–57.

B62 On May poems, see note to B17.

Songe en complainte, 450 Willow trees are most appropriate in this context, reminding us of the psalmist's lament over the Babylonian captivity: "Upon the rivers of Babylon, there we sat and wept: when we remembered Sion. On the willows in the midst thereof we hung up our instruments. For there they that led us into captivity required of us the words of songs" (Psalm 138:1–2, Douay).

B72, 34 "Faire son jubilé" was an expression which originated in the Church. "Jubilé" referred to a papal bull, originally issued once every 50 years, making a particular year one of remission in which plenary indulgence was granted if practices ordained by the pope were followed. In 1389 Urban VI reduced the interval to 33 years, so the two jubilee years in Charles's life would presumably have been 1422 and 1455. "Jubilé" is well attested in Charles's day with the meaning it still has: fiftieth anniversary. Taken literally this would mean the poem was written in 1444. However, the context indicates that a different meaning was intended. Why would celebrating his fiftieth anniversary lead to accusations that he was giving up without a fight ("sans coup ferir")? Champion (2:654) quotes two lines by Deschamps:

> Venez a mon jubilé
> J'ay passé la cinquantaine.

He does not, however, quote the next line: "Tout mon bon temps est alé . . ." which suggests that "jubilé" was viewed as heralding the end of the good times. Charles is saying in effect: "I am so full of melancholy that I might just as well be in my jubilee year, for I am no longer writing my love poems (lines 23–33), but I am not giving up and hope soon to start afresh." In the first line of the poem, the old word *chançons* is used, not *rondels* which largely replaced them on his return to France in 1440. The likelihood, therefore, is that he was writing this poem before 1440, possibly in 1437, the same year as the *Songe*, which precedes it.

B75, 24 *hasart*. A game of dice referred to already in the thirteenth-century *Jeu de St. Nicolas*. Here, literally, "On a game of dice I'll put . . .," i.e., "my 'Fortune,' good or bad, I'll risk some year or other on a game of dice," cf. B46, 27.

B76 When Charles was taken prisoner at Agincourt in 1415, the English domination in France was at its height, Henry V styling himself "King of England and France." French recovery began in 1429 with Jeanne d'Arc's taking of Orléans and crowning Charles VII king of France. Normandy was recovered by the French in 1449, Guyenne in 1453. Only two years later Henry VI lost his reason—hence Charles's *doubteuse balance* (26)—leading to the Wars of the Roses. Charles's failure to mention Jeanne d'Arc in his poetry seems strange, but he was still in English hands at the time. On his return to France he paid a pension to her relatives (see Intro., xxxiii, n. 50; de Laborde, #6698; Champion, *Vie*, 442–43).

14 *Taÿs*. Either the fourth-century B.C. Greek courtesan, Alexander's mistress, or the fourth-century A.D. prostitute who repented and became a saint. Villon has the same reference (*Le Testament*, 332), which R-H think is to the former (2:53).

19 *menoient leur sabat*. From its secondary meaning "witches' Sabbath" *sabat* came to mean "noise," "din," "racket," hence the translation: "the English wreaked their havoc."

B77, 8 *observance*. "Les religieux de l'Observance" was the title adopted by the *Cordelier* order to emphasize their strict observance of the Franciscan rule. The word was used metaphorically by Charles to indicate absolute loyalty to the God of Love. This use seems to have been adopted by the court at Blois, since it occurs several times in poems by others at his court as well as in Charles's later verse: R204, 1; R219, 1; R220, 1; R224, 3; R225, 6; and R227, 6. On two occasions it was used with the original meaning: B109, 26, and R218, 2.

B78 On Vaillant, see Appendix 3: Index of medieval authors.

B79 *Vidimus.* Latin "We have seen," implying "and approved." A *vidimus* is a letter following up on a letter by somebody else and rehearsing that earlier letter, wholly or in part. It is a note certifying the conformity of a text with the original.

> 5 *tabellion* is defined as follows by the *OED*, s.v.: "In France till the Revolution, an official scribe having some of the functions of a notary." Cp. Middle English *tabellioun*: "an official whose function was to authenticate signatures or to record in writing the intention of the unlettered." See also Rothwell, s.v. tabellion.

> 6 *Juré.* Originally applied to a vassal who had sworn allegiance to his overlord, later, as here, a title given to an official who had taken an oath in connection with his duties. *Contrauts de mariage,* "marriage contracts" is found (Godefroy, 9:197), hence the translation "registrar of love contracts."

> 12 *Queue* (double). This is characteristic of the quasi-legal vocabulary used by Charles in this pastiche. "Lettres scellées sur double queue" are defined by *Trésor de la langue française* (14:155) as "lettres dont le sceau est suspendu à une bande de parchemin traversant une incision pratiquée dans le repli de la pièce."

B80 On Jehan Caillau, see Appendix 3: Index of medieval authors.

Intendit derives from Latin *intendere* (lit. "he intends," or "he intends to"), which, in a legal context, meant "To bring or put forward a claim or plea . . ." (*Oxford Latin Dictionary,* s.v.). Huguet defines it as "Intention" and explains it as an "acte par lequel le demandeur énonce ce qu'il se propose de prouver" (4:662).

> 3 *Vous* is the lady.

> 9 The original expression was "frappé d'estoc et de taille," "struck with the point of the sword (*estoc*) and its cutting edge (*taille*)," hence the translation here "one way or another."

B84, 4 According to Champion (2:650), a cross was put opposite a soldier's name on parade (*montres*) when he was considered no longer fit for military service.

B85, 4 *En pris de Loyauté assise.* A difficult line. "Chosen for its loyalty value."

11 *pencarte.* Word with a variety of meanings throughout its history (modern "pancarte," sign, notice, placard). Daniel Poirion (*Le lexique de Charles d'Orléans dans les "ballades."* PRF 91, Geneva: Droz, 1967, 108) gives the meaning here as "un document qui . . . décrit les ports, les parages, les fonds et les marées." "Map" is obviously a suitable translation, even though, as Poiriot shows, it was not really a map in the modern sense.

B86 On Jacques, bâtard de la Trémoille, see Appendix 3: Index of medieval authors.

B88, 5 *percus.* "Pierced through and through," cf. "percus et exterminé" (Godefroy, 6:95) makes nonsense of the line, despite the poem's antithetical nature. Champion (1:172) reads "perclus," "paralysed," a mistaken reading according to Mühlethaler (711), but making better sense and more likely to be a deliberate correction, even though Champion does not record it as such.

B94 and R419 These two poems share a common theme and several expressions, suggesting the subject was of sufficient importance to Charles to have it represented in both the *ballades* and the *rondels*. Resemblances are such that the second, probably the *rondel*, cannot have been written without the first in mind. They share the following features:

(1) The first line: Escollier de Merencolie
(2) Des verges de Soussy batu (B94, 7, and R419, 2)
(3) A l'estude je suis venu (B94, 2, and R419, 3)
      Je suis a l'estude tenu (R419, 3)
(4) Es derreniers jours de ma vie (B94, refrain, and R419, 4)
(5) . . . moult fort m'y treuve esperdu (B94, 5)
      . . . me treuve tout esperdu (R419, 9)
(6) . . . j'ay mon temps mal despendu (B94, 25)
      Mon temps je pers et ay perdu (R419, 10)
(7) Fait l'ay par conseil de Follye (B94, 26)
      . . . rassoté en follye (R419, 11)

Melancholy personified appears in 54 of Charles's poems and is the principal subject in 25 of them. This emphasis may have been due in part to his temperament, but the circumstances of his life are enough to account for it. Now, in old age — *es derreniers jours de ma vie* — he imagines himself at school, but is bewildered (*esperdu*) saying he needs a straw (used as a pointer) to spell out the letters of learned works (*mondaine clergie*, B94, 3–4, literally "worldly knowledge, erudition"). On *mondain* Godefroy (10:168) specifies: "qui appartient à la vie du monde, par opposition à la vie religieuse." It appears, therefore, to be a confession of ignorance on all matters outside his own restricted circle. And why say he can neither read nor write (6)? Nowhere is there a hint of failing eyesight, though he did wear glasses in his later years. The remainder of the *ballade* shows this is a metaphorical way—characteristic of Charles—of saying that, in old age, he has become slow of wit and understanding. Being taken for a "donkeyman" (*asnyer*, l. 18, i.e., "fool, ass"), banished from good company, sunk in his *Nonchaloir* (17–20, i.e., "indifference," "sloth," see note to B7, 8 and to B10), this worries him, making him feel, as he puts it in allegorical fashion, "beaten by the rods of Worry" (7, and R421, 2). It will be up to somebody else to study in his place; he has left it too late (22–23). Both poems conclude by saying that he has wasted his time, and give the same reason: the influence on him of *Follye*. According to the *Songe en Complainte* (35–36), it was that particular counsellor who had kept him on the path of love ("l'amoureuse adresse"). So, he has wasted his time writing at such length on affairs of the heart, neglecting more serious subjects. Perhaps these regrets were real enough in old age, but in actual fact Charles was quite erudite, writing poetry as he did in French, Latin, and English and showing a knowledge of his mother's native tongue, Italian. In the speech he made at the duke of Alençon's trial (Champion, *Vie*, 532–48), he included over twenty Latin quotations from various sources, giving a translation for each one, evidently expecting that not all his audience would understand the Latin.

B97, 24 *faille. à la faille* is defined by Godefroy (3:699) as *en pure perte*, i.e., "to no avail," "in vain." According to Poirion, this does not fit the antithetical nature of the poem, which had its origin in the series with the initial line "Je meurs de soif auprès de la fontaine," but this is manifestly wrong, since the line can mean "I have been playing the whole year through, but to no avail." The game "quits or doubles," the sole meaning according to Poirion (*Lexique*, 79), may also be referred to in what is obviously a play on words.

B100 This *ballade* is attributed to Meschinot in BnF MS. fr. 9223 (ed. Raynaud, 107–8), and Champion follows Raynaud in attributing this lyric to him as well as 4 *rondels* (see note to R438). On Jean Meschinot, see Appendix 3: Index of medieval authors; see also note to R441.

B101 This is a very revealing poem. Who are these liars so resented by Charles that he would have them buried in the snows of Savoy? The reference, as Champion saw (*Vie*, 593–94), is to the Italians of Milan, who promised him support in reclaiming his dukedom of Milan inherited from his mother Valentina de

Visconti, yet prevaricated and did nothing to dislodge the usurper Sforza. In R187, particularly bothersome people are tax-gatherers—and the people of Milan (9). Charles's frustration and bitterness at the failure of his Italian campaign is also revealed later, in R272 (see note), a poem which gave rise to contributions by two others (see note to R393 and R394).

Jam nova The first of three contributions by Villon to Charles's manuscript (with B102 and B106), composed during a stay at Blois late in 1457 and early in 1458. All three are believed to be in Villon's own hand. Charles's daughter Marie d'Orléans, who is also the subject of B103 and B104, was born on 19 December 1457. The epigraph is a quotation from Virgil, *Eclogues*, IV:7: "Now a new-born child is sent down from high heaven." This is a particularly apt choice as an introduction to a poem on the birth of Charles's daughter Marie, the more so as it was looked upon at the time as a prophecy of the coming of the Virgin Mary and the Saviour. (Further information on these poems by Villon will be found in R-H, *Le Lais Villon*, 53–57.)

3 The lily was the emblem of the kings of France (see note to Intro., 167). Charles was the grandson of Charles V. His son, as yet unborn, was eventually to become Louis XII.

17 "Recovered" because it is the name of the Virgin Mary.

21 Clovis was king of the Franks 481–511 A.D. "Drawn from his right side" makes him the Adam of the royal dynasty, and Charles's daughter his direct descendant.

41–43 See Psalm 92:4.

50–51 There are several possible sources, none certain, according to R-H, 61.

57–61 See John 1:35–41.

71 See Luke 11:27.

78 Whether Charles did indeed save Villon from death or whether this is an exaggeration in this very fulsome adulation is not known for sure, but that the duke did receive Villon at his court and help him in some way is certain.

107–8 A well-known proverb according to R-H (62), who quote two passages as possible sources.

121–24 Names chosen as examples of supreme virtue (R-H, 64).

B102, 1 This first line ("Je meurs de soif auprés de la fontaine") is shared by 10 poems, 6 identified with their authors' names (Ballades 105, 108, 110, 111, 112, and 113), and 4 without (Ballades 102, 103, 107, 109). In addition, two begin with a similar line, "Je n'ay plus soif, tarie est la fontaine": B97 and B104. All of these, and the idea of juxtaposing contrasting and contradictory elements in each line, were inspired by Charles's B75, which begins "Je meurs de soif en couste la fontaine."

Thirteen of Charles's first lines were taken up in this way by other poets, the most frequently used of which, in addition to the *fontaine* poems, were "En la forest de Longue Actente" (11 poems: B81, R193, R194, R195, R196, R197, R244, R245, R246, R247, R251, and, as a ballade refrain line, B86) and "Jaulier des prisons de Pensee" (5 poems: R405, R406, R407, R408, and R411). Of the *fontaine* poems, the most frequently published is B103, by Villon, sometimes given the title "Ballade du Concours de Blois." In fact there is no indication that there ever was a competition as such, with this line or any other. The idea was to write variations on a theme originated by the duke, an idea which he no doubt encouraged. That there ever was a *concours* may be a rumour started by Champion (see *Vie*, 606).

B104, 8 "Between two waters, like a fish, I swim." *nager entre deux eaux* has the figurative meaning: *se ménager deux partis opposés* (*TLF*, 2:1299), "To take (equal) account of two opposing sides." The English equivalent would therefore be "to run with the hare and hunt with the hounds."

B105, 34 *les gaiges ravoir*. The various interpretations of this expression are summarised by R-H (68), who give the following meaning: "rentrer en possession des gages déposés," and view it as a joke, since, being penniless, Villon would have been incapable of redeeming his pledges. Possibly intended as a hint to the duke to redeem them for him.

B106 Fifteen of the poems in this collection are in macaronic verse, 12 mixing French and Latin, 3 French and Italian (R138, R272, and R393). All but 4 of the 15 (B106 [Villon], B143 [Fradet], R384 [Blosseville], and R393 [Damien]) are by Charles: B142, R131, R132, R135, R136, R137, R138, R139, R272, and R328, R383. On the 3 mixing French and Italian, see John Fox, "Glanures." In *Charles d'Orléans in England*, ed. Arn, 89–98.

12 *Ad ce mur!* R-H quotes several examples of this expression meaning: "Help!" (70–71). The origin is unknown.

B107, 23 Ogier the Dane was a mythical figure of medieval legend, akin, in some respects, to King Arthur. He is the national hero of Denmark.

B108 In this collection Montbeton records only one stanza of a lyric completed by Robertet, but four of his lyrics appear in BnF MS. fr. 9223 and six in BnF MS. nouv. acq. fr. 15771, of which three are common to both (Raynaud, xxvii–xxviii; Inglis, 47–48). On Montbeton and Robertet, see Appendix 3: Index of medieval authors.

B109, 25 *Complexion* was a term of rhetoric meaning a sentence which, to emphasize a particular term, both began and ended with it. *Incomplexif avant complexion* means the expression is missing from the beginning, hence the translation "having an end but no beginning," characteristic of the antithetical nature of the whole poem, based throughout on grammar and medieval rhetoric inherited from Latin. See note to B77, 8.

B110 (see also R388 and R394). On Villebresme, see Appendix 3: Index of medieval authors.

B111 On Caillau, see Appendix 3: Index of medieval authors.

B112 On Gilles des Ormes, see Appendix 3: Index of medieval authors.

B113 On Simonnet Caillau, see Appendix 3: Index of medieval authors.

Co3 The poet's *Balades de plusieurs propos* begin with B116, but starting with this *complainte* (followed by B113 and B114), we enter a world not much frequented by the God of Love. This *complainte* embodies the poet's feelings for his native land; the two *ballades* that follow it center on the duke's desire for peace.

29 *Montjoie.* Charles uses two of the three meanings of this word. Here it is the centuries-old battle-cry of the French crusading knights, believed to have originated in pilgrims' shouts of joy on first catching sight of their goal, in particular St. Denis and Jerusalem. The word was then applied to the piles of stones often surmounted by a cross, marking the many pilgrim routes of the Middle Ages, and from there came the meaning "heap," "pile," "abundance," which is Charles's second use in B124, 22 and R279, 5.

30–33 Three golden fleurs-de-lis on an azure background had been the coat-of-arms of the French kings since the 12th century (see note to Intro., 167 and *Jam nova*, 3). The oriflamme was the battle flag of the French kings, used for the last time by Louis XI in his war with the Burgundians in 1465, the year of Charles's death.

59 St. Louis was Louis IX (1215–1270), France's most renowned crusader king, who led the seventh and eighth crusades.

B115, 35–36 *la selle si vous blesse fort sur le dox.* Lit. "the saddle is hurting you very much on your back," i.e., you have a heavy burden to bear. The modern equivalent is "c'est là où le bât blesse," "that's where the shoe pinches." Cf. R12, 11.

B116 Just as the word "sonnet" was used in the early modern period, so was the word "balade" applicable to many verse forms, meaning in some cases nothing more than "lyric." The *Balades de plusieurs propos,* "lyrics on many subjects," contains both *ballades* and *complaintes.*

B116 and B117 As Jean de Garencières was killed at Agincourt, both of these poems predate 1415 (see note to Intro.), and are retained here by Charles under the heading *Balades de plusieurs propos,* along with poems written years later during his imprisonment, no doubt because they reminded him of happier times. Garencières (for whom see Appendix 3: Index of medieval authors) exercised a significant influence on Charles as a poet, and it is possible that the headings to both poems are in Charles's own hand. In B116, Charles teases Garencières whose healthy looks betray the unreality of his claims, in conventional mode, to be dying of love. B117 is a robust reply upbraiding this *enfant malicieux*—no doubt the young Charles—for philandering and thinking he can actually take the place of Cupid. Good fun, no doubt, in those pre-Agincourt days. (See Introduction, §6.)

B117, 34 *icellui,* like *cil* in B105, 23, was an archaic form by the fifteenth century.

B118 On May poems, see note to B17.

B121, 9, etc. "Encore est vive la souris" was a proverb. See Morawski, no. 638.

B123, 2 Jean, duc de Bourbon (1381–1434). There are two dukes of Bourbon named in Charles's manuscript. The reference here and in the following two *ballades* is to Jean I, duc de Bourbon, captured, like Charles, at Agincourt, and allowed to return several times to France in vain bids to secure the necessary ransom money. He died in London in 1434. For Jean II de Bourbon, see 3: Index of medieval authors.

> 25 Guillaume Cadier was the duc de Bourbon's secretary. For a lyric from his pen in praise of the duc d'Orléans, see Champion, ed., 2:603–4 (Champion, *Vie,* 621–22).

B124, On Bourbon, see previous note. 22 *Montjoye.* See note to Co3, 29.

B125, 2 *connins.* That Charles was not above using the occasional eroticism is shown by the two meanings here of *connins*: rabbit and female sex organ. The pun was not original, occurring already in the thirteenth-century *Roman de la Rose* (ed. F. Lecoy, 2:15110).

B126, 13 *escremie*. Modern French *escrime*, "fencing," no longer has the metaphorical sense it has here, and in R297, 11 of "to play tricks," again not an original use by Charles. Tobler defines this usage as *Fechten mit Worten*, "fencing with words" (3:994).

B127 Peace negotiations between England and France had been going on since 1436 when Charles was brought (closely guarded) to Calais in June 1439, in the hope that his presence would prove helpful, Philippe le Bon, duc de Bourgogne, who had already made his peace with Char.es VII of France and was as anxious as Charles d'Orléans to secure peace between the two kingdoms, was not far away, at St. Omer in the Pas-de-Calais. Little progress was made on this occasion, and Charles was returned to England in October, having received from Philippe a poem (B128) assuring him of his support. In B129 Charles's grateful thanks are directed towards the duke's wife Isabelle (28) as well as to the duke himself. In B130, Philippe declares there can be no peace until Charles is freed (19–22), and in B131 Charles reports from England that the king, Henry VI, looks favourably upon the idea of his temporary release to help the quest for peace — also to secure the necessary ransom money. In B135 — the last he was to write in captivity — only lack of the necessary funds prevents his release. He was freed at last in the autumn of 1440. Finally, in B136, Charles is back in France, but, relations between France and Burgundy being still cool, is pretending that he is hostile towards Burgundy and urges Philippe to keep their friendship well hidden. Charles translated into English one of these *ballades* from Burgundy, along with one of his own to Philippe (see note to B72, also Champion, *Vie*, 272–312; Arn, ed., *Fortunes Stabilnes*, 369–71).

B128 Philippe le Bon, duc de Bourgogne, is not otherwise known as a poet. Here and in B130 he responds to *ballades* addressed to him by the duc d'Orléans (who addressed 4 *ballades* to him: B126, B128, B134, and B135). See previous note.

B132, 3 Charles was forty-five years old in 1439, one year before his return to France.

> 11 *Trop seurement est rachassant*. A technical term referring to returning the ball in a game of "real tennis." Soussy, with Fortune's help, is putting Charles off his game, but Charles's good friend is Espoir, and it is only Soussy whom he fears.

> 18 *chasses*. Continuing the metaphor of the whole poem — a game of "real tennis" between Charles and Old Age — *chasses* here refers to the places where the

ball lands. Old Age will "mark" them (*merchera*, Modern French "marquera"), i.e., observe carefully where they land, to Charles's disadvantage.

22 *convenant*. "Agreement," "promise": if Bon Eur keeps the promise he made to me.

B133, 5 St. Martin's saint's day was 11 November, when the new wine was (and still is) ready, hence *le mal St. Martin* was drunkenness. See Glossary.

16 *loppin*. Lit. "a small amount." Still used in *un lopin de terre*, see Glossary. Charles's use of slang terms here and elsewhere shows he is by no means limited to courtly vocabulary and conventions.

B134, 15 *ce qui fait le ventre lever*. This shows, as in the preceding poem, that it is wrong to think of Charles as merely a poet restricted and restrained by courtly conventions, cf. R270, 6.

B135 and B136. *Beau frere*. lit. brother-in-law. On the Orléans-Bourgogne series, see note to B127.

B139, 29 *getoit*. According to Champion (ed., 2:653) this verb is related to the noun *getouers*, tokens of copper or lead used in calculations, hence the meaning here "calculated."

B142, 16 At the end of a complex and bloody story of rape and murder, recounted by Ovid in Book 6 of the *Metamorphoses*, Philomela (Philomena was an erroneous form common in Charles's day) was changed into a nightingale and her sister Procne into a swallow. The name Philomel is a poetic name for the nightingale.

B143 See previous note. See Introduction §6. This lyric is attributed to Fredet in the manuscript belonging to Marie de Clèves, Carpentras 375. On the macaronic lyrics, see note to B106.

Co4, 85 *Le débat du verre et du pot* is just one example of what was an extremely popular literary form in the Middle Ages (cf. B33), in this case evidently a debate between two equals, ending in stalemate.

96 See note to R416, 11.

Co5, 14 On Valentine's day, see Introduction, §6. On Fredet, see Appendix 3: Index of medieval authors.

Co6 See Introduction, §6. Nearly every verse ends with a proverb.

27 *se les couchez en despence*. *Coucher* with the sense "put down to," "attribute," also occurs in R239, 8. Here "if you put them down to expenses," i.e., accept them as inevitable.

63 *tenir par le doy*. "To hold on to, to hold firmly."

77 *sans reveiller le chat qui dort*. A proverbial expression common at the time, implying "without attracting undue attention."

100 *poys* is literally "weight" (modern "poids"). Here: "when I have weighed up these things," i.e., taken them into consideration.

Co7 See note to Co5 and Introduction, §6.

B144 For Charles's English poetry, see Arn, ed., *Fortunes Stabilnes*.

Ch1 From this point on, a note following each short lyric will indicate what the other portion of the page contains (if anything). There has been much critical discussion about the layout of the early *chançons* in this manuscript, a layout that was reproduced in two other manuscripts, both of them copies of the duke's English poetry (British Library MS. Harley 682 and the "Oxbridge" MS., a copy of Harley, for which see Arn, *Fortunes Stabilnes*, 106–9 and 119–23). Champion suggested, quite implausibly, that the space between the heading at the top of the page and the short lyric at the bottom was left for music, which was never added (an error repeated by a great many other scholars). Mary-Jo Arn has suggested that the spaces might have been intended for a series of miniatures (*Fortunes Stabilnes*, 108–9), on the model of some Machaut manuscripts (see also *The Poet's Notebook*, 77–84). Nancy Regalado has suggested that the blank spaces were a mark of the "libéralité qui manifeste la puissance et l'appartenance par la largesse" ("*En ce saint livre*," in *L'Hotellerie de Pensée*, ed. Michel Zink and Daniele Regnier-Bohler (Paris: Presses de l'Université de Paris-Sorbonne, 1995), 17). Finally, John Fox has suggested that putting the heading at the top of the page rather than immediately above the lyric was a way of reserving the space (though in the end it did not do so, for most of these spaces are filled with later lyrics). For note on May poems, see B17.

Ch9 In this lyric, the poet makes use of a double perspective, both addressing the lady in the second person and wishing he were someone else (who was actually close enough to his lady to see her), in the third.

Ch11 On May poems, see B17.

Ch40, 2 *la peneuse sepmaine*. Metaphorical: "enduring my torment."

Ch44, 2 See note to B36.

Ch50, 1 Medieval proverb in both French and English.

Ch55, 5 In the courtly tradition, *mesdisans* were the malicious people whose gossip threatened to expose lovers' secret affairs—still relevant, presumably.

Ch60 This poem seems out of place in a series devoted principally to the celebration of love. Disillusionment creeping in, perhaps? It appears to be all in the past: "when you have served Love as much as I have . . ." (12–13).

Ch63 This *chançon* appears to contain the germ of the idea for the "ballades de contradiction" (Ballades 75, 101–4, and 106, 12).

Ca1 Melancholy has taken the place of his lady's indifference as the chief source of Charles's complaints and is certainly less conventional, and more clearly personal.

Ca2 The counterpart to Ca1. Complaints to Melancholy are followed here by pleas to Hope.

R1 In this edition, the *rondel* form is distinguished from that of the *chançon* by the lack in the manuscript of a two-line refrain (whatever the scribal heading may say).

R2 and R193 On Charles de Nevers, see Appendix 3: Index of medieval authors.

R4, 1, 2 *herault, poursuivant.* From being an active follower of Love, Charles has become a mere herald concerned only with love and lovers in general. According to Galderisi (239), *poursuivant,* from the expression "poursuivant d'armes," can also mean a carrier of messages, although this hardly applies here, where the sense is clearly that, for Charles personally, love has lost all interest.

R5 *Cecile, Secile,* i.e., Sicily, referring to René, duc d'Anjou. See Appendix 3: Index of medieval authors.

R6 On St. Valentine's day, see Introduction, §6.

R8, 4 *reverdira leurs estomas.* Irony and metaphor are combined here. *Reverdir* literally means "to make green again," specially of springtime, cf. "toute chose reverdie [past participle] par les champs," (cp. R274, 3). Here, "rejuvenate," "reinvigorate," meaning of course the very opposite: the frost will numb their stomachs.

8–9 *Poulaines*, long narrow shoes with long points filled with padding, were high fashion in this period. Philippe le Bon was often depicted wearing them.

R9, 11 A unique example in Charles's poems of rhymes throughout on two syllables: *servy:desservy:serf vy:asservy; guerdonné:donné:habandonné:don né*. This dissyllabic rhyme distorts the usual meaning of *desservy*, "served." In the context it can only make sense as "deprived."

R10 On *Secile*, see note to R5.

R12, 1 The first line is a proverb, as is that of René d'Anjou's *rondel* which follows. Mühlethaler takes *vielle* as the musical instrument (401), despite recording another instance of the expression with *vieille*, not *vielle* (714). *Vielle* is a frequent spelling in the manuscript for *vieille* (e.g., "vielle rassoutie," B98, 25; "vielle rassottee," R276, 9; etc.) Hence "Every old woman . . ." Cf. B114, 35–36.

> 11 *Je sens ou mon pourpoint m'estraint.* A proverbial expression, lit. "I feel where my doublet is squeezing me," i.e., I know where the source of my trouble lies. The equivalent is "I know where my shoes are pinching." Modern French has "Je sens où le bât blesse." Cf. B115, 35–36.

R13 On *Secile*, see note to R5.

R14, 4 *Et que les fons vouler faisons.* Lit. "And make the bases fly," i.e., fully expose the bases of our arguments. Mühlethaler (403) suggests the expression is inspired by a hunting term "faire voler les faus" (falcons).

> 7 *billart.* Literally "billiard cue." Eroticism according to Champion, ed., 2:648 and Galderisi (158), cf. note to B125, 2. The ambiguity is retained in "And I have kept my end up very well."

> 8 *bons.* Godefroy (1:679) gives two meanings for this noun: "preuves," "dires," i.e., "proofs," "statements," which fit the context because the poem concerns a debate, hence: "it's a fine debate which contains two proofs" (i.e., sound arguments), but it can also mean "le plaisir dont on jouit avec une femme," and in view of the erotic undertones of *billart* and the subject under discussion, the ambiguity was doubtless intended.

R15 On *Secile*, see note to R5.

R16 One of the few *rondels* to which a date can be assigned. The truce referred to was agreed on 8 May 1444.

Ch64, 3 *pouoient*. See note to Intro., 164. From this point on, verse forms are sometimes mislabelled (see textual notes).

Ch70, 3 *Barres* (prisoner's base) was a game in which two sides played at catching members of the other side according to various rules.

Ch73 and Ch74 These two lyrics are anomalous in a number of ways. Besides being composed in English, they are copied together on the last leaf of a quire (BB) without heading. They are without any decoration, though the scribe has left space for the addition of decorative initials. Different in form from the English *rondels* (R360 through R365), they occur in an interesting part of the manuscript, surrounded by *rondels* and close to a group of bilingual *rondels*. Though the English term is "roundel" (see *Fortunes Stabilnes*, ed. Arn, 249–300), they match the form of the poet's early *chançons*, having two refrain lines at the midpoint of the lyric.

R21, 5 *aquilote*. "Petit oiseau de proie qu'on lançait sur le gibier" (Champion, ed., 2:647). Possibly a kestrel or small hawk. Godefroy (1:367) simply gives "oiseau de proie."

> 6 Old French *deduit* is usually an abstract noun meaning "distraction," "pleasure." A principal distraction for the nobility was hunting. The term "deduit de chasse" led to "deduit de chiens," "deduit d'oiseaux" (Huguet, 2:741). So *deduit* took on the meaning "hunt," as here. Beyond Charles's time it expanded further: "Equipage de chasse complet, avec veneurs, chiens, oiseaux etc." (*Grand Larousse*, 2:1174). *Sourdre*, normally intransitive (< *surgere*, to rise), is here transitive: "raised," i.e., started the hunt. *Remerchier* follows on from this, meaning "to mark" (i.e., find) the prey. All this is metaphorical. The hawk is Charles's memory, the prey the recollection it brings to mind, though the principal catch appears to have been "Hidden Hope," a reference, possibly, to some affair of the heart.

> 10 *peu* is first person singular, past historic, of *paistre*, "to feed," "to nourish."

R26, 4 *a la volee*. See note to Intro., 326–27. Very likely written about the same time as R27, clearly in a mood of depression, fed up with the Italians, the English, and anyone else he can think of.

R27, 6 The Mont Cenis is the Alpine peak and pass between Savoy and Piedmont in Italy. The poem may be a reference to Charles's campaign to reassert his claim to the dukedom of Milan (1447–1450). Writing about himself as he so often does, he habitually uses the first person, not the third. The reference may be to one of his ambassadors.

R28 and R29 On Estienne Le Gout, see Appendix 3: Index of medieval authors.

R30 On Jean, duc d'Alençon, see Appendix 3: Index of medieval authors.

1 *En la vigne jusqu'au peschier*, lit. "in the vine right up to the fishpond." Galderisi (273) quotes Cotgrave: "to step over head and eares into a vinetub," evidently one of the many picturesque French expressions down the ages for "drunk."

R31, 9–10. Godefroy lists two verbs *pigner* with different meanings: 1) *grincer, gémir en criant* (6: 156), "to howl" hence " the poor howling fellow" and 2) "to comb" (Modern French *peigner)*, which also had the extended meaning: *rosser, étriller* (Godefroy, 10:304) "to thrash" hence, l. 10, "given a sound thrashing." Littré, dating from the late nineteenth century, still lists *peigner* and *donner un coup de peigne à quelqu'un* as having the possible meaning *battre*, "to beat" (3:1029–30), nowadays archaic. The poem is therefore a clever pun on the two meanings of *pigner*.

R37, 5 Both Galderisi (227) and Mühlethaler (437) see *oblie* as a play on words: *pâtisserie/oubli*, but this is gratuitous as the following line indicates. There is no question of his presenting her with a *pâtisserie*. Mühlethaler (695) sees the same pun in R450, 2 but this means reading *oblie* as though it were plural. Here too it is an abstract noun: "forgetting," "oblivion."

R42 On Jehan Caillau, see Appendix 3: Index of medieval authors.

R46 On May poems, see note to B17.

R50, 6 *becz jaunes*. Here an abstract noun: "naïveté," "ignorance," "sottise" (see Huguet, 1:529, also *TLF*, 4:336). So the people who think they are so clever (but are not so in fact clearly implied) will have to answer for the practices resulting from their ignorance. The term became *béjaune* (now obsolete), defined as "jeune homme inexpérimenté" (*Grand Larousse*, 1:408), corresponding to English "greenhorn." Both Galderisi (158), and Mühlethaler (461) take the expression in this sense, but the reference throughout is specifically to these individuals who have too high an opinion of themselves, not to their offspring. (Plural *becz jaunes* offers no difficulty, cf. Modern French *sottises*.)

10–11 The legend of Melusine was written by Jean d'Arras in 1387. Charles had a copy in his library. Melusine was a normal woman, except for the unfortunate habit of sprouting a serpent's tail at weekends. She deceived all around her for many years until her husband found out, whereupon the rest of her became a serpent as well, and shot screaming through the window. The literal translation is "Melusine cannot lie about this, she knows them well by their faces." Not quite so literal: "Melusine realises the truth of this, having known such people," i.e., they were not so clever as to discover her secret.

R51, 10 *A lui je m'abutineray*. Not "partager un profit" as Champion says (2:647), followed by Mühlethaler (643). Godefroy (1:41) gives that as the meaning of the active verb (derived from *butin*, "booty"), but the reflexive verb is given as "s'abandonner à," "prendre part à," hence here lit. "I shall give myself up to Indifference," and the translation (with *butin* in mind): "I'll get my reward from Indifference." On May poems, see note to B17.

R52 On May poems, see note to B17.

6 *becz jaunes*.: "naïveté", "ignorance," "sottise" (see Huguet, 1:529, also TLF, 4:336). So the people who think they are so clever (but are not so clearly implied) will have to answer for the practices resulting from their ignorance. The term became *béjaune* (now obsolete), defined as "jeune homme inexpérimenté" (Grand Larousse,1:408), corresponding to English "greenhorn". Both Galderisi (1:158) and Mühlethaler (461) take the expression in this sense, but the reference throughout is specifically to these individuals who have too high an opinion of themselves, not to their offspring. (plural *becz jaunes* offers no difficulty, cf. Modern French *sottises*.

The legend of Melusine was written by Jean d'Arras in 1387. Charles had a copy in his library. Melusine was a normal woman, except for the unfortunate habit of sprouting a serpent's tail at weekends. She deceived all around her for many years until her husband found out, whereupon the rest of her became a serpent as well and shot screaming through the window. The literal translation is "Melusine cannot lie about this, she knows them well by their faces." Not quite so literal: "Melusine realises the truth of this, having known such people," i.e. they were not so clever as to discover her secret.

R55, 1 *De legier pleure a qui la lippe pent*. This proverb is recorded already some two hundred years earlier: "De ligier plore qui [=cui=a qui] la lippe pent" (No. 512 in Morawski, 19). It refers to a moody person easily moved to tears rather than an angry person as Galderisi says (212). Modern French still has "faire la lippe," "to sulk," "to be moody."

R59 The central refrain can be read with the first two lines of the poem or with the first line only, although that is the only one recorded by the scribe (see Note on the *Chançons* and *Rondels*). A consequential change in the punctuation may be needed read without the added refrain line.

R61 See note to R59.

R66 1 On this expression, see note to Intro., 272.

8 *corner prise.* A hunting expression, like "corner chiens," to call the hounds (with the hunting horn). Here, lit. "to blow the horn to announce that you have been captured," metaphorical like the entire poem.

R67, 9 *Chasteaux en Espagne*, with the meaning it still has, is found as early as the thirteenth century (Godefroy, 9:57). Why does Charles add *en France*? A reference, possibly, to dreams and ambitions of his which came to naught?

R70 On the central refrain, see note to R59.

R71, 5 Medieval proverb also used by Villon.

R74 On Valentine's day, see Introduction, §6.

R77, 11 Godefroy's definition of the meaning of "découvrir le pot aux roses" still applies today: "découvrir ce qu'on tenait mystérieusement caché" (10:386). The origin of the expression, according to him, is "le vase où l'on met le fard."

R79 See Introduction, §6: Note on *chançon* and *rondel* form. On the central refrain, see note to R59.

10 *traine ung festu* refers to the expression "Trainer un festu devant vieil chat," which Godefroy explains as "essayer de faire prendre le change, tendre un piège" (3:774), that is, attempt to play tricks on, to lay a trap for. Trail a piece of straw in front of a young cat, it will believe it is something alive and will jump at it. An old cat takes no notice. The sense of the passage is, "there's no point in trying to play tricks on me, I'm too old, I'm not taking any notice."

R80 On the central refrain, see note to R59. A close analysis of this poem, justifying the one-line central refrain instead of the two lines which Champion prints (2:328) is given by Defaux, "Charles d'Orléans ou la poétique du secret." *Romania* 93 (1972): 194–293.

R82 On Jean de Bourgogne, comte d'Étampes, see Appendix 3: Index of medieval authors.

R85, 5 *leurrer.* Eng. "lure," here "to tempt back," lit. "it will be in vain to . . . ." Hence "No point in shouting and tempting me back."

R89, 2 *gueines dorees*. According to Champion (*Poésies*, 2:654), these were gilded chains made by forgers of the period and sold as trinkets at pardons (see note below). The usual meaning of *gueines* (more commonly spelt "gaines") was "sheaths," "scabbards."

> 6 *livrees*. This is the same word, and has the same meaning, as English "livery": "The dispensing of food, provisions, or clothing to retainers or servants" (*OED*). Cp. Middle English *livere*, *MED* n.(3) 2.

> 8 *pardon*. A church festival at which indulgence (i.e., remission of sins) is granted.

R90, 1 This was a common saying at the time, still recorded by Littré (1:804) but absent from most recent dictionaries: "A qui vendez-vous vos coquilles, c'est-à-dire à qui vous jouez-vous? Prétendez-vous m'attraper?" Hence our translation. Scallop shells were a sort of badge of honor showing that one had taken part in the pilgrimage to Santiago de Compostela in northwestern Spain. A common fraud at the time was the sale of such shells supposedly coming from Compostela, but honest people rejected them with this saying, i.e., "Who do you take me for?"

> 2 *amans pelerins*. These pilgrim lovers were no more true lovers than those selling scallop shells were true pilgrims. In any case *pelerins* has the suggestion of "wandering" (< Latin *peregrinus*), hence "inconstant, unfaithful lovers."

> 4 French commentators are unanimous in seeing an eroticism here, no doubt rightly so as it fits the idea of "errant lovers."

> 11 Another regular expression in Charles's day. It is recorded in numbers of dictionaries, e.g., Littré (4:1426): "trousser son sac et ses quilles, s'en aller, décamper," hence, once more, our translation.

R92, 9 *baille lui bois*. Lit. "give him wood." According to Mühlethaler (539) this means "give him a lance," on occasions when jousts were fought with lances, whereas, according to Galderisi (156), it means "hit him with your lance," a cry of exhortation which seems more likely, since the two opponents would each have their lance at the outset.

R105, 10 *Karesme prenant*. This expression is still in some modern dictionaries. It refers to the days immediately preceding Lent, cf. Littré (1:488): "Les trois jours gras avant le mercredi des cendres, et particulièrement le mardi." Charles's days of good and carefree living are over, and now it is a matter of abstinence from all pleasure.

R109, 4 *donner le bont.* Taken by Champion (ed., 2:648) and Galderisi (160) as a tennis term, "return the ball." However, *bailler le bont* (*bailler* was a synonym of *donner* at the time, cf. R15, 11; R78, 11; etc.) is given by Godefroy as an expression meaning "planter là," "to abandon," while Lacurne de Sainte-Palaye adds more meanings: "Abandonner, se moquer, ou jouer un tour" (3:53), and one of his examples is with *donner*, not *bailler.* Hence "make fun of them."

R112, 11 *Qui de si finete me hourde.* Galderisi (204), following Godefroy (4:511), translates *hourder* as "garnir, charger," which seems too mild in this context. Champion (ed., 2:654) gives the more vigorous "flanquer," far more suitable, hence "Who lands me with such a sly creature."

R113, 10 *Fayete* and *Gouffier* are assumed to be the names of doctors, whether real or fictional is not known. *Villequier* too appears to be unknown. For Bourbon see Appendix 3: Index of medieval authors.

R114 For Clermondois see Appendix 3: Index of medieval authors. The count of Clermont was betrothed to Jeanne de France, daughter of Charles VII, in 1446, ten years before he was to succeed to the title duke of Bourbon. At the time she was eleven years old. The marriage eventually took place in 1452, hence the need for patience. Promised a massive dowry by her father, she was, as Charles calls her, "la riche" (see Champion, *Vie*, 618 n.).

R115, 6 *au plus savoir* was evidently a court game involving deception, pretending to know more than one did in fact. *Au plus sapere* in R272, 4, is an Italianized form of the term.

R118, 3 *baster aus corneilles.* Godefroy gives two examples of this expression with the translation "guetter" (1:594). This does not fit the context here, since it is clearly a matter of wives outwitting their husbands—a common enough theme at the time. Champion (ed., 2:648), followed by Galderisi (157), translates "envoyer promener," "to send packing," the same meaning as "l'erbe paistre," which still exists in "envoyer paître." The meaning is clearly different in R359, 6, where Mühlethaler (413) gives the expression "bayer aux corneilles," "to gape." See also R357, 6.

R123, 8 On the central refrain, see note to R59.

R124 On the central refrain, see note to R59.

R128 St. Valentine's Day and the first day of Lent coincided in 1453.

R130, 1 *Baillez lui la massue.* Nowadays meaning only "club," "bludgeon," in Charles's time *massue* meant also "fool's bauble."

R131, 1 *Ubi supra 5 annos* is an expression recorded by J. F. Niermeyer, *Mediae Latinitatis lexicon minus* (Leiden: Brill, 1976), s.v. *supra*, which he translates as French "il y a" (5 ans), and English "ago" (5 years ago). In this poem Charles is starting to complain about certain misdemeanors (*tours cornulz*), but then breaks off, saying, in effect, there's no point in it now (*non est cura*). Certainly he had much to resent in his past life, but, as so often, we cannot know his exact thoughts. Since he does not get as far as specifying a number of years, our translation is "Some time ago . . . Let us say no more about that . . ."

R132, 1 *Noli me tangere* are the words spoken by Christ to Mary Magdalene according to John 20:17.

R136, 11 *corda*, more properly *chorda*, is a Latin word of several meanings, one of which was "string of musical instrument," hence "lyre" (see Quicherat, *Thesaurus*, 211). The extended meaning here appears to be "emotions evoked by the music of a lyre," hence "feelings."

R138, 5 *jojo. Faire joujou*, "to play" is still in use referring to small children. For a full commentary on this poem see Fox, "Glanures," 89–91.

11 *gnogno.* The original French word, *gnognon*, has been Italianized by Charles to fit the rhyme. See Fox, "Glanures," 90.

R143 On Fredet, see Appendix 3: Index of medieval authors.

R146 On May poems, see note to B17.

R147 On May poems, see note to B17.

R151, 9 The expression *pois au veau* has caused difficulty. Champion (2:658) translates and comments "gros pois vert. Il y a sans doute une plaisanterie érotique." Galderisi (238) refers to Champion, but prefers a definition of the term given in *FEW*, "gens sans courage" without revealing how he would fit it into the context, introduced as the expression is by "ont," not "sont." Mühlethaler (459) translates "gros pois verts" and leaves it at that. A close look at the poem, and one other where the expression *pois au veau* is also used, can solve the problem. Line 2, "En ce temps nouveau" shows the poem is set in spring, the traditional time for the awakening of love, cf. "Amours et la saison nouvelle" (R95, 4). Charles, however, is quite indifferent (l. 4), and prefers to stay quiet in his "old skin." Numbers of his later poems tell of his loss of all interest in love, and even make fun of young lovers, who need their urine examined (R128, 2), so he says.

Turning now to poem R229, by Simonnet Caillau. Caillau tells us that, to be cured of the torments of love about which Fredet has been complaining in the preceding poem ("les grans dolours / Que seuffre pour ma tant amee . . .," R228, 4–5), it is necessary to keep away from "Esgrun de Dueil" (2), i.e., "bitter herbs of Grief" and "Les poix au veau te sont contraires" (3), i.e., "Peas with veal are bad for you" when "Les fleurs de plaisant viaire" (4), i.e., "flowers with pleasant faces," are boiled up in it—a typical medieval mish-mash, a more than usually substantial elixir of love, an aphrodisiac that would at least have met with the strong approval of Charles's contemporary François Villon, who complained that a famished belly was no good for love-making (*Le Testament*, 195). So it appears, then, that the main ingredients for this love potion were peas with veal. Accordingly, the "many" (this was the meaning of "plusieurs" in Charles's day) referred to in the poem who have "peas with veal" have the wherewithal for love-making, and no doubt they are younger than Charles, old as he tells us he is. It is springtime, young people are making love, but the poet is beyond it and really could not care less, hence our translation.

R153 The first line reads *Sil me pleust bien*, although initial *S* has been blotted out and can only just be deciphered. At its first repetition in line 7, *Sil* has given way to *Il* but has been restored in the last line of the poem. *Sil* has been corrected to *Il* in our edition for the following reasons: *sil* (more commonly *cil*) had become archaic by the late fifteenth century, having been replaced by *celui*. Nowhere else does Charles use *cil*, whereas *celui* he used many times. The scribes on the other hand, used to copying earlier texts as well as more recent ones, must have been familiar with *cil* and are no doubt responsible for its appearance here, though they reverted to Charles's reading in line 7. The Carpentras manuscript, a faithful copy of Charles's original text, reads *Il me pleust bien* on each occasion. The meaning is much the same, *Sil*, literally: "This man" while *Il* is quite simply "He."

R156, 1 Mühlethaler (468) reads "Hons, y fiez vous . . ." and comments *"Hons: Pierre Champion corrige en vous."* So, in fact, does the Carpentras manuscript. *Hons* was an archaic form in Charles's day, not used by him, though no doubt familiar still to the scribes of the time. Mistakes in initial letterings are frequent, and the word ends in *-ous* rather than *-ons*.

R160 On the central refrain, see note to R59.

R161, 5 This proverbial expression is no longer in current use. It is a metaphorical way of saying "with something agreeable you have to accept something disagreeable," i.e., things don't always go entirely your way. Modern French has "Il faut manger des vertes et des pas mûres" (you have to swallow insults).

R169 The first line echoes the second line of Villon's *Testament*. The poem is possibly intended as a reference to Villon, who was certainly known personally to

Charles. He is the author of three poems in the manuscript: *Jam nova*, B102, and B106 (four if one counts separately the *ballade* embedded in *Jam nova*).

R172 Mühlethaler (500–1) reads the poem interrogatively: "Qu'en faisons nous / De telles manieres . . .?" (How do we spend our time?). The emphasis being on fun and games, we have sided with Champion (2:407).

R173, R174 We have switched the manuscript order of these two lyrics, since the latter clearly responds to the former. On Clermondois, see Appendix 3: Index of medieval authors.

R180, 11 *prune*. Here "annoyance, tribulation." *Prune* is no doubt the implied noun in modern "avaler des vertes et des pas mûres," to swallow insults. "Pour des prunes" in Modern French means "to no purpose, for nothing." cf. note on R161, 5.

R181 On Clermont, see Appendix 3: Index of medieval authors.

R187, 1 *hanis*. The modern verb is "hennir," lit. "I don't neigh for any other oats except my return to Blois," i.e., all I want is to return to Blois. In this line Charles is a horse, whereas in the preceding poem he is a bird flying high in the sky.

6 *vins des Grois*. This was a local wine, Les Grois being in the Loir-et-Cher.

9 *generaulx et Millenois*. *Generaulx* were tax collectors, obviously no more popular then than now. *Millenois*, the people of Milan, is a reference to Charles's failed campaign in Northern Italy (see Champion, *Vie*, 358–79), so dating the poem to post 1450. On *jubilé*, see note to B72.

R193 On Nevers, see Appendix 3: Index of medieval authors. Champion omitted this *rondel* from his edition inadvertently (it is listed in his index of first lines).

R194 *Mgr.* The scribes' abbreviation for *Monseigneur* is retained in headings for layout purposes.

R195 and R242 On Madame d'Orléans (Marie de Clèves) see Appendix 3: Index of medieval authors.

R196 Charles replies to this poem by Fredet in R197.

R197, 8 *"vestu de vostre couleur,"* i.e., dressed in the duke's livery.

R201 This lyric can also be found in BnF MS. fr. 9223, where it is ascribed to Fredet (see Raynaud, xvii and 35–36). In this MS. it is unascribed.

R204, 1 On *l'Observance,* see note to B77, 8.

R210 On Jean d'Estouteville, see Appendix 3: Index of medieval authors.

R212 On Clermont, see Appendix 3: Index of medieval authors.

R214, 1, 7, 12 This is a modernization of a much older proverb: "Endementres que li fers est chauz le doit len batre" (Morawski, no. 645), cf. "strike while the iron's hot." On St. Valentine's day, see Introduction, §6.

R215 On St. Valentine's day, see Introduction, §6.

14 On *servir Amours,* see note to Intro., 326–327.

R217 On Daniel du Solier, see Appendix 3: Index of medieval authors.

R218 On Olivier de La Marche, see Appendix 3: Index of medieval authors.

2 On *l'Observance,* see note to B77, 8.

R219 On Vaillant, see Appendix 3: Index of medieval authors. 1 On *l'Observance,* see note to B77, 8.

R220 On George Chastellain, see Appendix 3: Index of medieval authors.

1 On *l'Observance,* see note to B77, 8.

R221 On Vaillant, see Appendix 3: Index of medieval authors.

1 *filé.* Nets were used for catching birds, hence the meaning here: "trap." The reference is interesting, the "trap" is apparently being married and not managing to have a mistress, prevented, perhaps, by a domineering wife from doing so, a situation which, according to Vaillant (l. 2), suits some men, but not him. "Dame" here is evidently "wife." In Charles's own poems it is often not clear if the word is referring to his wife, or to some lady-love, or is simply the usual courtly convention referring to no particular individual. There is an echo in Vaillant's poem of the contemporary *Quinze joyes de mariage,* in which each of the fifteen "joys" of the married man ends with the refrain "Or est en la nasse ou a tousjours voulu estre, et finira miserablement ses jours" (Now he's in the trap where he always wanted to be, and he'll finish his days in misery).

8 *bec affilé.* Sharp-tongued woman, cf. the refrain of one of Villon's *ballades: Il n'est bon bec que de Paris.*

R223, 8 Bourges was the seat of the king's court at this point.

R224 On Bouciquault, see Appendix 3: Index of medieval authors.

> 2 *creance.* A legal term still in use, it is an authorization. See Intro., l. 14: *lettre de creance,* where the authorization is to transfer guardianship from Enfance to Jeunesse.

> 3 On *l'Observance,* see note to B77, 8.

R225, 6 On *l'Observance,* see note to B77, 8. On Bouciquault, see Appendix 3: Index of medieval authors.

R226 On *l'Observance,* see note to B77, 8. On the author, see note to R224.

> 2 *meffait.* Misdeed, wrongdoing. The reference is to the preceding poem, where the only wrongdoing is hypocrisy, hence our translation.

R227, 6 On *l'Observance,* see note to B77, 8. On the central refrain, see note to R61.

R228 On Fredet, see Appendix 3: Index of medieval authors.

R229 On S. Caillau, see Appendix 3: Index of medieval authors.

> 3 *Les poix au veau.* See Glossary and note to R151.

R231 On Lorraine, see Appendix 3: Index of medieval authors.

R232, 3–4 *Ancollie* (aquilegia) recalls melancholy, while *Soussie* (marigold) recalls *souci* (care, worry). *Desplaisir* is apparently the allegorical vessel in which all the ingredients are mixed.

> 7 *poire d'Angoisse.* A village in the Dordogne whose very name has given the expression the meaning of "bitter fruit." In the fifteenth century it designated an instrument of torture placed in the mouth (see R-H, 2:111).

R236, 1 *Chose qui plaist est a demi vendue* is an old proverb recorded in Morawski (no. 392).

R238, R 239, R242, R243, 1 *l'abit le moine ne fait pas* This proverb has a long history, born of the custom of dressing in religious habit before (or sometimes without) making the profession that would constitute entry into a full religious life (see, e.g., Giles Constable, ed., *Three Treatises from Bec on the Nature of Monastic*

Life, trans. Bernard S. Smith. Medieval Academy books 109. Toronto: Toronto University Press, for the Medieval Academy of America, 2008, p. 24) Morawski records a version of the proverb: "Li abis ne fait pas le religious" (no. 1053). "L'habit ne fait pas le moine" is still a very well known French proverb. Cf. the modern English proverb, "clothes make the man," of which this is the opposite: appearances are deceptive.

R239, 2 *l'ouvrier se congnoist a l'ouvrage.* Morawski has nothing for the proverb, which survives to today (cf. modern English: "the workman is known by his tools").

R240 *De fol juge briefve sentence* is an expression that still exists, recorded by Larousse thus : De fou juge courte sentence, "L'ignorance de celui qui décide le rend trenchant et bref." In other words, "an ignorant arbitrator delivers a peremptory judgment."

R241, 8–9 In medieval French, verbs with multiple subjects normally agree in number with the noun closest to them, hence, here, *vient.*

R242 On Madame d'Orléans, see Appendix 3: Index of medieval authors.

R243 On Guyot Pot, see Appendix 3: Index of medieval authors.

R244 On Philippe Pot, see Appendix 3: Index of medieval authors.

R245 On Anthoyne de Lussay, see Appendix 3: Index of medieval authors.

R246 On Guiot Pot, see Appendix 3: Index of medieval authors.

R247 On Gilles, see Appendix 3: Index of medieval authors.

R249 On Fredet, see Appendix 3: Index of medieval authors.

R251 On Trimoille, see Appendix 3: Index of medieval authors.

> 6 *haye.* This means "wood" according to Champion (2:654), but nowhere is the word attested with that meaning. The proper meaning, as in Modern French, is "hedge." No doubt hedges were useful as windbreaks for tents, cf. this quotation given by Littré (2:1970): "Tout le monde estoit logé à l'estoille, et campoit à la haye, à faulte de trouver villages."

R252 On Le cadet d'Albret, see Appendix 3: Index of medieval authors.

R254 On Ormes, see Appendix 3: Index of medieval authors.

6–7 *On leur / Taille la broche sans couleur*: Champion (2:648) quotes a previous editor's suggestion that the reference is to "le bâton blanc qu'on donnait aux soldats renvoyés." This is quite certainly wrong, since "tailler [or couper, or rogner] la broche à quelque chose [or à quelqu'un]" was a regular expression. Godefroy (8:380) defines it as "couper court à une affaire," and Littré (1:424) as "empêcher qu'elle ne continue." *Couleur* is frequently found with the meaning "prétexte, ombre, apparence" (Godefroy, 9:216), so the meaning here is "(Once they have served) they are cast aside without any excuse."

R255 On Philippe de Boulainvillier, see Appendix 3: Index of medieval authors.

7 *Il ne faut pas clocher devant boiteux* is not recorded in Morawski, but has survived in modern French, explained as "Il ne faut rien faire devant les gens qui puisse leur rappeler un défaut naturel ou un souvenir fâcheux" (*Grand Larousse*).

R256 On Clermont, see Appendix 3: Index of medieval authors.

R257, 10 "De haulte lisse bonne ouvriere" was evidently a proverb, but does not appear to have been recorded elsewhere. *Haute-lice* contrasted with *basse-lice*. In the former, work on the tapestry, usually a large one, was done vertically, whereas in the latter the loom was placed horizontally. *Haute-lice* involved the more difficult work, hence the proverb.

R259, 9 The last letters of *conseilliez* have been scratched out, leaving the line a syllable short. The following word, *premier*, is written in a cramped hand, and can easily be misread as *prennez*. Whoever was responsible for the erasure had read "Conseilliez prennez entre vous," hence his correction to what he believed should have been "Conseil prennez entre vous," the *lectio facilior*, since adverbial *premier* in the original ("firstly" rather than "first") was rare though it does occur elsewhere in the manuscript. The Carpentras manuscript reads "Conseilliez premier entre vous."

R262 On le cadet d'Alebret, see Appendix 3: Index of medieval authors.

R263 On St. Valentine's day, see Introduction, §6.

2 *Bien et beau Karesme s'en va*. Lit. "Well and good, Lent (i.e., fasting) is on its way out." This was a game. Each day of Lent the first person to utter these words won whatever prize had been agreed upon (see Galderisi, 208).

5 *jouer a tintin*. The usual meaning of *tintinnare* was "noise," "racket," and that is how Champion takes it (2:660), but Galderisi (265) sees it as some

sort of game in which the loser has to give a pledge to the winner. (His reference is to *FEW*, s.v. *tintinnare*).

R266 On Benoit Damien, see Appendix 3: Index of medieval authors.

R269 On Benoit Damien, see previous note.

R270 Madame d'Angoulême is Marguerite de Rohan, wife of Charles's brother Jean d'Angoulême. Vaillant's signature survives in her copy of a work by Alain Chartier (BnF MS. fr. 2230) (Champion, *Histoire poétique*, 378–83).

6 see note to Co5, 15. On St. Valentine's day, see Introduction, §6.

R271 and R407 On T(h)ignonville, see Appendix 3: Index of medieval authors. On St. Valentine's day see Introduction, §6.

R272 On macaronic verse, see note to B106. The two languages mixed are usually French and Latin in Charles's case, but there is a special reason here for the second language being Italian. The poem is a bitter comment on the failure of his Italian campaign (1448–1450) to reclaim lands and title (duke of Milan) in northern Italy inherited through his mother Valentina Visconti. Contact had been lost as a result of Charles's quarter of a century imprisonment in England. The poem refers to the long-drawn-out and ultimately fruitless negotiations with the Italians. Line 1 *fenoches* (Italian *finocchio*) means "useless talk," while *nox buze*, lit. "empty nut," means much the same, "something of no value," "waste of time." For a full account of this poem see Fox, "Glanures," 93–96 (see also note to B101).

R273 On May poems, see note to B17.

R293 On S. Caillau see Appendix 3: Index of medieval authors.

R294 *Rondels* 366 and 372 share the same first line.

R295 On François Faret, see Appendix 3: Index of medieval authors.

R296 On Benoist Damien, see Appendix 3: Index of medieval authors.

R297 On Monseigneur de Beaujeu, see Appendix 3: Index of medieval authors. See also note to R255.

R305, 8 *paons*. The "voeu du paon" (lit. "peacock vow") is frequently referred to in medieval French romance and forms the title of one work: *Les Voeux du Paon*. The peacock was represented as the "noble oiseau," served up at table as the "viande des preux," a dish fit for knights, who each made a solemn vow on receiving his portion: to take part in a pilgrimage, crusade, etc. The vow had a special wording: "Je voue à Dieu, à la Vierge Marie, aux dames et au paon."

R309, 5 *almandé*. This word is found in no other text and is all the stranger in that pre-consonantal -*l*- had long since vocalised to -*u*-, cf. *aumosne*, B23, 19; *aumosnier* R201, 2; *autre* Intro., 394; etc. However, it may be intended as a compound of *mander*, since the first meaning of that word is "ordonner" (Godefroy, 5:139), which fits the context in the sense of "ordered," i.e., "conscripted," "against my will."

R311 Champion notes that Charles paid visits to Savonnières in August 1454, June 1457, June 1458, and July 1459 (590).

R313 On the central refrain, see note to R59.

R315 On Fraigne, see Appendix 3: Index of medieval authors.

R320 For May poems, see note to B17.

R325, 10 *maistre sebelin regnart*. Lit. "master sable fox," i.e., wearing a sable coat (Champion, 2:659; Galderisi, 256), that is, pretending to be something other, and better, than what he is (a sable coat is mentioned already in the 11th-century *Chançon de Roland*), hence "deceiving," and so the usual characteristic (attributed to the fox) of "sly," "cunning."

R335, 11 *Ainsi que fet qui met son eur en dez*. Lit. "like the man who puts his good fortune in dice," i.e., who gambles away his good fortune.

R337 Unusually, the central refrain here cannot be of two lines. It has to be either of one line only, the first, or the first three. See Introduction, §6: Note on the Chançons and Rondels.

R340 On the central refrain, see note to R59.

R343 On Gilles des Ourmes, see Appendix 3: Index of medieval authors.

R344 On Boulainvillier, see Appendix 3: Index of medieval authors.

R351 This poem is a *tour de force* in its restriction of all rhymes to the same two syllables: *passé(es)*.

R357, 6 For the expression *baster aux corneilles*, see note to R118, 3.

R359 On Bourbon, see Appendix 3: Index of medieval authors.

R360–R365 These English *rondels* are very difficult to place in the context of the whole collection. It has been argued elsewhere (Arn, *The Poet's Notebook*) that they may have been composed much earlier than they were copied (see note to R363, below) and so could be read immediately after the final two *chançons* (also in English). In this edition, however, we have printed them among the final (undecorated) *rondels*.

R360 On May poems, see note to B17. For Charles d'Orléans's English poetry, see Arn, ed., *Fortunes Stabilnes*.

R363 The name Anne Molins is spelt out in an acrostic. It has given rise to much speculation; see Eleanor Prescott Hammond, "Charles of Orléans and Anne Molyneux," *Modern Philology* 22 (1924–1925), 215–16. The reference might be to Anne Moleyns, first cousin of Alice Chaucer, the duchess of Suffolk, granddaughter of the poet. Charles was in the hands of the duke of Suffolk from 1433 to 1436. Adam Molyns, who may have been her father, was in the entourage of the duke (at that point, marquis) of Suffolk when they stopped at Blois in 1444, while escorting Margaret d'Anjou to England to marry the king.

R366 *Rondels* 294 and 372 share the same first line.

R369 On Lorraine, see Appendix 3: Index of medieval authors.

R369, 6 *pie*. There were two such words in Medieval French: (1) *la pie*, "the act of drinking" (related words were *pion*, "drinker," and *pier*, "to drink"), (2) *la pie*, "the magpie," as in Modern French. This identity led to certain popular expressions: *jucher la pie*, lit. "to put the magpie on its perch," i.e., "to sleep off one's wine," and *croquer la pie*, lit. "to crunch the magpie," another play on words, meaning "to drink" (see R-H, 2:183) Hence, here, *le desduit de la pie*, which could be understood as "the magpie's delight," in reality "the delight of drinking."

R372 *Rondels* 296 and 368 share the same first line.

R375 On Jehan Caillau, see Appendix 3: Index of medieval authors.

R377 l. 4 *karesme prenant*: see note to R105.

R379 On Bourbon/Clermont, see Appendix 3: Index of medieval authors.

R382 On Le Senechal, see Appendix 3: Index of medieval authors. In this poem the speaker pretends to be a priest hearing a girl's confession. He urges her not to spurn the advances of her loyal lover. In the next poem Charles continues the charade, pretending to be the girl confessing her arrogance and promising to repent. Then, in R384, Blosseville concludes the game by taking up the role of the confessor, absolving her on condition that she mend her ways.

R384 On Blosseville, see Appendix 3: Index of medieval authors. See also note to R382.

R385 On Bourbon, see Appendix 3: Index of medieval authors.

R388, 1 On Villebresme, see Appendix 3: Index of medieval authors. Atropos was one of the three Parcae, or Fates, in classical mythology. Clotho held the distaff, Lachesis spun the thread of life, Atropos cut it at life's end. Dyopee's life being cut short by Atropos is referred to a second time by Villebresme: "Tost print jadis Atropos Dyopee" (see Champion, 2:563). There is, however, no such name in classical mythology. The reference is probably to Dryope, whose beauty, and tragic life are described in Ovid's *Metamorphoses*, 9.330–393. On other Ovidian references, see note to B142.

> 5 Demophon was a legendary king of Athens. Phillis, daughter of the king of Thrace, fell in love with him and hanged herself when he abandoned her. Rhodope was a very rich and famous courtesan, subject of a number of legends.

> 8 Boreas was the mythological personification of the north wind; Zephirus, of the west wind.

> 14 Told by Ovid in the *Metamorphoses*, the story of Pyramus and Thisbe became very well known in the Middle Ages. Thinking that Thisbé had been killed by a lion, Pyramus fell on his sword.

R391 On Fraigne, see Appendix 3: Index of medieval authors.

R393, R394 The first line of R393 is that of Charles's French/Italian macaronic poem R272 (see note) complaining about the duplicity of his erstwhile subjects in Milan and the long-drawn-out but ultimately fruitless negotiations for his reclaiming his title, duc de Milan. It was not Charles's intention to criticize Italians in general—his mother was Italian after all. Damien (see note to R66) returns to this subject in a similarly macaronic poem, with even more Italian expressions than the duke had used. The basic message is this: in the face of this empty talk you have encountered (Charles's and Damien's first line) there is no need for you to mean what you say. Do one thing, but say another, because that is what they are all doing. In R394, Villebresme, who represented Charles on more than one occasion in Italy (see note to B110), expresses his utter disillusionment with *fenouches*, that is, endless Italian talk getting nowhere, and his consequent intention to retire altogether from public life (on these 3 macaronic *rondeaux* see Fox, "Glanures").

R394 On Villebresme, see Appendix 3: Index of medieval authors.

> 11 *faire le louche*, to look the other way, was used by Deschamps, *Oeuvres*, ed. Raynaud, 150, 4554, hence the meaning: Men seeing (wrongdoing) clearly (but) looking the other way. The failure of Charles's Italian campaign is reflected in this poem, where what Champion calls "la duplicité italienne" (*Vie*, 598) causes Villebresme to declare his wish to retire altogether from public life. That he was a man of considerable erudition, in addition to his ability as a poet, is shown by R388, and even more by a poem found in Marie's MS. (Bibl. de Carpentras 375, fol. 76r) and in BnF MS. fr. 1104, fol. 38v, that begins *Tost fut Priant puissant roy couronné* (see Champion, 2:563).

> 14 *souches*. Literally "tree stumps." Used metaphorically by Machaut: "j'estoie comme une souche delez ma dame" (Godefroy, 9: 484). Here, possibly, "nincompoops."

R395 On Bourbon, see Appendix 3: Index of medieval authors.

R402 On May poems, see Appendix 3: Index of medieval authors.

R406 On S. Caillou, see Appendix 3: Index of medieval authors.

R407 On Thignonville, see Appendix 3: Index of medieval authors.

R408 On des Ourmes, see Appendix 3: Index of medieval authors. Medieval prisons were unlike modern ones. Prisoners usually paid (generally a small amount) for their food and lodging there and were often allowed to leave the prison during the day in order to earn or beg the money to pay for them. At the other end of the social scale, the wealthy could negotiate all sorts of privileges, including better food and accommodation. See the following two *rondels* on the same theme.

R410 On Damien, see Appendix 3: Index of medieval authors.

R411 On H. le Voys, see Appendix 3: Index of medieval authors.

R412, 10 According to medieval monks there were no fewer than twelve sibyls, or prophetesses. Mühlethaler (671, q.v.) identifies this one with the Sibyl of Norcia.

R415, 1 *Baude* is usually assumed to be the name of a dog belonging to the duke: "nom d'un chien de Charles d'Orléans" (Champion, 2:610), though in his text the word is printed with a small b. "Répondait au nom de Baude un chien de chasse de Charles d'Orléans" (Gros, *Charles d'Orléans*, 411); "nom de chien" (Mühlethaler, 673). Galderisi gives two meanings "nom propre d'un chien de Charles, mais aussi le nom d'une race de chiens . . ." (157). This appears, however, not to be the whole truth. In addition to Charles's use of the word, Godefroy lists three others, in each of which Baude is associated with the verb *buissonner* and has the appearance of a name:

> Ainsi que Baude buissonnait . . .
> Adonc Baude buissonnera . . .
> Baude n'a tant sceu buissonner . . .

Baude appears, therefore, to have been used as a kind of generic name applied to this type of hunting dog: "Baud" is still in most dictionaries as a hound "propre à la chasse" (*TLF*, 5:294). The meaning would be lost on modern readers, hence our translation: Leave the hound to his hunting, This old dog is taking a rest . . . Charles, likewise a prisoner of "Vieillesse," obviously has much sympathy for the "vieil briquet." They are two of a kind.

R416 On Le Voys, see Appendix 3: Index of medieval authors.

R419 On the similarities between the two lyrics, see note to B93.

11 Up hill and down dale, i.e., utterly and completely See also C04, 96.

R420 On Le Voys, see Appendix 3: Index of medieval authors.

R425, 5 *barriere*. "a low fence running down the centre of the lists" (*OED*).

R426, 4 *faulx bourdon*. The first recorded use of this expression, corrupted to *faburden* in English, "one of the early systems of harmonizing a given portion of plainsong" (*OED*); cf. *MED* s.v. *faburdoun*. The correct translation would accordingly be "faburden of unhappiness," but since this would be obscure at best, we have introduced a new, but parallel meaning, in "burden of unhappiness," this having two meanings: "burden" in the sense of "refrain," since unhappiness was indeed a recurring theme with the older Charles, also in the sense of "load," "weight," which unhappiness certainly was for Charles, along with Care, Melancholy, etc. R427 On the identity of *Le grant seneschal,* see Appendix 3: Index of medieval authors. This *rondel* is not found in parallel collections.

R429 On Fraigne, see Appendix 3: Index of medieval authors.

R430 Champion attributes this lyric to Fraigne and notes "Cf. Lunettes des Princes" (2:593). See note to R315.

R431 On Fraigne, see Appendix 3: Index of medieval authors.

R433, 1 Daedalus was a legendary Greek character, father of Icarus and inventor of the Cretan labyrinth for the Minotaur (cf. Modern French "le dédale," "maze").

> 8 Tantalus was the son of Zeus in Greek mythology, punished for giving to mortals the secrets of the gods. Plunged up to his chin in a river of Hades with fruit hanging over his head just out of reach and the water receding every time he tried to drink, he was not a particularly happy individual (cf. ModE "to tantalize").

R434, R435, R436 On Anthoine de Cuise, see Appendix 3: Index of medieval authors.

R438 Pierre Champion tentatively ascribes this *rondel* and the three that follow (R439, R440, R441) to Jean Meschinot (see note to B100). He remarks that they are all transcribed in the same hand but that it is not the author's. He does not explain his attribution of them to Meschinot in his edition (593, note to CCCCXVI). He writes that "ces pièces [from the pen of the "rude Breton"] sont à écarter impitoyablement de l'œuvre de Charles d'Orléans" (*Vie*, 633–34; see 2:623–24).

R439, R440, R441 On the authorship of these lyrics, see note to R438.

R445 On S. Cailleau, see Appendix 3: Index of medieval authors.

R447, 1 *menteurs a carterons*. The only example of this expression, which Godefroy (6:486) translates as "menteurs impudents." This fits the context very well, but nowhere else has *carterons* (more usual spelling *quarterons*) this meaning. It is literally a quarter, either of a pound weight, or of a coin, which was a cent according to Godefroy. Just one other text suggests that the word was used loosely for "large number": "par cens et par quarterons" (Godefroy). Champion suggests "beaucoup" (2:648). Our rendering is "all you liars."

R448 On Gilles des Ourmes, see Appendix 3: Index of medieval authors.

R449 The pun is on marigolds and cares, worries. See note to R232.

R451 On Damien, see Appendix 3: Index of medieval authors.

9 Thetis was a sea-nymph of Greek mythology, most prominent amongst the fifty daughters of Nereus.

R452 On Benoit, see Appendix 3: Index of medieval authors.

R458 On Bourbon, see Appendix 3: Index of medieval authors.

R459 The heading refers to the previous lyric, by the duc de Bourbon.

8 There appears to be no record of the word *condet*.

11 *Mistodet* also appears to be unrecorded.

R460 On Pierre Danche, see Appendix 3: Index of medieval authors. *Fauveau* refers to the 14th century *Roman de Fauvel*, described, under the expression "to curry favour," as follows, in *Brewer's Dictionary of Phrase and Fable*: "a kind of counterpart to the more famous romance, *Reynard the Fox*. Fauvel, the fallow-coloured horse, takes the place of Reynard, and symbolizes cunning or duplicity: hence, to curry, or stroke down, Fauvel was to enlist the services of duplicity, and so, to seek to obtain by insincere flattery or officious courtesy" (for further details, see John Fox, *The Middle Ages*, London: Ernest Benn, 1974, 270–71). Sebastian Brant includes in his *Ship of Fools* foolish courtiers who "stroke the fallow horse" (*Das Narrenschiff*, chap. 100).

Glossary

This Glossary covers the entire collection of Charles's poems, also those of the various contributors to the MS. The principal concern is with the vocabulary of fifteenth-century French as well as with modern words with spelling variants (e.g. *sçavoir* for *savoir*). Italian and Latin terms are also included. Expressions needing explanation are referred to the notes. All verbs are represented by their infinitives. Where the infinitive does not appear in the text it is placed in square brackets.

Abbreviations

adj	adjective
adv	adverb
excl	exclamation
imp	imperative
nm	masculine noun
nf	feminine noun
pastp	past participle
personif	personification
prep	preposition
presp	present participle
pressubj	present subjunctive
pron	pronoun
num	numeral
vb	verb

A

[Abaisser], *vb* to lower, to reduce, abesse **Intro**, 110
Abandonné, *pastp* prodigal (with), **Co4**, 66
Abatre, *vb* to knock down, to subdue, **R65**, 11; m'abas, **R351**, 4
Abestir, *vb* to stupefy, **R50**, 2
Abregier, *vb* to abridge, to condense, **R73**, 10
[Abrier], *vb* to shelter, to conceal, abriee, **R416**, 2

[Absoudre], *vb* to absolve, absolz, **R389**, 5

Abstergo, Latin, *vb* I wipe out, cancel, **R137**, 8

[Abutiner (s')], *vb* to share booty, **R51**, 10, abutineray (je m') (see note)

Accez, *nm* coughing fits, **R229**, 11; **R231**, 11

Accident *nm* chance, **B105**, 14

Accointance, actointanses, *nf* acquaintance, **Intro**, 49; **B5**, 9, 18, 27; **R42**, 5; **R168**, 10

Accointer, *vb* to acquaint, to make the acquaintance of, **B17**, 28; accointa, **Ch2**, 9; accointé, **R261**, 1; acointeray, **R51**, 9; acointié, **Ch62**, 10; **R63**, 5

Accointes, *adj* acquainted, **B72**, 25

Accorder (s'), *vb* to agree to, to accept, **Ch17**, 16

Achoison, *nf* motive, occasion, **B44**, 17; *La departie*, 471

Acointance, see Accointance

[Acointer], see Accointer

Acoup, *adv* at once, **R425**, 6

[Acourser], *vb* to shorten, acourse, **R302**, 3

Acoustumance, *nf* custom, habit, **B92**, 16; **R53**, 8; **R67**, 6; **R240**, 4

[Acoustumer], *vb* to accustom, acoustumé(e), **R179**, 4; **R127**, 4

Acquester, *vb* to acquire, **B71**, 13; acqueste, **R284**, 8

[Acquitter], *vb* to pay one's debt, tribute to, to take the trouble to, acquittant, **B118**, 1; s'aquitte, **R140**, 8

[Acroistre], *vb* to increase, acroissent, **R215**, 5; acroist, **R350**, 4

[Actachier], *vb* to publicise, actache, **R116**, 4

Actaindre, *vb* to reach, to grasp, understand, **B91**, 21

[Actainer], *vb* to vex, to accuse, actainé, **B103**, 13; attaine, **B104**, 3; actaine, **B105**, 23

Actainte, *nf* aim, intent, **R426**, 6, see Attaintes

[Adeviner], *vb* to guess, adevinez, **R188**, 2

Adjournemens, *nm* summons, **R95**, 2

[Adjourner], *vb* to summon, adjourne, **B99**, 1; adjournez, **R160**, 8

Admortye, *pastp* dead, **R275**, 10

Adonc, Adonque (s), *adv* then, **Intro**, 241, 386; **B25**, 23; **B45**, 12; **Co4**, 38; **R267**, 10; etc.

Adoulee, *adj* painful, **R407**, 8

Adresse, *nf* way, path, **B29**, 21; *Songe*, 36; **B74**, 21; **Co3**, 65; **B115**, 4; **Ch5**, 5; **Ch21**, 3

Advenement, *nm* coming, arrival, **R430**, 1

A(d)venir, *vb* to happen, **B3**, 9; **B12**, 15; **B16**, 20; **B19**, 8; **B45**, 18; **B49**, 8; **B78**, 11; **B101**, 3; avint, *Songe*, 3; adviegne, *Songe*, 152

Advisemens, *nm* advice, **B142**, 24

Affaitee, *pastp* proper, serious, **B104**, 25 (demande affaitee, "demande qui exige une réponse précise," Champion, *Poésies*, 2:647)

Affamer, *vb* to starve, **B108**, 14

Affectueux, *adj* affected by ("qui éprouve tel sentiment," Godefroy, 1:136), **B110**, 7

[Afier (s')], *vb* to trust, affye, afie (je m'), **B12**, 21; **B64**, 17

[Afoler (s')], *vb* to madden, to go mad, to behave stupidly, l'afola, **R331**, 3; s'en afola, **R331**, 9

[Agraper], *vb* to catch, agrapé, **R31**, 11

[Agreer], *vb* to be agreeable to, m'agree, **B35**, 10

Aguet, *nm personif* Vigilance **Ch69**, 3; watch, lookout, **R387**, 10

Aguillon, *nm* spur, **R32**, 11

Aidier, *vb* to help, aid, m'aid **R99**, 4; **R106**, 5; aist, **R158**, 6; **R258**, 4

Aigret, *nm* thorn, **R220**, 13

Aille, elles, *nf* wing(s), **R32**, 9; **R85**, 2

Ainçois, ainçoys, *adv* rather, **B55**, 16; **Co4**, 19; **R293**, 11; ainçois que, before, *Jam nova*, 130

Ains, *adv* rather, **Co5**, 128; ains que, *conj* before, **R6**, 10

Ainsné, *adj* older, **B117**, 18

Aise, *nf* ease, comfort, **R369**, 10

[Aisier], *vb* to provide (with), aist, **R220**, 11

[Ajolier (s')], *vb* to make oneself pretty, s'ajolie, **R47**, 3

Alangoré, *pastp* langorous, feeble, **B110**, 10

Alans, *nm* (venans et alans) comings and goings, **R317**, 2

Alegeance, alegence, allegence, *nf* relief, help, **B77**, 18; **Co5**, 99; **Co6**, 44; **R114**, 11; **R337**, 14

Alegemens, allegement, *nm* relief, **B111**, 18; **R97**, 4

Aler, *vb* to go, **Intro**, 118; **B9**, 34; vois, **B103**, 6; **B108**, 7; **R215**, 4; voisent **B87**, 28; voys **R116**, 6

Allegier, *vb* to relieve, to lighten, **B128**, 25

[Almander], *vb* to conscript, almandé, **R309**, 5 (see note)

[Alouer (s')], *vb* to devote oneself to, s'aloua *Jam nova*, 63

Alquemye, see Arquemie

Ame, *nf* soul, living soul, person, **R429**, 6

Amende, *nf* amends, **R342**, 10

Amender, *vb* to correct, **B41**, 5; **B115**, 54; **Co3**, 66; **Ch21**, 5; **R140**, 9; **R276**, 4

Amendrir, *vb* to lessen, **B48**, 23

[Amer], *presp* to love, amant, **R279**, 9

Amolir, *vb* to soften, **B120**, 27; amolye **R302**, 8; **R333**, 3

[Amonester], *vb* to admonish, to warn, amoneste, **R460**, 10

Amont, see Bas

Amourettes, *nf* flirtings, trifling love affairs **Ch49**, 12

Ancollie, *nf* columbine, **R232**, 3; mere Ancolye, pun on Merencolie, *personif* Melancholy, **R163**, 3

[Anformer], *vb* to inform, anformé, **B141**, 10

Angoisse, see Poire d'angoisse

Anuys, *nm* troubles, pains, **B88**, 21

Anuyt, *adv* today, **R241**, 10; **R142**, 9

Apareil, appareil, *nm* readiness, preparation, *Songe*, 6; **B95**, 3; **R45**, 8; **R101**, 9

A part soy, apart soy, *adv* see Part

Apointement, *nm* adjustment, necessary change, **R55**, 4

Apostat, apostaz, *nm* apostate(s), **R224**, 10; **R225**, 2

Appareillier, *vb* to prepare, **B81**, 6; **R43**, 2; appareillee, **R366**, 3

Appellacion, *nf* court summons, **B109**, 5

Appointer, *vb* to decide, **R408**, 6

Appoticaires, *nm* apothecaries **R229**, 12

[Approprier], *vb* to appropriate, approprié, **B109**, 5

Approuver, *vb* to prove, to demonstrate, **Co3**, 48

Aprison, *nf* rancour, bitterness, **R280**, 13

Apuys, *nm* support, **B100**, 33

Aqueil, *nm* welcome, **R173**, 8

[Aquester], *vb* to acquire, to gain, aqueste, **R355**, 5

Aquilote, *nf* small bird of prey, **R21**, 5

Araisonner, *vb* to address, to reason with, **R77**, 3; araisonna, *Songe*, 17

Arbalestre, *nf* crossbow, **R20**, 4

Arc, see Destendre

Archier, *nm* archer, **R431**, 11

Ardre, *vb* to burn, **B27**, 13; ardy, **B65**, 25; **R261**, 10; arde, **Ch48**, 11; art, **R199**, 6; **R200**, 5; s'art, **R167**, 8

[Arguer], *vb* to argue, to claim, argue, **R130**, 4

Arquemie, *nf* alchemy, **R221**, 9; **R297**, 5; **R141**, 1

Array, arroy, *nm* order, array, **Intro**, 98; **R273**, 14

Arrerages, arreraiges, *nm* arrears, **B86**, 15; **R93**, 1

Arriereban, *nm* convocation of the nobility, **B84**, 7

Arrierefief, *nm* sub-fief, one depending on another, **R396**, 1

Arsoir, *adv* yesterday evening, **R460**, 3

[Artillier], *vb* to provide with artillery, artillié, **R22**, 8

Asnyer, *nm* ass, fool, **B94**, 18

Aspecte ung poco, *vb+ adv* Italian, wait a little, **R272**, 9

Aspresse, *nf* harshness, **Co3**, 68

Assavoir, *vb* to make known, **Co5**, 16

Assent, *nm* agreement, harmony, **B100**, 24

[Assentir (s')], *vb* to agree, s'y assent, **B100**, 22

[Asseoir], *vb* to sit, to place, asseray, **B46**, 27 (see note); assis **Ch56**, 2

Asservir, *vb* to enslave, **Ch53**, 5; **R385**, 4; asservy, **R9**, 8

Asseur, *adj* safe, secure, **B111**, 4

Asseuree, *pastp* confident one, **R165**, 12

Assommer, *vb* to add up, **Co6**, 38; assommoit, **B139**, 29

[Assortir], *vb* to get ready, to provide with what is needed, assortiz, **R22**, 10

Assotement, *nm* stupidity, **R136**, 6

Assotez, *adj* besotted, **R73**, 2

Assouagement, *nm* assuaging, relief, **R372**, 11

[Assoubtiver], *vb* to grow more subtle, assoubtivant, **Ch56**, 10

Assoulagier, *vb* to assuage, to relieve, **B128**, 15

[Assourdir], *vb* to deafen, assourdy **R443**, 1

[Assouvir], *vb* to assuage, assouvie, *La departie*, 416; **Co7**, 124; asso(u)vye, **B111**, 9; **Co5**, 35; accomplished, *Jam nova*, 129

Astronomians, *nm* astrologers, **B88**, 27

Atainte, *nf* assault, *Songe*, 32

Atante, *nf,* expectation, **R173**, 6

Atayne, *nf* effort, **B105**, 21; **B108**, 10

Atendre (s'a), *vb* to depend on, s'atent, **B37**, 28; s'atende, *Songe*, 93

A tergo, Latin, in the back, behind their backs, **R137**, 4

Atirer, *vb* to equip, to harness, used substantively, **R33**, 6

[Atiser], *vb* to stir up, atise, **B85**, 25; atisé, **Ch69**, 9

Atour, *nm* apparel, **R260**, 5

A tout (often written as one word: atout), *prep* with, **B94**, 4; **R240**, 8

Atraiance, *nf personif* Attractiveness, **B87**, 4

Atrais, *nm* attractions, *Songe*, 127; **R119**, 8

Atrayement, *nm* attraction, **R136**, 2

[Atremper], *vb* to moderate, atrempée, **B84** 10

[Attainer], *vb* to annoy, to harass, attaine, **B110**, 25; ataine, **B112**, 19

Attaintes, *nf* (venir aux attaintes) reach one's objective, **B72**, 14; actincte, **R435**, 13

Attargier, *vb* to delay, **B128**, 5

Attendre (s'en), *vb* to turn towards, to count on, s'en attent, **Co1**, 79

Aucunesfoiz, *adv* sometimes, **R295**, 11; **R402**, 2

Aucuns, *nm* some (people), **B122**, 4

Auffin, *nm* chess piece, bishop, **B58**, 15

Auffort, *adv* besides, after all, Au fort, **B64**, 17; **B82**, 10; **R13**, 3; **R146**, 2; **R159**, 5

Aumaires, *nf* cupboards, **R18**, 5

Aumosne, *nf* alms, **R280**, 2

Aumosnier, *nm* almoner, **R199**, 2; **R200**, 1; **R280**, 5

Autrier, *nm* the other day, **B37**, 1; **Co4**, 1; **Ch31**, 6; **R21**, 3

Avenir, *vb* to come, to happen, **R240**, 6; avendra, **Ch2**, 4; aviengne, **R69**, 5; avient, **R55**, 11; avint, **B114**, 2; **B124**, 7; to get there, **R198**, 10

Aventure d', *nf* peradventure, by chance, *Jam nova*, 105

Avilé, *pastp* vilified, traduced, **R221**, 5

Avisement, *nm* counsel, warning, **Ch20**, 11

[Aviser (s'), adviser], *vb* to consider, to reflect, to realise, je m'avisay, **B114**, 8; s'advise, **B90**, 28; s'avise, **R7**, 10; **R448**, 11; avisez, *Songe*, 29; mal avisé, ill advised, unwise, **Ch69**, 1; je vous en avise, I warn you, **R66**, 4

Avoglé, *pastp* blinded, **R36**, 1, 7, 12

Avouer, *vb* to acknowledge, **R371**, 6; [s'avouer], to acknowledge one has an overlord, m'avoue, **B113**, 6

[Avoyer], *vb* to put on the right road, avouyé, **B110**, 18

B

Baffe, *nf* slap in the face, **B133**, 1

Bagues, *nf* trinkets, **R319**, 14

Bailler, *vb* to give, **R224**, 9; bailla, **Intro**, 14; **R32**, 11; baillant, **R281**, 11; baillay, *Songe*, 357; *La departie*, 475, 480; baille lui bois, **R92**, 9 (see note); baille, **Ch65**, 9; **R322**, 1; baillé, **R15**, 11; baillee, *Songe*, 353; bailleroye, **R222**, 6; baillez lui la massue, **R130**, 1 (see note)

Bailleur de paroles, *nm* chatterbox, **R336**, 2

Baillie, ballie, *nf* jurisdiction, power, control, **B125**, 23; **R149**, 6; **R457**, 5

Baing, *nm* bath, **R25**, 8

Balais, *nm* balais, "A delicate rose-red variety of the spinel ruby" (*OED*), *Jam nova*, 106

Balance, *nf* uncertainty, unstable situation, **B76**, 26; **R340**, 4; au pois et a la balance **R93**, 5 (see note)

Bamme, *nm* see Basme

Banyere, *nf* banner, **R425**, 8

Barrez, *nm* (for barres) **Ch70**, 3 (see note)

Barriere, *nf* barrier in the lists (see note) **R425**, 5

Bas, *adv* en bas et amont, low and high, i.e., all over the place, **R287**, 8

Bas, *nm* burden, **R243**, 8

Basme, bamme, *nm* balm, **B103**, 25; **R439**, 9

Baster aus corneilles, *vb* **R118**, 3 (see note); **R357**, 6

Bastonnee, *nf* whacking, **R406**, 4

Baubans, *nm* excessive splendour, **B76**, 20

Baude, *n* **R415**, 1 (see note)

Baudement, *adv* boldly, **B4**, 10

Baus, *nm* woods, **R441**, 8

Baverye, *nf* chat, **R447**, 3

Bec affilé, *nm* smart aleck, wise guy, **R221**, 8; becz (jaunes), **R50**, 6 (see note)

Begnin, *adj* benign, **B102**, 15

Bescuit, *nm* biscuit, **R296**, 12

Besoingnier, *vb* to work hard, to be busy, **B123**, 4; **R235**, 5

Beste, *nf* fait en beste, behaved like a beast, **R289**, 4

[Betourner], *vb* to lead astray, betourna, *Jam nova*, 68

Bien, *adv* un bien matin, early one morning, **B66**, 3

Bienvueillans, *nm* well-wishers, **B25**, 2

Bigotz, *nm* bigots, **B77**, 25

Billart, *nm* billiard cue, **R14**, 7 (see note)

Billes, *nf* billiard balls, **R90**, 5

Bis, *nm* brown, **R40**, 11

Bise, *nf* North wind, **R71**, 10

Bissacs, *nm* bags, pouches, **B77**, 21

Blans, *nm* small coins, farthings, **Ch49**, 1

Bobo, *nm* spots, **R138**, 4

Boire, *vb* to drink, beuvra, **B82** 13; beues, **R169**, 1

Bois (baille lui), **R92, 9** (see note)

Bonde, *nf* barrier, limit, **R120**, 4; the Pillars of Hercules, **R451**, 4

Bonne(s), *nf* limit(s), **Co7**, 127; **R291**, 7 (modern borne)

Bons, *nm* **R14**, 8 (see note)

Bont, *nm* **R109, 4** (see note)

Bort, *nm* edge, **B91**, 29; **R423**, 14 (see Oultre)

Boucages, *nm* woods, **B86**, 21

Boulevers, *nm* bulwarks, ramparts, **R22**, 11

Bourde, *nf* untruth, **B105**, 28; joke, **R112**, 4; **R370**, 5

[Bourder], *vb* to lie, bourdent, **B105**, 24

Bourdon, *nm* faux bourdon (musical term), low accompaniment to a melody, **R426**, 4; cudgel, club, **B106**, 18

Bourgoise, *nf* bourgeoise, used pejoratively by the duke, dreadful woman, **R378**, 11

Bout(s), boutz, boux, *nm* end(s) **R156**, 11; see Cour(r)oye, tenir l'un des boutz, hold one of the ends, i.e., keep control of, **R164**, 6

Bouter, *vb* to push, to thrust, **B7**, 15; **B17**, 26; **B29**, 13; **B87**, 26; **B95**, 12; **B138**, 12; etc.; bouta **B65**, 23; boutasse, **R162**, 11; boute **B108**, 16; **Ch72**, 11; **R62**, 10; **R115**, 8; **R190**, 5; **R295**, 4; bouté **Ch17**, 13; **R225**, 7; **R430**, 4; boutent, **R447**, 11; bouteroye **R341**, 5; boutez **B91**, 7; boutons **R97, 6 R176**, 1

Boutons, *nm* (on ne vous prise deux), people care nothing for you, **R447**, 6

Boux, *nm* ends, **R156**, 11 (see Cour(r)oye)

Brahaing, *adj* sterile, **B103**, 11; **B110**, 4

[Brasser], *vb* to prepare, brasse, *Jam nova*, 8

Brider, *vb* to bridle, **R460**, 9

Brief, *adj* brief, short, *La departie*, 320

Brief, *adv* soon, briefly, **Intro**, 285; **B13**, 29; **B19**, 12; **B36**, 8; **B124**, 8; **Ch31**, 10; **R143**, 15

Briquet, *nm* spaniel, **R133**, 1; **R415**, 2

Broche (sans couleur), *nf* **R254, 7** (see note)

[Broder], brodé(e), *pastp* embroidered (with), bedecked (with), **R78**, 9; **R456**, 6

Brouderie, *nf* embroidery, **R44**, 3

Brouee, *nf* fog, **R81**, 6

[Bruire], *vb* to make a noise, a racket, bruit, **R260**, 8

Bruit, *nm* reputation, **R260**, 6

Buissonner, *vb* **R415, 1** (see note)

Bureau, *nm* paymaster's office, **R237**, 9

Butin, *nm* booty, **B127**, 19; **Co4**, 99; **R3**, 4; **R51**, 8; **R74**, 4; **R223**, 5, etc.

Buze Italian, *nf* **R272, 1** (see note)

C

Ça, *adv* Or ça, now then, **B92**, 1; **R57**, 9

Cabas, *nm* trickery, deceptions, **R434**, 16

[Cabuser], *vb* to cheat, cabuze, **R272**, 4

Cabuseurs, *nm* tricksters, cheats, **R161**, 3

Cadet, *nm* captain, **R459**, 4

Cameline, *nf* mustard sauce, **R298**, 5

Carreaulx, *nm* paving stones, **R19**, 5

Carterons, *nm* menteurs a carterons, **R447**, 1, (see note)

[Casser], *vb* to break, to remove, cassez, **R338**, 9; cassez, removed, dismissed, cancelled, **B40**, 32; **R204**, 6; **R338**, 9 (see Gages)

Cassés (gagez), *pastp* wages stopped, **R171**, 10; cassé des gaiges de Jeunesse, dismissed from Youth's payroll, **B84**, 5

Catoillier, *vb* to tickle, **Intro**, 222

Cautelle, *nf* ruse, trick, **B126**, 4; **R235**, 11

Cayement, caÿment, *nm* wretch, **R342**, 1; **R344**, 3; **R458**, 1

Cayers, *nm* registers, **B139**, 14

Ceans, *adv* in here, *La departie*, 466; **R281**, 5

Cedule, *nf* affidavit *Songe*, 156

Celer, *vb* to hide, **R435**, 1; cela *Jam nova*, 53; celes **R56**, 9; celle **B44**, 14; **B47**, 14; **Co5**, 70; **Ch8**, 6; **R64**, 3; **R212**, 5; cellee **R72**, 5; celles **B82**, 17

Celle, *adj* a celle fin que, to this end that (became in Modern French à seule fin que), **R88**, 8

Cendres, *nf* le jour des Cendres, Ash Wednesday, **R128**, 5

Cep, *nm* prison, **R411**, 6

Ceulx, *nm* thresholds, **R73**, 17 (see Sueil)

Chalenger, *vb* to demand, **B142**, 12

Chaloir, *vb* to matter, **Co7**, 156; **Ch55**, 11; **R257**, 8; chaille, **Ch 7**, 11; **R105**, 6; **R117**, 4; **R146**, 3; **R155**, 4; challoit **Intro**, 262; chauldroit, **Ch64**, 10; chault, **B11**, 15; **B91**, 15; **Co7**, 48; **Ch5**, 11; **Ch33**, 5; **R369**, 8; etc.

Change, *nm* exchange, **Intro**, 323; change, **B67**, 12

Chanterie, *nf* singing, **R47**, 10

Chanus, *adj* white, **R203**, 3

Chapperon, *nm* cloak, **R78**, 8; **R217**, 3

Charnaige, *nm personif* Shrove Tuesday, **R377**, 10

Chartre, *nf* prison, **B107**, 4; **R407**, 8

Chartreurs, chartreux, *nm* Carthusian(s), **R225**, 9; **R248**, 11; **R433**, 11

Chasser, *vb* to hunt, to move (from) **R274**, 10; **R376**, 10; fights, rails against, **R12**, 9

Chasses, *nf* **B132**, 18 (see note)

[Chastïer], *vb* to chastise, chastient, **R381**, 3

Chastoy, *nm* punishment, **B90**, 14

Chat (qui dort), *nm* (sans resveillier le chat qui dort), *proverb*, without waking the sleeping cat, i.e., surreptitiously, **Co6**, 77; **R18**, 2

Cheminee, *nf* chimney (eroticism), **R55**, 9

Cheres, see Chiere

Cherté, *nf* high prices, dearness, **R236**, 2

Chevalier, *nm* knight (chess), **B58**, 14

Chevance, *nf* profit, **R42**, 11; **R93**, 8; **R204**, 11; **R220**, 11

Chevilles, *nf* pegs, **R90**, 4

Chevir (se), *vb* to prevail, triumph over, **B68**, 15; **B101**, 23; **B116**, 29; **R399**, 2; **R421**, 2

Chiche, *nm* chiches, misers, *Jam nova*, 11

Chief, *nm* head mener a chief, to bring to a head, i.e., to achieve, **R277**, 8

Chiere, *nf* countenance, **B6**, 17; **B10**, 19; **R172**, 10; **R242**, 2; **R426**, 1; chiere marrie, sad countenance, **Bal 5**, 432; piteuse chiere, pitiful countenance, **R425**, 11; chiere lye (lie), lye chiere, happy countenance **Bal 7**, 484; **Co6**, 60; **B125**, 13; **R49**, 9; **R107**, 9; **R302**, 5; etc.; faire chiere lie, to rejoice, **B118**, 7; good fare **R1**, 1; bonnes cheres, good cheer, **R311**, 4

Chierir, *vb* to cherish, **B41**, 26

Chierté, *nf* esteem, value, **B30**, 25; **B32**, 2; **B35**, 11

[Choir], *vb* to fall, cheoit, **R154**, 1; (je) cheu **Intro**, 241; *pastp* **B55**, 7; cheust *pastp* **B113**, 26

Cil, *pron* (modern celui), the one who, **Co5**, 95

Clamer, *vb* to call, clame, **Co2**, 65

Clergie, *nf* knowledge, scholarship, **B94**, 3 (see note); **Co3**, 5; **B115**, 13; **R453**, 12

Cligniez, *pastp* closed, *Songe*, 125

Cliquant, *adj* flashy (with), **R234**, 7

Clochete, *nf* small bell, **R248**, 1

Cloichier, *vb* to err, falter, **R4**, 10

Clorre, *vb* to close, **R147**, 11

Coctidien, *nm* daily bread, **R219**, 4

Coessin, *nm* cushion, **B66**, 17

Coffin, *nm* casket, **R450**, 2

Coiaement, *adv* coyly, quietly, **R344**, 2

Coissin, *nm* cushion, **R270**, 8

Coissinés, *nm* small cushions, **R138**, 9

Combien que, *adv* however much, although, **B37**, 21; **B49**, 3; **B50**, 17; *Jam nova*, 49; **B114**, 6; **B120**, 12

Compas, *nm* par c., in regular fashion, **B91**, 16; skilfully, **R239**, 8; sans c., untidily, all over the place, **R242**, 8

[Compasser], *vb* to arrange, se compasse, is arranged **R184**, 12; compassé, ordered, ordained, **R349**, 10; faultes compassees, deliberate faults, **R349**, 11

Competent, *adj* appropriate, **B104**, 2

[Compiler], *vb* to arrange, to put together, compilé, **R221**, 4

Complexion, *nm* see notes to **B109**

[Composer], *vb* to arrange, to prepare, compose, **R375,** 6

Composte, *nf* compote, **B133,** 2

Compter, *vb* to tell, **B8,** 12; **B10,** 15; **B21,** 32; **B40,** 3; **R423,** 8; compte *Songe,* 337; comptee, **B54,** 42

Comptouer, *nm* cabinet, office, **B139,** 12

[Confire], *vb* to make, to compose, to preserve, confis, confit(e), confiz, *adj* permeated with, pickled in, soaked in, *Jam nova,* 34; **B133,** 2; **R140,** 1; **R332,** 2,

[Confondre], *vb* to confound, confus, **R249,** 5

Confrarie, *nf* brotherhood, **R297,** 1

Connins, *nm* **B125,** 2, 4 (see note)

Conseulx, *nm* advice, **Intro,** 332; **B68,** 8; **B69,** 27; **R73,** 9

Conquester, *vb* to acquire, gain, **B17,** 6; **B96,** 11; **R244,** 13; **R403,** 6; conquestoit, **R367,** 6

[Conseiller], *vb* to take counsel, conseil(lez) **R259,** 9 (see note); conseilles, **R345,** 11

Contenance(s), *nf* face, countenance, **Intro,** 133, 336; **B10,** 10; **B51,** 5; **Bal 5,** 423; **Ch54,** 1; **Ch57,** 9; **R121,** 11; appearance's sake, **Ch37,** 2

[Contendre], *vb* to strive, contens, **R335,** 9

Contens, contentes, *adv* in cash, "on the nail," **B79,** 25; **R335,** 2; **R428,** 5

Contens, *nm* contention, strife, **R335,** 6

Contens, *adj* contented, **Intro,** 415

Continuance, *nf* continuation, **B120,** 9

Contraire, *nm* opposition, **Ch29,** 1

[Contrarier], *vb* to contradict, contrarie, **R141,** 11

Contraux, *nm* contracts, **B79,** 6

Contrefaire, *vb* to imitate, **B107,** 22; **R239,** 6; contrefaisant, **R183,** 5; **R344,** 3; contrefait, **R287,** 10; contreffont, **R168,** 2; disguised, **R426,** 1

Contre(s), *nm* countertenor(s), **R47,** 11; **R426,** 8

Controuveurs, *nm* liars, **R448,** 8

Convenant, *nm* **B132,** 22 (see note)

Convoye(r), *vb* to accompany, convoie, **Ch69,** 3; convoye **Intro,** 80; **B70,** 13; *Songe,* 48; **Bal 6,** 440; **B103,** 14; **R96,** 10; etc.

Coquart, *nm* conceited rogue, **R125,** 10

Coquelourde, *nf* deceit, trickery, **R112,** 5

Coquilles, *nf* trinkets, **R90,** 1

Coquin, *nm* rogue, **B133,** 4

Corda, Latin, hearts, feelings, **R136,** 11 (see note)

Corneilles, *nf* rooks (baster aus c.), **R118,** 3 (see note); **R133,** 4

Corner, *vb* **R66,** 8 (see note)

Cornulz, *adj* peculiar, **R131,** 3

Cossy, Italian , *adv* thus, **R272,** 5

Coste, couste, *prep* near, beside, **B75,** 1; **B113,** 2 (see also Decoste)

[Coucher], *vb* couchez en despence, **Co6,** 27 (see note)

Couleur, *nf* pretence, lie, *Songe*, 234

Coulevrines, *nf* culverins (large cannons), **R22**, 9

Coulomb, *nm* dove, **Co3**, 38

Courage, couraige, *nm* mind, mentality, **Co7**, 40; **B129**, 3; **Ch61**, 10; **R50**, 4; **R233**, 9; **R239**, 10; etc.

Cource, *nf* rate, **R302**, 6

[Courcer, courcier], *vb* to grieve, to lament, cource, **B75**, 13; **R302**, 9; courcé, **R77**, 1; **R226**, 11; courcié, **Co4**, 110

Cour(r)oye, *nf* strap, . . . quant tenez le bout de la couroye, when you are in control, **B115**, 48; . . . du monde tenir Les deulx boux de la courroye, control the entire world, **B101**, 19–20 (see note); tenir les deux boux, hold both ends of the stick, **R156**, 11

[Courroucer], *vb* to vex, courrocee, **B96**, 22; courroucié, **Co2**, 22; courroussees, **R17**, 7

Courrous, courroux, *nm* annoyance, vexation, **Co4**, 104; **R206**, 11; **R250**, 2; **R282**, 4

Cours, *nm* run, **R215**, 11; way, path, **R216**, 11; **R254**, 8; **R285**, 6

[Couvenir], *vb* to be necessary, couvendra, *Songe*, 104; **Ch38**, 6; couvenu, **B116**, 26; couvient, **Intro**, 216; **B4**, 8; **B42**, 12; **B54**, 41; **B63**, 28; *Songe*, 146; etc.

Couvrechef, cueuvrechief, *nm* hat, **B32**, 6; **Ch59**, 1; **R217**, 4

Coy, quoy(e), *adv* quiet, tranquil, at peace, **B140**, 18; **Ch48**, 12; **R63**, 6; **R262**, 4; **R144**, 15; **R352**, 4

Coy, *adv* (modern quoi), what, **R262**, 5

Creance, *nf* belief, **Co7**, 77; **B116**, 24; **R178**, 5; **R224**, 2

Credatis, Latin, si me credatis, if you believe me, **R135**, 8

Cremir, *vb* to fear, **B117**, 16

Creue, *nf* increase (in price), **R237**, 4

Crier, *vb* to proclaim, to make public **R17**, 12; crié, cryé, **R248**, 1; **R380**, 12; criee, **R358**, 5; **R359**, 5

Crocheteur, *nm* thief, **R412**, 3

[Croire (s'en)], *vb* to be certain, je m'en croy **R24**, 8; to believe, j'en croy, **R54**, 13; m'en croy, **R262**, 11; **R352**, 11; créés, **R202**, 11; cru, **R226**, 3

Croizé, *pastp* **B84**, 4 (see note)

Croix, see Pille

Croq, *nm* de croq ou de hanche, by hook or by crook, **Co6**, 56

Cros, *nm* anchor, **R94**, 9

Croupir, *vb* to crouch, **B119**, 12

Crueux, *nm* cruel one, **B12**, 22; *adj* **B68**, 4; **Co7**, 76

Cry, *nm* noise, racket, **R316**, 8

Cuider, cuidier, *vb* to think **R218**, 4; **R239**, 11; **R244**, 8; cuidant **R216**, 4; cuiday, **R104**, 8; cuide, **B6**, 12; **B68**, 17; **B82**, 1; **B100**, 33; **R287**, 10; **R124**, 10; **R130**, 2; **R158**, 9; cuident, **B101**, 19; **R50**, 1; cuides, **B121**, 2; cuidés, **B99**, 21; cuidez, **Co1**, 16; **Co6**, 22; **R68**, 3; **R278**, 5; **R297**, 8; **R344**, 2; **R310**, 5; etc.; cuidoye, **Intro**, 247; **B16**, 21; **B17**, 17; **B64**, 9; **B139**, 33; **B140**, 14

[Cuire], *vb* to smart, to burn, cuise, **R71**, 7

Cum mestu, Latin, with regret (< *maestus*), **R328**, 11

Cum sensibus ebetatis, Latin, with dulled senses (ebetatis < *hebetare*, modern hébé-
ter), **R135**, 5

Cure(s), *nf* care, consideration, *Songe*, 18; **B87**, 30; **R33**, 6; **R174**, 2; **R203**, 4;
desservir deux cures, pursue two women at the same time, **R310**, 8

Cyens *adv* in here, **Intro**, 117

D

Da ly, Italian, *imp* give him, **R145**, 11; **R272**, 3

Danger, *nm personif* see note at the head of the translation

Danger, English, power, dominion **R364**, 6

Dangereuses, *adj* disdainful, **B118**, 22; coquette, **R168**, 2

Darde, *nf* dart, **Intro**, 178

Darder (contre), *vb* to fight against (lit. to throw spears at), **R183**, 10; darde, **Ch48**, 10

Dea, *excl* indeed, **Co4**, 40; **R283**, 1

Debat, *nm* debate (see note to **R14**, 8); debas, **R351**, 1; debatz, **B115**, 26

Debatre, *vb* to debate, to argue, **R65**, 5; **R214**, 11; debatu **R14**, 2

Debonnaire, *adj* kindly, sympathetic, **Co4**, 15; **Ch29**, 5

Debouter, *vb* to repulse, to repel, **Co6**, 93; deboutant, **B115**, 8; deboute, **B108**,
29; **R191**, 5; **R307**, 4; deboutee, **B95**, 23; **R452**, 9; deboutez, **B125**, 24;
deboutons, **R447**, 7

Deça et dela, *adv* here and there, **B139**, 13; par deça ne dela, on this side or
beyond, **Ch6**, 9; par deça, here, in this place, *Jam nova*, 66; **B128**, 5; **R27**, 6;
across **B33**, 13; **B131**, 5

Decepte, *nf* deceit, **R185**, 4; **R291**, 9

Decevance, *nf* deceiving, **R266**, 3

Decevement, *nm* deceiving, **B54**, 19

Decoppez, *nm* dandies wearing the latest cutaway fashion, **Ch60**, 2

Decoste, *prep* beside, **Intro**, 211 (see also Couste)

Decours (en or au), *nm* on the wane, **R285**, 3; **R334**, 10; **R379**, 10; **R427**, 4;
R436, 17; né en decours, born in misfortune, **R307**, 9; nostre decours, our
misfortune, **R436**, 17; mest au decours, brings to misfortune, **R379**, 10

Decy, *adv* from now, henceforth, **R347**, 1

Dedalus, *nm* Daedalus, **R433**, 1 (see note)

Deduire (se), *vb* to rejoice, *Songe*, 85, **B113**, 15; deduiray **R388**, 12; deduisant
B110, 22

Deduis, deduit, deduiz, desduit, *nm* pleasure(s), joy(s), **B40**, 32; **B101**, 5; **R21**, 6;
R299, 8; **R133**, 2; **R147**, 9; etc.; deduit de gibier, pleasure of the hunt, **R133**,
2; desduit de la pie, **R369**, 6 (see note)

[Defaillir], *vb* to fail, deffaille, **Co5**, 88; deffauldra, **Co5**, 96

[Defasser], *vb* to efface, undo, deffassant, **R46**, 5

[Deferrer (se)], *vb* to unshackle oneself, to free oneself, te defferre, **B121**, 31

Deffaire, *vb* to undo, to get rid of, **R343**, 9; *La departie* 545; deffait **Co7**, 8

Defferres, *nm* cast-offs, rejects, **R413**, 1

Deffrayement, *nm* costs, **R401**, 10

[Deffyer], *vb* to defy, to challenge, deffye **R304**, 11; deffié, **R380**, 9; deffiee, **R358**, 8

[Defrayer], *vb* to defray costs, defrayé, **R101**, 11

[Delaier], *vb* to leave, to bequeath, delairay, *Songe*, 174

Delaissier, *vb* to abandon, to leave off, **B41**, 12; **B43**, 21; **Bal7**, 472; **Co5**, 55; m'en delaisse, **Ch34**, 12

[Delitter (se)], *vb* to delight, **B125**, 18; delité, **R383**, 9

Demaine, *nm* domain, **B60**, 13

Demaine, *nm* thrall, slavery, **B75**, 17

Demener, *vb* to show, **B26**, 10; **Ch1**, 6; demené, **B9**, 5; demenee, **Co5**, 19; **R81**, 3; demaine, governs, controls, **B102**, 17; **B112**, 3; **Co6**, 34; **Ch40**, 6; *Jam nova*, 112

[Dementer (se)], *vb* to lament, dementé, **B17**, 29

Demourance, *nf* dwelling, **Co3**, 79; delay, **B114**, 17

Demouree, *nf* delay, **B23**, 21; abode, **B96**, 6

[Demourrer], *vb* to stay, to tarry, demourra, **R134**, 11; demourray, **R151**, 5; demourrés **R43**, 11

Denier(s), *nm* coin(s) of little value, sou, **R318**, 5; **R319**, 8; **R409**, 5; **R410**, 4

Denier a Dieu, *n* alms, **R237**, 3

Denombrement, *nm* total amount, **R397**, 1

Dentur, Latin (<*dare vb*), Let there be given (pl.), **R139**, 3

Departement, *nm* departure, **B34**, 20; **Ch9**, 14

Departie, *nf* departure, *La departie*, 421; **R286**, 8

Departir, deppartir, *vb* to share, to give, to distribute, **Intro**, 67, 296; **B23**, 19; **B37**, 17; **B49**, 22; **Co3**, 42; etc.; sans departir, without sharing, completely, without fault (see Poirion, *Le lexique*, 65), **B3**, 17; **B54**, 13; **B67**, 11; **R119**, 11; **R152**, 4; **R198**, 2; depars, **B102**, 6; depart, **B84**, 27; departie, **B70**, 21; departira, **B127**, 19; deppart, **B89**, 7; *n* Parting (from lady-love), **R229**, 14

Departir, *vb* to leave, *Songe*, 73; **Ch2**, 11; departirés, *Songe*, 63

Deport, depport, *nm* joy, pleasure, amusement, *Songe*, 206; **B91**, 11

[Deporter (se)], *vb* to have fun (with), deportés, **R281**, 3, 10

Deporter, Depporter (se), *vb* to abstain, **B10**, 23; **Co6**, 18; **R385**, 9; deporte, **B79**, 35; *Jam nova*, 93; take pleasure, deporté, **R284**, 3; deportés, **R284**, 3; deportez, **B126**, 22; se depporte, **R182**, 4; behaved, **R284**, 6; amused, **R284**, 3; vous deportez, you amuse yourself (with), **R292**, 11

Deppite, see Despiter

[Deprier], *vb* to beg for, depria, **Co4**, 36

Derrain (au), *adv* in the end, finally, **B46**, 7; **B60**, 13; **B64**, 5; **Bal 6** (*La departie*), 455; **B82**, 27; **Co6**, 11; etc.; last, derraine, **R408**, 11

Derrainement, *adv* lastly, recently, **B18**, 1; *La departie*, 535; **Co2**, 10

Derrenier, *adj* last, **B94**, 8, **R21**, 10; **R98**, 10; au derrenier, finally, in the end, **Ch69**, 11

Des cy et des ja, *adverbial expression,* here and now, **R81**, 5

Desaise, *nf* misery, **Intro**, 238

Desanuyer (se), *vb* to pass the time, to avoid getting bored, **R21**, 2

[Desavancer], *vb* to deny progress (to), to disadvantage, desavancee **R181**, 7

Deschans, *nm* descant, **R47**, 11

Descharger, *vb* to unload, **R321**, 11

Deschiquetee, *pastp* dagged, manche deschiquetee, sleeve the edge of which was cut in the latest fashion, **R8**, 6

[Desconfire], *vb* to overcome, to defeat, desconfira, **R353**, 1; desconfis, **R332**, 3; desconfit, **B97**, 18; **B118**, 12; desconfitz, **R87**, 11; desconfiz, *Jam nova*, 36

Desconfort, *nm* discomfort, par desconfort **Intro**, 231; *personif* **R425**, 3

Desconforter (se), *vb* to lose courage, **Ch22**, 5; s'en desconforte, **R147**, 4

Descogneu, *nm* stranger, **R395**, 8

Descort, *nm* discord, disagreement, *Songe*, 37

Descouverte (a), see Eschec

Descouverte, *pastp* see Eschec

Descouvreur, *nm* discoverer, scout, **R387**, 1

Descouvrir, *vb* to reveal, **B123**, 5; **R45**, 2

[Descrier], *vb* to decry coinage (i.e., declare it out-of-date), descriee, *pastp* **R414**, 1

Desduit, *nm* pleasure, **R250**, 2; see also Pie

Desencombrer (se), *vb* to rid oneself of, **R313**, 3

Desert, en *nm* wastefully, to no purpose, **R7**, 5

Deserte, *adj* destroyed, **R161**, 4

[Desgarnir], *vb* to empty, desgarny, **B66**, 27; desgarnie, **B115**, 43

Desirance, *nf* desire, **Co3**, 88; **B120**, 17

Desleauté, *nf* disloyalty, **R381**, 7

Deslier, deslyer, *vb* to untie, to release, *Jam nova*, 32; **R455**, 8; deslie, **R283**, 9

Deslogier, *vb* to dislodge, to remove from, **B128**, 23

[Desmettre (se)], *vb* to put aside, to rid oneself of, se desmect, **Co4**, 44

[Desnouer], *vb* to untie, desnoue, **R167**, 5

[Desnyer], *vb* to deny, desnye **B83**, 23

Despartir, *vb* to separate, **R300**, 5

Despens, *nm* expenses, **R101**, 2; despens contens, current expenses, **R428**, 5

Despencer, *vb* to squander, **R80**, 9

Despendre, *vb* to spend, **B115**, 42; despens, **R83**, 5

[Despenser], *vb* to dispense, despensee, **R428**, 3

Despeschier (se), *vb* to rid oneself of **R30**, 11; to hurry up, despeschee, **R178**, 11

[Despiecer], *vb* to shatter, despiece, **R347**, 5

[Despirer], *vb* to despair, despire, **B100**, 32

Despit, *nm* spite, **B8**, 19

Despit, despite, *adj* spiteful, **B43**, 3; **B40**, 15

[Despiter], *vb* to despise, despite, **R140**, 4; deppite, **R389**, 9

Despiteux, *adj* arrogant, **B102**, 5; **R255**, 10

Desplaisance, *nf personif* displeasure, **R356**, 1; **R337**, 6

Desployer, *vb* to display, **R455**, 9

[Despoillier], *vb* to strip, despoillié, **B94**, 15

Despourveu, *pastp* impoverished, **R261**, 5

[Despriser], *vb* to scorn, desprisant, **B9**, 49

[Desrober], *vb* to strip, desrobé, **B23**, 9

[Desserrer], *vb* to break, desserre, **R16**, 5

Desserte, *nf* deserts, **R161**, 1

Desservir, *vb* to deserve, **B38**, 2; **R424**, 6; desserviront, **R109**, 11; deserte, **R161**, 4; dessert, **R134**, 6; desservie, **B52**, 16; desservy, **B79**, 18; deprived, **R9**, 4; merited, **R9**, 11

Dessirer, *vb* to tear up, **R326**, 10

Destaindre, *vb* to extinguish, **B91**, 12

[Destendre], *vb* to stretch (of a bow), l'arc destendez, **R335**, 5

Destourber, *vb* to prevent, **B13**, 17; **B83**, 17; **Ch34**, 9; **R110**, 11; destourbe, *La departie*, 532; **B115**, 46; **R300**, 11; destourbé, **B114**, 24; detourbee, **B85**, 5

Destourbier, *nf personif* Trouble, **Ch48**, 10

Destre, *nm* right, **Ch67**, 9; dextre *adj* right, *Jam nova*, 21

Destruisement, *nm* ruin, **R397**, 11

[Desvoyer], *vb* to upset, desvoye, **B115**, 8

[Detenir], *vb* to detain, detient, **R254**, 5

[Detirer], *vb* to pull, detiree, **R374**, 5

Deul, *nm* grief, *La departie*, 84; **B107**, 9, **R163**, 4

Deulx, deux, *num* two, **R217**, 1; mener les gens de deux en trois, to trick, to deceive, **R278**, 6; le monde va de deux en trois, everything's going to pot, **R452**, 3 (see also Doloir)

Devers, *prep* towards, **Co5**, 97; **B117**, 5

[Devestir], *vb* to strip naked, devestu, **R328**, 10

Devier, *vb* to die, devie *Jam nova*, 131

Devis, *nm* liking, **B81**, 30; **Co2**, 61; **Co7**, 192; **R27**, 3; **R142**, 8

Devise, *nf* conversation, **R7**, 2

[Deviser], *vb* to describe, to chat, devise, **B85**, 12; **Ch58**, 3; **R71**, 1; **R98**, 6; **R202**, 1; **R152**, 5; etc.; devisant, **B9**, 34; devise, **R318**, 9; devisé, **Ch69**, 12; devisoye, **B139**, 1

[Devoir], *vb* to have to, doy, **Intro**, 10, 163; *Songe*, 315; doye, **R56**, 4; **R341**, 11; doyez **B5**, 20; **B83**, 19

[Devoyer], *vb* to wander (from the path), devoye, **B103**, 6

Dez, *nm* son eur met en dez, **R335**, 11 (see note)

[Diffamer], *vb* to defame, diffamés, **Ch68**, 9

Diffames, *nm* infamy, **R253**, 6

[Diffinir], *vb* to define, diffinient, **B109**, 21

Dire, *vb* to say, die, **R169**, 2; **R67**, 5; **R73**, 1; diz, *Jam nova*, 43; dye, **R99**, 11

Discordez, *pastp* people in disagreement, *Jam nova*, 30

Disposer (se), *vb* to get ready, **R181**, 12

Dodo, *nm* sleep (of children) **R138**, 1

Dolans, dolens, dolent, doulante, *adj* grieving, **B122**, 17; **Ch13**, 15; **R215**, 1; **R173**, 3

Dolendo de perpetratis, Latin, moaning about hardships, **R135**, 11

Doloir (se), douloir, *vb* to grieve, **B78**, 6; **B80**, 14; **R230**, 6; **R243**, 3; deulx, **B75**, 19; **B112**, 5; **R73**, 6; **R305**, 11; deulz, **B97**, 12; dueille, *Songe*, 100

[Donner], to give, doint, **B11**, 19; **B18**, 3; **B21**, 31; **B41**, 8; **B49**, 15; *La departie*, 496; etc.; donrrez, **R256**, 10

Dont, *adv* (=d'où) whence, **B97**, 12; **R52**, 6

[Donter], *vb* to overcome, donte, **R394**, 12

Doubtance, *nf* fear, **B25**, 24; **B50**, 23; **B87**, 5; **R121**, 5

Doubter (se), *vb* to fear, **B33**, 22; **B55**, 19

Doulcinés, *nm* sweet little children, **R138**, 6

Doy, *nm* finger, *Songe*, 47; teniez par le doy, **Co6**, 63 (see note); pris par le doy, hold firm **R82**, 1; **R143**, 13

Drame, *nm* drachm (a very small weight), **B103**, 10

[Dresser], *vb* to direct, to control, dresse **R180**, 6

Droicturiere, *adj* just, **B26**, 19; droicturiers, **B81**, 23

Ducatz, *nm* ducats, **R28**, 5; **R29**, 6

Duire, duyre, *vb* to lead, **B86**, 25; **B100**, 19; duit, **B86**, 22

Duresse, *nf* harshness, **Co7**, 111; **B120**, 27

Dya, *excl* Nennil dya, No, in truth, **B6**, 16

E

Ecce, Latin, behold, **R136**, 9

Echoicte, *nf* inheritance, **B105**, 19

Effray, *nm* fear, **R51**, 3

Electuaires, *nm* electuaries, **R229**, 8; **R230**, 7

Elle(s) (modern aile), *nf* wing(s), **Ch68**, 10; **R85**, 2

Embas, *adv* par embas, down below, **R8**, 11

Embasmer, *vb* to put to sleep, **Ch49**, 11, see Enbasmees

[Embattre (s')], *vb* to thrust oneself, to hasten, s'embat, **B76**, 38

[Embesoingner], *vb* to be busy, embesoingné, **B87**, 12; embesoingnez, busy folk, **R103**, 10

Emblee (par), *nf* stealthily, by surprise, **B96**, 11

Embler, *vb* to steal, **R234**, 5; **R344**, 2; **R412**, 4; s'emble, steals away from, emblé, **Ch33**, 3; **Ch55**, 2; emblent, **Ch20**, 10; embleray, **B68**, 5; embleroye, **Ch39**, 2

Embusche, *nf* ambush, **R111**, 5

Embuschié, *pastp* lying in ambush, **B87**, 21

Empescher, *vb* to block, **R376**, 1; empeschee, hindered, blocked, **R317**, 11; empeschier (s'), *vb* to get involved in, **R16**, 9; **R30**, 5

Empiece, *adv* for some time, **R347**, 11; **R375**, 3

Emplastre, *nm* plaster, **B73**, 1

Emprandre, *vb* to undertake, *Songe*, 108; empris, **Co4**, 45; emprist, **B117**, 23

Emprés, see Enprés

[Emprier], *vb* to beseech, empry, **Co1**, 7

Emprise, *nf* motto, **R7**, 6; undertaking, **R318**, 10; sign, **R325**, 4

Emptimeme, *nm* term used in medieval rhetoric, enthymeme, an argument based on probable premises, as distinct from a demonstration, **B109**, 14

Enbasmees, *pastp* scented, **R47**, 5

[Enchanter], *vb* to bewitch, enchanté **R327**, 13

Enchaperonné, *pastp* hooded (like a bird of prey), **R33**, 2

Enchere, enchiere, *n* auction, **B93**, 5; fole enchere, a reckless bid which cannot be honored, **R367**, 7

Encheu, *pastp* fallen, **Co1**, 27

[Enclore], *vb* to enclose, enclouse, **B76**, 16; encloz, prisoners, *Jam nova*, 31

Encombrier, *nm* encumbrance, **B58**, 11

Encontre, *prep* against, **R157**, 9

[Encresser], *vb* to grow, to increase, encresse, **Co3**, 40

Endormye, *nf* opiate drug made from poppies, **B82** 13

Enfanchonnés, *nm* little children, **R138**, 2

[Enferrer], *vb* to imprison, to capture, enferre, **R309**, 6

[Enforcir], *vb* to strengthen, enforcis **B50**, 3

Enforcy, *pastp* grown stronger, **Intro**, 12

Engigner, *vb* to deceive, **R325**, 9

[Engendrer (s')], to originate (from), s'engendre, **R345**, 9

Engin, *nm* intelligence, trickery, **B94**, 13; **R291**, 9

Engoisses, *nf* anguish, **R281**, 2

[Enhorter], *vb* to exhort, enhorte, *Jam nova*, 87; enhortez, **R292**, 5

[Enjoindre], *vb* to enjoin, enjoings, **R384**, 9

Enlasser (s'), *vb* to get involved in, **R123**, 11

[Enpirer], *vb* to worsen, enpire, **R392**, 2

Enprés, emprés, *prep* near, **B36**, 18; **B119**, 12; **Ch52**, 10; **R455**, 4

Enqueste, *nf* inquiry, mis en enqueste, subjected to an inquiry, **R355**, 4

Enquerir, enquerre, *vb* to ask, inquire, **R16**, 8; **R64**, 4; **R116**, 2

[Enroillier], *vb* to rust, enroillié, **B72**, 11

[Enrouer], *vb* to make hoarse, enroué, **B133**, 8

Ens, *adv* (hors et ens) outside and in, **R340**, 4

Enseigne, ensaigne, *nf* banner, **R84**, 5; (outre l'), beyond what one can say, **R213**, 5

Enserré, *pastp* shut in, surrounded, **R251**, 12

Ensevelir, *vb* to bury, **R45**, 9

Ensuïr, *vb* to follow, **Intro**, 40; *Songe*, 2; **B101**, 27

[Entamer], *vb* to broach, entame, **B103**, 15; **B108**, 13

Entendement, *nm* understanding, knowledge, **B9**, 22

Entendre, *vb* to pay attention (to), to give thought to, to understand, entende, **B104**, 10; **Co2**, 19; **R227**, 11; entens, **R278**, 1

Entente, *nf* intent, **Ch46**, 10; **R244**, 6

Enter (s'), *vb* lit. to graft itself onto, **Ch32**, 4

[Entonner], *vb* to set the tone, entonné, **R426**, 10

Entrejetteurs, *nm* dice throwers, **R161**, 9

Entremais, *n* dishes, desserts, **R108**, 11

Entremettre (s'), *vb* to interfere, **R119**, 5

Entretenir, *vb* to keep, to maintain, **R260**, 2

[Envahir], *vb* to attack, envaÿs, **B76**, 12

Envers, *prep* concerning, **Co4**, 23; **Ch29**, 4

En vers, *adv* on my back, **B105**, 17

Envis, *adv* regretfully, **Co7**, 189; **R49**, 4

[Envoier], *vb* to send, to despatch, envoiz, **R402**, 6

Epidimieux, *adj* epidemic, **B138**, 11

Ergo, Latin, therefore, **R137**, 11

Erigere, Latin, to raise up, to exalt, **R132**, 8

Erre, *nm* speed, **R16**, 11

Es, *prep* (=en+les), *Jam nova*, 26; **Ca1**, 3; **R16**, 9; **R40**, 10; **R111**, 9; etc.

[Esbaïr], see [Esbaÿr]

Esbanoys, *nm* people rejoicing, **B110**, 11

Esbas, esbat, *nm* pleasure, amusement, **B48** 21; **B62**, 15; **B76**, 21; **B100**, 7; **Co1**, 16; **B125**, 26; etc.

Esbatemens, esba(s)tement, *nm* pleasure, amusement, **B9**, 11; **B53**, 20; **B64**, 12; **B83**, 26; **B99**, 13; **B125**, 16; etc.

Esbatre (s'), *vb* to amuse oneself, to take pleasure in, to indulge in, **R65**, 1; **R214**, 4; m'esbas, **Co6**, 92; **R324**, 9; **R348**, 8; m'y esbas, **R152**, 6; s'esbat, s'y esbat, s'i esbat, s'ébat, **B35**, 17; **B49**, 13; **B101**, 1; **R112**, 3; esbatés, **R30**, 8; s'esba-toit, **Ca2**, 6

[Esbaÿr, (s')], *vb* to be amazed, to be terrified, esbahy, **R104**, 4; **R207**, 5; esbaïs, **R67**, 2; esbaÿs, **B75**, 16; esbaÿz, **R236**, 3; esbahissez, **Co6**, 9

[Esbluyr], *vb* to dazzle, esbluyst, **Ch57**, 2

Escadre, *nm* squadron, **R145**, 1

Escande, *nm* scandal, **B104**, 7

Eschaffault, *nm* raised platform at tournaments, **R4**, 3

Eschappee, a l', *pastp* fleetingly, **R416**, 14

Escharsement, *adv* avariciously, **R214**, 9

[Eschauder (s')], *vb* to burn oneself (fig.), s'eschauda, **Co4**, 61

Eschec, *nm* chess, eschec a descouverte, bad move in chess involving loss of a piece, **R161**, 11

Eschever, eschiver *vb* to eschew, to avoid, to abstain from, **R235**, 1; **R349**, 11

Escler, *nm* flash of lightning, **Ch57**, 6

Esclercie, *adj* bright, clear, **R326**, 5

Escondire, *vb* to refuse, to reject, *Songe*, 331; **R211**, 5; escondiriés, **Ch15**, 12; escondit, **Co6**, 52; **Co4**, 37; **R60**, 3; used as noun: rebuttal, dismissal, **R210**, 11

[Esconter (s')], *vb* to get into debt, escontant, *presp* **B97**, 8

Escot, *nm* cost, **Co4**, 88

Escoute, *nf* listening, **R293**, 8

Escremie, escremye, *nf* fencing, **R201**, 5; **R297**, 11 (see note to **B126**, 13)

[Escremier (s')], *vb* to fence, s'escremye **R162**, 6

Escrin, *nm* casket, *Songe*, 366

Escript, *nm* script, text, **R456**, 14

[Escrire], *vb* to write, escry, **R54**, 11

Escumeur(s), *nm* pirate(s), **B28**, 35; **B85**, 6

Escusson, *nm* escutcheon, shield, **B106**, 17

Esdenté, *pastp* toothless, **B107**, 12

[Esgarer (se)], *vb* to go astray, s'esgarent, **R399**, 4

Esgrun, *nm* bitter herb, **R229**, 2

Esjouyr, *vb* to cheer up, **R64**, 11

Eslargir, *vb* to free, **R405**, 10

Eslevance, *nf* promotion, **R220**, 6

Eslïesser, eslÿesser, *vb* to rejoice, to make happy, **Ch1**, 2; **Ch17**, 3

Eslire, *vb* to choose, **R392**, 11; esliroye, **R336**, 11; eslise, **B85**, 15

Eslongier, eslongner, *vb* to thrust aside, **B128**, 12; to move away, depart, **R92**, 10; m'esloingne, **R186**, 4; eslongnee, far away, **R72**, 11

Esmay, *nm* dismay, **R273**, 6

Esmayer, *vb* to surprise, **Ch11**, 11

Esmerillon, *nm* small falcon, **R32**, 8

[Esmovoir (se)], *vb* to be active, busy, s'esmeut, **Co6**, 80; to move (towards), esmouvoir, **B128**, 11; s'esmeuve, **R75**, 10

Espargnier, *vb* to spare, **Ch13**, 8; **R80**, 10; espergne, **R87**, 8

Espasse, *nm* space, interval, **R184**, 4

[Espeler], *vb* to spell, espelant, **B94**, 4

[Esperer], *vb* to hope, (j')espoir, *Jam nova*, 130; (j')espoire, **Ch29**, 5

Espergne, *nf* economy, **R213**, 1

Espidimie, *nf* epidemic, **B136**, 41

Espieu, *nm* hunting spear, **R165**, 13

[Esprendre], *vb* to incite, espris, **R438**, 2

[Esprouver], *vb* to put to the test, esprouvé, **R261**, 2

Essay, *nm* try, mect en essay, make an effort to, **B53**, 9

Esse (= est-ce), *vb* **R184**, 1; **R258**, 1, 8; **R279**, 10; **R292**, 1; **R299**, 11; **R327**, 10; etc.

Essil, *nm* exile, **R320**, 11

Essor, *nm* open air, freedom, **B120**, 10

Essorer, *vb* to take flight, **R85**, 4

Esteufs, *nm* tennis balls, **R90**, 5

Estoc, see Taillant

Estoffer, *vb* to reinforce, **B28**, 20

Estoup(p)er, *vb* to block, stop up, *Songe*, 385; **B138**, 13; estouppe, **R345**, 1; estouppant, *Songe*, 163; estouppees, **R400**, 1

Estourdie, a l'estourdie, *adv* irresponsibly, any old how, **R418**, 7

Estraine, *nf* gift, **B39**, 25; **B97**, 15

Estrangier, *nm* foreigner, **B107**, 15

Estre, *vb* to be, soye **Ch31**, 2; ou que soye, wherever I may be, **R279**, 4; **R122**, 1

Estrectement, *adv* expressly, **R303**, 5

Estrener, *vb* to give a present (to) (particularly a New Year present), **R222**, 4; estraine, **B103**, 9; estraynast, **B82**, 6; estrenee, **B59**, 13; estrené, **R6**, 5; **R37**, 1, 5; estreneray, **R37**, 9; **R72**, 3

Estrif, *nm* strife, **Co4**, 84

Estrilles (tours d'), *nf* tricks of the trade, deceit, **R90**, 8

Estrivance, *nf* striving, **R220**, 10

[Estriver], *vb* to fight, estrivant, **Co6**, 81

Estudie, *nf* study, **R326**, 8

Ethiques (maulx), *adj* feverish illness, **B88**, 22

Et reliqua, Latin, and the rest, **R131**, 11

Eueil, euil, eul, hueil, oeill, oueil, *nm* eye, **R34**, 2; **R41**, 2; **R174**, 8; **R350**, 1; **R367**, 3; **R430**, 6; **R431**, 1; **R440**, 11; a l'ueil, by sight, **R325**, 11

Eur(s), *nm* good fortune(s), **B85**, 23; **R454**, 11; **R456**, 11; Bon Eur *personif* Happiness, **B46**, 22

Exploit, *nm* result, **B139**, 36

F

Fa cossy, Italian, **R272**, 5 (see note)

Facteurs, *nm* agents, representatives, **R236**, 5

Fade, *adj* pale, **Intro**, 242

Faerie, *nf* fantasy, magic, **B111**, 31

[Faier], *vb* to enchant, bewitch, faee, **R26**, 11; faiee, **B75**, 6

Faille, *nf* game, **B97**, 24 (see note); **R146**, 10

Faillir, *vb* to fail, **Intro**, 324; **R124**, 11; faillant, **B80**, 17; faillent, **R371**, 8; failly, **R13**, 5, 11; see also Falloir

Faindre, *vb* to pretend, deceive, **B91**, 3; **R11**, 10

Faint(e), faynt *adj* false, pretended, **B27**, 17; *Songe*, 29; **B104**, 14; **R144**, 16; **R435**, 3; fains, **R268**, 6; Fainte, *personif* Pretence, **R426**, 3

Faintise, *nf* pretence, **B34**, 12; *Songe*, 172

Fais, *nm* (modern faix) burden, **Intro**, 59

Fais, *nm* (modern faits) features, goings-on, **Ch54**, 12; **R16**, 9

Faisant, *nm* pheasant, **R21**, 11

Faiseurs, *nm* makers, poets, **R264**, 2

Fait, *nm* manner, appearance, **R35**, 9

Faitiz, *adj* pain faitiz, coarse, home-baked bread, used in soups, **R142**, 5

[Falloir], *vb* to fail, fauldray, **Intro**, 198; **R368**, 5; fauldrez, **R25**, 1; fault, **R246**, 14; faulx, **R245**, 11; faulz, **R69**, 9; **R330**, 8; see also faillir

Fardeaus, *nm* heaps, **R18**, 11

Farder, *vb* to disguise, **R183**, 6; **R278**, 5

Farouches, *nm* savages, **R394**, 7

Faulcette, *nf* hypocritical woman, **R140**, 1

Faulte, *nf* en faulte du, for want of, **R341**, 1

Faulx bourdon, *nm* faburden, **R426**, 4 (see note); Faulx Semblant, false appearance, hypocrisy, **R257**, 4

Fausser, *vb* to act falsely, **B71**, 22

Fauveau, *nm* sly person, **R460**, 1 (see note)

Fayete, **R113**, 10 (see note)

Feaulté, *nf* fidelity, **R83**, 10; **R395**, 2; **R430**, 8

Fel, *adj* treacherous, **B68**, 4; felle, *n* treacherous one, traitor, **B41**, 3; **Ch54**, 9

Fellement, *adv* treacherously, **B6**, 5; **R397**, 10

Fenoches, fenouches, Italian, *nf* **R272**, 1 (see note); **R394**, 1

Ferir, *vb* to strike, to hit, **B4**, 18; **R314**, 5; ferant, **R25**, 11; ferez, **B5**, 12; ferra, **B45**, 15; feru, **Bal 1** (*La departie*), 282; **R14**, 10; feruz, **R99**, 2; fery, **B65**, 16; fiers, **B132**, 10; **R328**, 3

Fermer, *vb* to strengthen, reinforce, **Co3**, 32; **R208**, 4

[Ferrer], *vb* to shoe, ferré, shod, **R460**, 5

Festier, *vb* to celebrate, to hold a feast in honour of, to honour, to cheer up, **B48**, 11; **B104**, 6; **Ch37**, 12; **Ch43**, 3

Festu, *nm* a straw, **B94**, 4; **R76**, 3 (cf. modern tirer à la courte paille, to pull the short straw); traine un festu, **R79**, 10 (see note)

Feu gregeois, *nm* Greek fire (composition used for setting fire to enemy ships), **B27**, 12; il font . . . feu grejois, they make the sparks fly, **R260**, 4

Feurre, *nm* straw, **B120**, 8

Fïance, *nf* trust, confidence, *La departie*, 523; **B123**, 17; **R10**, 8; **R346**, 9; *personif* Trust, **R159**, 1

Fievre quartaine, *nf* quartan ague, **B107**, 11; **B110**, 27; fievre blanche, white fever, **R126**, 8 (not, evidently, scarlet fever!)

Filé, *nm* (craindre le), hunting term, **R221**, 1 (see note)

Finance, *nf* money, (ransom), **R405**, 11; **R408**, 8

Finement, *nm* ending, **B89**, 27

Finer, *vb* to end, **Co5**, 48

Finete, *nf* sly woman, **R112**, 11

Flebe, *adj* weak, **B102**, 13

[Fleurer], *vb* to be fragrant, fleurant, **B103**, 25

Foison, *nf* abundance, **R403**, 6

Fol, *adj* mad, folx **R277**, 7

Foleurs, *nf* follies, madness, **R132**, 10; **R384**, 5 (see also Fouleur)

[Folloyer], *vb* to act foolishly, folloye, *Songe*, 44; fouloye, **B137**, 18

[Fonder (se)], *vb* to rely on, **R451**, 5

Fons, *nm* fount, source, *Jam nova*, 6 (see note to **R14**, 4)

Fontaine, *nf* spring, line 1 in the following: **B75**, **B97**, **B102**, **B103**, **B104**, **B105**, **B107**, **B108**, **B109**, **B110**, **B111**, **B112**, **B113**

Forcenerie, forsenerie, *nf* lunacy, **B88**, 18; **B111**, 29

[Forclore], *vb* to shut off (from), to deprive, forclos, **Bal 2** *(La departie)*, 304

Foret, *nm* drill, **B133**, 24

[Forfaire (se)], *vb* to fail in one's duty, se forfait, **R395**, 5

[Forligner], *vb* to betray, to let down, forligne, **R31**, 6

Fors (que), *adv* except, **B123**, 22

Fort (au), *adv* after all, **B134**, 14; **R13**, 3; **R245**, 10 (see also Auffort)

Fort, je me fais, I am certain, **B9**, 39; je m'en fais, I am quite certain of that, **Intro**, 194; *Songe*, 94; **R425**, 2; se fait fort (fors), is certain, **B25**, 15; **R267**, 12; se firent fort, they were confident that, **B141**, 19

Forvoier, *vb* to go astray, to lead astray, **Bal 6** *(La departie)*, 449; forvoie **Ch69**, 10; forvoye, **B63**, 26; **B137**, 23; **R247**, 8; forvoyé, **B110**, 17; **R197**, 2

Fosse, *nf* jail, **R405**, 4; **R407**, 11

Foul s'i fie, *nm personif* Untrustworthy, Fickle, **B126**, 21

Foulé (du harnois), *pastp* tired, worn out, **R92**, 3; foulee (de foiblesse), overcome, exhausted (by weakness), **B84**, 2; **R404**, 4

[Fouler], *vb* to treat badly, foulez, **Co4**, 81

Fouleur, *nm* madness, **R254**, 2 (see also Folleurs*)*

[Fouloyer], *vb* to act the fool, fouloye, **B137**, 18 (see Folloyer)

Fourbir, *vb* to polish up, brighten, **B72**, 38

Fourcelle, *nf* breast, **B65**, 15; **B88**, 2

Fournir, *vb* to furnish, provide, accomplish, **R217**, 10; **R421**, 10; attend, participate in, **R340**, 9

Fourrez, *pastp* fur-clad, **Ch60**, 1

Fourriers, *nm* harbingers, **B81**, 5; **Ch62**, 1; **R43**, 1; **R341**, 3; **R390**, 3

Foy (de mon corps), *excl* by my faith! **B49**, 9

Frain, *nm* bit, **B107**, 12

Franchise, *nf* privilege, freedom, **R66**, 11; **R314**, 10

Francs, *nm* freemen, **B86**, 10

Frangere, Latin, *vb* to exhaust, to overcome (lit. to break), **R132**, 4

Fredaine, *nf* lie, **B108**, 21

Frein, *nm* see Runger

[Fremier], *vb* to tremble, fremie, **R221**, 10

Frenesie, *nf* frenzy, **B88**, 4; **B111**, 17

Frians, *adj* tasty, **R298**, 2

Frire, *vb* to tremble, **Co7**, 50; frit, **Ch65**, 4

Frise, robe de, *nf* thick woollen coat, **R71**, 11

[Froingner], *vb* to scowl, froigne, **R186**, 11

[Froisser], *vb* to shatter, froisse, **Co1**, 35

Frontiere, *nf* tenir frontiere, regular expression, "to oppose, to resist" (Godefroy, 4:163) me tenez frontiere, oppose me, **R425**, 4

[Fuir], *vb* to flee, füy, **R288**, 11

Furieux, *adj* frenzied, **Co7**, 64

G

Gage, *nm* gage (a challenge, usually a glove thrown down), de gage je vous appelle, I challenge (defy) you, **B44**, 29

Gage(s), gagez, gaige(s), *nm* wage(s), **B84**, 5; **B86**, 13; **B105**, 34 (see note); **Ch59**, 10; **B86**, 13; **R101**, 8; **R125**, 6; **R278**, 10; pledge(s); **R171**, 10; **R322**, 1; en gage, as a pledge, **Ch41**, 3; **Intro**, 392

Gaillerdement, *adv* boldly, **R145**, 10

Galee, *nf* galley, **B85**, 1; **R321**, 1

[Galer], *vb* to squander, galé, **R187**, 5; galerons, have a good time, **R311**, 13

Galimafree, *nf* gallimaufry, hotch-potch, **R26**, 8

Game, *nf* musical scale, **R331**, 1

[Garder (se)], *vb* to take up a defensive position in chess, me suy gardé, **B58**, 3; gard, gart, protect from, **Ch72**, 9; **R91**, 8; **R200**, 4

Gardon (for guerdon), *nm* reward, **B11**, 23; **Co4**, 43

[Garmenter (se)], *vb* to lament, me garmente, **R195**, 10; **R245**, 7; se garmente, **R247**, 2; s'en garmente, **R196**, 10

Garnison, *nf* reserve, storage, **B120**, 26

Gast, *adj* waste, **R273**, 10

Gaster, *vb* to ruin, **R390**, 6

Geline, *nf* chicken, **R298**, 8

Generacion, *nf* birth ("action d'engendrer," Godefroy, 9: 692), **B109**, 18

Generaulx, *nm* tax collectors, **R187**, 9

Gent, *nf* people, **R127**, 9; **R145**, 6

Gent, gente, *adj* nice, kind, **B2**, 20; **B11**, 6; **Ch5**, 4; **R251**, 7; **R112**, 4; etc.

Gentillesse, *nf personif* Gentleness, **B9**, 19; nobility, **B115**, 24

[Gesir], *vb* to lie, to rest, gis, **R379**, 1; gist, **R72**, 4; **R277**, 4

Gestu, Latin, *nm* gesture, **R328**, 14

[Geter], *vb* to calculate, getoit, **B139**, 29 (see note)

[Gibesser], *vb* to hunt, gibessant, **R21**, 1

Gibessiere, *nf personif* Huntress, appears to be Charles's name for Diana, goddess of hunting, **R21**, 8

Gietter (la chance), *vb* to have a lucky throw at dice, **B46**, 11; je vous giette mon gant, I throw down my glove, i.e., defy you, **B44**, 1

Glay, *nm* twitter, **B48**, 6

Glose, *nf* text, commentary, **R375, 11**

Gloser, *vb* to spell out, to explain, **R181, 8**

Gloses, *nf* remarks, comments, **R77, 4; R103, 5**

Glus, *nm* bird-lime, **R119, 9**

Gnogno, Italian, *nm* **R138, 11** (see note)

Gogo, a *nm* plenty, **R138, 8**

Gorge, *nf* (getter sa), to reject its food, (of falcons, used metaphorically), **R33, 8**

Gorgias, *nm* fops, dandies, **R8, 1**

Gouffier, **R113, 10** (see note)

Goute, *nf* gout, **R443, 3**

Goutte (ne . . . g.), *nf* drop (modern ne . . . pas), **B51, 8**

Gouvernement, *nm* control, power, authority, **B37, 26; B65, 22;** *Songe,* 63; **Bal 1**
  (*La departie*), 287; **B89, 21; B99, 5; R83, 4;** state, condition, circumstances,
  B125, 19; B127, 5; R146, 11

Gouverneur(s), *nm* butler, *La departie;* 463; governors, **Co1,** 61; administrators,
  R160, 6

Grandissime, Italian, *adj* greatest, extreme, **R272, 6** (see note)

Gravelle, *nf* gravel (disease), **B88, 19**

Gré, *nm* gratitude **R134, 6;** en gré, gladly, willingly, **Ch11, 6;** bon gré maugré,
  willy-nilly, **R340, 9; R418, 7;** see also Prendre

Gregoys, grejois (feu gregeois), *adj* Greek fire, **R260, 4; R278, 9; R308, 10;** see Feu

Greigneur, *adj* greater, greatest, **Ch26, 11; R178, 10; R253, 11; R264, 10**

Grevance, *nf* grievance, suffering, **B5, 16; B22, 21; B50, 15; B122, 10; Ca2, 12 ;**
  R58, 9; R220, 2; R337, 7; etc.

Grever, *vb* to harm, to grieve, **Intro,** 429; **Co7,** 106; **R106, 3;** greva, **R263, 10;**
  grevez, **R205, 11; R437, 2;** griefve, **Co7, 12**

Greveuse, *adj* grievous, **B11, 18**

Grezil, *nm* hail, sleet, **R320, 10**

Grieff, griefs, griefz, *adj* grievous, **B12, 8; Co4, 12; R212, 6; R440, 6**

[Groigner], *vb* to scold, groingne, **R186, 5**

Groings, *nm* (faire les groings) to sulk, complain, **R270, 11**

Grois, *nm* (vin des Grois) wine from the Loir-et-Cher, **R187, 6**

[Grossoyer], *vb* to magnify, grossoye, **B137, 11**

Gueines, *nf* **R89, 2** (see note)

Guerdon, *nm* reward, **B11, 23; B15, 14; B68, 25; B80, 6; Co4, 52; Ch41, 15;** etc.

Guerdonner, *vb* to reward, **R453, 1;** guerdonné *pastp* **Co2,** 96; **Ch24, 4;** guerdonnerons, **B121, 28;** (used as substantive) reward, *Jam nova,* 47

Guerredon, see Guerdon

Guerdonnement, *nm* reward, **B71, 14**

[Guerrier], [guerroyer], *vb* to wage war on, guerrie, **B60, 26; R148, 8; R301, 6;**
  guerroye, **B103, 22**

Guet, *nm* watch, **R293, 8;** Faictes bon guet, be on the lookout, **R339, 8**

[Guetter], *vb* to watch out, guette **R171, 1**

H

Habergier, *vb* to sum up, to abbreviate, **R431, 5**

[Haïr], *vb* to hate, hay, **R446,** 6; hayent, **B122,** 4; hé, **B108,** 4; **R148,** 11; hey, **B100,** 18

Haire, *nf* hair-shirt, **R218, 7**

Hale, *nm* bright sunlight, **Ch59, 4**

[Hanir], *vb* to whinny, hanis, **R187,** 1 (see note)

[Hanter], *vb* to frequent, hanté, **R381, 9**

Happer, *vb* to catch, seize, **R265,** 9; hapé, **R31, 4**

Hardement, *nm* boldness, **R387, 4**

[Harer], *vb* to set upon, hare, **R158, 11**

Harnaiz, *nm* armour, **B87, 7**

Harnoys, *nm* harness, **B84,** 1; armor, **R92, 3**

Hasart, hazart, *nm* throw of dice, **B75,** 24; **R53, 5**

Hasté, *nm* hasty (person), **Co4, 61**

Hau, *interj* Ha! **R171, 1**

Haultaine, *adj* high, **B107, 3**

Hay avant, *excl* Go on! **R256, 9**

Haye, *nf* wood, **R251,** 6 (see note)

Hayne, *nh* hatred, **B108, 3**

Hayneux, *nm* lit. hated one, hence "enemy," **B112, 7**

Herault, *nm* herald, **R4,** 2 (see note)

Herbergier, *vb* to take shelter, **B128, 18**

Heur, *nm* good fortune, **R264, 8**

Hoir, *nm* heir, **B105, 19**

Hors, *adv* outside, hors et ens, lit. out and in, hence all over the place, all the time, **R340, 4**

[Hourder], *vb* to encumber with, hourde, **R112,** 11 (see note)

[Hucher], *vb* to summon, hucha, **Intro, 111**

Hucques, *nf* short tunics, **R71, 11**

[Huer], *vb* to boo, hue, **R169, 5**

Huis, huys, huyz, uis, *nm* door, **B119,** 13; **B138,** 21; **R97,** 6; **R201,** 4; **R202,** 8; **R219,** 7; etc.

Hurt, *nm* shock, attack, **B104, 4**

Hutin, *nm* dispute, **B133,** 19; **B74,** 8; **R264,** 8; **R265,** 8; **R301,** 11; **R377,** 16; frenzy (erotic), **R270, 5**

I

Importun, *adj* importunate, **R182, 10**

In estu, Latin, aroused, enraged (< *aestus*), **R328, 7**

In questu, Latin, on the lookout, **R328,** 2 (*questu < pastp quaesitum*)

In tuo gestu, Latin, in your gesture, **R328**, 14
Incomplexif, *adj* see notes to **B109**
Intendit, *nm* intention, **B80** (title)
Ire, *nf* anger, **B100**, 34
Irer, *vb* to annoy, anger, **R326**, 9
Issir, *nm* issue, **R231**, 10; see also Yssir

J

Ja, *adv* ever, ne . . . ja, never, **B123**, 8; **R319**, 8; ja soit ce que, although *Songe,* 110
Jame, *nf* gem, **B69**, 14
[Jangler], *vb* to chat, jangle, **R234**, 12; **R267**, 6
Janglerye, janglerie, *nf* lying, bragging, **B116**, 8; **B136**, 36; *personif* **B117**, 18
Jangleur, *nm* slanderer, **R386**, 8
Jaulier, jaullier, *nm* jailer, line 1 (refrain) in **R405, R406, R407, R408, R411, R409**, 3; **413**, 10
Jeu lier, see Lier le jeu
Jeu party, *nm* an expression with a variety of meanings, here: dilemma, **B58**, 25
Jeusne, *nm* fasting, **R275**, 9
Jojo, *nm* **R138**, 5 (see note)
[Jouster], *vb* to joust, **B107**, 19
Jubilé, *nm* fiftieth anniversary, **B72**, 34
[Juner], *vb* to fast on, june, **R218**, 11
Jus, *adv* down, **R248**, 2; sa jus, down here, *Jam nova,* 2, 66
Jusques, *adv* until **R17**, 1; jusques a cy, this far, **Co1**, 46
Just, *nm* juice, **R232**, 3

K

Karesme (prenant), *nm* festive days preceding Lent, **R105**, 10; **R127**, 2; **R263**, 2; **R275**, 8; **R377**, 4

L

Lactz, laqs, las, *nm* snare(s), trap(s), **R283**, 9; **R388**, 11; **R434**, 3
[Laier], *vb* to leave, lairay, **B11**, 7; lairez, **Co1**, 14; lerrez, **Ch53**, 6
Lame, *nf* tombstone, **R331**, 8
Langagier, *vb* to chat, **B72**, 17
Langueurs, *nf* languor, **B88**, 17
Lardon, *nm* pork fat (used as bait), **R31**, 4
Largesse, *nf* generosity, **R288**, 8; a largesse, liberally, **R432**, 9
Larrecin, *nm* robbery, **Ch39**, 13; en larrecin, stealthily, **R301**, 8
Larron(s), *nm* robber(s), **Ch55**, 1; **R355**, 9; **R410**, 5; **R412**, 6

Las, *excl* alas! **Ch42**, 9; **R11**, 2

Las, *adj* weary, **Ch43**, 5

Las, *nm* snare, *Songe*, 147; **B126**, 6

Latin, *nm* language, **B66**, 11; **R265**, 11; **R377**, 13

Layz, *adj* gens layz, laymen, **R71**, 14

Leal, *adj* loyal, *Songe*, 220; **R228**, 12; **R323**, 2

Leans, *adv* within, inside, **Intro**, 113

Leauté, *nf* loyalty, **B35**, 23

Lëesse, see Lïesse

Legier (de), *adv* easily, **Intro**, 254; **B43**, 16; *Songe*, 9; **B82**, 23; **B96**, 19; **R235**, 7; etc.

Legierement, *adv* easily, **Intro**, 294; **B125**, 26

L'en, *pron* (modern l'on) one, **Ch70**, 12; **R169**, 2; **R213**, 8

Lesir, *nm* leisure, **R97**, 2

Lesse, *nf* leash, **Co7**, 115

Lettre (de retenue), *nf* retaining letter, contract, **Intro**, 388 (see note)

Leurrer, *vb* to lure, **R85**, 5 (see note)

Levee (d'escremie), *nf* assault, **R201**, 5

Levrier, *nm* greyhound, **R133**, 10

Lie, lye, *adj* happy, **B6**, 17; **B9**, 6; **B121**, 23; **Ca1**, 4; **R169**, 6; **R283**, 3; lÿee, **B44**, 38; chiere lie, happy mien, **R267**, 7; **B83**, 21

Liement, lÿement, *adv* joyfully, happily, **Intro**, 136, 385; **B53**, 28; **Co1**, 77

Lier jeu, *vb* to take up defensive position in chess, **B58**, 13

Lier (se), *vb* to bind oneself, to promise, me lie **R149**, 2; **Co6**, 61

Lïesse, lëesse, *nf* joy, **B1**, 14; **B24**, 26; **B38**, 17; **B54**, 28; **B82**, 6; **B110**, 3; etc. (see also Lëesse)

Ligement, *adv* loyally, *Songe*, 183

Lignage, *nm personif* Lineage, **R34**, 3

Limier, *nm* hound, **R133**, 9

Lippe, *nf* lip, **R55**, 1 (see note)

[Lire], *vb* to read, ly, **B98**, 12

Lis, *nm* lily (see note), *Jam nova*, 3

Lisse, *nf* tapestry, **R257**, 10 (see note)

Livree (s), *nf* **R89**, 6 (see note), **R366**, 9

Loiaulx, *adj* reliable, sound (advice), **B142**, 24

Loppin, *nm* small amount, pincé un loppin "taken a nip of Saint Poursain wine," **B133**, 16; see Poursain

Los, loz, *nm* praise, **B9**, 8; *Jam nova*, 97; **B103**, 7; **Co4**, 48

Losengiere, *nf* deceitful, **B26**, 22

Lotz, *nm* lots, fates, **R15**, 10

Louches, faisans les, *nm* looking elsewhere (pretending not to see wrongdoing), **R394**, 11 (see note)

[Louer (se l. de)], *vb* to follow someone's advice, loue, **B113**, 14

Lours, *nm* clumsy oafs, **R4**, 8; **R234**, 3

Lous, *nm* reputation, **R427**, 5

Loyaument, leaument, *adv* loyally, **B47**, 15; **Co1**, 74; **B143**, 23;

[Luire], *vb* to gleam, to shine, luyant, **R44**, 4

Luminaire, *nm* chandelier, **B69**, 6

Luxure, *nf* debauchery, **Co3**, 16

Lye, see Lie

Lyement, *adv* happily, gladly, **R127**, 6

[Lyer], *vb* to tie, to blindfold, lye, **R399**, 10

Lyme sourde, *nf* sly woman, **R112**, 1

M

Machier, *vb* to chew, **R180**, 10

Maille, *nf* coin of little value, half a denier, **R146**, 9; **R410**, 4

Main, *adv* in the morning, **B126**, 19; **R157**, 10; **R199**, 9; **R320**, 4

Main mise, see Mise

Maindre, meindre, *nm* lesser one, **Co7**, 143; **R11**, 3; **R264**, 10

Mains, maints (modern maint), *adj* many, **R299**, 9; **R160**, 11; **R335**, 3 (see also Manoir)

Mains (modern moins), *adv* less, **R121**, 11; **R261**, 5; **R279**, 9; **R288**, 1; a tout le mains, at the very least, **R268**, 11

[Mainsseer], *vb* to chop into small pieces, to mince, mainssee, **R298**, 10

Maintenement, *nm* appearance, manner, **B9**, 38

Maintesfoiz, *adv* many a time, **B35**, 13

Mais, *adv* evermore, more, mais, **Co7**, 82; **R108**, 5; a tousjours mais, for ever more, **R391**, 2; mes que, *conj* provided that, **B11**, 22; **B49**, 23; **B51**, 18; **B83**, 19; **Co3**, 23 etc.

Maistrie, *nf* domination, **B115**, 33; **B118**, 18

Mal, male, malle, *adj* bad, evil, maulx, **B86**, 14; **R53**, 4; **R163**, 2; *nm* troubles, **Co4**, 12; Que male part y ait on, A plague on, **R107**, 5; malles bouches, slanderers, **R394**, 10

Malassenee, *adj* badly married wife, **R270**, 10

Mal Saint Martin, *nm* drunkenness, **B133**, 5 (see note)

Mal talant, see Talant

[Malcontenter (s'en)], to be discontented (with), s'en malcontente, **R366**, 11

Maledicatur, Latin, *vb* may he be cursed, **R263**, 11

Malencontreux, *adj* unwelcome, disagreeable, **B112**, 18

Maleure(e), *adj* unfortunate, **R251**, 4; bringing misfortune, **R273**, 12

Malla jura, Latin, bad laws, **R131**, 8

Mallement, *adv* badly, **R123**, 4

Malvueillance, *nf* malevolence, **Intro**, 303; **B44**, 23

Mandement, *nm* command, **R277**, 9; **R387**, 3

Mander, *vb* to communicate, to make known, to summons, to tell, **B21**, 8; **B36**, 11; **B129**, 4; mande, **B37**, 15; **R377**, 10; **R422**, 3; manderay, **Ch21**, 9; mandons, **B79**, 4

[Manger], *vb* to eat, mengue, **B103**, 2; **B104**, 17

Manoir, *vb* to remain, **B18**, 29; *La departie*, 508; mains, **R332**, 5 (cf. Remanoir, **B19**, 20)

[Manyer], *vb* to handle, manye, **B136**, 29

Marchant (en Lombardie), *nm* usurer, **B135**, 9

Marché, *nm* bargaining, negotiation, **R83**, 1

Marmiteux (faictes le), *nm* (you) make a pretence of shame, **R255**, 6

Marry, marrie, *adj* downcast, **Ch22**, 6; **R36**, 5; **R193**, 4

Martire, *nm* suffering, **B113**, 5

Massue, *nf* clown's bauble, **R130**, 1

Mat, *adj* checkmated, **B58**, 8; beaten, **B109**, 9

Mau, *adv* badly, **R299**, 11

[Maudire], *vb* to curse, maudie, **R68**, 10

Maugracïeux, *adj* ill-disposed, ungracious, **Ca1**, 16

Maugré, maulgré, *prep* despite, **B37**, 16; **B123**, 14; **Ch25**, 12; **Ch33**, 3; maugré mien, despite myself, **Ch32**, 12; **R456**, 4; bon gré maugré, willy-nilly, **R340**, 9; ne m'en sachiez maugré, do not bear me ill-will, **B9**, 48

Mayne, see Mener

Meffaire, see Mesfaire

Meffait, *nm* wrongdoing, **R226**, 2

Meillieu, milleu, *nm* middle, **R305**, 4; **R307**, 1

Meller (se), *vb* to meddle with, **B134**, 4 (see Mesler)

Menasser, *vb* to threaten, **B84**, 23

Mener, *vb* to bring, to take, **Intro**, 27, 354; mayne, **B81**, 10; merront, **R196**, 8; see Chief, also Deux

Menus, *adj* small, trivial, **R49**, 8

Merancolie, merencolie, *nf personif* Melancholy, **R148**, 4; **R149**, 3; **R274**, 2; **R286**, 1; etc.

[Mercher], *vb* to mark, merchera, **B132**, 19 (see note)

Mercier, *vb* to thank, **B28**, 29; mercy, **Ch62**, 3

Mercier, *nm* merchant, **R318**, 1; **R319**, 3,

Mergo, Latin, *vb* I am sinking, **R137**, 1

Mes (modern mets), *nm* dishes, courses, **R231**, 4

Meschance, *nf personif* Misfortune, **B5**, 7; **R53**, 4

Meschans, *nm* unfortunate people, **B53**, 12

Meschantement, *adv* unhappily, **R342**, 4

Meschief, *nm* mischief, **B58**, 6; *La departie*, 289; **R277**, 6

[Mesconter], *vb* to misunderstand, mesconte, **R256**, 5

Mesdisans, *nm* evil gossips, **Ch55**, 5

[Mesfaire], *vb* to act badly, to mistreat, mefface, **R206**, 6; **R269**, 14; mesfacent, **Co1**, 88; mesfist, *Jam nova*, 59

Mesgnie, *nf* household, **B26**, 26

[Mesler], *vb* to mix, meslee, **B97**, 6 (see Meller)

Mesnagiere, mesnagiers, *nm* servant(s), worker(s), **R257**, 9; **R409**, 8

Mesnaige, *nm* household, **R306**, 4

Mesprison, *nf* wrong, injustice, abuse, **B120**, 6; **R280**, 10

Mestier(s), *nm* affair(s), business, **B119**, 2; **B139**, 42; **R129**, 3; **R369**, 11; necessity, **R235**, 2; sus le mestier, lit. on the business, i.e., ongoing, **R122**, 10

[Mestrier], *vb* to control, mestrie, **B136**, 26

Meur, *adj* ripe, **B104**, 17; **B120**, 4

Meure, *nf* blackberry, **R220**, 13

Mie (mye), *nf* crumb (ne . . . mie = modern ne . . . pas), **B64**, 9; *La departie*, 426; **B94**, 6; **B111**, 7; **R225**, 12; etc.

Mignons, *nm* fops, dandies, **R371**, 1

Mipartie, *adj* consisting of half, **B88**, 10

Mire, *nm* doctor, **B21**, 14; **R53**, 11; **R392**, 6

Mirer (se), *vb* to look at oneself, **B35**, 8; mirez, **R329**, 6

Mirlifiques, *nm* trinkets, **R319**, 1

Mise, *nf* expense, **B85**, 18; sans faire mise ne recepte, without incurring expense or income, i.e., having nothing to do (with the world), **R291**, 1

Mise, *pastp* de main mise, **Intro**, 272 (see note), **R66**, 1

Mitte, *nf* coin of little value, farthing, **B125**, 32

[Moillier], *vb* to wet, moillant, **B66**, 17; moilliez, **B56**, 27

Moisteur, *nf* moisture, **B102**, 14

Mommerie, *nf* masquerade, **B118**, 5; *personif* **R234**, 6

Mon (se faiz mon), *adv* for sure, **R78**, 5; **R217**, 6

Mondaine, *adj* secular, worldly, **B94**, 3 (see note)

Monnoye descriee, *nf* out-of-date coinage, **R414**, 1; **R416**, 1

Mont, *nm* a mont et a val, up hill and down dale, **Co4**, 95

Montjoye, *nf* **Co3**, 29 (see note); **B124**, 22; **R279**, 5

Montres, *nf* troop review, display, **B84**, 4

Mordre, *vb* to bite, to assault, **B112**, 28 "attaquer qq'un avec méchanceté," Godefroy, 10:134); mort, **B91**, 23; **R423**, 10

[Morfondre], *vb* to catch a cold, morfondez, **Ch70**, 11; downcast, miserable (with boredom), morfondus, **R43**, 8

Morisque, *nf* Morris dance, **R276**, 2

Mosnier, *nm* miller, **R300**, 8

Mouches, *nf* liars, informers, **R394**, 2

Moue, *nf* grimace, **B104**, 6; **B113**, 22

Mouldre, *vb* to grind, **R300**, 2

Moullié, *pastp* wet (with tears), **R40**, 8

Moult, *adv* much, **B21**, 7; **B64**, 2

Moustier(s), moutier, *nm* church(es), **B69**, 2; **B115**, 15; **R431**, 8

Moustrer, *vb* to show, **Co2**, 29; **Ch31**, 1; moustré, **Co2**, 42; moustrez, **B119**, 1

[Movoir], to move, put forward, propose, meuf, **B109**, 13; meu **Co7**, 13 (I move, etc.); se meuve, **R441**, 11

Moye, *pron* mine, **R100**, 6; **R212**, 11

Moyennant, *presp* in accordance with, **R271**, 4

Mue, *nf* moult, **B119**, 14; moulting cage, **R85**, 8

Mue, *adj* dumb, **R130**, 5

Muer, *vb* to change, **B136**, 22; **R48**, 13; mue, **B109**, 22; muee, **B54**, 45

Mur, *nm* Ad ce mur! Help! **B106**, 12 (see note)

Murdrir, *vb* to murder, to be murdered, **R177**, 9

Murtriés, *nm* murderers, **R410**, 5

Musart, *nm* simpleton, **R125**, 6

Muser, *vb* to waste one's time on, **R110**, 5; musoye, **R154**, 9

Musser, *vb* to hide, **Ch59**, 6; **R59**, 11; **R275**, 1; musse, **R239**, 10; mussee, *Songe*, 8; **R324**, 6; mussees, **R82**, 10; mussent, **R307**, 2; mussez, **R206**, 1; mussié, **Ch33**, 2

My partie, *pastp* in two equal portions, **R231**, 12

N

Nanyl, nay, **R256**, 11 *adv* (see Nennil)

[Na(s)vrer], *vb* to wound, nasvra, **B65**, 1; nasvré, **B65**, 26; navra, **R339**, 4

Natee, *pastp* carpeted, **R223**, 10

[Nayer], *vb* to drown, nayent (se), **R94**, 3

Necte, *adj* clean, **R326**, 5

Nef, *nf* ship, **R294**, 4; **R451**, 3

Neiz, *adv* same as, no less than, **R394**, 2

Nennil, nennyl, *adv* nay, **Co1**, 17; **R58**, 10; **R195**, 12; **R299**, 6; **R327**, 6

Nestre, *vb* to be born, **R130**, 10

Nesung, *pron* no one, anyone, **R182**, 9; **R266**, 10

Nettier (la dent), *vb* to clean, **B125**, 17; nettié, **B120**, 20

Neu, neux, *nm* knot(s), **B97**, 19; **R167**, 5; **R455**, 8

Nice, nysse, *adj* stupid, **Intro**, 305; **Ch66**, 9

Nicement, *adv* stupidly, **Intro**, 234; **B137**, 23

[Nier], *vb* to deny, nye **R282**, 6

Nigromance, nygromancye, *nf* necromancy, witchcraft, black magic, **B109**, 8; **R297**, 8

Nois (valoir une), *nf* to be worthless, **R194**, 8

Noise, noyse, *nf* annoyance, dispute, **Co6**, 91; **Ch55**, 10; **R378**, 4

Noli me tangere, Latin, do not touch me, **R132**, 1 (see note)

Nomper, *nf* peerless lady, *Songe*, 261

Non est cura, Latin, there is no interest, no point, **R131**, 5

Non obstant, Latin, notwithstanding, *Jam nova*, 52
Non semel sed bis, Latin, not once but twice, **R139**, 8
Non temptabis, Latin, you shall not tempt, **R136**, 1
Nonchaloir, *nm personif* Indifference, **B7**, 11; **B19**, 21; ne me mettez a nonchaloir,
      do not forsake me, **B52**, 19; mectre a nonchaloir, forsake, cast aside, **B80**,
      22; **Co6**, 25; **Ch12**, 9
Notoire, *adj* notorious, well known, **R416**, 12
[Nouer], *vb* to swim, noue **B104**, 8
Nourrir, *vb* to nurture, to bring up, **Intro**, 6; nourry, **R261**, 2
Nourriture, *nf* upbringing, **Intro**, 16
Nox buze, Italian, **R272**, 1 (see note)
Nuee, *nf* storm cloud, **R48**, 5
[Nuire], *vb* to harm, nuisans, nuysans, **R317**, 9; **R213**, 6
Nullui, nulluy, *pron* nobody, anybody, **B30**, 19; **Co7**, 150; **Ch69**, 2; **R24**, 2; **R276**,
      11; **R288**, 1; etc.
Nuysans, *adj* harmful, annoying, **R213**, 6
Nycement, *adv* stupidly, **R371**, 9
Nyent, *nm* nothing, in vain, **R287**, 4

O

Oberliques, *nf* trinkets, **R319**, 2
Oblie (see Oublie), *nf* forgetfulness, **R37**, 5 (see note)
Obliés mie (fleurs de ne m'), *nm* forget-me-nots, **R37**, 11; see Oublie
Obligation, *nf* obligation, legal undertaking, **B78** (title); **B79** (title)
Observance, *nf* Observant (strict Franciscan) Order, **B77**, 8 (see note); **B109**, 26;
      R204, 1; **R218**, 2; **R220**, 1; **R224**, 3; etc.
Obvier (a), *vb* to take precautions against, **B104**, 11
[Occire], *vb* to kill, occit, **R41**, 4; ocys, **R434**, 10
Octroy, *nm* concession, **B1**, 17
[Octroyer], *vb* to grant, octroye, *La departie*, 341; **B101**, 25; **Ch71**, 3; octroyez,
      R2, 11 (see also Ottrier)
Octz, *nm* bones, **R298**, 9
Oeill, see Eueil
Office, *nm* role, position, **R334**, 6
Oïr, see Ouïr
Oiseuse, *nf personif* Sloth, Idleness, **B87**, 8
Onc, oncques, oncquez, onques, *adv* ever (onques . . . ne = modern jamais . . .
      ne), **B64**, 21; **B100**, 5; *Jam nova*, 53; **Co1**, 51, 64; **Co5**, 24; **B117**, 21; etc.;
      oncques mais . . . ne, nevermore, **B72**, 20
Or, ore, *adv* now, **B129**, 34; **R237**, 6; Or ça, **B92**, 1; **R57**, 9; see Ça
Ordonnance, *nf* order, arrangement, orderly fashion, **B92**, 25; **Co4**, 31; **R67**, 10;
      R444, 6

Ordonner, *vb* to command, give orders, **B83**, 3

Orfaverie, *nf* gold work, **R44**, 10

Orine, *nf* urine, **R126**, 2

Ort, *adj* horrible, **B119**, 11

[Ottrier], (variant of Octroyer) *vb* ottrie, **B116**, 33; ottroit, *La departie*, 543

Ou, *prep* (=en+le) in the **B35**, 1; **B96**, 27; **Ch9**, 1; **R326**, 1; **R392**, 12

Oublie, oublye (see Oblie), *nf* forget-me-not, **B83**, 13; **R231**, 4; *personif* Forget-fulness, Oblivion, **R37**, 5; **R450**, 2

Oubliete, *nf* forget-me-not, **R229**, 6; prison, **R248**, 4

Oueil, see Eueil

Ouïr, oïr, ouyr, to hear, **B40**, 6; *La departie*, 495, 501, 504; **Co1**, 83; **R56**, 4; **R192**, 11; **R421**, 6; etc.; oit, **R343**, 4; oyt, **R343**, 1, 5; hoit, **R344**, 1; orra **B55**, 12; **R253**, 10; orroit, **R38**, 10; orrons, **B48**, 6; orroye, **B127**, 7; oüy, **Ch55**, 5; **R325**, 2; oy, **B71**, 1; *La departie*, 307; **B82**, 2; **B91**, 1; **Ch26**, 2; **R71**, 1; etc.; oÿ, **Ch2**, 5; oye, **B115**, 18; **Ch45**, 14; **Ch71**, 6; **R191**, 6; **R341**, 8; oyt, **B69**, 24

Oultrance (a), *nf* to excess, **R98**, 4; **R346**, 4; **R356**, 8; **R416**, 5

Oultre, *prep* beyond, **B91**, 29; **B114**, 17; **R126**, 5; **R423**, 14 (beyond the edge, i.e., too far); oultre plus, *adv* furthermore, **B70**, 19; *La departie*, 517, 533; **Co7**, 9; **R281**, 8; etc.

Oultrecuidance, *nf* pretentiousness, **B22**, 25; **B117**, 22

Oultrecuidyer, *nm personif* Presumption, **R241**, 3

Ouvrer, *vb* to toil, **B89**, 15; **R140**, 10; ouvree, **R21**, 8 motivated by (Pastime)

Ouvrier (jour), *adj* working day, **R318**, 8

Ouyl, *adv* yes, **R171**, 2; **R400**, 3

Oyes, *nf* geese, **R183**, 2

P

Paeur, paour, *nf* fear, **B68**, 3; **B105**, 17; **R358**, 11

Paillart, *nm* commoner, knave, **B107**, 22

Paintes, *pastp* specious, **B72**, 23

Paintures, *nf* deceptive words, **R310**, 5

Pestre, *vb* to feed, peu, I fed, **R21**, 10; l'erbe pestre, lit. to graze the grass, i.e., to dismiss, to send packing, **Ch67**, 5; **R118**, 4

Pansement, pensement, *nm* thought, **R42**, 3; **R205**, 10

Paons, *nm* **R305**, 8 (see note)

Papelart, *nm* religious hypocrite, Tartuffe, **R183**, 5

Par aler, paral(l)er (au), *adv* finally, after all, **B17**, 30; **B39**, 23; **B49**, 7; **B136**, 14; **R198**, 6; etc.

Parabolles, *nf* lies, deceitful words, **R336**, 3

Parachever, *vb* to complete, to conclude, parachevez, **R278**, 11; **R453**, 10

Parcial, *adj* special, private, a man apart, **B105**, 33

Parçonniers, *nm* participants, **Ch37**, 4

Pardon, *nm* pardon, **R89**, 8 (see note); **R281**, 11

[Pardonner], *vb* to forgive, pardoint, **R6**, 5; **R383**, 7

Parfaire, *vb* to carry on, to complete, **R318**, 10; parfait, **R214**, 6; parfaiz, **B76**, 35

Parfont, *adj* deep, **B49**, 2; **B106**, 1; **R324**, 2

Parfournir, *vb* to realise (profits), **B101**, 22

[Parler], *vb* to speak, je parle plain, I speak plainly, **R320**, 12

[Paroir], *vb* to appear, pert, **B133**, 12; **R7**, 4; **R116**, 8; **R374**, 4; parra, **B129**, 34; perra, **B82**, 20; **R346**, 2,

Part, a par(t) soy, *adv* alone, **B8**, 22; **B56**, 9; **R24**, 13; **R53**, 9; a par moy, **B63**, 2; **R67**, 8; a par elle, *La departie*, 398; on the French side, **B129**, 19; see also Mal

Partement, *nm* departure, **R401**, 1

Partie, *nf* court case, **B99**, 32

[Partir], *vb* to depart, to come from, part **R15**, 2

Partir, *vb* to share out, **Co4**, 99

[Partuer], *vb* to kill, partués **Intro**, 236

Party, *nm* cause, **B62**, 6; **B66**, 26; **Co2**, 52; **B129**, 31; **B132**, 24; plight, **B22**, 8; **B42**, 17

[Pasmer], *vb* to swoon, pasmé, **R405**, 3

Passee (a la), *nf* in passing, **R431**, 9; passees, lit. breaches, hence blunders, **R349**, 5

Passer, *vb* passer le pas, to cross the threshold, *Songe*, 151; vous en passez, you ignore it, **R338**, 6

Passion, *nf* suffering, torment, **B80**, 10; **B109**, 27

Pastis, *nm* thin pastureland, **B25**, 11 (see note)

Patins, *nm* rags and tatters, **R90**, 10

Paulme, *nf* real tennis, **B132**, 2

Pavais, *nm* large shield, **B4**, 11; pavaiz, **B87**, 6; paveis, **R339**, 5

Pavillon, *nm* trap (for catching birds), **R32**, 1; tent, **R416**, 3

[Peigner], *vb* to comb, to curry, peignez, **R460**, 11

Pelerins, *nm* pilgrims, **R90**, 2

Penance, *nf* penance, penitence, self-mortification, **B116**, 25; **R58**, 6; **R334**, 8

Pencarte, *nf* map, **B85**, 11 (see note)

Pener (se), *vb* to strive, take pains, **B33**, 20

Peneuse, *adj* painful, **B87**, 17; **R433**; 9

[Penser], *vb* to bandage, pensee, **R354**, 5

Pense levee, *nf* swollen belly, **R270**, 6; see note to **B134**, 15

Pension, *nf* reward, **Intro**, 410; **B77**, 19; **B80**, 15

Per(s), *nm* peer, equal, **B1**, 13; **B9**, 33; **Ch42**, 3; companion chosen on St Valentine's Day, **R3**, 2; **R129**, 11; **R128**, 2; **R264**, 9; New Year companion, **R223**, 2; une sans per, peerless lady, **R379**, 10; le non per, man without equal (in torment), **R385**, 8

[Percuter], *vb* to pierce through and through, percus, **B88**, 5 (see note)

Peresse, *nf* idleness, neglect, **B27**, 19

Pergo, Latin, I proceed, I go to, **R137,** 5

Pertuis, pertuiz, *nm* holes, **B138,** 13; **R90,** 4

Peschier, *nm* **R30,** 1 (see note)

[Peser], *vb* to weigh on, to grieve, poise, *La departie,* 512

Pesson, *nm* small coin, **R194,** 11, see Vente

Pestre, see Paistre

Peu, *adv* a peu que, almost, **R15,** 14

Phisique, *nm* physician, **R445,** 10

[Picquer], *vb* to prick, picque, **R423,** 10

Pie, *nf* magpie, desduit de la pie, pleasure of drinking, **R369,** 6 (see note)

Pieça, *adv* a long time ago, **B4,** 17; **B40,** 25; **B87,** 7; **B94,** 9; **Co3,** 22; **R111,** 11; etc.

Piece, *nf* (piece of) time, **R347,** 1; amount, **R347,** 4

Pigne, *nm* comb, **R31,** 10

[Pigner], *vb* to comb, pigne **R31,** 9 (this form is needed for the rhyme, but the context suggests, rather, peine, is suffering)

[Piler], *vb* to crush, pilé, **R221,** 11

Pille, *nf* side of coin opposite face, sans croix ne pille, penniless (lit. without heads or tails), **R412,** 9

Pïon, *nm* pawn (chess), **B58,** 14

Pipee, pippee, *nf* bird-trap, hunt for birds, **R8,** 2; **R388,** 11

[Piper], *vb* lit. to trap birds by imitating their call, pipant (en), **R119,** 9

Pis, piz, *adv* worse, worst, **R445,** 6; je les metz au pis, **B73,** 18; have the worst possible opinion of them (lit. I put them at their worst), worse **B83,** 14; **R12,** 10; **R57,** 1; **R140,** 10

Pitance, *nf* pittance, **B77,** 20

Piteux, *adj* compassionate, **B12,** 27; **B24,** 18; **B32,** 11; **B69,** 5; *Songe,* 70; **B88,** 1; **B102,** 7; **R255,** 2; pitiful, **B112,** 25; **R52,** 4; **R273,** 14; **R436,** 5; *n* compassionate people, **B86,** 9

Plain (a), *adv* fully, *Songe,* 137

Plainctureux, see Plantureux

[Plaindre], *vb* to complain, plains, **B100,** 16; **Co1,** 2; plaingnans, plaintive, causing complaints, **B88,** 9

Plains, *nm* complaints, lamentations, **Co1,** 63; **Co5,** 123; **R268,** 5

Plais, *nm* lit. cases, legal matters, tient avec Amour ses plais, discusses his (legal) affairs with Love **B49,** 19

Plaisance, *nf personif* Pleasure, **Co6,** 75; not personified, **Co7,** 80

Plangere, Latin, to complain, to lament, **R132,** 11

Planté, *nf* abundance, **Co4,** 75; **Ch25,** 3

Planter (une bourde), *vb* to tell a joke, **R112,** 4

Plantureux, plaintureux, *adj* abundant, **B68,** 25; **R436,** 19

[Plaquer], *vb* to stamp, plaque, *La departie,* 408

Plouvoir, *vb* to rain, **R147,** 10

Ploy, *nm* situation, **B7,** 25

Pluieux, *adj* rainy, **B138**, 9

[Poindre], *vb* to prick, point, **R162**, 5

Point, *nm* en point, in good health, **B112**, 21

Poire(s) d'angoisse, *nf* bitter pear(s), **Co1**, 33; **R232**, 7 (see note)

Pois, poix au veau, *nm* **R151**, 9 (see note); **R229**, 3

Poison, *nm* fish, **R31**, 3

Pompes, *nf* pomp, **B76**, 20

Port, *nm* pass, defile, **B3**, 22

Porte Baudet, popular name for one of the gates of Paris, properly Baudoyer, **R459**, 1

Pose, *nf* pause, spell, **R375**, 5

Posé que, *pastp* given that, **R427**, 9

Pot aux roses, *nm* secret, mystery, **R77**, 11

Pou, *adv* little **R204**, 9 (see also Peu)

Poulaine, *nf* long pointed shoe in fashion at the time, **R8**, 9

Pouldre de raisin, *nf* lit. grape dust, i.e., wine, or the sight or smell of it, **B133**, 9

Poupinés, *nm* little babies, **R138**, 10

Pource, *conj* accordingly, **B82**, 17; **B114**, 12; **B118**, 14; **R73**, 8; **R155**, 10; etc.; pource que, because, **R147**, 1

[Pourchacier (vers)], *vb* to urge, pourchacié, **Co3**, 17

Pourchas, *nm* quest, **Ch30**, 1; pursuit, **Ch44**, 3

Pourchassier, *vb* to pursue, to seek out, **Ch33**, 11; pourchassay, **Co6**, 48; pourchace, **R269**, 5; pourchacee, **R411**, 4, pourchassié, **Ca2**, 8

[Pourmener], *vb* to walk, to exercise, pourmaine, **Ch70**, 12 (see note to Barrez)

Pourpenser, *vb* to reflect, think about, **B59**, 1; pourpensee, **R334**, 11; **R428**, 9

Pourpensés, *nm* thoughts, **R49**, 8

Pourpoint, *nm* doublet, **R12**, 11 (see note)

Pourpos, *nm* intention, purpose, *La departie*, 306; **R26**, 6

Pourpris, *nm* enclosure, **R438**, 11

Poursain (Saint), *nm* name of a wine from the region near the village of Saint-Pourçain-sur-Sioule, **B133**, 17

Poursuivant (d'Amours), *nm* messenger, **R4**, 1 (see note)

Pourtraire, *vb* to portray, **B69**, 17

Pourveance, *nf* provision, **R98**, 8; **R159**, 4; **R272**, 6; **R443**, 10

Pourvoir (se), *vb* to prepare oneself, to provide, *Songe*, 112; pourverra, **R392**, 8; pourveu, *Songe*, 110; **R395**, 12; pourvoy, *Songe*, 115; pourvoye, **Co5**, 46; **Ch69**, 11; pourvoyent **R200**, 10

Pous(e), *nm* pulse, **B83**, 9; **R3**, 9; **R166**, 8

Povair, povoir, *nm* power, ability, **Intro**, 164, etc. (see note)

[Povoir], *vb* to be able to, puet, **B88**, 25; **B90**, 4; etc.; puist, **B41**, 8; **Co3**, 87; **R118**, 1; pouair, pouoient, etc., see note to **Intro**, 164

Poy, *adv* (a) little, **R151**, 4; **R155**, 4; **R171**, 5; **R429**, 4

Poys, *nm* weight, **Co6**, 100 (see note)

Precieuses, *nf* precious, worthy, **R168**, 3

[Prendre], *vb* to take, Tout prens en gré, I take all in good heart, **B11**, 21; je prens en gré, **B108**, 6; en gré prens, **R238**, 10; prangne en gré, put up with, **Ch21**, 11; en gré le preigne (qui poura), take it in good heart (whoever is able to do so), **B92**, 17; prenant en gré, **B98**, 15; putting up with, en gré prendray, **B81**, 17; I shall welcome, make do with, en gré prengnent, **B90**, 25; Let them be happy with, prengne, **B95**, 20; **R189**, 10; prenez en gré, **R2**, 9; deign to accept, prenez l'en gré, **Co4**, 107; put up with it, prent en gré, **Co7**, 136; puts up with, preigne, **R213**, 4; prisse, **R96**, 4

Pres (en), *prep* close to, **R242**, 6

Presse, se mettra souvent en, *nf* will often strive to, **B51**, 21; mettre en presse, to enclose, **B120**, 15; throng (of admirers), **Ch10**, 10; sans presse, alone, in private, **Ch39**, 7

Prestement, *adv* swiftly, **B127**, 25

Preu, *nm* advantage, **R167**, 11

Prier, *nm* request, **B20**, 2

Pris, *nm* price, value, **B85**, 4 (see note); reward, **R23**, 1

[Priser], *vb* to value, to esteem, prise, **R257**, 11; prisez, **R105**, 2

Privee, *adj* familiar, **R422**, 4

Priveement, *adv* secretly, **R72**, 3

Probacion, *nf* testing, confirmation, **B79**, 32

Probavi te, Latin, I have put you to the test, **R136**, 5

Procul a nobis, Latin, far from us, **R139**, 1

Propos, *nm* intention, **Co4**, 73; **Ch56**, 4; **R202**, 1; **R285**, 2; **R322**, 1; **R368**, 11

[Proscrire], *vb* to proscribe, exile, proscript, *Jam nova*, 67

Proveheur, *nm* purveyor (official charged with the supply of requisites, evidently a suitable task for Desire), **R219**, 11

Prune, *nf* plum, **R180**, 11 (see note)

Puis, *adv* puis deux jours, for the last two days, **R13**, 9 (modern depuis)

Q

Quanque, *pron* whatever, **B10**, 9; **Co7**, 145; **Ch45**, 2; **Ch52**, 11; **R37**, 2; **R155**, 5

Quans, *adj* large number of, **R162**, 11

Quarantaine, *nf* forty, **B102**, 3

Quartaine, *nf* see Fievre

Quartiers (par), *nm* in military quarters, lodgings, **B81**, 14

Quas amatis, Latin, which you love, **R135**, 4

Querelle(s), *nf* cause(s), **B28**, 25; **B31**, 19; **B33**, 21; **B41**, 11; **B58**, 15; **B82**, 19; etc.

Querir, querre, *vb* to seek, **Intro**, 323; **B23**, 17; **B25**, 1; **B101**, 13; **Co4**, 55; **R280**, 2; **R309**, 3; **R340**, 6; etc., querant **B108**, 7; **R442**, 3; querez, **B36**, 13; **R310**, 3; **R344**, 5; queroye, *La departie*, 456; quier, **B33**, 5; **B49**, 23; **B100**, 7; quiere, **R322**, 3; quiers, **B77**, 25

Queu, *nm* chef, **R370**, 8

Queue (double), *nf* B79, 12 (see note)

Quicte et quicte, *adj* quits, R389, 2

Quieulx, *pron* (= modern quels), what, R73, 18; R401, 11

Quilles, *nf* skittles, a variety of bowling R90, 11 (see note)

Quintaine, quintayne, *nf* tilting, R92, 1; tilting-block, B104, 9; B109, 9; R459, 10; target, B110, 9

Quoy(e) (see Coy, also Tenir), *adj* tranquil, unruffled B140, 18; R164, 4; R205, 4; R330, 4

R

Rabat, *nm* lower price, R237, 4; rabat joie, killjoy (old age), Bal 6 (*La departie*), 451

Rabat, *nm* in tennis, rebound of the ball, B76, 36

[Rabatre], *vb* to cast down, to reduce, rabas, R351, 8

[Rachasser], *vb* rachassant, B132, 11 (see note)

Raençonné, *pastp* ransomed, Ch18, 10

Raison, *nf* address, Co7, 195; qui me fera de vous raison, who will help me get the better of you, B44, 4

Ralier, *vb* to reconcile, *Jam nova*, 30

[Ramener], *vb* to bring back (to), to return (to), to recall, ramaine, *Jam nova*, 115; B109, 19

Ramentevoir, *vb* to remind, B127, 27; ramentoit, B60, 1; ramentoive, B54, 6

Rans, see Rendre

[Rapaiser (se)], *vb* to relax, rapaise, Ch58, 9; R304, 3; rapaisons, R172, 11

[Rapeller (se)], *vb*, to change one's mind, se rapelle R271, 9

Rapport, *nm* information, news R279, 6

Rapporter (se), *vb* to count on, to rely on, Co6, 19; R250, 6; m'en rapporte, *Jam nova*, 99

Rassiz, *pastp* firm, settled, composed, *Jam nova*, 109

Rassoter, *vb* to be stupid, to act stupidly, B134, 2; rassoté, R419, 11; rassotez, R234, 2; rassottée, R276, 9; rassoutee, R163, 3; rassoutie, B99, 25; rassotiz, R39, 8; rassoty, R36, 11

[Ravaler], *vb* to lower, to humble, ravalé, **Intro**, 252; ravalle, Co6, 97; ravallee, R416, 10

Ravir, *vb* to carry off, to delight, Ch72, 5; raviz, B77, 10; ravye, Co7, 129; ravy en trance, R444, 10

Raviser (soy), *vb* to change one's mind, B41, 4

Ravoir, *vb* to recover, to redeem, B105, 34 (see note)

[Rayer], *vb* to strike off, rayé, R101, 8

Rebaillier, *vb* to restore, to give back, *Songe*, 229; rebaillant, *Songe*, 60; rebaillié, *Songe*, 378

Rebours (tourner a), *nm* the wrong way, the opposite **B58**, 21; **B78**, 17; *Jam nova*,
    11; **Co1**, 29; **R38**, 6; **R192**, 6; etc.; riens a rebours, anything wrong, **R4**, 5;
    au rebours, **R160**, 4

[Rebouter], *vb* to repel, reboutant, reboute, **R295**, 11; reboutant, **R275**, 4;
    rebouté, **B32**, 15; reboutee; **B95**, 7; Jamais ne m'y rebouteray, lit. Nevermore
    shall I thrust myself, i.e., fall into (your trap), **R283**, 8

[Recevoir], *vb* to receive, reçoit (receives, i.e., understands, gets) **B106**, 7

Reclamer, *vb* to acclaim, to invoke, to call upon, to summon, **B108**, 20; reclamés,
    Ch68, 1

Reclus, *nm* recluse, **B42**, 32; **R119**, 10; **R248**, 11; **R249**, 4; **R433**, 11

Reclusaige, *nm* isolation, reclusion, **B76**, 17

Recors, *nm* witnesses, *Songe*, 411

Recours, *nm* recourse, **R254**, 4; **R379**, 11; **R436**, 16

Recous, see Rescorre

Recouvrance, *nf* recovery, **B116**, 22

Recouvrer, *vb* to recover, **Ch38**, 11; recouvreray, **R216**, 10; recouvré, *Jam nova*,
    17 (see note)

Recoy, see Requoy

[Recroire], *vb* to weary, recreu, *Songe*, 111; **R261**, 8

Recueil, *nm* reception, welcome, **R238**, 10; meditation, **R387**, 7 (see also Requeil)

[Recueillir], *vb* to receive, to get, to have, recueil, **Co2**, 76; **R184**, 14

Redire, *vb* to criticise, **B113**, 18; **R15**, 3

Redite, *nf* repetition, **R140**, 5

[Redresser], *vb* to repair, to put right, redresse, **R442**, 14

[Reffaire], *vb* to reassure, to comfort, refait, **Co7**, 12

Reffraindre, *vb* to refrain, to hold in check, **B91**, 19; **R102**, 9; refrain, *Jam nova*, 95

[Refuir], *vb* to flee, refuy, **B17**, 21

Regere, Latin, to rule, **R132**, 5

[Regiber], *vb* to rebel, regibe, **R130**, 8

Regnart, see Renart

Regnon, *nm* reputation, **R386**, 6

Relacion, *nf* copy of a juridical act, **B79**, 10

[Relaisser], *vb* to release, relaissera, *La departie*, 343

Relievement, *nm* relief, **R397**, 5

Relique, *nf* relic, **R292**, 10

Remanoir, *vb* to remain, to restore to, **B19**, 20; remaine, **R325**, 9; remains, **R347**,
    11; remaint, **Co6**, 28; **R427**, 12

Remerchier, *vb* **R21**, 6 (see note)

[Remettre], *vb* to restore, to give back to, remiz, **R403**, 11; wearied, remis, **R40**, 8

Remoustrer, *vb* to show, **B31**, 21

Renart, regnart, *nm* Reynard the fox, sly, cunning individual, **R183**, 1; **R125**, 3

[Rencheoir], *vb* to fall ill again, rencheez, **R231**, 13

Risee, *nf* laughter, **R48**, 10; *personif* **R366**, 2

[Robber, Rober], *vb* to rob, robbé, **R197**, 4; robez, **R301**, 9

Robeurs, *nm* robbers, pirates, **B28**, 35

Rocq, *nm* rook (chess piece), **B58**, 15

Rompre sa teste, to strive in vain, to rack one's brains, **R141**, 5; **R289**, 1; romperoye, **R154**, 10

Ronde, *nf* en la ronde, round about, all around, **B92**, 10

[Ronger], *vb* to chafe, en roingeant mon frain, champing at the bit, **R186**, 11

Rongneux, *adj* mangy, scabby, **B133**, 3

Roussin, *nm* horse, **R376**, 11; ronssin, **B133**, 23

Route, *nf* band, company, **Ch72**, 10; **R191**, 8; **R307**, 8

Route (< Lat. *pastp. ruptum*), *adj* broken, defeated, **R145**, 1; **R190**, 11

Rouz (coups), **Co6**, 24 (see note)

Rubis, *nm* ruby, *Jam nova*, 106

[Ruer], *vb* to kick, rue, **R130**, 8; **R460**, 6; rué jus, lit. kicked down, hence ruined,
R343, 6

Runger, *vb* frein runger, champ at the bit, **R55**, 6

S

Sabat (mener le), *nm* to ravage, to destroy, **B76**, 19 (see note)

Sachant, *presp* knowing, wise, **B9**, 16

Sacquement, *nm* pillage, sack, **R145**, 2; **R314**, 3; **R315**, 3

Sage, *nm* wise man, fais que sage, do what a wise man would do, i.e., act wisely,
R233, 3; fait que sage, **R249**, 9; fera que sage, **R290**, 8

Saichans, *presp* **Ch69**, 5, see under Sachant

Saichans, *nm* wise men, **B75**, 4

Saillir, *vb* to leap, to jump, to sally forth, **R340**, 10; saille, **R412**, 11; saillent,
R46, 10; saillez, **R343**, 8; saillirent, **R165**, 6; sailliroit, **R113**, 8; saillit,
R111, 5; sailly, **R13**, 4; sauldray, **B136**, 20; sault, **R79**, 2

Sainte, *pastp* girded on, **R165**, 13

Sang (de moy), *excl* by my blood! **R378**, 11

[Sangler], *vb* to strap up, to tie, sanglé, **R457**, 13

Sans croix ne pille, see Pille

[Santir], (see Sentir), *vb* to be aware of, sans, **Ch60**, 3

Sapere, Italian, **R272**, 4 (see note)

Saquement, see Sacquement

Sas, *nm* sieve, **R238**, 4

Satis, satis, plus quam satis, Latin, Enough, enough, more than enough, **R135**, 1

Saufconduitz, *nm* safe conduct, **R203**, 11

Sault, saulx, *nm* leaps, **Co4**, 33; **R19**, 4; **R28**, 11

[Saulter], *vb* to jump, sault, **R79**, 2; **R130**, 9

Saussoye, *nf* willow plantation, *Songe*, 450 (see note)

Sauva(i)ge, *adj* wild, **Intro**, 206; strange, **R179**, 3
Sauves, *prep* except for, **R115**, 1
Savance, *nf* wisdom, **R220**, 14; **R272**, 9; non savance, folly, **B114**, 8
[Sçavoir], *vb* to know, sceu (modern je sus), **R389**, 8
Se, *adv* if, **B121**, 16, etc.
Se suis je (= Ce suis je), it is I, it's me, **R377**, 2
Seau, *nm* seal, **R151**, 10 (see note)
Sebelin, *adj* **R325**, 10 (see note)
Sebille, trou Sebille, the Sibyl's grotto, **R412**, 10
[Secourir], *vb* to help, secourray, **R144**, 5 (see also Sequeurir)
Segrés, *nm* secrets, **R212**, 4; **R435**, 5; *adj* secret, **R213**, 10
Seigneurir, *vb* to overcome, **Co3**, 33
Sejour (estre a), *nm* rest, leisure, **R125**, 5
Selle, *nf* saddle, **B115**, 35 (see note)
Selle, *pron* (modern celle), **R134**, 10
Semblance, *nf* appearance, **B11**, 17
Semblant, *nm* appearance, **B102**, 15 (see also Faulx)
Sen, *nm* sense, sen dessus dessous, higgledy-piggledy, **R282**, 11
Sente, *nf* path, **Ch32**, 1; **R194**, 5; **R195**, 2; **R197**, 2; **R244**, 7; **R246**, 2; etc.
Sentence, *nf* judgment, discernment, **R241**, 8
[Sentencer], *vb* to pronounce sentence, sentence, **R241**, 4
Sentine, *nf* boat, **R94**, 6
[Sentir (s'en)], *vb* to be aware of, to realize, Je m'en sens et m'en suis sentu, **B94**,
    27; s'en sente, **R246**, 5; me faictes sentir, make me aware of, i.e., inform me
    of (your good news), *La departie*, 499
Seoir (se), *vb* to sit, **Co3**, 49; seioit (se), **R305**, 4; seit toy, **R262**, 8; siet, **Ch54**, 2
[Sequeurir], *vb* to help, sequeure, **R124**, 10; **R143**, 11; **R390**, 11 (see also Secourir)
Sergent, *nm* law officer, prosecutor, **R160**, 1
Serre (tenir en), *nf* prison, **Co6**, 8; **B121**, 9
Servage, *nm* service, *Songe*, 61
Seur, *adj* sure, **R246**, 13; **R252**, 11
Seure, *adv* on, at, me courent seure, run at, i.e., assault me, **R143**, 8
Seurement, *adv* safe, **R75**, 6
Seurté, *nf* security, *Songe*, 171
[Seurvenir], *vb* to come about, seurvient, **R286**, 9
Siche (modern chiche), *adj* niggardly, **B107**, 25
Sicut "pax vobis," Latin, (words) such as "peace to you," **R139**, 5
[Sillogiser], *vb* to make syllogisms, sillogisant, **B109**, 12
Simplesse, *nf* childish behaviour, naïveté, **B137**, 20; *Jam nova*, 34
[Singler], *vb* to sail, singloient, **B140**, 5
Soiller, *vb* to besmirch, **R224**, 12
Solacer, see Soulacer
Some, *nf* summit (of perfection), *Jam nova*, 91

Sommeilleux, *adj* asleep **B97**, 5
Sommiers, *nm* pack animals, **B81**, 13
Son, *nm* bran, **R300**, 6
Songnieus, *adj* concerned about, occupied with, **R30**, 4
Sonner (mot), *vb* to utter (a word), **B112**, 25; **R51**, 2
Sort, *nm* luck, **B122**, 22; spell, **R96**, 12; **R350**, 9
Sorte, *nf* company, friends, **R411**, 9
Sotye, *nf* stupidity, **R154**, 8
Soubrement, *adv* soberly, **B89**, 23
Souches, *nf* lit. tree stumps, simple folk (?), **R394**, 14 (see note)
Soucies, *nf* marigolds (with pun on soucis, cares, worries), **R449**, 1
Soudart, *nm* soldier, **B84**, 8 (refrain)
Soudoiers, *nm* soldiers, **B125**, 31; souldoyers, **R424**, 5
Souffisance, *nf* sufficiency, enough for one's needs, **B17**, 11
[Souffrir], *vb* to tolerate, seufre, **R351**, 3
Soufreteux, *nm* invalid, **B24**, 23
Souhaidier, *vb* to wish, to desire, **B123**, 23
[Soulacer] (se), *vb* to find solace, m'y solace, **R206**, 9; me soulace, **R269**, 11; se soulace, **Intro**, 106
Soulas, *nm* solace, **Ch43**, 4; *personif* **R40**, 5
[Souloir], *vb* to be accustomed to, to be in the habit of, souloit, **B53**, 28; **B59**, 1; **B62**, 5; *Songe*, 392; **B100**, 2; **R247**, 11; etc.; souloye, **B59**, 1; **B62**, 5; **B114**, 4; **R40**, 9; **R210**, 8; etc.; sueil, **R121**, 10
Soulz (vieux), *nm* lit. out-of-date coinage, **R258**, 9
Sourde, see Lyme
[Sourdre], *vb* to arise, sourde, **R112**, 8; sourt, **R366**, 2; sourdent, **R56**, 8; sourdoit, **R21**, 6
Soussie (chapel de), *nf* marigold (garland of), **R232**, 4
Soussïer, *vb* to worry, **Ch1**, 3, **R108**, 4
[Soustenir], *vb* to sustain, to tolerate, soustiengne, **R386**, 11,
Soutivement, *adv* stealthily, **B65**, 20
Soutiveté, *nf* skill, en soutiveté, skilfully, **R75**, 4
Soutte, *nf* hold (of ship), **R296**, 7
Souventesfois, *adv* oftbetimes, **Intro**, 339; souventesfoiz, **R404**, 3
Soy, *pron* (for a part soy, see under Part) fera de soy, will do as he pleases, **R117**, 11
Sta fermo, Italian, **R272**, 8 (see note)
Substantament, *nm* support, mainstay, *Jam nova*, 10
Sueil, *nm* threshold, **R174**, 5; **R325**, 5
Suïr, süyr, *vb* to follow, *Songe*, 118; **Co3**, 6; **Ch21**, 3; **R124**, 8; **R333**, 11; suient, **Ch10**, 9; süy, **R288**, 10; suyt, **R146**, 8
[Surmonter], *vb* to dominate, to overcome, surmontent, **B115**, 24
Sus, *prep* above, *Songe*, 25; *adv* up, get up, **R49**, 5; cours sus, run at, assault, **R203**, 2; **R165**, 10

Sus et jus, *adv* up and down, **R248**, 2; **R312**, 2

[Suspeçonner (se)], *vb* to suspect, suspeçonné, **R6**, 8

Suye (plus amer que), *nf* soot, **B111**, 19; **B112**, 27

Sy (sans), *adv* if, **R54**, 5

T

Tabellion, *nm* notary, **B79**, 5 (see note)

Tables, *nf* backgammon, **B46**, 1

Tabliers, *nm* gaming tables, **R311**, 10

Tabourin, *nm* drummer, **R51**, 1; **R444**, 5

Taillant (de), *nm* d'estoc et de taillant (taille), with cut and thrust, **Co6**, 57; one way or another, **B80**, 9 (see note)

[Tailler], *vb* taille **R254**, 7 (see Broche)

[Taindre], *vb* to lose colour, tains, wan, **R441**, 9

Talant, *nm* wish, desire, **B44**, 33; *Songe*, 259; a vostre talant, **R69**, 10; mal talant, dislike, hatred, **B136**, 17

[Talenter (se)], *vb* to desire, s'en talente, **R193**, 5

Tanné, *pastp* wearied, "browned off", **R6**, 1; brown (symbolizing sadness), **R52**, 2; **R426**, 2

Tanser, tenser, *vb* to scold, to complain, **R186**, 6; **R289**, 2; tenser, **R303**, 1; tance, **R219**, 11; tancee, **R181**, 5; tanse, **R86**, 9; **R306**, 10; **R399**, 6; tense, **B73**, 15; tence, **R337**, 10; s'en tence, **R241**, 5

Tant (ne) ne quant, *adv* not one little bit, **R26**, 6; **R257**, 5

Tantalus, *nm* **R433**, 8 (see note)

Tantost, *adv* at once, **R272**, 2 (see note)

Tarder, *vb* to delay, to hold back, **R278**, 8; tarde, **Ch48**, 6 (see also Tirer)

[Tarir], *vb* to dry up, tarie, **B104**, 1; **R326**, 4

Tatin, *nm* blow, **R223**, 8; **R263**, 8; **R376**, 5; **R377**, 12

Taye, *nf* opaque spot in eye, **R40**, 10

Tellement quellement, *adv* as well as I may, **R123**, 1

[Tempester], *vb* to torment, tempeste, **R289**, 8

Teneur, *nm* tenor, **R426**, 8

Tenir, *vb* to hold, **R156**, 11; see Cour(r)oye, tenir pié, *vb* to resist, *Songe*, 103; s'en tendroit, **R274**, 1; s'en vous ne tient, providing you don't resist, have no objection, **R198**, 9; tenir coy, tenir quoy, lie low, **R164**, 4; **R330**, 4; **R414**, 6; see Quoy

Testu, *adj* stubborn, **R328**, 6

Theologie, *nf* theology, difficult subject, **R62**, 11

Tieuls, tieulx (modern tels), *adj* such, **B83**, 22; **B137**, 15; **Co7**, 82; **R57**, 4; **R76**, 8; **R105**, 11; **R351**, 3 etc.; tieulx quieulx, according to their whim, willy-nilly, **R454**, 11

Tintin, *nm* game, **R263**, 5 (see note)

Tire (de), *nf* at once, **B21**, 24; **Ch50**, 10; d'une tire, at one go, all together, **Co7**, 55; de grant tire, rapidly, **R440**, 10

Tirer, *vb* to advance, to bring forward, to draw (of water), **Co5**, 80; **R278**, 8; **R326**, 2; tire, **Ch53**, 15; **R59**, 4; **R392**, 10; **R440**, 7; tirez vous la, **R255**, 1; tirez autre part, go elsewhere, clear off, **R325**, 6; tirez avant, go ahead, **R257**, 8; tirer et tarder, shove one way or another (lit. advance and retard), **R278**, 8; se tire arriere, withdraw, **R377**, 11

Tison, *nm* ember, **B120**, 14

Tolir, *vb* to take away, to rob, to rid of, **B16**, 7; tollir, **B38**, 18; **B40**, 17; **Co2**, 86; **Ca2**, 16; **Ch11**, 9; **R268**, 12; etc.; tollu, **B63**, 20; tolt, **Co7**, 61; **Ch44**, 1; toult, **B103**, 9; toust, *Jam nova*, 92

[Tondre], *vb* to cut the hair off, tonde, **R120**, 8

Tonnellet, *nm* barrel, **B133**, 6

Touches, *nf* clump of trees, **R394**, 6

Touppet, *nm* top of head, **B133**, 13

Touppin, *nm* (spinning) top, **B133**, 11

Tourbes, *nf* clouds, *Jam nova*, 60

Tour(s), *nm* trick(s), **R4**, 4; **R10**, 5; **R17**, 8; **R153**, 2

Tout (du), *adv* entirely, **Co1**, 18, 54; **B125**, 24

Trailles, *nf* trellis, arbour, **R118**, 9

[Trainer], see Festu

Traire, *vb* to attract, to draw (towards), **B69**, 28; *Songe*, 245; trait, **B9**, 2; **Co6**, 21; drawn from, taken from, trait, **R453**, 13

Trait, *nm* blow, shot, harmful act, **B87**, 2; **B104**, 21; **Ch51**, 1; **R20**, 1, 4; **R75**, 1

[Traitier], *vb* to negotiate, traictié, **Co4**, 93; governed, traictez **R378**, 10

Transporter (se), *vb* to bring oneself (to), me transporte, *Jam nova*, 95; yielding, **R385**, 4

[Transsir], *vb* to transfix, to penetrate, transsi, **B103**, 20; transy, **Co7**, 31; **R374**, 9

Travailler, *vb* to strive, to make an effort, to suffer, travaillier **Co6**, 69; travaillons, *La departie*, 452; traveille, **R286**, 2

Traveil, travail, *nm* travail, suffering, toil, **B95**, 17; **Co3**, 61; **R67**, 3; **R332**, 8

Travers, a *adv* thoroughly, completely, **R435**, 6

Tresdespite, *adj* very spiteful, **B43**, 3

Treshastis, *adj* impetuous, **B73**, 16

Tresleaument, *adv* very loyally, **Ca3**, 19

[Trespasser], *vb* to die, trespasse **R184**, 8; trespassé, **R204**, 10; transgresses, trespace, **R242**, 6; transgressed, trespassé, **R349**, 2; trespassans, passing along, **R165**, 5

Trespiteuse, *adj* very pitiful, **R444**, 2

Tresplus, *adv* far more, **R268**, 7

Tresque, *adv* until, **R430**, 6

Tressegret, *adj* very secret, **R348**, 4

Tressoingneux, *adj* very earnest, eager, **B36**, 22; **B117**, 3

Trestout, *adv* entirely, **R255**, 5
Treu, trou, *nm* hole, **R455**, 11; trou Sebille, Sibyl's grotto, **R412**, 10 (see note)
Triacle, *nm* electuary, **R229**, 10
[Trocter], to trot, to wander, troctent, **R303**, 6
Trompeur, *nm* deceiver, A trompeur trompeur et demi, proverb still current, every rogue has his match, **R129**, 1
Trouver, *vb* to find, treuve, **B81**, 30; **B94**, 5; **B108**, 2; **B129**, 16
Truages, *nm* dues, toll, **B86**, 23
Truchement, *nm* interpreter, **R129**, 10; **R178**, 1; **R179**, 1
Truffes, *nf* mockery, **R169**, 8
Tutelle, *nf* guardianship, protection, **R234**, 1; **R235**, 4; **R413**, 9

U

Ubi supra, Latin, (some time) ago, **R131**, 1 (see note)
Ueil, hueil, see Eueil
Uis, uys, see Huis
Umbrages, *nm* concealments, **Ch59**, 3
Usance, *nf* custom, habit, **B44**, 9
Ut (ré, mi, etc.), *n* do, re, mi, etc., **R331**, 2

V

Vade retro, Latin, go back, withdraw, **R136**, 3
Vaillance, *nf* valiance, **Co3**, 61; **R98**, 11
Vaillant, *adj* valiant, **B76**, 35; *n* worth, value, **B80**, 3; **Ch26**, 11
[Vaincre], *vb* to overcome, vaint, **Co7**, 109; **R427**, 13
Val, *nm* lit. vale, a val le vent, downwind, **R146**, 5
[Valoir], *vb* to be worth, vaillant, **B76**, 35; vaulzit, **R63**, 6
Vantance, *nf* boasting, **B116**, 12
Vengement, *nm* revenge, **B54**, 49
Vente, *nf* lit. tax (on goods) to collect, pesson ne vente, fig., benefit small or big, **R194**, 11
[Venter], *vb*, to blow, vente, **R294**, 1; **R296**, 8; **R366**, 1
Veoir, *nm* **Co5**, 114, see Voir, *nm*
Verba pro verbis, Latin, words for words, **R139**, 4
Verdeur, *nf* prime, *Songe*, 175
Verges, *nf* rods, **R381**, 5
Vert gay, *nm* bright green, **B48**, 14; vert perdu, dull, dark green, **R52**, 2; **R426**, 2
[Vestir], *vb* to clothe, veis, **R238**, 2
Veu, veulx, *nm* vow(s), *Songe*, 209; **R305**, 8 (see note)
Veufve, *nf* widow, **R75**, 9
Viaires, *nf* faces, **R229**, 4

Viande, *nf* food (not necessarily meat), **B104**, 2

[Vider], *vb* to dispatch, to send away, vidés, **R94**, 5

Vidimus, *vb* Latin, we have seen (certificate giving approval), **B79**, title

[Vilipender], *vb* to inveigh against, to insult, vilipende, **B104**, 5

[Virer (se)], *vb* to transform oneself, viray (for viré), **R388**, 8

Visee, *nf* sight, **R431**, 10

Vivres, *nm* provisions, **R311**, 10

Vo (modern votre), *pron* your, **B128**, 4

Voir, *vb* to see, veez me ça, just look at this! **R128**, 1, veoye, **B62**, 4; **Co2**, 82; vissiez, **B141**, 11; voy, **R201**, 2; vy, **B139**, 31

Voir, voire, *nm* truth, **Intro**, 10; *Songe*, 384; *La departie*, 460; **B7**, 5, **B122**, 30; **B126**, 11; etc.; *adv* voire? really? **R258**, 4; really! **R283**, 1; **R370**, 9

Voise (see Aller), *pressubj* **Intro**, 54; *La departie*, 511; **R378**, 1; voisent, **B87**, 28; **R74**, 8

Volage, *adj* flighty, **R290**, 4

Volee (a la), *nf* any old how, **R26**, 4

Volte route! *excl* about turn! **R145**, 5

Vouer, *vb* to swear (allegiance, etc.), **R114**, 8

Vouler, *vb* **R14**, 4 (see note)

[Vouloir], *vb* to want, veil, **R356**, 10; **R350**, 5; veuil, **R62**, 1; **R211**, 11; **R255**, 8; vieulx, **R440**, 4; voulsist, **B41**, 18; voult, **B115**, 19; **R271**, 6; (je) veul, **B107**, 18; (je) vueil, **Intro**, 303; **B56**, 25; **Co3**, 12; **R269**, 3; **R286**, 5; etc.; vueille, **B56**, 14; vueilliez, **B68**, 7; weil, **R39**, 10

Vueil, *nm* wish, **B70**, 16; **B123**, 5; **R42**, 1; **R121**, 3; **R174**, 4

Vuit, vuys *adj* empty, **Ch21**, 10; **R70**, 12

W

Widyer (se), *vb* to rid oneself (of), **R241**, 6

Y

Ydropisie, *nf* dropsy, **B88**, 21

Yer (Modern hier), *adv* yesterday, **R241**, 10; avant yer, **B116**, 14; devant yer, the day before yesterday, **Ch2**, 9

Yssir, *vb* to exit, to go out, **B54**, 3; **B119**, 13; ist, **R372**, 6; *transitive*, to pull out, **R240**, 3; see also Issir

Yssue, *nf* freedom, *Jam nova*, 31; exit, **R408**, 4